Lecture Notes in Computer Science 1357

Edited by G. Goos, J. Hartmanis and J. van Leeuwen

Springer
Berlin
Heidelberg
New York
Barcelona
Budapest
Hong Kong
London
Milan
Paris
Santa Clara
Singapore
Tokyo

Jan Bosch   Stuart Mitchell (Eds.)

Object-Oriented Technology

ECOOP'97 Workshop Reader

ECOOP'97 Workshops
Jyväskylä, Finland, June 9-13, 1997
Proceedings

 Springer

Series Editors

Gerhard Goos, Karlsruhe University, Germany

Juris Hartmanis, Cornell University, NY, USA

Jan van Leeuwen, Utrecht University, The Netherlands

Volume Editors

Jan Bosch
Department of Computer Science and Business Administration
University of Karlskrona/Ronneby
S-372 25 Ronneby, Sweden
E-mail:jan.bosch@ide.hk-r.se

Stuart Mitchell
Department of Computer Science, University of York
York, YO1 5DD, UK
E-mail: stuart@cs.york.ac.uk

Cataloging-in-Publication data applied for

Die Deutsche Bibliothek - CIP-Einheitsaufnahme

Object oriented technology : ECOOP 97 workshop reader ;
proceedings / ECOOP 97 workshops, Jyväskylä, Finland, June 9 - 13,
1997. Jan Bosch ; Stuart Mitchell (ed.). - Berlin ; Heidelberg ; New
York ; Barcelona ; Budapest ; Hong Kong ; London ; Milan ; Paris ;
Santa Clara ; Singapore ; Tokyo : Springer, 1998
    (Lecture notes in computer science ; Vol. 1357)
    ISBN 3-540-64039-8

CR Subject Classification (1991): D.1-3, H.2

ISSN 0302-9743
ISBN 3-540-64039-8 Springer-Verlag Berlin Heidelberg New York

© Springer-Verlag Berlin Heidelberg 1998
Printed in Germany

Typesetting: Camera-ready by author
SPIN 10661353   06/3142 – 5 4 3 2 1 0   Printed on acid-free paper

Preface

Jan Bosch

University of Karlskrona/Ronneby
Dept of Computer Science
SoftCenter, S-372 25, Ronneby, Sweden
Jan.Bosch@ide.hk-r.se

Stuart Mitchell

University of York
Dept of Computer Science
York, United Kingdom
Stuart@minster.cs.york.ac.uk

1 Introduction

Although it is becoming more accepted in software industry, object-oriented technology still is an active field of research with many issues remaining to be addressed. This workshop reader, in a way, presents the width of the ongoing research activities in object orientation. One can classify these activities into three categories:

- *Domain-specific*: Several activities focus on a single application, e.g., telecommunication, or computer-science, e.g., real-time and mobility, domain. Research tries to address the domain-specific problems of object-oriented technology.
- *Design issues*: Object-oriented design has been an issue for at least a decade, but one can identify an increasing focus on formal approaches and on the evolution and re-engineering of existing object-oriented software.
- *Beyond object orientation*: The object-oriented paradigm will, at some point, be replaced by a subsequent paradigm and several research efforts investigate alternative or extended approaches. Examples include extended language expressiveness for design patterns and frameworks, component-oriented programming, and aspect-oriented programming.

2 Contents

The remainder of this book is a selection and re-iteration of the contributions to 12 workshops (of a total of 15) held during the ECOOP'97 conference. The workshops generally relate to one of the above categories.

Part I is concerned with the use of object-oriented technology in the telecommunications domain, in particular service engineering. Due to the breaking of the monopoly of traditional telecommunication providers, competition has increased rapidly. Since the competitive edge is in services rather than connections, the organisers predict a shift to a service-driven telecommunication market. To develop new services with short time-to-market, low complexity, high reusability, etc., the object-oriented paradigm is considered to be the most suitable candidate.

Reflective real-time object-oriented programming and systems are discussed in Part II. Real-time systems have traditionally been very static, which results in changes to system behaviour during the software lifecycle being very costly. An important area of real-time research is how to make systems flexible and adaptive whilst retaining guarantees about their temporal properties. Reflection, i.e., the ability to perform computation on the system itself, is seen as a potential mechanism for achieving these goals.

Part III discussed the problems of conventional languages for the implementation of design patterns and object-oriented frameworks and new approaches to describing and implementing design patterns and frameworks. One can identify three categories of approaches: design environment support, visualizing otherwise implicit structures; the generative approach, generating a code skeleton that can be filled in with application-specific code; and programming language extensions that provide first-class representations for design patterns or framework concepts.

Part IV discusses the semantics of object-oriented modelling techniques. The participants, among others, reacted against the traditional signature-based way of describing standards: In addition to a precise syntax, also precise semantics needs to be specified. This would include allowance for detecting inconsistencies and inaccuracies and for comparing descriptions for their semantic equivalence.

Part V is concerned with distributed object-oriented computing, in particular methodological and implementation-oriented models and formal modelling techniques. The participants concluded that enabling technologies such as CORBA and Java RMI still lack a firm ground since no de-facto standard of distributed OO computing exists. On the other hand, it is unclear how formal notations such as Petri nets, Estelle, and Lotos can support the object-oriented paradigm. Finally, methodological support for these systems is still in the early stages.

Part VI studies the evolution and re-engineering of existing object-oriented software. Even though the object-oriented paradigm is often thought to be superior to older approaches with respect to maintenance, the large body of complex and expanding object-oriented software is placing an increasing burden on software engineers. The evolution and re-engineering of object-oriented software is a complex and multi-faceted problem that needs to be studied from several perspectives.

The modelling of software processes and artifacts is discussed in Part VII. The relation to object-oriented technology is twofold. First, object-oriented software development requires explicit modelling of its processes and artifacts. Secondly, software processes and artifacts can be modelled using object-oriented principles.

Part VIII is concerned with component-oriented programming (COP). COP is often referred to as the next step beyond OOP. Among other things, COP differs in its focus on constructing systems from independently developed components. Research issues include the relation to software architecture, the non-functional requirements that components should fulfil, and the glueing of components during application construction.

Part IX presents the doctoral students' workshop. Unlike the other workshops that focus on a technical topic, this workshop presents a wide variety of research topics, in which the common denominator is the current occupation of its participants. Nevertheless, the part presents an excellent overview of ongoing research activities in object-orientation.

The topic of Part X is object-oriented real-time systems. Despite early scepticism, object-oriented technology has become more widely used in real-time systems. However, there remain several research issues such as generating code from RT specifications, validation and testing of dynamic behaviour, and the relation between object-oriented real-time software and conventional kernels. In this part, the focus is on the modelling of object-oriented real-time systems and on implementation techniques.

Aspect-oriented programming is discussed in Part XI. One can identify a general awareness that code tangling reduces the quality, e.g., maintainability and reusability, of software. AOP is concerned with approaches to separately describe the various aspects of a component or software system and to compose them at a later stage. However, various approaches to achieving this separation of concerns can be identified and the part defines a characterisation of AOP and identifies research issues.

Part XII is concerned with operating systems. Modern operating systems must, in addition to the traditional requirements of performance and usability, fulfil additional requirements such as flexibility, adaptability, and scalability. The object-oriented paradigm provides properties that help achieve these requirements. Operating system issues discussed in this part are, among others, reflection, configuration of adaptable operating systems, and virtual machines.

3 About the diversity of the submissions

A workshop reader is, by its nature, very diverse in its contributions. This reader is by no means an exception to that rule. The contributions have a wide diversity in topics as well as the form of presentation. Some workshops are represented only by a workshop report whereas other workshops primarily present the participants' papers and spend limited effort on summarizing the workshop. As editors, we have given the organisers much freedom in the presentation of their workshop. We considered the contents of the parts more important than their uniformity and we do not believe that this would decrease readability.

4 Acknowledgements

An incredible number of people have been involved in creating this workshop reader, in particular all authors and workshop organisers. As editors, we merely composed their contributions. This workshop reader presents an important contribution to object-oriented research and we would like to express our sincere appreciation to everyone involved.

Table of Contents

XI: Aspect-Oriented Programming

XII: Object-Orientation and Operating Systems

Workshop 1: Object Oriented Technology for Telecommunications Services Engineering

June 9th 1997
Jyväskylä, Finland
Organisers : Simon Znaty, Jean-Pierre Hubaux

The demand for advanced telecommunication services has increased enormously the last few years. This has led to situations where the network operators have clashed new services into their networks at high speed to satisfy the customer needs. Today, when the telecommunication monopolies are breaking up, the fight for market shares has become hard. Moreover the demand for more and more specialised end-user services will continue to grow, and there will be an increasing demand for having the new services in shorter and shorter time frames. Thus, the structure and function of the switching systems will change to
accommodate the need for rapid deployment of more and more customised services.
The telecommunications industry which has been interconnection-driven will, in the future, be service-driven!
A new discipline called "telecommunications services engineering" is now emerging to cover the specification, design, implementation, management and validation of telecommunications services and their deployment and exploitation over current and future network architectures.
One of the main technology that has to be applied to master the service engineering complexity is object orientation. This can be easily explained: reusability of service class libraries, easy customisation of services, encapsulation for hiding implementation specific solutions and thereby gaining manufacturer independence as well as network independence, object modeling, etc.

In spite of this consensus, many issues still need to be investigated. For this reason, this year, a workshop has been organised on this specific topic in the framework of ECOOP.
Around 20 people attended this workshop; thanks to the limited size of the group and to the commitment of the participants, the sessions were highly interactive.
8 papers were presented in this workshop. All papers result of the call for papers and were carefully reviewed. The presented papers can be roughly put into 4 areas.

In the area of methodological support, Arve Meisingset addresses the problem of graphically representing a management information model specified with GDMO by using the well known OMT object-oriented methodology.

The second area is about behavior formalisation of objects.
Dominique Sidou deals with the important features of a behavior model intended for the specification and validation of distributed applications.

Jorge Luis Tellez Portas, David Watrin and Tayeb Ben Meriem focus on the use of the B method for specifying unambiguously managed objects. They also show its application for the specification of a WDM management information model.

The third paper of this group, by Lisandro Granville, Luciano Gaspary and Janilce Almeida proposes the OST development tool based on a new object oriented methodology called NSOMA which is intended to help the designer of protocols and services in the formal
definition of specifications.

A third area which has been addressed is the object-oriented development of telecommunications protocols and services.

In their paper, Jarmo Harju, Bilhanan Silverajan and Ilkka Toivanen propose an object oriented development environment called OVOPS, for protocol and distributed applications implementation. The tool supports the design, implementation and prototyping steps by providing an object oriented framework. The authors describe TCAP and GSM BTS implementation experiences.

The paper from Luca Deri deals with rapid network management development and presents his tools that are able to mask the complexity of network management.

The fourth area is about quality of service provisioning in a CORBA environment.

Zied Choukair and Antoine Beugnard focus on the integration of quality of service with real-time constraints and present the COREMO prototype which implements their approach.

As we have seen, the different papers address quite hot topics of the area of service engineering. In the near future, we can expect that issues such as CORBA, ODP, and TINA will be seriously investigated by our community.

In any case, the saga of the application of object oriented technology to telecommunications services engineering is far from being over. We hope that this workshop has been successful in helping the participants to get a better insight on the different facets of this exciting area.

Simon Znaty and Jean-Pierre Hubaux

Telecommunications Services Engineering : Principles, Architectures and Tools

Simon Znaty[1], Jean-Pierre Hubaux[2]
[1]ENST-Bretagne, RSM Department, France, Simon.Znaty@enst-bretagne.fr
[2]EPFL, TCOM Laboratory, Switzerland, hubaux@tcom.epfl.ch

Abstract
This paper introduces telecommunication services engineering through a definition of services, of network architectures that run services, and of methods, techniques and tools used to develop services. Emphasis is put on the intelligent network (IN), the telecommunication management network (TMN) and TINA architectures.

Key words : telecommunications services engineering, network architectures, methods, techniques

1. Introduction to Telecommunications Services Engineering

The previous decade has been devoted to the deployment of complex heterogeneous networks. Today, the new trend is toward services with quality of service requirements increasingly stringent. There is a need of a global reply to master and meet the requirements of the different stakeholders of this complex area. The proposed discipline to tackle these issues is *Telecommunications Services Engineering*.
Telecommunications services engineering is becoming strategic with the advent of broadband networks and mobile communications that enable to think of a large variety of services. Moreover, because of deregulation expected for 1998 in Europe, competition will lead to a market pressure to propose services increasingly reliable and cheap.

1.1. Service definition
Telecommunication services is a common name for all services offered by, or over, a telecommunication network.
The word service is used in several different contexts. In the ISDN (Integrated Services Digital Network) world, three types of network services can be distinguished [1] :
Support services define the transmission capabilities between two access points, including routing and switching across the network. They correspond to « bearer services ».
Teleservices include capabilities for communication between applications. Teleservices are supplied by communication software in the terminals. Telephony, audio, fax, videotex, video telephony are examples of teleservices.
Supplementary services also called features, complement support services or teleservices. Most well known supplementary services are related to the telephony

teleservice (Call forwarding, three party conference, etc.), but they could of course be generalised to other teleservices.

Value added services is a term often used for advanced supplementary services, especially services that can be offered and marketed as stand-alone products. Examples of such services are freephone, premium rate, virtual private network and televoting. Many value added services can be offered by special service providers connected to the network.

1.2. Service engineering definition

The concepts, principles and rules of service engineering have been first borrowed from those of software engineering. With years, the work of researchers in the service area have shown that the telecommunication services sector has specific requirements and should also integrate results from some other disciplines such as security, verification and validation, database management systems, communication management, etc.

Service engineering can be defined as the set of methods, techniques and tools to specify, design, implement, verify and validate value added services that meet user needs and deploy and exploit these services in the current or future networks. Service engineering is a young discipline, but a discipline, as is protocol engineering.

Three important components are considered (Figure 1):

• the *service creation environment* which may be compared to a software engineering platform specialised for the development of telecommunications services,

• the *telecommunication network* which corresponds to a black box that offers an application programming interface (API). This latter may be a signalling or management interface.

• the *network architecture* which is in charge of controlling the execution of the service within the network. It is positioned between the service creation environment and the network.

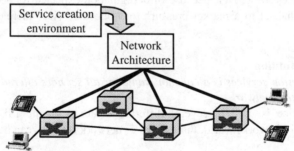

Figure 1: Components of Telecommunications Services Engineering

Service engineering covers three important domains, namely :

• *Service creation*, where the service is considered as a distributed application running on the multiple nodes of a telecommunication network,

• *Service management*, which should be studied during service analysis and design,

• *Network management*, which concerns the management of network resources used to provide telecommunications services.

Therefore two kinds of services are involved, telecommunications services and management services.

2. Network Architectures

2.1. The Intelligent Network (IN)
Telecommunications organisations have first defined the Intelligent Network (IN) that allows a rapid, smooth and easy introduction of new services in the network [2]. These services may be customised according to customer needs.

The architecture chosen is based on a centralised control. Service control is completely separated from call control. It is based on the existence of a signalling network linking all the switches. In the modern digital telephone network this signalling network does exist : it is called Common Channel Signalling n°7 (CCS7) network.

Figure 2 shows the IN architecture. It is based on a central node, the Service Control Point (SCP) , which controls the execution of a service in the network. The SCP is the master, while the switches, called Service Switching Points (SSP), are the slaves. Such an architecture is well adapted to services needing a centralised database like the green number (sometimes called Freephone) service. The IN will play a major role in the provision of mobile services.

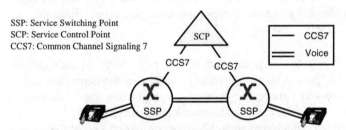

Figure 2 : Simplified IN Architecture

2.2. The Telecommunication Management Network (TMN)
Parallel to the IN standardisation, telecommunications organisations have defined the Telecommunication Management Network (TMN). TMN enables to federate the equipments that constitute the telecommunication network, produced generally by different telecommunication vendors, to enable their control in a uniform, global and efficient way [3].

Management of telecommunication networks may be defined as the set of activities of monitoring, analysis, control and planning of the operation of telecommunication network resources to provide services to customers with a certain level of quality and cost.

The main functions supplied by TMN, named functional areas are fault, configuration, performance, security and accounting management.

The set of capabilities necessary for network management relies on a reference structure which identifies the main TMN components and interfaces. The TMN architecture may be considered according to three views: information architecture, functional architecture and physical architecture.

The information architecture provides a data representation of the network resources fo the purpose of monitoring, control and management. The approach considered for the specification of the information model is object oriented.

The information architecture also defines management layers which correspond to levels where decisions should be made and where management information reside. ITU-T has proposed a generic network information model. Genericity enables the model to be applicable to different network technologies (ATM[1], SDH[2], PDH[3], etc). The model is currently applicable to both network element and network management layers.

The functional architecture describes the realisation of a TMN in terms of different categories of function blocks and different classes of interconnection among these function blocks called reference points.

The TMN physical architecture corresponds to the physical realisation of the functional architecture. Every function block becomes a physical block or a set of physical blocks (OS, Operation System) and reference points are transformed into interfaces. The TMN is seen as a set of connected physical blocks, every of them executing a set of TMN functions. To ensure interoperability, the specification of an interface requires the use of compatible communication protocols and compatible data representation. The exchanges of information between two management systems are performed by means of management operations and notifications through the CMIS[4] service and CMIP[5] protocol.

Figure 3 shows the physical architecture of a VPN (Virtual Private Network) configuration management system [4]. VPN is a telecommunication service that provides corporate networking between geographically dispersed customer premises based on a shared public switched network infrastructure.

The configuration management architecture consists of a set of OSs, namely, the CPN OS that manages the CPN resources, the PN OS that manages the public network resources, the PN-service OS which is responsible of the management of the services offered over the public network (e.g., a virtual path service in an ATM network), the CPN-service OS which role is to administer the services provided over the CPN, and finally the VPN-service OS for the management of the VPN service. The X interface enables interactions among the VPN service actors, i.e., the customer, the service provider and the network provider . The Q3 interface takes place between OSs of a given management domain.

---

[1] ATM : Asynchronous transfer Mode
[2] SDH : Synchronous Digital Hierarchy
[3] PDH : Plesiochronous Digital Hierarchy
[4] CMIS : Common Management Information Service
[5] CMIP : Common Management Information Protocol

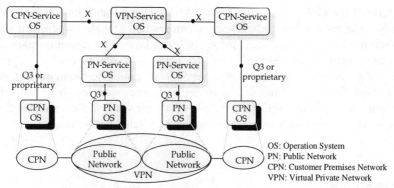

Figure 3: VPN Physical management architecture

Obviously, the IN and TMN architectures overlap. For instance, one TMN application such as billing and one IN application such as virtual private network must be tightly related because VPN billing should be handled in a consistent way with TMN billing. This shows that unless both IN and TMN architectures are made more consistent, the interconnection of IN and TMN applications would be very difficult. Moreover, it will be difficult to support two independent architectures while applications of both architectures must interoperate. The TINA architecture encompasses an integrated IN/TMN architecture.

2.3. Telecommunications Information Networking Architecture (TINA)

The evolution of the IN calls for new facilities such as flexible control of emerging multimedia, multisession, multipoint, broadband network resources, and services interoperability across diverse network domains. To meet these requirements, the TINA consortium has defined a global architecture that enables the creation, deployment, exploitation and management of services worldwide [5].

The goal is to build a reference model for open telecommunication architectures incorporating telecommunication services and management services, integrating the IN and TMN domains. TINA makes use of the latest advances in distributed computing (Open Distributed Processing, ODP [6] and Object Management Group, OMG [7]), and in object orientation to ensure interoperability, software reuse, flexible distribution of software and homogeneity in the design of services and their management.

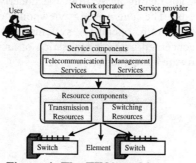

Figure 4: The TINA architecture

The layers of the TINA architecture (figure 4) divide application objects into different domains : The service layer where service components provide value added services with their management integrated, and the resource layer where resource management components provide an abstraction of the network resources used to supply the service (e.g., components that enable services to establish, maintain and release connections). Service and resource management components run over a distributed processing environment (DPE) [8]. At the lowest layer of the architecture, we can find the physical resources such as transmission links, switches and terminals.

3. Techniques

The advanced information processing techniques are playing a major role in the realisation of telecommunications services and underlying network architectures. Among these techniques, we can find object oriented methods for the specification phase, open distributed processing for the design phase, and the agent technology which provides a suitable support for the control and management of telecommunications systems.

3.1. Open Distributed Processing

A telecommunication service is a distributed application that runs over the multiple nodes of a telecommunication network. This statement leads to consider an information network (e.g., TINA) as an open distributed system, and to apply open distributed processing (ODP) concepts [9] to its design. The ODP reference model jointly defined by ISO and ITU-T provides a framework for the design of distributed systems with the introduction of viewpoints. Each viewpoint represents a different abstraction of the original system. Informally, a viewpoint leads to a representation of the system with emphasis on a specific concern. Five viewpoints are identified: enterprise, information, computation, engineering and technology (figure 5).

The *enterprise* viewpoint is concerned with the overall environment within which an ODP system is to operate. The *information* viewpoint focuses on the information requirements of the system, and deals with information object types, together with their states and permitted state changes. The *computation* viewpoint shows processing functions and data types, abstracting away from the underlying hardware structures via transparency functions. The *engineering* viewpoint establishes transparency services utilising concepts from operating systems and communications. The *technology* viewpoint is concerned with the realisation of an ODP system in terms of specific hardware and software components.

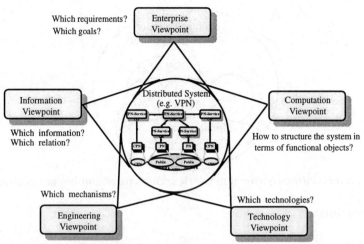

Figure 5: ODP viewpoints: different projections of a system

3.2. Mobile agents

An agent is a program, which, with a certain degree of autonomy performs tasks on behalf of a user or an application. An agent may move between network sites and cooperate with other agents to achieve its goals.

Agent development finds its roots in two research domains : intelligent agents stemming from artificial intelligence, which studies the capabilities of learning and decision making of cooperative autonomous entities ; mobile code technology that enable programs to migrate from a machine to another, while preserving their execution environment. This latter domain is evolving at a fast pace ; this is due to the emergence of languages such as Tcl [10] and Java [11], and of their portable execution environment.

The use of agent technology for telecommunications services engineering is a very hot topic. It lies within the boundaries of areas such as telecommunications, artificial intelligence and software engineering. This can be seen as an advantage since it promotes the convergence of research results from different communities.

3.3. Other techniques

Among the other techniques not detailed in this survey, we can mention formal methods for the verification, validation and test of telecommunication services before deploying them ; the goal of formal methods is to improve the reliability of these services.

Figure 6 summarises the interrelations among the different network architectures of telecommunications services engineering and the impact of techniques on these architectures.

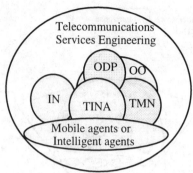

Figure 6: interrelations between network architectures and impact of techniques

4. Conclusion

To conclude, telecommunications services engineering takes several important aspects into consideration:
• An aspect related to methods, techniques and tools for the analysis, design, implementation, verification, and validation of telecommunications services. These methods , techniques and tools rely heavily on the object oriented approach and open distributed processing.
• An aspect related to the network architecture which is in charge of executing the service in the network.
Experimentation and prototyping are the only means available today to show the feasibility of the proposed concepts and scenarios.
Anyhow, telecommunications services engineering is an important research domain at the boundaries of software engineering and telecommunication systems. It draws much attention from network operators and telecommunication vendors since it is an important source of income. We hope that the scientific community will significantly contribute to this emerging area.
Specifically, the way the Internet will develop within or in parallel with these architectures is still an open question.

References

[1]   ITU-T Rec. I.210 : Principles of Telecommunications Services supported by an ISDN and the means to describe them, 88.

[2]   ITU-T Recommendations Q120x, Q121x, Q122x: The Intelligent Network, 93.

[3]   ITU-T Rec. M.3010: Principles for a Telecommunications Management Network, 93.

[4]   J-P. Gaspoz. « Object Oriented Method and Architecture for Virtual Private Network Service Management», PhD Thesis N° 1446, EPFL, Nov 95.

[5]   W.J. Barr, T. Boyd, Y. Inoue. "The TINA Initiative". IEEE Communications Magazine, March 93, pp 70-76.

[6]   ITU-T Rec. X901 : Basic Reference Model of Open Distributed Processing - Part1: Overview and Guide to Use", 94.

[7]   OMG, The Common Object Request Broker : Architecture and Specification. OMG Document N° 91.12.1, Rev. 1.1, Dec. 91.

[8]   TINA-C, « TINA Distributed Processing Environment (TINA-DPE)», TINA-C Deliverable N° TB_PL001_1.0_95, July 95.

[9]   J-B. Stefani, R. Kung, Y. Lepetit. « L'architecture à long terme Sérénité ». L'écho des Recherches, N°157, 3ème trimestre 1994, pp 45-52.

[10]   J. K. Ousterhout. "TCL: An Embeddable Command Language". Conf. Winter USENIX'90, pp 133-146.

[11]   Sun Microsystems : « The Java Language Environment : A White Paper », 1995. http://javasoft.com/whitePaper/java-whitepaper_1.html.

Difficulties with Mapping OMT Specifications into GMDO

by Arve Meisingset
Telenor Research and Development
PO Box 83 2007 Kjeller Norway
tel. +47 6384 8400, fax: +47 6381 0076
arve.meisingset@fou.telenor.no

Rumbaugh's OMT [1] notation is frequently proposed as a candidate 'conceptual' language for the Information viewpoint of the Open Distributed Processing framework, ODP [2]. Guidelines for the Definition of Managed Objects, GDMO [3], is a notation used for defining 'information' for the Telecommunications Management Network. This definition is considered to belong to the Engineering viewpoint of ODP. OMT is a pure graphical language, while GDMO is a pure alphanumeric language. This paper identifies difficulties with using OMT in combination with GDMO.

1 Background

The Standardization Sector of the International Telecommunication Union, ITU-T, Study Group 10 on Languages and general software aspects for telecommunication systems is - as one of its tasks - developing Recommendations on design of human-machine interfaces to Telecommunications Management Network applications, TMN, see e.g. ITU-T M.3010 [4]. Data communicated over the interfaces between TMN applications are specified by means of GDMO. Therefore, GDMO specifications are used to extract information to be presented at the human-machine interface. In this context, note that the ODP framework from ISO does not provide 'viewpoints' to specify the human-machine interface. Also, the human-machine interface is kept outside the TMN boundary of the TMN functional architecture. However, it is the human-machine interface that matters to the operator at his terminal and to the operator organisation. They will not be satisfied with unharmonised presentations of the same or different information by software from different vendors. Hence, ITU-T SG10 is addressing harmonisation of presentation of information at the human-machine interface to TMN applications, and are developing specification techniques, i.e. reference models, methods, languages and guidelines [5, 6, 7, 8], to this end.

Alphanumeric GDMO specifications are inherently hard to overview. Therefore, SG10 has developed Recommendation Z.360, Graphic GDMO [9], to provide an overview of GDMO specifications. Rumbaugh's OMT notation has been evaluated for this use, however, has not been found appropriate, as explained in this paper.

2 Formalisation

OMT has no formal definition. GDMO has a definition of the syntax, but not of its semantics. The implication of these deficiencies is that you do not know what notions in one language can be mapped into notions in the other language. Aggregation in OMT may either be mapped into Name Binding, an attribute stating a reference to the subordinate object, an attribute stating a reference to the superior object, a GRM [11] relationship or other combinations of notions. GRM, General Relationship Model, can be considered to be an extension of GDMO. The problem is that you do not know what is the right mapping between OMT and GDMO/GRM, and you cannot know, as long as the languages are not formally defined.

3 Graphic versus alphanumeric languages

OMT is a pure graphical language, while GDMO is a pure alphanumeric language. GDMO specifications are hard to overview, and this is a reason for supplying GDMO specifications with graphical illustrations. Entity Relationship (ER) graphs with extensions have been used for this purpose. Frequently these graphs are misleading and/or wrong compared to the alphanumeric specifications:

- The graphs frequently use classes which do not exist in the GDMO specifications
- The class labels in the graphs, informal texts and GDMO specifications are frequently different for the same class
- Inheritance of Name Bindings by the 'and subclasses' sub-clause is not depicted in the graphs, while it is essential for the understanding of the alternative naming structures and pointers
- Pointer attributes are in the informal texts frequently said to refer to informal classes which do not exist in the GDMO specifications
- Pointer attributes from class A to class B are incorrectly believed to be inhereted to subclasses of B
- The symbols used are misleading as to whether they represent one template statement, several template statements or a reference between template statements

The OMT graphics come closer than ER to the expressiveness of GDMO, as both languages are object oriented. However, the basic problem, that they are different, remains. Therefore, ITU-T has developed Recommendation Z.360, Graphic GDMO, which provides a graphic notation for GDMO/GRM. The basic requirement for this notation is that 'The Graphic GDMO shall be true to the Alphanumeric GDMO'.

4 Conceptualisation

OMT provides no indication of naming attributes, while GDMO defines the naming attribute within the context of a Name Binding. OMT provides an association notion similar to but not identical to the ER relationships. Pure GDMO use pointer attributes only, while GRM provides an advanced relationship notion. These observations indicate that OMT is intended for conceptual specifications, while pure GDMO is for syntactical definition of data. The detailed definitions of data values in GDMO are provided by the use of Abstract Syntax Notation One, ASN.1 [11]. However, the informal text on GDMO is misleadingly mentioning information trees of instances from GDMO specifications. Neither of the languages provide means to state denotation mappings from terms to entities or assertion mappings from statements to propositions. Therefore, the notions of modelling, information and conceptualisation are naivistic in both languages.

5 Aggregation versus Name Binding

OMT uses aggregation of object classes, while GDMO provides Name Binding of managed object classes. These notions are similar, however, not identical. In the following we will investigate if aggregation can be mapped into Name Binding, and vice versa:

1. OMT provides no indication of how to associate a (Name Binding) label with aggregation, as aggregation has no label. Therefore, there is no way to refer from the graphics in OMT to GDMO statements; in most cases this is no big problem, but sometimes it is.
2. OMT provides no means to state explicit inheritance of aggregation, similar to 'and subclasses' of the superior class of a Name Binding in GDMO. Many of the mistakes in GDMO specifications are associated with the use of the 'and subclasses' sub-clause.
3. OMT allows branching from one aggregation symbol to several components. We think this is just a way of drawing, without any extra semantics.
4. The OMT aggregation diamond is associated with the superior class. This assymmetry of the symbol may be interpreted as an indication of an attribute or constraint on this class, ref. point (2) on inheritance of aggregation. The assymmetry is misleading as to the GDMO interpretation, since Name Binding in GDMO is a separate template, i.e. a kind of association, and not a reference from one managed object class to the other.

6 Generalisation versus Derived From

OMT uses a Generalisation notion between object classes, while GDMO uses a Derived From reference from a subclass to its superclasses. These notions are similar, however, not identical. In the following we will investigate if Generalisation can be mapped into Derived From, and vice versa:

1. While OMT is intended to be a conceptual language, GDMO has an extra syntactical dimension not provided by OMT. In GDMO: Suppose A is Derived From B, and C is Derived From B, as well. If A and C have different (distinguished) naming attributes, then they have different name spaces; if the distinguished names are identical, then the name spaces are overlapping. OMT does not allow for this distinction.
2. OMT and GDMO allow multiple inheritance, but resolution of conflicts is left for the implementations.
3. The discriminator notion of OMT has no parallel in GDMO.
4. GDMO has not the same restriction on what classes can be instantiated as in OMT. While all classes in GDMO may be instantiated, in OMT only leaf classes can be instantiated.
5. GDMO does not provide means to constrain the attributes of a subclass relative to its superclass, except by conditional packages and informal behaviour specifications.
6. OMT allows branching from one generalisation triangle to several subclasses. GDMO has no similar notion.

7. OMT uses a filled triangle to state that an object can be an instance of several nondisjoint subclasses of a superclasses. GDMO has no similar notion, but can obtain the same result by defining a (sub-)subclass of the subclasses.
8. OMT uses a relational triangle symbol to indicate generalisation. However, in GDMO inheritance is stated by a Derived From statement (reference/pointer) from a class to (several) superclasses. The different statement styles and branching of the two languages may mislead the users.

7 Associations versus pointer attributes

In OMT a link is a physical or conceptual connection between object instances, while an association describes a group of links with common structure and common semantics. An association can be reinterpreted as a class. The 'multiplicity' of associations can be: Exactly one (no mark), Many (Zero or more) (filled dot), Optional (Zero or one) (open dot), one or more (1+), Numerically specified (1-2, 4). Pure GDMO uses pointer attributes only. The informal text of each attribute indicates which managed object classes this attribute can point at - due to provisioning of multivalues and rich ASN.1 syntaxes, one attribute can point at more than one managed object class. GRM provides complex relations, which can be inherited and reinterpreted. In the following we will investigate if associations can be mapped into pointer attributes, and vice versa:

1. The OMT text on "Implementing associations" clearly indicates that GDMO references/pointers are not covered by OMT.
2. GDMO pointer attributes are directed, similar to relational mathematics, while OMT associations are undirected, similar to the relational model.
3. GDMO references/pointers are one-way, and no cardinality is indicated. However, in ASN.1 an attribute can be defined to be multivalued. This allows for one attribute having several values which can point to many objects. This 'multiplicity' is in OMT indicated by a filled dot at the pointed at side. GRM provides cardinality constraint parameters similar to, but different from the multiplicity notion of OMT.
4. Some GDMO references/pointers can refer to objects of alternative classes. This is in Graphic GDMO represented by branching arrows. OMT has no similar notion. In OMT a binary association is between two classes only - while a GDMO pointer attribute can point to more than two classes.
5. Also, the mappings from several binary OMT associations to the GDMO branching references become difficult, as they all have to be assigned different labels.
6. The label of a GDMO attribute acting as a pointer is interpreted as the role label of the object pointed at. OMT associations will have to be assigned both association labels and role labels which are mapped to the GDMO labels.
7. In (Graphic) GDMO the attribute label <package label, attribute label> is used to indicate the full path to the attribute in the alphanumeric GDMO specification. OMT has no similar means of identification. Hence, OMT and GDMO labels will be different and explicit mappings are needed between the labels.

8. OMT supports n-ary relations, and so does GRM (and Graphic GDMO), but not GDMO. GRM is not (yet) used in most TMN specifications. GRM supports inheritance of relations; this is not supported by OMT. OMT supports attributes of associations (without assigning an object class label); this is not supported by GRM. Both OMT and GDMO support reinterpretation of an association/relation to become a (managed object) class.
9. We observe that a realistic OMT graph becomes cluttered and does not convey the same information as in (Graphic) GDMO.

8 Conclusion

Currently, most TMN specifications are using GDMO supported with informal, and frequently, incorrect ER-like illustrations. Existing GDMO specifications are difficult to represent in OMT. The mapping from OMT to GDMO is somewhat simpler. However, GDMO and OMT are two different languages. Therefore, sometimes many-to-many mappings are needed between statements in the two languages. The mapping statements can only be done if OMT is supplied with an alphanumeric notation, to which the mapping statements can refer. Due to the differences between the languages, OMT is neither a suitable tool to depict the contents of GDMO specification nor to validate the contents of these specifications.

Due to the problems mentioned above, ITU-T has developed Recommendation Z.360, Graphic GDMO, to provide an overview of GDMO specifications. To ensure the compatibility, the development of Graphic GDMO was based on a carefully developed Requirement document [9].

If OMT/UML is used for some viewpoint and GDMO for another viewpoint of a total specification, then the developers have to carefully address and validate the mappings between these specifications. Automatic tools to ensure the compatibility are preferable.

References

1. Rumbaugh J et al. *Object-Oriented Modeling and Design.* Prentice Hall, 1991.
2. ISO/IEC. *Information technology - Basic reference model of Open Distributed Processing.* Part 1: Overview (ITU-T X.901), Part 2: Foundations (ITU-T X.902), Part 3: Architecture (ITU-T X.903). ISO/IEC DIS 10746-1, 2, 3.
3. ITU-T. *GDMO.* Recommendation X.722.
4. ITU-T. *Principles for a Telecommunications management network.* Recommendation M.3010.
5. ITU-T. *Data oriented human-machine interface specification technique - Introduction.* Recommendation Z.351.
6. ITU-T. *Data oriented human-machine interface specification technique – Scope, approach and reference model.* Recommen-dation Z.352.
7. ITU-T. *Extensions to the HMI specification technique.* http://www.itu.int/SG10/reports/
8. ITU-T. *Questions allocated to ITU-T Study Group 10 for the Study Period 1997-2000.* ITU-T COM 10-1, 1996.
9. ITU-T. *Graphic GDMO.* COM R-4, 1996.
10. ITU-T. *GRM.* Recommendation X.725.
11.ITU.T. *Abstract Syntax notation 1 (ASN.1).* ITU-T Recommendation s X.700-X.790.

Towards a "Good" Functional and Executable Behavior Model

D. Sidou, Institut Eurécom, France (sidou@eurecom.fr)

The objective of this paper is to present the more important features of a behavior model intended for the specification and the validation of distributed applications or distributed application components. Distributed application components are the basic building blocks that are directly useful for the procurement of working distributed applications, e.g. telecommunication management network (TMN) applications, electronic commerce applications.... Such distributed application components are typically built on top of distributed object computing (DOC) systems that basically provide the communication infrastructure. Among the existing DOC systems we are particularly interested in the OSI Systems Management (OSI-SM) framework [13] typically used for TMN applications and the general purpose OMG-CORBA [12] DOC system. There is an important requirement for a better specification of distributed application components. Indeed, without a precise, unambiguous and correct specifications it is difficult to build a truly interworking distributed application. To this end, it is necessary to go far beyond the communication infrastructure for which a reasonable level of maturity is available. The challenge is to provide effective specification and validation frameworks for application oriented issues, e.g. what is the meaning or semantics of each interaction occurring between a client and a server. As a matter of fact, organizations such as the network management forum (NMF) and the OMG have proposed new concepts to allow the standardization of application oriented issues. In the NMF we have *Ensembles* [11], in the OMG we have *Object Frameworks* [17]. A NMF-Ensemble defines a coherent grouping of object interfaces and utilization scenarios corresponding directly to a given network management application. However an Ensemble does not include any behavior specification of involved managed objects. Object frameworks are a more recent proposal by the OMG intended to cover behavior issues. In this paper, the goal is to define a suitable behavior model based on executable specifications to allow the validation of distributed object frameworks.

In terms of expressiveness of the specification framework, nondeterminism and dynamism are considered as the two important features in the behavior of distributed applications. Section 1 gives a more precise description of these features and presents the way they are considered in the proposed behavior model. In terms of validation involvement of users is the key point. Section 2 presents some motivations for this statement and describes also the way usability is achieved for validation issues.

1 Specification Framework

1.1 Nondeterminism

Nondeterminism is a natural consequence of distribution. In a distributed system, actions[1] may execute concurrently (concurrency), actions may execute in an undetermined order (unordering), or actions can be selected for execution in a non-determined way (choice). As a result, the overall behavior of the system can not be uniquely determined a priori. Consequently, a behavior model for distributed applications has to allow the modeling of nondeterminism. In fact two approaches can be distinguished depending on the use of control abstractions to organize the specifications of actions in the system.

1.2 Transition Systems

In this section the notion of *transition* and *state* are defined. Putting this two notions together defines in its turn the concept of *transition system* which can be viewed as a low level representation for the behavior of any distributed system. Transitions in the system are merely its atomic actions, i.e. steps that can be observed in a single and coherent phase. The configurations of the system between its atomic transition steps define naturally its states. The overall behavior of the system can be defined either by all the sequences of transitions or states the system can go through from a given initial state s_0. This defines the concept of *transition system*. Though the behavior of a system can always be given as a transition system, such a representation is rather impractical because it is too low level. Most of the time transition systems are used by verification tools as a backend representation [2]. Because specification is a human activity the availability of higher level abstractions is mandatory to allow the specification of state and transitions – even if validation is typically performed at the low level representations based on transition system.

1.3 Using Control Abstractions

In many notations dedicated operators are introduced to model the causes of nondeterminism, e.g. concurrency or nondeterministic choice operators. These operators are applied to some rather sophisticated control abstractions such as processes as in process calculi [9], or automatas as in automata based specification languages [16]. Processes and automatas are intended to give a suitable partitioning of the control state of the system into well identified and manageable pieces. Actions are typically organized on such control structures, i.e. actions are specified based on the local (control) states that are defined in each process / automata in the system. Because of the emphasis that is put on control issues in the configuration of the system such models are referenced as control oriented models.

---

[1] An action is defined as in RM-ODP2 [15] very generally by anything happening in the system. One important point is that the granularity of actions is a design choice. An action need not be atomic, so actions may overlap in time.

1.4   Declarative Specification of Actions

In this approach, each action is declared one by one. Each action is self contained in the sense that it contains both a specification of the conditions required for its activation, a specification of its effects, and a specification of any other constraint that it may observe. It is important to note the key role played by the underlying data state of the system. Effects are typically specified as data state changes, and constraints are assertional conditions on data states that have to be verified at well identified places, e.g. pre- and post-conditions or general assertions. The enabling condition is based on a condition related to the data state. However it may also include a triggering event used to model interactions of the systems with its environment. For instance, a client that makes a request on a server object, or more basic things such as data state changes. Since the configuration of the system is defined only w.r.t. data abstractions, such models are referenced as data oriented models.

1.5   Synthesis

One of the first models proposed for the specification of concurrent systems was Dijkstra's guarded command language (GCL) [1], which is a typical example of a data oriented model. The semantics of such languages is based only on nondeterminism. For instance in Dijkstra GCL at each step one guarded command among the enabled guarded commands is nondeterministically selected to be fired. In general instead of atomic commands actions of any granularity are used, it follows that the execution model is typically based on the nondeterministic interleaving of enabled actions. In contrast, control oriented models can be viewed as refinements of data oriented models intended to model specific features of the real world. For instance, automata based languages are particularly adapted to the modeling of communication protocols. At each step, the local control state in each automata / process defines the set of enabled actions. The execution model then follows as before the same principle of nondeterministic interleaving of enabled actions. Detailed modeling of control is useful if related knowledge is available and relevant at a give stage of specification. This implies that the actual distribution of actions in the system is established as well as their relative sequencing within each process or automata. In ODP terms this implies that a significant part of the engineering viewpoint issues are fixed. A model of the actual distribution might be required if real time constraints are to be checked that typically depend on the parameters associated to the communications channels (e.g. network links) existing between the execution threads in the system. However, if one is only interested in the specification of functional issues, an engineering viewpoint model is absolutely not required. In fact this would overspecify the problem [7]. Therefore a behavior modeling framework, based on the declarative specification of actions, where control issues are specified minimally is more adapted for the purpose of functional modeling.

1.6   Dynamic Nature

Role Modeling   In contrast to interfaces that are object centric, behaviors are of collective nature [8]. This is a natural consequence of modeling application oriented issues where the contexts of utilization of objects has to reflect the application requirements. Within an object framework basic objects are typically composed to form composite objects or object configurations. Each object is intended to fulfill a well identified role in the configuration. The role can be used as an identifier for objects [15] involved in specification of behavior, but this identifier has a high level semantics value w.r.t. the application. In other words, a role represent a view of an object for a particular purpose or context of utilization. So roles, by capturing utilization contexts provide a suitable modeling abstraction to take into account application requirements. In addition, role modeling allows dynamic subtyping, which is as shown below a very important feature of distributed applications.

Subtyping A role defines a subtype for an object in the sense that an object fulfilling a role is still compatible with the core specification of the object itself, i.e. it still observes the interfaces defined on the core object. However, the behavior resulting from the interactions on such interfaces with other objects is defined w.r.t. the role. For instance specific state information may be associated to a role and updated according to the purpose of this role. In addition, in the behavior of an object in a given role interactions with other objects are specified using object references based on the role identifiers available in the object configuration, e.g. an object in the *client* role interacts with an object in the *server* role. So behavior gains to be promoted at the role subtype level. The advantages are that (i) much more expressive and readable behavior specifications are obtained, and (ii) core object are kept as simple as they are, i.e. most of the time limited to their mandatory interfaces and attributes.

Dynamic Subtyping The dynamic subtyping character of role modeling results merely from the fact that roles may be associated dynamically to objects. ODP states clearly that in a composite object, the association of a component object with a role may result from the actualization of a parameter [15]. An object can in fact play several roles, and this set can change over time according to its evolution in the distributed application. An important point is that a usual object oriented mechanisms such as (static) inheritance is clearly not satisfactory to model the different variants of an object just because these variants need to be dynamically available. Note that the set of roles fulfilled may have to be kept consistent. For instance an object is usually not allowed to play the *reviewer* and *reviewed* role at the same time. Such inconsistencies are not caused by role modeling, they merely reflect properties of real life systems. Interestingly, role modeling provides very expressive means to specify such constraints. This has typically been used to model and analyze management policy conflicts [10].

1.7 Relationships

The concept of relationship follows directly from the need to model configuration of objects. However, this is only one way to do so, and in fact some authors prefer not to use relationships because they want to keep the emphasis on roles. A typical example is the *role model collaboration view* of the object oriented role analysis and modeling (OOram) software engineering method [14]. One problem with relationships is that they are often used for other purposes such as graph modeling and navigation on object graphs. Though relationships is an overloaded concept, in the context of TMN applications it turns out that the generic relationship model (GRM) [5] is suitable to define roles for the purpose of dynamic subtyping. Note that as in [4] only GRM templates related to information modeling viewpoint issues are used. The computational viewpoint issues in GRM are not usable as such. For instance relationship operation mappings can not be defined precisely using GRM. In addition they are defined only using CMIS services.

2 Validation Framework

Validation of a specification consists to check the correspondence between informal requirements and the formal specification. Three techniques are commonly used :

1. *inspection* consists merely for the people involved to cross-read their respective specifications.
2. *reasoning* consists to prove properties about a specification.
3. *execution* proceeds by executing series of tests and by observing their outcome.

Though inspection is a technique that can always be used because it is always possible, it suffers from severe limitations because it is a manual process directly limited by the capacities of humans. In contrast execution and reasoning provide some assistance for validation. However, in the end the quality of the validation depends only on the relevance of either the executed test cases or the properties that were proved. So in both cases all depends on the users involved in the validation process. Execution and reasoning have been opposed for ages. Executable specifications are often qualified as less abstract and less expressive that non-executable ones. In addition, it has also been argued [6] that, though executing individual test cases is useful, it is less powerful than proving more general properties. However, with declarative specifications it can be shown [3] that a comparable level of abstraction and expressiveness can be obtained. In addition, executable specifications are much more prone to the involvement of users. They allow a direct *touch-and-fell* approach about the features of a system. This provides an excellent communication vehicle between users, specifiers and developers. In contrast reasoning has not yet reached a satisfactory level of usability, because theorem provers still need intelligent indications from users to achieve complex proofs. Even then other important issues are the manageability, the presentation... of such proofs, which is still a difficult problem in the currently available tools. Note that to allow for the executability of declarative specifications of actions a precise execution semantics based on the nondeterministic interleaving of the execution of actions has been devised.

3 Conclusion

By deliberately limiting our ambitions to the specification and validation of functional behavior properties, we have come up to a behavior model particularly adapted to information and computational viewpoint modeling. The declarative specification of actions is intrinsically nondeterministic. Thus there is no problem to model nondeterminism, which is a basic feature of distributed applications. Another important feature of distributed applications is their dynamic nature. To this end it has been shown how roles provide a powerful information modeling abstraction to capture application oriented requirements. Roles define object subtypes dynamically available, object configurations and behavior labels, all that being directly linked to high level application issues. Finally, validation is based on the principle of executable specifications. This is a pragmatic approach that has been felt more usable than reasoning. The resulting behavior model is "good" because it allows to model the intended distributed application features, moreover it is reasonably usable for distributed application domain experts such as telecom engineers both in terms of specification and validation.

References

1. E. W. Dijkstra. *A Discipline of Programming*. Prentice-Hall, 1976.

2. J-C. Fernandez, H. Garavel, A. Kerbrat, R. Mateescu, L. Mounier, and M. Sighireanu. Cadp (cæsar/aldebaran development package): A protocol validation and verification toolbox. In *CAV*, 1996.

3. Norbert E. Fuchs. Specifications are (preferably) executable. Technical Report 92, University of Zurich (CS Dept.), 1992. Available at ftp://ftp.ifi.unizh.ch/pub/techreports/.

4. Management of the Transport Network – Application of the ODP Framework, ITU-T G851-01, 1996.

5. ISO/IEC JTC 1/SC 21, ITU X.725 : General Relationship Model.

6. I.J. Hayes and Jones C.B. Specifications are not (necessarily) executable. Technical Report 90-148, University of Manchester, 1990. Available at ftp://ftp.cs.man.ac.uk.

7. H. Jarvinen and R. Kurki-Suonio. DisCo Specification Language: Marriage of Action and Objects. In *Int. Conf. on Distributed Computing Systems*, 1991. Available at www.cs.tut.fi.

8. H. Kilov, H. Mogill, and I. Simmonds. *Invariants in the Trenches in Object Oriented Behavior Specifications*, pages 77–100. Kluwer, 1996.

9. LOTOS : A Formal Description Technique based on the Temporal Ordering of Observable Behaviour, ISO / IEC 8807, 1987.

10. Emil Lupu and Morris Sloman. Conflict Analysis for Management Policies. In *Integrated Network Management*, 1997. available at ftp://dse.doc.ic.ac.uk.

11. Ensembles: Concepts and Format, 1992. Network Mangement Forum.

12. Common Object Request Broker Architecture, 1996. Available at http://www.omg.org.

13. The OSI Systems Management Standards, ITU-T X.7xx Documents.

14. Trygve Reenskaug. *Working with Objects : The OOram Software Engineering Method*. Manning Publications, 1996.

15. Basic Reference Model of ODP – Part 2: Foundations, ISO 10746-2, ITU X.902.

16. C. C. I. T. T. Functional Specifications and Description Language (SDL). Rec. z.100-z.104, Geneva, 1984.

17. Bryan Wood. Draft green paper on "object model for services", 1997.

The Formalization and Simulation of a Network Management Model

Jorge L. Tellez Portas[1] **& David Watrin**
Institut National des Télécommunications
Tel : (33) (1) 60-76-47-25
[tellez, watrin]@int-evry.fr

Tayeb Ben Meriem
France Telecom
Tel : (33) (1) 44-44-27-54
tayeb.benmeriem@francetelecom.fr

Abstract

The actual standards used in network management to represent managed equipment or networks are not totally satisfying. To solve this problem we propose a new FDT, the B method. We believe that B method has advantages over its counterparts and will bring new ideas on subjects such as ODP concepts. To confirm our assertions, we have tested this method on a real case study, the management of a WDM network based on the TMN.

Keywords

Network management, behaviour formalization, B method, TMN, ODP, WDM

1. Introduction

GDMO is the standard used in network management to represent managed equipment or networks. It is well established but it is not totally satisfying, since the specification process is still ambiguous. The identification of this problem is not new and many solutions have been advanced. In such a context, we propose a new FDT, the B[10] method. Indeed we believe that B method has advantages on its counterparts and in any case, it will bring new ideas on the subject such as its conformance to ODP concepts. Moreover, we use different tools that allow us to reduce significantly the amount of work to be done. To confirm the use of B method as a FDT for network management, we have tested this method on a real case study.

2. The purpose of formalization

2.1 The OSI Management Model Ambiguities

GDMO is a widely used standard in the industrial and normative world. However the people involved in the specification process are not totally satisfied with GDMO because it is only a semi-formal language.

This characteristic appears in the behaviour template that is used in six templates over the nine defined by GDMO. The three main problems consist of:

- The use of natural language (English). It introduces several interpretation ambiguities at the moment of code development.

---

[1] Supported by a grant from the Mexican National Council for Science and Technology (CONACYT)

- Non standardized behaviour field content. Sometimes it deals more with a description of the class rather than a description of a behaviour.
- Non standardized placement of the behaviour description. It can be filled in several templates and depends on the logic of each modeler. For instance, let us consider a parameter defined in an action. Some people would fill the behaviour description in the MOC[2] template, others in the action template and others in the parameter template. In such context, it is very hard to find the needed information, and once again the global behaviour interpretation depends on the programmer expertise.

To understand the importance of the formalization behaviour, we can point out some of the major advantages using FDT. Formal system modeling is closer to the real world. Moreover, these methods present rigorous languages, mainly based on first order predicate logic. Once the formal specification is written, there is no possibility of misinterpretation since these methods offer proof mechanisms which enable to verify that further development stages are consistent with the previous ones. Thus, it allows a better understanding of the specifications before beginning the development stage. In consequence, this improves the test scope and the reliability in the model.

2.2 Investigated Solutions

The main solutions to this problem are based on FDTs, such as: the Z formal notation[7] supported by the SG15 of the ITU-T based on the translation of the GDMO specification to Z; LOBSTERS[13] of the INRIA based on IBM's CRS; the TIMS[3] platform of the Eurecom Institute based on Scheme and dedicated to the information point of view; and SDL[5,8,12]. SDL is the most widespread FDT in telecommunications. However, the finite state machines concept does not really fit to object models. Even the latest version of SDL[3] does not support multiple inheritance, moreover the SDL frontier between specification and executable code is not very clear.

As another example, we have GDMO+ [9] that is not based on an FDT. It is aimed to be an extension of GDMO, defining new templates dedicated to the behaviour. GDMO+ is also already engaged in a standardization process. Nevertheless we believe that it is too much dedicated to CMIP which is not in the ODP spirit, concerning the independence of the different viewpoints, i.e. information and engineering.

To our knowledge, none of these approaches really gives a totally satisfying solution. We may be tempted to give up GDMO for a more rigorous language. This solution is not very good because it does not take into account the great amount of

---

[2] Managed Object Class
[3] SDL'92 which is object oriented

work already done in GDMO. Another idea is the translation of all GDMO models in certain formalism but this is not cost effective since it is a purely manual task. Under the circumstances, we believe that the best approach is to integrate a formalization of the behaviour in the GDMO models using B method.

3. Why B?

3.1 From Z to B

As previously mentioned, various solutions based on Z have been explored [7,13]. Z is a FDT based on the first order predicate logic which offers great possibilities of abstraction. However Z has an important problem that lies in the absence of tools producing a machine executable code.

At this stage, B method can be helpful. B is the natural continuation of Z. Both formalisms have been originated by the same person: Jean Raymond Abrial[10]; and they share practically the same mathematical language; It is mainly the language structures and their manipulation that differ: Z uses the scheme concept and B the abstract machine one. Moreover, the weakness of B holds in the fact that it is not yet standardized, but it should be in the next two years. Indeed, it benefits from the BUG[4][4] dynamism, and most of all from the support of various industrials such as British Petroleum, Matra, French Metro & Railways, Aerospatiale, GEC-Alsthom, and GEC Marconi Avionics Ltd.

3.2 Executable code production

The B refinement technique enables to progressively determine the different choices of implementation during the specification stages. This is achieved thanks to the formal proof concept that assures whether the concrete specification really performs what was first specified in the abstract one. The concrete specification can be automatically translated into machine executable code. This ends with the ambiguity problem that arises during the code development. These concepts are implemented in industrial tool like the *atelier B*[3], developed by Steria Méditerranée, that produces C or ADA executable code and has been used in large industrial projects such as the development of METEOR[5][] security systems.

4. Our strategy to validate the use of B

In order to validate the use of B we will analyze a real system that we are currently developing at our TMN laboratory.

The B method offers the possibility to specify the whole model. But, as we said before, we should only concentrate our efforts on the GDMO behaviour template formalization.

---

[4] B user group
[5] An new all-automatic underground line in Paris

4.1 Specification of a WDM model based on TMN and ODP

WDM[6] is an optical technology based on the multiplexing of various wavelengths over the same medium. This new layer is complementary to the SDH[7] transport layer, and will increase the capacity of the transport network, providing higher network flexibility and additional capacities in terms of routing, reconfiguration and protection. Thanks to new equipment such as the OADM[8] we can insert or extract a chosen wavelength from SDH ring networks. The WDM networks and equipment remain experimental and thus, there is not yet any standardized management model available today. Our mission is to define a new model based on TMN standards and ODP principles in order to manage SDH coloured sections rings[1,2]. Our functional model is based on the ITU-T G.805 and G.681 functional architecture that divides the WDM the optical network into three client-server layers optical channel(oCH), optical multiplex section(oM) and optical amplifier section(oA). Thus, our information model is a specialization of the ITU-T M.3100 model. To illustrate our WDM network management model, *figure 1* shows the whole inheritance tree.

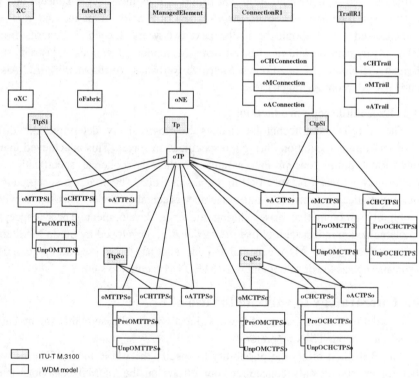

Figure 1. WDM model inheritance tree

---

[6] Wavelength Division Multiplexing
[7] Synchronous Digital Hierarchy
[8] Optical Add/Drop Multiplexer

The B machine representing the behaviour of the optical fabric class is shown in *figure 2*.

```
MACHINE
    OFABRIC
SEES
    STATES, CONNECT, DISCONNECT, CTPPROTECTED
INCLUDES
    Ctp.CTPPROTECTED ...
OPERATIONS
    CriticalAlarmTreatment(Ctp)
    PRE    (Ctp ∈ Ctpprotected)∧ severity⁻¹ (Ctp) = critical∧ OperationalState(Ctp) =
    Disabled ∧ OperationalState(Ctp.protectedby) = Enabled ∧ AdministrativeState
    (Ctp.protectedby) = unlocked∧
    THEN ANY
    OXCprotection
    WHERE
    OXCprotection ∈ OXCinstanciated
    THEN
    aCTp = Ctp.protectedby || OXCid = Ctp.pointerOXC || zCTp
    =Ctp.connectivitypointer || Odisconnect(OXCid) ||
    Connect(aCtp,OXCprotection,zCtp)
END
```

Figure 2. Optical fabric objet specification in B

4.2 Simulation

We simulated an experimental SDH/WDM ring with three OADM. To reach this goal, we use the tool NEMOT.X[12]. It simulates the managing part as specified in the TMN NML[9]. At this level, it knows the WDM network components and topology, at the agent level, it simulates the three agents and their respective MIBs as specified by the TMN NEML[10]. These MIBs evolve independently according to TTCN[6] scenario.

The abstract machine of the MOC optical fabric(oFabric) is shown in *figure 2*. This machine is part of the scenario that simulates the agent and manager levels, the establishment of a connection, followed by a link breakdown and the triggered corrective actions. The manager, who has a global network vision, sends a connection request between the nodes A and Z linked by the wavelength $\lambda 1$. The agents receive a connection indication and execute it, modifying the attributes of their MIBs corresponding to the A-Z link connection. When the operation is achieved, they send a response connection to the manager and wait for any new event or problem in the network or in the equipment. The manager receives the connection confirmation and waits for any event or any other request from the agents or the upper-level network manager.

A link breakdown is simulated by changing the MIB attributes that trigger the Loss of Signal (LOS) notification. When the agent detects the *LOS*, it decides to send an *event-report* to the manager. Since it is a critical error, the manager decides to send a *protection-node-request* to the agent. The agent executes it and sends the response to the manager. This last request means that the agent has to consider the signal that

---

[9] Network Management Level
[10] Network Element Management Level

goes through the protection path. This is done by the MO[11] oFabric[12] of the node Z that destroys the normal connection object oXC[13], and creates a new oXC that links the protection path taking into account the final destination of the signal.

5. Conclusion

This work is not finished yet, since we still have to validate an architecture for a distributed behaviour integration, identifying what really needs to be formalized. Then, we will have to find out how to improve our TTCN tests. For instance, we can determine the optimal behaviour from one MIB state to another in a distributed environment.

At the present time, thanks to the different B method refinement levels, we can take into account the behaviour along the different development viewpoints, like it is done in ODP. This improves significantly the model reliability, scalability and reusability. Moreover, the great amount of research done on Object-Oriented B and Distributed-B methods let us envision new horizons. The major problem that we have to face now is that B method data structure doesn't cover the whole ASN.1 range and that data handling with write permission is not directly possible in all contexts, thus sometimes we can not have direct solutions.

References

[1] A. Hamel, V. Troley, A. Sutter, D. Laville, J. Stoschek et P. Lann. *First results of an experimental Coloured Section Ring*. ECOC'96, September 15-19, 1996.
[2] A. Hamel, V. Troley, A. Sutter, L. Blain, et F. Chatter. *Increased capacity in a MS protection ring using WDM technique and OADM : "The coloured section ring"*. Electronic Letters, 1st. February 1996 Vol. 32 N 3 pp234-235.
[3] Atelier B from Steria Méditerranée. Http://www.atelierb.societe.com
[4] B. Mermet, *Spécification de services et gestion des interactions*, Lettre B, Publication Steria Méditerranée, April 97
[5] D. Sidou, S. Mazziotta, R. Eberhardt, TIMS: a TMN-based Information Model Simulator, Principles and Applications to a Simple Case Study. http://www.eurecom.fr/~sidou/
[6] ISO 9646-3. Tree and tabular Combined Notation.
[7] ISO/IEC JTC1/SC21 N 9982, Liaison Statement to ITU-T Question 30/SG15 Concerning the Use of Formal Techniques for the Specification of Managed Object Behaviour, November 1995
[8] ITU-T Recommendation Z.100 SDL Specification and Description Language
[9] J. Keller. An extension of GDMO for formalising Managed Object Behaviour, CNET Lannion, 1995.
[10] J.-R. Abrial. *The B-Book: Assigning Programs to Meanings*, Cambridge University Press, 1996. ISBN 0-521-49619-5.
[11] L. Andrey, O. Festor, E. Nataf, A. Schaff et S. Tata. *Validation des bases d'information de gestion. Experience multi-FDT sur un modèle de gestion configuration d'interconnexion des commutateurs*
[12] NEtwork Manager Object Tester. Http://www.semagroup.com
[13] O. Festor , Formalisation du comportement des objets gérés dans le cadre du modèle OSI. PhD Thesis, Université Henri Poincare, Nancy I, Centre de Recherche en Informatique de Nancy (CRIN), octobre 94.
[14] S. Traverson, Methodological guidelines for B formal method. PhD Thesis, Ecole Nationale Supérieure des Télécommunications, Paris France, July 11 1997.

---

[11] Managed Object

[12] Optical Fabric

[13] Optical Cross Connect

OST - An Object-Oriented Computer Networks System Specification Tool

Lisandro Granville   Luciano Gaspary   Janilce Almeida

Universidade Federal do Rio Grande do Sul - UFRGS
Instituto de Informática
Pós-Graduação em Ciência da Computação - CPGCC
Campus do Vale, Bloco IV - Bento Gonçalves, 9500 - Agronomia - CEP 91591-970
Porto Alegre, RS - Brasil
E-mail: {granvile, paschoal, janilce}@inf.ufrgs.br

Abstract

With the purpose of lessening the software production efforts in computer networks area, the use of tools that help the system specification and implementation process is needed. This work presents a development tool based on the NSOMA methodology, intended to help the designers in the formal definition of specifications. It is composed of a graphical editor, an animation module that allows the visualization of specification dynamic behavior and a source code automatic generating module.

Key Words: computer networks, specification tool, NSOMA, object-orientation, animation, source code generation.

1 Introduction

The use of tools for developing software is currently a fact, due to advantages such as reduced production time and easy system maintenance, documentation and expansion. The use of a number of features available for each tool provides help for the various stages of software developing.

There are many system specification and implementation environments designed for computer networks. Most designers, though, still use primitive, user-unfriendly methodology, as these environments are usually based on complex *Formal Description Techniques* (FDTs) [COH86]. An *Object-Oriented Specification Tool* (OST) has been developed at Universidade Federal do Rio Grande do Sul bearing this difficulty in mind. OST associates a modeling and developing methodology to a formal specification technique. This tool allows better comprehension and organization of the system components and thus becomes a very efficient way to produce easy-to-use tools regardless of the programming language they are based on, which are only a few and mastered by few designers.

OST is based on the *Network System Object Modeling Approach* (NSOMA) (see item 2 below), integrating object-orientation concepts to SDL (*Specification and Description Language*). OST is composed of three modules: a *graphic editor*, which allows creating and editing a specification from NSOMA's graphic grammar, an *animation module*, which provides instruments to visualize the dynamic behavior of the specifications, and an *automatic source code generator*. These modules are presented in items 3, 4 and 5, respectively.

2 Network System Object Modeling Approach (NSOMA)

The goal of NSOMA is to make SDL easier to use, associating it to the object-orientation paradigm under the *Object Modeling Technique* (OMT) method [ALM94] [RUM91]. As the human mind can see the world as a series of inter-related objects, the use of this concept furthers comprehension. Thus, the real world is brought closer to the computing world. It also allows the possibility of reusing previously developed entities in the creation of new software.

Because NSOMA specifications are hierarchically defined, this approach is broken into three specification levels. These levels allow the designers to start from a more abstract level and then refine their specification, bringing it closer to the implementation.

The following are NSOMA specification levels:

• *Abstract structural level*: at this level, classes' behavior and relations are determined.

• *Detailed structural level*: at this level, each class' behavior is determined. Ports, internal signals, attributes and operations are defined.

• *Operation level*: at this level, each previously defined operation is detailed.

The abstract structural level description is based on OMT concepts. It allows the definition of highly abstract classes that form a network system and the relations between them. Their corresponding objects represent elements of a network system - protocols, functions, services, entities. These classes are described and identified by their type, name, attributes and operations.

A class can be defined from another's definition. In such case, one says the first *inherits* from the second and calls it a subclass, which may inherit attributes and operations from the parent class totally or partially. In addition, a class can be defined as a combination of other classes, though preventing the latter from inheriting attributes or operations from the former. A class can inherit classes that were defined by combination. In such case, the subclass inherits all classes that compose the parent class.

The detailed structural level is where attributes, operations and internal signals are actually defined for a given class. Every class modeled at the abstract structural level is refined at the detailed structural level. The internal signals allow communication between operations of the same class. They can be synchronous or asynchronous.

Ports and external signals supply communication between elements of different classes. It can also be synchronous or asynchronous. Communication is considered synchronous when the source operation enters a hold state for a response signal, thus being blocked indefinitely, whereas asynchronous communication does not hold and therefore is not blocked. External signals are defined outside classes' behavior, which allows their further individual use.

The operation level allows every previously defined operation to have its behavior diagramed, thus determining the system's control flux. Hierarchically, it is the closest level to implementation and it is strongly based on SDL. Graphically, this level is described by diagrams that represent a state machine of the operations.

3 The Graphic Editor

This editor implements all functions necessary to system specification in NSOMA. The software uses NSOMA's graphic syntax to help the user interact more naturally. Specifications are created through the manipulation of the graphic grammar [GAS95]

[GRA95]. The textual approach is not neglected, though, allowing the user to textually visualize the specifications being built.

The editor was built according to an object-oriented programming approach. The basic classes that were implemented can be divided into two separate groups, database class and graphic class. The database classes (*Data_ob*) are responsible for the semantic consistency of a given specification. Each new element added to the diagram is actually a database object. If it cannot be created, some database rule violation can be assumed. Further information on how database elements interrelate to keep specification consistency can be found in [GAS95] [GRA95].

On the other hand, the graphic classes are responsible for the implementation of all graphic functionality. There are basically a window class (*TDragDropWindow*) and a graphic object class (*TShape*). These two primitive classes work together to implement drag-and-drop and multiple selection functions, among others. Window classes for each specification level were derived from *TDragDropWindow*. All graphic symbols used in the editor were derived from *TShape*.

The basic classes are divided into two separate groups for the sake of comprehension. Actually, there is high interaction between the two groups. In fact, any graphic element is a database object and a graphic object at the same time. It must be consistent to its specification as well as have all the necessary graphic functionality. The basic classes, in their turn, are also derived from a library set (OWL, which accompanies Borland C++).

4 Animation Module

The animation of a system's dynamic behavior is a basic need to its definition and specification [ALL95]. It fosters the understanding of the description being specified, translated as reduced construction cycles since a number of problems can be verified during the early development stages [VER94]. OST provides an environment to visualize animation, in addition to plenty of statistic data and some deadlock-detection facilities. This kind of functionality can be found in verification systems.

The animation was implemented using, basically, symbols from the operational level and operation representation structure [GAS96]. The animation controls were implemented in two new classes called *AnimOL_Sym* and *AnimOperation*, which relate to the editor's structure. *AnimOL_Sym* associates every animation-relevant symbol to a count variable, in order to provide statistics on the use of this symbol. Also, it has a drawing method for the symbol being run, so that it can be highlighted. *AnimOperation* implements an input signal queue for each operation, which keeps the signals from being lost. Using the same pattern as for symbols at the operational level, a drawing method for the highlighted operation symbol should follow.

OST's animation provides the following operations: *Start, Next Step, Previous Step, Auto, Next Stop* and *Stats* [EIJ88]. These operations enable a larger and clearer view of the specification being developed. Furthermore, the user can assess specific situations and decide if they perform as expected.

5 Code Generator

The language hierarchy provides instruments for automatic code generation [FRÖ93]. The classes defined at the abstract structural level are mapped to C++ classes.

Each defined class is coded in a separate module, containing the definition of the operations and attributes that are converted, respectively, into functions and variables.

When a class is initialized, each operation is run as a process and its descriptor is stored as an internal attribute to the class, like user-defined attributes. The ports, in their turn, become the methods visible externally to the class. Each method receives messages from external operations to the class and forwards them to their corresponding destiny processes.

6 Conclusions

OST is a very powerful specification tool. It provides any users, either computer networks programmers or information systems designers, with a tool based on a standard FDT, such as SDL, and then improves this tool using an object-oriented paradigm, which is known as a potential productivity booster in software development.

The many modules that form OST offer a more efficient way to specify systems. Its editor allows the creation of a specification using NSOMA's graphic grammar, furthering comprehension and interaction. OST's on-line syntax check avoids user errors. In addition, classes can be reused, which makes the construction process ever evolving, incremental, fast and efficient. Under the computer networks area jargon, classes can represent the basic concepts of model, layer, protocol, service and entity.

OST's animation feature increases comprehension of the systems developed. This is fundamental for a software developing team where a single and clear idea of what is being done is a must. Also, errors associated to the dynamic behavior of the specification (deadlocks and livelocks, for instance) can be detected. Furthermore, automatic code generation avoids the manual codification of a whole system. Consequently, the source code is free of lexical and syntactical errors.

OST can be further expanded, including specification verification and validation mechanisms that will assure even better correctness. Even though the editor is syntax-oriented, no lexical consistency is performed. This reflects on source code generation, which becomes undesirably linked to errors from the specification stage. Such lexical consistency is also to be included in future expansions.

Bibliography

[ALM94]   Almeida, Maria Janilce. *Especificação de sistemas na área de redes de computadores: uma abordagem orientada a objetos*. Porto Alegre: UFRGS, 1994. (tese de doutorado).

[ALL95]   Allende, Jesús Sánchez. *GLAv2.0 - Graphical Animation for LOTOS - Quick reference*. Technical University of Madrid. Spain, 1994.

[COH86]   Cohen, B. et al. *The Specification of Complex Systems*. Great Britain: Addyson Wesley, 1986.

[EIJ88]   van Eijk, Peter Herman Johan. *Software tools for the specification language LOTOS*. Twente University, 1988.

[FRÖ93]   Fröberg, M. W. *Automatic Code Generation from SDL to a Declarative Programming Language*. Proceedings of SDL Forum, 1993.

[GAS95]   Gaspary, Luciano Paschoal. *Editor gráfico do nível operacional do SDL OO*. Porto Alegre: UFRGS, 1995. (trabalho de diplomação).

[GAS96]   Gaspary, Luciano Paschoal. *Estudo de Simulação e Animação em Ambientes de Especificação de Redes*. PortoAlegre: UFRGS,1996. (trabalho individual)

[GRA95]   Granville, Lisandro Zambenedetti. *Editor gráfico dos níveis estrutural abstrato e estrutural detalhado do SDL OO*. Porto Alegre: UFRGS, 1995. (trabalho de diplomação).

[RUM91]   Rumbaugh, James. *Object-oriented modeling and design*. New Jersey: Prentice-Hall-Englewood Cliffs, 1991.

[VER94]   Verilog Corporation. Geode - *Technical Presentation. Preliminary Version*. July, 1994.

Experiences in Telecommunications Protocols with an OO Based Implementation Framework

Jarmo Harju [a], Bilhanan Silverajan [b], Ilkka Toivanen [b]

[a] Dept. of Information Technology, Tampere University of Technology,
P.O. Box 553, FIN-33101 Tampere, Finland
email: harju@cs.tut.fi

[b] Dept. of Information Technology, Lappeenranta University of Technology,
P.O. Box 20, FIN-53851 Lappeenranta, Finland
email: {bilhanan I toivanen}@lut.fi

Abstract: In this paper, an object oriented development environment, OVOPS, for protocol implementation is described. Object oriented tools have been gaining ground quite slowly in the field of protocol engineering. By providing special support for this particular branch of software engineering in the form of an implementation framework, together with a class library, the deployment of new techniques can be made easier. Description of the use of OVOPS to implement 2 non-trivial protocol stacks (TCAP and GSM BTS protocols) illustrates the methods and practices available in this environment.

Keywords: protocol engineering, software tools, protocol implementation

1. Introduction

The concept of a layered protocol architecture has had a significant influence on communications software structure by increasing modularity and forcing designers to use clean interfaces between the modules. Currently protocol standards contain both the specification of abstract service interfaces and the specification of the protocol itself. Yet, the communications software products resulting from the multi-layer specifications are large and complex, and modularity achieved by applying traditional methods of structured programming in the layered protocol architecture has been considered insufficient. To ease the deployment of object oriented methods in protocol engineering, an object oriented framework for implementing protocol software is described in this paper. Experiences and details about an application of this framework to implement 2 protocol stacks including the TCAP (Transaction Capabilities Application Part) and the GSM BTS (Base Transceiver System) protocols are also reported.

2. OVOPS

OVOPS [1] supports the design, implementation and prototyping of protocols and distributed applications by providing an object oriented framework with class libraries and tools, that are often needed in the development of communications software. The basic structure of OVOPS is described in Fig. 1. With OVOPS, implementations can be made largely independent of the operating system so that they can be ported to any system supported by OVOPS.

In short, the basic services and tools provided by OVOPS libraries include:
- scheduling of OVOPS tasks either with the default or user implemented scheduler
- asynchronous message passing between tasks through the usage of port classes
- I/O handler, interfaces to devices and other operating system services
- graphical and textual protocol tracers for message tracing and debugging
- hierarchical symbol interface to support user interactions in a symbolic form
- efficient, flexible and controllable memory management
- timers, frames and other useful classes.

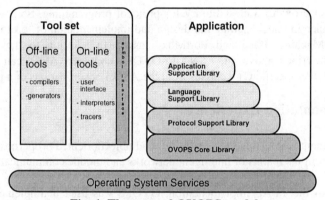

Fig. 1. The general OVOPS model

Above the core library there are specific services for protocol engineering, described in more detail in Section 3. Support for specification languages can be built on top of these levels, as there is no built-in high-level specification method implied by OVOPS. Experiments with the integration of Kannel language [2] to OVOPS have been reported in [3]. On the topmost level OVOPS provides support for the development of distributed applications via the component library containing protocol modules that can be used by applications.

3. Protocol support library

The three important parts in any protocol specification are the service definitions described by a set of primitives, the definition of the PDUs used to communicate with the peer entity, and the functionality with which the protocol behaves and responds to each event (arrival of a service primitive or PDU, timer expiration). The service access point (SAP) defines the primitives of the protocol as well as the user and provider interfaces for the passing of primitives.

The OVOPS Protocol Toolbox (PTB) supplies code generators to produce OVOPS specific C++ code from a set of specifications, which are the following [4]:

- SAP definition. The service access points are described and compiled into class libraries for utilisation of protocol layers.

- PDU definition. The protocol data units of the layer are described and declarations of the PDU classes with necessary data structures are generated.

- State machine definition. The structure of the state machine of a protocol is described and the state machine class for executing the corresponding handling functions is generated. Description at this level is rather simple, leaving the details of the actions to be carried out by the handling functions, which are manually coded in C++.

The PTB also provides a class library for protocol programming. Some classes that bear importance in understanding the design and implementation of protocols are the Ptask, StateMachine, Iface and PortMux classes. In addition to the three code generators described above, an ASN.1-to-OVOPS compiler, ACO, can be used to generate OVOPS specific C++ classes from the ASN.1 specifications of a protocol.

4. Implementation Experiences

The environments for testing the capabilities and object oriented properties of OVOPS were taken from the realms of intelligent networks and mobile communications.

In the case of the TCAP implementation, OVOPS was used to implement the core elements of a service control point (SCP): the SCCP layer to provide connections to service switching points (SSP), TCAP protocol for transporting the application layer messages between the SCP and SSP and an INAP multiplexer to take care of forwarding incoming INAP requests to proper service logic programs (SLP) and multiplexing responses to use the common TCAP service. The SSP simulator and the SLPs were provided as external elements, and the peer entities of INAP, TCAP and SCCP protocols at the SSP simulator were provided by a non-OVOPS based commercial software. For simplicity, TCP/IP sockets were used to connect the SCP process and the SSP simulator below the SCCP layer, instead of the SS7 message transfer protocols (MTP 1 - 3) as shown in Fig. 2.

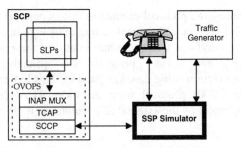

Fig. 2. First environment for the test implementation

In the case of the GSM BTS implementation [5], OVOPS was used to implement the core elements of the BTS protocol stack: for simplicity, drivers working at the Physical layer provide TCP/IP socket connections and communications with non-OVOPS MS (Mobile Station) and BSC (Base Station Controller) simulators, while the upper layers provide logical signalling channels (LAPDm and LAPD), connection radio resources (RR'), and handling of signalling transfer between the BTS and the BSC (BTSM), as shown in Fig. 3.

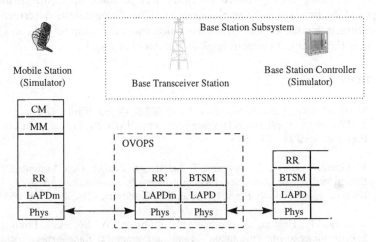

Fig. 3 Second environment for test implementation

The aim of the implementations can be summarised as follows:
- test thoroughly the protocol toolbox (PTB)
- evaluate the ASN.1 class library and the ASN.1 compiler (ACO)
- evaluate buffering techniques of OVOPS
- evaluate multiplexing and multiple connection handling facilities
- apply the OO paradigm to protocol development.

Bearing the last item in mind, the design decisions reflected here largely arise from undertaking an object oriented approach during the analysis and design phases of the project. The study of how the protocol could be designed with 'object orientedness' was favoured over making the protocol execute as fast as possible. Thus, the protocol stack and the individual protocols were broken into units high in cohesion and low in coupling. Well defined interfaces were introduced between these units. Encapsulation was used effectively, and a key principle for managing complexity was communication and interaction using message passing. This has an important impact, e.g., in updating the TCAP protocol from the older TCAP'88 [6] specification (mandated in this experiment by the external SSP simulator) to the newer TCAP'92.

5. Conclusion

OVOPS provides a framework and a set of tools for object oriented implementations of protocols and distributed applications in general. Class libraries facilitated the reuse of elements typically utilised in protocol engineering, and a wide selection of tools assisted the protocol engineer in routine work. Off-line tools including code generators for building interfaces, PDUs and state machines were beneficial in the implementation of the protocol stacks. On-line tools such as textual and graphical protocol tracers work in the higher level of abstraction as compared to the C++ debugger, and hence they provided an easier way to catch up errors in the early prototypes of the protocol stack implementations The thorough tests described in this paper confirmed that the OVOPS implementation framework can provide an efficient environment for the object oriented implementation of protocols.

References

[1]   Martikainen O., Puro P., Sonninen J.: 'OVOPS, Object Virtual Operations System for Distributed Applications Development'. *Proc. INDC 94,* Funchal, Madeira Island, Portugal, April 18 - 21, 1994.

[2]   K. Granö, J. Harju, T. Järvinen, T. Larikka, J. Paakki: Object-oriented Protocol Design and Reuse in Kannel. Proc. Euromicro 95, Como, Italy, Sept. 4 -7, 1995. IEEE Computer Society Press, Los Alamitos, California, USA, 1995, pp. 465 - 472.

[3]   J. Harju, P. Heinilä, T. Kotonen, J. Kuittinen, A. Sopanen: From protocol Specifications to implementation - combining graphical Kannel-specifications with the OVOPS implementations framework. Proc. of the INDC'96, Trondheim, Norway, June 17 - 19, 1996 Chapman & Hall, London, 1996, pp. 101 - 116.

[4]   J. Harju, B.Silverajan: OVOPS - an Object Oriented Implementation Framework for Protocol Engineering. Proc. 9th Euromicro Workshop on Real-Time Systems, Toledo, Spain June 11 - 13, 1997. IEEE Computer Society Press, Los Alamitos, California, USA, 1997, pp178.

[5]   Toivanen, I: OVOPS GSM BTS Implementation v1, Lappeenranta University of Technology 1996. http://ovops.lut.fi/docs/

[6]   ITU: Recommendations Q771 - 775, Specifications of Signalling System No. 7. Blue Book, Geneva 1989.

Rapid Network Management Application Development

Luca Deri

IBM Zurich Research Laboratory, University of Berne[1]

Whereas the recent hardware innovations brought increasingly powerful computers to the market at constantly lower prices, the development cost and time of software applications has not decreased at all. In the field of network management, applications and tools are usually large, expensive and difficult to build and maintain, preventing their diffusion.

This paper proposes a new method for rapid application development based on tools developed by the author. Reducing development time, complexity and cost gives developers the chance to create their own management applications without having to be network management experts or highly skilled developers.

Keywords: Network Management, Rapid Application Development.

1. Introduction

Network management application development is usually considered a task for highly specialised developers. This is because developers must have the necessary skills in both network/system management and application development for a certain platform in order to fulfil this task. In case the application being developed has a graphical appearance, the developer should also be familiar with the windowing toolkit present on the target platform. If the application has to be ported on different platforms, aspects such as portability and performance must also be taken into account.

Quite often, network management platforms [IBM_TMN] offer facilities for application development. Developers can take advantage of class libraries or collections of routines which simplify the interaction with the managed resources and which allow them to exploit desired services provided by the management platform. Although this way to develop management applications is widespread, management platforms offer nearly no facilities for prototyping applications, nor provide a development environment that would allow the development process to be simplified. From another perspective the process of application development is even more complicated because developers create applications tightly coupled with a specific environment which cannot be run outside it. Additionally, management platforms are rather complex preventing them from being updated frequently and hence from keeping pace with the evolution of the computer world. For instance none of the best-selling management platforms have provided real facilities for developing Internet-aware[2] applications nor they have offered tools for developing applications capable of exploiting a distributed and mobile environment.

---

[1] Current affiliation: Finsiel S.p.A., Via Matteucci, Pisa, Italy. Email: l.deri@tecsiel.it.

[2] An Internet-aware application is such if it has an Internet visibility, i.e. if supports Internet protocols such as HTTP or Gopher.

The aim of this paper is to present a new method for building network management applications in a short amount of time and at low cost without having necessarily to rely on large management platforms. Some (class) libraries for network management have been developed in order to allow rapid application development (RAD) tools, such as IBM VisualAge™ or Borland Delphi™, to be used for network management application development which can run stand-alone or exploit the services of the corporate management system. This paper demonstrates that the creation of management applications is no longer a task for very skilled developers but that average programmers can build outstanding applications by exploiting the power of RAD tools which are now mature and widely available on the market for many platforms.

2. Rapid Application Development and Network Management

In the past few years one of the most frequently used terms in the software engineering field, and even in the network management field [Schmidt95], has become the word 'visual'. This term is often used to identify packages which allow a certain task to be performed efficiently and easily by visually performing a certain activity in an interactive way. Although this term has often been misused, it frequently refers to how rapidly applications can be built using a certain tool. This is because:
- visual development is interactive and hence faster than classic edit-compile-run application development: it allows one to immediately see the effects of a certain operation immediately without the need to build and run the application;
- visual tools are simpler to use and more powerful than traditional tools/languages, so average programmers can build very complex applications in a limited amount of time without having to be software gurus.

RAD tools provide a rich set of basic components ranging from visual interface to remote application communication. Quite often the component one needs has already been built by someone and put on a public repository. Although RAD is becoming increasingly important in the software industry, the network management world is apparently uninterested in this new technology probably because RAD is mainly diffused throughout the PC industry, whereas most of the network management applications run on UNIX boxes. Nevertheless the increasing use of PCs for everyday business that contributed to the replacement of many UNIX terminals and demonstrated that a graphical interface can quite often substitute the shell interface. The obvious consequence of this trend is that many old-fashioned character-based applications have acquired a graphical interface in order to be used not only by administrators but also by advanced end-users who need to control certain critical resources for their activity.

In conclusion, it is becoming necessary to rapidly and easily develop simple yet powerful management applications that run primarily on PCs, because:

- average end-users are accustomed to simple graphical user interfaces whilst administrators can still use the shell interface, which is more powerful and faster but more difficult to use;
- average developers must be able to develop and maintain the application their company needs without being experts of both PC application development and network management;
- mobile computing demands simple applications that can run from remote locations over slow links.

3. Rapid Management Application Development using Liaison

Webbin is a research project which aims to simplify the way network management is performed. Webbin is based on the idea that the complexity of protocols such as CMIP or SNMP has to be hidden by the system and that the users have to rely on the services provided by the system and to reuse them every time a new application has to be developed instead of replicating them (craftsman paradigm, i.e. everything has to be custom built for a certain task). The core element of Webbin is a software application called *Liaison*[3] [Deri96a], a proxy application [Shapiro86] which allows end-users to manage network resources through HTTP using CMIP [CMIP] and SNMP [SNMP], the two dominant network management protocols.

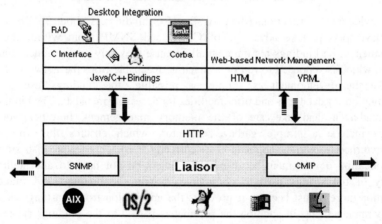

Fig. 1. Liaison's Overview

Liaison is written in C++ and allows client application to issue HTTP requests, which are translated into CMIP/SNMP protocol requests according to a defined mapping [Deri96b]. Although client applications communicate with Liaison using a

---

[3] A version available for public download can be found at http://www.alphaworks.ibm.com/.

standard network protocol, Liaison has been designed to be portable in order to facilitate its integration into an existing computing environment. Liaison is based on a special type of software component called *droplets* [Deri95], which can be added and replaced at runtime without having to stop the application. Each droplet provides one or more services which can be reused by other droplets. Among those services, Liaison includes droplets that allow CMIP/SNMP resources to be managed using HTML/VRML. Additionally Liaison provides the *External Bindings* (available in Java/C/C++) that communicate with further droplets by enabling programmers to develop decentralised management applications/applets [Meyer95] based on the services provided by Liaison. *C External Bindings* are used to glue Liaison with a RAD environment.

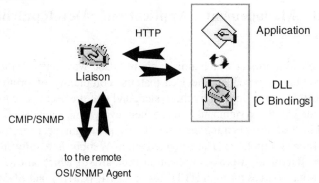

Fig. 2. Liaison's C External Bindings

They provide a set of functions (the total size of C bindings is about 30 Kbytes) that allow developers to take advantage of CMIP and SNMP from within the RAD environment. The bindings are quite small because they rely on the functionality of Liaison, which is supposed to run on a machine reachable from the network. In order to make the development as simple as possible, the bindings use a string representation for datatypes and offer facilities for accessing metadata. The bindings are multithread-aware and take care of the memory management. In other words the bindings include a simple garbage collector, which ensures that the strings passed/returned from/to the application are correctly freed. This feature also simplifies the application development because programmers do not have to allocate/free the memory of the strings used to communicate with the bindings and makes the application more robust because it prevents the application from crashing due to bad memory management. In addition the parameters passed to the bindings are carefully verified in order to eliminate the risk of crashing the entire application in case a bad value is passed to the bindings.

In order to demonstrate how easily and fast applications can be developed using RAD tools, an example is shown in the following figure.

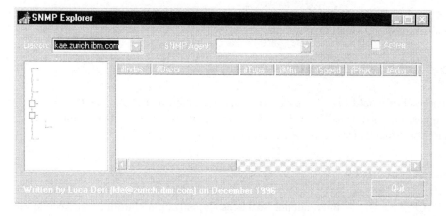

Fig. 3. Simple SNMP MIB Explorer

This simple SNMP MIB explorer allows one to manipulate the SNMP MIB of a remote host by exploiting the services of Liaison, which can run on a local or a remote host. Similar applications which support the CMIP protocol have been also developed by the author. This application has been written by an average programmer in a couple of hours and it has the look and feel of the operating system on which it runs. The same application written using different tools or a different language would have been much more difficult to write and it would have required a much more skilled programmer with deep knowledge of the underlying operating system.

The integration in the desktop environment has several advantages. Functions such as cut and past, move, drag and drop are immediately available at no extra cost and the application behaves and looks as any other application running on the same operating system. Additionally it is possible to script the application or to use it as building block for a more complex application.

4. Final Remarks

This work attempted to demonstrate that the development of management platform is no longer an expensive task requiring highly skilled programmers and that it can be used for generic application development employing appropriate tools able to mask the complexity of network management. The era in which "one management platform does everything" is about to end and will be replaced with one that enables developers to build needed management applications easily. This does not mean that large and powerful management platforms will disappear because these applications constitute the backbone of corporate management systems. It means that in the future, end-users will increasingly demand tools that allow them to write the applications they need, tuned to their environment instead of delegating this task to specialised and expensive developers. One of the reasons for the limited diffusion of management tools lies with the cost of the tools and their extreme complexity. This work is a small contribution towards the construction of simple and powerful network management tools that can be used by many people and not only by rich or large organisations but also by universities and small institutions.

5. Acknowledgments

The author would like to thank Eric Van Hengstum and Dieter Gantenbein for their suggestions and valuable discussions other than the users of *Webbin'* who have greatly stimulated with all their comments and suggestions.

6. References

[CMIP]   International Standards Organization, Information Technology - OSI, *Common Management Information Protocol (CMIP) - Part 1: Specification*, CCITT Recommendation X.711, ISO/IEC 9596-1, 1991.

[Deri95]   L. Deri, *Droplets: Breaking Monolithic Applications Apart*, IBM Research Report RZ 2799, September 1995.

[Deri96a]   L. Deri, *Network Management for the 90s*, Proceedings of ECOOP '96 Workshop on System and Network Management, Linz, Austria, July 1996.

[Deri96b]   L. Deri, *HTTP-based SNMP and CMIP Network Management*, Internet Draft, November 1996.

[IBM_TMN]   IBM Corporation, *IBM TMN Products for AIX: General Information, Release 2*, GC 31-8016-00, March 1996.

[Meyer95]   K. Meter, M. Erlinger, J. Betser, C. Sunshine, G. Goldszmidt and Y. Yemini *Decentralizing Control and Intelligence in Network Management*, Proceedings of Int. Symposium on Integrated Network Management, May 1995.

[Schmidt95]   *C. Schmidt and M. Sevcik,* Do-It-Yourself TMN Applications by Visual Programming Methods, *IEEE Communications Magazine, November 1995.*

[Shapiro86]   M. Shapiro, *Structure and Encapsulation in Distributed Systems: the Proxy Principle*, 6th Int. Conference on Distributed Computing Systems, Boston, Mass., May 1986.

[SNMP]   J. Case, M. Fedor, M. Schoffstall and C. Davin, *Simple Network Management Protocol (SNMP)*, RFC 1157, May 1990.

Real-Time Object-Oriented Distributed Processing with COREMO

Zièd Choukair & Antoine Beugnard

ENST de Bretagne
Département Informatique
Technopôle de l'Iroise
29285 Brest cedex France
Zied.Choukair,Antoine.Beugnard@enst-bretagne.fr

Abstract. This paper presents our COREMO (COrba Real-time Extension MOdel) model [2]. It aims to conciliate real-time with openness so that CORBA compliant applications will benefit from real-time concepts and reciprocally real-time application developers will take advantage of the CORBA concepts and facilities. We will introduce a real-time extension that will allow application developers to specify end-to-end temporal characteristics for their requests. COREMO objectives are to maximize the temporal previsibility of CORBA compliant applications and to improve their performance. Our model includes the definition of real-time policy behavior for servers so that the clients gain previsibility and time. We also recommend an associated framework for the development of distributed soft real-time components and for their utilization in the context of open systems.

The implementation we did of the model and the experimentations gave convincing results concerning the feasibility and the utility of such an extension. We will end this paper with a presentation of our planned research activities for the future. Those activities concern real-time and synchronization issues and target to improve the quality of service from the client's point of view.

1 Introduction

CORBA [4] (Common Object Request Broker Architecture) is a model released by the OMG (Object management Group). The OMG's aim was to provide a standard for interoperability between heterogeneous objects. The underlying concepts are distribution and heterogeneity transparency. CORBA is a kind of *middleware* which allows objects to interact with each other even if they are written in different languages and run on different hardware/software platforms. In this way, an application developer can focus exclusively on the aspects directly concerning his application.

We involved ourself in CORBA and we developed a minimal CORBA in Ada 95 since March 1995. Our objective was to study if we can manage to integrate the *Quality of Service with Real-time Constraints* (RT-QoS) as there was nothing for

CORBA concerning real-time at that time. RT-QoS, in our approach, consists in guarantying a client that when his request is accepted by the targeted server, it will be processed in time. Otherwise, he will be informed on the fly of its rejection so that he can start alternatives. COREMO compliant applications offer the clients the possibility to specify an end-to-end deadline for their requests as well as other temporal preferences.

In this paper, we will present the retained category of real-time which we think is adapted to CORBA. Next, we will develop the real-time extension model and some convincing experimental results. We conclude with our future research directions concerning the evolution of COREMO and new experimentations planned.

2   The integration of RT QoS to CORBA

CORBA is intended for open systems. The characteristics of such systems are rather unpredictable : a set of servers and a group of clients which communicate, the request arrivals being unknown. On the server side, the event's timings and precedences are unknown *a priori*. All those unknowns make the CORBA application unpredictable and so unadapted for critical hard real-time applications : those application are conceived off-line with a deterministic known *a priori* system.

From now on, we will consider only soft real-time applications for which missed deadlines are to be avoided but will not cause serious damage [1]. A typical soft real-time application is a multimedia display, where a missed deadline might cause distortions but would not cause the display to be interrupted. The idea in soft real-time systems is then to support the so-called *best effort* and *least suffering* approaches [3]. For such kind of applications, missing some deadlines is undesirable but bearable, in opposition with hard real-time applications.

Our CORBA real-time extension model is then usefull for applications which need a plateform for distribution and interoperability in conjonction with soft real-time. Multimedia applications, bank financial applications, travel agency reservation applications could improve their openness and QoS using such combination.

2.1   The design of COREMO

The idea for COREMO is therefore to provide an environment which supports the *best effort* and *least suffering* approaches concerning real-time. We will then design and develop a real-time level with pluggable modules offering such support when needed. We discarded the *time polymorphic* and the *imprecise calculus* approaches for the following reasons :

– they are dedicated to specific applications.

- they return degradated functional results.
- they keep accepting requests even if the system is overloaded.
- the client may not understand the semantic of the returned service.

The retained approach is based upon the idea of *schedulable invocation* for timed constrained methods. The server scheduler retains on the fly only requests feasible in time and guaranty the respect of their deadline. For non feasible requests, their clients are informed promptly of their rejections and thus avoid wasting time waiting for free.

In this way, COREMO maximizes the temporal previsibility of CORBA compliant applications and improves their performances. For such COREMO real-time applications, we defined a performance metric slightly different from usual hard real-time performance metrics. It consists in a major metric which measures the rate of the requests that are correctly processed in time. We also developed a minor metric which measures the average delay the late requests. The improvement in performance starts by maximizing the *In Time Rate* and ends by minimizing the *Average Tardiness*.

A COREMO real-time request is characterized by four additional temporal constraints. The client may specify for a request a *Deadline*, a *Temporal Tolerance Rate* as the allowed time overstepping, a *Request Criticality* and an *Estimate Criterion* among *pessimistic*, *optimistic*, and *mean*.
When a COREMO compliant server receives such a request, its scheduler evaluates its deadline moment from the server perspective, the computation duration of the targeted method, its criticality, its priority and its start time. Those values will help the scheduler to estimate promptly the feasibility of the request to know whether it is to be accepted for waiting or to reject it and inform the caller.

We introduced the concept of server Policy Vectors to give servers a behavior concerning real-time aspects. Those vectors combine *Priority*, *Feasibility* and *Concurrency Control*.

$$PV = \begin{pmatrix} \text{Priority\_Policy} \\ \text{Feasibility\_Policy} \\ \text{Concurrency\_Control\_Mode} \end{pmatrix}$$

The priority policy is among *EDF*, *Relative EDF*, *Least Slack Time First*, *Least Flexibility First* and an *Heuristic Policy*. *EDF* privilegiates the requests which have the smaller duration between arrival time and deadline. *Relative EDF* estimates the deadline duration between the start-time of the request, instead of the arrival-time, and the deadline moment and then traduces better the urgency than *EDF*. The Slack Time is the duration between the end of the execution and the deadline. Flexibility is defined as the ratio between the method run-time duration and the *Relative EDF*. The *Heuristic Policy* is a linear combination between the best two policies.
The feasibility policies are *Probably Feasible Request* and *Probably Schedulable*

Extended Request Set. PFR retains the requests which respect their own deadlines whereas *PSERS* retains the requests which respect their own deadlines and also preserve the feasibility of all the requests already scheduled.

The concurrency control policies are among serial execution mode where requests are ordered in a unique file or parallel execution mode where a pool of tasks run to process the queued requests. Concurrency raises synchronization issues which we solved by developing a synchronization protocol based on mutual exclusion rings (MER) [2].

2.2 The model use and mechanism

Having the appropriate IDL file, a client can generate a stub or construct a request on line. In the case of COREMO, real-time servers export real-time IDL files to their potential clients. Real-time IDL files will contain additional real-time information such as server PV and method execution duration at installation time. A client is then able, according to those interfaces, to choose an object on which to make a request not only based on functional criteria but also on temporal needs. Hence, a client can invoke the stub service by passing the object reference, the parameters, the deadline duration and optionally the tolerance, the criticality and the data selection criterion.

The *Response_Status* parameter returns the status of the reply among *Timed-_Out, Rejected, Correct* and *Dl_Too_Short*. A request is timed out if the reply is not returned in time. A rejected status is obtained if the server scheduler estimated, due to its policy vector (behaviour), that the request will not be executed in time and then promptly informed the client. The *Dl_Too_Short* status corresponds to a request where the deadline will not be met even if the server is not requested for other jobs. In this last case, the request is rejected by the local *RT_Stub* which has in its possession enough information on the run-time of the targeted method as well as the round-trip duration to decide whether or not the deadline is definitely not reachable.

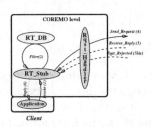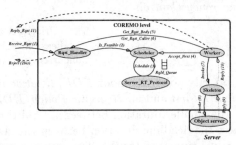

From the server side, upon reception of a request, the server will decide , according to its own policy, whether to queue the request or to drop it. This decision results from the temporal feasibility of the request. As infeasible requests are rejected immediately, this approach will unload the server, so that its performance is improved. It will also avoid penalizing the client since he will not wait for free : he is informed as soon as possible that his request is not feasible in the assigned temporal constraints.

When a request is detected by the BOA, it activates an available request handler or creates a new one and then tranfers the request data and control. The BOA is then available to receive other requests or process other tasks. The *Rqst_Handler* extracts real time information and asks the method associated scheduler to insert the request inside the waiting queue according to the server policy. If the request is infeasible, the request handler is informed promptly and then extracts the request caller ID to send back the rejection status. Otherwise, the request is accepted and scheduled inside the waiting file associated to its method. When it is its turn, the associated method *Worker* will get the request body and the request caller Id, execute the request and then return the result to the caller.
More details on the mechanisms of the model or the implementation approach is available in [2]. This dissertation also includes additional information about the performance evaluation and gauging of the server and an approach to finding an appropriate PV.

Knowing that COREMO maximizes the previsibility of the system, we experimented the effect of this previsibility improvement on the performance of the system according to the primary criterion and the secondary criterion. We experimented different server policies with an increasing request's arrival frequency or *load*.

Our experimentations show that restrictions on feasibility improves the performance criterion. PFR performs a little better than $PSERS$ but we opted for $PSERS$ as it keep the guaranty on already scheduled requests. We also experimented the relative influence of scheduling policies. HP gives usually the best result when the combination coefficient is well tuned, whereas EDF gives the worst one as it expresses urgency less than the other policies. We thought that the other policies would give results proportional to the way they express urgency, but this is not always the case. For example, LFF expresses better the urgency than $LSTF$ but for some specific servers, the primary performance of $LSTF$ is better.

3   COREMO future extensions

It would be interesting for clients to launch consulting requests and to know whether their global temporal characteristics will be guaranteed. We mean by consulting requests, the requests for periodical information consultation. If the server accepts such requests, he must guarantee that each specified period of time, a message containing the requested information will be sent to the client with respect to the temporal characteristics specified by the client. The difficulty stands at the scheduling, as the server must optimize its resources by translating the reserved temporal gaps so that he accepts the maximum new arriving requests.

We are also working on the extension of this model to take into account complex requests composed of a pool of simple requests runnable in a serial or a concurrent way that have not only individual temporal constraints but also a global constraint. Complex requests will access services on different objects. This will necessitate the development of new synchronization and scheduling algorithms that take account of distribution.

Another interesting point to investigate is how to deduce the requested quality of service for each simple request, knowing the requested quality of service required by the client for the complex request and vice-versa.

4 Conclusion

We have developed a CORBA real-time extension model which is optimistic in comparaison with other newly developed models based on *a priori* negociation of the QoS concerning real-time. Instead of starting a negociation systematically, we send the request and the server estimates its feasibility. In this way, in the case of an acceptance, we gain the duration of the negociation message and in the case of rejection, the client waste the same time. The purpose was to offer real-time application developers the CORBA paradigms and also to provide the CORBA compliant applications with real-time sensibility. We developed the design and the mechanisms of COREMO. We advise the reader to refer to [2] for more details. We ended with encouraging results of our experimentations. Those results show that, not only the temporal previsibility of the system is maximized, but also the global performance of the system.

Providing QoS concerning temporal constraints, seems important to us in an open context. Such quality of service will make the difference between two similar service providers in such a context from the client's point of view. Our work already shows that soft real-time can be conciliated with open distributed systems and aims at highlighting the feasibility of such an offer.

References

1. B. Adelberg, H. Garcia-Molina and B. Kao. *"Emulating Soft Real-Time Scheduling Using Traditional Operating System Schedulers"*. IEEE Real-Time System Symposium, 1994.
2. Z. Choukair. "Inter-opérabilité des objets distribués : extension temps-réel du modèle CORBA et application avec Ada 95". PhD thesis, ENST de Bretagne et Université d'Orsay, 1997.
3. J. A. Stankovic and K. Ramamritham, editor. "Advances in Real-Time Systems". IEEE Computer Press, 1993.
4. OMG. "The Common Object Request Broker Architecture and Specifications", July 1995. revision 2.0.

Reflective Real-Time
Object-Oriented Programming and Systems

Introduction to ECOOP'97 Workshop #3

June 10th, 1997
Jyväskylä, Finland.

S. E. Mitchell,
Department of Computer Science,
University of York, UK

R. J. Stroud,
Department of Computer Science
University of Newcastle, UK

1   Introduction

This was the first workshop to be held on this topic at ECOOP and was attended by approximately 15 participants from around the world.

The workshop was organised into two sections – the morning session contained paper presentations followed by in-depth discussion in the afternoon session. This report first presents some background to the workshop and explores its terms of reference and then briefly summarises the afternoon's discussion. The remainder of this chapter then includes the papers presented at the workshop

1.1   Reflection and Real-Time

Reflection [1, 2] within a computing system can be defined as the process of performing computation on an internal representation of the system and, by doing so, changing the underlying system in a controlled manner. Conversely, changes in the system are reflected in changes in the internal representation with a causal link between the two ensuring they remain consistent.

A reflective system can thus divide its computation into two separate parts – computation about the system (non-functional computation) and that about the problem itself (functional computation). This separation has been termed a separation of concerns.

The real-time properties of a system are an example of a non-functional system requirement. Many other non-functional properties are possible, for example fault-tolerance or security, and a system may include any combination. Non-functional properties are *orthogonal* to functional properties they may be, at least in theory, 'mixed-in' to a system without requiring modification to functional code.

Real-time presents a number of unique challenges due to the introduction of another axis of measurement – time. The concerns of a real-time programmer require temporal guarantees of behaviour (in addition, and separate from, existing guarantees of functional behaviour). These temporal guarantees have traditionally been provided through static analysis of the system to arrive at *a priori* guarantees that the system is schedulable even in the event of worst case behaviour [3]. This can give rise to severe problems, for example, it may not be possible to check schedulability until the final stage of development at which point any required changes are expensive.

Consequently, there is considerable demand for flexible systems that can adapt to changing environments, unexpected faults, etc. The ability to mix-and-match requirements and the potential for compile and run-time adaptation offered by a reflective system is very appealing and has lead to a number of reflective real-time systems and also prompted the motivation for this workshop

2 Presentations

There were six presentations at the workshop, five of which are included in this report:

- *Implementing Real-Time Actors with MetaJava*, Michael Golm & Jürgen Kleinöder University of Erlangen-Nürnberg, Germany.

- *Weak Protection for Reflective Operating Systems*, Shigeru Chiba, Takeshi Nishimura, Kenichi Kourai, Atsushi Ohnoki & Takashi Masuada, The University of Tokyo, Japan.

- *Reflective ORBs: Supporting Robust, Time-critical Distribution*, Ashish Singhai, Aamod Sane and Roy Campbell, University of Illinois at Urbana-Champaign, USA.

- *Adaptive Scheduling using Reflection*, Stuart Mitchell, Alan Burns and Andy Wellings, University of York, UK.

- *Adaptive Fault-Tolerant Systems and Reflective Architectures*, Jack Goldberg and Robert J. Stroud, University of Newcastle upon Tyne.

The sixth paper, which is not included in this report, was on the workshop organiser's project, *Design for Validation* [4], and was used as an introduction to the workshop and also to present the organisers research background.

3 A Summary of Workshop Discussions

As a result of the discussion session, participants at the workshop created a list of eleven points for consideration. This section lists each of these points in turn and outlines the motivation for inclusion on the list and also some results of discussion undertaken at the workshop. Some of the points were discussed in depth and a consensus reached, others remain more open research questions.

3.1 What do we need to reflect upon for real-time?

There are many properties upon which one may wish to reflect (monitor and possibly influence) in a real-time system. Apart from the obvious such as CPU time used, a flexible real-time system will also require such properties as the current "value" of a task. The consensus reached by the workshop participants was that a complete list would be impossible to compile since there are an infinte possible properties. However, this was not seen as a problem since using a combination of compile and run-time reflection one can open-up the run-time system to obtain the required information

3.2 Run-time vs. Compile time Reflection

Ashish Singhai commented that components in a system which appear at first sight to have similar semantics and are thus candidates for adaptation may not be, logically, compatible – for example switching between spin locks and priority inheritance. Discussion at the workshop concluded that some sort of "type error" for erroneous composition was required but it was unclear how this would work especially in the case of redefined semantics.

3.3 Reflection vs. encapsulation

The potential in a reflective system to open up the run-time system for examination and modification by a program raised concerns over protection and breaking of encapsulation. For example, in his presentation Shigeru Chiba made the point that meta-objects need to access the kernel but illegal access needs to be trapped.

3.4 Do we need policy objects?

A policy object can be used to implement (encapsulate) a scheduling, admissions, migration polices etc. It was generally agreed that such objects would be necessary for flexibility and that their reification permits run-time change and adaption.

3.5 Adaptation vs. Validation

A recurring theme in the discussion was a requirement for some form of type system for meta-objects that can be checked for correctness. There was also a desire that this be extended to cover the semantics of the meta-object – for example, the scheduler object. This would enable a real-time reflective system to have some confidence that a change to a policy object either at compile or run-time would leave the system in a consistent, correct, state.

3.6 What level is reflection for?

This point represents a feeling that reflection has yet to be "sold" to the real-time community. One cannot allow infinite adaptation in a real-time system and maintain the temporal guarantees

3.7 OS vs. Application vs. Library vs. Middleware

This point illustrates that there are a number of points at which reflection can occur.

3.8 How do we program the meta-level?

There were three programming roles identified by workshop participants – base (application) level programmer, meta-level programmer and integrator. These roles are perhaps best performed by different people and involve different degree of abstraction.

3.9 What impact will reflective design have on application structure?

It is perhaps obvious that a reflective system cannot be designed without clear reference to its reflective properties. However, the implications that this would have for the resultant structure of an application are unknown and await further research and the development of tools and methods for design support.

3.10 What is the cost of reflection?

The cost of reflection, how to measure the cost and how to place bounds on it were of special concern to workshop participants. To be accepted and used by the real-time community there must be clear bounds on the run-time costs and how to impose these remains an open question. Presentations at the workshop outlined some initial approaches – for example, grouping operations – but it was clear that considerable work remained in this area.

3.11 Can the concurrency model be reflective?

One presentation introduced the idea of a *metathread* object that is responsible for the structure and behaviour of a base-level thread in much the same way a metaobject controls a base-level object. Further discussion turned on whether or not the concurrency model itself could be reflective, and if so, how this could be achieved.

4 Acknowledgements

The organisers of the workshop would like to thank all those who contributed their time and efforts to its preparation. We would especially like to thank Dr. A. Romanovsky and Professor B. Randall from the University of Newcastle and Professors A. Wellings and A. Burns from the University of York for their helpful comments on both the original call for contributions and on the submissions received.

We would also like to thank all those who attended the workshop, whether as participants or presenters, and hope that they found it as useful and enjoyable as we did.

5 References

[1] P. Maes, "Concepts and Experiments in Computational Reflection," *ACM SIGPLAN Notices - Proceedings of OOPSLA'87*, 22(12), pp. 147-155, 1987.
[2] G. Kiczales, J. d. Rivières, and D. Bobrow, *The Art of the Metaobject Protocol*: MIT Press, 1991.
[3] A. Burns and A. Wellings, *Real-Time Systems and Programming Languages*, Second Edn.: Addison-Wesley, 1996.
[4] DeVa Project, "Design for Validation Proposal Document," : http://www.newcastle.research.ec.org/deva/index.html, 1995.

Reflective ORBs: Supporting Robust, Time-Critical Distribution

Ashish Singhai, Aamod Sane, and Roy Campbell

University of Illinois, Department of Computer Science
1304 W. Springfield Ave., Urbana IL 61801 USA
http://choices.cs.uiuc.edu

1 Introduction

Modern applications of computers such as video-on-demand require real-time response and need distributed implementations. Object Request Brokers(ORBs) [9] provide a solution to the distribution problem by allowing method invocation on remote objects. However, mere remote method invocation is not enough in a distributed setting: application programs also require features like fault-tolerance and load-balancing. Integrating all possible functionality into an ORB would result in a complex, monolithic program, so we need a modular architecture for ORBs. In this paper, we show how reflection enables the construction of a composable ORB that can be customized to support new features.

After reviewing Common Request Broker Architecture (CORBA [9]), we discuss reflection [5] and its application to ORBs. Then we consider the requirements for a real-time ORB and show how we use reflection to build real-time support in our ORB. Later we address other services like fault-tolerance and show that systematic application of reflection can result in a plug and play system. We conclude with initial performance results and discussion of future work.

2 Standard ORBs

A minimal ORB architecture (Fig. 1) has the following elements. (The names in the parentheses refer to Object Management Group (OMG) terminology.)

- Servers (Implementation): Servers implement desired behavior. The ORB facilitates client access to the servers.
- Object References (ObjRef): Remote representations of objects that enable communication with servers.
- Client-side Invocation (Stubs): Stubs located on the client side package and transmit the method invocation (method-id, parameters) to the server.
- Server-side Invocation (Skeleton): The server-side ORB receives the client request and calls the server. The "Skeleton" objects perform this function.

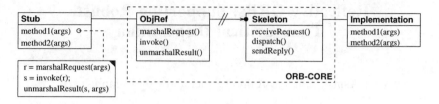

Fig. 1. A minimal ORB architecture

A client application gets an object reference to a server through the ORB. Servers register themselves with the ORB to allow clients to access them. Thus, the primary user interface to the ORB[1] consists of methods for registering and querying about services.

We provide an extended interface that allows applications to adjust various aspects of the ORB.These include method dispatch, memory and concurrency management, object creation and destruction, object reference management and marshaling. The resulting reflective architecture supports a variety of features without changing the basic ORB architecture.

3 Reflection in ORBs

A reflective system gives a program access to its definition and the evaluation rules and defines an interface for altering them. In an ORB, client method calls represent the 'program', the ORB implementation the 'evaluator' and evaluation is just method invocation. A reflective ORB lets clients redefine the evaluation semantics.

For instance, in a real-time ORB, a client must transmit method completion deadlines to the server. The server uses the deadline to schedule the method call. Except for scheduling the method call and (un)marshaling the deadline, rest of the ORB remains unaffected.

Our reflective ORB accommodates these changes by reifying method call processing in the form of *Invoker* and *Dispatcher* objects. Client programs supply a subclass of *Invoker* that knows about marshaling with deadlines. This provides a reflective control interface allowing application programmers to interact with the reified objects and modify the functionality. Figures 2 and 3 show the client-side and server-side architecture, respectively, of our ORB with the reified objects.

As another example, consider incorporating fault-tolerance by replicating client method calls and merging their responses. In our ORB, the *Invoker* objects control method dispatch on the client-side. Applications can install a specialized *Invoker* that replicates calls and merges results.

---

[1] In the CORBA parlance, the application environment contains a *pseudo object reference* to the ORB. This reference may be used to access naming services that return object references.

4 Real Time Support in ORBs

Real time support in an ORB entails the following requirements.

- Timing: For all methods, we must know the estimates for the worst case execution time, memory requirements and I/O bandwidth requirements. For all method calls, clients must indicate start and end deadlines.
- Priority: The ORB must support prioritized use of resources. In particular, blocking and synchronization must preserve priorities [1].

These requirements mean changes to service registration, access to object references and method execution.

- Service Registration: Services must express estimated resource requirements (memory, threads, I/O bandwidth) to the ORB.
- Access to Object References: In order to gain access to a service, clients specify parameters, e.g., priority, type of service (periodic, aperiodic.)
- Method Invocation: Client method calls have to transmit additional parameters such as deadlines. This changes the format of the network packets.
- Method Execution: Servers schedule incoming client method calls depending on the service (periodic or deadline driven.) Therefore, servers must provide their own scheduling policies.

The Reflective Interface The reflective interface of our ORB allows applications access to method invocation, execution, and registration components to implement these changes.

- On the client side, programmers can set *Marshaler* and *Invoker* objects on a per-service basis. Thus programs may add support for deadlines.
- Clients can specialize *Invoker* objects to handle rejected invocations (e.g., by retrying with a more relaxed deadline.)
- *Dispatcher* objects optionally interpose schedulers with different policies in the dispatch path.

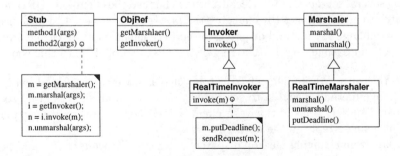

Fig. 2. Client-side ORB architecture for our RT-ORB

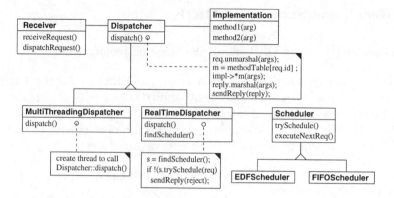

Fig. 3. Server-side ORB architecture for our RT-ORB

Operating System Interface Besides the changes in the external ORB interface, a real-time ORB also requires a different interface from the operating system.

- To facilitate controlling resource utilization, the operating system should support page locking, thread and process priority control, real-time timers [3].
- Operating system supported synchronization constructs within the server-side ORB require new queuing disciplines that prevent priority inversion [1].
- Server scheduling policies such as rate monotonic scheduling [7] require operating system support for fixed priorities and preemption.

Our ORB accesses operating system services provided by the ACE [11] library. While our ORB is predictable in its memory and CPU usage, it can support real-time applications only if the operating system provides required facilities.

5 Supporting Fault-Tolerance and Load Balancing

We implement fault-tolerance and load balancing using the same reflective interface developed for real-time support.

Load Balancing Load balancing is implemented by distributing client requests among several servers [12, 14]. Recall that we changed the client-side ORB method dispatch to add deadlines (by changing the *Invoker* object, Sec. 4.) In the present case, we change the method dispatch to send the client requests to one among a group of compatible servers. The rest of the ORB is oblivious to this change.

Fault-Tolerance We implement fault-tolerance as a variation of load-balancing. We change method dispatch to send client requests to all servers in a group of replicated servers. In addition, the client side ORB merges multiple replies to present a single reply to the client.

Apart from changing method dispatch, we create *ClientInteraction* and *Server-Interaction* interfaces to implement policies for managing server groups, evaluating load metrics and failure detection.

6 Preliminary Performance Results and Status

Our ORB currently supports basic object distribution, real-time scheduling of client calls, and simple fault-tolerance by replicating objects. The following table shows the timing for null method calls on the basic ORB, ORB with real-time scheduling using Earliest Deadline First (EDF) and First In First Out (FIFO) algorithms, and a server duplicated on two machines: These numbers are averaged over 5000 iterations of null calls, with a single client (to avoid contention.)

ORB type	Time (μs)
Basic	1962
Real Time (EDF)	3172
Real Time (FIFO)	3227
Replication	2616

Figure 4 exhibits the results from an experiment, which changes scheduling policies at run-time. The first phase uses the EDF policy. The second and third phases change it to FIFO and NONE (No Scheduling) respectively. In each phase, we have 10 clients, 5 of them requiring 3 seconds of processing time every t seconds, and the other 5 requiring 7 seconds of processing time every t seconds. We adjust t to change the targeted CPU utilization. EDF scheduling [2] performs the best. FIFO and NONE exhibit similar behavior at lower CPU utilizations since enough capacity is available. But with increasing contention, performance of the NONE scheme deteriorates.

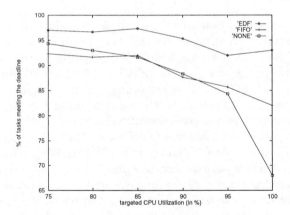

Fig. 4. Performance of various scheduling policies in our RT-ORB.

We plan to use the adaptive capabilities of the ORB to build a video server, operating in a dynamic, heterogeneous environment. Using the reflective capabilities of the ORB, it will use different communication protocols and adapt to varying network conditions.

7 Related Work

The OMG special interest group on Real-Time CORBA is studying the issues involved with real-time processing in CORBA; but there is no concrete specification from OMG yet. The Electra [8] ORB supports fault-tolerance using reliable multicast. Instead of using reflection to implement fault-tolerance, it introduces the notion of "group object reference" as a separate construct and uses the group communication facilities of the underlying system (ISIS or HORUS.) No commercial ORB has any real-time features to the best of our knowledge.

Real-time method invocations in CORBA has been considered by Wolfe, et. al. [15]. Their approach involves transmitting the timing information using the *context* field from the CORBA specification. Takashio, et. al. [13], have mentioned Time Polymorphic Invocations (TPI) using their Distributed Real-Time Object (DRO) model. They assume existence of multiple implementations of the same method with different resource requirements and at run-time execute the one that is feasible according to the timing constraints.

Honda and Tokoro [4] develop a language with timing specifications and schedulers at the meta level. This is similar to the way we reify marshaling, unmarshaling and scheduling using *Invoker*, *Marshaler*, and *Dispatcher*.

Schmidt, et. al. [10], develop an architecture for real-time additions to CORBA. They discuss optimizations for high performance, the development of a real-time inter-orb protocol and real-time scheduling. However, their architecture does not appear to be explicitly targeted to support fault-tolerance and load-balancing.

8 Conclusion

We have shown how reflection allows us to build a modular ORB that may be customized to support real-time processing, fault tolerance, and load balancing. Reflective facilities created for one feature help us in supporting additional features without drastically changing the initial architecture. We support changes by reifying the structure and evaluation strategy in the ORB; as a result, changing the ORB amounts to creating new subclasses and using the corresponding objects, so system performance is practically unaffected.

In our ORB, we use reflection in a limited way. The underlying language and the fine-grained features of the ORB are not reflective. We explicitly choose the entities we reify, and it is possible that additional changes will need new objects.

Moreover, the changes we consider largely leave the semantics of the programs unchanged. Real time processing has the most impact on the ORB because it changes the semantics to the greatest degree. For instance, we must expose the synchronization structure of the ORB and allow users to change the queue disciplines. Fault-tolerance and load balancing required relatively benign changes.

This mild form of reflection has been practised in many domains with considerable success [5]. It is interesting to speculate about language support for such limited reflection. A language with explicit support for frameworks might allow programmers to specify the parts of the framework structure and processing that would be reified. Support for Aspects [6] would achieve the same effect.

Acknowledgements We gratefully acknowledge the help provided by Mallikarjun Shankar, Amitabh Dave and Zhigang Chen.

References

1. Özalp Babaŏglu, Keith Marzullo, and Fred B. Schneider. A formalization of priority inversion. *Real-Time Systems*, pages 285–303, 1993.
2. Thomas H. Cormen, Charles E. Leiserson, and Ronald L. Rivest. A task scheduling problem. In *Introduction to Algorithms*, chapter 17.5. The MIT Press, 1992.
3. Bill O. Gallmeister. *POSIX.4: Programming for the Real World*. O'Reilly & Associates, Inc., 1995.
4. Y. Honda and M. Tokoro. Time-dependent programming and reflection: Experiences on R2. Technical Report SCSL-TR-93-017, Sony CSL, 1993.
5. Gregor Kiczales. Towards a new model of abstraction in software engineering. In *Proc. IMSA'92 Workshop on Reflection and Meta-level Architectures*, 1992.
6. Gregor Kiczales, John Lamping, Anurag Mendhekar, Chris Maeda, Cristina Lopes, Jean-Marc Loingtier, and John Irwin. Aspect-oriented programming. Technical Report SPL97-008 P9710042, XEROX PARC, 1997. http://www.parc.xerox.com.
7. C. L. Liu and J. W. Layland. Scheduling algorithms for multiprogramming in hard real-time environment. *Journal of the ACM*, 20:46–61, 1973.
8. Silvano Maffeis and Douglas C. Schmidt. Constructing reliable distributed communication systems with CORBA. *IEEE Communications Magazine*, 14(2), 1997.
9. Object Management Group. *The Common Object Request Broker: Architecture and Specification*, 1996. Document PTC/96-08-04, Revision 2.0.
10. Douglas C. Schmidt, Aniruddha Gokhale, Timothy H. Harrison, David Levine, and Chris Cleeland. TAO: a high-performance endsystem architecture for real-time CORBA. (RFI response to OMG-SIG Real-Time CORBA), 1997.
11. Douglas C. Schmidt and Tatsuya Suda. An Object-Oriented Framework for Dynamically Configuring Extensible Distributed Communication Systems. *IEE/BCS Distributed Systems Engineering Journal*, 2:280–293, 1994.
12. Ashish Singhai, Swee Lim, and Sanjay R. Radia. The SCALR framework for internet services. submitted for publication, 1997.
13. Kazunori Takashio and Mario Tokoro. Time polymorphic invocation: A real-time communication model for distributed systems. In *Proc. 1st IEEE Workshop on Parallel and Distr. Real-Time Systems*, 1993.
14. Y. T. Wang and R. J. T. Morris. Load sharing in distributed systems. *IEEE Transaction on Comptuers*, C-34(3):204–217, 1985.
15. Victor Fay Wolfe, John K. Black, Bavani Thuraisingham, and Peter Krupp. Real-time method invocations in distributed environments. In *Proc. HiPC'95 Intl. Conf. on High-Performance Computing*. IEEE, 1995.

Weak Protection for Reflective Operating Systems

Shigeru Chiba   Takeshi Nishimura
Kenichi Kourai   Atsushi Ohnoki   Takashi Masuda

Department of Information Science, The University of Tokyo.
Email: {chiba,takeshi,kourai,ohnoki,masuda}@is.s.u-tokyo.ac.jp

Abstract. A customizable scheduler for real-time computing is a typical example of the advantage of extensible operating systems. We have applied the reflection technique to a traditional operating system and experimentally implemented a customizable scheduler for real-time computing. This paper reports this experience and discusses the limitation we encountered. Then this paper presents a new mechanism we call *weak protection* and mentions that it is useful to make a reflective operating system workable. We are currently developing this mechanism for our DECADE operating system.

1 A Reflective Operating System

Although there are various definitions of reflective systems, a typical reflective system can be expressed as a system that exposes part of modules in the system and makes it possible for the users to replace the modules. The interface to the exposed module is designed in an object-oriented method, and hence the modules are often called *metaobjects*. Also, (1) the reflective systems should enable scope control by the users so that they can control the scope where the substituted module is effective, and (2) the interface should provide higher-level abstraction that hides implementation details for easy of use.

The two design criteria presented above are effective in most of reflective systems such as the CLOS MOP [4] and OpenC++ [2], but they are not sufficient for designing reflective operating systems. We need the third design criterion, which is *protection* from malicious or wrong metaobjects. Since an operating system must protect the whole system from a malicious or wrong user program, a reflective operating system also needs to prevent a metaobject from destroying other user programs or the system kernel.

Implementing this kind of protection is not straightforward because most of metaobjects of operating systems exist in the system kernel, where all programs are trusted and running without any restriction or audits. A naive approach to this issue is to run a metaobject in a user process. This idea is found in the Mach operating system [5] if we regard a user-level pager as a metaobject for the paging mechanism. The user-level pager determines a page-replacement algorithm instead of the kernel but runs in a user process. Since it is completely isolated from other processes and the kernel, it cannot destroy other user programs or the kernel. However, the Mach project and other research activities have revealed that the approach adopted by Mach has a serious performance problem. Assigning a user process to a metaobject is extremely expensive since this approach causes frequent context-switches between user processes and hence decreases system performance.

In-kernel Interpreter

To avoid serious performance overheads, our experimental reflective operating system did not take Mach's approach. It instead uses an interpreter running in the kernel for isolating a metaobject from the others. The metaobjects are programmed in a simple C-like language and interpreted by the in-kernel interpreter. Since the interpreter prohibits invalid access, the operating system is protected from malicious metaobjects. Although the interpretation still implies performance penalties, the total costs of the protection is significantly reduced against the Mach's approach. This is due to the fact that most of user-defined metaobjects are short programs and the costs of the interpretation is not high.

The operating system we developed is a preliminary version; the reflective feature is implemented as an extension to NetBSD, a traditional Unix operating system. We extended NetBSD to support kernel threads and asynchronous I/O, and we developed a thread scheduler on top of it. This scheduler is exposed to the users as a metaobject and thus the users can customize it, for example, to schedule threads to satisfy real-time constraints.[1] Moreover, the users can implement a scheduling policy depending on not only time constraints but also kernel information such as the I/O status and the virtual memory status because our reflective system allows the metaobject to access such information.

To examine the benefits of our customizable thread scheduler, we implemented three different scheduling policies on top of it. The first policy uses time constraints and the I/O status. The scheduler executes a thread with the earliest deadline or a thread that accesses an idle device. The second policy accepts a hint about dependency between threads. The users can specify time constraint on a thread and also which thread should be scheduled before that thread. The third policy is an extension to the second one. Besides time constraint and dependency, the third policy examines how many memory pages for the thread actually reside on physical memory.

We measured the execution time of a micro benchmark under the three scheduling policies. For comparison, we also ran the micro benchmark with a simple earliest-deadline-first policy, which is the default policy of our scheduler. This policy is directly embedded in the scheduler and hence no interpretation is involved. The micro benchmark that we ran was written to simulate the behavior of a continuous media server, which handles video frames and so forth. The benchmark runs two threads; one thread periodically reads a certain amount of data on a disk and transfers the data to network, and the other thread simultaneously writes the data on the same disk.

Figure 1 shows the results of our measurement. The horizontal axis means the amount of data transferred at a time. The line marked "default" is the elapsed time by the default earliest-deadline-first scheduler. The line marked "I/O" is by the scheduling with time constraints and the I/O status. The line marked "dependency" is by the scheduling with concerning about dependency. The line marked "VM" is by the scheduling with dependency and the number of pages on physical memory. The micro benchmark was executed on our extended version of NetBSD 1.1 running on Pentium 75MHz and 32Mbyte memory.

---

[1] Because of the limitation of the base operating system, the user can implement only pseudo real-time scheduling.

Elapsed time (sec.)

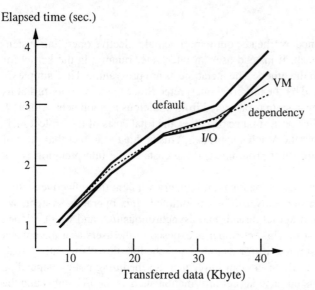

Fig. 1. Execution time of the micro benchmark

We can see that the customized thread scheduler performs better scheduling than the default earliest-deadline-first scheduler despite overheads by the interpretation. This is obviously because the gain by better scheduling policies is bigger than the performance penalty by the interpretation of the scheduler. The result of our experiment shows that, if the implemented scheduling policy is significantly better than the default one, the in-kernel interpreter is effective.

2 Weak Protection

Although the protection by using an in-kernel interpreter is workable in the case of real-time scheduling presented above, its inefficiency due to interpretation limits the applicability of reflection to operating system design. With an in-kernel interpreter, reflection is effective only if the gain by customization is sufficiently large. In fact, another experiment with our extended NetBSD showed that a scheduler implemented as a new metaobject is about 4 times slower than an equivalent scheduler directly embedded in the kernel, although it is still twice faster than the scheduler implemented by a user process as in Mach.

To overcome this limitation, the DECADE operating system we are currently developing adopts another protection mechanism for metaobjects. The new mechanism that we call *weak protection* cannot protect the operating system from malicious metaobjects, which attempt to destroy the system or steal protected information on purpose, but rather it is supposed to protect the system from accidental access violation of wrong metaobjects. Since metaobjects for extending an operating system are usually written by privileged users such as "root", we believe that an expensive protection mechanism from malicious metaobjects is not necessary in practice. Metaobjects are similar to device drivers and "OS patches" and hence the users would carefully choose installed metaobjects. The mechanism that we really need is for protecting the system from accidental wrong accesses by a metaobject and making it easy to develop and debug the metaobject. Our observation is that, considering the trade-off between security and efficiency, the protection for metaobjects does not need to be as strict as that for user programs, which may be malicious.

Currently, we have two different implementations of the weak protection. The first exploits language or library supports, and the other implementation uses a 64-bit address space. In the rest of this section, we present these two implementations.

Language or Library Supports

One of the reasons of the inefficiency of the Mach's approach is that a metaobject is completely isolated in a user process and cannot directly access the kernel address space. Hence, if the metaobject needs to access kernel information such as the I/O status for better real-time scheduling, the interaction between the metaobject and the kernel seriously decreases the execution performance.

Our idea is to allocate shared memory between the kernel and the user process that the metaobject is running in. This enables the metaobject to quickly access kernel information. On the other hand, to protect the shared memory from invalid accesses, we have the metaobject call a library function whenever accessing the shared memory (Figure 2). The shared memory is usually write-protected, but the library function removes the protection, copies the kernel information on the shared memory to local memory, and set the protection again. The caller metaobject receives the data structure copied on local memory. It reads and modifies this data structure and calls a library function again if it needs to write the modified data structure back to the shared memory. The coping might seem redundant but it is necessary to hide inappropriate kernel information and avoid invalid accesses. Although the metaobject can also remove the protection and directly access the kernel information without calling the library function, we believe that this mechanism provides adequate security for our ends.

The shared memory between the metaobject and the kernel can be also protected by using language supports instead of library supports. For example, if we use a language like Modula-3 that is safer than C and C++, we can prohibit invalid accesses to the shared memory by the protection mechanism of that language. This approach is more efficient than the library approach, but it restricts the kind of possible programming language. Another disadvantage is its less flexibility; if the shared memory is protected by library functions, the security level of the shared memory can be adjusted by substituting different library functions. No change of the program of the metaobject is needed. This feature makes it possible, for example, to decrease the security level and run the metaobject more efficiently after debugging is finished.

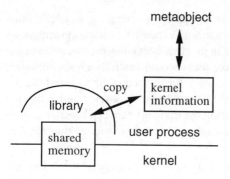

Fig. 2. Weak Protection by Library Supports

64-bit Address Space

Another idea for implementing weak protection is to use 64-bit addressing. Since a 64-bit address space is extremely large, a metaobject can be efficiently isolated from the other kernel modules in the kernel address space if the metaobject and the kernel modules are placed at a random address. A 64-bit address itself can be an capability [6]. It is so large that the probability that the metaobject accidentally accesses and destroys other kernel modules is practically negligible. Especially, since most of memory pages are not used or associated to physical memory, a wrong memory access mostly causes a page fault and the wrong metaobject can be terminated before it destroys other kernel modules.

Although this protection mechanism provides only "probably safe" security, its advantage is that it needs significantly small runtime penalties. For inter-metaobject calls, it does not need TLB flush or a system trap but only a special calling convention. In a regular calling convention, the return address and the stack pointer are passed to the callee function, but these values can be accidentally used to derive the address of the caller function. To keep low probability of successful invalid accesses, all inter-metaobject calls should be performed through dispatch routines that exist on execution-only memory and encrypts the return address and so forth. Also, for the same reason, any pointer to a kernel data structure such as a process queue should not be passed to a metaobject. A copy of the kernel data structure should be passed instead. This can be a performance penalty if the metaobject handles tight real-time constraints, but it is considerably less expensive than traditional protection mechanisms.

Our uniqueness is that we use 64-bit addressing for isolating a metaobject. Another literature [6] have already suggested the possibility of a general protection mechanism based on 64-bit addressing, but its "probably-safeness" is a serious problem for the general purpose. We think that weak protection is one of the best applications of the protection by 64-bit addressing.

3 Related Work

There are several related activities in the operating system area. First, the SPIN operating system [1] uses an idea similar to our weak protection by language or library supports. It allows the users to write an extension program (i.e. a metaobject) in Modula-3 and directly run it in the kernel address space. The security of running the extension program depends on the protection mechanism of Modula-3.

Another related activity is Exokernel [3]. Exokernel is an operating system kernel that provides very low-level primitives such as TLB-entry control, and traditional operating system services are implemented as a library on top of that kernel. It gives significant flexibility to the users since they can customize the library and build their own version of operating system. However, the Exokernel users have to customize the whole library; Exokernel does not provide a protection mechanism for isolating only a customized module, that is, a metaobject, from other correct library code.

References

1. Bershad, B. N. et al, "Extensibility, Safety and Performance in the SPIN Operating System," in *Proc. of ACM SOSP-15*, pp. 267–284, December 1995.
2. Chiba, S., "A Metaobject Protocol for C++," in *Proc. of ACM OOPSLA'95*, no. 10 in SIG-PLAN Notices vol. 30, pp. 285–299, ACM, 1995.
3. Engler, D. R., M. F. Kaashoek, and J. O'Toole Jr., "Exokernel: An Operating System Architecture for Application-Level Resource Management," in *Proc. of ACM SOSP-15*, pp. 251–266, December 1995.
4. Kiczales, G., J. des Rivières, and D. G. Bobrow, *The Art of the Metaobject Protocol*. The MIT Press, 1991.
5. Loepere, K., *Mach 3 Server Writer's Guide*. Open Software Foundation and Carnegie Mellon University, 7 1992.
6. Yarvin, C., R. Bukowski, and T. Anderson, "Anonymous RPC: Low-Latency Protection in a 64-Bit Address Space," in *Proc. of the 1993 Summer USENIX Conference*, pp. 175–186, June 1993.

Implementing Real-Time Actors with MetaJava

Michael Golm, Jürgen Kleinöder[1]

University of Erlangen-Nürnberg, Dept. of Computer Science IV
Martensstr. 1, D-91058 Erlangen, Germany
{golm, kleinoeder} @informatik.uni-erlangen.de

Abstract. Actors are a suitable abstraction to manage concurrency in real-time applications. Meta-level programming can help to separate real-time concerns from application concerns. We use reflection to transform passive objects into active objects. Then we extend the meta-level implementation of the actors to be sensitive to soft real-time requirements.

1 Introduction

Meta-level interfaces allow the service provided by a base-level API to be adjusted to specific application needs and run-time environments. MetaJava [4] extends the Java Virtual Machine by a meta-level interface (MLI). The MetaJava MLI allows metaobjects to modify the interpreter's object model. We show, how the meta-level interface can be used to implement active objects. Active objects, or actors, are an appropriate abstraction to manage concurrency in real-time systems. Most real-time systems have a reactive nature. They respond to signals from sensors and do control actuators. The signal/response behavior of real-time systems maps well with the message/reply scheme of actors. To be useful in an environment with real-time constraints the originally developed actor system must be extended. The proposed actor implementation is not intended for hard real-time systems. To satisfy hard real-time constraints, it is necessary to find out worst-case execution times, use incremental garbage collection, use resource negotiation, etc. This was investigated in RT-Java[8].

The paper is structured as follows. Section 2 introduces relevant concepts of MetaJava. Section 3 discusses the actor model. Section 4 explains the actor implementation and Section 5 the real-time extensions to this implementation. Section 7 discusses related work and Section 8 concludes the paper.

2 MetaJava

MetaJava is an extension to the Java Virtual Machine [6] that supports structural and behavioral reflection [2] in Java. The base-level object model is the Java model. MetaJava provides mechanisms to modify this object model and to add extensions—for example, persistent objects, remote objects, replicated objects, or active objects.

---

1. This work is supported by the *Deutsche Forschungsgemeinschaft DFG* Grant *Sonderforschungsbereich SFB 182*, Project *B2*.

Base-level objects and meta-level objects are defined separately. Meta-level objects that inherit from the class MetaObject can be attached to base-level objects. After a metaobject is attached, it can register for events of the base-level computation (lines 3,4 of Fig. 1). Operations that can raise an event include method invocation, variable access, object creation, and class loading. An event description contains sufficient information about the event and enables the metaobject to reimplement the event-generating operation. A method-event description, for example, contains the following information:

- a reference to the called object
- the method name and method signature
- the method arguments

An event is delivered to the event-handler method of the attached metaobject (line 5 of Fig. 1). This method is responsible for an appropriate implementation of the operation. It could continue with the default mechanism or customize it. The default mechanism for method executions is provided with the method continueExecutionVoid (line 6 of Fig. 1).

```
1   public class MetaObject {
2       protected void attachObject(Object baseobject) { ... }
3       protected void registerEventMethodCall(Object baseobject) { ... }
4       protected void registerEventMethodCall(Object baseobject, String methods[]) { ... }
5       public void eventMethodEnterVoid(Object o, EventDescMethodCall event) { ... }
6       protected void continueExecutionVoid(Object baseobject, EventDescMethodCall event) { ... }
7       ...
8   }
```

Fig. 1 The MetaObject class

When attaching a metaobject to a base-level object, base level and meta level are visible. During this process information about the semantics of the base-level object can be passed to the metaobject. This information consists of details about methods, instance variables, and other object properties. As the current version of MetaJava uses a standard Java compiler, there is no linguistic support for reflective programming. This means, that the names of those methods or instance variables must be passed to the metaobject as strings.

Once the metaobject has been attached, the meta level is transparent to the base-level object.

3 Actors

The actor model, developed by Hewitt [3] and Agha [1], is a approach to manage concurrency. Recently, it has been applied to the domain of real-time programming [10], [9].

One advantage of the actor model is the easy synchronization. In the original actor model, there is exactly one thread active in one actor and thus there is no need to synchronize inside an actor. However, in multiprocessor real-time systems it can be beneficial to have more than one thread executing in an actor—for example, if the threads execute read-only methods.

Our actor model differs from the original actor model in two points: message passing is not asynchronous and there can be an arbitrary number of threads executing in an actor.

The use of actors leads to a very dynamic and adaptable system. Actors are a means to implement a *best-effort* real-time system—that is, a system that tries to meet timing constraints but cannot guarantee this a priori. Actor systems are not intended for hard real-time systems with guaranteed timing behavior.

4   Implementing Actors at the Meta Level

Active objects are an extension of the passive object model. A passive object implements the functional aspect of the actor. The actor behavior is implemented at the meta level, as shown in Fig. 2. The *MetaActive* metaobject transforms a

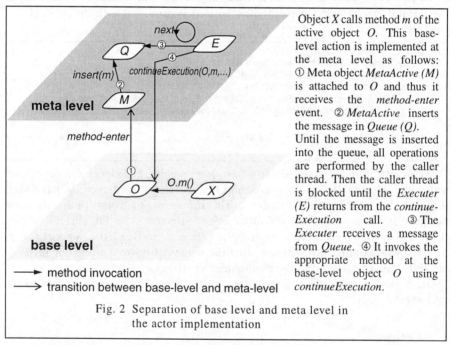

Object *X* calls method *m* of the active object *O*. This base-level action is implemented at the meta level as follows: ① Meta object *MetaActive (M)* is attached to *O* and thus it receives the *method-enter* event. ② *MetaActive* inserts the message in *Queue (Q)*. Until the message is inserted into the queue, all operations are performed by the caller thread. Then the caller thread is blocked until the *Executer (E)* returns from the *continueExecution* call. ③ The *Executer* receives a message from *Queue*. ④ It invokes the appropriate method at the base-level object *O* using *continueExecution*.

Fig. 2 Separation of base level and meta level in the actor implementation

passive object into an actor. The constructor of MetaActive configures its state according to the parameters and attaches itself to the base-level object.

Fig. 2 shows a part of the implementation of the MetaActive metaobject. The constructor initializes the active-object execution environment, consisting of *Queue* and *Executor* and attaches itself to the base-level object. MetaActive reimplements the method-call mechanism to support the actor behavior.

```
1   public interface Queue {
2       public void insert(Object event);
3       public Object next();
4   }
```

Fig. 3 The QueueManager interface

When receiving a method-enter event MetaActive creates a new message object and inserts it into the message queue. Then the caller thread blocks until it is notified by the Executor. The

Executer object continuously obtains messages from the Queue. To enable different message scheduling policies, MetaActive and Executer merely use the interface Queue (Fig. 3).

5 Real-time Extensions to the Actor Metaobject

To handle real-time requirements, the actor metaobject developed in the previous section must be extended to include temporal considerations. We consider the following real-time related aspects of actors:

(1) *The policy to accept messages and insert them into the message queue.* This includes the policy to assign priorities to messages. Priorities can be based on the message name, the message sender or the message receiver.

(2) *The policy to map messages to methods and execute them.* Some methods may need wrapper functions that check pre- and post-conditions. In special situations it is possible to use a separate thread to execute the method.

(3) *The synchronization policy.* If multiple threads are active in one actor, a synchronization policy for these actors is needed.

(4) *The policy to control method execution.* It is possible to specify a maximum time quantum for method execution. If this quantum is exceeded, the method execution is aborted. Aborting a method could lead to an inconsistent object state. Therefore, after aborting a method, another method to clean up must be invoked.

These considerations are implemented by a different actor metaobject. This metaobject is parametrized with information about message properties. A message property consists of

– the message name
– the name of methods that must be invoked before and after the called method
– the message priority
– the maximum time quantum of the message, including wrapper functions

As shown in Fig. 4, only the metaobject constructor must be reimplemented to initialize a new execution environment for active objects with real-time properties.

```
1    public class MetaRTActive extends MetaActive
2    {
3        public MetaRTActive(Object obj, MessageProperties props) {
4            // init real-time active object execution environment
5            queue_ = new RTQueue(props);
6            RTExecutor executor = new RTExecutor(queue_,obj, props);
7            (new Thread(executor)).start();
8            // establish base-meta link
9            attachObject(obj);
10           registerEventMethodCall(obj);
11       }
12   }                          Fig. 4 The MetaRTActive class
```

The priority in the message-property specification is used by the insert method of RTQueueManager for a placement decision. The RTExecutor (Fig. 5) uses the message property to execute the wrapper functions (lines 19 and 21 of Fig. 5) and to control maximal execution times. To control maximal execution times, a watch-dog thread is started, which blocks until the time quantum is over and then sends the thread a stop signal. This causes the thread to throw a ThreadDeath exception. The exception is caught (lines 22 to 25 of Fig. 5) and this way it triggers the clean-up function.

```
1    class RTExecutor extends Executor
2    {
3        MessageProperties props_;
4
5        public RTExecutor(QueueManager queue, Object o, MessageProperties props) {
6            super(queue,obj);
7            props_=props;
8        }
9
10       public void run() {
11           EventDescMethodCall event;
12           for(;;) {
13               ActorMessage msg = (ActorMessage) queue_.next()
14               EventDescMethodCall event = msg.getEvent();
15               MessageProperty prop = props_.getProperty(event.methodname, event.signature);
16               ... prepare the wrapper event descriptions ...
17               ... initialize and start the watchdog thread ...
18               try {
19                   doExecute(obj_, pre_wrapper_event);
20                   continueExecutionVoid(obj_, event);
21                   doExecute(obj_, post_wrapper_event);
22                   ... terminate watchdog thread ...
22               } catch(ThreadDeath e) {
23                   ... prepare the cleanup_event description ...
24                   doExecute(obj_, cleanup_event);
25               }
26               msg.notifyAll();
27           }
28       }
29   }
```

Fig. 5 The RTExecutor class

6   Related Work

The main difference between our work and other implementations of real-time actors is, that we do not need any support for actors from the run-time system. We solely rely on a minimal object model with reflective capabilities.

The actor model described in this paper was inspired by the Real-Time Object-Oriented Modeling language ROOM [10]. ROOM's primary focus lies on the design of actor-based real-time systems. The actor model is predefined in the ROOM virtual-machine layer and can not be extended by applications.

DROL [11] is an actor implementation based on the ARTS kernel. It relies on kernel support for active objects, but can control the execution of actors with metaobjects. MetaJava provides means to implement an object model that supports active objects. This way, different active object semantics can co-exist within the same program.

RTsynchronizers [9] extend an actor model with real-time constraints. These constraints on message executions are defined separately from the actor definition and thus the actor can be reused in a different environment. RTsynchronizers define conditions over time variables. These conditions must be fulfilled before a message is scheduled for execution.

7 Conclusion and Future Work

We described a scheme to implement real-time sensitive actors using the reflective Java interpreter MetaJava. More work needs to be done to support well-known policies for real-time–sensitive actors. This includes message schedule times, periodic tasks, etc. It would be interesting to investigate the possibilities of combining the actor meta system with other metaobjects, such as *MetaRemote* [4] or *MetaReplication* [5].

8 References

1. G. Agha. *Actors: A Model of Concurrent Computation in Distributed Systems*. MIT Press, 1986.
2. J. Ferber. Computational Reflection in class based Object-Oriented Languages. *OOPSLA '89*, New Orleans, La., Oct. 1989, pp. 317–326.
3. C. Hewitt. Viewing control structures as patterns of passing messages. *Journal of Artificial Intelligence*, 8(3) 1977, pp. 323-364
4. J. Kleinöder, M. Golm. MetaJava: An Efficient Run-Time Meta Architecture for Java. *IWOOOS '96*, October 27-18, 1996, Seattle, Wa, 1996.
5. J. Kleinöder, M. Golm. *Transparent and Adaptable Object Replication Using a Reflective Java*, TR-I4-96-07, University of Erlangen, IMMD IV, Sept. 1996
6. T. Lindholm, F. Yellin. *The Java Virtual Machine Specification*. Addison-Wesley, Sept. 1996.
7. S. Matsuoka, A. Yonezawa. Analysis of Inheritance Anomaly in Object-Oriented Concurrent Programming Languages. in G. Agha, A. Yonezawa, P. Wegner. *Research Directions in Concurrent Object-Oriented Programming*. MIT Press, 1993. pp. 107-150
8. K. Nilsen. Issues in the Design and Implementation of Real-Time Java. in *Java Developer's Journal*, June 1996.
9. Ren, G. Agha, Saito. A Modular Approach for Programming Distributed Real-Time Systems. Special Issue of the *Journal of Parallel and Distributed Computing* on Object-Oriented Real-Time Systems, 1996.
10. B. Selic, G. Gullekson, P.T.Ward. *Real-Time Object-Oriented Modeling*. John Wiley & Sons, Inc., 1996.
11. K. Takashio, M. Tokoro. DROL: An Object-Oriented Programming Language for Distributed Real-Time Systems. *OOPSLA '92*, pp. 276-294

Adaptive Scheduling Using Reflection

S. E. Mitchell, A. Burns and A. J. Wellings,
Real-Time Systems Research Group, University of York, UK

Abstract. This paper presents a model for adaptable scheduling for hard and soft real-time systems that are designed to cope with a variety of situations including unexpected faults, imprecisely defined environments, reconfiguration etc. The model uses scheduling groups (derived from meta-groups as used in ABCL/R) that are responsible for managing shared resources within a set of components. Each group has an independent schedule (for simultaneous soft and hard groups) and many factors can be modified at run-time.

1 Introduction and Motivation

Historically, the properties required of real-time systems (RTS) have been guaranteed by *a priori* analysis. This has led to systems that are fixed and therefore unable to adapt to a changing environment or unexpected failure. The motivation for this work, therefore, is a requirement that systems become more adaptive. This requirement can arise at design time (e.g. delay of method binding – polymorphism), compile time (re-configuration) or run-time (an evolving system) to cope with changes in the environment. System modifications can be used to cope with unexpected faults or with an imprecisely defined environment, etc. In addition, we want to support flexible scheduling to allow the introduction of optional components into the system at run-time with some guarantee of schedulability. The ability to determine characteristics of a system late in the development lifecycle also has great potential to reduce or eliminate the high economic cost normally associated with modifications required at a late stage.

The above aims lead us to consider integrating contemporary real-time research with (object-oriented) reflective systems [1, 2]. Whilst many of our aims do not *require* reflection to be implemented in a real-time system, we believe a reflective system has advantages for both disciplining/controlling run-time change and as a mechanism for system structuring. The clear separation between computation about the problem (application level) and computation about the system itself (meta-level) acting as a strong factor influencing system structure. We also consider that a reflective real-time system will permit both the desired flexibility (e.g. run-time modification of the task set) while also producing an extremely adaptable system (e.g. modify or replace the scheduler).

1.1 The Concurrency Model

Before discussing reflection and metaobject protocols it is helpful to describe the concurrency model. Our model has been heavily influenced by TAO [3, 4] and adopts the concept of (multiple) tasks encapsulated within objects to form *active objects*. Tasks in an active are created with the encapsulating object and executed in conformance with the system schedule. When an object is destroyed any encapsulated threads are terminated; however, should a task terminate before the object is destroyed the object enters a passive (purely reactive) state.

This approach allows for the dynamic creation and destruction of tasks via their encapsulating object and for concurrency control and task monitoring via the relevant metaobject.

2 Requirements

The primary motivation for this work is to expand the available dynamism within RTS to promote their ability to cope with an ever-changing environment possessing varying demands and faults. We consider than an (object-oriented) reflective system will give us the ability to implement both compile-time and run-time change while also imposing a strong influence on system structure by separating computation on the problem from computation about how to go about solving the problem.

A key design decision when developing our model is that we want to be able to localise change within our system. This is desirable so that a change in one part of the system (for example, introduction of a new or replacement component) does not invalidate any guarantees made with regard to the remainder of the system. For this, we require that our model support a single meta-object per application object. However, a many scheduling policies require knowledge about the state of the entire system prior to making a decision so we also require a facility for joint decision making.

The most readily identifiable characteristic of a RTS is the particular scheduling policy in use – for example, cyclic scheduling, fixed-priority etc. If hard real-time guarantees are required many of these policies need the schedules to be fixed at design time before any code is written and therefore subsequent changes during a project development can be costly both in economic terms and in terms of development time. The requirement that available CPU (or other resources) be distributed amongst components early also makes the use of optional components to absorb any slack-time available difficult or impossible.

Therefore the ability to modify the scheduling policy is one of the most desirable candidates for the introduction of dynamism within a system and this change must occur without causing a "great leap backwards" in the lifecycle. Depending on the degree of temporal criticality required a number of dynamic scheduling policies exist, e.g. best effort [5], which allow for modifications of the schedule and the introduction of optional components. The use of these within a reflective framework will further extend their dynamism by allowing modifications to elements of the schedule, and indeed the scheduler itself, to be made at run-time along with a repeat computation of temporal guarantees. The introduction of dynamic scheduling requires that the model support the introduction of optional components at run-time with some guarantee of their temporal behaviour (in that once introduced the system remains schedulable).

Many RTS involve competitive concurrency where components compete for limited resources so that each can achieve their goal. The problem of priority inversion [6] where a task with low importance can prevent a more important task from reaching its goal has been well known for some time. The creation of a replaceable scheduler introduces another variant of this problem whereby a component could replace the scheduler with one that would give it a more favourable allocation of resources. We thus also need to be able to limit the degree of change so that a program cannot introduce a change in schedule without agreement. In our model we consider that the best way of doing this will be to limit change to switching between a set of possible schedulers. This will permit much greater adaptive behaviour – for example switching from fixed priority to best-effort to maintain some functionality in the event of an unexpected failure – while retaining confidence that a single component cannot adversely affect the entire system.

3   A Reflective Model for Adaptive Scheduling

3.1   Meta-groups in ABCL/R2

We have chosen a model based on the notion of meta-group first used in the reflective object-oriented language ABCL/R2 [7]. In ABCL/R2 objects possess an individual reflective tower as well as belonging to a particular *meta-group* with a group reflective tower. Objects in a group share a group object manager, GMgr, present in the meta-group and that the metaobjects ↑x and ↑y share an evaluator from the meta-group. Each group also includes a *metagen* object that is responsible for the creation of new objects/metaobjects within a group. ABCL/R2 models the use of shared limited resources through *group kernel objects* shared amongst the application-level objects within the same meta-group. The use of two reflective towers allows for both individual modification and group wide modification.

3.2   Using Metagroups for Adaptive Scheduling

The two key components for an adaptive scheduler are the admissions policy (governs the acceptance of new entities into the system) and the scheduler (controls execution of entities at run-time). Therefore, the first task is to map these components into the meta-group structure. The role of admissions policy will be implemented by *metagen* since in the ABCL/R2 model it already controls object creation within the group. The scheduler will likewise be implemented in the GMgr manager object. Within ABCL/R2 group kernel objects are non-reified (have no meta-object) and are therefore hard to change. For a dynamic, adaptive, system we would like to be able to modify these objects at both compile and run-time and so our model introduces a *third* reflective tower for this operation. The metaobjects of metagen and GMgr are members of the meta-meta-group.

Guaranteeing the temporal properties of a task set to ensure that it is schedulable even in the worst case is NP hard. Hence it is not practical to allow complete freedom for hard real-time groups – for example simply trying to recalculate the schedule after admitting a new component would invalidate the temporal guarantees to the existing components in the group. Instead there must be increasing restrictions on the groups as their temporal properties harden. We will use a two-phase process for group creation – start-up and run-time. The initial phase allows *all* groups to accept object admission while the second allows hard real-time groups to put a block on further admission and so maintain their fixed schedule. Such an approach allows for the dynamic reconfiguration of soft real-time schedules at run-time with whatever online guarantee of schedulability they can provide while retaining the guarantee that a hard real-time group will remain schedulable.

The act of scheduling, whether soft or hard real-time, involves the distribution of resources, e.g. memory and CPU, to components within the group. Each scheduling group receives an allocation of each resource that the GMgr object manages as a shared resource on behalf of the component objects. For CPU time this distribution is of the form "*X in Y*" (e.g. 100ms in every 500ms). This leads on to how the amount allocated to each group should be calculated. On one level this is not of particular importance – it could be round robin, handled by a meta-meta-group, etc. but it does illustrate that one may want to change the distribution policy. We propose to use the meta-meta-group for this activity – it will be responsible for implementing the second level scheduling by distributing resources among groups as well as its role of modifying the scheduler. It is therefore here that we will control the change possible within a group to limit

A hard real-time group must acquire all resources during the start-up phase to ensure that the schedule will remain valid at run-time. This means that such a group cannot share resources with other groups (since they must be available at all times) and that objects that require shared access must be present in the same group. Conversely, a group that only enforces soft real-time guarantees can acquire any additional resources, such as communication links, during any phase as required. It should be noted that even this two-phase strategy could be made more rigorous if *absolute* guarantees of schedulability are required. For example, after a system has adapted to a reconfiguration or changed environment we may not know how many components will attempt to join a HRT group during the start-up phase. This may lead to some (lower priority) components being rejected to retain group schedulability and having to seek entry into alternative groups so possibly leaving the whole system without a valid schedule. In such a case we would need to be able to either explicitly specify which components will join a group and then have these constraints validated during compile time or have the system develop some appropriate validated distribution. The existing restriction on run-time migrations to hard real-time groups would then ensure that the system retained schedulability.

Component objects become part of a scheduling group when they are created. However, group membership is not static and components can move to another group. Reasons for migration are diverse but fundamentally voluntary migration will occur if a resource is required which is not available in the current group. For example, if a component cannot get a resource since it is held for exclusive use by another group it can elect to attempt to migrate to access the resource rather than waiting till it can be pulled into the current group. The corollary of this is that a group manager may, in certain circumstances, *force a migration* if this would improve either the schedulability of the group or the system as a whole. For example, consider a group with hard real-time characteristics with a number of optional components which at run-time are never or rarely) able to complete due to lack of CPU resource within the group. A forced migration to another group with spare CPU (possibly on another node) would therefore be an alternative to a rescheduling of meta-groups by the meta-meta-group. Such an approach will need some means valuing a task so the group can decide what to migrate– this decision could be based on task priority or on a notion of value when complete.

3.3 Metalevel Control of Application Level Active Objects

We now want to consider when to perform computation at a metalevel. A *scheduling group* is not itself a meta-object - it is more akin to a collection of (reified and non-reified) active objects at the meta-level responsible for managing shared attributes. Thus there is no direct relationship between an event at the application level triggering metalevel computation and the analogous base level event triggering group computation. However, one exception that we have identified is an event that may require the scheduling of any active component base level objects (i.e. context switch, task termination or task arrival).

To resolve this, we propose to place *GMgr* and *metagen* at a notional *metathread level.* Consequently, just as metaobjects deal with base level objects, we can consider that a new group level object, which we term the *metathread,* will deal with a base level thread. This new object performs actions analogous to a metaobject but instead acts upon a base level task and may describe both its structure and behaviour. However, with an active object model the distinction between objects and threads can be rather blurred (e.g. we have assumed a concurrency model in which threads are embedded within a base level object). Hence, in our model the metathread controls behaviour but the structure of the thread is determined by the metaobject that "contains" the base level object.

It is now appropriate to consider the interaction behaviour between *metaobject* and *metathread.* The base level task is embedded in an active base level object so its structure/behaviour should therefore determined by the metaobject/metathread. Consequently each significant event in a task's life (context switch, etc.) can be made to trigger a switch to metaobject computation which can communicate the change in state to *GMgr* or *metagen* as appropriate. This approach is appealing since it yields a mechanism for unifying two elements – objects and threads – with (effectively) different metaobject and *metathread* objects handling their structure/behaviour and controlling their execution respectively. We thus have two, distinct, areas of group/meta-level computation – metaobject and metathread – in which each a different area of base level computation is addressed.

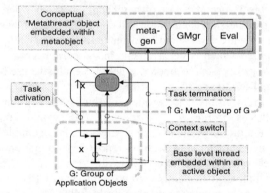

Figure 1: Interaction between thread, "metathread" and group objects

Fig. 1 illustrates the interaction between a thread in a base level object "x", its metaobject "↑x", the metathread portion of "↑x" and the group shared objects within a group "G" and meta-group "⇑G". The metathread for active object "x" is embedded within "↑x" and encapsulates the behaviour of the metaobject related to control of thread execution. This object serves as the interaction point between GMgr and the base level thread. At thread creation a jump is made to the metalevel through the metathread object and *metagen* invoked to add the thread to the group's schedule.

Finally, on termination a jump through the metathread is made causing any necessary updates the group's schedule to occur.

4   Summary and Conclusions

The model presented here is able to support different levels of dynamism within a single system depending only on the hardness of the temporal guarantee that is required. We have decided not to attempt to create new real-time scheduling policies but rather to seek to explore how existing techniques could be married with reflective implementations. The model allows for many characteristics of a system to be modified either at compile time or at run-time.

Reviewing the requirements presented in Section 2, the presented model uses scheduling groups to permit both compile-time and run-time change with the benefit that such change is localised placing boundaries any effects. In addition, the group scheduler can be changed, but only within a pre-defined set which satisfies the requirement for *safe* change. The ability of a metaobject to perform different activities based on current resources (e.g. trading execution cost against accuracy at run-time) further enhances the dynamic scheduling possibilities.

5   References

[1] T. Watanabe and A. Yonezawa, "Reflection in an Object-Oriented Concurrent Language," *ACM SIGPLAN Notices - Proceedings of OOPSLA '88*, 23(11), pp. 306-315, 1988.

[2] P. Maes, "Concepts and Experiments in Computational Reflection," *ACM SIGPLAN Notices - Proceedings of OOPSLA '87*, 22(12), pp. 147-155, 1987.

[3] S. E. Mitchell, "TAO - A Model for the Integration of Concurrency and Synchronisation in Object-Oriented Programming," Department of Computer Science, University of York, UK, 1995

[4] S. E. Mitchell and A. J. Wellings, "Synchronisation, Concurrent Object-Oriented Programming and the Inheritance Anomaly," *Computer Languages*, 22(1), pp. 15-26, 1996.

[5] C. D. Locke, "Best-Effort Decision Making for Real-Time Scheduling," Computer Science Department, CMU, 1986

[6] L. Sha, A. R. Rajkumar, and A. J. P. Lehoczky, "Priority Inheritance Protocols: An Approach to Real-Time Synchronisation," *IEEE Transactions on Computers*, 39(9), pp. 1175-1185, 1990.

[7] H. Masuhara, S. Matsuoka, T. Watanabe, and A. Yonezawa, "Object-Oriented Concurrent Reflective Languages can be Implemented Efficiently," *ACM SIGPLAN Notices -- Proceedings of OOPSLA '92*, 27(11), pp. 127-144, 1992.

Adaptive Fault-Tolerant Systems and Reflective Architectures

Jack Goldberg[1] and Robert J. Stroud,
Department of Computing Science,
University of Newcastle upon Tyne, UK
Email: goldberg@csl.sri.com, r.j.stroud@ncl.ac.uk

ABSTRACT

As the environment of a fault-tolerant system increases in complexity, the system's performance may be degraded if it has to respond to all conditions in the service range at any time. The performance may be improved if the system is able to adapt its structure to changing environmental conditions. Adaptation may be valuable not only at run time but over the entire life-cycle. At run time, adaptation should be automatic, but during design and configuration, it may be manually driven. We examine the benefits of adaptation at different times of the life-cycle, and discuss issues of structure and control. We review several architectural approaches to adaptive system design and recommend using reflective architectures because of their power and generality.

1 Introduction

Every system is designed to operate over some range of operating conditions and user requirements. Operating conditions may vary in workload, type of data, type of fault, and availability of resources, and user requirements may vary in operator skill and preferences with regard to performance and dependability.

As the range and complexity of operating conditions and user requirements widens, the efficiency of resource utilization in a fixed design may degrade; for example, resources needed for performance may have to be reserved to provide high fault coverage for a very wide range of fault types. While conditions at any given time may fluctuate within a narrow range, a fixed design must be able to deal with any condition within its design range. With adaptation, a system's resources can be configured so that it gives optimum service for the actual current range of conditions. The improved service can be realized in fault coverage, throughput, response speed, or user support.

The benefits of adaptability may be realized not only during run time, but also during design and during system configuration. During design, decisions are always in flux. If there are several design teams, one team may find that its portion of a design cannot meet the assumptions made about it by another team. In some cases, a design may depend on an externally supplied component or technology that is not available when the design effort begins.

Similar variations occur during a system's configuration and reconfiguration. Component subsystems with previously unknown characteristics may have to be integrated in a system, and growth in system size may introduce new points of contention and overload.

---

[1] Visiting research fellow, SRI International (retired)

Adaptation may be beneficial for a wide variety of concerns, including service objectives, operating conditions, system composition, and user behavior, as suggested by the following examples. Most of the examples are meaningful at design, configuration and run-time phases:

- **Service objectives** – Different, situation-dependent requirements for dependability and performance
- **Operating conditions** – Changing fault types (permanent, transient, physical, design, etc.) and fault rates, changing workload types (text, images, streams) and workload distributions (frequencies and ports), and changing process and object distribution in multi-level client-server systems
- **System composition** – Varying amounts of system resources and their capabilities, new configurations of equipment, software and data, growth in system scale and geographic extension and growth in the types of services and functions
- **User behavior** – User expertise (error rate, use of multimedia,) and patterns of user interaction (duration, breadth of demand for data and resources)

2   Adaptation for Fault Tolerance

The effectiveness of various fault tolerance mechanisms is very sensitive to a variety of operating conditions, including level of available resources, type of fault, fault rate, workload distribution and user priorities for performance and dependability. Following are examples of how variations in these conditions can call for different fault-tolerance techniques [Goldberg *et al.* 1993]:

- **Response to variations in available resources** – Change the level of redundancy within a given fault-tolerance scheme, or change the fault tolerance scheme to exploit available resources. For example, change from fault masking (three or four-fold redundancy) to fault detection (two-fold redundancy)
- **Response to variations in fault types and rate** – Change from retrying the same process (for a transient fault) or pausing (to allow dissipation of an overload) to shifting to a new process (for a permanent fault), or change from voting (for a simple fault) to Byzantine agreement (for a complex fault)
- **Response to variations in workload distribution** – Change from load balancing (sufficient resources) to load shedding (insufficient resources)
- **Response to variations in user requirements** – Change from a balance of reliability and performance objectives to a requirement (perhaps short-term) for maximum reliability

2.1   Managing Run-time Adaptation of Fault Tolerance

Adaptation is a new mode of system operation that requires special design and control. Important concerns are *effectiveness*, including how much improvement is achieved and how fast, and *correctness*, including avoidance of minor and major errors during adaptation. Following are some requirements for managing adaptation.

Correct design – The following functions must be designed and verified:

- A set of alternative fault-tolerance implementations
- Diagnostic algorithms for determining the current fault types and fault rates, and for assessing the availability of resources

- Mechanisms for making transitions between alternative implementations and for assuring that the transitions are error free and that state information is preserved

Run-time control – The following functions must be executed at run-time:

- Observe and analyze real-time fault tolerance for success and performance
- Identify the most appropriate fault tolerance method and decide if a change is warranted and has acceptably low risk of failure
- Execute the change to new fault tolerance method
- Evaluate the new behavior and revise as needed

3 Detailed Issues of Run-time Adaptation

Adaptation is a process that itself has numerous design issues that have been studied at length in the field of process control. The following discussion is an interpretation of such issues in the context of fault-tolerant computing.

3.1 Control algorithms

Several control algorithms are well known, and reflect different situations of predictability and aspirations for optimality. These include:

- **Trial and error** – The adaptation controller periodically tries some adaptation method and evaluates its benefits. If the benefits are minor, the system reverts to the previous mode of operation.
- **Static or dynamic probabilistic decisions** – The adaptation controller computes an estimate of the benefits of changing to different implementations. The computation may be based on static system models or on run-time behavior.
- **Model-based prediction** – The adaptation controller predicts future behavior for the present and alternative implementations on the basis of a dynamic model of faults, input data flow and system capabilities. Model based prediction has the greatest potential for accuracy and speed of adaptation.

3.2 Risk management

Making changes entails risks of error and failure. The primary sources of such risks are inadequate information or incorrect analyses of faults and system capabilities. Errors are inevitable. It is therefore necessary for the adaptation strategy to allow for such errors. There are two general strategies for dealing with risks in adaptation:

- **Incremental change** – Changes should be made in several steps that are small enough to permit assessment and reversal. The steps may be in the fraction of the system or in the fraction of system functionality that is modified.
- **Correctable change** – Changes should be correctable if they are found to be ineffective or incorrect. The correction may be by reverting to a previous configuration state or by moving to a new configuration state that is safer or more effective.

3.3 Stability

A common problem in process control is the need to avoid unstable control. Examples of instability are

- **Thrashing** – If the system changes too slowly, it may lag behind the driving force it is trying to track. It may then spend all of its working time making changes that never stabilise.
- **Circularity** – In a multi-stage system, adaptation in one stage may induce adaptation in a second stage (the first stage may act as part of the environment of the second stage). Such changes may eventually return to cause an adaptation in the first stage. Such circular changes may fail to stabilise.
- **Unbounded change** – In a large network such as the Internet, if the nodes are tightly coupled, it is possible that an unlimited wave of adaptations may be triggered.

Familiar solutions to stability problems are

- **Change threshold** – The adaptation force must exceed a managed threshold.
- **Hysteresis control** – A higher level of an adaptation criterion is needed to leave a configuration state than to enter it.
- **Change-isolation boundaries** – For spatial adaptation effects, a system may be partitioned in regions, with boundaries that block the spread of adaptation. Subsystems within the region exchange resources and work obligations with some level of slack in resources and job assignment.

3.4 Time-sensitive diagnosis and analysis

Good adaptation requires good diagnosis of faults and system capabilities. Given the uncertainties of fault diagnosis, which are uncertain inferences from error observations, and of system capabilities, which may depend on unobservable data, it is very desirable to have the best possible access to system data and the best possible diagnostic and analysis algorithms. In run-time adaptation, there is an intrinsic conflict between accuracy of diagnosis and speed of diagnosis. For less than infinite-time diagnosis, some inaccuracy is inevitable. Diagnostic algorithms should be designed to produce an adequate diagnosis in real time rather than an optimal diagnosis in arbitrary time.

3.5 Control policy

Given the benefits of adaptation and the risks of inadequate and erroneous adaptation, the decision to adapt should be subject to a policy that properly weighs the benefits and the risks. Such a policy may be built into a system at design or configuration time, or it may be subject to change during operation. For example, a user may decide to take a risk of adaptation if none of the current operations are critical. Alternatively, an experienced user may have sufficient confidence in the system to initiate adaptation to meet a severe workload.

3.6 Separation of adaptation concerns

We note here that the various concerns about the adaptation process (diagnosis, error recovery, risk management and control policy) are design concerns that may have many solutions. Having them expressed as separate classes will help in the evolution of a successful adaptation capability.

4 Architectures for Adaptive Fault Tolerance

Adaptivity can be realized in a variety of architectural structures. Some generic structures are:

- **Monolithic** – A single algorithm may be designed with several modes, and with decision functions to invoke one mode or another for different operating environments. A fixed structure of this kind can exhibit adaptive behavior, but it is difficult to modify and enhance. For example, enriching the adaptive control functions may require rewriting the entire algorithm.

- **Distributed** – An adaptive system might be built from a set of communicating modules that achieve adaptation by changing their interpretation of interface messages. For example, a given configuration would consist of a set of contracts for services between modules; adaptation would be achieved by modifying the contracts. This scheme has some merit as a flexible medium for changing structure, but it is only a fragment of a system; issues such as diagnosis, representation of alternate structural modes, risk management and adaptation policy are not addressed.

- **Delegation** – Delegation is the run-time binding of alternate object representations. As in the preceding technique, this method has potential as a mechanism for accomplishing change, but it does not address system issues.

- **Reflective** – This architecture is attractive because it provides a general framework for incorporating various adaptation concerns as separate meta levels, an effective means for communicating information and a convenient means for invoking alternate structures [Maes 1987].

4.1 Benefits of Reflective Architectures

The two key ideas underlying a reflective architecture are

- **Reflection** – Reflection is the ability of a program to modify its own structure based on observed behavior or more concretely "the ability of a program to manipulate as data something representing the state of the program during its execution".

- **Meta level structure** – A simple meta level structure involves associating one or more meta level objects with each application object so that the implementation of each application object is controlled by its corresponding meta level objects [Kiczales *et al.* 1991]. This relationship may be recursive, so that a given meta level structure may itself be controlled by a higher meta level. The result is an upward-going hierarchy. When the hierarchy provides reflective control of lower levels based on the feeding upward of data about lower-level behavior (a process called Reification), the structure is called a Reflective Tower.

This structure offers the following benefits for adaptive system design:

- **Separation of concerns** – The hierarchical structure provided by a recursive use of reflection allows a very convenient separation of behavioral concerns, such as application function, fault tolerance technique, security technique, and operating policy. Such separation reduces the interdependence of design solutions, and thus increases flexibility.

- **Flexible support for late binding** – Allowing the way in which functionality is realized to be modified ("Design for Modifiability") makes it easier to defer the binding of design decisions. This extends the long-term trend in computer engineering to manage binding time, and to allow binding decisions to be delayed until information is obtained that will improve the quality of the decision.

- **Intrinsic support for run-time adaptation** – The principle of reflection provides, in a way that is intrinsic to the architecture, the feedback from behavior to control of structure that is needed for run-time adaptation. The flow of information that reflective structure provides from lower to higher levels of control also provides a convenient mechanism for invoking alternative control structures.

A convenient heuristic for establishing the relationship between levels is to consider the lower level to specify *what is to be done*, and the upper level to specify *how it is to be done;* for example, a lower level may define a user function, while an upper level may define a particular fault-tolerance technique that is to be used to provide reliable service [Fabre *et al.* 1995]. The what/how relationship can be extended upward; for example, a higher level might be used to evaluate the effectiveness of a given fault tolerance technique and govern the change to an alternate technique.

4.2   A Simple Reflective Architecture for Fault Tolerance

Figure 1 illustrates a simple reflective architecture for fault tolerance

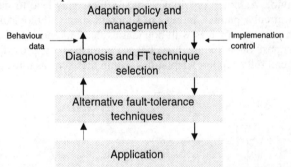

Fig. 1: A Reflective Tower for Fault Tolerant Computing

The possibility of separation of concerns is evident from the figure. This separation simplifies the enrichment of various concerns, since, for example, the risk management functions can be increased in power without necessarily changing the fault tolerance methods. Similarly, as new fault modes are discovered, additional fault-tolerance techniques may be added without necessarily changing other functions.

4.3   Extensions of the ArchitectureThis simple architecture may be extended in several ways, in both monolithic and distributed systems, as follows:

- **Monolithic systems** – Reflective architecture may be applied to monolithic systems, either by treating the module itself as the lowest layer of a tower, or by applying towers to individual layers of a hierarchical structure. A tower can serve to adapt the functions of a given layer for optimal behavior in a changing environment.
- **Distributed systems** – In a system composed of communicating subsystems, each subsystem may be structured using a reflective architecture. If it is desired

that the communication between subsystems be subject to reflection, the usual technique for realizing hierarchies in distributed systems may be employed, that is, a virtual upper level may be created by providing each subsystem with a higher-level stage, and then ensuring that communication enforces the identity between the stages in state and output, as illustrated in Figure 2.

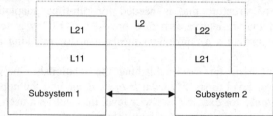

Fig. 2: Virtual Reflective Tower for Communicating Subsystems

Adaptation in distributed systems faces the problem that subsystems comprise part of each other's environment. An adaptation in one subsystem may then stimulate adaptation in neighboring subsystems; for example, the result of an adaptation in one subsystem—say due to a loss of resources—may be that the subsystem cannot fulfill its contract for service with an adjacent subsystem. That subsystem may then have to adapt its behavior. As noted previously, such effects may lead to instability, such as oscillations in circular paths. One way to suppress such pathological behavior would be to establish adaptation zones with boundaries that hide non-local adaptations from neighboring zones. Such hiding may be accomplished by providing a reserve of resources that can fully support adaptations within the zone, as illustrated in Figure 3.

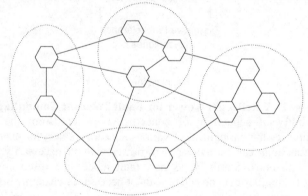

Fig. 3: Adaptation boundaries in distributed systems

5   Open Questions

At this early stage in development of the architecture, questions arise as to novelty, generality, designability and difficulty of realization. We offer the following brief answers.

- **Novelty** – The issues of flexible structure, provision of alternative modes of implementation of a functional requirement, the decision process for making changes, and the need to evaluate new modes, are all either explicitly or implicitly present in the design of practical adaptive systems, such as modems and mathematical software. What is new in our approach is not adaptivity, but the architectural structure for designing it. The contribution of the architecture is separation of concerns and strong support for feedback of behavior data to structure control.

- **Generality** – Reflection seems to be applicable to both monolithic and distributed systems, and may be flexibly applied to elements of a design hierarchy. A critical issue is the overhead requirement for the various communication mechanisms. Various authors have observed that the performance load of inter-level communication can be made very small when compared to the load of the levels themselves. These observations need further verification.

- **Designability** – The additional mechanisms used in fault-tolerant architectures introduce complexities that may create new failure modes. We think that the separation of concerns allows an orderly approach to design and design verification. Alternative fault tolerance mechanisms can be designed and verified separately, as in ordinary fault-tolerant designs. Several new process types will have to be verified, such as assurance that no data is lost during adaptation, and that adaptation is incremental and reversible. Designs for those processes must be effective and easy to verify. Diagnosis in real-time is a challenge, but incrementality and reversibility reduces the need for high diagnostic precision.

  We reject the view that adaptive fault tolerance requires special machine intelligence. None of the issues we have discussed imply anything other than ordinary engineering solutions.

- **Difficulty of realization** – The issues of risk management, continuity, mode switching, and recovery are potentially open-ended in complexity. Nevertheless, they may have very simple expression if the environmental challenges and the goals for optimality are modest. The existence of various practical adaptive systems encourages us to believe that useful, well-structured, adaptive systems can have acceptably low complexity. The separation of concerns provided by the architecture should make it possible to enrich a simple design.

6 Summary

Adaptation offers a way to cope with the increasing complexity and dynamism of modern systems. It is needed to provide acceptable system performance for a broadening range of requirements for fault tolerance, resource management, load management, and service trade-offs.

Adaptation has value at all points of the life cycle, from design, to configuration, to operation. It may be seen as a form of managed binding time, a major trend in computer engineering.

Adaptation is common in practice. Our approach makes use of new ideas in object-oriented systems to extend it to fault tolerant systems. We believe that reflective architectures offer a general and effective design framework.

7 Acknowledgements

This work was partially supported by an EPSRC visiting research fellowship and also by the CEC as part of the DeVa "Design for Validation" Long Term Research Project no. 20072.

88

8 References

[Fabre *et al.* 1995] J.-C. Fabre, V. Nicomette, T. Pérennou, R. J. Stroud and Z. Wu, "Implementing Fault-Tolerant Applications using Reflective Object-Oriented Programming", in *Proc. 25th Int. Symp. on Fault-Tolerant Computing (FTCS-25)*, Pasadena, CA, USA, pp. 489-498, June 27-30, 1995

[Goldberg *et al.* 1993] J. Goldberg, I. Greenberg, T. Lawrence, "Adaptive Fault Tolerance", in *Proc. IEEE Workshop on Advances in Parallel and Distributed Systems*, Princeton, NJ, USA, pp 127-132, Oct 6, 1993

[Kiczales *et al.* 1991] G. Kiczales, J. d. Rivières and D. G. Bobrow, *The Art of the Metaobject Protocol*, MIT Press, 1991

[Maes 1987] P. Maes, "Concepts and Experiments in Computational Reflection", in *Proc. Conf. on Object-Oriented Programming Systems, Languages and Applications (OOPSLA'87) (ACM SIGPLAN Notices, 22,10)*, pp.147-55, 1987

Workshop on
Language Support for Design Patterns and Frameworks (LSDF'97)

Introduction

Jan Bosch

University of Karlskrona/Ronneby
Dept of Computer Science
SoftCenter, S-372 25, Ronneby, Sweden
Jan.Bosch@ide.hk-r.se

Görel Hedin

Lund University
Dept of Computer Science
Box 118, S-221 00 Lund, Sweden
Gorel.Hedin@dna.lth.se

Kai Koskimies

University of Tampere
Dept of Computer Science
Box 607, FIN-33101, Tampere, Finland
koskimie@cs.uta.fi

There is growing interest in the role of languages in employing reusable OO architectures. In particular, OO frameworks and design patterns can be related to languages in various ways. More concretely, we recognise the following topics where languages, patterns and frameworks come together:

- Language support for design patterns: Design patterns are primarily used as a design technique and only limited attention is paid to their implementation. A number of researchers have investigated different ways of providing language support for design patterns, e.g. by representing them as language constructs or by template code generation. However, the issue is far from solved and should be investigated further.

- Framework instantiation languages: Lately, some authors have proposed the use of specific instantiation languages for frameworks. Especially black-box frameworks in well understood domains could benefit from such languages, since they simplify instantiation of the framework considerably. However, the actual design and implementation of such languages is not well understood and needs to be further investigated. Also, when composing frameworks for use in an application, the instantiation languages may conflict with each other.

- Framework extension support: A well-known problem with white-box frameworks is that they are difficult to extend. One may need quite detailed understanding of the implementation of framework classes in order to know how they should be subclassed. Language techniques might be able to lessen these problems by giving support for checking the extensions and giving framework-specific editing support for doing correct extensions.

- Domain specific language extensions to support frameworks: When constructing or using framework in a particular domain, there may be domain concepts that are not easily expressed as classes or objects. Such domain concepts can often be expressed as language constructs and reused as such. Traditionally, software engineers have dealt with this through, for example, the use of macros and preprocessors, but more integrated and structured approaches are required.

- Framework-based language implementation: Frameworks provide an interesting basis for implementing domain-oriented languages: general domain concepts, presented as abstract classes, can be specialized into concrete language structures and reused in many languages, allowing fast development of domain-oriented languages. Although there are tools supporting this, the process of deriving languages from abstract concepts is not well understood.

The goal of this workshop was to bring together researchers active in the aforementioned areas and to provide an interactive forum for the exchange of ideas, results, and open problems in this area. 14 submitted papers were selected for presentation and, when combined, they cover most of the identified topics.

To obtain a high degree of interaction at the workshop, the presentations were kept short, and after each session consisting of 2-4 papers, a 15 minute panel discussion with the session authors was held. At the end of the workshop, an "open-mike" session was held, allowing also non-author participants to initiate a discussion on related topics. This scheme worked out very well, giving good discussions and an interactive informal atmosphere.

In this Workshop Reader 3-4 pages summaries of all the papers are presented. The full papers are available electronically at http://www.ide.hk-r.se/~bosch/lsdf/.

The papers were presented in five sessions, briefly introduced below.

Message Interception for Design Pattern Implementation
This session contained two papers discussing the implementation of design patterns. *Bosch* introduced the session and the workshop by describing the problems, approaches and requirements of providing language support for object-oriented frameworks and design patterns. As examples, the solutions developed in the layered object model were discussed. Also *Ducasse* intends to describe design patterns as first-class entities. These entities are specified as templates and their instances intercept messages between objects involved in the design pattern.

Relations of General-Purpose Languages, Frameworks and Design Patterns
This session was introduced by a paper by *Gil* and *Lorenz* discussing the relationships between design patterns and programming languages, and how far patterns in different categories are from being actual language features. The following paper by *Agerbo* and *Cornils* made this discussion more concrete by looking in detail how the programming language BETA supports particular design patterns. The final paper in this session, by

De Volder and *De Meuter*, discusses how type systems from the functional programming community might help in constructing reusable OO frameworks.

Specification, consistency and implementation of design patterns

The first paper in this session, by *Eden* and *Yehudai*, presented an approach where pattern solutions, "lattices", can be specified by the use of a hierarchy of "tricks", defining lower level pattern solutions. *Hedin* presented an approach based on attribute grammars for supporting automatic checking that the patterns are applied consistently in source code, with the aim of supporting framework usage and maintenance of source code using patterns. *Jacobsen* proposed the use of an "extract level" to view program code at a more abstract conceptual level, for example to view design pattern applications.

Framework definition languages

Matthijs, *Joosen*, and *Robben* reported on experience from defining a special language for a framework for concurrent distributed programming, with the goal of simplifying framework usage. To provide an open implementation, the framework objects were made available as meta objects in the new language. *Bjarnason* discussed a technique for supporting framework-specific language extensions, based on APPLAB, an integrated language-design environment. *Peres*, *Malcolm*, *Vortman*, and *Zodik* present an example of a specialization language; their language defines specializations for a GUI framework. *Nowack* proposes the notion of a framework component. A framework can be described as a set of interrelated framework components, each describing an abstraction over a part of a framework. A framework component organizes a framework into more understandable units providing explicit collections of adaptable hotspots.

Language implementation frameworks

The last session discusses the relations of frameworks and languages from the perspective of languages: how could the framework concept be exploited in the implementation of textual or visual languages. In the paper by *Harsu, Hautamäki and Koskimies* an architecture is presented for a framework supporting analysis of textual languages. The framework and the accompanying graphical tool (TaLE) is based on a flexible top-down parsing scheme which allows the free combination of classes representing various language structures, thus facilitating high degree of reusability of language components. *Tuovinen* presents a similar framework for visual languages based on the atomic relational grammar model. This approach makes use of a grammar specification of the visual language to be implemented. The framework allows fast development of various diagram editors supporting the construction of structures from visual elements. Implementing languages with frameworks is an attractive approach especially in situations where the language is constantly evolving or growing. This may be the case for framework specialization languages: if a framework is specialized into a more narrow framework, its specialization language may also have to specialized.

Implementing GoF Design Patterns in BETA

Ellen Agerbo and Aino Cornils

Dept of Computer Science, Aarhus University, Denmark.

e-mail: {lnx | apaipi}@daimi.aau.dk

Abstract

In this paper it is investigated how well the BETA supports the Design Patterns presented in [GoF 95]. We go through the language constructs in BETA to show which prove especially useful when implementing these Design Patterns. It is a fact that several of the Design Patterns found in [GoF 95] can be implemented in a simpler and more straightforward way in BETA than in ordinary OO-languages. This leads us to consider whether it is true that the more advanced OO-language one uses, the more of these Design Patterns are included directly in the language constructs.

1   Introduction

In this paper we investigate how BETA supports the Design Patterns described in [GoF 95]. Comparing our implementation solutions with those of [GoF 95], we discovered that several of the Design Patterns would be implemented in a simpler and more straightforward way in BETA.

In [Cornils97] a detailed discussion of all the Design Patterns and a categorisation consisting of the following four categories have been made: The ones that are implemented in the same way in BETA as in most other OO-languages, those that are covered more or less directly from BETA's special language-constructs, the ones that are partially improved in BETA and finally those that lack support in BETA. The most interesting category is of course the one containing those Design Patterns that are easier or more elegantly implemented in BETA. If we look at the language constructs found in every OO-language, like sub-classing and virtual procedures, one might say that these are so commonly used that if they were not already in the languages one used, they could be thought of as Design Patterns. It now seems obvious, that when working with OO-languages, these constructs are considered fundamental and will certainly be found in any new OO-language. But what about the Design Patterns of today? Will they continue being considered Design Patterns or will they eventually be subsumed as natural language constructs in every OO-language?

2   Special Beta-constructs

During this discussion on Design Patterns in BETA one should be aware that BETA has unified abstraction mechanisms such as class, procedure, function, process type, exception type, etc. into one language construct called a *pattern*. Therefore we will in the following use the term *pattern* interchangeably with classes and/or methods, using the latter terms whenever the need for clarification arises. The term *pattern* should not be confused with the term *Design Pattern*. The following list of BETA constructs is in no way exhaustive; it is only meant for illuminating how BETA is applicable in implementing the [GoF 95] Design Patterns:

Nested Classes
In many modelling connections it is an advantage to restrict the existence of an object and its description to the environment where it has meaning. This is possible in BETA, where a class can contain declarations of other classes; this mechanism is called *nested classes* ([Madsen 95], [Rapin 95], [Einarson 97]). In BETA an object of a nested class will at runtime execute in the context of the enclosing class, and methods of the nested class can access members of the outer class. Consequently the BETA notion of nested classes must not be confused with the mechanism of 'nested classes' in C++, where it is impossible for a nested class to access local members of the enclosing class, and the nesting thus has no effect on objects at runtime. BETA's version of nested classes has recently been adopted by JAVA [JAVA] under the name *inner classes*.

An obvious Design Pattern to benefit from BETA's nesting of classes is **Facade**, where the idea is to provide a unified interface to a set of interfaces in a subsystem by placing a **Facade**-class "between" the subsystem classes and the client classes. Explicitly placing the subsystem as classes nested into the Facade class clearly solves the intent of the pattern.

Patterns to benefit from the enforced locality of the nested classes, but where the intent of the pattern is not fully covered by this mechanism, are for instance **Iterator** and **State**. The idea of **State** is to have the different states of an object in a given context represented by classes, where the change of state is represented by what class the object is an instance of. Since it only makes sense to talk about a state of the object within the given context, it is from a modelling point of view logical to declare the State class as a nested class of the Context class. Nesting of classes would be enhancing the modelling aspects of **Iterator** in an analogous way.

Singular Objects
In BETA it is possible to describe an object directly, without it being an instance of a class. This is typically done when dealing with a situation where there is only one single object to consider. A consequence of making a singular object is that it is ensured that there is never more than one object of this type.

From a modelling point of view it is obviously an advantage to be able to denote that an object is one-of-a-kind and not an instantiation of a concept of which any other number of objects can exist. The Design Pattern **Singleton** has been made to ensure this property in a class - that only one object can ever exist as an instance of the class. In C++ and in SMALLTALK there is no language support for this but a work-around has been proposed in the (so-called) Design Pattern, where the constructor is redefined to return the already existing object or create it if it doesn't already exist.

Virtual Classes

The virtual patterns in BETA have two aspects: The virtual procedure patterns and the virtual class patterns. The virtual procedure patterns correspond to the use of virtual procedures in C++ or methods in SMALLTALK. The virtual class pattern is the BETA construct corresponding to class parameters of generic classes in Eiffel and template classes in C++.

In one use of virtual patterns, it can be nested into another pattern, P. The virtual pattern can then in subclasses of P be *further extended* or *further bound* to subclasses of the virtual pattern. Virtual patterns can thus not be overwritten, only extended. This kind of constrained genericity is not possible in C++, where a template class has the same type in the subclass as in the superclass.

Virtual classes has been proposed as a language construct in JAVA [Thorup97]. Having virtual classes as part of the implementation language will eliminate the need of the Design Pattern **Factory Method**, where the purpose is to create objects whose exact classes are unknown until runtime. This is in [GoF 95] done by instantiating the objects in virtual methods. In BETA the product class would simply be declared a virtual class, which in different subclasses could be bound to the wanted classes of products. Since the language construct of virtual classes in this way covers **Factory Method** it follows that all Design Patterns in which it is a part will be more simply implemented in BETA. Examples are **Abstract Factory** and **Iterator**.

Coroutines

In BETA objects may execute their actions alternating with other objects. Such objects are called components and are used as symmetric coroutines. The coroutines show their usefullness in a Design Pattern **Iterator**, where the Iterator's can be implemented as coroutines, which are executed, suspended and eventually resumed in appropriate places in the code. Iterators implemented like this will not need methods like First and Next. The construct can also be of use in some variations of the State pattern.

Inner versus Super

In most languages a method from a superclass may be redefined in the subclass, and there a notation for executing the method in the superclass exists. In BETA a method may not be redefined in subclasses, but only extended, and the inner mechanism is used for expressing this. It is the responsibility of the superclass designer to insert inner where the subclasses may need to extend the behaviour. The motivation for this is to ensure that all properties that hold for the superclass should also hold for the subclasses, which is ideal from a modelling point of view. This is useful in connection with the Design Pattern **Template Method** in the cases where there is only one hook method. Here the template method will simply be a virtual method extendible where the inner is placed.

Pattern variables

Patterns in BETA are first-class values, which means that they can be assigned to variables and passed around as parameters to methods. This is possible because of the notion of a *pattern variable*, which is a construct that contains a pattern, from which a new object can be initialised. This can be used to implement the Design Pattern **Prototype** where the use of pattern variables will eliminate the need of all the involved classes implementing a copy procedure.

3 Conclusion

When using BETA as implementation language the Design Patterns suggested in [GoF 95] are for the most part easily implemented, and to some extent BETA supports these Design Patterns better than other OO-languages.

Many of the Design Patterns in [GoF 95] come close to be considered language constructs in BETA and several other Design Patterns being so well supported that the complexity of each of these is considerably reduced. This indicates that several of the Design Patterns found in [GoF 95] are solutions to shortcomings of the C++ language, and perhaps the greatest part of them solutions to shortcomings of OO-languages in general.

This leads us to the assertion that some of the Design Patterns, if not most of them, will be integrated in the OO-languages as language constructs in the years to come.

References

[Cornils97] E. Agerbo and A. Cornils (1997): *PreThesis on Design Patterns in* BETA. http://www.daimi.aau.dk/~apaipi/workshop/gof.ps

[GoF 95] E. Gamma, R. Helm, R. Johnson, J. Vlissides (1995): *Elements of Reusable Object-Oriented Software*. Addison-Wesley Publishing Company.

[BETA 93] O. L. Madsen, B. Møller-Pedersen, K. Nygaard (1993): *Object-Oriented Programming in the* BETA *Programming Language*. Addison-Wesley Publishing Company.

[JAVA] http://www.javasoft.com:80/products/JDK/1.1/docs/guide/innerclasses

[Thorup97] K. K. Thorup (1997): *Genericity in* JAVA *with Virtual Types*. Proceedings of ECOOP '97 pp. 444-469. Springer-Verlag.

[Madsen 95] O. L. Madsen (1995): *Open Issues in Object-oriented Programming – A Scandinavian Perspective*. Software – practice and experience, Vol. 25(S4), S4/3-S4/43 (December 1995) John Wiley & Sons, Ltd.

[Rapin 95] C. Rapin (1997): *Block Structured Object Programming*. Sigplan Notices. ACM Press, Vol. 32 No 4, April 1997

[Einarson 97] D. Einarson (1997) : *Using Inner Classes in Design Patterns*. Draft (June 1997) e: daniel@dna.ith.se

Message Passing Abstractions as Elementary Bricks for Design Pattern Implementation: An Experiment

Stéphane Ducasse
Software Composition Group, University of Bern
ducasse@iam.unibe.ch, http://iamwww.unibe.ch/~ducasse/

1 Introduction

Design patterns (DPs) are becoming increasingly popular as a way to describe solutions to general design problems [GHJV94]. Most design pattern authors consider that DPs should stay independent of the implementation language to keep their abstraction. However, the problems that occur during DP implementation in traditional object-oriented languages - loss of the DP, class proliferation, increased code complexity and impossibility to reuse the DP implementation lead - to the question of providing language support for DPs in languages themselves.

The experiment presented here is based on design pattern implementation using the connectors of the FLO language - explicit entities that represent the interactions between objects [DR97]. The evaluation of such a experiment - by comparing it with similar approaches - shows that elementary message passing abstractions are a flexible way to represent design patterns. In contrast to approaches based on the systematic introduction of new constructs in the language for each new DP [Bos97], connectors based only on message passing control give the same expressive power and a greater flexibility.

2 Implementation Problems and Solutions

In the implementation of design patterns in traditional object-oriented languages the following problems occur [BFVY96,Bos97,Sou95] :

Loss of the design entity. DPs are lost and spread into the code of the participant classes. There is no easy mapping between design and implementation entities. BOSCH called it the *traceability* problem [Bos97].

Class Proliferation. DP implementations need new class definitions that often specify only trivial behavior such as message forwarding. Moreover, the code of the participants has to be modified thus increasing the application's complexity and leading to a proliferation of classes [BFVY96]. SOUKUP stated that the composition of design patterns can produce mutually dependent class clusters [Sou95].

Difficult Reusability. BOSCH identified a problem due to the lack of reusability of DP implementation [Bos97]. Although DPs are reused at design level, their implementation is not reused. Each time a DP is used, the software engineer needs to re-implement it.

Solutions for Design Pattern Support.

Environments. DPs are taken into account by design or programming environments. One way is to generate code from design models that include DP representations. Specific code can be added in the generated code. The limits are that the original design is difficult to extract from the generated and modified code [BFVY96]. Another way is to provide support in the programming environment. DPs are represented at a meta-level and the environment is able to link them to the code. For example, [EGY97] defines a DP as a set of elementary operations on the code. Only the effect of the code manipulation represents the DP at the code level.

Language extensions. This approach introduces DPs in the programming language itself. This can be done by means of macros [Sou95], message control using composition filters [Bos97], code annotation (Hedin in [Wec97]). Our experiment, presented below, belongs to this category.

3   The FLO model

Before presenting how DPs are implemented by means of FLO's connectors, we quickly present the FLO language. More information can be found in [DR97].

Objects and classes. In FLO, three entities are distinguished: objects, classes and connectors. An object is black box entity defined by its behavior and not its structure. Objects communicate by message passing only. Classes define intrinsic structure and behavior of a set of instances.

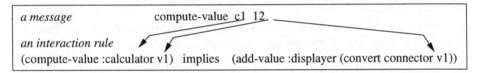

Fig. 1. An interaction rule: when the message `compute-value` is received by object with role `calculator`, the method is executed and the message `add-value` is sent with new values computed from the second argument of the call `value`.

Connectors. Connectors are explicit entities that express locally and declaratively how the behavior of a group of objects, named its *participants*, can change during message exchange. A connector is defined given a *name*, a *name role list* and a *dynamic behavior* that specifies the exchange of messages between its participants. The dynamic behavior is specified by *interaction rules*. An interaction rule allows one to define how a message received by a participant should be handled. Inhibition, propagation and delegation are proposed using respectively operators `permitted-if`, `implies` and `corresponds`. During the connection of objects, a connector enforces the dynamic behavior by controlling message passing. Moreover, during message passing control calling arguments can be manipulated as shown by the figure 1. The order of the arguments can be changed or new arguments can be computed.

4   Flo's Connector as DP Implementation

We now present two DP implementations. Due to the lack of space, we refer to [GHJV94] for their description.

Adapter. The implementation is based on the use of the delegation operator (`corresponds`) and the definition of a connector named `AdapterForGraphObj` with the role name adaptee. Messages (mess1, mess2 and mess3) sent to the participant named adaptee will be changed and forwarded to the adaptee. Moreover, the connector can adapt calling argument order or compute new ones (e.g. fct line 3).

```
(defconnector  AdapterForGraphObj (:adaptee)
 :behavior
   (((mess1  :adaptee a1 a2) corresponds (newMessA  :adaptee (fct a2) a1))
    ((mess2  :adaptee a1 a2) corresponds (newMessB  :adpatee a1))
    ((mess3  :adaptee a1 a2) corresponds (newMessB  :adaptee a1))))
(make AdapterForGraphObj :adaptee graph)
```

Note that to implement a Facade messages sent to the connector itself can be controlled and forwarded to the other participants.

Observer. A first simple implementation of the Observer is the following one. When the subject receives a message that changes its state the connector ensures that the observers are notified. Note that the notification mechanism is specified outside of the participant classes.

```
(defconnector  Observer (:subject :observers)
  :behavior (((setState :subject val) implies (map update :observers))))
(make Observer :subject suj1 :observers (list obs1 obs2 obs3))
```

With a second implementation based on the control of methods that directly change the subject and update the observers, methods such as setState and update are no longer necessary. The definition of the update can be specified in the connector itself [DR97].

5   Comparison and Evaluation

A comparison with LAYOM is appropriate because LAYOM and FLO are both extended models that are based on message passing control [1] [Bos97,DR97].

A Design Pattern Implementation in LayOM: Adapter.

Basically each new DP introduced in LAYOM is defined by a new layer. We present the Adapter implementation to give a flavor of LAYOM. A new layer is introduced that represents the Adapter DP.

```
class  AdapterForGraphObj
    layers
       adapt : Adapter( accept mess1 as newMess1,
                        accept mess2, mess3  as newMessB);
       inh : Inherit(Adaptee);
```

Comparison between FLO and LayOM.

Message passing. LAYOM, in contrast to FLO, controls both sent and emitted messages. However, LAYOM does not provide a generic mechanism for the

---

[1] LAYOM (Layered Object Model) was inspired by Composition Filters and is based on layers that encapsulate an object state and control messages.

manipulation of calling arguments. This last point is a real drawback for the DP implementation used in LayOM.

Shift of Level. In LayOM, the new layer definition is mandatory for the definition of a new DP. This means that a new parser and associated compiler have to be described. Such a definition should be done by a meta-programmer. Thus the definition of a new DP is not at the same level as the implementation language used by the software engineer. In FLO, the definition of a new DP can be done by the software engineer himself by composing interaction rules.

Flexible and minimal. LayOM provides a well defined DP semantics. However, a software engineer may want to have a slightly different semantics than the one offered by the constructs. In such a case he has no way to change the semantics of the DPs except by asking the meta-programmer to introduce a new DP in LayOM. This can lead to a proliferation of layers. In contrast FLO offers a flexible approach based on a filter mechanism and a minimal set of elementary abstractions of message passing (delegation, propagation...) that can be composed. Thus the software engineer can define his own DP semantics.

Conclusion.
Similar to the LayOM's approach, our approach offers abstractions of DPs at the implementation level. DPs are explicit entities whose semantics is no longer spread into participant classes. Moreover, trivial forwarding classes or participant class modifications are not necessary. Though we have successfully implemented several DPs (Facade, Observer, State, Mediator, Adapter), not all the DPs can be implemented using this approach.

As many of the DPs result from the lack of traditional object-oriented languages to support object interactions, it is not surprising that connectors support implementation of DPs such as the one presented. Moreover, we only consider such an experiment as proof of concept that message passing control can support DP implementation. However, the comparison with LayOM tends to prove that introducing only language constructs is not sufficient to capture the inherent flexibility of DPs.

References

[BFVY96] F. Budinsky, M. Finnie, J. Vlissides, and P. Yu. Automatic code generation from design patterns. *IBM Systems Journal*, 35(2), 1996.
[Bos97] J. Bosch. Design patterns as language constructs. *Accepted to JOOP*, 1997.
[DR97] S. Ducasse and T. Richner. Executable connectors: Towards reusable design elements. 1997. Accepted to ESEC'97.
[EGY97] A. Eden, J. Gil, and A. Yehudai. Precise specification and automatic application of design patterns. *JOOP*, may 1997.
[GHJV94] E. Gamma, R. Helm, R. Johnson, and J. Vlissides. *Design Patterns: Elements of Reusable Object-Oriented Software*. Addison-Wesley, 1994.
[Sou95] J. Soukup. Implementing patterns. In *Patterns Languages of Program Design*, pages 395–412. Addison-Wesley, 1995.
[Wec97] *Ecoop'97 Workshop on Languages Support for Design Patterns and Object-Oriented Frameworks*, 1997.

Patterns of the Agenda

Amnon H. Eden[1]

Amiram Yehudai[1]

Abstract: *Most of the study of patterns has been restricted to the composition of "new" patterns. These authors, however, believe that the investigation of design patterns is ripe for an endeavor at an underlying formal conceptual framework. In this article we address future directions in the investigation of design patterns and stress the significance of precise specifications. We also propose our own approach at precise specification of design patterns.*

Keywords: Tool support for design patterns, formal methods, metaprogramming

1. Introduction

Patterns and design patterns have been attracting great interest within the OOP community and the general software industry. Their research is, however, yet at its cradle, and effort is mostly constrained to the definition (or discovery) of new software patterns (see pattern mining [GoV 96]). It is the humble opinion of these authors that much benefit can be gained from the study of other questions that would typically be classified as second-order or reflexive reasoning about patterns.

It is often claimed that generalizations about design patterns cannot be validated without having a solid body of patterns; there seems to be no dispute in this point. Nonetheless, we believe that with the accumulated publications of design pattern papers [GoF 96; Coplien & Schmidt 95; Vlissides, Coplien & Kerth 96; GoV 96] there is no longer a justification to defer treating design patterns with what are widespread scientific techniques. We conclude that the investigation of design patterns is apt for a fundamental, comparative, and formal analysis.

2. Open Questions

This section discusses topics in the understanding of design patterns that are yet to be studied. These questions will serve us later in measuring the adequacy and usefulness of a theory of design patterns. The questions we present are the following:

1. Is it possible to formalize the specification of a design pattern? In particular, the problem described? Its solution?

2. What are the constraints that rule the application of each design pattern? The outcome of such application? The composition of different patterns?

3. Among the activities related to design patterns are:

   * The **implementation** (application) of a design pattern

[1] The Department of Computer Science, School of Mathematics, Tel Aviv University, Tel Aviv, Israel. Email: {eden,amiram}@math.tau.ac.il

- The **recognition** of a design pattern, i.e., tracking the "existence" of a known pattern in a certain program

- The **discovery** of a new design pattern, i.e., tracking a repeated formation of behavior and/or structure in a certain program

How, if possible, can these activities be automated? For instance, can they be supported by a CASE tool?

4. How can design patterns be effectively indexed or classified?

We believe that precise specification of design patterns is a prerequisite to their analysis and the automation of their implementation.

3. Elements Of The Specification Of Design Patterns

The purpose of this section is to distinguish the role of the generic solution proposed by each pattern from the problems it attempts to solve.

Problems vs. solutions

Two basic elements partake in the specification of design patterns: *problem* and *solution*. The problem (usually accompanied by descriptions of *forces*, *context*, or *applicability*) part is usually defined in vague terms, demonstrated using one or two examples. This is followed by (code and diagram) examples that serve as an approximation to the complete problem domain. The solution is mainly described using natural language specification that attempts to circumscribe its applicability.

To characterize the recurring motifs in structure and behavior specified by a particular design pattern, we designate this construct as *lattice*[2]. Principally, a *lattice* is the "scaffolding" of class fragments and specialized relations among them as indicated by a solution proposed in a design pattern[3]. The term *lattice* distinguishes the generic solution from the rest of the pattern.

Many justly object to referring exclusively to the pattern's lattice; it is claimed that doing so allegedly abolishes the very purpose of patterns: to disseminate good design and experience gained in solving recurring problems. Indeed, this purpose (the dissemination of solutions) is best served by the contemporary nature of design patterns, as the overwhelming success of the [GoF 96] book and other patterns' literature indicates. Nonetheless, it is the lattice that most effectively sets off one design pattern from another. To stress our point we quote the following two definitions for design patterns:

---

[2] No connection to the respective mathematical term.

[3] A precise definition would be possible when a formal foundation is provided, such as the one proposed in section 4.

"Description of communicating objects and classes that are customized to solve a general design in a particular context [GoF 95]"

"Design patterns capture the static and dynamic structures of solutions that occur repeatedly when producing applications in a particular context [Coplien & Schmidt 95]"

Both definitions emphasize the solution element of the pattern form, and appear as synonyms to *lattice* as defined above.

A design pattern is best identified with the respective lattice. Note, for instance, that the set of problems a particular design pattern address may change without affecting the identity of the pattern. For example, pattern "sequels" (such as [Kim & Benner 95; Rohnert 96]) elaborate only on the description of the original problem, leaving the description of the solution intact[4]. Also observe that the lattice cannot change without radically effecting the pattern. Finally, a design pattern never proposes more than a single lattice, while it may address various problems.

We believe the reasons listed above justify a formal treatment of the *lattice* concept in separation from its respective design pattern.

4. The Metaprogramming Approach

According to the metaprogramming approach, a design pattern's lattice is represented by a sequence of operations performed over elements of a program, such as classes and relations, as prescribed by this pattern. In other words, the description of a lattice is transformed to the application algorithm, by which it is represented.

Two programming languages partake in the metaprogramming scheme: The *metalanguage* is the language by which the manipulation of programs is phrased; for this purpose we used Smalltalk in our prototype, as an expressive and flexible language with a powerful class library. The *object language* is the language of programs to which lattices are introduced. We used Eiffel for our prototype as a convenient, static object oriented programming language (OOPL).

The metaprogramming approach incorporates also a class library, designated "the internal representation", or the abstract syntax, instances of which classes represent programs in the object language. The combination of the abstract syntax with the Smalltalk language is an example to a *pattern specification language* (PSL), forming an API to the user who wishes to specify how a lattice is implemented.

A lattice is represented as a routine in PSL with arguments, often existing constructs in a program that are manipulated and adjusted to incorporate the lattice. The routine's body specifies the necessary modifications to the program's and possibly

---

[4] At least in the sense listed above, i.e., recurring motifs in structure and behavior.

introduces new constructs to it. The result of the enactment of the routine is the program modified to incorporate an implementation of the respective lattice.

We implemented a prototype for a tool that supports the specification and application of design patterns in PSL, the 'pattern's wizard.' The Smalltalk-80 environment, combined with the abstract syntax, provides a convenient, dynamic metaprogramming apparatus. The wizard's role is also to support the application of lattices in the object language.

Definition: A *trick* is an operator defined over elements of the abstract syntax; in other words, it is a unit of modification of a program. A *trick* is defined as a PSL routine, the body of which may comprise other tricks of the same abstraction level or lower. Tricks may have more that one version, each of which has a distinct *synopsis*.

The specification of each trick defines a respective lattice, as the abstraction of the result of the application of this trick. For example, the lattices prescribed by the *Visitor* and the *Decorator* patterns [GoF 95] can be induced by the enactment of suitable tricks. In [Eden, Gil & Yehudai 97] we demonstrate the specification of the tricks that ultimately induce the *Visitor* pattern and additional design patterns.

Our Ultimate intent is to define a hierarchy of *tricks* of different abstraction levels. At the first level we introduce *micro-patterns*, tricks of small scale that are defined as routines in PSL, each of which must be decidable. We strive to define a finite, small set of micro-patterns that is sufficiently expressive to identify the lattices of distinguished design patterns at the next levels, such as the *Visitor*, the *Abstract Factory*, and the *Observer*..

Recognizing Occurrences of a Lattice

The decidability of tricks is a condition that is necessary to allow their recognition. It remains to be solved whether, given a "fundamental" set of "suitable" (i.e., decidable) micro-patterns, it is possible to find the sequence of specific trick enactments (or the their manual equivalents) that lead to a given program. A possible problem is that this search process may result in more than one solution, each of which is a valid sequence of enactments of tricks of the given set. We, however, consider this particular case an example to an insight gained by the recognition process.

5. Conclusions

We claimed that a suitable, small set of micro-patterns, can account for lattices of most design patterns. We have proved that the specification of tricks allows the implementation of various lattices in source code. It remains to be proved whether the use of tricks forms a foundation for the definition of lattices and for their recognition. The results so far indicate that this method of formalization of patterns has the potential to address what we posed at the beginning of this article as open questions that the research of patterns has yet to resolve.

104

Acknowledgments

We are grateful to Dr. Gil for his useful remarks and to Prof. Hirshfeld for his contribution. This research was enabled in part by the German Israeli Fund (GIF).

References

Beck, K. and R. Johnson (1994). Patterns Generate Architecture. European Conference on Object Oriented Programming. Berlin: Springer-Verlag.

GoV: Buschmann, F., R. Meunier, H. Rohnert, P. Sommerlad, M. Stal (1996). *Pattern-Oriented Software Architecture-A System of Patterns*. Wiley & Sons.

Coplien, J. O. and D. C. Schmidt (1995), eds. *Pattern Languages of Program Design*. Addison-Wesley.

Eden A. H., J. Gil and A. Yehudai (1997). *Precise Specification and Automatic Application of Design Patterns*. Automatic Software Engineering - ASE'97. Also available at:
http://www.math.tau.ac.il/~eden/precise_specification_and_automatic_application_of_design_patterns.{ps.Z,rtf.zip}

Fowler, M. (1997). *Analysis Patterns: Reusable Object Models*. Addison-Wesley.

GoF: Gamma E., R. Helm, R. Johnson, and J. Vlissides (1995). *Design Patterns: Elements of Reusable Object Oriented Software*. Addison-Wesley.

Johnson, R. & W. Cunningham (1995). *Introduction*, in: [Vlissides, Coplien & Kerth 96].

Kim, Jung J and Kevin M. Benner (1995). *Implementation Patterns for the Observer Pattern*, in: [Vlissides, Coplien & Kerth 95].

Rohnert, H. (1996). *The Proxy Design Pattern Revisited*, in: [Vlissides, Coplien & Kerth 96].

Vlissides, J. M., J. O. Coplien, and N. L. Kerth (1996), eds. *Pattern Languages of Program Design 2*. Addison-Wesley.

Design Patterns as Program Extracts

Eyðun Eli Jacobsen

Department of Computer Science, Aalborg University, Fredrik Bajers Vej 7E,
DK-9220 Aalborg Ø, Denmark, E-mail: jacobsen@cs.auc.dk

Abstract. We present a view on software systems, which emphasizes that a software system shapes the user's conceptual model. Regarding a software developer as a user, we point out the existence of a gap between the model of programs represented by a software development system and the software developer's conceptual model of programs. To minimize this gap, we motivate an extension of software development systems to support architectural abstractions, and we propose a two level model consisting of a program level and an extract level.

1 Introduction

Traditionally software has been designed with a focus on the algorithms and on the components making up the program. Today software is to a great extent being designed with a focus on the user's experience of the software. Attention is paid to the nature of human-computer interaction and the metaphorical spaces that users inhabit when using a piece of software—the design of software is the design of the user's conceptual model [3].

A software developer is a user who uses software to develop new software. If a development system is to be comfortable and efficient in use, we must pay attention to the user's conceptual model when designing the software development system.

2 Architectural Abstractions and Development Systems

A software development system can be based on various sets of concepts; examples include classes and objects, functions, and logical assertions.

A software developer's *design language* is the set of abstractions over structures in a program. Software development with classes and objects is now so well-understood that software developers are extending their design languages. The concepts finding their way to the software developers' design languages express archetypical patterns of class and object relations and collaborations. One kind of archetypical patterns are termed design patterns [1]. Design patterns are not dependent on a specific program, but occur across many programs.

The patterns of class and object collaborations can be regarded as examples of *architectural abstractions* where the notion of an architectural abstraction is a general concept regarding abstraction over structures in software systems in [2].

The arrival of new architectural abstractions increases the distance between a software developer's design language and the program model represented by his software development system.

We are interested in understanding design patterns, and to describe a software development system in which design patterns are part of the program model presented by the software development system.

3   Program Level and Extract Level

We regard design patterns as abstractions over programs—they group aspects of the program and consider these as a whole—and we regard programs and design patterns to reside at two different levels. The overall idea is that programs themselves are expressed at the *program level*, and the developer's additional understanding of programs is expressed at the *extract level*.

3.1   Program Level

A programming language is a language for describing a computational process. The structure of a program is given by an abstract syntax, and the program can be understood as a series of elements arranged in accordance with the abstract syntax. A program can also be understood independently of the abstract syntax—patterns for organising elements and their relations can be identified and understood at an abstract level. The design patterns are examples of these general patterns [1]. These patterns will of course contain elements that are part of the abstract syntax of the language, but the *organisation* is different to that dictated by the abstract syntax. A program element can be understood through several patterns, and hence the patterns become perspectives on a program. These different understandings of a program are what we want to capture at the extract level.

3.2   Extract Level

At the extract level we want the developers to be able to express how they perceive a program. The main element at the extract level is the *extract abstraction* of which design patterns are special cases. The idea behind extract abstractions is that we group together *relevant* program elements and treat these as a whole. In this way the software development environment will be capable of supporting the work with the developer's abstractions over programs. The extract level narrows the gap between the developer's conceptual model of programs and the model of programs supported be the development environment.

An extract abstraction can either be atomic or composite. An atomic extract abstraction represents an indivisible programming element, and a composite extract abstraction represents a group of extract abstractions. Extract abstractions are instantiated to mark where in the program they are used. An instance of an extract abstraction is a manifestation of the fact that in the developer's conceptual model, selected parts of the program exist as a unit described by the specific extract abstraction.

Two kinds of operations are relevant for extract abstractions:

1) Operations on extract abstractions themselves, such as manipulating single extract abstractions and defining new extract abstraction from existing ones. In creating new extract abstractions desired operations include aggregation, decompostion, generalisation, and specialisation.

2) Operations on the relations between extract abstractions and program elements. This is related to connecting program elements and extract abstractions, creating program elements from extract abstractions, and creating extract abstractions from program elements.

a) Creating program elements from extract abstractions. The elements in the extract abstraction are copied and possibly renamed. The extract abstraction functions as a template for the program code.

b) Creating program elements from extract abstractions where the new elements are coupled to already existing program elements. The existing program elements are extended by (a subset of) the elements in the extract abstraction.

c) Marking existing program elements as instances of an extract abstraction. This is to realise that something existing can be seen as an instance of an extract abstraction. In practice, however, something existing will rarely fit to an extract abstraction, so some support or guidance for adjusting the program elements to the extract abstraction will be needed.

4 Summary and Acknowledgements

We presented a motivation for supporting higher level abstractions than object and classes in software development environments. The motivation was rooted in the idea of the user's conceptual model. We suggested a two level view on software—the program level contains the operational description of the system, and the extract level contains descriptions of the architectural abstractions and their relations to the parts of the system.

We thank Bent Bruun Kristensen for inspiring discussions.

References

1. Gamma, E., Helm, R., Johnson, R. E., and Vlissides, J.: Design Patterns Elements of Reusable Object-Oriented Software. Addison-Wesley. (1995)
2. Kristensen, B. B. Architectural abstractions and language mechanisms. Proceedings of the Asia Pacific Software Engineering Conference '96. (1996)
3. Winograd, T., editor: Bringing Design to Software. Addison-Wesley, Reading, Massachusetts. (1996)

Design Patterns vs. Language Design*

Joseph Gil   David H. Lorenz

The Faculty of Computer Science,
Technion—Israel Institute of Technology,
Technion City, Haifa 32000, ISRAEL;
Email: { yogi | david } @CS.Technion.AC.IL

Abstract. This report investigates the relationships between design patterns and programming languages. A comparison is carried out between the usual track of programming languages development and the discovery of patterns. We argue that there are fundamental differences between the two. We offer a taxonomy of patterns based on how far they are from becoming actual language features. An observation is made that many patterns are in essence a set of rules governing the relations between two objects in run time. An initial multi-dimensional classification of such relationships is proposed.

1   Introduction

Abstraction, a fundamental objective of good software development, is the process of identifying commonalities and then capturing them by what we may call *abstraction mechanisms*. This paper puts aside the *manner* of identifying an abstraction (a cognitive intellectual activity, which therefore is beyond the domain of discourse of exact sciences.) We concentrate instead on the *mechanisms* themselves, and use these as a base point for analyzing and understanding design patterns and their relationship to programming languages.

A programming language is essentially a toolbox of abstraction mechanisms. Nonetheless, the abstraction mechanisms of current object-oriented programming languages are still too low-level. Here design patterns come to the rescue. Design patterns elevate the level of available object-oriented abstractions by capturing a relationship among the language-level abstraction mechanisms.

Our main hypothesis is that in many ways, design patterns are nothing but "puppy language features". That is, patterns could (sometimes even should) grow to be language features, although they are not yet implemented as such. One evidence for this hypothesis comes from considering language-independence. Many design and analysis methodologies and notations pride themselves for being "language independent". Design patterns candidly admit they are not. *"Point of view affects one's interpretation of what is and isn't a pattern. One person's pattern can be another person's primitive building block"* and *"the choice of* programming language *is important because it influences one's point of view"* [2,

---

* The full version of this paper is available as Technical Report LPCR9703, Computer Science Dept., Technion–Israel Institute of Technology.

Ch. 1]. In essence, we adopt this observation and take it a step further, postulating that many patterns can be found as a feature of some language, but not the one in which the pattern is being applied.

We present a taxonomy of patterns based on how far they are from becoming actual language features. In this taxonomy, low-level patterns are mere *clichés*. *Idioms* are patterns mimicking features found in another language. More concretely, idioms sometimes cater for the absence of these features in the current language. *Cadets* are patterns which are candidates for making their way into a programming language. We distinguish between two kinds of cadets. *Relators* are those patterns which capture the relation between a small number (typically two) of lingual entities such as objects, classes, etc. *Architects*, on the other hand, are patterns which describe the architectural structure of a large number of entities. Architects grow out of their lingual infancy into new language paradigms. For example, data-flow languages can be thought as a more mature form of the *pipeline* [3, 1] concept.

2   Clichés

Clichés are trite pieces of programming. Everybody is familiar with them; nobody can claim rights over them. In short, tools of the trade.

For example, the following cliché tells you that *"it is all right"* to write

```
for (*s++ = *t++)
        ;
```

in order to duplicated a buffer in C. Everybody does it this way. No one stops to think any more why it works (e.g., to verify that the operators precedence is right.) It will work for sure.

Object-oriented clichés are no different. They reassure you that is acceptable and all right to do this and that with object-oriented programming.

Definition 1. Clichés are straightforward and common uses of prevalent mechanisms.

The patterns that fall in this category are characterized by being captivating to the novice and obvious to the expert. COMMAND: it is desirable to use classes and objects for non-physical things, for operations, and for very abstract notions. TEMPLATE METHOD: if a method calls other methods, then by overriding these methods the calling method changes its behavior. Null object [4]: it is desirable to code conditional if-statements as inheritance. FACADE: it is desirable to encapsulate complex, ugly, inadequate for your needs, things.

3   Idioms

A design pattern maps a recurring object-oriented problem to its solution in terms of objects and classes. In principle the solution is independent of its precise implementation. In practice, the choice of object-oriented programming language affects what is and is not a "pattern". For example, the GoF catalogue assumes Smalltalk and C++ -level features ([2, page 4]). Hence, *Inheritance*, as an extreme example, is not a pattern because it's a builtin language construct, but VISITOR is a pattern because *multi-methods* are not. We call patterns of this level of abstraction, *idioms*.

Two balancing forces are involved here. If it's a natural object-oriented recurring phenomenon, then it's a sure candidate to become a pattern. Specifically, a feature of some well-established object-oriented programming language is almost certainly an idiom (e.g., the VISITOR mimics CLOS multi-methods.) But if it's so natural, as *inheritance* is, that it is part of most object-oriented programming languages, then not much is left to be gained by cataloging it. Hence, we must conclude that

Definition 2. Idioms are what other languages, but not the main-stream ones, have as builtins.

Class and *type* separation is a good example. Abstract class serves as type definition and concrete class provides implementation. In a language which distinguishes between class and type, there must be a mechanism for creation of an object which would reveal its type, but not its class. Unfortunately, in Java, the best known language in which such a separation exists to a limited extent, there is no such mechanism. ABSTRACT FACTORY and FACTORY METHOD deal exactly with this. The following patterns are also idioms. SINGLETON: module. PROTOTYPE: deep copy; and MEMENTO: persistence.

4 Cadet Patterns

Patterns which are neither clichés nor idioms fall in the category of plain patterns.

Definition 3. Cadets are abstraction mechanisms not yet incorporated in any programming language.

We show further subcategories according to the number of objects: a single object, two objects (pseudo-inheritance), and a system of objects (pseudo-composition).

Relators Viewing design patterns as a mapping from a recurring problem to object structures with static and dynamic inter-relations, we refine our classification by investigating the nature of two object relations. We list six independent criteria along which two object relationships enforced by patterns can reside: *coupling strength* (how strong is the connection?), *coupling time* (when is the connection established?), *features export* (is the connection exported?), *overriding prior to export* (may the connection be overridden?), *internal dynamic binding* (delegation or forwarding?), and *external dynamic binding/substitutability* (is the connection const?). Patterns in this group include: ADAPTER, BRIDGE, DECORATOR, PROXY, CHAIN OF RESPONSIBILITY, MEDIATOR, MEMENTO, OBSERVER, STATE, and STRATEGY.

Architects While relators are pseudo-inheritance, pseudo-composition patterns are basically all architectures that revolve around the tree of objects. Note that this division is only approximate, and that we are talking objects, not classes here. Some of the patterns that fall into this category are: COMPOSITE of course, BUILDER, VISITOR (unless you agree it's an idiom), and the INTERPRETER.

5 Conclusions

We subscribe to the belief that the success of exact science comes from the concentration on the *how*—the rules governing the working of any abstraction, rather than the *what*—the intent and context of its application. Examining the inner working of design patterns we found that they vary widely in terms of how well their inner working is defined. Therefore it was difficult to classify patterns based on their mechanics. [2]

What we were able to do instead was to classify patterns based on the cohesiveness of the definition of their mechanics. Clichés can be thought of as sophisticated macros of using an existing feature(s), i.e., mechanisms which are so trivial that are not worthy to implement as a feature. Idioms are just a matter of emulating a language feature by a language that misses it. Cadets are the "real patterns", i.e., abstractions which are not yet sufficiently mature and/or important enough to be language features. Still, the know-how they capture is important enough to be collected and recorded as patterns. Cadet relators are expected to develop into being single language feature. Cadet architects are expected to develop into a programming language paradigm. We observed that cadet relators are the largest group, and further, many of them can be thought as variations of mechanics of the relation between two objects in run time.

References

1. F. Buschmann, R. Meunier, H. Rohnert, P. Sommerlad, and M. Stal. *Pattern-Oriented Software Architecture–A System of Patterns*. John Wiley & Sons Inc., 1996.
2. E. Gamma, R. Helm, R. Johnson, and J. Vlissides. *Design Patterns: Elements of Reusable Object-Oriented Software*. Professional Computing. Addison-Wesley, 1995.
3. M. Shaw and D. Garlan. *Software Architecture. Perspectives on an Emerging Discipline*. Prentice-Hall, 1996.
4. B. Woolf. The null object pattern. In *PLoP '96*, Robert Allerton Park and Conference Center, University of Illinois at Urbana-Champaign, Monticello, Illinois, Sept. 3-6 1996. PLoP '96, Washington University, Technical Report WUCS-97-07. Group 5: Design Patterns.

---

[2] Even in [2] the patterns are ordered by alphabetical order!

Multi-level Patterns

Frank Matthijs, Wouter Joosen (+), Bert Robben (*),
Bart Vanhaute, Pierre Verbaeten
Dept. of Computer Science - K.U.Leuven, Belgium
E-mail: Frank.Matthijs@cs.kuleuven.ac.be
(*) Research Assistant for the Belgian National Fund for Scientific Research
(+) Researcher for the Flemish I.W.T.

Abstract

It's no secret that instantiating frameworks can be a tedious process. In this position paper, we propose our solution to the problem, which consists of providing an application programmer with a language that supports high level abstractions, and automatically instantiating the underlying frameworks based on the code written in that language. Application programmers use only the language, not the underlying frameworks. While this hides the frameworks' abstractions, we can maintain the open architecture of the frameworks by making the interesting objects from the hidden frameworks available again as meta-objects at the language level. This leads to a system where objects (e.g. pattern participants) live at three different levels of abstraction: the objects that are hidden in the underlying frameworks, the base-level language objects, and the meta-level language objects that are incarnations of the interesting objects from the underlying frameworks.

1. Introduction

Frameworks are important to leverage the benefits of object technology, and allow for reuse not only of code, but also of analysis and design. However, complex frameworks are difficult to use, because the programmer has to know the framework at hand very well. Moreover, following all the necessary steps for using the framework can become tedious. A possible solution we propose in this position paper is to provide the programmer with a language that supports higher level abstractions. The code that is written in this language is automatically translated into an instantiation of the underlying frameworks.

Our main area of expertise is in developing object support systems for distributed computer architectures (e.g. [Bijnens]). In our development prototypes, the underlying object support system consists of a set of different frameworks that are written in C++. We have currently built a prototype of the object support system running on Dec Alpha, Sun Solaris and SGI.

This position paper is structured as follows: we first highlight in section 2 a typical pattern used in the object support system (the Active Object pattern), and we illustrate in section 3 the higher level language interface we use to exploit the framework. Section 4 discusses how we can maintain the open architecture of the framework, despite the fact that it's hidden for an application programmer. This approach leads to multi-level patterns where some participants live in the support framework, hidden for the programmer, and the appealing participants live at the language's meta-level, available for customization by an application programmer. We conclude in section 5.

This paper is a shorter version of the original paper, which can be found in the LSDF workshop proceedings.

2. Active Objects as an Example

The aim of our object support system is to support concurrent, object oriented, distributed applications. To this end, the system is built as a framework incorporating many patterns commonly used in such systems, such as variations of Thread Pool [Schmidt], Thread Specific Storage [Schmidt], Proxy [Gamma], Command [Gamma], State [Gamma], and Active Object [Schmidt].

In this section, we will illustrate the use of the framework, specifically related to the Active Object pattern. Note that the Active Object patterns as described in [Schmidt] is concerned only with non-distributed concurrent programming. Since we specifically target distributed concurrent programming, many of the patterns we use (including the one we illustrate here) are variations of "off the shelf" patterns.

The Active Object pattern essentially allows an object to execute a method in a different thread than the one that invoked the method. This is achieved by giving the active object an activation queue that stores pending invocations, and by supplying the active object with a thread of its own, that continuously retrieves an invocation from the activation queue according to some synchronization constraints, and executes its associated method.

In order to create an active object in our framework, the user has to go through the following steps (essentially dictated by the pattern):

1. For each method X in the active object's interface, create a class so that method objects that represents the invocations on X can be instantiated from it. Each method object contains the parameters of the invocation.
2. A method call on another object is implemented by creating an instance of the corresponding method class and putting it in the destination object's activation queue. It is the client's responsibility to perform these steps.
3. Unlike Schmidt's Active Object pattern, where synchronization code specific to an active object has to be incorporated in the active object's dedicated scheduler object, our active object pattern uses a generic Scheduler object that defers the testing of the precondition (guard) to the method objects. Of course, the specific synchronization code still has to be written.

We believe that active objects are key abstractions in a concurrent, object oriented environment. However, the process of defining active objects as described above gets tedious when the application program uses more than just a few active classes and methods. In the next section, we show how language features can be used to alleviate the problem we have illustrated in this section.

3. Introducing the CORRELATE Language

CORRELATE is the language we use to exploit our object support system. This language emerged as a natural successor to our early purely framework-based approach. Key abstractions from the framework (such as active objects) are present in the language, where they can be manipulated and used at a higher level.

CORRELATE is a class-based concurrent object-oriented language. While CORRELATE looks a lot like C++, its computational model, unlike that of C++, is based on concurrent objects. Due to space constraints, we don't cover CORRELATE features such as autonomous methods or synchronization, but instead we focus solely on support for active objects. We refer to [Joosen] for a more elaborate CORRELATE overview.

A CORRELATE application consists of active objects that interact by sending messages (invoking operations). CORRELATE supports both synchronous and asynchronous message passing. Because we believe that active objects are key abstractions in a concurrent, object oriented environment (exactly the environment targeted by CORRELATE), active objects are available at the language level. The declaration of an active class in CORRELATE looks like the code example to the right.

```
active Server {
interface:
  void Method1(int a);
};
```

An immediate benefit is that this form makes it much easier for an application programmer to actually use active objects. In the CORRELATE run-time, we still use the Active Object pattern to implement these active objects. The run-time contains the "fixed participants" of the pattern, notably Activation Queue and Scheduler, while the "variable parts" of the pattern (such as the various method objects and the synchronization code) are automatically generated from the above CORRELATE code.

At the client's side, invocations on active objects no longer require creating method objects. The application programmer can simply write code like the fragment on the right for

```
_my_server @ Method1(x);
```

an asynchronous invocation of Method1 on _my_server, using x as parameter. This is automatically translated in the creation of a method object, as in the previous section. Thanks to the location transparency offered by CORRELATE, the method object automatically reaches the destination active object, where it is put in the latter's activation queue.

CORRELATE programs are thus translated into an instantiation of the underlying support framework. The result is that programmers programming in CORRELATE never use the basic abstractions of our framework directly. They even aren't aware of the framework, and don't need to know its interface. As far as the CORRELATE programmers are concerned, the language with its concurrent objects is their API.

4. Reopening the System

One problem with automatically generating an instantiation of a framework by translating CORRELATE code, is the danger of losing the open architecture of the framework. Indeed, programmers don't even get to see the framework in the application. To solve this problem, we expose the important abstractions of the framework by introducing them as concurrent objects in the CORRELATE language. The result is that, while in general CORRELATE programmers are not aware of all the abstractions of the framework, they are explicitly aware of the important ones, because these are available as objects with which they can interact and whose behaviour they can alter.

Two such important abstractions are the Scheduler and the Activation Queue (both participants of the pattern described in section 2). Together with a number of other important aspects of the underlying run-time system, they are available in the CORRELATE language as MetaObject objects. In CORRELATE, each object can have its own individual metaobject. A metaobject is responsible for creation and destruction of its base-level object, for managing the activation queue, for determining which method will be executed, and for forwarding invocations. Each metaobject can be specialized in the CORRELATE language.

Using this approach, we not only obtain an open environment, but we can very explicitly control the degree of openness, by identifying the components we want to expose. In our Active Object pattern example, we only expose part of the participants, namely the activation queue and the scheduler.

Another example of this approach is the RoutingProtocol class in the I/O sub-framework of our system. This class encapsulates the protocol that determines the routing tables that are used to route the invocation messages to their destination. The application programmer can customize this protocol to create a routing protocol that is optimised for a specific application [Matthijs].

5. Discussion

A trivial advantage of our approach is that it becomes much easier for an application programmer to use our framework. The programmer can concentrate on the difficulties of the application domain, without having to remember how to use the framework.

A second advantage is that the language level interface can remain stable even while the underlying frameworks evolve. This is mainly an advantage in environments such as ours where the frameworks themselves are subject to study, which sometimes results in changes to interfaces and functionality.

A potential problem with the approach is that, by exposing more and more components at the language level, we may end up with a complex meta-level framework: the base level framework is conveniently hidden, but all appealing objects are exposed at the language level, and they themselves interact and may form a framework of their own. Our experience shows that the framework at this level will not be as complex as the original one, but the aspects and implications of this approach are certainly subject to further study.

6. References

[Bijnens]   Stijn Bijnens, Wouter Joosen, and Pierre Verbaeten. A Reflective Invocation Scheme to Realise Advanced Object Management. In Object-Based Distributed Programming, Lecture Notes in Computer Science 791, 1994.

[Gamma]   Erich Gamma, Richard Helm, Ralph Johnson, John Vlissides Design Patterns, Elements of Reusable Object-Oriented Software. Addison Wesley, 1994.

[Johnson]   Ralph Johnson. Documenting Frameworks using Patterns. In Proceedings of OOPSLA '92.

[Joosen]   Wouter Joosen, Bert Robben, Johan Van Oeyen, Frank Matthijs, Stijn Bijnens and Pierre Verbaeten. Developing Distributed Applications using the CORRELATE MOP. Dept. of Comp. Science, KULeuven Belgium, technical report.

[Matthijs]   Frank Matthijs, Yolande Berbers, Wouter Joosen, Johan Van Oeyen, Bert Robben and Pierre Verbaeten. Towards flexible I/O sypport in parallel and distributed systems. In Proceedings of PDCS '96.

[Schmidt]   Douglas Schmidt. Design Patterns for Concurrent, Parallel, and Distributed Systems. http://www.cs.wustl.edu/~schmidt/patterns-cpd.html

Architectural Abstractions for Frameworks

Palle Nowack

Department of Computer Science, Aalborg University
Fredrik Bajers Vej 7E, DK-9220 Aalborg Ø, Denmark

Abstract. *In order to improve possibilities for language support for the development and use of object-oriented frameworks, we propose to elaborate on the conceptual understanding of frameworks with focus on architectural issues. In particular we propose the idea of framework components and connectors*

The *software architecture* [3] level of design is concerned with the description of elements from which systems are built, interactions among those elements, patterns that guide their composition, and constraints on these patterns. In [7] *design patterns* [2] and *frameworks* [5] are described as being two different examples of categories of *architectural abstractions*. The categories are characterized differently in the universe of architectural abstractions according to a set of dimensions, including Level of abstraction, Degree of domain specificness, Level of granularity, and Degree of completeness. To manage the complexity of object-oriented frameworks themselves, we propose to use architectural abstractions as means for decomposing them into more conceivable and reusable units.

1 Framework Architecture

An object-oriented framework represents knowledge about a certain domain, a reusable design for applications within that domain, as well parts of a reusable implementation for such applications. We believe that the major benefit of using a well-designed and mature framework is the implicit reuse of a high-quality and proven software architecture. This architecture can be seen as the partitioning of an overall abstract design into a set of abstract classes, i.e. the abstract classes in a framework specifies it's architecture.

A framework architecture imposes some restrictions on the application specific code to be provided by the application developer, and a problem with conventional frameworks is that these architectural constraints are invisible. The rules and patterns of collaborations that objects must follow in order to adhere to the framework architecture are not made explicit. As an example, typically when adapting a framework, the application developer have to specialize a framework provided class, and maybe then in relation to this change, register the new class with some other part of the framework in order for the application to behave correctly. These kind of logical interdependencies among different classes are very hard to detect and thus conform to. Hence proper framework documentation (for example documentation patterns [6]) is very important. Indeed, we believe that much of the complexity of frameworks is caused by the lack of intermediate abstractions, and in general this can be seen as part of the reason why different notions of patterns have been successfully applied in framework development, documentation, and use, as they provide this abstraction level. Because patterns in general describe certain perspectives on software, different notions of patterns can be applied in different stages of a framework life-cycle for different purposes [4]. Specifically some patterns deal with the architectural level of object-oriented design [1]. Still, being used as perspectives, patterns are not made explicit in the software.

The software architecture level of system design suggest the use of components and connectors as basic units [3]. Components and connectors are used to describe the high-level composition of systems independent of the individual components' and connectors' representations. We believe that a software architecture perspective on frameworks would be very useful, as it could provide inspiration for hypotheses about how to make the architectural guidance provided by frameworks explicit.

2 Components & Connectors

In our perspective a framework component describes a class hierarchy, i.e. a (typically abstract) superclass and its subclasses. Currently we are not considering multiple inheritance, although we believe that this is indeed a feasible approach for developing frameworks. In the description of the class hierarchy other framework components can be applied, thus resulting in the possibility of composite framework components. A composite framework component is typically composed of two types of part components; the components specifying the abstract behavior of the whole-component, and the components specifying alternative concrete behaviors of the whole-component. Each individual framework component contains information about where and how to adapt it, i.e. it clearly specifies the adaptable hot-spots [8] that it contains. This can eventually be expressed in terms of a component's constituent components, i.e. their hot-spots. In this a way a family of related hot-spots within a class hierarchy can be described. Dedicated framework components exists; e.g. one component must contain the class from which the first object to be executed is instantiated. This object basically performs a template method [8] invoking the different objects of the framework and in turn the application specific objects (through hook methods [8]. Furthermore many frameworks consists of two sets of components; components facilitating the expression of a wide range of similar problems (in the framework domain) to be solved, and components used to express different solution strategies applicable to those problems.

Framework components are related by framework connectors. Types of connectors include nesting (whole-part composition as described above) and client-supplier relationsship. Connectors can also be composite, i.e. enabling complex associations between components to be specified. Typically connectors encapsulate the specification of references between objects. Like framework components provide templates and possible substances for classes, connectors provide templates and possible substances for relationships between different class hierarchies, i.e. a connector is an abstract relationship between components, which can be made concrete in different ways.

It is important to note that while objects and classes are applied in order to model a problem domain and describe a *program execution* based on that model, framework components and connectors are applied to describe and organize a partial *program description*.

3   Status & Future Work

The current work is concerned with providing software developers with abstractions for reusable framework parts that are applicable to framework source code, i.e. a static and partial description of a program execution. The goal is to reduce the complexity involved in framework development and use. Currently the conceptual framework for such a perspective is being developed together with alternative description techniques for object-oriented frameworks. A possible next step will be to provide abstractions for runtime entities, i.e. descriptions of the structure and interplay between framework-provided and application-specific code in terms of components and connectors. This would include the possibility of specifying patterns of collaborations between components as connectors.

References

1. Buschmann, F., Meunier, R., Rohnert R., Sommerlad P., Stal, M.: Pattern-Oriented Software Architecture: A System of Patterns. John Wiley & Sons, 1996.
2. Gamma, E., Helm, R., Johnson, R.E, Vlissides, J.: Design Patterns Elements of Reusable Object-Oriented Software, Addison Wesley, 1995.
3. Garlan, D., Shaw, M.: Software Architecture Perspectives on an Emerging Discipline. Prentice Hall, 1996.
4. Jacobsen, E.E., Kristensen, B.B., Nowack, P.: Patterns in the Analysis, Design, and Implementation of Frameworks. Proceedings of the Twenty-First Annual International Computer Software and Application Conference, Washington, USA (COMPSAC'97), 1997.
5. Johnson, R.E., Foote, B.: Designing Reusable Classes. Journal of Object-Oriented Programming, 2(1), 1988.
6. Johnson, R.E.: Documenting Frameworks using Patterns. Proceedings of Conference on Object-Oriented Programming Systems, Languages, and Applications (OOPSLA'92), 1992.
7. Kristensen, B.B.: Architectural Abstractions and Language Mechanisms. Proceedings of Asia Pacific Software Engineering Conference (AISEC'96), 1996.
8. Pree, W.: Design Patterns for Object-Oriented Software Development. Addison-Wesley, 1995.

A Framework for Processors of Visual Languages

Antti-Pekka Tuovinen*

Dept. of Computer Science, P.O. Box 26, 00014 University of Helsinki, Finland

Abstract. The initial design of a framework for processors of visual languages is presented. The concept of visual language is discussed and the framework-based approach to implementing visual languages is motivated. The main features of the proposed framework are presented. The framework combines declarative grammar-based language specification techniques with inheritance and dynamic binding of language entities.

1 Introduction

Visual programming means using compositions of graphical objects to give instructions to the computer. Visual programming systems are usually quite complex employing a specialized GUI and an execution engine that interpretes the user's actions according to some computational model, e.g. the data-flow model. Spreadsheets and visual CASE tools are examples of such systems.

The research interests in the field of visual programming concern not only the interaction part but also the form of visual programs. The graphical objects constituting a visual program can be seen as elements of a language. For example, consider the flowchart in Fig. 1. Notations like this have a graphical *vocabulary* and explicit *rules* for composing and arranging basic graphical elements to acquire more complex structures: the vocabulary and rules define a *visual language*.

Although basic research has been done for many years, a generally accepted model for specifying visual languages has not yet emerged. The language models that have been developed display a great deal of variance in language structures and computational models. The impact of these models on practical language engineering has been negligible.

In visual programming systems, the language environment (program editor) and the language analyzer (interpreter) are closely coupled. If a formal grammar is used, the language analyzer can be generated automatically. However, using a grammar to specify and generate also the editor is cumbersome. Framework-based approaches seem more appropriate for developing complete, modular and extensible visual language systems.

This research aims at developing practical specification and implementation methods for diagram-like visual languages based on a formal language model. As the model we have chosen Wittenburg's *atomic relational grammars* (ARG) [7] which belongs to a family of constraint-based grammatical models for multi-dimensional languages.

---

* Antti-Pekka.Tuovinen@cs.helsinki.fi

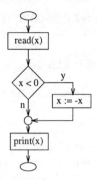

Fig. 1. A flowchart.

We combine the grammar- and framework-based approaches in an object-oriented framework for specifying ARGs. Our approach is motivated by the existence of frameworks for graphical editors [2, 4, 6] and by the reuse techniques associated with frameworks. While a new grammar is specified by deriving new classes from our framework and writing new methods, declarative meta-language expressions are used to make specialization easier. Existing grammar specifications can be reused through inheritance.

The current stage of the research concentrates on the language processing part and on its framework-based specification. A prototype of the framework has been implemented in Smalltalk.

2 The Framework

ARGs are specified in a BNF-like formal notation with additional elements in the productions: constraints between the right-hand-side symbols as well as special attribute assignments. The associated parsing method is a generalization of a parsing algorithm for context-free string languages. The sentences of the languages specified by ARGs are characterized as networks of terminal objects connected through (relational) constraints.

The OMT/UML class diagram in Fig. 2 describes the main classes of the framework and the associations between them. The specialization interface of the framework consists of two partially abstract classes, *Grammar* and *AST-Node*, and a concrete class, *Production*.

The interface of *Grammar* consists of methods for defining the elements of the grammar. To build a grammar, the *buildGrammar* method in *Grammar* calls user-defined methods in a concrete subclass, say *G*, to build the symbol sets and productions of the language. All the grammar building operations check the validity of the result.

The methods for specifying the symbol sets (nonterminals, terminals, relation names, and attributes) return lists of symbols. Obviously, the bulk of the

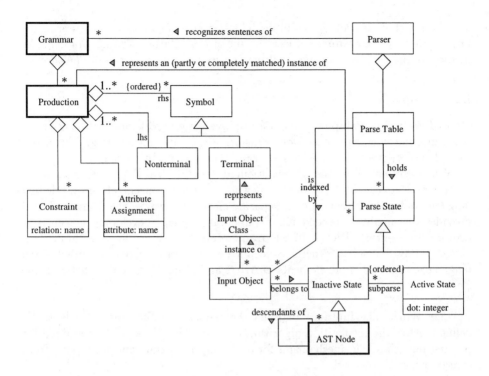

Fig. 2. The OMT/UML class diagram of the central classes of the ARG framework.

grammar is in specifying the productions. For each production of G, a method specifying the structure of the production must be defined in class G. Then, the G object must know which methods to call to actually create the productions. In the prototype we implement this by naming each method that defines a production as *<nonterminal><n>* where n is an integer ranging from 1 to the number of productions having *nonterminal* as their left-hand-side symbol. Then the *build-Productions* method (defined in *Grammar*) simply checks for each nonterminal whether methods for that nonterminal are defined in G and calls them. The methods defining the symbol sets and productions may be overridden in subclasses of G. Also, productions may be incrementally added in subclasses and even deleted from the grammar.

The interface of *Production* consists of methods for defining the parts of a production (left-hand-side, right-hand-side, constraints, and attribute assignments). The parts are defined in a symbolic meta language which the *Production* class parses.

The main mechanism for defining the operational semantics of a language is to subclass *ASTNode* which represents abstract syntax tree nodes. For instance, in the specification of production P, method *inactiveStateClass* is used to define the actual class of the syntax tree node that the parser creates when it has parsed a P.

The interface of *Parser* is simple. The parser receives as parameters of the *analyze* method the grammar object and the object-relation network (input). The method returns the root of the resulting syntax tree composed of *ASTNodes*.

Discussion

Related Work The Vampire system [5] employs a framework for developing visual programming languages based on transformation rules on iconic graphical objects. However, there is no notion of grammar as in our approach.

When compared to the object-oriented systems TaLE [3] and delegating compiler objects (DCO) [1], our framework does not concentrate on modelling language-independent concepts as separate classes. However, the framework still provides the flexibility needed for incremental language development even if at a more coarse-grained level. In our framework, reuse is confined within a language family instead of general concepts because, in comparison with textual languages, there are more elements in ARGs and more dependencies between the elements.

Further Work The interface between the parser and the editor needs to be defined. Also, the recognition algorithm presented in [7] has to be modified for parsing purposes, e.g. mechanisms for detecting, reporting, and recovering from syntax errors are needed.

References

1. Jan Bosch. Tool support for language extensibility. In Lars Bendix, Kurt Nørmark, and Kasper Østerbye, editors, *NWERP'96 Nordic Workshop on Programming Environment Research*, pages 3—17, Aalborg, Denmark, 1996.
2. John M. Brant. Hotdraw. Master's thesis, University of Illinois at Urbana Champaign, 1995.
3. Esa Järnvall, Kai Koskimies, and Maarit Niittymäki. Object-oriented language engineering with TaLE. *Object Oriented Systems*, 2(2):77—98, 1995.
4. William A. Jindrich, Jr. Foible: A framework for visual programming languages. Master's thesis, University of Illinois at Urbana Champaign, 1990.
5. David W. McIntyre. Design and implemetation with Vampire. In Margaret M. Burnett, Adele Goldberg, and Ted G. Lewis, editors, *Visual Object-Oriented Programming: Concepts and Environments*, pages 129—159. Manning Publications Co., Greenwich, 1995.
6. John M. Vlissides and Mark A. Linton. Unidraw: A framework for building domain-specific graphical editors. *ACM Transactions on Information Systems*, 8(3):237—268, July 1990.
7. Kent Wittenburg. Predictive parsing for unordered relational languages. In Harry Bunt and Masaru Tomita, editors, *Recent Advances in Parsing Technology*, volume 1 of *Text, Speech and Language Technology*, chapter 20, pages 385—407. Kluwer Academic Publishers, 1996.

Type Oriented Programming

Kris De Volder and Wolfgang De Meuter

Vrije Universiteit Brussel, Departement Informatica, Pleinlaan 2, 1050
Brussels(Belgium)

Abstract. We will argue that usage of type information still has a lot
of unused and unexplored potential towards supporting frameworks. In
the functional programming community the usage of static type systems
successfully supports highly abstract, modular and reusable frameworks
in the area of language interpreters [3]. We will illustrate with an example how similar type systems in OO languages allow more active usage of
type information. We claim that this facilitates a more direct expression
of the framework's domain theory, thus helping both framework developer and user.

1 Introduction

It has already been argued [1] that two kinds of polymorphism should be supported to facilitate reuse: *subtype polymorphism* and *parametric polymorphism*.
Subtype polymorphism is well supported in current day production level OO languages. However, support for parametric polymorphism is usually totally absent
or very ad-hoc.

Parametric polymorphism can be elegantly incorporated into statically typed
OO languages. Examples of this are Theta [1] and Pizza [4]. However, drawing
upon the work in the functional community we feel that things can still be ame-
liorated. *Type classes* in the functional language Haskell [2] enable the writing
of highly generic code on a set of abstract types. The Haskell type system was
the cornerstone for the implementation of modular interpreter frameworks [3].

2 Type Oriented Programming

To give a feeling for the style of generic programming possible with type
classes and to show that it can be carried over into OO, we present an example written in a fictional extension of Java with parametric polymorphism as in
Pizza. Figure 1 shows a few interfaces that are used to structure a collection hierarchy and outlines the implementation of a concrete `Vector` class implementing
some of these interfaces. The language also allows using `interfaces` in a manner similar to Haskell's type classes by writing `any` clauses. An `any` clause is a
declaration resembling a logic Horn clause that infers an implementation of an
interface depending on a logical expression. Figure 2 shows a clause implementing the `Searchable` interface on any `Enumerable` and `Finite` class. The type
system may use this definition to infer a concrete implementation for `Searchable`

```
interface Collection<El> {}
interface Enumerable<El> extends Collection<El> {
  void beginEnumerating();
  Boolean hasMoreElements();
  El next();
  void put(El val); }
interface Finite<El> extends Collection<El> {
  int size(); }
interface Searchable<El> extends Collection<El> {
  Boolean contains(El);}
interface Equality<This> {//For elements comparable for equality
  Boolean equal(This); }

class Vector<El> implements Enumerable<El>, Finite<El> {
  /**Vector specific functionality*/
  private El[] contents;
  Vector<El>(El[] initWith) { ... }
  El get(int index) { ... }
  void put(int index, El val) { ... }
/**Enumerable*/
  private int position = 0; //Current position in enumerating
  void beginEnumerating()   { position = 0; }
  Boolean hasMoreElements() { return (position < this.size()); }
  El next()                 { return ( this.get(position++) ); }
  void put(El val)          { contents[position] = val; }
/** Finite */
  int size()                { return(contents.length) } }
```

Fig. 1. Part of a collection hierarchy

on any collection class that meets the constraints in the whenever expression. This means that we can now send contains to a Vector if its elements implement Equality. Note that the Finite interface is not accessed explicitly, but is included to ensure that the end of the enumeration is always reached. An any clause allows to inject method implementations into a class hierarchy in several places that do not share a common parent. It might seem better to restructure the class tree so that classes sharing functionality have a common parent, but this is not always possible without using multiple inheritance which is in itself very debatable. Forcibly trying to factor out code into abstract parent classes will usually lead to a convoluted class tree.

This example shows that type systems have greater potential than merely type checking. A more active usage of types is possible. One can write generic code depending on a set of interfaces and let the type system automatically insert them into classes conforming to the requirements. We call this kind of programming *type oriented programming*. The type system presented here is not intended as a final and dogmatic proposal. Nevertheless we feel that combining

```
any X implements Searchable<El> whenever
  X   implements Finite<El>, Enumerable<El> ;
  El implements Equality<El> ;
{ Boolean contains(El e) {
    Boolean found = false;
    while (this.hasMoreElements() & !found)
      found = this.next().equal(e);
    return (found); } }
```

Fig. 2. An abstract implementation of the `Searchable` interface.

parametric polymorphism and type class like features into a statically typed OO language is a very good starting point.

3 Conclusion

We illustrated with a short example the idea of *type oriented programming*, i.e. relying actively on types to infer implementations of interfaces onto classes that meet certain type requirements as described by a simple logic expression. We feel that this yields extra expressive power that can benefit both framework development and instantiation because it facilitates a more direct expression of the domain theory without convoluting the class hierarchy to factor out abstract code.

We know of no currently existing OO language that supports active usage of types the way type oriented programming proposes. We feel that type oriented programming is a valuable addition to the arsenal of tools and techniques that can help framework developers and users.

References

1. Mark Day, Robert Gruber, Barbara Liskov, and Andrew C. Meyers. Subtypes vs. where clauses: Constraining parametric polymorphism. In *OOPSLA '95 Conference Proceedings*, volume 30(10) of *ACM SIGPLAN Notices*, pages 156–168, 1995.
2. Cordelia V. Hall, Kevin Hammond, Simon L. Peyton Jones, and Philip L. Wadler. Type classes in Haskell. *ACM Transactions on Programming Languages and Systems*, 18(2):109–138, March 1996.
3. Sheng Liang, Paul Hudak, and Mark Jones. Monad transformers and modular interpreters. In *Conference Record of POPL '94: 21st ACM SIGPLAN-SIGACT Symposium on Principles of Programming Languages, San Francisco, California*, pages 333–343, January 1995.
4. Martin Odersky and Philip Wadler. Pizza into Java: Translating theory into practice. In *Conference Record of POPL '97: The 24th ACM SIGPLAN-SIGACT Symposium on Principles of Programming Languages*, pages 146–159, Paris, France, 15–17 January 1997.

A Framework Registration Language

Yardena Peres, Jerry W. Malcolm, Pnina Vortman, Gabi Zodik

IBM Haifa Research Lab, Matam, Haifa 31905, Israel

{gabi, yardena, pnina}@vnet.ibm.com

IBM Austin, 11400 Burnet road Austin, TX 78758

jmalcolm@austin.ibm.com

Abstract

In order to maintain a framework generic, one must provide means that will allow the framework users (application developers) means to extend and adapt it to their specific needs. This implies that some kind of registration mechanism is needed in order to keep the framework neutral of any specific application. The registration mechanism is needed in order to allow the framework to become aware and be able to control the user objects/extensions. To overcome this need we have introduced a framework registration language that allows developers to register and maintain their framework extensions. Moreover the registration language allows the developers to render dialog controls and many UI related behaviors, such as drag/drop and menu items, without any code. As an outcome of these capabilities the language enabled developers to develop fast prototypes based on the registration language only.

1.0 UIFW Overview

The User Interface FrameWork (UIFW) provides applications with a framework of GUI objects, a registration language and a registration process. This framework type tool is not a class library. The result of this differentiation causes applications to inherit from it not only code but design as well. UIFW is based on Model-View-Controller paradigm while the Controller enables dynamic connection between them [1].

UIFW begins where GUI builders or classlibs end; meaning it provides connectivity between application data objects and generic presentation objects. Unlike a GUI classlib or a GUI builder, in UIFW, it is not the application which invokes the GUI objects and methods but vice versa. With UIFW, the GUI framework invokes the application methods. Developers can then concentrate mainly on the application-dedicated code while relying on UIFW to manage the user interface.

All presentation-type actions, such as minimizing a window, maintaining multiple-consistent views of the same object, closing and canceling dialogs, sorting and filtering containers, are provided by UIFW for any application. Moreover, it provides a registration language in which to define the correspondence between dialogs, controls (widgets) and application data. All of this is without requirement for any code. These impressive features and enhancements are achieved by use of a novel independent attributes' design and novel memory-to-stream algorithms.

The strength and the advantages of the OO design and its reusability were proven during the development of actual products such as Lan Server 4.0, LAN Netview/2, GUI for DCE [3,4] [6], SOM Visual IDL Editor and IR Browser [5] shipped with SOM 3.0, GUI for DFS, OpenDoc resource editor and LAN Server Enterprise.

2.0 Framework registration language

2.1 Motivation

Frameworks provide generic mechanisms for specific application domains. Applications can use these mechanisms as is, but more important they should be able to extend them or adapt them to their specific needs as well. All frameworks need to support some kind of registration mechanism in order to gain full control over the application objects. In general, there are two known ways to support this kind of mechanism: one is via an application registration language, as it is in our case; the other is by "coding in" the registration information as part of the application code. Extensibility achieved by sub classing ("coding in") ,framework classes, usually requires an in-depth understanding of the framework design. Moreover code maintenance, as we all know, is a burden we all would like to avoid.

2.2 Goals

2.2.1 Declare as much as possible without coding

This goal has been selected for several reasons. First, the code that is used to perform these tasks is generic and resides in the framework, this implies that it is robust and stable as it serves many applications. Secondly having the ability to change the application behavior without code changes allows faster edit/debug/run turnaround times. Moreover it allows non developers to make changes in the appearance and behavior of the application

2.2.2 Fast prototyping

Over the last few years, one of the greatest obstacles developers have been faced with is in demonstrating a product while simultaneously writing the code to support its GUI. UIFW is a revolutionary GUI development tool that meets the needs for easy, code less implementation of GUI demos and prototypes. With little effort or time, a development team can assemble a running demo of their future product leaving resources for other areas of technical development. No longer will demos struggle to be completed due to lack of code. Moreover, presentations do not lie on top of untested, possibly bug infested code, giving a clean, accurate GUI demonstration.

2.3 Overview

The registration language extends the object-oriented methodology of the GUI objects and actions. It provides the ability to dynamically register new classes and supports new applications using only the registration language. The registration language supports rendering of dialogs, menus, drag & drop actions and even methods. The language supports inheritance of these elements, which follows the object oriented hierarchy, enables developers to create portable windows, menus, drag & drop actions and views.

2.4 Requirements

- *Application declaration:* The main task for which we have introduced the registration language is to allow application developers to declare their objects so that the framework will be aware of them. This information is vital for frameworks as it provides them full control over them. With this information the framework is able to create/destroy and invoke methods on the application objects while no interfering is required from the application side at all.
- *Domain specific extensions:* Once the registration mechanism is in place, it can be extended to support additional tasks, such as registration of domain specific information, which otherwise would have been part of the application code. Applications can use the registration language to declare as much about themselves as possible without coding.
- *Simplicity:* The golden rule to keep in mind when designing an registration language is that registering information should be a simple process, much simpler than coding.

3.0 Conclusions

We have introduced a registration language that allowed us to develop a generic UI framework on one hand, and still provided means for application developers to extend and adapt the framework to their specific needs on the other hand. In addition the ability to define with this language many of the UI application behavior and dialog definitions, extended further the reuse of the framework, as all these UI activities are spared from the application developer code. Both these capabilities of the language saved code that had to be part of the application, not only does this saves the development effort but more important the management of it. Moreover the code that is used to perform these tasks is generic and resides in the framework, which makes it robust and stable as it serves many applications.

4.0 References

[1] Object-Oriented Software Engineering: A Use Case Driven Approach, by I. Jacobsen, Magnus Christerson, Patrik Jonsson, Gunnar Overgaard et al, Addison-Wesley 1992. B2303
[2] LAN Systems User Interface Framework Object Registration Tag Reference by Jerry W.Malcolm
[3] Yardena Peres, GUI for DCE Demo at DCE Solutions Showcase, OSF European Symposium, Paris, September 1995.
[4] Pnina Vortman, Aviella Angel and Shimon Yanai, GUI Framw Work, in6th IBM Conference on Object Oriented Software Development, Toronto July 19-23, 1993
[5] Pnina Vortman, Gabi Zodik, A Visual SOM IDL Editor and IR Browser, at IBM OO Conference, San Francisco - June 16-21 1996
[6] Pnina Vortman, GUI for DCE and GUI for DFS Demos at OSF/DCE Conference, Boston August 1995
[7] WMS 2.2 Control Definition Document, *GUI Common Services, Austin 1992*
[8] WMS 2.2 Programming References, *GUI Common Services, Austin 1992*

Tool Support for
Framework-Specific Language Extensions

Elizabeth Bjarnason and Görel Hedin

Dept of Computer Science, Lund University
Box 118, SE-221 00 Lund, Sweden
e-mail: {Elizabeth.Bjarnason I Gorel.Hedin}@dna.lth.se

Abstract. The conventions connected to the use of object-oriented frameworks can be described by framework-specific language extensions. The programmer is then aided in writing more correct programs. In an integrated structure-oriented language-design environment such language extensions can be supported internally.

1 Introduction

White box frameworks are known for being hard to use since they require detailed knowledge of the internal structure of the framework[Joh88], and that a number of programming conventions[Hed97] must be adhered to when using the framework. Failure to follow these conventions may lead to unpredictable errors which are often left undetected until run-time. Framework-specific language extensions which capture these conventions allow such errors to be detected and reported to the programmer before the program is executed. This is especially useful when working in an integrated programming environment since editing support for the framework-specific syntax and semantics can then be supplied. Also, in such an environment debugging can be supported in terms of the extended language rather than in terms of the internal code of the framework. The design and implementation of framework-specific extensions can be made easier by supplying support for such language extensions in an integrated structure-oriented language-design environment. The syntax, static-semantics, and code generation for the language extensions are then defined in terms of a base language. The proposed techniques for handling such language extensions are intended to be used in our language-design environment, APPLAB [Bja96, BHN97], to support the interactive design, development and use of framework-specific language extensions.

APPLAB currently supports the interactive development of languages. A language can be designed by editing a grammar description, and an example program can simultaneously be edited in the new (changing) language. The editor used, both for grammars and programs, is structure-oriented and based on grammar interpretation. That is, it interprets the current grammar descriptions in order to supply language-specific behaviour to the program editor. Editing is performed on the abstract syntax trees of the programs, and not at the text level. Text editing of subtrees is supported by invoking a grammar-interpreting parser. The static-semantics and code generation is expressed by standard AGs using an object-oriented specification language.

2 Support for Language Extensions

Figure 1 shows how the grammar for a base language, G_{BL}, is extended for a framework, FW. The framework is programmed in the base language, whereas the application program AP is programmed in the extended language G_{BL+FW}. The grammar for the extensions, G_{FW} can access the framework to implement the code generation of the new language constructs. Because the extended language imports the base language, rather than copying its definition, changes made to the base language can be automatically incorporated into the extended language. Such changes of the base language may be fairly frequent in an interactive language-design environment such as APPLAB.

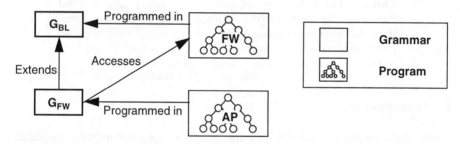

Figure 1. The dependencies between the language descriptions of the base language, G_{BL} and of the framework-specific language extensions, G_{FW}, the framework, FW, and an application program, AP, expressed in the extended language, G_{BL+FW}.

2.1 Subclassing Existing Language Constructs

When extending a language with new constructs it is desirable to reuse as much as possible of the existing implementation, as well as being able to add new features. In a declarative system using an object-oriented grammar notation this can be done by subclassing existing grammar rules. The new language construct then inherits the attributes and rules of the inherited grammar specification. New features can be added by defining additional attributes, and existing features can be modified by reimplementing the existing rules in the grammar specification of the new language construct.

Consider an example taken from robot programming where a base language is extended by adding a construct for moving the robot arm. The new construct, MoveTo, is declared as a subclass of the existing Statement declaration. Part of the specification of the extended language, G_{ROBOT}, is as follows:

```
MoveTo::=Statement ( "move" "to" Exp) (* Statement for moving the robot arm. *)     (1)
{  (* expansion definition:                                                           (2)
        equations defining the expansion tree(see below) implementing the MoveTo
        construct in terms of the framework *)
    (* static semantics:                                                             (3)
        equations which check that Exp is a Coordinate object (defined in the framework) *)
    (* code generation:                                                              (4)
        equations which compute the code to generate by using the expansion tree*)
};
```

131

The abstract and concrete syntax (1) are specified, introducing the new keywords move and to, and stating that a MoveTo-statement contains an Exp-part. Static-semantic rules that ensure that the expression (Exp) represents a coordinate are added (3). The code generation for the MoveTo-construct (4) involves generating a call to the framework using the defined expansion tree (2).

2.2 Expansion Trees

A programmer using an extended language is only interested in seeing the new language constructs and their syntax. The system, on the other hand, needs to consider how the new constructs are implemented in terms of the base language and the framework, in order to correctly perform code generation and static-semantic checking. In a system whose internal representation of programs is based on abstract syntax trees, ASTs, *expansion trees* can be used for representing the new language constructs. Similarly to macros which are not expanded until compile time, expansion trees are not constructed until an attributed syntax tree is evaluated. This can be done by using *Higher-Order Attribute Grammars*[VSK89] which allow a node in the tree to be defined by the value of an attribute. We want such nodes to be invisible to the user, but used by the system to perform attribute evaluation, and thus code generation and static-semantic checking. Since the structure of an expansion tree follows the base language the system can evaluate its attributes in the same way as for the other parts of the program tree.

Part of the AST for a program using the extended language G_{ROBOT} is shown in Figure 2. The expansion tree connected to the MoveTo-node contains a procedure call of the MoveLinear-method of the framework. Note, that a reference back into the program AST is used to access the user-defined coordinates, while the other coordinates are defined by the language extension.

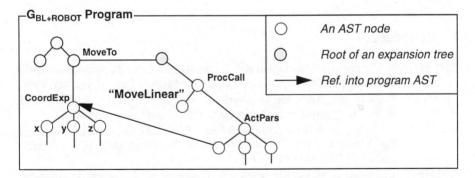

Figure 2. Part of the abstract syntax tree for a program expressed in the extended language $G_{BL+ROBOT}$.

3 Conclusions and Future Work

Framework-specific language extensions which supply framework-specific syntax and enforce the conventions of the framework make it safer and easier to use object-oriented frameworks. An object-oriented grammar notation allows new language constructs to be added by subclassing existing grammar rules. The new constructs can either reuse the properties, like syntax and semantics, of the existing language constructs, or specify new syntax, semantics etc.. When working in a programming environment which represents programs as abstract syntax trees, *expansion trees,* based on higher-order attribute grammars, can be used to implement new language constructs in terms of a framework. Static-semantic checking and code generation, as well as source code debugging, can then be supplied for the extended language. Such support for the design and implementation of framework-specific language extensions is being added to our language-design environment, APPLAB.

There are several interesting issues to look into connected to the use and implementation of framework-specific language extensions. For example, when a base language is changed this affects languages implemented as an extension of that base language, and programs expressed in the changed language. A mechanism is then needed for transforming the affected languages and programs into consistent versions according to the new version of the base language, by for example using techniques like those in the TransformGen system [GKL94]. It is also desirable to be able to allow multiple language extensions. That is, to combine several language extensions into one extended language. There may then be combinations of language constructs which contradict each other. Can such clashes be avoided or resolved automatically?

A lot of work remains to be done in this area. Both in implementing the proposed techniques and in doing further research into the area. Due to its declarative nature we believe APPLAB is a suitable platform for performing such research, and trying out new ideas in practice.

4 References

[BHN97] E. Bjarnason, G. Hedin and K. Nilsson. APPLAB-An Application Language Laboratory. Techn Report, Dept. Computer Science, Lund University, 1997.

[Bja96] E. Bjarnason. APPLAB: User's Guide (version 1.2). Techn. Report LU-CS-IR:96-01, Department of Computer Science, Lund University, 1996.

[GKL94] D. Garlan, C. W. Krueger, and B. Staudt Lerner. TransformGen: Automating the Maintenance of Structure-Oriented Environments. *ACM TOPLAS,* 16(3):727–774, May 1994.

[Hed97] G. Hedin. Attribute Extension - A Technique for Enforcing Programming Conventions. *Nordic Journal of Computing* 4(1997), 93-122. 1997.

[Joh88] R. E. Johnsson and B. Foote. Designing Reusable Classes. *Journal of Object-Oriented Programming,* 1(2):22-35, June/July 1988.

[VSK89] H. H. Vogt, S. D. Swierstra and M. F. Kuiper. Higher Order Attribute Grammars. *Proceedings of the ACM SIGPLAN '89 Conference on Programming Language Design and Implementation,* ACM Sigplan Notices, 24(7), 1989.

Design Patterns & Frameworks: On the Issue of Language Support

Jan Bosch

University of Karlskrona/Ronneby, Department of Computer Science and Business Administration, S-372 25 Ronneby, Sweden, e-mail: Jan.Bosch@ide.hk-r.se, www: http://www.pt.hk-r.se/~bosch

Abstract. Object-oriented frameworks and design patterns are useful abstractions that are relatively new to the object-oriented paradigm. The implementation of these abstractions, however, suffers from a number of problems due to the fact that insufficient language support is provided by traditional object-oriented languages. In this paper, we analyse these problems, study the different approaches for providing extended language support that can be identified and specify the requirements that have to be fulfilled by such approaches.

1 Introduction

In this paper, the problems, approaches and requirements of providing language support for design patterns and frameworks are investigated. The object-oriented paradigm has been extended with these abstractions, but the traditional object-oriented languages have not evolved and incorporated support for these abstractions. Whenever a programming language provide no support for a particular paradigm concept, the software engineer is forced to translate the concept into multiple language constructs which causes, among others, diminished tracability of the design in the implementation. In the next section, the problems of traditional languages associated with the implementation of design patterns are investigated. The various approaches that exist today to address these problems are discussed and the requirements one should put on language support for design patterns are defined. Section 3 repeats the process for object-oriented frameworks. The paper is concluded in section 4.

2 Design Patterns

Since the beginning of the '90s many patterns have been proposed, but the probably best known collections of design patterns are provided by [6] and [5]. Design patterns can be categorised into general patterns, application-domain specific patterns (e.g. patterns for fire-alarm systems) and computer science-domain specific patterns (e.g. patterns for distributed computing). Initially design patterns were proposed primarily as a design concepts, but during recent years the importance of corresponding language concepts has been recognised and several efforts to provide this can be identified.

2.1 Problems

When implementing design patterns in a traditional object-oriented language, we have experienced a number of problems:

- **Traceability**: The traceability of a design pattern is often lost because the programming language does not support a corresponding concept. This problem has also been identified in [10].
- **Self problem**: The implementation of several design patterns requires forwarding of messages from an object receiving a message to an object implementing the behaviour that is to be executed in response to the message. The resulting problem is known as the *self problem* [8].
- **Reusability**: The implementation of a design pattern can generally not be reused and the software engineer is forced to implement the pattern over and over again.
- **Implementation Overhead**: The software engineer often has to implement several methods with only trivial behaviour, e.g. forwarding a message to another object or method.

2.2 Providing language support

Providing language support for design patterns may prove difficult because the semantics of design patterns generally is orthogonal to that of the elements of object-oriented programming languages. Despite this difficulty, three categories of approaches to providing this support have been developed:

- **Design environment support**: During design the software engineer makes use of design patterns that have a representation in the environment. After implementation, the environment is able to make the code related to a design pattern visible in the code.
- **Generative approach**: Another approach is to generate code from a design model that comprises design patterns. After code generation, the application-specific code for the class can be added to the class specification. An example of this approach is presented in [4].
- **Programming language extensions**: The most complete approach is when the programming language itself provides direct support for representation of design patterns. An example of this approach can be found in [1].

2.3 Requirements

Based on the described approaches to providing language support for design patterns, we have identified the following requirements that should be taken into account when developing language support: *first class representation, reusability, configurability* and *behaviour superimposition*.

3 Frameworks

Despite the (sometimes dramatically) improved reusability resulting from using object-oriented frameworks, there still remain considerable problems to be addressed. In [2] technical, life-cycle, management and economical problems of frameworks are discussed. In this paper, the problems that can be addressed by providing more powerful language support are discussed.

3.1 Problems

A number of problems related to object-oriented frameworks can, at least partially, be addressed by providing more powerful language support. Below, the problems that we identified when using conventional languages are described:

- **Implicit architecture**: The architecture of the framework often disappears in the implementation details and is very hard to identify by the software engineer.
- **Cross-framework dependencies**: Dependencies between remote classes in the framework requires considerable understanding of the internal workings of the framework.
- **Framework instantiation**: The instantiation of a framework, be it white-box or black-box, generally requires considerable effort from the software engineer to understand the internal framework structure.
- **Legacy components**: Among others due to typing rules it is generally difficult to combine legacy components with object-oriented frameworks.
- **Framework composition**: As we identified in [9], framework composition may suffer from several problems, related to, among others, composition of framework control, legacy components and framework entities.

3.2 Providing language support

Three approaches to providing language support for frameworks can be identified:

- **Design environment support**: This approach would allow for visualizing cross framework dependencies and the framework architecture.
- **Generative approach**: Two generative approaches that can be identified are *architecture description languages* and *domain specific languages*.
- **Programming language extensions**: The third approach is to extend the programming language in which the framework is defined with language concepts that provide solutions to the aforementioned problems.

3.3 Requirements

Based on the different approaches to providing language support for object-oriented frameworks, we believe that the following requirements should be fulfilled: *explicit architecture representation, architecture adaptation, role-component association* and *cross framework dependencies*.

4 Conclusion

The topic of this paper was the issue of language support for design patterns and object-oriented frameworks. A number of problems were identified related to the implementation of design patterns using a traditional object-oriented language, related to traceability, the self problem, reusability and implementation overhead. To address these problems, different approaches to providing language support can be identified, i.e. design environment support, generators and programming language extensions. From these approaches, the requirements that have to be fulfilled can be distilled: first-class representation, reusability, configurability and behaviour superimposition.

With respect to the implementation of object-oriented frameworks using traditional object-oriented languages also a list of problems can be identified, related to the implicit architecture of the framework, cross framework dependencies, framework instantiation, legacy components and framework composition. Again, three main approaches to providing language support can be identified, design environment support, generators and language extensions. The requirements that we believe should be put on language support are that the framework architecture can be specified explicitly and adapted for application architecture, roles and components can be associated to each other in an expressive way and the cross framework dependencies can be represented explicitly.

References

1. Bosch, J.: Design Patterns as Language Constructs, Accepted for publication in the *Journal of Object-Oriented Programming,* November 1996.
2. Bosch, J., Molin, P., Mattsson, M., Bengtsson, PO.: Object-oriented frameworks - Problems and Experiences, *submitted,* March 1997.
3. Bosch, J.: Towards Reusable, Composable and Expressive Specification of Architectural Fragments, *submitted,* April 1997.
4. Budinsky, F.J., Finnie, M.A., Vlissides, J.M., Yu, P.S.: Automatic code generation from design patterns, *IBM Systems Journal,* Vol. 35, No. 2, 1996.
5. Buschmann, F., Meunier, R., Rohnert, H., Sommerlad, P., Stal, M.: Pattern-Oriented Software Architecture - A System of Patterns, *John Wiley & Sons,* 1996.
6. Gamma, E., Helm, R., Johnson, R., Vlissides, J.O.: Design Patterns - Elements of Reusable Object-Oriented Software, *Addison-Wesley,* 1994.
7. Johnson, R.E., Foote, B.: Designing Reusable Classes, *Journal of Object-Oriented Programming,* Vol 1, No. 2, June 1988.
8. Lieberman, H.: Using Prototypical Objects to Implement Shared Behavior in Object Oriented Systems, *Proceedings OOPSLA '86,* pp. 214-223, 1986.
9. Mattsson, M., Bosch, J.: Framework Composition: Problems, Causes and Solutions, *Proceedings TOOLS USA '97,* 1997.
10. Soukup, J.: Implementing Patterns, *Pattern Languages of Program Design,* J.O. Coplien, D.C. Schmidt (eds.), pp. 395-412, Addison-Wesley, 1995.

Language Support for Design Patterns Using Attribute Extension

Görel Hedin

Dept. of Computer Science, Lund University
Box 118, S-221 00 Lund, Sweden
Gorel.Hedin@dna.lth.se

Abstract This paper presents a technique based on attribute grammars for formalizing design pattern solutions. The technique allows design pattern applications to be identified in the source code, and supports automatic checking that the pattern is applied correctly. We expect the technique to be particularly useful when specializing frameworks built using design patterns.

1 Introduction

Design patterns in catalogs like [Gamma et al. 1994] and [Buschmann et al. 1996] describe recurring structures of collaborating objects. Each pattern involves a number of participating objects playing different roles in the pattern. Although the design pattern solutions are based on semi-formal class diagrams which allow for many implementation variations, they are sufficiently precise so that when selecting a particular implementation, the pattern can be formalized and form the basis of programming language support.

When a design pattern is applied, this can be viewed as a introducing a number of rules, i.e. subsequent updates to the program should be done without breaking the rules of the pattern. For example, the Decorator pattern uses a clever way of adding functionality to Component objects: a Decorator object "wraps" a Component, i.e., all clients of the Component refer to the wrapping Decorator instead of directly to the Component. The Decorator forwards all messages to its Component in addition to possibly adding some behavior of its own. An application of the Decorator pattern implies some rules, for example that whenever a new operation in introduced on Components, each Decorator must implement this operation and forward it to its Component.

Thus, we can think of a pattern application as a kind of language construct which identifies the objects that play the particular roles in the pattern, and which specifies some rules that these objects must follow.

Patterns are evolving concepts. New patterns and variations on how to implement specific patterns are reported every year at conferences, in books and journals, and in discussion groups on the net. For this reason, it is not sufficient to support a number of predefined patterns by built-in language constructs. Instead, we need a mechanism which allows new patterns to be both specified and applied. I.e., if we view each pattern as a language construct, we need a mechanism for extending the language.

In this paper, we propose the use of *attribute extension* [Hedin 1997 a] to support the specification and application of design patterns. Attribute extension allows the static-semantics of a language to be extended, allowing programming conventions to be enforced, but keeps the syntax of the base language. A key advantage of this technique is that it is easy to integrate with existing languages and environments.

Attribute extension is based on attribute grammars, describing conventions by declarative semantic rules. A convention checker can be automatically generated from an extension grammar in a similar way as an attribute evaluator can be generated from an attribute grammar. The technique makes use of three kinds of specification: 1) A *base grammar interface*, which is a context-free grammar for the base language, extended with functions for basic static-semantic information such as name bindings and type information. 2) An *extension grammar*, which is an attribute grammar describing the programming conventions, making use of the base grammar interface to avoid specifying basic information from scratch. 3) *Attribute comments*, which are special comments used to annotate an application program.

In the following we give an overview over how the attribute extension technique can be used to formalize design pattern solutions. For a detailed example and a more thorough discussion of the technique, the reader is referred to the full paper [Hedin 1997 b].

2 Language support for a pattern

To support a pattern at the language level, we need first of all to identify the different roles in the pattern and then to formulate the rules for these pattern roles.

2.1 Pattern roles

The most important roles are played by classes, but some roles may also be played by methods or variables. For example, in the Decorator pattern [Gamma et al. 1994], we can identify the following roles: COMPONENT (class), OPERATION (method), CONCRETECOMPONENT (class), DECORATOR (class), DECORATEDCOMPONENT (variable), CONCRETEDECORATOR (class), DECORATINGIMPLEMENTATION (method).

To support the identification of a pattern in the source code, we annotate the source code with pattern roles, using attribute comments. However, it is not necessary to mark *all* the roles in the source program, because many of the roles can be derived from the other roles. For the decorator, it is sufficient to explicitly mark the COMPONENT, DECORATOR, and DECORATEDCOMPONENT roles. We call these roles the *defining roles*. Other roles are called *derived roles*. It is possible to formalize the pattern using more or fewer defining roles, but too few defining roles may give a too restrictive implementation (for example relying on naming conventions of classes), and too many defining roles may put an unnecessary burden on the programmer to explicitly identify the roles.

Pattern applications often cross module boundaries. In particular, it is common that a framework implements some of the roles in a pattern application and that the applica-

tion program using the framework supplies the other roles. For example, the COMPO-
NENT and the DECORATOR may be part of a window-system framework, whereas the
CONCRETECOMPONENTS and the CONCRETEDECORATORS may be part of an application using the framework. We expect language support for design patterns to be particularly beneficial for frameworks since it allows rules for how to use the framework to
be formalized and checked automatically.

2.2 Pattern rules

The rules for applying a pattern can be expressed in terms of the pattern roles. The
identified roles must be consistent with each other. We refer to rules which express
such consistency as *role rules*. For example, in our formalization of the Decorator pattern we will have a role rule stating that a DECORATOR must be a subclass of a COMPO-
NENT.

If the role rules are satisfied, the pattern application is sufficiently complete to
make it possible to go on with checking *collaboration rules*. For example, to formalize
the Decorator pattern we could have a collaboration rule stating that a CONCRETEDEC-
ORATOR must have a DECORATINGIMPLEMENTATION for each OPERATION declared in
the COMPONENT. The DECORATINGIMPLEMENTATION may be declared in CONCRETE-
DECORATOR or in any of its superclasses.

The collaboration rules are usually more interesting than the role rules in that they
are more easily broken by mistake, and therefore more interesting to enforce. For
example, if we are working with a window system applying the Decorator pattern, it is
easy to forget to update the CONCRETEDECORATOR classes with delegating operations
each time a new OPERATION in the COMPONENT is added. This error might not show up
immediately, since applications which do not make use of the decorating objects will
work fine. A system which enforces the pattern rules would detect such errors at compile-time.

2.3 Specifying a pattern

To specify the roles and rules for a pattern, an extension grammar is written which
extends the base grammar interface with attribute declarations and equations defining
the attribute values. For each defining role, a special "program-defined" attribute is
declared, whose default definition can be overridden by an attribute comment. A
derived role is represented by a synthesized attribute. Finally, the role rules and collaboration rules are represented by special string-valued "error" attributes. The value of
an error attribute is defined as an error message if the rule is violated, and the empty
string if the rule is satisfied. To allow the definition of these attributes, additional synthesized and inherited attributes may be introduced.

3 Conclusion

The language support for design patterns we have outlined here supports both the identification of patterns in source code (traceability), and automatic checkability that the patterns are applied consistently, according to given rules. The technique requires that the programmer annotates the source code with some defining pattern roles.

The use of formalized patterns naturally has a cost in flexibility: Any pattern formalization will pin down precise rules for the pattern, and it might be difficult to foresee all reasonable implementation variations of the pattern. However, just as standardized libraries and frameworks are developed for a given implementation language, we expect standardized pattern specifications to be developed for a given language.

We expect one of the most beneficial uses of formalized patterns to be for frameworks where the framework supplies some roles, and the application program the other roles. It is then very important that the application program follows the pattern rules, because otherwise the complete system may fail. It is well known that frameworks are difficult to use and that application programmers need to have detailed knowledge of the framework implementation in order to be able to use it correctly. An aid in solving this problem could be to formulate the requirements on using the framework in terms of patterns, and to formalize and enforce these pattern rules as discussed in this paper.

References

[Buschmann et al. 1996]
Buschmann, F., Meunier, R., Rohnert, H., Sommerlad, P., and Stal, M. *Pattern-Oriented Software Architecture. A System of Patterns.* Wiley. 1996.

[Gamma et al. 1994]
Gamma, E., Helm, R., Johnson, R., and Vlissides, J. *Design Patterns. Elements of Reusable Object-Oriented Software*, Addison-Wesley, 1994.

[Hedin 1997 a]
Hedin, G. Attribute Extension - a Technique for Enforcing Programming Conventions. *Nordic Journal of Computing* 4 (1997), 93-122.

[Hedin 1997 b]
Hedin, G. Language Support for Design Patterns using Attribute Extension. In Proceedings of LSDF'97, *Workshop on Language Support for Design Patterns and Frameworks*, held in connection to ECOOP'97. Full paper available electronically at http://www.ide.hk-r.se/~bosch/lsdf/.

A Language Implementation Framework in Java

Maarit Harsu, Juha Hautamäki and Kai Koskimies
Department of Computer Science
University of Tampere, Box 607, FIN-33101 Tampere, Finland
e-mail: {csnima, csjuha, koskimie}@cs.uta.fi

Abstract
An object-oriented language implementation environment called TaLE is presented. TaLE consists of an OO framework that provides basic language implementation mechanisms, and of a graphical editor that supports visual syntactic specifications and various kinds of language-oriented specializations, generating the desired subclasses for the framework. Parsing is based on a model in which parsing information is distributed at runtime among the metaobjects representing language structures. The TaLE approach facilitates the reuse of both syntactic and semantic classes.

1 Introduction

Language implementation is perhaps not generally regarded as an area amenable to object-oriented frameworks. This is probably due to the fact that language implementation techniques are traditionally based on an idea of a global language definition and various techniques (or phases) working on the global language. Hence the primary architectural design of language implementation is usually phase-oriented rather than language-oriented. We argue that the idea of having a monolithic language which is the target of phases is not particularly amenable to framework-based design because this makes the system rather coarse-grained and essentially rules out language-oriented modularization. For example, it is usually then not possible to combine the implementations of individual language structures belonging to different languages, to reuse semantic concepts, or to implement and test a language piecewise.

In general, there are several aspects in language implementation which favour framework-based architectures:

- Language implementation techniques, especially scanning and parsing, are generic and specialized for each particular language. Some aspects of the techniques can be even specialized for individual language structures.
- Abstract language notions are specialized into concrete syntactic structures. In this way the abstract and the concrete language specification can be naturally fused, avoiding the need to have two separate specifications for abstract and concrete syntax, and an explicit mapping between them.
- The same abstract (semantic) concept can be used in many languages, and specialized into different concrete language structures. At the semantic level, languages share many concepts in common.
- Language structures are hierarchically organized according to syntactic alternation: a certain language structure (say, statement) can appear as several specializations (say, procedure call). Hence syntactic alternation can be naturally presented using inheritance.

In the sequel we show how these aspects can be exploited in the architecture of a framework supporting language implementation. We also show how the producing of appropriate specializations for the framework can be supported with a graphical tool.

The framework and the tool described here have been implemented in Windows/NT. The system is called TaLE (Tampere Language Editor).

We believe that a system like TaLE is especially useful when its support for reuse can really be exploited - only in that case the unavoidable loss of efficiency pays off when compared to traditional systems like, say Yacc/Lex. Typically, the processing speed of language analyzers produced using the TaLE framework is 2-3 times slower than using conventional techniques. Hence, it does not make sense to use TaLE for production-quality compilers of general-purpose languages: in such applications the efficiency demands are high and the prospects for reuse are low. In contrast, the support for reuse offered by TaLE is an essential advantage if 1) a language has several variations; 2) a prototype language making use of many standard language concepts must be developed fast; 3) different subsets of the same base language are used; 4) new languages are rapidly constructed as combinations of "language modules"; or 5) a language is constantly evolving and expanding. Some of the objectives mentioned above can be easily transformed into motivations of frameworks for graphical user interfaces. Indeed, we argue that frameworks for textual languages could be as useful and popular as frameworks for GUIs are today.

TaLE supports both C++ and Java; we will here discuss the Java version. The design process of the basic architecture of the TaLE framework has been discussed in [KoM95]. An overview of the C++ version is presented in [Hau96]. TaLE has been used as an implementation tool for a PL/M-to-C converter [Har96]. TaLE is freely available via anonymous ftp from cs.uta.fi/pub/tale.

We proceed as follows. Basic design principles of the TaLE framework are considered in the second chapter. In the third chapter, we show how a graphical tool can support various kinds of specializations of the framework.

2 Basic design of the TaLE framework

A main principle in designing TaLE has been support for fine-grained reuse. In particular, we have aimed at an implementation model in which individual language concepts, represented as classes, can be specialized and combined as freely as possible. Reusable concepts are hence, for instance, various standard notations like lists, expressions, constant denotations, etc., semantic concepts like conditionality, iteration, representations of data types, subroutines, etc., and supporting mechanisms like symbol tables. The language implementer/designer develops an implementation for a language by giving language-specific subclasses for the classes of the framework. Roughly speaking, the language implementor defines a class for each nonterminal in the grammar and for each semantic concept that can be associated with a language structure, reusing existing classes for these purposes as much as possible.

Incrementality is another important design principle of TaLE. The requirement of incrementality means that each class knows only the information directly associated with the language structure in question. This makes it possible to develop and test a language piecewise one structure at a time. As far as the syntactic aspects are concerned, modification of a single class requires recompiling only that class. For example, the syntactic pattern of a language structure class can be modified without any need to recompile other classes than the modified class. On the other hand, if language specific semantic interfaces of the classes are changed, all the affected classes have to be recompiled in the usual way.

The runtime representation of the source text is an interrelated collection of objects (roughly an abstract syntax tree) which are instances of *language classes*. These classes include e.g. the basic classes provided by TaLE for specifying general interfaces and for implementing certain standard language features, language-specific classes defining the semantic properties of the language, and language-specific classes defining the concrete syntax and parse time actions.

The language classes need various kinds of background facilities provided by *service classes*. The required instances of service classes are created automatically during the initialization of a language analyzer, and calls for their operations are generated automatically by the specialization tool discussed in chapter 3. Hence service classes are usually not interesting for the language implementer, unless they need to be specialized. The creation of the instances of the language classes is taken care of objects of a third class category, the *metaclasses*. The metaclasses constitute a separate class hierarchy implementing the cornerstone of the TaLE framework, metaobject-directed parsing. This is a variant of recursive descent parsing in which each language class is associated with a unique runtime representative, a metaobject. A metaobject is an instance of a metaclass. Several language concept classes may share the same metaclass, but each language class has its own metaobject. All the metaclasses are produced automatically by TaLE, and they are invisible for the user of TaLE. A metaobject has two important operations, one for matching input stream with syntactic pattern of the metaclass, and another for answering whether the language structure represented by the metaobject appears to be coming next in the input stream or not (the lookahead operation).

3 User interface support for specialization

One of the obstacles in using frameworks is that the reuser must understand the framework fairly well to be able to specialize it for a particular application. Since frameworks are often exceptionally complex software systems evolved gradually towards the optimal architecture, understanding their structure and function is in many cases too demanding for an average reuser. Hence a framework should always be accompanied by a careful documentation or - if possible - by a tool that assists in specializing the framework.

In general, there are at least the following three aspects that should be supported by such a tool:

- A tool should provide the user with a visual view of the application domain, if such a visualization can be naturally given.
- A tool should support constructing initialization code for an application, including the creation of the basic objects constituting the application. This can be based on the visualization technique mentioned above.
- A tool should support constructing subclasses for the framework classes. If possible, a tool should generate subclasses on the basis of high-level descriptions. Again, this feature can exploit the visualization of the application domain.

In the case of TaLE, one could think of visualizing (1) the static structure of a language, i.e. the grammar, and (2) the dynamic structure of a language, i.e. the representation of a program. The latter could be useful mostly for debugging or animation purposes. For the first one, there is indeed a fairly popular visualization technique for grammars, namely so-called railyard syntax diagrams. We have adopted this notation for syntactic specifications in a somewhat simplified form. The dynamic structure is not visualized in TaLE.

For TaLE, the initial set of objects is the set of metaobjects, organized through the starter lists. Note that the set of metaobjects and the contents of the starter lists eventually determines the language to be analyzed, not the language classes themselves. The initialization code is produced in TaLE in a separate tester window. In this window, the user selects the language classes for which a metaobject will be created (and which are thus included in the language). The superclasses and the used classes of the selected classes are automatically selected, but it is possible to select only a subset of the leaf classes. In addition, the user selects the class used as a start symbol; i.e. the class whose metaobject's make operation will be called after the initialization. The tester window also allows the user to compile the classes and execute the resulting analyzer.

The support for constructing subclasses of the framework classes is rather rich in TaLE. The specialization tool provides currently e.g a Smalltalk-like class browser, with specialized editor windows for different (sub)class categories provided by TaLE, special editor windows for standard token categories (e.g. identifier), automatic generation of skeletal semantic processing functions traversing the object representation of the source, automatic generation of code required for symbol table management and graphical tools for giving abstract components and associating them with concrete components in subclasses.

4 Concluding remarks

TaLE represents a new language implementation paradigm which is so far not very well understood - even by us. In particular, the idea of more or less independent components implementing various features of a language seems to contradict with the conventional idea of a monolithic language. This opens up new avenues to language design, encouraging reuse at the level of both semantic and syntactic concepts.

On the other hand, TaLE is a representative example of an OO framework and of a tool supporting its use. In particular, we feel that many aspects in the tool could be generalized and employed in other kinds of frameworks as well. To make this idea more concrete, assume that the TaLE specialization tool is itself implemented as a specialization of another framework. What kind of framework would this be? In other words, what are the characteristics of a tool which the TaLE tool is a specialization of? For example, the possibility of refining component classes and the tool for configuring the application (tester window) are clearly generalizable. We feel that TaLE could be used as a starting point for the design of a generic framework tool.

References

[Har96] Harsu, M.: Automated construction of source-to-source translators. Department of Computer Science, University of Tampere. Ph. Lic. thesis, Report A-1996-3.

[Hau96] Hautamäki, J.: Language Implementation with TaLE. Department of Computer Science, University of Tampere. M.Sc. thesis, 1996.

[JKN95] Järnvall, E., Koskimies, K., Niittymäki (at present Harsu), M.: Object-oriented language engineering with TaLE. Object Oriented Systems 2 (1995), 77-98.

[KoM95] Koskimies K., Mössenböck H.: Designing a framework by stepwise generalizaton. In: Proc. of 5th European Software Engineering Conference (ESEC '95), Sitges, Spain. Lecture Notes in Computer Science 989, Springer 1995, 479-498.

Precise Semantics for Object-Oriented Modeling Techniques

Summary of ECOOP'97 Workshop #5
Jyväskylä, Finland

He had bought a large map representing the sea,
Without the least vestige of land:
And the crew were much pleased when they found it to be
A map they could all understand.

"What's the good of Mercator's North Poles and Equators,
Tropics, Zones, and Meridian Lines?"
So the Bellman would cry: and the crew would reply
"They are merely conventional signs!

"Other maps are such shapes, with their islands and capes!
But we've got our brave Captain to thank:
(So the crew would protest) "that he's bought us the best--
A perfect and absolute blank!"

This was charming, no doubt; but they shortly found out
That the Captain they trusted so well
Had only one notion for crossing the ocean,
And that was to tingle his bell.
(Lewis Carroll. The Hunting of the Snark.)

The first ECOOP workshop on "Precise Semantics for Object-Oriented Modeling Techniques" can be regarded as a success. With 22 accepted submissions of high quality a variety of opinions has been represented and discussed among the 24 participants. During the workshop a set of conclusions has been drawn, which is included later within this summary. It probably serves as a good starting point for the next workshop.

The articles following this summary have been selected for the LNCS Workshop Reader. They are revised versions from the workshop submissions, which have been collected in the workshop proceedings [1]. We thank the department of computer science of the Technische Universität München for their kind permission to reuse the earlier versions of the contributions published in [1].

Scope of the Workshop

Object-oriented modeling techniques (OOMTs) are a way to produce various specifications. Business specifications (the "what"s) are refined into business designs (the "how"s), from where refinements into various information system (software) specifications and implementations are possible.

Currently there is an ongoing standardization process for object-oriented modeling techniques (OOMT) initiated by the OMG. Standardization of OOMTs does not only include a precise syntax, but a precise semantics as well. This is essential for unambiguous understanding of business and system specifications modeled with OOMTs.

Precise specification of semantics – as opposed to just signatures – is required not only for business specifications, but also for business designs and system specifications. In particular, it is needed for appropriate handling of viewpoints which exist both horizontally – within the same frame of reference, such as within a business specification – and vertically – within different frames of reference. In order to handle the complexity of a (new or existing) large system, it must be considered, on the one hand, as a composition of separate viewpoints, and on the other hand, as an integrated whole, probably at a different abstraction level.

A precise semantics allows us to detect inconsistencies and inaccuracies both in OOMTs themselves (meta-modeling), and in specifications written using these OOMTs (modeling). It is essential if we want to compare (and use) different OOMTs, with perhaps quite different syntaxes (notations), based on their meaning (semantics). This not only may improve the notations and make them more convenient, but also will enable interoperability between different OOMTs.

Moreover, precise semantics allows us to use a notation in a more standardized way, thus leading to better and unambiguous understanding and therefore supporting true reuse of specifications and design, including a more accurate definition of context conditions or (code) generators. And precise semantics provide the only way to trace requirement decisions, often through several intermediate steps, to produced code.

The scope of the workshop includes, but is not limited to:

- Precise semantics for OOMT
- Integration of semantics for a heterogeneous set of OOMT
- Formal development and refinement techniques for OOMT
- Comparisons of existing semantics models
- Ways to achieve preciseness
- Concurrency and OOMT
- Tool support
- Existing standards (e.g., ISO) and OOMT

The workshop is intended to contribute to an infrastructure that supports both desirable practice and future research and should document progress made.

This is not the first semantics workshop at OO conferences. The five OOPSLA workshops (with Proceedings, 1992-96) on behavioral semantics are reasonably well-known; and led to the publication of a book [2]. In addition, conclusions of these OOPSLA workshops have been published in the OOPSLA Addenda to the Proceedings. We hope to establish a similar tradition at ECOOP.

The submissions to this workshop represent a productive mix of academia and industry, and have a clearly international flavor. This statement is also applicable to the organizers of the workshop (we have done everything electronically!). We want to note, with great pleasure, that many if not most of the submissions emphasize the need to specify semantics in an abstract and precise manner, and use various rigorous and formal approaches to do just that. Important practical (and hopefully reusable) results have been achieved. Finally, we want to stress that the workshop is not about any particular product or methodology, but about concepts and constructs needed for better understanding and for building better systems. Thus, we will avoid situations described by Lewis Carroll above, "for avoydance of scandall is Divine law" (John Donne).

The workshop proceedings have been published as technical report by the Faculty of Computer Science of the Munich University of Technology [1]. The technical report is provided by the SysLab project, which is chaired by Manfred Broy, under grant of the DFG (German Research Community) under the Leibnizprogramme and by Siemens-Nixdorf.

Conclusions drawn during the workshop

The following list of conclusions has been drawn during the workshop by collecting statements from the participants. These statements have been discussed at the workshop and widely agreed upon. The list should be seen more as a good starting point for future workshop discussions, and less as final conclusions.

Some items below may be perceived as being "trivial", "obscure", or "contentious".

The trivial stuff is well-known, but too many projects (in industry) fail just because this "trivial" stuff has not been taken into consideration (e.g., "no time", "this is abstract crap, and we need to get the code out", and so on).

The obscure stuff needs refinement and is especially suited to form the starting point for future workshop discussions.

And we tried to delete all contentious points if anyone at all tried to reject them in Jyväskylä.

- Simplicity (with correctness) is the most important aspect of human communication.
- Scalability and abstraction are explicitly needed.
- You may get insights from a picture.
- Precision:
    - Precision and ease of understanding are needed for a specification. Two approaches are possible for precise specification of semantics:
        - formalize OO modeling techniques [make more precise], or
        - add "warm" features to formal specification languages [make easier to understand].
    Merging as the result would be great.

- Semantics of basic generic concepts should be made precise. To use terms like "aggregation" and "subtyping", they have to be formally defined
- Any notation (textual or graphical or ...) has to have a precisely defined semantics.
- Precise semantics of a graphical notation (e.g., in Z) is used:
  - to rely upon in cases of doubt
  - to provide feedback to the (more or less) rigorous specifications using the notation
  - to detect inconsistencies and incompletenesses
  - and to acquire much better (analyst's and client's) understanding, not just a "warm and fuzzy feeling".
- Explicitness:
  - Decisions have to be made explicit (and explicitly).
  - Explicit extraction of evidence of conflicts:
    - articulation of business specifications, including defaults and hidden information
    - notation must allow that
  - Extensibility has to be dealt with explicitly
  - Appropriate aspects of the environment have to be specified explicitly
  - How to combine different components of "OO" specifications should be stated explicitly. This is not trivial.
- Composition:
  - Composition is not an operator, it is an intellectual act (emergent properties appear here)
  - Composing different viewpoints is possible and often required
  - Abstraction is a result of composition
  - Implementation is composition (of specification and platform) [composing a given specification with an implementation-oriented context]
  - Objects (components) to be composed often belong to different layers (not only different frames of reference at the same layer)
- A tool (for specifications) may comprise a word processor and hypertext facility.
- Approaches have to be used in their frame of reference, and not everywhere

The gap between the semantics of the models and the semantics of the code has to be recognized and filled in. It is relatively easy if the semantics are explicitly specified and impossible otherwise.

- For precise (informal) specification notations, how do we achieve that
  - the users have a mutually consistent intuitive understanding of symbology (can't be resolved without a rigorous specification)
  - the users' intuitive understanding of semantics is the same as provided by the formally specified semantics.
- Trying to localize behavior in objects leads to pathological results and is difficult to understand; global description is very useful. Objects (and components) do not

exist in isolation: collective state and behavior is essential. Closed system = isolated component.

- What to show the user?
  - Different levels of detail
  - Abbreviations
  - Different presentations for different users (e.g., graphical vs. linear)
  - Explicit conflicts should be shown
  - How to deal with the learning curve?
- Appropriate education and reward systems are needed to solve many of these problems.

Literature

[1]   ECOOP'97 Workshop on Precise Semantics for Object-Oriented Modeling Techniques. Editors: Haim Kilov, Bernhard Rumpe. Technical report TUM-I9725, Institut für Informatik, Technische Universität München, 1997.

[2]   Haim Kilov and William Harvey. *Object-oriented behavioral specifications*. Kluwer Academic Publishers, 1996. ISBN 0-7923-9778-9.

Organizers

Haim Kilov (haim_kilov@ml.com)

has been involved in all stages of information management system specification, design, and development. His approach to information modeling, widely used in telecommunications, financial, document management, and insurance areas, has contributed clarity and understandability to enterprise and application modeling, leading to business (and system) specifications that are demonstrably better than traditional ones. It has been described in *Information modeling: an object-oriented approach* (Prentice-Hall, 1994). Haim Kilov is using and extending his approach in customer engagements, and does research and consulting in the areas of business specifications and information modeling. He is a member of and active contributor to several international standardization technical committees, as well as an invited speaker at OMG task force meetings. He co-chaired five OOPSLA workshops on object-oriented behavioral specifications, and co-edited their Proceedings. He also co-edited a book (recently published by Kluwer) based on the first four of these workshops. He has been a speaker and a program committee member at numerous national and international conferences. He has a significant number of publications in journals and conference proceedings. His interests are in the areas of information modeling, business specifications (including business patterns), and formal methods.

Bernhard Rumpe(rumpe@informatik.tu-muenchen.de)

is working in his research group to narrow the gap between formal methods and practical modeling techniques. In his Ph.D. thesis he has developed an approach for an integrated formalization of object-oriented modeling techniques that capture structure as well as behavior. He contributed to several papers on related topics, including a submission to the ECOOP'97, that contains an analysis of the UML description concepts. He also contributed to several workshops about similar themes, and recently organized a workshop with a similar theme within the working group ``Foundations of Object-Oriented Modeling" (GROOM), organized in the German Computer Science Community (GI, FG 2.1.9). Within the SysLab project he contributes to the development of a tool, that focuses less on simple editing functions, but more on the concrete use of the refinement and composition techniques for object-oriented description notations like class diagrams, state transition diagrams, and sequence diagrams.

Ontology-Based Layered Semantics for Precise OA&D Modeling

Jean Bézivin[1], Richard Lemesle[1,2]

[1]Laboratoire de Recherche en Sciences de Gestion, Université de Nantes,
2 rue de la Houssinière BP 92208 Nantes cedex 03, France
email : jbezivin@acm.org
[2]société Soft-Maint, 4 rue du château de l'Eraudière BP 588 44074 Nantes cedex 03
email : lemesle@iae.univ-nantes.fr

Abstract. OSMOSIS [Bézivin1995] is a research platform intended to investigate the various forms of products and processes in object-oriented software production. The kernel of this system is made of a minimal representation support called sNets, a typed, reflective and modular kind of semantic network. Each model represented in this network is composed of a number of typed entities (nodes) and relations between these entities (links) i.e. each model is a partition in the sNet called a *universe*. For each such universe, there is another one called its semantic universe defining the corresponding ontology. In short, an ontology specifies the concepts that may be used and the possible relations between these concepts. Our kernel sNet notation may be qualified of a NOON (Non Object-Oriented Notation) because the concepts of class or object are not built-in in our system. One reason for this choice is to cather with many different semantics for classes, objects and instanceOf/isA relations. We stress here some of the consequences of these choices on the architecture of meta-levels and show the strong relation between this architecture and the precise definition of the instanciation relations in different contexts. Our illustration will be based on CDIF [Ernst1997].

Introduction

The arriving to industrial maturity of object technologies is opening a new period that should see narrowing the differences of concerns between the software engineering and the knowledge representation communities. The announced arrival of the unified modeling language UML [Booch1995] by OMG strengthen this feeling. This compromise between standardization and openness may only be expressed within a framework where models and ontologies are considered as essential notions. The likely choice of CDIF in the OMG efforts as well as the layered architecture of metamodels, clearly opens the debate on the key contribution of modeling and knowledge representation techniques in this new deployment period of object technology. This paper presents some of the practical problems resulting from the multiplicity of models and ontologies in the current forms of software systems development. More particularly it adresses the important problem of model semantic interoperability and shows how an adequate architecture of meta-levels may allow to define with precision the different kinds of instantiation relations that may be found in a practical system.

Meta-modeling : How Many Layers ?

A classical problem is the number of layers used in meta-modeling. The first layer, always present and usually known as the meta-meta-model, is the base of this layered architecture. The second always represents meta-models. And the third layer always represents models. At this point, you can either consider the architecture complete, or you can also add another layer to describe data. Some proposals uses an unlimited number of layers to represent these data. But one has to keep in mind that the number of layers depends on the instantiation relation used between entities from each of these levels (or layers). In order to explain how these different layers are identified. Let's take the example of a common architecture using four layers.

A Four Layer Common Architecture

This is the architecture used by CDIF. The four layers are presented below :

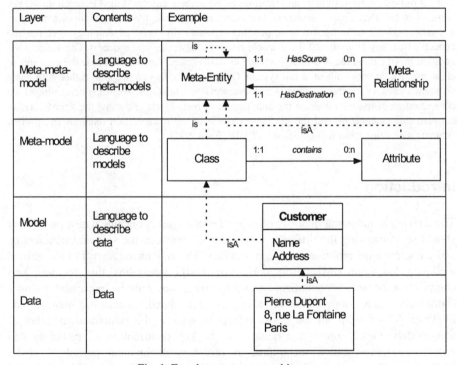

Layer	Contents	Example
Meta-meta-model	Language to describe meta-models	
Meta-model	Language to describe models	
Model	Language to describe data	
Data	Data	

Fig. 1. Four layer common architecture

Layered architecture is associated to a given instantiation relationship [Odell1995] (called *«isA»* there).

153

Accordingly, we have the following predicates :

- A layer contains entities.
- Stating that an entity belongs to a layer means that this entity has an instantiation link to an entity from the previous layer.

So, there must be a precise and unique definition of this instantiation relationship in order to determine to which layer any entity belongs to. The previous figure seems to be consistent with these predicates. But does all the *isA* links have the same meta-definition ? Attempting to represent these meta-definitions, the following scheme is obtained :

Layer	Contents	Example
Meta-meta-model	Language to describe meta-models	
Meta-model	Language to describe models	
Model	Any entity of a type defined in the meta-model	

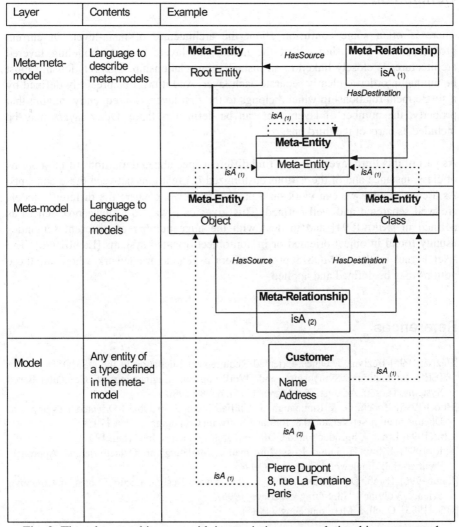

Fig. 2. Three layer architecture with instanciation meta-relationship represented.

In this figure, bold lines represents an inheritance relation used to make the $isA_{(1)}$ meta-definition unique. This figure shows that there is two differents instanciation relations. The first one, used to identify meta-modeling layers, is called $isA_{(1)}$ there. The second, called $isA_{(2)}$, should be defined in a meta-model which corresponds to a specific given object paradigm based on a specific definition of classes. Such a paradigm defines an instanciation relation between an object and it's class, but this relation is totally different from the $isA_{(1)}$ relation. Obviously there are several of these $isA_{(2)}$ relations as there are several notions of classes in different definition spaces (semantic universes).

Conclusion

There is often some confusion about the architecture of meta-levels in current proposals. We have shown that the number of layers in meta-modeling layered architectures is closely linked to an instantiation relationship. This relationship must be unique in order to clearly separate each layer. And it must be precisely defined by a single meta-relationship which belongs to the first layer. Consequently, having that property, the number of layers that can be defined is three. Other layers may be included as parts of the third one.

As part of this third layer, we may find different specialized definitions of the notions of class, instance and of the various customized *isA* relations between these concepts. As a consequence we can work on a precise framework where the different models are well separeted and well defined. This gives us a way to achieve preciseness as defined in [Kilov1994] and to deal with the huge number of different semantics usually found in object-oriented or in non object-oriented systems [Lamb1996]. The sNet kernel in the OSMOSIS project offers a general framework where all these notions may be defined and applied.

References

[Bézivin1995] Bézivin, J. Object-Oriented Requirement Elicitation in the OSMOSIS Project IEEE International Symposium and Workshop on Engineering of Computer-Based Systems, Tucson, Arizona, (6-9 March 1995), p. 289-298.

[Booch1995] Booch, G. & Rumbaugh, J. Unified Method for Object-Oriented Development Documentation Set Version 0.8, Rational Software Corporation, (Oct. 1995).

[Ernst1997] Ernst, J. Introduction to CDIF, Integrated Systems, Inc., (Jan. 1997).

[Kilov1994] Kilov, H. James Ross. Information Modeling: an Object-oriented Approach. Prentice-Hall, Englewood Cliffs, NJ, (1994).

[Lamb1996] Lamb, D.A. Editor, Studies of Software Design, Lecture Notes in Computer Science, Volume 1078, Springer Verlag, (1996).

[Odell1995] Odell, J. Meta-modeling, (1995).

Formalising Object-Oriented Models in the Object Calculus

J.C. Bicarregui, K.C. Lano, T.S.E. Maibaum

Dept. of Computing, Imperial College, 180 Queens Gate, London SW7 2BZ, UK

Abstract. This paper identifies how object models, statecharts and interaction diagrams can be given a semantics in the Object Calculus of Fiadeiro and Maibaum. A compositional interpretation of object model and statechart diagrams is developed, with separate theories constructed for object instances, class managers and associations which are then combined using categorical constructions to yield a formal interpretation of complete systems.

We use this semantics to identify some problematic features of these notations in the Syntropy method.

1 Introduction

The three core OO modelling techniques of *object models, statecharts* [7] and *object interaction graphs* are common to many OO methods, including the current version of the UML [10]. Defining a unified axiomatic mathematical semantics for these notations which will support reasoning is therefore a valuable step towards enhancing the rigour of OO methods[1].

We will look in particular at the versions of these notations used in Syntropy [3], which also includes some degree of formal specification based on Z-like [11] annotations.

In this paper we define a compositional approach to the interpretation of Syntropy statecharts and interaction graphs. We interpret diagrams as logical theories in the Object Calculus [4]. As far as possible separate diagram elements are interpreted as separate theories which are then combined via the categorical constructors of the Object Calculus. This incremental approach makes the interpretation suitable as a basis for a support system which would provide a formal basis for the validation and verification of system specifications.

1.1 The Object Calculus

The Object Calculus [4] is a formalism based on structured first order theories composed by morphisms between them.

An object calculus theory models a component of a system. It consists of a set $\mathcal{S}$ of constant symbols, a set $\mathcal{A}$ of *attribute symbols* (denoting time-varying data)

---

[1] an operational semantics already exists for statecharts.

and a set $\mathcal{G}$ of *action symbols* (denoting atomic operations). Axioms describe the types of the attributes and dynamic properties of the actions.

A global, discrete linear model of time is adopted and axioms are specified using temporal logic operators including: $\bigcirc$ (in the next state), $\square$ (always in the future), and $\diamond$ (sometime in the future). The predicate **BEG** is true exactly at the first moment.

The temporal operators are also expression constructors. If **e** is an expression, $\bigcirc$e denotes the value of **e** in the next time interval, etc.

In the style of [6], theories are composed by morphisms to yield a modular definition of a whole system. The Object Calculus defines a notion of locality which ensures that only actions local to a particular theory can effect the value of the local attributes. For each theory we have a logical axiom

$$\bigvee_{g_i \in \mathcal{G}} g_i \; \vee \; \bigwedge_{a \in \mathcal{A}} a = \bigcirc a$$

We need to extend the Object Calculus with a concept of durative actions, which may overlap in their executions [8], in order to capture the semantics of interaction graphs and implementation models. In this case "next" refers to the next initiation time of an action. Actions α have associated initiation times $\uparrow(\alpha, \mathbf{i})$ and termination times $\downarrow(\alpha, \mathbf{i})$ of their **i**-th invocations.

The interpretation of object types, associations and aggregation in the Object Calculus is given in the papers [9, 1]. Here we will present the interpretation of statecharts and interaction graphs.

2 Interpreting Statecharts

Statecharts are the most complex and semantically rich notation employed by Syntropy. Based on [7], they depict the state space of an object, partitioned according to "those states which distinguish the possible orderings of events" ([3], p.91). We will focus on the essential model level, but many of the semantic interpretations also apply to the specification and implementation levels.

State classes, depicted by boxes with a diagonal line in their top left hand corner, represent varying subsets of the objects of the superclass where an individual instance can move between the subtypes. Statecharts define the transitions which take instances from one state class to another.

In Syntropy, the effect of transitions is specified by preconditions and postconditions similar to those used in Z or VDM. For example, $e_1[\mathbf{P}]/\mathbf{Q}$, indicates that transition e_1 can only occur if the predicate **P** holds and that the two-state predicate **Q** must hold between the before and after states of each occurrence of e_1.

Further semantics is given by **Events** listed in the textual part at the bottom of the statechart. Events are system-wide, but can be targeted at particular objects by the use of parameters and filters. Typically, events effect a state transition in a single object of the class and have the same name as a state transition in the diagrammatic part of the statechart.

We make a syntactic distinction between the event and its associated transitions by capitalising the event name and indexing the transition names.

2.1 Interpreting State Types and Events

The information in the class diagram is interpreted as in [9, 1]. The statechart defines the actions of the classes which replace the white box actions of the instance theory. Each arrow in the statechart represents a class of possible state transitions and is interpreted as an action of the instance theory.

Filters More generally, events are of the form $\mathbf{E}(\mathbf{p[F]})$, where the parameter $\mathbf{p}$ is a list of object or value parameters and the filter $\mathbf{F}$ is a predicate involving the parameters, self and the class constants. Object instances that satisfy the filter will undergo the corresponding transition (depending on their state and precondition), whereas objects for which a filter fails to hold ignore the associated event.

Interpreting Preconditions Preconditions in the Syntropy essential model are intended to specify that certain transitions "cannot occur" in given circumstances. Thus we interpret preconditions as (blocking) guards which prevent execution of the transition they annotate. Consider a transition $e_1[\mathbf{P}]/\mathbf{Q}$ from state $\mathbf{B}_1$ to state $\mathbf{B}_2$. We define a *permission axiom* in the instance theory:

$e_1 \Rightarrow \mathbf{P}$

which expresses that e_1 can only occur when $\mathbf{P}$ holds.

Note, that this interpretation prevents preconditions from being weakened in refinement, that is, such transformations do not yield theory extensions. Thus subtyping form 5 of Chapter 8 of [3] (weakening preconditions) is not valid in essential models[2].

At the class level, each transition is also guarded by the state from which it occurs, for example, we have $\mathbf{a}.e_1 \Rightarrow \mathbf{a} \in \overline{\mathbf{B}_1}$ where $\overline{\mathbf{C}}$ denotes the set of currently existing objects of class $\mathbf{C}$.

Postconditions Postconditions are expressed in terms of the change between attribute values of the current state and those after the transition. Modifications to associations which result from postconditions defining a change to one end only are assumed to be made explicit in the postcondition.

For the above transition with postcondition, $\mathbf{Q}$, we have the *state-transition* axiom

$e_1 \Rightarrow \mathbf{Q}^{\bigcirc}$

where $\mathbf{Q}$ is a predicate in attribute symbols $\mathbf{f_i}$ and $\mathbf{f_i'}$ and we replace $\mathbf{f_i'}$ with $\bigcirc \mathbf{f_i}$ in $\mathbf{Q}^{\bigcirc}$.

At the class level, the event additionally moves the targeted instances to state $\mathbf{B}_2$:

$\mathbf{a}.e_1 \Rightarrow \mathbf{a} \in \bigcirc \overline{\mathbf{B}_2}$

---

[2] In specification models, on the other hand, preconditions are to be interpreted as assumptions: any behaviour is valid if a transition is executed when its precondition is false. So preconditions *can* be weakened in specification models.

Generated actions Generated actions **act** of e_1 (in specification model state-charts) are required to eventually occur:

$$\textbf{a.P} \land \textbf{a.e}_1 \land \textbf{a} \in \overline{\textbf{B}_1} \Rightarrow$$
$$\bigcirc(\neg\,(\textbf{ext}_1 \lor \ldots \lor \textbf{ext}_k)\,\mathcal{U}\,\textbf{act}(\textbf{a}))$$

where the $\textbf{ext}_i$ are all external input actions of the model: this asserts that $\textbf{act}(\textbf{a})$ must occur in the same *macro* step of the execution of the state machine model as $\textbf{a.e}_1$.

3   Mechanisms

Mechanisms are a form of interaction graph showing objects and messages between them. They are relatively informal, so only a loose semantics is attached to them. Nevertheless this semantics allows a check to be made against the implementation model statecharts which describe the allowed behaviour of the system in complete detail.

A generalised fragment of a mechanism is shown in Figure 1. The **l**, **n** and **m** are

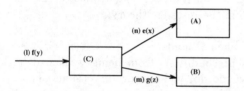

Fig. 1. General Interaction Graph

indices such as 1.1, 1.1.2 and 3 – they have a natural lexicographical ordering $<$. We interpret this figure as saying (if **n** and **m** are of the form **l.t**) that some execution of $\textbf{f(y)}$ on an object **c** of **C** leads to calls of $\textbf{e(x)}$ on an attached **c.a** object and $\textbf{g(z)}$ on a **c.b** object. The order of these calls is given by the indices:

$$\exists\,\textbf{c}:\overline{\textbf{C}}\cdot\exists\,\textbf{i},\textbf{j},\textbf{k}:\mathbb{N}_1\cdot$$
$$\uparrow(\textbf{c.f(y)},\textbf{i}) \leq \uparrow(\textbf{c.a.e(x)},\textbf{j})\ \land$$
$$\uparrow(\textbf{c.f(y)},\textbf{i}) \leq \uparrow(\textbf{c.b.g(z)},\textbf{k})\ \land$$
$$\downarrow(\textbf{c.a.e(x)},\textbf{j}) \leq \downarrow(\textbf{c.f(y)},\textbf{i})\ \land$$
$$\downarrow(\textbf{c.b.g(z)},\textbf{k}) \leq \downarrow(\textbf{c.f(y)},\textbf{i})$$

With

$$\downarrow(\textbf{c.a.e(x)},\textbf{j}) \leq \uparrow(\textbf{c.b.g(z)},\textbf{k})$$

if $\textbf{n} < \textbf{m}$.

It is possible to extend this semantics to cover the synchronisation notations of the UML *collaboration diagrams* [10].

159

4 Refinement

The relationship between the models of Syntropy is not formalised in [3], however a number of examples of techniques for transformation between models are given, and systematic transformations for *subtyping* within a model level are provided. We can formalise refinement and subtyping by theory morphisms: model $\mathbf{D}$ represents a refinement or subtype of model $\mathbf{C}$ if there is an interpretation σ of symbols of $\mathbf{C}$ into symbols of $\mathbf{D}$ which preserves the theorems of $\mathbf{C}$:

$$\Gamma_{\mathbf{C}} \vdash \varphi \quad \text{implies} \quad \Gamma_{\mathbf{D}} \vdash \sigma(\varphi)$$

where $\Gamma_{\mathbf{C}}$ is the theory of $\mathbf{C}$, etc.

Using this, all the forms of subtyping described in [3] can be shown to be refinement steps in addition, with the exceptions that arbitrary redefinition of generated actions on transitions is not valid, and that *target splitting* of transitions is only valid if the target state was unstructured in the abstract model.

This definition of refinement can also be applied between the specification and implementation models, using the techniques for relating theories at different levels of granularity described in [5]. For example a standard form of refinement in Syntropy is to replace broadcast events by point-point message sending (Figure 2). For this transformation to be valid we must require that the messages

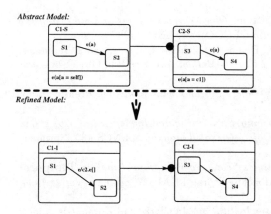

Fig. 2. Forwarding Transformation

forwarded to objects of $\mathbf{C}_2$ are executed within the "secured" part of the execution of $\mathbf{a.e}$, where $\mathbf{a}$ is the target object in $\mathbf{C}_1$. Otherwise, $\mathbf{a}$ could respond to $\mathbf{a.e}$, send $\mathbf{e}$ to an associated $\mathbf{C}_2$ object $\mathbf{b}$ in the relaxed part of the transition for $\mathbf{e}$, and enter a new state, different to $\mathbf{S}_2$, by the time that this forwarded event is responded to by $\mathbf{b}$, which contradicts the abstract specification axioms

$$\mathbf{a} \in \overline{\mathbf{S}_1} \wedge \mathbf{e}(\mathbf{a}) \Rightarrow \bigcirc(\mathbf{a} \in \overline{\mathbf{S}_2})$$
$$\forall \mathbf{y} \in \overline{\mathbf{S}_3} \cdot \mathbf{y}.\mathbf{c}_1 = \mathbf{a} \wedge \mathbf{y}.\mathbf{e}(\mathbf{a}) \Rightarrow \bigcirc(\mathbf{y} \in \overline{\mathbf{S}_4})$$

Refinement between the essential and specification models is more complex, since elements (outside the software boundary) of the essential model may be omitted from the specification model, and because of the change in interpretation of transition "preconditions" described above.

5 Conclusions and further work

The formalisation given here is of benefit as a means of making precise the diagrammatic notations involved and to support reasoning about specifications. We have used it to identify some potential enhancements of and problems with Syntropy – these issues are also relevant to UML and other related methods.

Syntropy attempts to reconcile the traditional object-oriented style of localising behaviour and properties in classes with the need to represent a system without prematurely fixing its design or partitioning into classes. It uses broadcast message-passing and navigation expressions in its essential and specification models in order to achieve this, but this results in a loss of compositionality and some convoluted and un-natural specifications on occasion (see, for example, the "radio button" example of [3]).

References

1. J C Bicarregui, K Lano and T Maibaum. *Objects, Associations and Subsystems: a hierarchical approach to encapsulation.* ECOOP 97, LNCS, 1997.
2. D Coleman, P Arnold, S Bodoff, C Dollin, H Gilchrist, F Hayes, and P Jeremaes. *Object-oriented Development: The FUSION Method.* Prentice Hall Object-oriented Series, 1994.
3. S Cook and J Daniels. *Designing Object Systems with Syntropy.* Prentice Hall, 1994.
4. J Fiadeiro and T Maibaum. *Describing, Structuring and Implementing Objects*, in de Bakker *et al.*, *Foundations of Object Oriented languages*, LNCS 489, Springer-Verlag, 1991.
5. J Fiadeiro and T Maibaum. *Sometimes "Tomorrow" is "Sometime"*, in **Temporal Logic**, D. M. Gabbay and H. J. Ohlbach (editors), LNAI 827, Springer-Verlag 1994, 48–66.
6. J Goguen and R Burstall. *Introducing Institutions.* In Clarke and Kozen, eds. Logics of Programs, pp. 221-256, Springer-Verlag, 1984.
7. D Harel. *Statecharts: A Visual Formalism for Complex Systems.* Sci. Comput. Prog. **8** pp. 231-274 (1987).
8. K Lano, S Goldsack, J Bicarregui and S Kent. *Integrating VDM^{++} and Real-time System Design.* Z User Meeting, LNCS, 1997.
9. K Lano. *Semantic Frameworks for Syntropy.* BIRO project document GR/K67311-1, Dept. of Computing, Imperial College, February 1996.
10. Rational Co., *UML Version 1.0*, http://www.rational.com, 1997.
11. M Spivey. *The Z Notation: a reference manual*, Prentice-Hall, 1989.

Set Theory as a Semantic Framework for Object Oriented Modeling

Prof. B. Cohen,
Centre for Interoperable Systems Research
City University, London (bernie@soi.city.ac.uk)

Abstract: The author has modeled complex systems in a variety of business contexts, from healthcare to telecoms, using a variant of Z. The notation, like Z itself, is a syntactically sugared form of ZF set theory but it permits the use of weak post-conditions — a small, but crucially important, semantic device. The style of construction is very similar to that employed in Object-Oriented modeling, but it illuminates many dark corners of that paradigm, especially as concerns: composition, (multiple) inheritance, concurrency, invariance, inconsistency, emergence, modalities of interpretation, and the clinical aspects of enterprise modeling. This paper describes some of the author's work-in-progress in these areas, and provides references to several models that have been published.

Introduction

In this paper, the author reflects on his experience in object-oriented modeling using the style and notation developed by Professor S. A. Schuman at the University of Surrey [Sc1][Sc2]. No models are presented here, there being plenty in the literature already [Co1], [Co2], [Co3], [Gly]. The intent is to draw from this experience some insights into the practice of systems modeling that pertain whenever the object-oriented paradigm is invoked. These insights are mainly semantic in character but they also shed light on problems that frequently arise in praxis and in the mathematical foundations themselves.

We start with a brief, technical introduction to simple (*isolated*) systems [Bun]. This is followed by a discussion of complex (*composite*) systems, where *interaction*, which is regarded as *concurrent* composition, can yield either emergent properties or inconsistency. Section 3 considers some other interpretations of composite models as their projections into different modalities. Implementation is then considered as the complex model formed by composing a model of a *service* with a model of a *platform*, which suggests that the traditional concept of *refinement* is not applicable. In section 5, we consider some of the problems raised by the modeling of *anticipatory* systems [Ros] from both mathematical and clinical perspectives.

1. The principles of systems modeling in set theory

The subject of a set-theoretic model is the class of systems defined by:

- the *name* of the class;
- its *state space*, expressed as the product of some
  - *state components*, each of a set-theoretic type, mutually constrained by an
  - *invariant*, a first order predicate that is satisfied only by *valid* states;

- its *initialisation*, an assignment of values to the state components that defines the state of any newly created system of the class;

- the *events* (or *operations*) in which any system of the class may participate, each with
  - its *name*, unique to the class,
  - zero or more *parameters*, each of a type declared in the state space;
  - its *precondition*, a first order predicate governing the values of the parameters and state components for
    which the event is enabled; and
  - its *postcondition*, a first order predicate relating values of the state components after the event has
    terminated to values of the state components and parameters when the event occurred.

Note that the invariant expresses a 'global law' — a property of the state space that may not be violated by any event in which the system participates. The pre and postconditions, on the other hand, express 'local constraints' — obligations imposed on the occurrence of each event.

Such a model is *consistent* only if the local constraints guarantee the global law, i.e. no behaviour (sequence of events starting at the initial state) of any system of the class may ever reach a state that violates the invariant, which can be proved inductively by discharging the following *proof obligations* [Co5]:

- that the invariant is satisfied by the initialisation.
- for each event, that whenever it is enabled, it may terminate — i.e. that for every value of the state components (before the event occurs) and parameters that satisfy the invariant and the precondition, there exists at least one value of the state components (after the event occurs) that satisfies the invariant and the postcondition.

Notes

1. The semantic domain here is entirely set-theoretic, i.e. the type of every state component and parameter is a set. However, sets of arbitrary structural complexity may be used, including powersets, relations, functions, and set-theoretic models of such familiar types as sequences, bags, graphs, etc.

2. It is considered good style to express all invariants as relational constraints on, and between, state components and avoiding explicit quantification.

3. A clear distinction is drawn between *types*, which range over sets of *values*, and *classes*, whose instances are *objects*. Values are eternal and unchanging whereas objects retain their identity while changing their state. Thus, we eschew the practice of Smalltalk and several other O-O programming languages in which everything is an object.

4. We do not construct *generic* classes (or *meta-models*) even though some class structures, such as the *name space*, frequently recur. The main vehicle for reuse is set theory itself: it is the *types* that are generic, not the *classes*.

5. We do not quantify over events. Behavioural properties are derivable from the model, but we cannot represent event sequences in it. These semantic restrictions allow us to remain strictly within the domain of first order logic, but also exclude consideration of the evolution of the system itself (see nr. 5).

6. Throughout the construction of a class we assume that its instances will be *isolated* systems. This assumption is fictional but essential for intellectual manageability (as it is in all of science). Under it, interaction among systems is modeled by the explicit *composition* of their classes.

2. Composite Systems

In order to model the interaction of two or more isolated systems, we must construct a class whose state space includes all the state components of each of the subsystems, together with any additional state components and invariants needed to express the additional interrelationships and constraints involved in their interaction [Bun].

That is, we take the product of their state components and the conjunction of their invariants. The events in which a composite system may participate may similarly be composed from its subsystem's events, possibly extended with further parameters, pre or post conditions.

Statically, this denotes the conjunction of all their preconditions and of all their postconditions. Dynamically, it can be thought of as *synchronising* the subsystems' events, or as *decomposing* the event in the composite system.

Notes

1. Clearly, in this framework, composition is an intellectual act, not an *operator* . All the consistency proof obligations must therefore be redischarged for each composite model, because the consistency of the composite system's model is not guaranteed by the consistency of its subsystem's models. These proofs are all still first order, but are not mechanically constructable from the proofs of the components.

2. If event postconditions are 'strong' — that is, if they insist that the values of all state components that are not affected by the event 'remain unchanged' after it — then the composition of such events is guaranteed to be *inconsistent*. This is the case with Z itself, which therefore cannot be used to construct models of composite systems in this way. The style developed at the University of Surrey allows weak postconditions, but imposes certain conditions that ensure the well-foundedness of the models [Sc3].

3. This form of model composition corresponds to both *subtyping* and *multiple inheritance* in the object-oriented paradigm. However, there is no equivalent structure to the O-O concepts of *message passing* and *object relations*, which are simply not needed.

4. The *repair* of an inconsistent composite model also requires an intellectual act. There is no known *unification theorem* for set-theoretic models. Such inconsistencies reveal defects either in the enterprise being modeled or in the modeler's understanding of that enterprise [Co4]. In either case, the resolution of the inconsistency requires the participation of the appropriate enterprise *stakeholders*, to whom the model's consequences must be presented via one or more of its *interpretations*.

3. Interpretations

Since the models are not generic, each has a specific *frame of reference* — that is, some system-in-the-world of which it purports to be a theory. In the set-theoretic style, the names of classes, state components and events are chosen to suggest this intended frame of reference, which is further elaborated in informal comments attached to the model. The names of the types of components, however, are drawn from set theory itself and are independent of the frame of reference.

Often, the model's frame of reference is an *enterprise*, a part of the world in which *agents* offer their *services* to each other with a view to achieving some collective *purpose* [Co6]. In this kind of context, the parts and consequences of a model may usefully be interpreted in several different *modalities*, including:

- *temporal* , the normal interpretation in which the model denotes *behaviour*, the set of sequences of events that it induces;
- *deontic* , in which pre and post conditions on events are interpreted as the *contractual* obligations and responsibilities of agents who offer the service defined by the model.
- *linguistic* , in which the state components and invariant are taken to define the *semantic domain* of the language comprising the set of sequences of events, and of the *communicative* acts from which these sequences arise.

Notes

1. Under the temporal interpretation, all the usual properties of concurrent systems may be investigated, including liveness, safeness and fairness. It is very straightforward to translate a set-theoretic model into the notation of a temporal logic or a process algebra (although the converse does not hold). Of course, the decidability of any of these properties will depend on the domain structure, but as many models have finite domains, this is not usually a problem.

2. The resolution of inconsistency that arises from model composition often involves the imposition of constraints on subsystem models that are stronger than those to which they were subject when isolated. Under the deontic interpretation, this is tantamount to contract renegotiation, the parties having to find some compromise in which the new constraints are mutually acceptable. Of course, the model arising from any such agreement need not necessarily be consistent. The proof obligations here are essential checks on the fairness and validity of negotiated settlements.

3. The resolution of inconsistency often enriches the system state space which, under the linguistic interpretation, introduces additional complexity into the semantic domain which, in turn, increases the *cognitive* complexity of each of the services involved. The wise modeler therefore monitors the topological structure of the state space, and seeks frequently to simplify it — i.e. to endow it with 'nice algebraic properties' — for the sake of the eventual users of the services. It can be more effective to tackle cognitive issues at this stage than to wait for the 'Human Computer Interface' to become available.

4. The invariants of a composite model may be interpreted as the *purpose* of the enterprise and the pre and post conditions of its events as its *business rules*. Consistency proof therefore demonstrates that the rules achieve their purpose.

5. The interpretation of a subsystem model as a service description is particularly valuable when services are to be acquired from outside the enterprise, as in *outsourcing* and *open systems*.

6. In both deontic and temporal modalities, a distinction is often sought between an *obligation* (a *triggering* condition) and a *permission* (an *enabling* condition). In set theory, preconditions are naturally interpreted as permissions and there is no obvious way of denoting triggers. However, most systems modeling formalisms, from classical systems theory to Petri Nets, suffer from this same limitation — an inability to capture, in Aristotelian terminology, *efficient cause*

[Bu2]. This is a technical mathematical problem rather than a pragmatic one. The closure of a model that defines enabling conditions for an event, but does not insist that the event occur as soon as the conditions are satisfied, includes all the behaviours of the system in which the event does or does not occur when enabled. This stance accounts for an arbitrary delay between the enabling of an event and its occurrence thereby accommodating both relativity and failure, neither of which sits comfortably with the concept of an absolute trigger.

4. Implementations

The notations of most object-oriented modeling techniques derive from computational (programming) languages. Systems satisfying models in such notations are usually implemented by *compiling* the language onto a suitable *host*. It is actually possible to translate any set-theoretic model directly into an executable logic program [], but the resulting programs are usually extremely inefficient and must be optimised by property-preserving transformations.

The implementation of a set-theoretic model therefore requires an additional step, in which the intended target *platform* is itself modeled (as an *unpopulated* computational system) and composed with the service model to produce an *interaction model* [Hol]. This act of composition must explicitly relate the resources of the platform to the state space of the service, each events of the interaction model being decomposed into a pair of events, one in each 'subsystem', if possible. This composition defines all the integrity constraints that the implementation must maintain, but it also reveals the purposes of the service/enterprise that the computer system cannot itself guarantee.

A common phenomenon in implementation is the temporary violation, and subsequent repair, of an invariant. For example, in distributed databases, global integrity constraints may be violated during update of individual fields and restored after all the updates have been completed (*coend*), access to the affected fields being locked out for the duration of the disturbance. It is clear from this formulation that such events are *durative*, that is, occupy, and potentially overlap with each other in, time. In an interaction model, this phenomenon would manifest as a composition of the update events in the distributed platform with the abstract event in the service model, the proof obligation being to to demonstrate that the abstract invariant be satisfied by all traces of the update events, operating *concurrently*. This kind of proof would typically performed over an interpretation of the model in a *temporal* modality, but such an interpretation is not, in general, possible in set-theoretic models in which the post-conditions are 'strong', i.e. where those state components not directly referred to by an event are explicitly stated to 'stay unchanged'. The variant of Z developed by Schuman et al [Sc3] uses 'weak' postconditions precisely for this reason.

Notes

1. This view of implementation challenges some basic tenets of computing, particularly those concerned with the *refinement* of specifications into code. A fundamental assumption of refinement is that it commutes over composition, i.e. that the composition of correct implementations of two specifications will satisfy the composition of the specifications. The problem arises because the composition of services in an enterprise usually requires those services to interact with each other. Their models cannot therefore be *orthogonal* and their

composition is not necessarily *conservative* (otherwise the collection of services would be a mere *aggregate*, not a *system* [Bu1]). In other words, the composition of service descriptions introduces additional constraints on each. However, implementation involves the composition of a service description with a platform model, which also introduces additional constraints on each — not necessarily the same ones as those imposed by service interaction. Clearly, implementation does not commute over composition. So much for 'open systems'!

2. An effective treatment of service composition will require that every service, and every platform, be provided with a public model, expressed in forms that admit composition and the discovery of inconsistency. This has serious implications for the OMG, CORBA, and Java communities, where external service descriptions are not expressed as formal models, and platforms (such as Java) are not provided with formal semantics.

3. These problems are not imaginary. They have been occurring for over 30 years in the telecommunications industry, where they are known collectively as *feature interaction* [Ca1]. Composition seems to impact feature interaction in at least five different ways, which can be used to provide a useful classification of known pathologies [Ca2].

5. Open Questions

All modeling techniques, including set theory and O-O, that take the system state space as their subject, suffer from similar analytical limitations which, although clearly visible in set theory, are obscured (sometimes deliberately) in most commercial O-O tools. These limitations are strongly related to open problems that have already been identified in other disciplines. Two of the most important are *anticipatory systems* and *clinical intervention*. The enterprises that we are called upon to model often belong to that class of systems known as *anticipatory* [Ros]. Such a system behaves as if it has internal models of itself and of its environment that it consults before deciding on its response to an event. These models are, of course, just theories which eventually must bifurcate with the reality to which they refer. In the context of business enterprises, this is known as *strategy*.

The modeler encounters strategy in two different ways: as an attribute of the system itself; and as a consequence of the act of modeling. Both require structural operations on the model itself which an algebraist would recognise as *theory morphisms*. Set theory provides no mathematical assistance for modeling systems that can alter their own models. The search for a suitable mathematical framework is currently being pursued [Dub]. Such systems bear some resemblance to those in the continuous world that classical systems theory treats with *tensor calculus*, but the question remains open.

For many years, systems analysts have drawn attention to their clients' annoying tendency to change their minds while analysis is in progress. It is clear from our earlier discussions of composite systems that such changes might well be stimulated by the modeler's revelation of inconsistencies among the purposes, services and agents of the enterprise itself. Here, the modeler's relationship to the enterprise is not that of the objective scientist to an unconscious reality (which has itself been a questionable philosophical stance since Heisenberg). As the demand for enterprise-wide integration increases, so do the scope of the model, the complexity of its state space, and the likelihood that it will reveal conflicts (and opportunities) that the enterprise itself had failed to detect.

Under these circumstances, modeling becomes a *clinical* act — the modeler must diagnose, and attempt to treat, the subject's neuroses and psychoses. The relationship becomes much more similar to that between psychoanalyst and patient, confronting both parties with many of the potential analytical pitfalls identified by the likes of Freud and Lacan [Box]. One aspect of this relationship has been identified with the tendency of software to 'construct the reality' of its users [Flo], but the problem arises well before software is constructed.

This similarity between psychoanalysis and theory morphism is anathema to many practitioners on both sides of the disciplinary divide. It is therefore a totally unexplored field of research, but one that might have results of unexpectedly wide applicability.

References

[Box] Boxer, P. and Cohen, B. *Analysing the* lack *of Demand Organisation*, Proc CASYS '97 (to appear).

[Bu1] Bunge, M. *Treatise on Basic Philosophy* (8 vols.), D. Reidel, 1974-80.

[Bu2] Bunge, M. *Causality*, D. Reidel, 1986.

[Ca1] Cameron, J. and Velthuijsen, H: *Feature Interactions in Telecommunications Systems*, IEEE Communications Magazine, August 1993.

[Ca2] Cameron, J. and Cohen, B. *Formal Approaches to Feature Interactions*, Tutorial Notes, FORTE/PSTV'96, Kaiserslautern, 1996.

[Co1] Cohen, B. and Mannering, D., *The Rigorous Specification and Verification of the Safety Aspects of a Real-Time System*, Proc. Compass '90, 1991.

[Co2] Cohen, B. *The CBM Co.: A Formal Model of a Dataflow Design*, Proc. "Putting into Practice Theories and Tools for Formal Specification", Université de Nantes, 1992.

[Co3] Cohen, B. *Formal Modelling of the Principles Governing the Confidentiality of the Patient Record*, Proc. 'Toward an Electronic Patient Record', Nashville 1997 (to appear).

[Co4] Cohen, B. *Models and Modelling Frameworks in Health Care Informatics*, Proc. 'Toward an Electronic Patient Record', San Diego and London, 1996.

[Co5] Cohen, B. and Pitt, D. *Proof Obligations 2: State-Based Systems*, Proc. Colloq. on High Integrity Systems, University of Warwick, 1990.

[Co6] Cohen, B. *The Description and Analysis of Services as Required and Provided by their Agents*, http://www.cs.city.ac.uk/homes/bernie/services.html

[Dub] Dubois, D. *Concept and Method of Incursion and Hyperincursion*, Proc. CAST '96.

[Flo] Floyd, C. et al, *Software Development as Reality Construction*, Springer Verlag, 1991.

[Gly] Glykas, M., Wilhelmi, P. and Holden, T. *The Combination of Object Oriented Design Techniques with Object Oriented Formal Methods: ORML + Schuman Pitt*, CAISE 93, Paris.

[Hol] Holland, J., Sønksen , P., Carson, E. and Cohen, B. *The Directorate Information System at St. Thomas' Hospital*, Intl. Conf. on Requirements Engineering, Colorado Springs, 1994.

[Ros] Rosen, R. *Anticipatory Systems*, Pergamon, 1987.

[Sc1] Schuman, S.A. and Pitt, D.M. *Object Oriented Subsystem Specification*, in *Program Transformaion and Transformation* (ed. Meertens), Proc. IFIP Working Conf., North-Holland, 1987.

[Sc2] Schuman, S.A., Pitt, D.M. and Byers, P.J.*Object Oriented Process Specification*, in *Specification and Verification of Concurrent Systems* (ed. Rattray), Springer-Verlag, 1990.

[Sc3] Schuman, S.A. and Pitt, D.M. *Object Oriented Formal Specification and 'the rest stays unchanged'*, BCS/FACS Workshop on Formal Aspects of Object-Orientation, London, 1993.

Unification of the Models for Types, Classes and State Machines

Gary W. Daugherty, Rockwell International, gwdaughe@cca.rockwell.com

Abstract– The static model, specified formally, and the dynamic model, represented by hierarchical state machines, are intimately related. By defining a mapping between the two, we are able to provide a definition of inheritance, multiple inheritance and behavioral subtyping for state machines based on that for formally specified types and classes, and provide a graphical representation for formal specifications in terms of state machines. The state machine notation is based on statecharts. It, however, supports both a declarative style, appropriate for types, and an imperative style, appropriate for classes. State machines may be parameterized and may be viewed from different perspectives, based on an arbitrary choice of state predicates. *And* states are interpreted not as an expression of concurrency, but result from a choice of independent state predicates.

1 Introduction

This paper presents a mapping from hierarchical state machines to formal specifications, and a corresponding inverse mapping from formal specifications to hierarchical state machines. As a result a formal specification may be presented graphically from a variety of perspectives, each based on an arbitrary choice of state predicates.

Conversely a hierarchical state machine may be converted to a formal specification and combined with other similarly converted state machines using the conventional rules for inheritance, multiple inheritance and behavioral subtyping. The resulting formal specification may then be presented as a hierarchical state machine, potentially from a different perspective, i.e. with a different choice of state predicates.

The approach applies equally well to types/classes which represent classical event–driven, reactive components and those that do not. All that is required is a degree of rigor in the definition sufficient to make an association between operations and states.

Event detection and event processing are regarded as distinct/separate. In this context, state machines then specify how the system reacts to events without specifying how they are detected.

2 Notation

Formal specifications are given in a simple text notation, and in a pre/post/invariant style with explicit specification of the frame condition (although any comparable notation would do). Attributes in this notation are regarded as abstract queries on the state of the object. The predicate *frame (e)* asserts that 'with respect to the current definition, e is true and nothing else has changed'. Specifically, no attributes or roles associated with the current definition (including those inherited from its parents) and no objects accessible via its roles are changed unless explicitly changed by *e*. When inherited, *frame (e)* recursively applies to any attributes introduced by the subtype/subclass.

State machines are drawn using a variation of Harel's statechart notation. They differ from Harel's original definition [4] most significantly in that:

1.   An invariant is associated with the diagram as a whole and an explicitly stated predicate is associated with each state.

2.   Inner transitions are assumed to override outer ones (rather than vice versa).

3.   Event names and parameters appear on initial transitions, which are distinguished notationally from other default transitions.

4.   State machines (like types) may be parameterized.

5.   To allow for the overloading of operations, each event is defined by its signature rather than by its simple name.

6.   Events which return a value (*observers*) include the return type following a ':', e.g. A: Boolean, B: Boolean and C: Boolean.

7.   A condition (the *delta condition*) enclosed in square brackets is permitted after the / on transitions to allow the effect of a transition to be stated declaratively.

8.   Information not captured by the statechart itself (the invariant, state predicates, state machine parameters, event parameters, descriptions of the state machine and events, and its roles in associations with other objects) is included in a table following the diagram itself.

9.   There is no 'behind the scenes' support for history or history connectors.

10.   The actions associated with a transition are executed in the order given.

11.   No assumption is made regarding the atomic (uninterruptable) nature of transitions.

12.   No assumption is made regarding the time required to execute a transition.

3   Mapping

The mapping between events and operations is based on a strict interpretation of transitions as *predicate transformers* [2, p. 109] as defined by the following principles.

P1.   States are defined as predicates over the values of the attributes and roles defined by the formal specification.

P2.   Each choice of state predicates leads to a different *view*.

P3.   The state predicate for a substate implies that of any superstate.

P4.   An *xor* decomposition corresponds to a set of substates for which every pair of state predicates is contradictory, i.e. substates are mutually exclusive.

P5.   An *and* decomposition corresponds to a set of substates for which no pair of state predicates is contradictory, i.e. substates are independent and the associated substate predicates are equal to that of the associated *and* state.

P6.   Operations directly correspond to events.

P7.   Operations indirectly correspond to the set of transitions triggered by the associated event.

P8.   Nondeterminism is a natural by-product of abstraction.

P9.   State diagrams may be drawn for either types or classes (implementations of types).

Algorithms for mapping between formal specifications and state machines given in [1, section 8]. By default unprocessed events are considered undefined. The same basic approach, however, applies if some (or all) unprocessed events are ignored.

4 Examples

Due to space limitations, it is impossible to include any significant examples in this version of the paper. A large number of such examples, however, may be found in [1], and at the web site http://jml–pc.risc.rockwell.com/Gary/epapers.html. These examples include a number of variations on the alarm clock problem posed in [5], a variety of other examples from the literature, a number of examples involving nondeterminism, etc.

5 *And* decompositions and orthogonal states

Although commonly presented as a representation of *concurrency* [4, p. 242][5, p. 10], orthogonal decomposition is more accurately interpreted as an expression of logical independence. Specifically the decomposition of an *and* state into orthogonal substates indicates that the substate predicates of orthogonal components do not contradict one another, and nothing more.

This view is reinforced by the observation that the same state machine may be represented in terms of either orthogonal or mutually exclusive substates. The state machine in Fig. 2, for instance, is equivalent to that appearing in Fig. 1. Both are derived from the same formal specification [1, sections 9.1 and 9.2]. In the latter, however, our choice of states and state predicates is different, i.e. S1 and S2 represent true, S1.1 represents ~A, S1.2 represents A, S2.1 represents ~B, and S2.2 represents B.

6 Comparison

Unlike other approaches, we do not deal with inheritance and subtyping in terms of restrictions on and orthogonal composition of the state machines themselves. Instead we use the definition of inheritance with respect to the formally specified types to combine the parent types, directly check the result against the subtyping rules of [3], then present the result graphically as a state machine, possibly viewed in terms of a different set of state predicates.

As a result of this approach we can easily deal with complex cases involving the duplication (rather than the sharing) of repeatedly inherited features along different paths [6, p. 167, chapter 11], the independent redefinition of features from a common ancestor along separate paths][6, p. 169], the joining of features from separate type hierarchies [6, p. 156], the merging of features [6, p. 158], the constrained generic parameterization of types/classes, the use of *matching* in lieu of subtyping, etc.

7 References

[1]   Daugherty, Gary. *Formal Specifications and State Machines*, technical report, Rockwell International, December 1996.

[2]   Gries, D. *The Science of Programming*, Springer–Verlag, Berlin and New York, 1981.

[3]   Liskov, B. and J. Wing. "A behavioral notion of subtyping", *ACM Transactions on Programming Languages and Systems,* vol. 16, no. 6, November 1994, pp. 1811..1841.

[4]   Harel, D. "Statecharts: A visual formalism for complex systems", in *Science of Computer Programming*, vol. 8, pp. 231..274, 1987.

[5] Coleman, Derek, Fiona Hayes and Stephen Bear. "Introducing Objectcharts or How to Use Statecharts in Object–Oriented Design", *IEEE Transactions on Software Engineering*, vol. 18, no. 1, pp. 9..18, January 1992.

[6] Meyer, Bertrand. *Eiffel: The Language,* Prentice–Hall, Englewood Cliffs, NJ, 1992.

Fig. 1. Xor decomposition

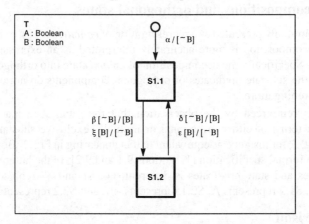

Invariant	True
Frame condition	Implicit
Unprocessed events	Undefined

State name	State predicate
S1.1	~A
S1.2	A

Fig. 2. Equivalent orthogonal decomposition

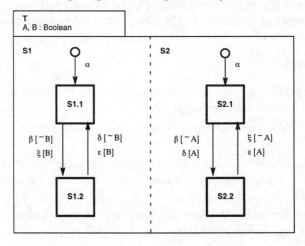

Integration of $\mathcal{Z}$-Based Semantics of OO-Notations

Jürgen Ebert, Roger Süttenbach
University of Koblenz-Landau, Institute for Software Technology
{ ebert, sbach }@informatik.uni-koblenz.de

Abstract. This paper shows how an integrated and formalized description of the abstract syntax and the semantics of the notations of object-oriented methods can be produced by extending EER/GRAL descriptions of the syntax by an operational semantics notated in $\mathcal{Z}$.

Keywords: operational semantics, EER/GRAL, object-oriented methods, declarative modeling, abstract syntax, integrity conditions, $\mathcal{Z}$.

In order to formalize the semantic aspects of an object-oriented method its (textual and visual) languages have to be described precisely. Here, we develop an operational semantics based on abstract syntax. Therefore, we will present the description of the abstract syntax at first.

1   Abstract Syntax

The abstract syntax of a notation used in an object-oriented method can be described by a *metamodel*. The set of instances of this model is the set of *abstract syntax graphs* of the documents (usually diagrams) which are used for modeling real systems using that method.

For every document there is one corresponding syntax graph. This graph can be checked whether it is correct with respect to the metamodel or not. A diagram is a correct diagram if its corresponding syntax graph is an instance of the metamodel of the method.

We use the *EER/GRAL approach* of modeling to achieve a formal description of syntax graphs as described in [EWD+96]. Here, graph classes – sets of graphs – are defined using *extended entity relationship (EER) descriptions* [CEW94] which are annotated by integrity conditions expressed in the $\mathcal{Z}$-like *assertion language GRAL* (GRAph specification Language) [F97].

Example: Figure 1 is an example of an EER/GRAL description which shows a small part of the Booch metamodel [SE97]. Roughly speaking, it defines two kinds of diagrams – ClassDiagrams and StateTransitionDiagrams. Class diagrams describe the class structure of a system and state transition diagrams describe the sequences of operations which are possible for a given class.

In the example, GRAL predicate CD4 demands that the names of classes in

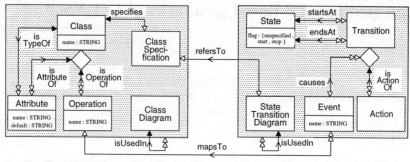

For G in *Booch* **assert**

. . .

CD4 : $\forall\, c_1, c_2 : V_{Class} \mid c_1 \neq c_2 \bullet c_1.name \neq c_2.name$;

. . .

STD9 : $\forall\, e : V_{Event};\ o : V_{Operation} \mid e \xrightarrow{\ }_{mapsTo} o$

$\bullet\ e \xrightarrow{\ }_{isUsedIn} \xleftarrow{\ }_{refersTo} \xrightarrow{\ }_{specifies} \xleftarrow{\ }_{isOperationOf} o$;

Fig. 1. Metamodel of the Booch Method (Part from [SE97])

a system have to be unique, and GRAL predicate **STD9** demands that an event which is mapped to an operation of a class must belong to the state transition diagram of the respective class[1].

The EER/GRAL description of the notations underlying a method formalize their (context free and context sensitive) syntax. It is proposed to formalize different notations separately, in order to integrate the descriptions into an overall description afterwards. The approach has successfully been applied to the Booch method [SE97] and to OMT [ES97].

2   Semantic Description

The semantics of a notation can be described by an operational semantics based on abstract automata, called *semantic bases*. Such an automaton has *states*, which describe possible configurations, and a *transition relation*, which describes possible transitions from one configuration to another. Furthermore, there is an *initial state* from which the computation starts.

A semantic basis corresponds to some $\mathcal{Z}$-text and some $\mathcal{Z}$-schemata. We propose to describe the semantic basis SB_N of a graphical notation N in four parts:

- some global definitions,
- a schema $Config_N$ to model the states,
- a schema $Init_N$ to model the initial state, and
- a schema $Delta_N$ to model the transition relation.

---

[1] The predicate **STD9** is an example for *regular path expressions* in GRAL. In this case the long predicate states that there exists a path from e to o consisting of four edges with the respective type and direction.

We will give an example by describing a semantics of both parts of our metamodel in Figure 1.

A ClassDiagram is used in Booch's method to describe what objects can be found in a system. The universe of objects is given by the set $OBJECT$. An object is either existent on its own (like e.g. the integers, strings, etc.) in which case it has a value assigned to it by the partial function $objectValue$, or it may be an instance of a – user-defined – object class given in the diagram.

$[OBJECT, VALUE]$

$$
\begin{array}{|l}
objectValue : OBJECT \nrightarrow VALUE \\
classOf : OBJECT \nrightarrow V_{Class} \\
\hline
\langle dom(objectValue), dom(classOf) \rangle \text{ partition } OBJECT
\end{array}
$$

Objects of classes may change over time. An object carries the attributes of its class and each attribute has a (changing) value, which is again an object (given by the type of this attribute).

$$
\begin{array}{|l}
\underline{Config_{CD}} \\
objects : \mathbb{F}\, OBJECT \\
objectAssign : OBJECT \nrightarrow (V_{Attribute} \nrightarrow OBJECT) \\
\hline
objects \subseteq dom(classOf) \\
objects = dom(objectAssign) \\
\forall\, o : OBJECT;\ c : V_{Class} \mid c = classOf(o) \\
\quad \bullet\ (dom(objectAssign\ o) = c \leftharpoonup_{isAttributeOf} \\
\qquad \wedge\ (\forall\, a : V_{Attribute};\ c_1 : V_{Class} \mid c \leftharpoonup_{isAttributeOf} a \leftharpoonup_{isTypeOf} c_1 \\
\qquad\quad \bullet\ c_1 = classOf((objectAssign\ o)(a)))
\end{array}
$$

The initial configuration of a class diagram is an arbitrary instantiation for each class of the diagram.

$$
\begin{array}{|l}
\underline{Init_{CD}} \\
Config_{CD}
\end{array}
$$

Since a class diagram alone has no restrictions on the changes of its instantiations the transition relation $Delta_{CD}$ is reduced to a very simple one.

$$
\begin{array}{|l}
\underline{Delta_{CD}} \\
\Delta Config_{CD}
\end{array}
$$

A StateTransitionDiagram describes the state space of a given class, the events that cause a transition from one state to another, and the actions which are triggered by these events. The $Config$ of such a diagram is the actual state.

$$
\begin{array}{|l}
\underline{Config_{STD}} \\
s : V_{State}
\end{array}
$$

The inital state of the semantic basis corresponds to the start state of the state transition diagram.

$$
\begin{array}{|l}
\hline \textit{Init}_{STD} \underline{\hspace{10cm}}\\
\textit{Config}_{STD}\\
\underline{\hspace{5cm}}\\
\textit{s.flag} = \textit{start}\\
\hline
\end{array}
$$

A *Delta* is made due to an event which enables the transition and triggers the action.

$$
\begin{array}{|l}
\hline \textit{Delta}_{STD} \underline{\hspace{9cm}}\\
\Delta\textit{Config}_{STD}\\
e? : V_{Event}\\
a! : V_{Action}\\
\underline{\hspace{11cm}}\\
\exists\, t : V_{Transition} \bullet s \stackrel{\frown}{\,}_{startsAt} t \stackrel{\frown}{\,}_{endsAt} s' \wedge e? \stackrel{\frown}{\,}_{causes} t \stackrel{\frown}{\,}_{isActionOf} a!\\
\hline
\end{array}
$$

3 Semantic Integration

At this point, we have only given a syntactic integration. For example, a State-TransitionDiagram always refersTo a ClassSpecification and therefore to a Class. We will now describe the semantic integration of both diagrams. In order to do this we use some *meta operations* which operate on semantic bases and adapt them depending on the extended semantics of the integration.

To integrate the semantics given above we use the idea that each user-defined object in the system gets additionally assigned a state of its corresponding state transition diagram. We put this idea into action by using the meta operation

$$\underline{addToSchema} : Schema \times Declaration \times Predicate \to Schema$$

which extends a given schema in its declaration and its predicate part:

$\underline{addToSchema}(\textit{Config}_{CD}, objectState : OBJECT \nrightarrow V_{State},$
$\quad dom(objectState) = objects$
$\quad \wedge\ \forall\, o : objects;\ s : V_{State} \mid objectState(o) = s$
$\quad\quad \bullet\ s \stackrel{\frown}{\,}_{isUsedIn} \stackrel{\frown}{\,}_{refersTo} \stackrel{\frown}{\,}_{specifies} (classOf(o)))$

Using this integration, the initial configuration specification and the delta specification have to be adapted in order to reflect the fact, that states of the objects shall behave according to the corresponding state transition diagram.

$\underline{addToSchema}(\textit{Init}_{CD},,$
$\quad\quad \forall\, o : objects;\ s : V_{State} \mid objectState(o) = s \bullet \textit{Init}_{STD})$

$\underline{addToSchema}(\textit{Delta}_{CD},,$
$\quad\quad \forall\, o : objects;\ s, s' : V_{State} \mid objectState(o) = s \wedge objectState'(o) = s'$
$\quad\quad\quad \bullet\ (\exists\, e? : V_{Event};\ a! : V_{Action} \bullet \textit{Delta}_{STD}))$

These three changes lead to a modified version of SB_{CD} which reflects the integrated semantics.

4 Conclusion

These short (and simplified) examples should have shown, that a formal $\mathcal{Z}$-based semantics of object-oriented (oo) methods might be achieved:

1. The formalization of the *abstract syntax* of the notations of oo-methods can be made properly and concisely by using the EER/GRAL approach.
2. These metamodels have several parts, which are then *syntactically integrated* into one model. This is usually done by introducing a relationship or by adding generalizations between two entities of different diagrams.
3. The *semantics* of the individual notations may be described operationally by defining semantic bases.
4. When considering the *semantic integration* these semantics may be combined by meta operations on the semantic bases.

Here still a lot of work has to be done. Up to now about seven different meta operations on semantic bases have been identified [F96] and applied in examples. These operations, when combined, enable us to realize the semantic integration in several cases. We hope that some more experience will help to understand the main approaches for integration using this technique.

It is interesting to note, that syntactic and semantic integration seem to be only loosely coupled. We expected that the choice of a syntactical integration operation in step 2 above would determine the semantic integration operation in step 4. But we did not find such a result. The meta operations used to integrate the semantic bases are only determined by the intention of the considered object-oriented method but not by the syntactic approach.

Acknowledgement
The authors thank Alexander Fronk for his work on the Subject.

References

[CEW94] Carstensen, M. ; Ebert, J. ; Winter, A. ; *Entity-Relationship-Diagramme und Graphklassen.* in german Koblenz: Universität Koblenz-Landau, Report, 1994.

[EWD+96] Ebert, J. ; Winter, A. ; Dahm, P. ; Franzke, A. ; Süttenbach, R. ; *Graph Based Modeling and Implementation with EER/GRAL.* In: B. Thalheim [Ed.]; 15th International Conference on Conceptual Modeling (ER'96), LNCS 1157, p. 163-178. Berlin: Springer, 1996.

[ES97] Ebert, J. ; Süttenbach, R. ; *An OMT Metamodel.* Koblenz: Universität Koblenz-Landau, Fachbericht Informatik 13/97, 1997.

[F97] Franzke, A. ; *GRAL 2.0: A Reference Manual.* Koblenz: Universität Koblenz-Landau, Fachbericht Informatik 3/97, 1997.

[F96] Fronk, A. ; *Software Engineering: Semantik von Entwurfssprachen.* Master's thesis in german. Koblenz: Universität Koblenz-Landau, 1996.

[SE97] Süttenbach, R. ; Ebert, J. ; *A Booch Metamodel.* Koblenz: Universität Koblenz-Landau, Fachbericht Informatik 5/97, 1997.

Integrated Informal Object-Oriented and Formal Modeling Techniques

Robert B. France[1]* and Jean-Michel Bruel[2]

[1] Department of Computer Science & Engineering
Florida Atlantic University
Boca Raton, Florida 33431, USA. Email: `robert@cse.fau.edu`
[2] Laboratoire IRIT/SIERA, bat. 1R1
118, rte de Narbonne
31062 Toulouse, FRANCE. Email: `bruel@irit.fr`

Abstract. One approach to making graphical object-oriented methods
(OOMs) more precise and amenable to rigorous analysis is to integrate
them with suitable formal specification notations. The integration we
outline in this paper provides a bridge from the OOM modeling constructs to the formal notation. We used the Z formal notation and its
related tools to provide a well-defined model of the system.

1 Introduction

The *Methods Integration Research Group* (MIRG)[3] at Florida Atlantic University
has worked primarily on formalizing object-oriented (OO) modeling techniques,
in particular, the Fusion method [3], and, more recently, the Unified Modeling
Language (UML) [1]. We used the formal notation Z [6] in our work because of
its maturity and expressiveness, the availability of analysis tools, and its apparent compatibility with OO analysis modeling concepts. Our work on integrated
methods focuses on providing a formalization that can be used to directly support validation and verification activities. For this reason, we have used only
formal notations for which there exists a sound set of analysis tools. The Z notation we use is supported by typecheckers, animators, and theorem proving
environments. We are also investigating the use of other formal notations, in
particular, B [5] and Object-Z [4], for formalizing OO models.

The integration model shown in Fig. 1 captures the essence of the integrated
methods that we have developed. In the figure, boxes represent documents and
ovals represent activities. The model is generic in the sense that it can be adapted
for use at various stages of software development. For example, at the requirements specification and analysis stage of development the model can be used
to develop a precise specification of functional behavior. Similarly, at the design
stage, modeling of a solution can start with the creation of an informal model

---

* This work was partially funded by NSF grant CCR-9410396.
[3] See *http://www.cse.fau.edu/research/MIRG/*

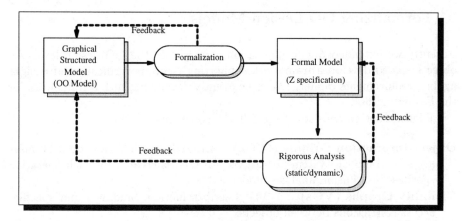

Fig. 1. An integration model.

which is then formalized and analyzed. For iterative design, the model describes the formalization and analysis activities in a single iteration.

The formalization activity can be viewed as a process in which critical assumptions and imprecise concepts are made explicit and more precise. This process is very likely to uncover inconsistencies, ambiguities, and missing information in the informal model, and should highlight any deficiencies in the modelers' views of the problem or solution domain. The result is a more complete model of behavior that can be rigorously analyzed and that can be used as the basis for further development.

2 Formalizing Object-Oriented Analysis Models

The primary model at the analysis stage in most OOMs is the type structure. A type structure consists of types and their associations. Formally, we view a type structure as a characterization of a set of instance structures, that is, structures consisting only of linked instances of depicted types. Denotationally, the meaning of a type structure is a collection of instance structures that conform to the type structure (i.e., the structures all satisfy the properties expressed in the type structure). We call such instance structures *configurations*.

We have developed a formal set of rules for transforming Fusion Object Models [3] and UML type structures [1] to Z specifications characterizing their set of configurations. The MIRG web site has more details on the formalization of Fusion analysis models and on the current form of our UML type structure formalizations.

3 Formalizing OO Design Models

Recently we extended our formalization attempts to the OO design level. An objective is to develop a framework supporting rigorous verification of designs against requirements models. We are currently developing such a framework for the Fusion method.

A Fusion design consists of the following elements:

Object Interaction Graphs (OIGs) : An OIG describes how objects interact to accomplish system operations. An OIG is created for each operation specified in a Fusion analysis model.

Visibility Graphs (VGs) : A VG describes lifetime bindings, and specifies access restrictions between objects.

Inheritance Graphs : The inheritance graphs describe the inheritance structure of the solution.

Class Descriptions : Class descriptions are textual descriptions of classes. Information in the other models are assembled in Class Descriptions.

In our current approach to formalizing Fusion Design we use information in the OIG and the Class Descriptions. Information in the Class Descriptions is used to obtain a design-level Object Model. The formalized Object Model characterizes the design configurations that are manipulated by the system operations described by OIGs.

In [2] we give rules for transforming OIGs to Z specifications. The formalization is based on the promotion mechanism of Z. This allows one to define interactions in a local context and later extend them to a more global context. We have recently developed an alternative approach to formalizing OIGs that produces Z specifications that are easier to analyze.

In general, formalization of an OIG proceeds as follows:

1. For each child operation emanating from the controller, do the following:
   (a) Formalize the effect of the leaf messages.
   (b) Working back from the leaf messages, formalize the effect of non-leaf messages. The sequence numbers are used to relate child messages to parent messages. Typically, formalization will start with the formalization of the interaction labeled with the sequence number 1 (starting with its leaf messages and working backward to interaction 1), then formalization of interaction 2, and so on.
2. Define the effect of the invoking operation (e.g., *enter_test_request*) on the controller. The resulting schema includes variables representing the before and after design states, and conjuncts relating the effects defined for the suboperations to effects on the design state.

The formalization of the OIG, unlike the formalization of the Object Model, requires considerable human effort. The schemas defining the effect of interactions on objects are based on the informal descriptions of methods found in

Class Descriptions. Formalizing these descriptions requires significant human effort. We are currently developing a formalism for method descriptions that will reduce the effort of going from informal to formal descriptions.

We have also developed techniques for transforming state machine models to Z specifications. Currently, analysis of behavior involves animating the Z specifications with ZANS to dynamically explore the behavior described by a formal model. This type of analysis can uncover problems related to ambiguous, imprecise, and incomplete descriptions of behavior. For complex systems, dynamic exploration is seldom exhaustive enough to provide assurance that a system has the desired properties. For such assurance one needs the support of theorem proving tools. We plan to supplement animation with theorem proving and model-checking capabilities.

4 Conclusion

The primary objective of integrating FSTs and OOMs is to create precise and analyzable graphical OO models. The integration we outline in this paper allows one to use Z type checkers and animation tools to analyze OO models. In our experiments, we found that doing such analyses can reveal additional problems with the Fusion models (as well as with the formalization of the problem). Another benefit of the formalization is that it uncovers deficiencies in the modeling technique. When such deficiencies are addressed, a well-defined notion of well-formed models can be formulated and used to drive the analyses of the models in CASE tools.

References

1. Grady Booch, James Rumbaugh, and Ivar Jacobson. Unified Modeling Language. Version 1.0, Rational Software Corporation, Santa Clara, CA-95051, USA, January 1997.
2. Jean-Michel Bruel, Robert B. France, Maria M. Larrondo-Petrie, Bharat Chintapally, and Gopal K. Raghavan. CASE-based Rigorous Object-Oriented Modeling. In *Proceedings of the Northern Formal Methods Workshop*, Bradford, UK, 23–24 September 1996.
3. Derek Coleman, Patrick Arnold, Stephanie Bodoff, Chris Dollin, Helena Gilchrist, Fiona Hayes, and Paul Jeremaes. *Object-Oriented Development: The Fusion Method*. Prentice Hall, Englewood Cliffs, NJ, Object-Oriented Series edition, 1994.
4. Roger Duke, Paul King, Gordon A. Rose, and Graeme Smith. The Object-Z specification language. In Timothy D. Korson, Vijay K. Vaishnavi, and Bertrand Meyer, editors, *Technology of Object-Oriented Languages and Systems: TOOLS 5*, pages 465–483. Prentice Hall, 1991.
5. Kevin C. Lano and H. P. Haughton. Formal development in B Abstract Machine Notation. *Information and Software Technology*, 37(5):303–316, May 1995.
6. J. Michael Spivey. *The Z Notation: A Reference Manual*. Prentice Hall, Englewood Cliffs, NJ, Second edition, 1992.

Semantics Through Pictures

Stuart Kent, Ali Hamie, John Howse, Franco Civello, Richard Mitchell[1]

Division of Computing,
University of Brighton, Lewes Rd., Brighton, UK.
http://www.biro.brighton.ac.uk/biro/index.html, biro@brighton.ac.uk
fax: ++44 1273 642405, tel: ++44 1273 642494

Abstract. A diagrammatic approach to the semantics of OO modelling notations is proposed. This is based on an innovative and expressive notation dubbed "constraint diagrams", which can be used to precisely characterise a range of sophisticated, static constraints on OO models. Other notations, such as those found in UML, can be viewed as projections of constraint diagrams. Work on using constraint diagrams at the core of a 3D modelling notation is also briefly described as a means of similarly providing the semantics of diagrams imposing constraints on dynamic behaviour.

1 Introduction

This paper outlines a pictorial approach to constructing a precise semantics for object-oriented modelling notations. There are at least four reasons why one might want to build a precise semantics:

1. To clarify meaning leading to refinements of the notation.
2. To clarify meaning for developers using the notation.
3. To clarify meaning for tool developers, thereby increasing the likelihood of inter-operability between tools at a semantic level (e.g. code generated from different tools for the same model has the same behaviour).
4. To support semantic checking of models, automated if possible. This includes checking that implementations meet their specifications, checking internal consistency of components, and checking for inconsistencies and conflicts between components.

(1) just requires the semantics to be written down in a precise form. (2) and (3) require it to be written down in a form which developers and tool developers can easily understand. In addition, it would be desirable for (3) to provide a semantics in a form which directly assists the construction of tools, e.g. the automation of (4).

We propose that the semantics is given in terms of an expressive and innovative diagrammatic modelling notation, dubbed constraint diagrams, which can be used to precisely characterise a range of sophisticated, static constraints on OO models and which is particularly targeted on (2) and (3) (with some impact on (1) and (4)). A 3D notation based on constraint diagrams may be similarly used to characterise the semantics of dynamic behaviour. In essence, our notation is rich enough to characterise a model that would otherwise require many different kinds of diagram. The latter can then be viewed as projections of this model.

---

1. This research was partially funded by the UK EPSRC under grant number GR/K67304

Section 2 briefly surveys some of the notations used for describing OO models found in UML (UML) and Catalysis (d'Souza and Wills, 1997). Section 3 introduces constraint diagrams and contract boxes. Section 4 outlines how these could be used to give a semantics, and discusses how the approach could be extended to other diagrams in UML.

2 Generic Descriptors: Perspectives on a Model

In essence an OO model *is* the set of states it is allowed to enter, where a state can be visualised as an object diagram (*snapshot*), together with the set of allowed paths through those states. These sets are in general infinite, or at best very large, so impossible to enumerate. Therefore modellers need notations that are able to define very large sets in only a few diagrams. UML calls these notations *generic descriptors*. Essentially generic descriptors provide ways of writing rules or constraints which determine whether any particular snapshot or filmstrip is allowed in a model or not. Here we consider type and state diagrams (from UML) combined with invariants and action specifications (from Catalysis).

2.1 Type Diagrams

Type diagrams define most of the language that can be used in snapshots and constrains cardinalities of links between objects. The type diagram for the specification of a library system is given in Figure 1.

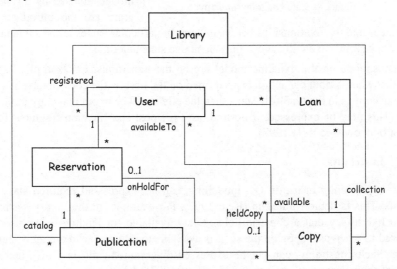

Figure 1: Type model for library

Only types and association rolenames appearing in the type model may appear in snapshots. Furthermore the number of links in a snapshot corresponding to a particular association may not exceed the cardinality constraints declared on the type model, for any objects of the types associated. For example, focusing on the (unlabelled) associations between **Loan** and **User** and **Loan** and **Copy**, a loan object may be linked with only one user and one copy, though user and copy objects may be linked to many loan objects.

2.2 State Diagrams

A state diagram places constraints on both the static and dynamic models. The state diagram for the type Copy, in the context of the Library, is given in Figure 2.

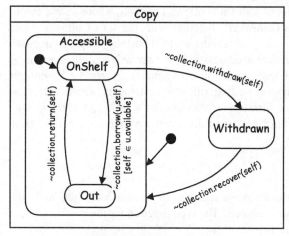

Figure 2: State Diagram for Copy

This is essentially UML notation, though we allow navigation expressions labelling the transitions. For example the diagram indicates that when the action borrow is performed on the object identified through ~collection with self as the copy argument, then, provided self is in the OnShelf state, the effect will be to move it into the Out state.

The constraints on the static model imposed by a state diagram are the introduction of new states and the relationships between them. In particular, states at the same nesting level are disjoint, so an object can only be in one state at a time.

The constraints on the dynamic model are on the transitions: for example, Figure 2 says that when a borrow action is performed on the library, the copy involved is self, and that copy is in the onShelf state, then the effect will be to put that copy in the Out state. This may be expressed, if desired, as a pre/post specification fragment for the action borrow (see Kent 1997).

2.3 Invariants

Diagrams currently in use in OO modelling, can not express all required static constraints. This is demonstrated in (Kent 1997). For example, in the library system we would like to say that a copy on hold is only available for lending to the user who reserved it, whereas a copy on the shelf is available to all users who are registered and active. Such constraints can not be expressed diagrammatically in UML, and some form of textual annotation is required. (Kent 1997) shows how this and other constraints may be written using the mathematical language of Catalysis.

2.4 Action Specifications

Similarly, diagrams in UML can not express all constraints on dynamic behaviour. For example, in the case of borrow, the state diagram of Figure 2 does not say that a new, loan object must be created recording the fact that the copy has been loaned out to the user. Again such constraints have to be written using a textual notation. In Catalysis they are expressed precisely as pre/post conditions or *contracts* written in the mathematical language.

3 Constraint Diagrams and Contract Boxes

Constraint diagrams (Kent 1997) are a diagrammatic notation for expressing static constraints on models. They build upon the effectiveness of snapshots in illustrating the import of constraints on a model. They may be viewed as a generalization of snapshot notation (i.e. UML object diagrams) – one constraint diagram represents a set of snapshots, which is more expressive than type diagrams. They make use of Venn diagram notation, with some extensions, to show relationships between the values of navigation expressions. They also show types and states as the sets of objects of that type or in that state, respectively.

Figure 3 is a constraint diagram for the invariant stated in Section 2.3 on page 3. Reading the diagram starting from the object x, part of that invariant is read off as follows: for all libraries x, and for all copies y in the collection of x that are on hold, y is available for lending to the (single) user associated with the reservation that y is on hold for.

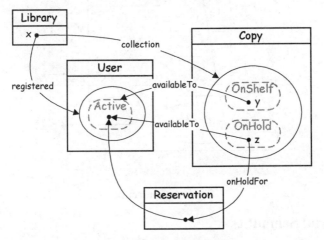

Figure 3: Constraint Diagram

The state diagram of Figure 2 with transitions removed is also a constraint diagram, showing the relationships of sets of objects in different states: onShelf and Out are disjoint, so an object can't be in both states at the same time; they are contained in Accessible, so if an object is onShelf or Out it must be accessible.

Contract boxes (Gil and Kent 1997) are a diagrammatic notation for showing dynamic constraints, that would otherwise be expressed textually using pre/post conditions (contracts). A contract box is shown in Figure 4. It is a pair of constraint diagrams linked by object lifelines. The constraint diagrams show constraints on the objects involved in or affected by the action associated with the box (in this case borrow). The top diagram is a general characterisation of the pre-state, and the bottom of the post-state. The lifelines are a visual aid to identifying how specific objects are affected by the action. For example, in Figure 4 a lifeline makes it clear that the copy object is moved from being available to out.

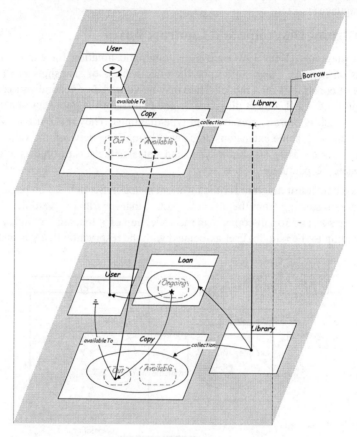

Figure 4: Contract Box

4 Pictorial Semantics

It appears that constraint diagrams and contract boxes can be used to express most, if not all, static and dynamic constraints that can be expressed with invariants and contracts. This includes constraints imposed by type diagrams – cardinality constraints are just a particular form of invariant; and constraints imposed by state diagrams, which contribute to the type model (dynamic types) and action contracts.

Thus using one notation – constraint diagrams and contract boxes (which are just pairs of constraint diagrams), it is possible to express a model with a rich set of constraints, that otherwise requires a range of different diagrams and textual annotations in other notations. This suggests that constraint diagrams and contract boxes could be used to give a semantics to the other notations. This could help to make the semantics easier to understand, and provide an alternative approach to tool support for semantic checking, through the direct comparison of diagrams (see Kent, 1997 and Gil and Kent, 1997, for more specific ideas). The semantics could be formalised by grounding the semantics of constraint diagrams and contract boxes in a formal language such as Larch (Guttag & Horning 1993), adopting an approach similar to (Hamie & Howse, 1997).

In terms of the meta-model semantics currently proposed for UML, a model of (the abstract syntax of) our notations would have to be built, with well-formedness rules (as invariants or operations) to describe the mapping of all the UML diagrams (whose abstract syntax is also encoded as OO models) into this model. Then, when the state of the meta-model was instantiated with a particular system model, all parts concerned with UML diagrams could be stripped away and no information would be lost.

Contract boxes are just one part of a series of 3D notations currently under development (Gil & Kent 1997). Not only can these notations be used in their own right for modelling, it emerges that they can also be regarded as a visualisation of a single underlying semantic model, of which 2D notations such as sequence, collaboration and activity diagrams are just projections. An important result of this work is the identification of other projections (some 3D, some 2D) which are more precise and richer than current notations, but just as simple and intuitive. Indeed, it may be that this work results in a general improvement to existing 2D notations, which was one of the reasons stated in the Introduction for doing semantics work.

Much work remains to be done. The details need to be worked out for the mappings between our notation and standard 2D notations such as UML. The precise semantics of the former also need to be worked out, to ensure the integrity of the notation and to explore its expressiveness, as well as help with provision of tool support. Tools envisaged include assistance with: 3D visualisation; derivation of 2D and 3D projections; generation of the complete 3D model from projections; use of the complete model to perform integrity checks on the projections; and checking the integrity of the complete model itself.

References

Cook S. and Daniels J. (1994) *Designing Object Systems*, Prentice Hall Object-Oriented Series.

D'Souza D. and Wills A. (1997) *Component-Based Development Using Catalysis*, book submitted for publication, manuscript available at http://www.iconcomp.com.

Gil Y. and Kent S. (1997) Three Dimensional Models, submitted to ICSE98, available at http://www.biro.brighton.ac.uk/biro/index.html

Guttag J. and Horning J. (1993) *Larch: Languages and Tools for Formal Specifications*, Springer-Verlag.

Hamie A. and Howse J. (1997) *Interpreting Syntropy in Larch*, Technical Report ITCM97/C1, University of Brighton, available at http://www.biro.brighton.ac.uk/biro/index.html.

Kent S. (1997) *Constraint Diagrams: Visualising Assertions in Object-Oriented Models*, to appear in Procs. OOPSLA97, ACM Press.

UML (1997) *Unified Modelling Language v1.0*, Rational Software Corporation, available at http://www.rational.com.

Business Rules:
From Business Specification to Design

Haim Kilov   Ian Simmonds

haim_kilov@ml.com, isimmond@watson.ibm.com[1]

A "business rule" precisely describes communities of business things:

> *A business rule is a proposition about business things, relationships between them and operations applied to them, from the business enterprise viewpoint. [X3H7-96]*

> *A proposition is an observable fact or state of affairs involving one or more entities, of which it is possible to assert or deny that it holds for those entities. [RM-ODP95]*

The emphasis in the understanding, specifying, and reusing business rules is on their semantics rather than on (many different) ways of expressing their syntax. Similarly, understanding of a program (and reuse of programming constructs) is possible only based on semantics rather than on a syntax used to express this semantics.

A business rule is defined in terms of the (mathematical) notion of "proposition" showing that precision is essential when formulating business rules. An imprecise notion of "business rule" is of no use because it can be applied to almost anything (for example, "business rules are those things supported by mechanism ZYX, which is a business rule mechanism"). When used in this way, the term "business rule" is merely a buzzword, whose value is determined by current fashion.

The definitions of business rules do not mention computers, software, programming languages, databases, or any other technological notion. A business rule has to be made explicit even if the rule is "get approval for XYZ from a competent, trusted business expert". Explicitly documented rules were followed by businesses (and, as legislation, by entire societies) many centuries before computers were invented.[2]

Kinds of business rules

The diagrammatic specification[3] below shows that a (business) rule can be subtyped (exhaustively) into an invariant, a triggering condition, a precondition, a post-

---

[1] Authors' current addresses are: Haim Kilov, Merrill Lynch, Technology Strategy and Planning, World Financial Center, South Tower, New York, NY 10080-6105; Ian Simmonds, IBM T J Watson Research Center, 30 Saw Mill River Road, Hawthorne, NY 10532, USA

[2] For example, the business rule "Policies of insurance and reversionary contracts are void, if the person whose life is insured shall die upon the seas, or upon any of the great lakes, ... or shall ... visit those parts of the United States which lie south of the southern boundaries of the States of Virginia and Kentucky ..." appeared in a business specification in 1835 [M1835].

[3] These specifications are rigorous and precise in the following sense: for each diagram indicating concepts and relationships, there exists an equivalent set of formulas of first-order or higher-order logic. Each diagram should be read in the following manner. The boxes represent things (concepts). The labeled triangles, together with lines that connect those triangles and boxes, indicate the relationships between these things. The kind of relationship is indicated by the label in the triangle. These kinds of relationships are elementary generic ones (such as

189

condition, and perhaps something else. This subtyping is not overlapping: each rule belongs to (satisfies) only one of its subtypes in this subtyping hierarchy. The (business) operation is a composition-assembly (CA) of a signature, a triggering condition, a precondition, a postcondition, and so on. Due to being a composite in a composition, some properties of an operation are determined by properties of its components; and some properties of an operation are independent of properties of its components (this is a fragment of the invariant that defines a generic composition relationship). The decomposition of the (business) operation is an assembly because an operation can exist only if its

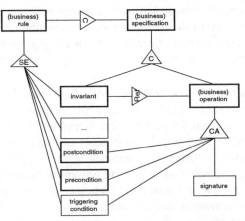

components — a signature, a triggering condition, a precondition, a postcondition, and so on — exist. In addition, the reference relation-ship (Ref) between an invariant and a (business) operation shows that some properties of an operation are determined by its invariant (as required by the definition — invariant — of the reference relationship).

Finally, a business specification is composed of invariants and operation specifications; and in another composition — of business rules. This information model [KR94] presents in-variants for collections of things. Operations exist only in a *context* specified by the invariants that describe properties of things and relationships which are true "no matter what" at a particular level of abstraction.

This business (rule) specification tames complexity by identifying only pure business "things", relationships, constraints, and the behaviors of collections of these "things". It relies upon explicitly defined concepts and semantics rather than meaning presented only implicitly, either in "meaningful" names or informal descriptions. Implicit semantics result in the need for each reader to "interpret" — that is, invent a meaning for — the named concepts; each reader inevitably invents a different meaning, and the resulting system fails to meet the needs of the business, which were never explicitly captured. The major part of a business specification — the deliverable of business analysis — is a structured representation of all rules that govern the business (see, e.g., [KMS96]).

composition) encountered in virtually all applications. The semantics of each kind of relationship is precisely defined (using invariants); this definition is reused for each of its application-specific instantiation. The definitions of generic relationships provide their distinguishing characteristics and are also used to specify typical, generic, *operations* applied to the related things.

Conceptual similarity

Many *concepts* used in system specification have counterparts (and even origins) in business. For example, transactions, locks, data, concurrent processing, monitors, compensating transactions, abstraction, all exist in business, although only some of these *terms* predate computer systems. From the business point of view, the execution mechanism for these notions is not important. Similarly, it is not important how a computer system works – "electronically, pneumatically, or by magic" (EW Dijkstra).

Similarity of concept names can be both good and bad. When done properly, the semantics of concepts in the system context satisfies the semantics of those in the business context, thus allowing direct correspondences between system and business. This direct and visible traceability makes both initial development and future maintenance significantly simpler. However, assuming correspondence when slight differences exist can be catastrophic; system mechanisms tend to prevent or banish human discretion and human decision making in general, even when employee discretion can lead to substantially increased customer satisfaction.

Business specification, business design, and system specification

To improve understanding, it is essential to separate the concerns of business specification (the "what"), business design (the "how"), and system specification (the "automation"). The need for clarity and elegance in understanding was explicitly stated — for the programming frame of reference — in the 1960s [D62], and in more modern terms in [P95]. To understand a complex system, appropriate abstraction has to be used: irrelevant details have to be suppressed. For a business specification these details include (in particular) everything related to possible automation. ("What is to be automated" belongs to the business design frame of reference, and "how to auto-mate" belongs to the system specification frame of reference.)

Business design refines a business specification into a detailed strategy for conducting business. Thus, it *refines existing and adds new business rules*. It determines the operations to be automated, possible outsourcing of some operations, workflow-related issues, and so on. For a particular (fragment of a) business specification, there is a choice between several possible business designs, each determined by a business design strategy and the environment in which the business fragments (*communities*) operate. A business design has to satisfy its business specification.

For the parts of a business design being automated, a system specification is required. It must satisfy[4] both the business specification and the business design. As with business designs satisfying a business specification, the choice between several system specifications satisfying a given business design and its business specification is again determined by a system specification strategy and the environment.

Analysts and what they do

Analysts write specifications.

---

[4] Satisfaction is a generic business pattern precisely defined in [KS96, KS96-2].

Business analysts write business specifications and business designs; systems analysts write system specifications. This role separation is analogous to the distinction between architects and master builders in building. Neither business nor systems analysts work in isolation: the former work in close cooperation with subject matter experts (real business people) and sometimes with systems analysts; the latter work in close cooperation with technology experts and sometimes with business analysts.

A deliverable of a business analyst is a business specification — the collection of relevant business rules described in a precise, explicit and abstract manner. A business specification is declarative: it describes "what is true about the business" rather than "how the business is run". Except for rules evidently beyond the scope of that particular business domain, *all* rules must be gathered whether or not they will ultimately be realized by, or even known to, a computer system. After a business analysis activity, decisions may be made to change the business by some combination of changes, additions or abandonment of business processes and/or computer systems. Since the goal of business analysis is not to design or implement a computer system, it should not be constrained by constructs (or tools!) appropriate for system design.

Analysts must be explicit about everything they do.

Classifications of rules governing the business

The following diagrammatic specification shows several mutually orthogonal ways of classifying the rules that govern a business. The subtyping of rules into preconditions, postconditions, invariants and so on (shown above) also obviously applies. Each of the four shown subtyping hierarchies effectively subclassifies all elementary rules. Different components of a single composite rule may belong to different subtypes within the same subtyping hierarchy.

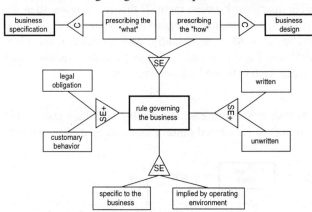

These subtypings are mostly self explanatory and straightforward. However, a particular rule need not permanently belong to a fixed set of subtypes (as for most things, the classifications into which a particular rule falls are time-dependent). Note that in some operating environments most rules may belong to a particular subtype in a certain subtyping hierarchy. The most striking examples are at the level of an entire society which may rely almost exclusively on one of custom or legislation [F97].

Discovery of "rules of interest"

Some rules may seem irrelevant to the application under consideration. This especially applies to rules describing things, relationships or operations that are not intended to be automated. However, contexts are essential. For example, understanding and automating "back office" underwriting operations is possible only if (perhaps more general) rules governing "underwriting" are understood and made explicit. For another example, an automated passenger transit system should be aware of occasional usage of its rail network by vehicles that are not controlled by the system.

Analysts can only document rules that have been explicitly made available to them. Of course, part of the skill of the analyst is to uncover business rules, the technical term for which is elicitation (see, e.g., [KR94], Chapter 6).

Not all business rules have to be given to system developers, although a business analyst needs to document all relevant rules. When for some part of the business being automated a coherent and reasonably complete set of rules exists, it can form the basis of the corresponding part of the system specification and subsequent system design and coding.

Analysis should start with the production of an initial, high-level domain specification. This should be used to structure the more detailed analysis activity, allowing to proceed by successively concentrating on coherent fragments of the domain in isolation, with thin and visible interfaces between them. If this is not done, then so-called "analysis paralysis" may result, leading to many thick volumes of probably useful but ill-structured specifications. Most importantly, such monolithic specifications are both difficult to understand and navigate, and prevent system development activities — and therefore, initial system usage — from commencing.

Rules in business design

Business design involves (but is not restricted to) making decisions about what rule enforcement will (or will not) be performed (and/or audited) by a computer sys-

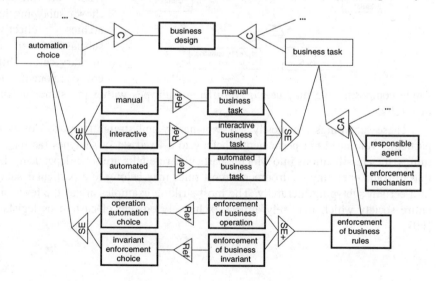

tem. It is typically performed in terms of larger units than individual elementary business rules. In particular, when a business specification is structured in terms of business operations and invariants constituting an information model (as presented above), it is possible to work in terms of these higher-level structures.

The diagram shows two viewpoints on what business design accomplishes. The first (automation choice and its two subtyping hierarchies) is largely about making choices, while the second (business task and its subtyping and composition) is about producing a design that satisfies these choices. Automation choices are made about the enforcement[5] of business operations and business invariants. Observe that a business invariant — specified declaratively in a business specification — has to be enforced ("operationally") in a business design; and so a business task will have to be created for this purpose, in the same manner as a business task is created to enforce a business operation. Often a business task will be able to enforce both operation rules and invariant rules, which is why the subtyping is overlapping.

Business tasks correspond to operation or invariant automation choices. The reference relationships explicitly show property determinations, including those corresponding to the component automation choices of the business design which satisfy the business rule and business operation components of the business specification. Another reference relationship (not shown) specifies that properties of a business task are in part determined by the business invariant. It is possible to specify several business tasks for a single business operation and — perhaps more often — for enforcement of a business invariant.

References

[D62] E W Dijkstra. Some meditations on advanced programming. *Proceedings of the IFIP Congress 1962*, North Holland, 1963, pp. 535-538.

[F97] Damn Yankees (by Stephan Herrera), *Forbes* Magazine, March 10 1997, pp. 22-3.

[GRM95] ISO/IEC JTC1/SC21. Information Technology - Open Systems Interconnection - Management Information Systems - Structure of Management Information - Part 7: General Relationship Model, ISO/IEC 10165-7, 1995.

[KMS96] Haim Kilov, Helen Mogill, Ian Simmonds. Invariants in the Trenches. In: *Object-oriented behavioral specifications* (Ed. by H.Kilov and W. Harvey). Kluwer Academic Publishers, 1996, Chapter 6. ISBN 0-7923-9778-9.

[KR94] Haim Kilov, James Ross. *Information Modeling: an Object-oriented Approach*. Prentice-Hall, Englewood Cliffs, NJ, 1994.

[KS96] H. Kilov, I. Simmonds. Business patterns: reusable abstract constructs for business specification. In *Implementing Systems for Supporting Management Decisions*: Concepts, methods and experiences, Ed. by P. Humphreys et al, Chapman and Hall, 1996, pp. 225-248.

---

[5] The term "enforcement" does not convey — in its normal English and American usages — the semantics that we want here. The correct term is probably "implementation", in accordance with the Oxford English Dictionary: "to fulfill, satisfy (a condition)". We hesitate to use "implementation" because of its strong perceived associations in the context of "producing code from a spec" (in one context) and "putting a system into production" (in another context).

[KS96-1] Haim Kilov, Ian Simmonds. Business patterns and viewpoints. *Proceedings of the Workshop on Viewpoints*, ACM Symposium on Foundations of Software Engineering, San Francisco, USA, October 1996.

[KS96-2] Haim Kilov, Ian Simmonds. How to correctly refine business specifications, and know it. *Proceedings of the Fifth OOPSLA Workshop on Specification of Behavioral Semantics*, San Jose, USA, October 1996, pp. 57-69, ISSN 1089-7143.

[M1835] Proposals of the Massachusetts Hospital Life Insurance Company, to make insurance on lives, to grant annuities on lives and in trust, and endowments for children. James Loring printer, Boston 1835.

[P95] David Lorge Parnas. Teaching programming as engineering. In: *ZUM '95*: The Z Formal Specification Notation (Lecture Notes in Computer Science, Vol. 967). Ed. by J. Bowen and M. Hinchey, Springer Verlag, 1995, pp. 471-481.

[RM-ODP95] ISO/IEC JTC1/SC21/WG7. Open Distributed Processing - Reference Model: Part 2: Foundations (IS 10746-2 / ITU-T Recommendation X.902, February 1995).

[X3H7-96] Business rules for the Enterprise Viewpoint of RM-ODP. ANSI X3H7-96-07R2, 7 December 1996.

Liberating Object-Oriented Modeling from Programming-Level Abstractions

Reino Kurki-Suonio and Tommi Mikkonen

Software Systems Laboratory, Tampere University of Technology
P.O. Box 553, FIN-33101 Tampere, Finland

Abstract. Encapsulating methods in objects requires design decisions that complicate specification and modeling of object systems. To allow modeling at a higher level of abstraction, we outline a rigorous theory for dealing with patterns of generalized object systems. Unlike "classical" object-oriented extensions of specification formalisms, the approach is based on a reactive rather than transformational view of computations. It allows dynamic modeling at an intermediate level between logic and direct implementability, with a simple relationship between operational models and logic. Support is provided for early modeling of temporal properties, systematic use of rigorous refinements, and for composition of patterns.

1 Introduction

Conceptual understanding of software has mainly developed through an abstraction process, which allows to view well-structured software artifacts in terms of high-level programming concepts. Object-oriented programming is commonly acknowledged as a successful step in this process.

Associated with the evolution of programming concepts, there has been a widespread belief that these would provide a suitable level of abstraction not only for the implementation of programs but also for their specification. As ease of modeling is an explicit goal in object-oriented languages, their developers may consider them sufficient as such (see e.g. [12]). Some others have complemented them with language-independent, often vague notations, in which the conceptual level of abstraction is, however, the same.

There is also an opposite direction of developing abstractions, rising from the logical foundations for reasoning on program-like models. Such abstractions have been of much academic interest but have not yet affected practical design methods. The theory outlined in this paper reflects the view that both ends should meet in operational modeling and design, and that the theory should be kept sufficiently simple to be practical.

2 Evidence of Complexity

In principle, object-orientation seems to simplify modeling. However, even seemingly simple programming concepts turn out to be complex when one tries to understand them in detail. Object-oriented programming concepts are no exception, as evidenced by efforts to give formal meaning to them:

- Integration of object-orientation into formal methods (mainly Z) has been surveyed in [11]. Complexity is reflected in the lack of well-defined semantics for several formalisms, and in subtle semantic differences.
- Using abstract data types, Willis has analyzed theoretical problems with inheritance and multiple inheritance [15]. His conclusion is that multiple inheritance leads to a contradiction.
- Achuthan *et al.* have investigated object-oriented modeling of embedded real-time systems, based on an extension of IO automata [1]. Their analysis leads to three different notions of inheritance, since preservation of behavior does not ensure substitutability.

One cannot avoid the impression that any attempt to model truthfully the mechanisms in object-oriented programming languages leads to undesirable complexity. Also, sharing their view to model individual objects and classes in isolation, formal methods only add precision to what can already be done considerably well in programming. In particular, these formalizations fail to assist effectively in the area where complementary support would be needed most, i.e., in specification and modeling of collective behaviors.

Further evidence of complexity in conventional concepts is that they have not succeeded in providing a commonly accepted basis for the modeling of concurrency, even though at first sight this might be expected of them.

3 Need for Higher-Level Abstractions

With growing size and behavioral complexity of software, programming-level abstractions are inadequate for specification and modeling. Design notations like OMT [13] provide valuable help in practice, but they lack precision and do not help in modeling of collective behaviors.

One consequence of keeping to the conceptual level of programming languages is that collective behaviors cannot be addressed rigorously in early stages, where mistakes and misunderstandings cost most. Scenarios and use cases are helpful in discussing behavioral properties, but their semantics are vague, and they fail to provide means for effective modeling.

Need for higher-level abstractions is also shown by the fact that all logically rigorous approaches to software design, initiated by the seminal work of Dijkstra [4], have led to theories where specifications and programs are all part of a larger "iceberg," in which executable programs are only the visible tip.

The main source for programming-level bias in "classical" object-oriented models is the principle that "behavior" is encapsulated in objects as "methods" invoked by "messages" [8]. This principle is natural when one needs to indicate *how* responsibilities are divided between objects, and *how* objects communicate. For high-level modeling it is, however, sufficient to specify *what* the objects do in cooperation, and *which* objects are needed for this. Further details can be superposed on a high-level model as design decisions.

"Generalized object models" have therefore been proposed, in which single-object methods are generalized into *multi-object actions*, and communication mechanisms are abstracted away. Such models have been advocated and used independently in the specification of reactive systems [5, 17] and in information systems modeling [7]. Their need has also been recognized in the standards work on object models [16].

Multi-partner actions were proposed in [2] for distributed systems, to allow design and reasoning in terms of collective behaviors of cooperating processes. Subsequently they were adapted to object systems in a form where action participants are objects belonging to specified classes [5]. Assuming that an action may be executed whenever suitable participants are ready for it, the mechanism is symmetric with respect to participants, and no explicit invocations are needed. Handshake communication between prospective participants can also be abstracted away, as well as the partitioning of the action itself between them.

4 Action-Oriented Execution Model

Obviously, appending multi-object actions to an ordinary programming language would only increase its complexity. Fortunately, in specification and high-level modeling it is possible to use a simple execution model with no explicit processes or control threads, with actions as atomic units of execution, and with nondeterministic selection between alternative actions as the only "control."

At first sight this may seem like a huge step backwards from the sophisticated control structures in programming languages. This sophistication has, however, been designed for implementation of sequential processes; logical simplicity and independence of superfluous control assumptions are more important in specification and modeling. Primitive action-oriented execution models have, in fact, been used successfully for concurrent and reactive systems, as shown by experiences with UNITY [3], Temporal Logic of Actions (TLA) [10], and DisCo [17], for instance. Similarly, such simplicity has not been an obstacle in constructing generalized object models for information systems [6], or in using production system languages in expert systems.

Besides providing a simple basis for reasoning, an action-oriented execution model allows interleaved modeling of concurrency in a natural manner, and is eminently suited for formal refinement. Concurrency requires to pay attention to atomicity of execution – an issue that has been blurred by languages where concurrency is an add-on feature. Atomic units of execution are therefore essential in high-level descriptions, while process structure can be addressed later. As for refinement, it is easier to append new detail to actions that have been given as syntactic entities, or to insert totally new actions, than to make corresponding insertions to process behaviors.

5 Outline of a Rigorous but Practical Theory

Based on experiences with DisCo [17], fundamentals for object-oriented modeling with multi-object actions have been presented in a language-independent form in [9]. As discussed in [14], the classical algorithmic paradigm is unsatisfactory for modeling interactive systems. Therefore, the theory is based on a reactive paradigm, where all interacting partners can contribute to temporal behaviors.

The theory covers three closely interrelated areas: a simple execution model for object-oriented models, a logic for reasoning on collective temporal behaviors in these models, and language principles for constructing such models. Some of its main principles are as follows:

- Temporal behaviors exist only in the presence of an environment. Therefore, the *closed-system principle* is adopted, where objects are always modeled in connection with their assumed environments.
- Absence of implicit "program counters" for control threads is essential for the logical simplicity of the approach. Instead of explicit invocation of actions, their execution is controlled by "guard" expressions associated with actions.
- The execution model is *nondeterministic*, allowing modeling without complete information. This is crucial, for instance, in environment modeling.
- Models are given as generic *patterns*, which cover all possible instantiations where objects of the given classes can appear.
- TLA [10] is used as the logical basis, giving precise (state-based, linear-time) semantics in terms of *temporal behaviors*. The execution model gives a natural match between operational models and canonical TLA expressions.
- Reasoning can be based on an *interleaving model*, where actions are executed in some sequential oder. Still, all temporal properties hold also in concurrent implementations, where concurrency is restricted only by the atomicity constraint that no object can participate in more than one action at a time.
- *Incremental* construction of models is supported. At each stage, a model exhibits precisely determined temporal behaviors, which can be subjected to both rigorous reasoning and to validation by animation.
- In *composition* (or synthesis) of models, each component represents an incomplete view of temporal behaviors in the total system.
- Facilities for incremental specification and composition support *formal refinement*, where all temporal properties are preserved. Preservation of safety properties is guaranteed by construction; proof obligations are obtained for liveness properties.
- Subclasses are defined as logical refinements of their superclasses. Thus an object of a subclass satisfies all temporal properties of its superclasses, even in the presence of multiple inheritance.

6 Concluding Remarks

Developers of rigorous program design methods have always been worried about the complexity of programming languages, and have advocated the power of logical simplicity. In high-level modeling this concern is even more justified.

Operational modeling should be affected both by programming notions and by logics for reasoning. Generalizing single-object methods into multi-object actions allows object-oriented modeling at a level where communication aspects have been abstracted away. On the other hand, ease of reasoning on temporal behaviors and practical applicability of formal refinements require an essentially simpler basis than that offered by traditional programming language concepts. Challenged by these concerns, a simple operational basis has been developed for a rigorous but practical theory, as outlined in this paper.

References

1. Achuthan, R., Alagar, V.S., Radhakrishnan, T., A formal methodology for object-oriented development of real-time reactive systems, *Workshop on Object-Oriented Real-Time Systems (OOPSLA'94)*, Oct 1994.
2. Back, R.J.R., Kurki-Suonio, R., Decentralization of process nets with a centralized control, *Proc. 2nd ACM SIGACT-SIGOPS Symposium on Principles of Distributed Computing*, Aug 1983, 131-142.
3. Chandy, K.M., Misra, J., *Parallel Program Design, A Foundation*, Addison-Wesley 1988.
4. Dijkstra, E.W., *A Discipline of Programming*, Prentice Hall 1976.
5. Järvinen, H.-M., Kurki-Suonio, R., Sakkinen, M, Systä, K., Object-oriented specification of reactive systems, *Proc. 12th Int. Conf. on Software Eng.*, 1990, 63-71.
6. Kilov, H., Mogill, H., Simmonds, I., Invariants in the trenches, *Object-Oriented Behavioral Specifications* (Eds. H. Kilov and W. Harvey), Kluwer 1996, 77-100.
7. Kilov, H., Ross, J., *Information Modeling: An Object-Oriented Approach*, Prentice Hall 1994.
8. Korson, T., McGregor, J.D., Understanding object-oriented: a unifying paradigm, *Comm. ACM 33*, 9, Sep 1990, 40-60.
9. Kurki-Suonio, R., Fundamentals of object-oriented specification and modeling of collective behaviors, *Object-Oriented Behavioral Specifications* (Eds. H. Kilov and W. Harvey), Kluwer 1996, 101-120.
10. Lamport, L., The temporal logic of actions, *Transactions on Programming Languages and Systems 16*, 3, May 1994, 872-923.
11. Lano, K., Haughton, H., (Eds.), *Object-Oriented Specification Case Studies*, Prentice Hall 1994.
12. Madsen, O.L., Open issues in object-oriented programming – a Scandinavian perspective, *Software – Practice and Experience 25(S4)*, Dec 1995, 3-43.
13. Rumbaugh, J., Blaha, M., Premerlani, W., Eddy, F., Lorensen, W., *Object-Oriented Modeling and Design*, Prentice Hall 1991.
14. Wegner, P., Why interaction is more powerful than algorithms, *Comm. ACM 40*, 5, May 1997, 80-91.
15. Willis, C.P., Analysis of inheritance and multiple inheritance, *Software Engineering Journal*, July 1996, 215-224.
16. ANSI X3H7 OODBTG Reference Model, Available at <http://info.gte.com/ftp/doc/activities/x3h7/by_model/OODBTG.html>.
17. DisCo, Available at <http://www.cs.tut.fi/ohj/DisCo/DisCo-english.fm.html>.

Discovering, Displaying and Agreeing Semantics in an Environment of Conflicts

by Geoff Mullery, Systemic Methods Ltd., email geoff_mullery@dial.pipex.com

Introduction

For many years we have improved tools for specification and implementation, but the problem of delivering unsatisfactory systems persists. A major reason is failure to discover what is really wanted/needed. There are differences of view which contribute to this - differences between: what is wanted and needed (required design rather than requirement); the contractual customer and end-user customers; different types of end-user customers; individual customers of any given type; the views of a given person at different times

The larger and more complex the environment the greater is the difficulty of producing a specification reflecting these views and implementing it without delivering unpleasant surprises. There are several factors to be dealt with:

- Discovery of what is really wanted/needed.
- Illustration of wants/needs so that they can be recognised by all relevant agents.
- Discovery that *and remembering where* the wants and needs conflict.
- Illustration of conflict so it can be understood and assistance in its resolution.

None is well-served now and this paper discusses problems to be addressed in handling them and notes technologies available to achieve improvements.

Discovery of What is Wanted/Needed

It is widely recognised that there are numerous views of any large system (a recent workshop [1] was devoted to requirements Viewpoints). Discovery of *all* wants/needs relevant to a large system is not the simple interview/document analysis process once assumed (e.g. the author's CORE method [2]). For many projects a practical interview process is impossible. Instead one must examine many documents about the environment, assisted by pseudo-user authorities whose views are not necessarily representative.

There are cultural differences between developers and customers and within the customer community. This results in invalid disagreements/agreements because of different interpretations across cultural boundaries - e.g. some believe a fact is obvious (axiomatic and need not be explicitly stated) while others (e.g. system developers), not sharing the axiom set do not recognise its existence.

Cultural problems are compounded by hidden "agendas" among specification stakeholders. This is manifest as a conscious effort to get something included or excluded when it should not be. It is often done for reasons of local "politics" or personal "empire building" within the customer organisation.

Specification is more than fact expression and checking for notational consistency. There is a need to consider *meaning* - e.g. a potential difference in meaning is the notion of *working for* someone. *X works for Y* may mean Y supervises X or it may mean X performs a service used by Y or even Y is an objective X seeks to fulfil.

Cultural/organisational boundaries mean that some sources of relevant information are not known when specification starts. Some remain hidden even through to system installation. Information is dispersed across boundaries and it is not always appreciated by those in possession that it is relevant to a given project or team.

For large projects, particularly involving legacy components there numerous documents of varying quality, produced under varying issue control policies. It is unclear which parts of which documents are relevant. In a long-standing environment the terminology may change over quite short periods. It is unsurprising that for some systems only people who have served the environment for years are trusted to enhance or modify its systems.

Document analysis is then enormously complicated. It is necessary to establish relevance and linkages among documents, in spite of cultural differences between them. Linkages are not necessarily only by referencing pointers. The nature (meaning) of a linkage needs to be clear - and often is not, because of pointer imprecision or changes of terminology or interpretation.

Illustration of Wants/Needs

Analysts often use diagrams to express requirements, but the notation is unnatural to their customers. In one case in the author's experience a requirement was never seriously reviewed by user-authorities, who found the notation too opaque, walking out of a course to familiarise them with it. Checkland [3] advocates avoidance of strict formalisms, permitting stakeholders to use any notations convenient for expressing and discussing requirements. This can encourage user authorities to co-operate in production and analysis of the requirement, but suffers from two problems.

First, though the meaning may seem clear to the originators, it may not be as clear to later users. The argument that later users should be involved in its derivation is fanciful on anything but a short, small project. On large, long-running projects staff turn-over will render useless the insights of the original specifiers.

Second, though agreement may be reached, there is no guarantee with an ad hoc notation that it is justified. Everyone applies a personal interpretation, which may differ from that applied by others. Even with a defined notation some will ignore the definition, applying another interpretation. If the interpretation is not well defined then the opportunity for this type of problem is far too great.

A compromise between use of defined/formal notations and ad hoc notations is to map between them. This is not a one-time, one-way mapping - from ad hoc to structured/formal. When analysis of the formalism shows a need for change this often needs reflection to the customers, who resist learning the formal notation.

An analyst mind-set says if they will not learn the notation the work should not be done for them. What if the medical profession, which makes heavy use of Latin, asserted their customers were not to be served unless they learn Latin? If I have an ailment I should not be forced to learn Latin before diagnosis and treatment starts.

A customer mind-set is that they should not have to be bothered with niggling detail. What if I tell a doctor I have a pain I want treated and resist answering further questions? I must answer questions about its nature, location and related symptoms or causes if I am to get the right treatment. The doctor and I negotiate towards a precise statement of my problem. The doctor manages translation from me to/from medical terminology.

In computing such negotiation is needed and analysts should manage the mapping to/from the formalism. When the formalism changes analysts should identify where and how the ad hoc representation might change. Then there will be re-negotiation of the ad hoc form to ensure that all relevant authorities agree the change.

Discovery and Recording of Conflicts

In large systems conflict is a certainty. Large projects commonly have long-running conflicts due to weak management or contractual difficulty (introduction of change is difficult and expensive) or technical complexity (the best option for resolution can not be agreed) or politics (someone delays a decision until unwanted options becomes infeasible).

Frequently pressure is applied to resolve a conflict and it is resolved with inadequate study. Later the decision is reversed with greater cost and greater delay. Occasionally the resolution is later over-turned as a result of company politics not visible to the analysts, but going on as the original decision is applied.

Problems arise when conflicts are not detected or not resolved or resolved wrongly. A conflict may be missed through ignorance (nothing said indicates its presence), politics (someone deliberately hides it to avoid a resolution in a way they do not want) or negligence (analysts miss the evidence). It is very important to use analysis techniques which promote the probability of detection of conflict.

Conflicts must be sought, detected, recorded, analysed and resolved when possible. The most important factors are the first three. Unanalysed, unresolved conflicts can be carried for some time without causing too much damage. A conflict resolved with inadequate analysis can be carried through design as long as its existence is known. Designers can protect against the chance that the decision may change.

Architectural Models can assist analysis and discovery of conflicts. They propose what a domain should look like. Their virtue is that they facilitate discovery of facts about an environment and probable areas of conflict within it (e.g. by detecting mis-positioned components). This is a big advance over simple reflection of what user-authorities say, with analytically detectable problems in what has been said.

Computing has tended to identify only low level architectural models (the ISO 7 layer model is aimed only at communications between systems/sub-systems). From the 1960's a more general model of a system architecture, the Viable System Model (VSM) [4] was produced in the OR/Cybernetics community. More recently computing has taken notice of external influences, proposing Business/Behavioural Models (e.g. [5]) for analysing the environment when specifying requirements.

Another aid to conflict detection comes from the Artificial Intelligence community. They use natural language analysis and reasoning in an uncertain environment, producing tools to investigate agreement/divergence between people with different cultural backgrounds (e.g. [6]). A general view of how techniques like this and the VSM might be integrated into an Enabling Network System [7] to support system development for distributed sites, organisations and cultures is presented in [8].

Illustration and Resolution of Conflicts

The CORE method used Constructive Redundancy, which aimed to get information from more than one route and use differences between the results to illustrate inconsistencies - and thence conflicts. That however was based on a defined notation and the need for non-structured/formal notations has been pointed out.

This requires study of such specifications for less obvious evidence of conflict. Different sources must be examined for disagreement even when using the same, or similar phrases to describe the same or similar things. For example *John Smith works for peanuts* may be interpreted literally by a farmer and as a statement of poverty by a stockbroker.

A conflict expressed in ad hoc representation may say too little to allow its illustration (or even detection). Hence there is need to persuade people using ad hoc representation, to say sufficient about the terminology used to test for disagreement. This requires *starting* the process of mapping to a formalisation without seriously distorting the chosen terminology. One approach is described in [6] and an approach to comparison once some formalisation has occurred is provided by [9].

Unresolved conflicts can be carried for some time (even into implementation) but it is usually more cost/time-effective to find as soon as possible a resolution of conflict which is practicable and acceptable to all parties. Some conflicts can be carried into the run-time system, because they will not cause system failure or yield damaging results. Preferences for user interface styles can be argued as an either/or choice, but yielding in other areas like cost and time would permit several styles to be included, with end-users selecting the styles they prefer.

Other conflicts require resolution before the system goes into service, since they will be damaging to the environment. The CORE approach to this used mediation, recommendation and accountability but there are occasions when its approach is counter-productive – either by introduction of an element of personal confrontation or by forcing a poor/inadequate solution just to remove the pressure only to see it surface as a future problem with need for an expensive re-work.

In resolving conflict the more that confrontation and pressure can be eliminated the better. An approach to reducing this personal element in conflict resolution is being researched via the AI community (e.g. [6]). Something derived from this and used on an Enabling Network System has considerable potential for improvement.

What is Still Needed?

It is difficult to keep up with all relevant approaches. Many have only laboratory experience and use isolated support. Some use such weaknesses as a reason for not applying a published approach, but it is not a reason to do nothing to "systematise" the specification process. This paper cites techniques and research pointing a way to improvement. Rather than choose a "least bad" published approach, a combined approach is needed, which can be evaluated, refined and improved.

For OO development, questions raised in this paper about how an environment for supporting Object Oriented system development will deal with key problems are:

204

- How will you map from an informal, piecemeal, multiply redundant, inconsistent customer environment to the precise semantics and (presumably) non-redundant, internally consistent support environment you aim to use?

- How will you demonstrate to the originators that your mapping validly captures their views as expressed in ad hoc conversations/documents in their multiple informal terminologies?

- How will you ensure that problems found in analysis of formal specifications are reflected to the customer environment in a form they can understand - i.e. in their multiple informal terminologies?

- How will you make sure that the evidence of conflict is properly understood by the customer environment with sufficient supporting evidence understandable to all who must participate in resolving it?

- How will you handle the presence of inconsistency and other forms of conflict you are forced to carry on through the process of design and development?

- How will you control/avoid the distorting effects of confrontation and coercion on the conflict resolution process?

- How will you ensure that conflict resolution leaves evidence that the conflict occurred, to ensure that down-stream users of the specification can protect against the possibility that the decision is later over-ruled?

- How will you ensure your support tools can interact (exchanging data in both directions) with other tools which deal with factors not covered by you (e.g. AI tools supporting terminology comparisons and conflict resolution)?

References

[1] Vidal, Finkelstein, Spanoudakis and Wolf (Editors Joint Proceedings of the SIGSOFT '96 Workshops: ACM, 1996

[2] Paul and Siegert (Editors). Distributed Systems. Methods and Tools for Specification, An Advanced Course, Chapter 3: Springer-Verlag Lecture Notes in Computer Science 190, 1985

[3] Checkland and Scholes. Soft Systems Methodology in Action: Wiley, 1990

[4] Espejo and Harnden (Editors The Viable System Model: Wiley, 1989

[5] Kilov and Harvey Object-Oriented Behavioral Specifications: Kluwer Academic Publishers, 1996

[6] Shaw and Gaines. Group Knowledge Elicitation over Networks : Knowledge Science Institute, University of Calgary, Alberta, Canada (summarised for a seminar to the BCS RESG at Imperial College, London)

[7] Harnden and Mullery Enabling Network Systems: System Practice, Vol 4, Part 6, Dec 1991

[8] Mullery. Joint Proceedings of the SIGSOFT '96 Workshops, pp 227-231: ACM, 1996

[9] Leite and Freeman Requirements Validation through Viewpoint Resolution: IEEE Transactions on Software Engineering, Dec. 1991

Towards a Precise Semantics for Object-Oriented Modeling Techniques*

Ruth Breu, Radu Grosu, Franz Huber,
Bernhard Rumpe, Wolfgang Schwerin

Institut für Informatik
Technische Universität München
email: {breur,grosu,huberf,rumpe,schwerin}@informatik.tu-muenchen.de

Abstract In this paper, we demonstrate how a precise semantics of object-oriented modeling techniques can be achieved, and what the possible benefits are. We outline the main modeling techniques used in the SYSLAB project, sketch, how a precise semantics can be given, and how this semantics can be used during the development process.

1 Introduction

The development of complex software systems is a subject of great technical, economic and scientific importance. A software development method can be defined as a unified approach incorporating multiple description techniques, characterising a system from several points of view. Most of these description techniques currently used, however, lack a formal semantics. While recent research works on *formal methods* aim at the formal foundation of separate description techniques, less emphasis is put on the formal integration of the multiplicity of description techniques used in a single method. Yet, integrated description techniques are the basis for a systematic design and for vast tool support during the development process.

Besides the use of description techniques in specific methods, one has to consider them in a more general scientific context. Their importance for modeling software systems might turn out to be comparable to the importance of mathematical techniques, invented in the second half of the 19'th century to model physical processes. Therefore, a scientific foundation of description techniques seems to be of great significance.

It is the aim of the SYSLAB project to develop a mathematically founded modeling technique for distributed, object-oriented systems, based on UML [BRJ96] description techniques. The modeling technique will offer a systematic set of steps for enhancing, refining, and transforming *documents* of the description

---

* This paper originates from the SYSLAB project, which is supported by the DFG under the Leibnizprogramme and by Siemens-Nixdorf.

techniques used in SYSLAB. It supports the systems development process from analysis to implementation.

2 The SYSLAB Description Techniques

2.1 Modeling Method

A modeling method roughly defines the process of software development. It turns out that the description techniques used and their usage order are rather orthogonal. It therefore makes sense to develop the description techniques and their precise semantics independently of the modeling method, as, e.g., done in UML 1.0. However, the semantics has a severe impact on the possible transformation steps for documents. These transformation steps are the connection between the description techniques and the method. A method can be seen as a set of guidelines and heuristics that tell the developer when and why to use a sequence of transformations. The method tells what the prerequisites are, what the benefits are, and what pitfalls should be avoided (quite similar to design patterns [GHJV94]).

Description techniques used to define different views of a system, play a central role within a modeling method. Documents describing a system using these techniques are used and transformed until the whole system is described by a set of executable documents. Basically, we use the following description techniques originating from UML, but adapted and specialized to allow the definition of a precise semantics:

- Informal Text and Diagrams (ITD)
- Message Sequence Charts (MSC)
- State Transition Diagrams (STD)
- Object Model (OM)
- Specification Language (SL)
- Programming Language (PL)

Documents of these kinds are provided with a semantics based on a *mathematical system model* (MSM). Through this semantic foundation, we not only get a precise semantics for documents, but also an integrated one, which allows us to define transformations between documents as well as rigorous context conditions within and between different description techniques.

A transformation step takes a finite set of documents (often one) and produces new documents. The set of possible transformations is to be chosen carefully, to ensure systematic and correct manipulation of documents. Then it is, e.g., possible to inherit the STD-based behaviour description of a class to its subclasses using a refinement calculus, as, e.g., given in [Rum96, RK96], which is similar to refinement calculi, like, e.g., the work of C. Morgan [Mor90].

The development of a system is captured in a *development graph*, which contains documents as nodes and dependencies between them as directed arcs. Each document has a state which, e.g., captures whether a document is still necessary or already redundant, because its successor documents contain all information of the document. Such information for documents is necessary, on the one hand, to trace requirements and design decisions through the development process, and, on the other hand, to allow requirement changes in a systematic way.

2.2 Description Techniques

For software engineers it is extremely important to describe complex structural and dynamic dependencies in a clear, structured, and systematic way. Therefore, several description techniques, providing different *views* as well as different *abstraction levels*, are used.

Based on existing object-oriented modeling techniques like UML or OMT [BRJ96, RBP+91] we use the following techniques as core of the SysLab-method:

Informal Text and Diagrams (ITD) comprise any kind of text, diagrams, tables and graphics. Whenever desired or necessary, ITD can be used, thus allowing scalability of formal techniques. It is escpecially useful to capture requirements in early phases, comments and annotations not yet fully explored, and to store reasons for design decisions. Despite its informal character, ITD can be used in a systematic way, e.g., to extract classes and attributes from requirements descriptions. We also attach a state to informal documents, capturing, e.g., the validation or redundancy state of a document.

Message Sequence Charts (MSC) describe separate flows of communication or subsets of communication flows in a system. Emphasis is put on communication between separate parts (objects or groups of objects) of a system. Constituting a high level of abstraction, MSCs are well suited to capture a system's requirements. Moreover, MSCs can be used for and generated by simulation respectively. Our MSC variant is based on the message-oriented model and allows us to define different layers of abstraction, repetition, choice and hierarchy of MSCs.

One of the main and still not completely explored problems is the semantics of an MSC in the presence of underspecification and nondeterminism. It seems that some kind of completeness assumption could be necessary to allow a set of MSCs to be given a semantics. Furthermore, a starting part (usually the first message) will be considered as a starting trigger.

State Transition Diagrams (STD) describe the lifecycle of objects. In STDs, descriptions of state and behaviour are combined. Different levels of abstraction allow both the specification of an object's interface as well as the specification of methods. Refinement techniques enable not only inheritance of behaviour but also stepwise refinement of abstract STDs, resulting in an implementation.

To describe a detailed behaviour of transitions, it is necessary to use a specification language that relates input and source state with output and destination state. This specification language (SL) is characterised below.

Object Model (OM) describes the static structure of a system. The OM encompasses the description of classes and of relationships between classes: association, aggregation, and generalization. It includes the signature of objects, given by their operations and attributes.

To describe structural invariants that have to be maintained, we use the same specification language as for transitions in STDs.

Specification Language (SL) is an axiomatic specification language based on predicate logic, resembling Spectrum [BFG+93]. SL allows declarative definition of properties. Particularly, SL is used for the definition of pre- and post-conditions of transitions and for the definition of state invariants not only in single objects but also between several objects in the OM. In order to enable automatic testing of verification conditions, SL is also oriented towards functional programming, resembling Gofer [Jon93] in this concern. As an effect, the step from high-level descriptions towards executable code is facilitated, which again makes prototyping easier.

Programming Language (PL) is an executable implementation language. System descriptions formulated in an executable language are the target of any software development process. Therefore the integration of PL in our method is a must. Designing PL as a subset of the object-oriented language Java [Fla96] seems to be reasonable. Besides others, Java has the advantage of being architecture-independent. In order to fully integrate PL into the development process, assigning PL a formal semantics is necessary.

For each description technique, except informal documents (ITD), a formal *abstract syntax*, a *concrete diagrammatic or textual representation*, and a complete set of *context conditions* for the correctness of documents will be supplied. Furthermore, a *formal semantics* based on the MSM will be given.

3 Mathematical System Model (MSM)

3.1 Informal Description of MSM

The mathematical system model serves as a basis for the creation of the semantics of the description-techniques. The MSM describes the universe of systems $\mathbb{SM}$ that can be specified by the SYSLAB-method. The MSM is formalized using mathematical techniques [RKB95, KRB96]. However, for an understanding of the SYSLAB method it is not necessary to know the formalization of the MSM. For this reason, we only roughly sketch the MSM below.

A system consists of a dynamically changing set of *objects*, each with its own *identity*. The *objects* are grouped by a finite set of *classes*. A *state* is assigned to each object. Both the object's *attributes* as well as the set and states of its active operations determine the object's state. A *signature* describes the set of incoming and outgoing *messages*, which can be classified into *method calls* and *return messages*.

3.2 Formalisation and Usage of MSM

Let $\mathbb{SM}$ be the set of systems that we are interested in. Let us assume that we have formalised the syntax for the description techniques, resulting in a set of context correct documents $\mathbb{DOC}$. The semantics of one document $d \in \mathbb{DOC}$ is given by a set of systems that obey the restrictions of this document. Formally, we define the semantics function as:

$$[[.]] : \mathbb{DOC} \rightarrow \mathbb{P}(\mathbb{SM})$$

If, for example, d is an object model, each class mentioned in d has to exist in each system $s \in [[d]]$. Classes not mentioned in d may exist, but need not. A canonical minimal system may be implemented containing only mentioned classes, but adding new classes is a perfect refinement. This "loose", set based semantics [BBB+85] for documents allows a very simple and powerful extension of the semantics function to sets of documents $D \subseteq \mathbb{DOC}$:

$$[[D]] \stackrel{def}{=} \bigcap_{d \in D} [[d]]$$

This definition captures the idea that adding documents, and thus refining the existing information about the system in development, rules out more and more systems, until only the system to be implemented remains as semantics.

We now can define the notion of redundancy. A document d is redundant with respect to another document d', if the semantics of the latter is a precision of the former: $[[d']] \subseteq [[d]]$. Any redundant document does not need to be considered in the development any longer, as the semantics of the complete set of documents is the same as of the non redundant subset, here: $[[d, d']] = [[d']]$.

However, a document being redundant in this formal sense can still be important for documentation reasons. For example, the abstract and therefore redundant version of a document may omit details which are irrelevant for human understanding.

We also define the notion of refinement $\models$. Document d' refines d, is defined by:

$$d \models d' \stackrel{def}{=} [[d']] \subseteq [[d]]$$

This definition immediately shows, that the refined document d becomes redundant, and only the refinement d' has to be considered furthermore.

This notion of semantics allows us to classify different kinds of transformations of documents. We can, for example, distinguish between transformations that add information and are therefore true refinements or semantics preserving transformations.

On the one hand, these transformations must grant as much freedom as possible to the developer. On the other hand, a systematic development of correct systems has to be ensured.

4 Conclusion

In this paper, a coherent set of description techniques based on UML and used in the SYSLAB project has been presented. Documents, created using these description techniques specify a set of systems in a loose manner. The development of a system can be understood as the repeated transformation, e.g., refinement, of documents. The introduction of a mathematical system model assigns not only an *integrated* formal semantics to the set of description techniques, but also to the set of transformations.

References

BBB+85. F.L. Bauer, R. Berghammer, M. Broy, W. Dosch, F. Geiselbrechtinger, R. Gnatz, E. Hangel, W. Hesse, B. Krieg-Brückner, A. Laut, T. Matzner, B. Möller, F. Nickl, H. Partsch, P. Pepper, K. Samelson, M. Wirsing, and H. Wössner. *The Munich Project CIP, Vol 1: The Wide Spectrum Language CIP-L*. LNCS 183. Springer-Verlag, 1985.

BFG+93. M. Broy, C. Facchi, R. Grosu, R. Hettler, H. Hußmann, D. Nazareth, F. Regensburger, O. Slotosch, and K. Stølen. The Requirement and Design Specification Language SPECTRUM, An Informal Introduction, Version 1.0, Part 1 and 2. Technical Report TUM-I9312, Technische Universität München, 1993.

BRJ96. G. Booch, J. Rumbaugh, and I. Jacobson. The Unified Modeling Language for Object-Oriented Development, Version 1.0, 1996.

Fla96. David Flanagan. *Java in a Nutshell: A Desktop Quick Reference for Java Programmers*. O'Reilly & Associates, Inc., 1996.

GHJV94. E. Gamma, R. Helm, R. Johnson, and J. Vlissides. *Design Patterns*. Addison-Wesley, 1994.

Jon93. M. P. Jones. *An Introduction to Gofer*, 1993.

KRB96. C. Klein, B. Rumpe, and M. Broy. A stream-based mathematical model for distributed information processing systems - SysLab system model - . In Jean-Bernard Stefani Elie Naijm, editor, *FMOODS'96 Formal Methods for Open Object-based Distributed Systems*, pages 323–338. ENST France Telecom, 1996.

Mor90. C. Morgan. *Programming from Specifications*. Prentice-Hall, 1990.

RBP+91. J. Rumbaugh, M. Blaha, W. Premerlani, F. Eddy, and W. Lorensen. *Object-Oriented Modeling and Design*. Prentice Hall, 1991.

RK96. B. Rumpe and C. Klein. *Automata describing object behavior*, pages 265–287. Kluwer Academic Publishers, Norwell, Massachusetts, 1996.

RKB95. B. Rumpe, C. Klein, and M. Broy. Ein strombasiertes mathematisches Modell verteilter informationsverarbeitender Systeme - Syslab Systemmodell. Technical Report TUM-I9510, Technische Universität München, Institut für Informatik, March 1995. http://www4.informatik.tu-muenchen.de/reports/TUM-I9510.ps.gz.

Rum96. B. Rumpe. *Formale Methodik des Entwurfs verteilter objektorientierter Systeme*. Herbert Utz Verlag Wissenschaft, 1996. PhD thesis, Technische Universität München.

Formal Definition and Refinement of UML's Module/Package Concept

Andy Schürr, Andreas J. Winter
Lehrstuhl für Informatik III, RWTH Aachen, D-52056 Aachen
[andylwinter]@i3.informatik.rwth-aachen.de

Abstract. UML is the first OO modeling language with a useful modularization and information hiding concept which supports nesting, import, and refinement. This paper translates UML's informal package definition into predicate logic formulas and solves some open problems concerning the visibility of exported and imported elements.

1 Introduction

After about 20 years of development, object-oriented (OO) modeling methods and notations are widely accepted for the analysis and design of software systems. Popular OO methods - like Booch [1], OMT [9], or OOSE [4] - are used to develop systems of continuously increasing size and complexity. Keeping analysis and design documents consistent or reusing generic parts is a nightmare without any module concept.

These problems are familiar for software developers of the late 60ies. Well-known software engineering concepts like "abstract data types" and "programming-in-the-large" have been invented to overcome them. They have lead to modular programming languages like Modula-2 or Ada and software design languages like HOOD [8] or EMIL [2]. For a long time these ideas did not have any significant impact onto the development of OOA/OOD notations. Their approaches offered ad hoc solutions for partitioning diagrams into surveyable pieces. OMT [9] offers so-called "modules", which allow to decompose unmanageable diagrams into a number of related diagrams. But there are no means to construct export or import of modules. As a consequence any two elements in different diagrams with the same name have to be identified. Even more elaborate concepts like categories in Booch [1] or collaborating subsystems with contracts inWirfs-Brock [13] do not study interactions between information hiding, module boundary crossing associations, and inheritance.

The *Unified Modeling Language* [7] as a successor of Booch, OMT, and OOSE, is the first OO notation addressing all facets of a state-of-the-art module concept. Its *packages* build shells around arbitrary types of diagrams (static structure diagrams, collaboration diagrams etc.). Their information hiding concept is strongly influenced by C++:

(1) *Explicit import* relationships have to be used to access *public* elements of one package within another package,
(2) *refinement* (generalization) relationships provide access to *protected* elements, and
(3) *friend* relationships reveal even *private* (but not *implementation*) elements of one package to another package.

Furthermore, UML supports nesting of packages with visibility rules derived from nested scope rules of programming languages à la Modula-2 or Ada.

Our main problems with UML's module concept are as follows:

(1) All concepts are defined in natural language only. This makes it difficult to determine the precise semantics of introduced terms.
(2) Import, refines, and friend relationships between packages are indirect subclasses of *Element* and inherit a *Visible* attribute with values from the ordered set {*public* > *protected* > *private* > *implementation*}. But we did not find a single line that ex-

plains the consequences of dependency visibilities for connected packages, although the usage of import and refines relationships with varying visibility values makes sense from the software engineering point of view.

(3) Many strictly necessary constraints like "a client A of another (imported/referenced) package B should not add (own) an import relationship from B to another package C" are not part of the UML semantics definition.

This paper is an attempt to translate the natural language definition of UML's packages into eleven predicate logic formulas that give precise answers to points (1) and (2) above. We will suggest more formulas addressing point (3) above in a forthcoming publication. Within all formulas the following (all-quantified) variables are used:

$P, P', P'' \in$ *Package is_a Element, $E \in$ Element, dep* $\in$ *{exp_imports, refines, friend}*
$\omega, \omega', \omega'' \in$ *{public > protected > private > implementation}*

2 Aggregation of Elements and Packages

Any UML document contains a number of top-level packages which represent the regarded system model. Each package defines a visibility shell around a number of elements, which are either (a) basic constructs of a certain type of diagrams or (b) nested packages or (c) dependencies between nested packages. A package P contains an element E if it owns or references (uses) E, which belongs to another package P'. In the latter case, where P references E, E must be visible inside P. This situation is captured by the following predicate logic formulas. Note that formula (5a) considers only *visibility of nested package elements*. The interactions between visible elements and (explicit) import relationships as well as refinement are subject of sections 3 and 4.

The following formulas cannot be explained in detail. We do hope that almost all of them are self-explanatory as soon as the role of ω variables is clear. Terms like

P *owns* ωE or P *references* ωE or P *contains* ωE or   ...

have to be interpreted as "package P owns/references/contains/... element E with associated visibility $\omega \in$ *{public > protected > private > implementation}*". Please note that the concepts *owns*, *references*, and *sees* (visibility) are defined in UML, whereas *contains* and *offers* are our own inventions in order to keep formulas as simple as possible.

(1) *Owner of element is unique:*
   P *owns* $\omega E \wedge P'$ *owns* $\omega' E \rightarrow P = P' \wedge \omega = \omega'$

(2) *Elements (from other packages) may be referenced if visible:*
   P *references* $\omega E \rightarrow P$ *sees* $\omega' E \wedge \omega \le \omega'$

(3) *Contains relationship is union of owns and reference relationship:*
   P *contains* $\omega E \leftrightarrow P$ *owns* $\omega E \vee P$ *references* ωE

(4) *Offers relationship is transitive closure of contains relationship:*
   P *offers* $\omega E \leftrightarrow P$ *contains* $\omega E \vee \exists P': P$ *contains* $\omega P' \wedge P'$ *offers public E*

(5a) *Visibility of elements (of nested packages) is determined as follows:*
   P *sees* $\omega E \leftrightarrow P$ *offers* $\omega E \vee ...$

The most important consequence of the definitions above is that a package sees all public elements of nested packages (visibility is transitive), where nested packages are either locally defined packages or imported (referenced) packages. A surrounding package has no possibility to hide public elements of nested packages at its own interface, except by owning or referencing nested packages themselves with restricted visibility.

3 Export/Import of Packages

We have seen that nesting of packages gives surrounding packages access to the public elements of enclosed packages. Therefore, UML says that owns and reference relationships establish a kind of *implicit import*. Using implicit imports only, packages would never be able to reference elements of sibling packages. Therefore, UML has introduced the concept of *explicit import* as a dependency relationship between packages that belong to the common surrounding package of the related client (target) and server (source) package. These import dependencies have their own visibility attributes. *Public import* represents, for instance, a kind of interface import, which is visible for all clients of the surrounding package. An *implementation import*, on the other hand, is an always hidden import, which represents local analysis or design decisions.

The following formulas are our attempt to formalize imports and exports of packages. Please note that packages do not have any means to define sets of exported elements explicitly. Their *public/protected/... exports* are always implicitly determined as their sets of public/protected/... visible offered elements. As a consequence, packages do not only export own elements, but also referenced elements from other packages. This takes from client packages the cumbersome burden to import all those elements of other packages which are used in the interfaces of already imported packages.

(6) *Implicit import are all indirectly owned or referenced elements:*
$P \ imp\_imports \ \varpi \ E \leftrightarrow \exists \ P': P \ contains \ \varpi \ P' \wedge P' \ offers \ public \ E$

(7) *Import is the union of explicit and implicit import:*
$P \ imports \ \varpi \ E \leftrightarrow P \ exp\_imports \ \varpi \ E \vee P \ imp\_imports \ \varpi \ E$

(8) *Export is set of all offered nonimplementation elements:*
$P \ exports \ \varpi \ E \leftrightarrow P \ offers \ \varpi \ E \wedge \varpi > implementation$

(5b)*Visibility of elements across packages is extended as follows:*
$P \ sees \ \varpi \ E \leftrightarrow P \ offers \ \varpi \ E \vee (\exists \ P': P \ exp\_imports \ \varpi \ P' \wedge P' \ exports \ \varpi \ E)$

4 Refinement of Packages

The previous two sections introduced the "classical" modularization concepts of programming languages like Modula-2, i.e. the construction of export interfaces for packages (with varying degrees of visibility inherited from C++), nesting of (local) packages, and the establishment of visible or hidden import relationships between packages. These import relationships permit access to public interface elements of server packages, only. The remaining two visibility values (for interface elements) — *protected* and *private* — are only useful in combination with refinement (generalization) and friend relationships between packages. The concept of friends is not discussed in this paper, whereas the concept of refining/generalizing packages will be explained here.

The main motivation for introducing the *refinement (subtype)* relationship between packages is that the important OO concept of *inheritance* should not only be available for defining single classes, the basic elements of static structure diagrams, but also for defining and refining arbitrarily complex subdiagrams.

It is not at all difficult to come up with a precise definition of the consequences of refinement (generaliziation) relationships for the visibility of package elements as well as with a formal definition of the constraint "*generalization relationships do not build cycles*". It is far more difficult to translate the meaning of sentences like "*... an instance* *of the subtype is substitutable for an instance of the supertype"*. The latter constraint cannot be defined for packages in general, but must be studied for each language of UML diagrams, separately. Such a precise definition of the term "substitutability" is not part of UML. Therefore, our formulas will only take the consequences of public refinement relationships for the visibility of (public) interface elements of related packages into account. For further details concerning the formal treatment of subtyping from an algebraic point of view the reader is referred to [3] and from a type-theoretic point of view to [6]. It is an open question whether similiar constraints have to be added for the case of non-public refinement relationships and interface elements.

(9) *SubtypeOf relationship is transitive closure of refines relationship:*
   $P\ subtypeOf\ P' \leftrightarrow \exists\ P", \varpi: P\ refines\ \varpi\ P" \wedge P" = P' \vee P"\ subtypeOf\ P')$

(10) *Refines (generalization) relationship is acyclic:*
   $\neg(P\ subtypeOf\ P)$

(11) *Public export of refining package has refined package's export:*
   $P\ refines\ public\ P' \wedge P'\ exports\ public\ E \rightarrow P\ exports\ public\ E$

(5c) *Visibility across package boundaries is extended as follows:*
   $P\ sees\ \varpi\ E \leftrightarrow ...$ *(* see Def. (5b) *)*
   $\vee \exists\ P', \varpi', \varpi" \geq protected: P\ refines\ \varpi'\ P' \wedge P'\ exports\ \varpi"\ E \wedge \varpi = min(\varpi', \varpi")$

Please note that formula (5c) above is just an extension of formula (5b) of the previous section. It takes refinement relationships with different degrees of visibility into account, ranging from a kind of *public subtype inheritance* to pure *implementation inheritance*. It says that a refining (subtype) package sees all public elements of the refined (supertype) package as public elements (if the refinement relationship is public, too). It states furthermore that a refining package sees all protected elements of the refined package as $\varpi \leq protected$ visible elements (if the refinement relationship is ϖ visible, too). It is an open question, whether it makes sense to have four different visibility cases for refinement relationships, instead of the usual distinction between interface preserving subtype inheritance and the hidden inheritance of implementations.

5 Summary

This paper presented a compact definition of the UML notation's modularization concept. Together with a number of useful extensions we could avoid obvious incompletenesses in its natural language definition or represent additional policies for the definition of import, refinement, and friend relationship between packages. We have omitted the consideration of the friends concept here, the value of which is doubtful for object-oriented analysis and design. The precise definition of a OOA/OOD module concept is not an isolated activity at our department, but an integral part of the following projects:
(1) The module interconnection language EMIL has been developed at our department offering different types of modules, nested (sub-)systems, import/export relationships between modules and (sub-)systems, inheritance for abstract data type modules as well as genericity in the sense of generic Ada packages [5,2].
(2) Our formal background are logic-based graph rewriting systems [10]. They are used—in the form of the visual specification language and environment PROGRES [12]—to define graphical software engineering languages and to prototype tools for them. We are about to specify a significant subset of UML in PROGRES.

(3) Graph rewriting specifications for complex languages like UML tend to be too large to be written down as a single unstructured document. Therefore, we have started to develop a module concept for PROGRES similiar EMIL and UML [11]. To summarize, neither UML's module concept itself nor the considerations presented here concerning its formal definition and necessary modifications are restricted to a single object-oriented analysis and design method. On the contrary, the presented *module concept may be added to other analysis, design, or specification languages* or it may even build the basis for a separate module interconnection language. This is due to the fact that presented formulas make no assumptions about the semantics of basic elements in packages. It is their exclusive purpose to explain the impact of packages and relationships between packages on the visibility of package elements. As a consequence, this paper complements the rapidly growing number of publications which have either the formal definition of module interconnection languages (architecture styles) or certain OO diagram types as their main topic. Both categories of papers assume either very simple visibility rules or neglect this aspect due to the absense of a module concept.

References

[1] Booch G.: *Object-Oriented Analysis and Design*. Series in Object-Oriented Software Engineering. Benjamin Cummings, Redwood City, CA, 1994.

[2] Börstler J.: *Programmieren-im-Großen: Sprachen, Werkzeuge, Wiederverwendung*. Dissertation (RWTH Aachen), TR UMINF 94.10, Department of Computer Science, Umeå University, Sweden, 1994.

[3] Breu R.: *Algebraic Specification Techniques in Object-Oriented Programming Environments*, LNCS 562. Springer-Verlag, 1991.

[4] Jacobson I.: *Object-Oriented Software Engineering: A Use Case Driven Approach*. Addison-Wesley, Reading, MA, fourth edition, 1994.

[5] Nagl M.: *Softwaretechnik: Methodisches Programmieren im Großen*. Springer-Verlag, 1990.

[6] Palsberg J., Schwartzbach M. I.: *Object-Oriented Type Systems*. John Wiley, New York, NY, 1994.

[7] Rational Software Corporation: *UML Semantics, Version 1.0*. http://www.rational.com, 1997.

[8] Robinson P. J.: *Hierarchical Object-Oriented Design*. Prentice Hall, Englewood Cliffs, MA, 1992.

[9] Rumbaugh J., Blaha M., Eddy W. P. F., Lorensen W.: *Object-Oriented Modeling and Design*. Prentice Hall, Englewood Cliffs, NJ, 1991.

[10] Schürr A.: *Logic Based Programmed Structure Rewriting Systems*. Fundamenta Informaticae, XXVI(3/4), 1996.

[11] Schürr A., Winter A. J.: *Modules and Updatable Graph Views for PROgrammed Graph REwriting Systems*. TR AIB 97-3, RWTH Aachen, Germany, 1997.

[12] Schürr A., Winter A. J., Zündorf A.: *Graph Grammar Engineering with PROGRES*. In Schäfer W., Botella P. (eds.): Proc. 5th European Software Engineering Conf. (ESEC'95), LNCS 989, pp. 219–234. Springer Verlag, Berlin, 1995.

[13] Wirfs-Brock R., Wilkerson B., Wiener L.: *Designing Object-Oriented Software*. Prentice Hall, Englewood Cliffs, NJ, 1990.

Experience with Formal Specification of CMM and UML

Jos Warmer, IBM (jwarmer@nl.ibm.com)
John Hogg, ObjecTime Limited (hogg@objectime.com)
Steve Cook, IBM (sj_cook@uk.ibm.com)
Bran Selic, ObjecTime Limited (bran@objectime.com)

Abstract. A simple specification language (OCL) was used to specify and analyze metamodels and metametamodels as part of the OMG OOA&D standardization process. Significant benefits were seen from a small investment in "user-friendly" formality.

1 Introduction

This paper discusses the IBM/ObjecTime Limited experience with using OCL (Object Constraint Language) to specify and verify the CMM (Common Metamodel) and UML (Unified Modelling Language) submissions to the OMG (Object Management Group) for an OOA&D (Object-Oriented Analysis and Design) interchange standard. A key discovery was that a small amount of formality can have a large payback in a practical application.

In 1996 the OMG released a Request for Proposals for a standard for interchange of Object-Oriented Analysis and Design models. Several groups replied. Among the submissions were Rational's UML proposal and the CMM proposal by IBM and ObjecTime Limited.

UML was put forward not only as a unification of the Booch and OMT models, but also as a "universal modelling language": it was intended to be general enough to use for all analysis and design modelling.

The UML 1.0 submission was specified in a mixture of the UML notation itself and "precise English". The authors wanted the document to be accessible to a large audience and were concerned that a more formal treatment would be hard to read.

IBM and ObjecTime Limited saw a need for more flexibility: the CMM proposal was intended as a framework within which metamodels could be built. UML, ROOM, OORam, Catalysis and any other modelling languages could be built on the CMM base. An immediate result of this paramount requirement for extensibility was a way of unambiguously defining extensions, and English (precise or otherwise) was not considered sufficient. IBM therefore provided their Object Constraint Language technology as a way of specifying semantics of both extensions to CMM and the CMM core itself.

Both parties recognized value in the other's contributions and in March the CMM and UML proposals were merged. The joint proposal uses the notation of UML and the formality and extensibility of CMM. It is anticipated that it will be approved by the OMG in September.

2 OCL Overview

OCL (Object Constraint Language) is a simple language for specifying properties of elements and models. It has been used on CMM and UML and can be applied to any metametamodel having appropriate element and association properties.

The definition of OCL semantics is informal, using no mathematical notation. This has been adequate in practice for two reasons. First, the language itself is small; there is not much to define and therefore there are fewer possibilities for obscure interactions and contradictions. Secondly, it has not been used for any formal proofs of system correctness. There is nothing in OCL that makes a formal semantics difficult. Such a definition may be written in the future.

The OCL syntax is well defined and has been implemented as a parser for syntax checking.

OCL constraints are boolean expressions on model elements and their relationships. OCL has a set of basic valuetypes (Boolean, Integer, etc.) and the usual set of basic operations on these valuetypes. An OCL constraint typically applies to a collection of elements and the Collections Set, Bag and Sequence are a part of the core language. Operations such as forall(expr), exists(expr) and union(set) allow common idioms to be expressed easily. Queries that are not boolean-valued frequently return collections for use in further expressions.

To permit recursive constraints (and also to make constraints more readable) parameterized operations can be specified and used in later constraints.

The CMM used OCL as part of the metamodel definition mechanism. A new metamodel is defined as a scheme. A scheme creates new model elements by adding properties to existing model elements and defining new stereotypes on them. A stereotype is a model element whose behaviour is constrained by OCL expressions.

An example may be useful. The following is a fragment of a scheme for the ROOM (Real-Time Object-Oriented Modelling) language.

```
Scheme ROOM_design_models
...

Stereotypes      ROOMSignalRefSet
      applies to Specification
      invariant
            -- [1] only in ROOMProtocolClasses...
            self.container.stereotypes.includes(ROOMProtocolClass);
            -- [2] ... and contains only ROOMSignalRefs
            self.topElements.forAll( elem |
                  elem.stereotypes.includes(ROOMSignalRef))
      end
...
end scheme
```

A core model element Specification has been stereotyped to give a new model element, ROOMSignalRefSet. This new element can only be contained in another new element, ROOMProtocolClass, and can only contain elements of another new stereotype, ROOMSignalRef. (Container is a navigable role from the metametamodel element ModelElement to Composite in CMM.)

This small fragment of the overall scheme is fairly typical of OCL use. Each model element has a property stereotypes which is typically heavily used in constraint definition. The properties container and topElements from the CMM are set-valued representations of containment relationships. Most constraint expressions assert that some property holds over a collection of elements.

3 Results

OCL has been used in two different applications in the OOA&D process: as an essential component of the CMM submission, and as a tool for reviewing UML 1.0. It is now being used again in the merged submission.

Within the CMM submission, OCL had two uses. The first was as a mechanism by which CMM users could create metamodels. The second was in the specification of CMM itself (i.e., the metametamodel).

In this second application, OCL played a crucial role. Due to the language's simplicity and familiar notation, writing constraints was easy, as was reading them (with judicious use of textual explanations). The hard part was designing the metametamodel itself. OCL made this harder in the sense that it brought ambiguities and contradictions to the surface much more quickly; they wouldn't go away with handwaving. The result was a much faster convergence on an unambiguous and consistent design. Other authors in similar circumstances have reported this experience.

The use of OCL did *not* result in a flawless design; the authors are keenly aware of various shortcomings in the CMM submission. OCL in no way provides a "proof of correctness". Its value comes from the improvement gained compared to the amount of effort needed to use it.

OCL was next used to understand UML 1.0. After the proposals had been submitted, they were circulated for review. The CMM team had some trouble understanding the "precise English" of the UML 1.0 document, and how UML 1.0 and elements were related to one another. The lead author clarified a number of questions by representing about half of the UML 1.0 Semantics document in OCL.

In rough numbers, about 60 out of 100 pages of UML 1.0 English text and diagrams were represented as about 20 pages of OCL. A total of 23 assumptions had to be made, 13 points were otherwise unclear and there were 7 contradictions between different parts of the English text which became obvious when they were captured more formally.

Again, an OCL representation did not catch all potential problems in the UML 1.0 design. However, it provided a very clear and effective way to identify a large number of issues.

In summary, OCL was found to be effective in catching a large number of errors at source in CMM, and in identifying problems in UML 1.0. It is now being used to specify the revised UML, which will be submitted to the OMG for a final adoption vote.

4 Tools

IBM has implemented a parser for OCL that does syntax checking. This was found to be useful during CMM design. All OCL was mechanically checked, and a number of "finger trouble" problems were found. It was particularly valuable because the language evolved slightly while the CMM submission was written. The document was manually changed, but the parser picked up a few anachronisms that were missed.

OCL did not have and does not have any tools for consistency checking or any analysis at a deeper level than syntax. Such tools would certainly be useful, but they are far from essential. OCL is a means of communication between humans, and if the reader and the writer can both interpret a piece of specification unambiguously, it has succeeded in its purpose. The first benefit comes when writers are forced to clearly state something that they may think they understand, but don't. The second benefit comes when another human can read a fragment of OCL and understand what the writer meant. Any gains from automated verification would be minor in comparison.

5 Problems

The main open question we found when using OCL was, "How much is enough?" Any model element could always be described more precisely by the addition of more constraints. There was no clear notion of "doneness", in part because there were no stopping criteria in the form of properties to be proved. This highlights the difference between a communication mechanism and a proof mechanism. The general answer was, "Enough to satisfy the reader." When a design stood up to a sufficient level of review, it was declared done.

A second issue is more of an observation than a problem: neither OCL nor any other conceivable magic bullet can create good designs. Tools like OCL can highlight bad design, but they can't tell a human how to do things right in novel situations. (Cookie-cutter variants on a theme are outside the domain of this discussion.) This is just another recurrence of a universal truth in software.

A minor problem with OCL has been its dependence on the system being modelled. OCL is in part defined by the metamodel it represents in the areas of entities and the relationships between them. Therefore, changing the metametamodel can require redefinition of OCL.

A *non*-problem was the lack of a formal, mathematical base for OCL. There is no reason why one could not be created, but there is little reason to do so. OCL is simple and it has not been used for formal proof construction. Therefore, there are few deep issues and they have not come to the surface.

6 Conclusions

OCL is formalism at a simple level. It is a classic example of getting 90% of the benefits for the first 10% of the work. In practice, the additional effort required to specify constraints using OCL was minimal compared to the effort required to create an English specification, and the payback was obvious and early.

Our key lessons are:

- simple formality comes almost "for free"
- mathematical elegance is not necessary
- extensive tool support is not necessary
- human readability is vital

A parting thought: the Canadian Department of Transport has just changed regulations regarding lifejackets. Previously, an approved lifejacket had to be red, orange or yellow, so that it would be visible in the water. Unfortunately, 85% of drowning victims were not wearing lifejackets. The DOT wisely decided that if more stylish (but still highly visible) colours encouraged greater use, this would outweigh the theoretically superior performance mandated by the old regulations.

Formal techniques are like lifejackets. Let's focus on usability, not ultimate power. Think "Formality for the masses."

References

Steve Cook, Bran Selic et al., *OMG OOA&D RFP Response* Version 1.0, 10 January 1997.

S. J. Cook & J. Daniels, *Designing Object Systems: Object-oriented modelling with Syntropy*, Prentice-Hall 1994.

Bran Selic, Garth Gullekson and Paul T. Ward, *Real-Time Object-Oriented Modelling*, Wiley 1994.

UML Semantics Version 1.0, Rational Software Corporation, 13 January 1997.

Jos Warmer, *UML 1.0 Semantics Scheme*, Version 0.1, 1997.

Models, Formalisms and Methods for Object-Oriented Distributed Computing

Rémi Bastide[1] and Didier Buchs[2] (Organizers)

[1] LIS, Université de Toulouse I, Place Anatole France, 31042 Toulouse, France
Remi.Bastide@cict.fr
[2] LGL-DI, Swiss Federal Institute of Technology, CH-1015 Lausanne, Switzerland
Didier.Buchs@di.epfl.ch

1 Introduction

This report is a presentation of the contributions to the workshop on Models, Formalisms and Methods for Object-Oriented Distributed Computing. The goal of the workshop was to bring together researchers interested in the the foundations and in the practice of concurrent and distributed object-oriented computing. Two main directions of concurrent system description have been studied during the workshop: the methodological and implementation oriented models and the formal modeling techniques. In order to compare the various approaches the organizers have proposed to share a common case study: A Distributed Diary which was presented by the contributors as an illustration of their respective approaches. The workshop was divided into three part, first a summary of all approaches was given, then according to the kind of approaches two sessions were simultaneously organized for presenting the respective contributions, finally summaries of the discussions were given at the end of the workshop.

1.1 Topics

The emergence of enabling technologies such as CORBA or Java RMI makes it possible to develop industrial scale object-based distributed systems at a fraction of the cost that they would require using more conventional techniques.

However, it seems that these technologies still lack a firm ground to develop on : no model of distributed object-oriented computation is widely agreed upon. It is not quite clear how existing formal notations for distributed and concurrent systems (such as Petri Nets, Estelle, LOTOS, ...) can support the object paradigm, and methodological practice for this kind of systems is still at its early stages. Furthermore considering the growing interest in distributed embedded critical systems, the extent to which object-orientation can be used to develop reliable systems remains to be asserted.

The purpose of this workshop was to bring together researchers interested in the foundations and in the practice of concurrent and distributed object-oriented computing. Specific areas of interest included, but were not limited to :

- Fundamental models of concurrent and distributed object systems

- Formal notations for the analysis, design, validation and verification of concurrent and distributed Object-Oriented systems.
- Methodological issues, notably the inclusion of formal approaches within semi-formal methods such as OMT, Fusion, UML, ...

1.2 Plan of the report

The plan of this report is as follows : a reminder of the objectives of the workshop is given, the case study is presented, the various approaches are presented according to a predefined presentation skeleton, and finally we conclude.

2 Case Study: A Distributed Diary

2.1 Introduction

The aim of this case study was to serve as a reference example for the working sessions of the ECOOP'97 workshop on Models, Formalisms and Methods for Object-Oriented Distributed. Contributors were expected to exercise their formalism, modeling approach or tool on this problem, in order to demonstrate how it may deal with the specification of a software of reasonable size.

The use of a common example can make it easier to compare the various proposals presented at the workshop. The working group's discussions focused on this case study, and one of the expected outcomes of the workshop was to produce this report on the discussions.

2.2 Statement of the problem

The system to model is a simple collaborative diary, for members of a 'software engineering laboratory'. This diary assists in the management of meetings in the laboratory conference room by letting several users view and modify its contents simultaneously from their individual workstations, while preventing conflicts, i.e. planning of overlapping events. The diary allows the following services: Consultation, addition, cancelation and replacement of events. An event structure is simply composed of a day, a beginning and ending time and a comment line.

The system should allow for a "real-time", simultaneous edition of the diary, where a group of users can actively contribute to the construction of a consistent meeting schedule, and where each user is constantly informed of the current state of the diary and of the activity of the other users.

To ensure a maximum reliability, the system should present a distributed, peer-to-peer architecture, and should be built in such a way that the failure of any single workstation does not hamper its global functioning.

There is a need to guarantee consistency between the replicas of the diary. To this end, we propose a very simple mechanism: When a user modifies its copy of the diary, the corresponding event modification must be accepted by the other participants. If by misfortune another user wants to validate at the same moment a conflicting event, then the problem should be detected, and both updates should be rejected. We will not bother specifying here how the conflict is actually solved: Let us just imagine that the interface signals the error, and that the humans are able to communicate by other means to arrive at an agreement.

From an algorithmic point of view, the validation of an event is implemented by an atomic three step operation: First broadcast the wish to validate an event, and then wait for all participants to acknowledge by a vote. If a single answer is negative then broadcast an abort, otherwise a commit order. This algorithm is called the two-phase commit protocol (2PC) [29]: The first phase consists of the two first steps above, and the second phase is the communication of the final decision.

2.3 Treatment of the case study

The idea was to come to the workshop prepared to explain in which ways each approach can contribute to the modeling, design, formal verification or implementation of such a system, and to give a short presentation explaining each view of this problem.

One of the purposes of the case study is to explore the extent to which a formal specification may further the completeness of these requirements. It was possible to deviate from those requirements if necessary, to highlight some feature of the approach proposed, but in this case you it was expected to state precisely the reason for this deviation.

It was free to undertake this case study at whichever level it was appropriate for the approach (e.g. to deal only with requirements engineering, or with the software architecture), or to focus only on one precise aspect of the problem that is most relevant. However, it was important to make precise the scope of each treatment of the case study.

3 Workshop contributions

Contributions may be divided into two distinct groups: the contributions focusing on the methodological and model aspects of the software development and the contributions focusing on the formal model aspects.

The first group gathers the contributions of Berger, Diagne, Demartini, Restrepo, Sadou, while the second group is composed of the contributions of Robben, Smith, Vachon and Peter. The original texts of the contributions to the workshop are available on-line at 'http://lis.univ-tlse1.fr/ecoop-ws'.

Contribution 1 : Interaction and Communication Models

Laurent Berger, Anne-Marie Dery, Mireille Fornarino, Olivier Jautzy
ESSI - Université de Nice Sophia-Antipolis - 650 route de colles 06903 Sophia-Antipolis

Introduction to Interaction and Communication Models Few works deal with the way to express and to manage interactions between remote objects independently of their intrinsic behavior [32,56,26,52,34,66] . However in these approaches the programmer may implement the interactions in the method code, link the objects at the class level, mixing intrinsic and communication knowledge. Then, the problem we address is : can we define a model outside the objects to express and manage interaction between remote objects? This model should be appropriated to specify Interaction and Communication Managers (ICM). Their role is to allow, by specifying interaction properties and network communication properties to keep inside the interacting objects only their intrinsic functionalities.

Interaction properties : In this section, we resume the essential properties expected from an interaction manager. The *reactivity* seems to be a fundamental paradigm required for such a manager. For example, a client software component that displays real-time data usually needs to be updated as soon as the information changes on the source side. Reactivity consists in sending messages before or after the asked message. That is, an ICM prescribes what should be done in response to some message requests, but it also has to initiate actions on the interacting objects. *Own properties and behavior* are then needed by the interaction model. In particular, automata are often used to design the internal states of communications. The introduction of a *condition* such as an *if-then-else* instruction is also necessary for expliciting contextual reactions. The reactions can indeed depend on the state of the communication and a condition has to be checked on the state of the interaction to determine how to react.

Network communication properties : The main goal of platforms such as Corba or Java RMI is to achieve object distribution transparency, which means that the interaction between a client component and a server component through the server interface is independent of their physical location, access path[56]. Our aim is to give to our model this level of transparency of the communication constraints. We also have to consider *failure* cases : what happens if an object cannot answer because the machine where it is localized is down ? What happens if the network communication loses messages ? The manager must be able to detect failures and to signal or correct them. The integration of *transaction* in our model has also to be studied [49,30,13]. At present, we are not able to statuate if the notion of transaction has to be explicitly managed by the ICM or if the proposed meta-protocol is sufficient to implement transactions. Morover, object distribution implies to design *synchronous* or *asynchronous* reactivity. That is, if a message m is received by an interacting object, according to the interaction model we will react before or after the execution of the corresponding method (synchronous) or in parallel (asynchronous). The main difficulty of the ICM specification is to decide which minimal set of properties has to be included in the model in order, for example, to detect and manage deadlocks.

Presentation of the case study First let start with the distributed architecture proposed for the case study: each user is supposed on a separate workstation but an user and its local diary are on the same wokstation. A diary is an entity able to respond to messages like *add, delete,replace* and *consult*. As it becomes a local copy of a shared diary, the accesses to this object have to be controlled in order to maintain the global consistency of the system. In particular it has to be notified about "changes" and to accept or reject them.

An Explicit Atomicity Modelling : We specify an interface object, inherited from the *diary* class, which is viewed by the user as his local diary but contains additionals and overloaded behaviors for the management of network transfers.

```
IObject inherit from Diary(D)
    Consult(...)      = D::Consult(...).
    Add(Event)        = D::Add(Event).
    Delete(Event)     = D::Delete(Event).
    Replace(E,E')     = D:: Replace(E,E').

    Notify(Event,Action,Sender)   = if (...)
                                    Sender::NotifyOK(self,Event,Action)
                                    // if (Action == 'add') D::Add(Event).....
                                    else Sender::NotifyKO(self,Event,Action).
    Abort(Event,Action)           = if (Action == 'add') D::Delete(Event) ...
    Commit(Event,Action)          = .
```

The ICM is used to react when a modification is made in one of the local diary for validation through the interface object. The following ICM implements the two-phase-commit for the atomicity of an event validation by asynchronous message sending. This ICM is able to catch the messages received by an interface object to associate automatically a reaction (->), essentially to broadcast to the others interface objects that a modification as occured and has to be validated. The interface objects will answer by sending *NotifyOK* or *NotifyKO*. When all the notifications are received (see the use of the ObjList variable), the ICM broadcasts a *Commit* or an *Abort* message to the interface objects. The global functionning is hampered if a workstation is in failure case due to the promise of an answer (see the *FuturMessage* operator). We must assure that the ICM receives a notification, if no answer is received before a time-out the deduced answer is *NotifyOK*.

```
ICM(DiaryList)
    var ObjList, IsCommit
    FuturMessage(Notify,[NotifyOK,NotifyKO],NotifyOK).
```

```
Forall InterfaceDiary of DiaryList
Add(E) -> WaitUntil(self::Release());
           InterfaceDiary::Add(E);ObjList:=(InterfaceDiary);IsCommit:=true;
           Forall IDj of DiaryList - InterfaceDiary
           IDj::Notify(E,'add',ICM).
...
NotifyOK(U,E,A) = ObjList := ObjList + U ; Ack(E,A).
NotifyKO(U,E,A) = ObjList := ObjList + U ; IsCommit:=false;Ack(E,A).
Ack(E,A)        = if ObjList == DiaryList
                     if IsCommit Forall InterfaceDiary of DiaryList
                                    InterfaceDiary::Commit(E,A)
                     else Forall InterfaceDiary of DiaryList
                                    InterfaceDiary::Abort(E,A)
                     Release().
```

Others modelling : The model is open to allow the definition of the semantics of new operators such as *atomic* for example. The semantics of *atomic* is to assure the atomicity of a group of messages and to execute a correction given by the user if this operation fails. We can also add an operator to simulate the notion of concurrent reception : which time is associated to the same time. This model is evoluting but we want a minimal model to be able to make proof and we have difficulties to statuate about the add of operators in the model such as *time-out* and *atomic* for example...

Particularities of the approach In our modelling, each object keeps its own semantics (behavior, properties and internal automaton) and an ICM describes more precisely the inter-automata and communication. We think that we will be able to exploit the set of intra and inter automata to verify the correctness of the written code and also to determine failure or deadlock cases. Several experimentations have already be done to validate our ideas. At the origin of this study is the FLO model. With FLO, objects can be linked in a synchronous way, in a monolithic platform[22]. The implementation of synchronous ICM in Open C++ [31,14] offers a test platform for the communication aspects. This implementation is based on Open C++ meta classes allowing Remote Procedure Call communication. Actually this experimentation is limited to a bidirectional implementation of managers allowing only Client Server communication via RPC. This is not sufficient and we are developping Corba metaclasses and extended models.

Contribution 2 : Integration of Semi-Formal and Formal Approaches

Alioune Diagne [†], *Jean-Michel Ilié*[†] *& Daniel Moldt*[††]
[†] *Université Pierre & Marie Curie, 4 Place Jussieu, 75005 Paris, France.*
[††] *Universität Hamburg, Vogt-Kölln-Str. 30, 22527 Hamburg, Germany.*

Introduction to OO Approaches and Petri nets The development of traditional methodologies like OMT [61], Booch [9], and Jacobson [38] towards UML [10] shows that object oriented approaches still have not reached a stable state like e.g. Structured Analysis. The main reason is that the approaches still do not provide the desired models. The techniques lack certain concepts like concurrency, distribution or co-ordination mechanisms.

The formal foundation of the techniques and the already present features and concepts are not sufficient. Furthermore, due to missing concepts of the techniques, some methods like prototyping are not offered. Overall, it can be noted that validation and verification are not supported in an appropriate way. All of these problems can be tackled by nets. However, to improve the quality of the models, more sophisticated development environments are required. Also the widely distributed knowledge in the area of nets about validation and verification has to be carefully adopted to improve the object oriented approaches. There are many different attempts to combine object orientation and Petri nets (see [3] or [4]. Here three different approaches, which cover different areas, are integrated. Each of them has different advantages and constraints. The main difference lies in the chosen grads of support of formality and level of preciseness toward the previously raised topics. All the three approaches are combined to form an overall one.

The approaches are briefly presented and their integration to an overall approach will be sketched. A short discussion shows the advantages and further requirements on approaches.

Available Support for OO Approaches Each of the following paragraphs emphasizes special parts of the development process covered by one of the approaches. In this section three different levels of formal support are presented. The notions of validation and verification are used to refer to the matching of the intention of the customer by the system and to the formal and complete confirmation that a model meets its requirements respectively (see [8]).

Prototyping and Validation of OO Models. The first part is directed to the more informal aspects of a specification (see also [48]). For this the usual semi-formal techniques of object oriented approaches like object/class diagram, statecharts or data flow diagrams are replaced by Colored Petri Nets ([39]). This replacement is done on a formal basis to provide a consistent and correct operational semantics. This allows us to totally replace the former techniques or to use them as some kind of interface (with a precise meaning). The operational semantics not only improves the quality of the specifications and reduces the number of misunderstandings, it also allows to execute the models. Therefore simulation, animation, and code generation (and execution) become possible. This again provides the means for prototyping. Prototyping can be seen as the overall approach as well as only one kind of method used during system specification. Overall this allows a very good integration with usual object oriented approaches like UML.

Formal Verification of Control Models of OO-Specifications. Control aspects of object-oriented specifications are split among many representations. Individual objects have methods and operations which model their internal control. This intra-object control can exhibit concurrency e.g. in presence of aggregation. State diagrams show the allowed intra-object control flow. The interactions between objects are represented by the control flow diagrams. They model the inter-objects control. The inter-objects control represents many aspects like coordination, communication and synchronization. Scenarios or event traces can be given to characterize some operating cycles of a system or their traces on some objects. All these aspects are given in different models but they are strongly related. For instance a scenario must be verified against the control flow models. On another hand, intra and inter-object controls must be consistent versus each other. Basic questions which can be answered using nets are liveness, deadlock-freeness and conservation of values borne by attributes. These questions can be answered by classical techniques in nets, like invariants computation (places and transitions) or model checking based on reachability graph construction. These properties can be considered as implicit expectations that are always worth to be verified on a specification because they constraint its correctness. Scenarios and event traces can be verified with more elaborated techniques. These can be considered as explicit expectations the modeler has to ensure on a specification. The construction of the reachability graph is achieved using modular techniques in order to hide non-relevant details, like the firing of autonomous actions in an object (see [67,50,16]). These techniques allow to stress on the most important aspects or parts of a model and by the way allow to avoid the state explosion inherent to net analysis.

Formal Verification for Design and Architectural Models. Standard approaches to formal verification techniques are mainly based on the analysis of the reachability graph in which the system states and their changes are represented. Because of the state explosion problem for a system, it is a challenge to reduce the representation of reachability graph while improving span algorithms used in verification processes. Earlier research showed the value of exploiting the intrinsic symmetries that exist between some objects within the system [39]. The existence of such symmetries causes redundancies of information in the reachability graph, that is sub-graphs having the same structure and expressing similar behaviors. Thus, the verification process can be restricted to only analyzing non-redundant structures in the graph. Currently, the building of reduced graphs based on symmetry concepts is performed automatically from the system specification using a colored Petri net formalism called Well-formed Nets [15]. Moreover, general properties can be checked automatically on such graphs with respect to a convenient (but static) analysis of the specified property [37]. In contrast to standard approaches of verification, questions can be asked symbolically in order to test the behavior of any element of a group of symmetrical objects.

Integration and Discussion In this section, the integration of the former approaches within one overall approach is shown. This is done by sketching the way a modeler has to proceed when building a system. It is important to notice that there is not only one optimal approach. Depending on many different aspects each project has to use a special (set of) approach(es).

The assumptions for the overall approach are minimal. However, the main advantages of the approach lie within the area of distributed and concurrent systems with the demand on high quality. Concerning the life cycle models are no limitations, even when prototyping and iterative proceedings are recommended. Verification activities assume that the input model is correct and do not consider any eventual misconception. They should be accompanied by a validation procedure to ensure that the proved model can be traced back to users expectations on the target system.

The first step of the proceeding is to start with parts which are small enough to be handled in a first attempt. Fast presentation of an executable model is a central goal for the modelers. The execution can be realized by simulation, animation and/or code generation. At each stage, the modeler is provided with net-based verification and validation means which allow him/her to tune and refine the models. Once again, verification and validation should be mixed as to prove the correctness of models and their conformance to users expectations.

The advantages of the overall approach presented here is that for different levels of abstraction and preciseness along a system life cycle, nets are used for verification and validation. While the validation purpose is quite general, the verification is concentrating on the control view of the system. Behavior represents a central problem when specifying systems. Nets provide a good means to support both processes. It is important to notice that there is a concentration on the control aspects of systems, the further the process within a life cycle is evolving. Especially for complex systems, the behavior is the most difficult aspect to be predicted early. Therefore, the emphasis is laid on the control issues. This fact is taken into account by restricting the investigated and covered models. Especially co-ordination, communication and synchronization raise important questions for control systems.

A highly iterative approach is followed. Modeling, validation, verification are tasks to be performed. Depending on the progress of the modeler, the model reaches a level, where the cycles get more restricted to each approach. The larger a model becomes, the more time goes into the related activity of validation or verification. Modeling usually becomes a less time demanding task. This is due to the increase in testing and debugging of the model.

Presentation of the case study For sake of place we can not present the case study into details. We proceed using an object-oriented approach like OMT or UML but we enhance it by verification and validation means for its different models. The static object is mad executable by the first approach and stands as a prototype. The dynamic and functional models implementing the $2PC$ are verified by the second approach. Specific scenarios can also be simulated and checked. With the third approach presented above, we manage a notion of *teams of diary owners*. Such groups of objects can be accessed as a whole through a dispatcher. The requests are sent to the dispatcher and thus to the teams. Each dispatcher offers the coordination means necessary to handle it. Many coordination policies have been tried for the coordination (at least one positive answer from a team member, a given quorum of positive answers, etc.). This allows us to apply the notion of symmetries to reduce the reachability graph which supports the verification activities.

Contribution 3 : Supporting the Development of Multithreaded and Distributed Applications in Java

Claudio Demartini, Riccardo Sisto
Dipartimento di Automatica e Informatica, Politecnico di Torino, corso Duca degli Abruzzi n. 24, 10129, Torino, Italy

Introduction to The Automaton Object The Automaton Object model is a simple extension of the traditional object model [18] [62], with an architecture based on a couple of hierarchical layers. The lower layer represents the Base Automation Object, involved in the description of real entities, while the upper one provides those objects necessary to support the control of base object interactions. In order to support object interaction, which takes place according to events management, the message passing mechanism is used in the model, and the client server approach is taken to implement the interactions. The interaction model that is used is an extension of the java RMI model [28], supporting both synchronous and asynchronous interaction. When a Automation object, working as a client, requires interaction with another Automation Object, a message is sent to it, and the latter will act as a server object. The execution on the client side can be halted until a reply message is received from the server object, which is responsible for the execution of a specific method related to that message or for rejection of the request. The client is halted only when a synchronous mechanism has to be implemented, otherwise it can resume its operations and examine the reply at a later time. To the outer layer in the Automation Object is left the role of processing incoming requests, and of converting each of them into the execution of a specific method made available by the base object. Sending a message required by an operation carried out by the base object is also handled by appropriate meta objects placed in the outer layer of the Automation Object. These basic communication mechanisms can be implemented in java either relying on the RMI facility (in fact, they are an extension of the RMI model), or directly by means of the java socket interface. A class library is proposed in order to provide the user with the structural and essential mechanisms the Automation Object should make available for the specification and development of real system software elements on behalf of the user.

Presentation of the case study The case study is implemented using an AO called "Diary" having seven public methods that can be remotely accessed. Each Diary can handle a vector of events and each event is also a remote class. A copy of the Diary is available on each station. One of the workstation plays the role of the primary copy provider, so that all requests from clients are addressed to a unique destination which has the responsibility to forward those requests to all other sites. When a new workstation wants to join the group it creates its own diary and invokes the Consultation method made available by the server and populates its own copy with up to date information. To find out on which workstation the server is running, the client examines an ordered list with all possible workstations that are or can be connected in the network. The list is replicated on each node. The station which is on top of the list and that is still working plays the server role. If no reply for the client request is received from that server, then the first node in the list is unavailable. In this case it will be removed from the top of the lists in all the stations. The client will apply the same procedure with the second station in the list and so on until the server is identified.

Static analysis of concurrent software generally follows the paradigm of deriving a simplified abstract formal model of the application to be analyzed [71], in which the details not relevant to concurrency are removed, and then using some tool to perform the analysis. We selected for the case study the on-the-fly verifier SPIN [35], designed at AT&T Bell Labs, because it is considered to be one of the fastest tools available to date for analyzing concurrent systems [19] SPIN accepts input descriptions expressed in a guarded command language called Promela, which features a C-like syntax, dynamic creation of processes, and various inter-process communication models (shared memory, message-based, synchronous, and asynchronous). The analysis engine of SPIN implements the technique known as reachability analysis, powered with a partial-order reduction aimed at mitigating the state-explosion phenomenon. The first stage in the analysis process is the derivation of a simplified abstract model of the given application. A common approach consists in abstracting away from the actual contents of variables, and considering only a reduced control flow graph in which nodes represent sequences of statements not relevant to inter-process communication, and arcs represent the meaningful statements. This kind of reduction features the interesting property of preserving concurrency errors like deadlocks, in the sense that the reduced model contains any errors that were present in the original application. A reduction of this kind, applied to the java language, leads to the formulation of reduction rules like the following: * Within each method, only concurrency-related statements such as calls to the wait(), join(), notify(), and notifyall() thread methods are kept; * Methods not containing synchronized blocks, nor concurrency-related statements, that call only other methods with the same features, are not relevant and are removed. The same applies to objects containing only non-relevant methods. The next stage consists in mapping the reduced application into a Promela model, that is then fed to the analyzer. The mapping principles can be summarized as follows: * Threads are modeled in Promela by means of processes; * The behavior of a Promela process is the translation of the run() method of the corresponding thread into Promela code, where method invocations are replaced by their in-line expansions; * Synchronized methods and blocks are modeled by representing explicitly the correspond-ing object lock and wait-set mechanisms, by means of global variables.

As an example, here is how an object lock and some of the related operations can be described in Promela:

```
byte nwait=0;
chan lock = [1] of {bit};
chan notify = [0] of {bit};          if \
#define lock(lock) lock?0            :: (nwait>0)-> atomic{notify!0; nwait-- }\
                                     :: (nwait==0)-> skip \
#define unlock(lock) lock!0          fi
                                     #define notifyAll(notify, nwait) \
#define wait(lock, notify, nwait) \  do \
nwait++; lock!0; notify?0; lock?0    :: (nwait>0)-> atomic{notify!0; nwait--} \
                                     :: (nwait==0)-> break
#define notify(notify, nwait) \      od
```

Validation Results In this section we show some results regarding deadlock analysis of the case study with varying number of nodes. For the validation a simplified model has been generated from the java source code. Computations have been performed for 2, three and four nodes. In the first case, SPIN evaluated 1582 states with 4056 transactions in 0.1 sec, while in the second case the states number increased to 170228 involving 572315 transactions which required 20 seconds. In both cases, SPIN declared a full search. The third evaluation has been processed for four nodes featuring 2.9E+06 states and 1.3E+07 transactions in 268 sec. In this case SPIN did not perform a full search.

Contribution 4 : Combining OOP and Behavior Modeling: Case Study Using sC++ and CORBA

Antonio José Restrepo-Zea, Claude Petitpierre
Laboratoire de Téléinformatique, EPFL,1015 Lausanne, Switzerland

Introduction to Modeling with sC++ and CORBA Our approach to resolve the Distributed Diary Case Study is based on a concept of active object that allows us to merge OOP and concurrency. The relationships between con-currency and OOP can be highlighted by taking a look at the object-oriented development method OMT/ Rumbaugh (Object Modeling Technique) from a particular angle. According to this method, the creation of application software should proceed along three phases: analysis, design and implementation. The analysis phase produces three models, namely the object model, the dynamic model and the functional model; while the design phase builds on these mod-els to prepare the implementation phase. The object model specifies the data components pertinent to the application, their attributes, relationships and the operations that characterize them. The dynamic model specifies the sequences of the operations, which are often triggered by events. Thus this model describes the behavior of the objects and uses state diagrams. The third model uses data flow diagrams to specify the inputs and outputs of data, their sources and sinks, and from where to where the data must be transmitted. These aspects are closely related to message passing and parallelism. Thus, the first model describes the data, while the two last ones describe aspects that are usually related to concurrency.

Object-oriented languages such as C++ provide good support to implement the object model, but the implementation of the aspects described by the dynamic and functional models requires much involvement from the programmer. We have defined an extended version of C++, named sC++, that introduces the concept of active object and makes the implementation of the two latter models a straight forward task. The syntax of the definition, instantiation, reference, call, inheritance and deletion of an active object is identical to the syntax of the same operations on a standard object (called henceforth passive). An active object contains an internal activity, named body, that runs in parallel with the activities of the other active objects. It can delay the executions of its methods, when they are called from outside, until it is ready to accept them. The latter aspect is derived from the Hoare monitor. The execution of the method of an active object is thus atomic. It is not interleaved with other executions of the same method, nor with executions of other methods in the same object.

The usefulness of the active objects is not limited to applications that share a common memory space. It can be extended both to implement an underlying middleware as CORBA and to structure and implement distributed applications using this last. We have implemented our own ORB using active TCP objects and obtained, without any additional work, a multithreaded environment with the possibility of having several clients and servers in the same UNIX process. We also have access to Motif graphical interface, the possibility to add easily other protocols, e.g., SNMP, TCP channels, and a good support for modeling, etc. The adaptation of an IDL (Interface Definition Language) compiler to generate the stubs and the skeletons was easy. Finally, it has been verified that this environment can communicate with different commercial ORBs.

Presentation of the case study Functional and Dynamic Models Figure 1 defines the Functional Model of the Distributed Diary showing the local and distributed data flow between the DiaryControl and the PropositionSender entities. Figure 2 specifies the protocol that guarantees the consistency between the replicas of the diary in the Dynamic Model. This protocol has been defined according to the problem definition. The behavior of each entity is represented by a Finite State Machine (FSM), which can be analyzed by the Calculus of Communications Systems (CCS), a well known theory about concurrent systems. Each transition arrow is labeled with a word that represents a method acceptance or with an overlined word that represents a method call. To indicate that some action must be executed after a method acceptance, the name of the action is written under a line attached to the corresponding transition.

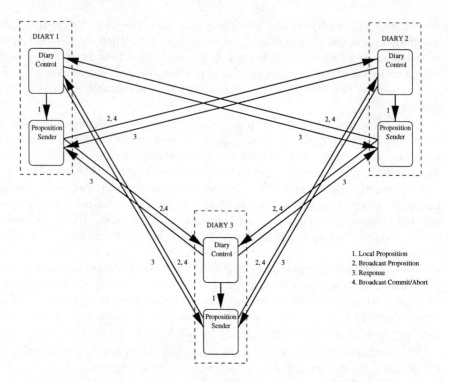

Fig. 1. Functional Model

1. Local Proposition
2. Broadcast Proposition
3. Response
4. Broadcast Commit/Abort

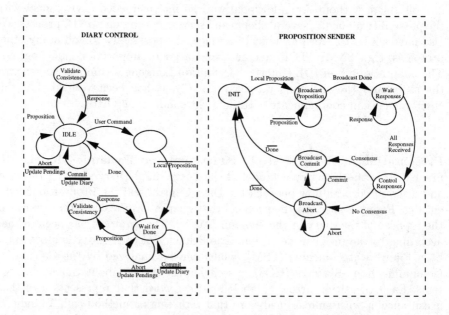

Fig. 2. Dynamic Model

The protocol specified in the FSM of Figure 2 is the following: The DiaryControl gets the new proposition from the user and sends it locally to its PropositionSender. The latter broadcasts it to the DiaryControl of all the other users and waits for their responses. If all responses are positive, it broadcasts the commit order to all the DiaryControl. If this is not the case, it broadcasts the abort order.

When a broadcasted proposition arrives from another user, the DiaryControl checks if it appears among the entries already registered in the diary or in the pending propositions waiting for the commit or abort orders. If the new proposition does not meet anyone, a positive acknowledge is sent back and the proposition is stored in the pending list. Otherwise a negative acknowledge is sent back to the sender and the proposition is dropped.

The DiaryControl and the PropositionSender entities are carried out by two active objects. The body of each one implements the behavior specified by the FSM in the Dynamic Model. Both objects are embedded in the CORBA environment in order to add the distributed capabilities.

Characteristics of the approach This contribution has shown a new approach using the models derived from OOP as a starting point both for the analysis of the behavior and for the implementation application. sC++ has the characteristics that allow the merging of analysis and implementation which is essential for the professional development of reactive applications.

A point to highlight in this solution is the capability to combine CORBA client and server in the same object. The DiaryControl object acts as a server when it receives either a proposition, a commit order or an abort order from the other Diaries. It acts as a client when it sends a response to a received proposition. On the other hand, the PropositionSender object acts as a client when it broadcasts either a local proposition, a commit order or an abort order, and acts as a server when it receives the responses to a local proposition. This characteristic is much easier to manage in this environment than in the commercially available ORBs.

Our solution could have been developed with any other multithreaded environment. However, the use of active objects, from the design of the application down to the details of the middleware, provides developers with an homogeneous methodology that eases the design, the implementation and the debugging of the applications. Initially, the system has been developed, tested and debugged in a single UNIX process running a simulated CORBA bus, which was much easier than in the distributed situation. The distributed version has been realized as the last step of the implementation phase.

Contribution 5 : Competence Pool Abstraction and Dynamic Re-use

Salah Sadou, Gautier Koscielny
ORCADE - VALORIA, Université de Bretagne Sud
BP 561, 56017 Vannes Cedex, France

Introduction to The Competence Pool Abstraction It often happens that objects (which differ by their type and/or their owner) contain the features linked to the same area of application without those being linked. For instance, various objects may have different features about conversion of image formats. The role of the Competence Pool Abstraction (CPA) is to gather these features processing in the same area of application to provide users with only one interlocutor who would still be rich in possibilities. The CPA is a factorization of objects know-how and not of their type, as it is the case with existing systems [44].

Let us come back to the idea of dynamic re-use, objects participating to the constitution of the CPA are servers. The features provided by these servers will be called "active services".

In an environment organized in CPA, the programming of a new application must be made with and for other applications. The whole idea is to use "active services" already existing in the system to build an application rather than to create new objects.

So that this can actually work we have to set rules and to define means of construction. Let us quote a few as examples :

- The rules : each inventor of a new server object must check if some his methods do not correspond to a CPA. If this is the case, he should not include them into this CPA. Client objects have to go through CPAs for their requests ;
- The means : a CPA administrator is necessary for the creation of new pools and so as to avoid doubles, two CPAs are merged into one and the same field of application. An other means which is necessary during the construction of an application, is the CPA seeker. This is what is actually going to allow inventors to know what already exists.

The client no longer communicates directly with object servers. It is a constraint for communication performances , but going through competence the pool provides an abstraction which proves to be quite helpful to programmers of clients object. The server object associated to a service of the CPA can change without the client being affected. Moreover, several object servers can be associated to a same service. Thereby, the parallelization of the requests and the tolerance to faults can be achieved at the level of the competence pool in a way that is transparent to the client.

Modeling the CPA needs a concept that is little more flexible than the traditional object approach. Contrary to the object model, the competence pool has a dynamic interface : during execution the number of services which are

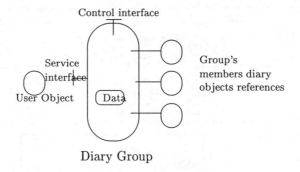

Control interface

Service
interface

User Object

Data

Group's
members diary
objects references

Diary Group

Fig. 3. The global view of the diary group

provided by the pool may change, according to the arrivals and departure of servers object; And services correspond to the redirection and leave the actual processing, of the requests to servers object. The CPA is before anything an element of organization.

An example of the CPA modeling is the group of objects. The group abstraction allows us to facilitate the interaction with a logical group of entities [6]. Instead of separately addressing each of the entities meeting the same property, one address the whole via the group.

We can now give a general definition of the group of objects :

A group can be defined as a non void totality of objects from which one or several relationships $\langle R_1, ..., R_n \rangle$ are defined.

For the CPA, these relationships express the fact that objects have the methods concerning a same area of application.

Objects belonging to a group are called "members" of the group.

An object x is member of a group G if and only if $\exists y \in G$, $\exists (R_i)_{i \in [1,n]}$ so that $R_i(x, y)$.

A same object may belong to separate groups, *i.e.* the object may have features linked to different areas application. We then speak *recovery* of groups.

Presentation of the case study   In our case one group represents de distributed diary. The members of the group are objects sharing the diary (one per user) (Fig3). So, these objects are both clients and servers.

A user creates an event by invoking the group. So, the group manages the data linked to this event.

The group is duplicated so that each machine gets its own view of this group (Fig4). There is only one local view per machine. Consequently, only one copy of the diary's events per machine. Concretely, data are stocked in a distributed memory managed by the group.

We use a modified algorithm of the two-phase commit protocol. In the classic one there is only one coordinator. Or, in our case each local view of the group

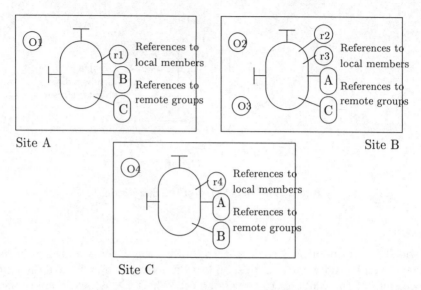

Site A

Site B

Site C

Fig. 4. The local view of the diary group

may be a coordinator. So, we us a token ring algorithm for concurrency control between local groups.

Sharing active objects We have discussed a possible model of distributed applications so as to take into account the possibilities brought by the distribution to object oriented programming. We have focused mainly on the active re-use of the dynamics service. We got to the conclusion that principles of the objects technologies are not sufficient. The lack is mainly focused on the organization aspect of the distributed objects.

We have proposed the CPA approach, implemented by the group of objects, to deal with this lack. In addition to the abstraction which simplifies the application programming, this approach has the advantage to throw a bridge between the development and the execution of objects. Thereby, crew working organization can be easily mapped onto internal organization of objects.

What we have presented corresponds to what has to be shared between several applications. However, each application needs to define an organization of its own objects. We think that the abstraction "Activities" [41] is more adequate for the definition of this organization. This abstraction aims the round up of a coherent task continuation (generally towards the organization) to define an activity. The Activity can very well be represented by the group of objects. In this case, the combination of this approach (application level) and the CPA (environment level) seems to be very promising for the construction of cooperative distributed applications.

239

Contribution 6 : Formalizing Correlate through the Pi-calculus

Bert Robben[1], Frank Piessens[2], Wouter Joosen[3]
K.U.Leuven, Dept. of Computer Science   Celestijnenlaan 200A, B3001 Leuven - Belgium

Introduction to Correlate and the pi-calculus Correlate is a concurrent object-oriented language developed at the distributed systems group of K.U.Leuven. One of the aims of our research team is to develop system software with an open implementation: while applications are developed, system software is being customized to match the application's needs. The practical goal of the Correlate language is to offer a powerful programming environment in which both application and system software can be described using the paradigm of concurrent objects. We have gathered experience in using the prototype with applications in the areas of High-Performance Computing (Molecular Dynamics simulation, PDE solvers), network applications (routing) and multi- agent systems. This iterative process of experimenting with real-world applications has been driving the continuous improvement of the language.

As a statically typed, class-based, object-oriented language, Correlate much resembles Java or C++. The focus of the language is however on high-level support for developing distributed concurrent object-oriented applications. On the on hand this is realized by a meta-level[53] architecture that gives the application programmer control over the execution environment of the application. On the other hand and orthogonal to it, new language features are introduced to enable the description of the application as a set of concurrent objects.

Recently, a formal description of Correlate in the π-calculus[60] has been developed. The π-calculus[47] is an elementary calculus for describing and analyzing concurrent systems as collections of independent processes that communicate through named channels. The semantics of the Correlate language are precisely specified by a layered translation to this calculus. A first part defines a generic runtime architecture supporting active objects. The second part is built on top of this generic runtime and specifies all Correlate-specific semantics.

In our experience, formalization is a crucial ingredient in the design process of a practical language, even though not every detail (in our case, only Correlate's language elements, not its architecture) has been (and can be) modeled. We believe that our work is a complement to the formal work that is produced with simple, yet pure, languages where formalization is the main goal.

Presentation of the case study The Correlate environment is built to develop applications like the distributed diary. This section gives a brief overview of this process and shows the role the recently developed formal semantics can play in this.

---

[1] Research assistant of the Belgian National Fund for Scientific Research (N.F.W.O.)
[2] Postdoctoral fellow of the Belgian National Fund for Scientific Research (N.F.W.O.)
[3] Research assistant of the Belgian I.W.T.

In Correlate, programmers develop write their applications in two separate phases. First, the application developer must describe her/his application guided by a computational model. The result is a description corresponding to the problem domain of the application. In this phase, hardware architecture aspects (like distribution scheduling, threading) are completely hidden for the application programmer, who models the natural abstractions of the application's problem domain as a set of active objects. [68] describes this phase for a distributed agenda similar to the case study. Secondly, an optimal execution environment must be described to target the application to the specific architecture it is running on. In this phase, the programmer uses a so-called meta-interface[53], which is a separate interface, for fine-tuning the support system to application specific requirements. Through the meta-interface, the programmer can e.g. construct a replication policy to enhance reliability and availability.

The formal specification of the language unambiguously defines the different language entities, thereby indirectly specifying applications written in it as well. This is one of the major benefits we perceived of the formalization process. Formerly, the language was in fact defined through the implementation of the execution environment. No clear distinction was made between specification and implementation leading to possibly ambiguous interpretation. As an example, the semantics clearly state that no ordering on message acceptance is guaranteed in case of asynchronous invocations. The current implementation however delivers all messages in the same order as they were sent, but only because of a set of implementation decisions concerning scheduling and network communication which can and most probably will change in a future implementation.

Current research is taking this one step further and tries to use the specification to prove properties of the architecture and of certain objects. Object encapsulation can serve as a simple example. It should not be too hard to prove, that an object only has access to its own internal state and cannot directly modify the state of other objects. More ambitious, through the concept of unique bearing of names[47] it might be possible to prove that no spoofing (i.e. impersonating another object) will happen during execution. The notion of (bi)similarity is another opportunity for further study. Through this concept it might be possible to construct a kind of behavioral type where not only the static structure of a class determines its type but also its dynamic interaction pattern.

Benefits of the specification process As already mentioned in the previous section, a major benefit was the clear separation of language semantics and execution environment implementation. But this was not the sole benefit. As the π-calculus allows very fine grained concurrency, a clear grasp is obtained on the synchronization possibilities of the language while writing the specification. E.g. in our case, synchronization of interface operations through preconditions was already well studied before creating the π description. Object construction and destruction however were given only ad hoc semantics; e.g. synchronizing on the creation of destruction of an object was not supported. In the formal description, this lack of synchronization clearly showed and a more expressive alternative could be formulated. Hence the formal specification of the language influences the language design itself.

Since the π-calculus has an operational semantics, the specifications have the advantage that they can be executed by an appropriate execution engine. However, the π-calculus is a very abstract formal system and although execution engines exist, extracting meaningful information is not always easy as the gap with a high-level notation suitable for general-purpose concurrent programming is considerable. A lot of work has been done however to close this gap. Pict[55] is a formal concurrent language related to the π-calculus, as LISP is to the lambda-calculus. A compiler and execution environment is available. It turned out that our π-calculus semantics could be implemented in Pict with relatively little effort. The benefits of the Pict implementation of the formal semantics were twofold: first, it served as a fine test bed for the specification. Both the type checker at compile-time and executing simple programs at run-time are great tools to find hidden faults or confirm a correct specification. A second benefit was that the Pict program is a valid prototype execution environment. As such it can be more easily used to test some new language features than the actual execution environment which is a much bigger program (in C++).

Contribution 7 : Integrating Object-Z and CSP for the Specification of Object-Oriented Concurrent Systems

Graeme Smith
Technical University Berlin, Franklinstrasse 28/29, 10587 Berlin, Germany

Introduction to the Object-Z / CSP notation Formal specifications of concurrent or distributed object-oriented systems need to encompass two distinct points of view. The first, which we will call the *structural* or *internal* view, describes the classes in terms of their attributes and methods. This view also incorporates the inheritance relationships between classes. The second, which we will call the *behavioural* or *external* view, describes the system in terms of the behaviour of the concurrently executing objects and their interactions.

Process algebras such as CSP, CCS and (Basic) LOTOS are ideal for specification of the external view. The behaviour of an object can be specified by a process and a system of objects by a parallel composition of such processes. This approach has been advocated using Basic LOTOS by both Mayr[45] and Cusack *et al*[20]. However, process algebras are not suited to modelling the internal view. Hence, extending these approaches to model inheritance has proved more difficult[7].

Object-oriented extensions of state-based techniques such as Z and VDM[65,42], on the other hand, are ideal for modelling the internal view. Classes are specified by encapsulating state variables with the operations which may affect them and inheritance by "merging" of class definitions. They can also be used to model the external view of a concurrent system. However, the resulting specifications are generally far less elegant than those using process algebras.

A more effective way of specifying concurrent object-oriented systems, therefore, is to combine an object-oriented state-based language with a process algebra. Such an approach using Object-Z[23], an object-oriented extension of Z, together with CSP is presented in [63]. The basis of the integration is a semantics of Object-Z classes identical to that of CSP processes. This enables classes specified in Object-Z to be combined directly with CSP operators.

The specification of a system comprises three phases. The first phase involves specifying the components of the system using Object-Z. Inheritance may be used in this phase enabling components to be specified incrementally and the specification to reflect the desired object-oriented structure. In the second phase, the interfaces of the components are modified using Object-Z inheritance. This is necessary for the components to synchronise and communicate as desired when combined, in the final phase, using CSP operators.

The approach uses the existing languages without altering their syntax or semantics making it accessible to users who are already familiar with the languages. This also enables the use of existing methods of verification and refinement developed for the languages as shown in [64].

Presentation of the case study   The case study was completely specified at two levels of abstraction. The first (abstract) specification was devoid of the algorithmic details of the two-phase commit protocol. The second (concrete) specification included these details and a proof of the refinement relation between the specifications was performed.

– Abstract specification

- The first phase of the specification involved specifying the shared diaries which comprise the system. To separate the diary concerns from those of communication between the distributed diary entities, a class *Diary* was specified with only the following operations: *Add*, *Cancel*, *Replace* and *Consult*. The specification of this class was facilitated by first defining types, corresponding to events and user requests, and various relations on these types, e.g. a relation which associates events which overlap.

  The class *Diary* was then inherited in a class $SharedDiary_0$ which added the operations *SendRequest*, *ReceiveRequest*, *Commit* and *Abort* corresponding to the system communication. Since the class *Diary* is devoid of these operations, it could also be reused in other specifications such as that of a personal (non-shared) diary.

- The second phase involved the specification of a class *SharedDiary* which inherited $SharedDiary_0$ and added a constant corresponding to the diary's identity. Inputs and outputs corresponding to diary identities were added to inherited operations to ensure the correct communication and synchronisation in the CSP system specification.

- The final phase involved using CSP to specify the system as a parallel composition of a collection of shared diaries: one for each diary identity.

- Concrete Specification

  - The first phase of the concrete specification reused the *Diary* class of the abstract specification and specified a class *SharedDiaryImpl$_0$* which inherited it and added the operations required for the two-phase commit protocol.

  - The second phase followed the same approach as the abstract specification to ensure correct communication and synchronisation: a class *SharedDiaryImpl* which inherited *SharedDiaryImpl$_0$* and added a constant corresponding to the diary's identity was specified.

  - The final phase also followed the same approach as the abstract specification. However, the operations corresponding to the sending and receiving of acknowledgements (votes) were hidden in the resulting system as these are not part of the system's externally visible behaviour.

Refinement and proofs One of the main advantages of specifying a system at several levels of abstraction is that proofs can be performed at the most abstract level rather than the lower, more complex levels. This requires, however, proofs of refinement between the specifications.

Refinement in Z is usually defined in terms of *simulation* rules which relate the initial states and operations of specifications. A set of such rules is defined for Object-Z classes in [64] such that if a class A is refined by a class C then $f(A) \sqsubseteq f(C)$ where $\sqsubseteq$ is CSP refinement and $f(x)$ is any CSP specification in terms of a process x. This allows specifications in the Object-Z / CSP notation to be refined by refining the individual classes of the system components.

The abstract and concrete specifications of the diary system, however, could not be related using these rules because of the hiding in the latter. That is, we need to relate classes A and C such that $f(A) \sqsubseteq f(C) \backslash X$ where X is a set of operations to be hidden. An approach to this problem involving *weak* simulation rules is presented for the Object-Z / CSP notation in [25]. These rules require, as well as the initial states and operations of the classes A and C to be related, that

- the hidden operations in X do not affect the parts of C's state which correspond to the state of A and
- the hiding of the operations in X does not cause *divergence*, i.e. where an unbounded sequence of operations is hidden.

The proof of the latter relies on finding a finite bound on the number of hidden operations which can occur consecutively. For the concrete specification of the diary system this bound is one less than the number of diary identities (since each diary receiving a request for an event modification sends exactly one acknowledgement). This number was finite in the specification since the number of diaries had to be finite to enable the CSP composition to be defined.

Since there are no hidden operations in the abstract specification, it is obviously free from livelock. Therefore, the concrete specification, because it introduces no divergences, is also free from livelock. While this may not be surprising for a protocol as simple as the two-phase commit, in general the absence of livelock is an important property of a concurrent or distributed system.

Equally important is the absence of deadlock. The simulation rules ensure that any such properties holding in the abstract specification also hold in the concrete specification. Once again proving the absence of deadlock for the abstract diary specification is relatively straightforward. In general, such properties can be proved using a combination of the existing proof systems for CSP and Object-Z as outlined in [64].

Contribution 8 : Subtyping as a Support for Incremental Development

Julie Vachon, Didier Buchs
Laboratoire de Génie Logiciel, EPFL, 1015 Lausanne, Switzerland

Introduction to Subtyping and CO-OPN/2 In today's concrete applications, reuse and incremental development are key principles which must be supported and applied through the use of a well-defined methodology. During the incremental development process, one may want specifications to preserve certain objects properties – be they semantical, syntactical or pragmatical – all depending on the needs to be fulfilled by the specifications. These properties are usually specified through objects types. According to the specification formalism used, these types are described by objects behaviors (axioms), signatures or implementation definitions.

Incremental modification, be it horizontal or vertical, may therefore give rise to different kinds of compatibility relations between specified entities. From the most to the less permissive, we can identify the three following kinds of relations: name, signature and behavioral compatibilities. Depending on the specification requirements, one or the other may be especially sought after.

Until now, most of the work has been addressing name and signature compatibilities. Much less results have been obtained for the third form of compatibility; according to its strong definition, behavioral compatibility should ensure the preservation of all the behavioral properties of an object. Hence, we can think of an associated *behavioral subtyping relation* which could guaranty the following substitutability principle:

Principle of substitutability: An instance of a subtype can always be used in any context in which an instance a of a super-type was expected. (*Wegner and Zdonik*,[69])

Specifications should facilitate the reuse, the extension and the verification of systems components by providing appropriate information. In particular, specifications should be helpful for the validation of object substitution and for checking that it doesn't generate errors. Behavioral compatibility, and its associated subtyping relation respecting the substitutability principle, should help achieving this.

To be applicable, formal behavioral subtyping relations should rest on a concise and well-defined model of objects. Former work on behavioral compatibility and subtyping ([57], [43], [51]) have often omitted giving such a model and thus led to more-or-less unclear definitions.

These last years, several formalisms based on P/T-nets with structuring capabilities have been developed, and most of them have adopted the object-orientation paradigm. Among these is found the CO-OPN (Concurrent Object-Oriented Petri Net) [11] and its new version, called CO-OPN/2 [5] , which is based upon two fundamental formalisms: order-sorted algebras (OSA) [27], for the specification of data structures, and algebraic nets (AN) [59], to deal with operational and concurrent aspects. In CO-OPN/2, the type attributed to a class is a transition system representing the semantics of this class, that is to say, the possible behaviors of objects belonging to that class.

Presentation of the case study : A model of the collaborative diary in CO-OPN/2 The diary must allow the following services: consultation, addition, cancelation and replacement of events. An event structure is simply composed of a day, a beginning and ending time, and a comment line. Each site has a diary for each member. Each diary is specified by four components:

- The **ADR** (Abstract Document Representation), keeps all information concerning the diary definition.
- The **DSA** (Distributed Synchronization Algorithm), ensures that the replicated information is consistent.
- The **DAL** (Data Access Layer), filters accesses to the ADR.
- **Network** is a model of the services expected from the communication medium.

The abstract data types required in this system specification are defined in the following modules: **Message, ID, Action, Event, ListEvent, Decision** and **Vote**. This architecture described in Figure 5 is inspired from [40].

The role of the **DSA** is to guarantee consistency between the replicas of the diary. To this end, we rely upon a very simple mechanism: When a user modifies its copy of the diary, the corresponding event modification must be accepted by the other participants. If by misfortune another user wants to validate a conflicting event at the same moment, then the respective **DSAs** implementing the two-phase locking protocol will detect the problem and reject both updates.

Figure 6 is the textual specification of **ADR**: the associated Petri net described by this specification is not represented here. In the interface of the object

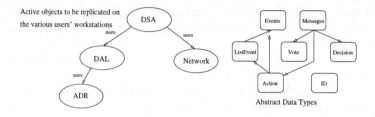

Fig. 5. Architecture of the diary: Hierarchy of Components classes and of ADTs' modules

ADR, the **Use** list reports the other objects with which we perform synchronizations and the ADTs used in the specification. In the **Body** of object **ADR**, the keyword **Where** introduces the declaration of local variables. Although strongly typed, they should be considered as logic variables.

Two kinds of transitions are proposed. First, there are the internal transitions (usual transitions of P/T nets) which correspond to the spontaneous reactions of the objects and, secondly, there are the parameterized external transitions, or methods, which are the visible events from the outside. Cooperation between the objects is realized by means of a synchronization mechanism, i.e. each object event may request synchronizations with the methods of one or of a group of partners by using synchronization expressions. Three synchronizations operators have been provided: '//' for simultaneity, '..' for sequence and '+' for alternative or non-determinism. Thus, a behavioral axiom is established as follows:

$$[Cond \Rightarrow] EventName [\text{With } Sync] \, Pre \rightarrow Post$$

Cond is an optional equality condition on algebraic values. *EventName* event tells which specific event the axiom defines. The synchronization expression is given in *Sync*. It states the methods which are called for establishing rendez-vous. The *Pre* axiom precondition and *Post* axiom postcondition parts establish the links to the input and output places of the event in the sense of Petri nets, and state with algebraic expressions the additional conditions to establish or the transformations to perform on the tokens.

Use of the subtyping relation It must be noted that the model defined for component **ADR** provides a first simple specification of the diary data structure. An incremental evolution of this modeling can introduce additional behavioral features. This is for instance the case of the class **ADR_concur** in Figure 6, which introduces additional concurrent behaviors to the behavior of **ADR**. **ADR_concur** models a more sophisticated agenda which allows a more efficient access to its resources by authorizing two concurrent consultations of the diary. The new behaviors of **ADR_concur** correspond to the additional arrows found in the illustration of **ADR_concur**'s behavioral type in Figure 7. In order to be able to substitute **ADR_concur** to **ADR** it is necessary to establish that

```
CLASS ADR                                    CLASS ADR_concur
INTERFACE                                    INTERFACE
   USE Booleans, ListEvent, Event;              USE Booleans, ListEvent, Event;
   METHODS                                      METHODS
      Consult _ : listevent;                        Consult _ : listevent;
      AddEvent _: event, event;                     AddEvent _: event, event;
      Update _ _: event, event;                     Update _ _: event, event;
      Cancel _ : event;                             Cancel _ : event;
BODY                                         BODY
   PLACES                                       PLACES
      diary: listevent;                            diary: listevent;
   INITIAL                                      INITIAL
      diary [];                                    diary [], diary [];
   AXIOMS                                       AXIOMS
      Consult(l) : diary l → diary l;              Consult(l) : diary l → diary l;
      AddEvent(e) : diary l → diary (e+l);         AddEvent(e) : diary l1, diary l2 →
      e1 isin l = true ⇒                                        diary (e+l1), diary (e+l2);
         Update(l) :                               e1 isin l = true ⇒
            diary l → diary (e2 + (l-e1));            Update(l1) :
      e isin l = true ⇒                                   diary l1, diary l2 →
         Cancel(e) : diary l → diary (l-e);               diary (e2 + (l1-e1)), diary (e2 + (l2-e1));
                                                  e isin l = true ⇒
WHERE                                                 Cancel(e) : diary l1, diary l2 →
   e, e1, e2 : event;                                     diary (l1-e), diary (l2-e);
   l : listevent;                            WHERE
END ADR;                                        e, e1, e2 : event;
                                                l : listevent;
                                             END ADR;
```

Fig. 6. The CO-OPN/2 Specification of **ADR** and its Enrichment **ADR_concur**

ADR_concur is a subtype of **ADR**. In our simple view of behavior preserving subtype relation, a superclass and a subclass are related by a subtype relation if and only if all existing behaviors of the superclass can be found in the subclass (like it is the case of the example given in Figure 7). This subtyping principle necessitates that the classes using the class **ADR** will not use new services of the subclass **ADR_concur**. In particular, that all methods will respond to clients in the same way for the class and its subclass.

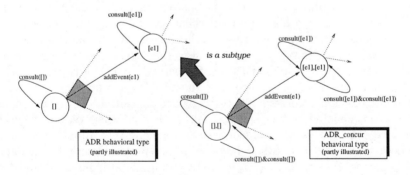

Fig. 7. The Transition Systems of **ADR** and **ADR_concur** Related by the Subtyping Relation

This strong view of the subtype relation is used in CO-OPN/2. We are currently exploring a way to weaken this relation in a new generalized relation. We call this subtyping relation: observer-based subtyping. This relation shall take into account specific classes of clients for which substitutability is required.

Contribution 9 : Static Type Checking and Deadlock Prevention with Asynchronous Message Passing

Christof Peter and Franz Puntigam
Technische Universität Wien, Institut für Computersprachen
Argentinierstraße 8, A-1040 Vienna, Austria

Introduction to Process Types In concurrent and distributed systems it is more difficult to deal with type errors detected at run time than in sequential and centralized systems. An erroneous argument may already have caused effects in various places that cannot be undone by aborting a single call. Models like CORBA support static type checking for distributed systems. However, their rather simple notions of type consistency are not sufficient in concurrent systems.

Usually, a server's type specifies a constant set of understandable messages. A type is a signature and a type checker ensures statically that clients send only messages specified in the server's signature.

The acceptability of messages can depend on the server's state. In general, in distributed systems, clients do not know the server's current state and the messages they can safely send. With conventional type models this problem can be solved only by delaying the handling of unexpected messages (or by dynamic type checking). But delaying messages may cause deadlocks and the handling of messages in wrong contexts.

The process type model [58] eliminates this problem by giving the clients information about the server's state. All messages are handled in the logical order they were sent. A process type describes an abstract state and how this state changes after handling a message. Each client has its own image of the server's type and sends its messages according to this image. After sending a message, a client has to update its type image. The server has to accept all messages from the clients in arbitrary interleaving, i.e. the server's type is a super-imposition of all clients' type images. It is possible to split a type image into two images so that the old image corresponds to the super-imposition of the new images. This concept, denoted by type splitting, has to be used whenever a new client is introduced. The process type model ensures statically that all messages sent to an object are understood, although the set of acceptable messages can change.

The process type model cannot prevent all undesired kinds of deadlocks: It does not ensure that the server returns an answer to a message as expected by the client. If the server does not send the answer, the client can wait forever. This problem can be circumvented by checking that the server sends an answer after a finite number of actions: The server is allowed to wait only for a guaranteed answer to some message.

With guaranteed answers, the process type model prevents all undesired kinds of deadlocks if (1) objects communicate only through asynchronous message passing, (2) the size of message buffers is unlimited, and (3) each object handles received messages while waiting for a guaranteed answer. The last condition is necessary because we don't want to prevent call-backs, where the server is asking the (waiting) client for a service.

Presentation of the case study Syntactically, a process type consists of two parts: The activating set describes an abstract state of the type's instances, and the behavior descriptor the acceptable messages, depending on the activating set. When an object's behavior changes, the activating set also changes, but the behavior descriptor remains unchanged. The activating set is a multi-set of state descriptors. States are distinguished by the presence or absence of state descriptors. For each supported message, the behavior descriptor contains a message descriptor. The type Diary specifies the interface of a (local) diary:

$$
\begin{aligned}
\text{Diary} = \quad & \{\} \mid \text{consult(Time, Back)} + \text{add(Time, Event, Succ)} + \\
& \text{cancel(Time, Succ)} + \text{replace(Time, Event, Succ)}. \\
\text{Back} = \{!\text{one}\} \mid & \text{back(Event)}\{!\text{one}\} + \text{failed()}\{!\text{one}\} \\
\text{Succ} = \{!\text{one}\} \mid & \text{prepared(Decision)}\{!\text{one}\} + \text{failed()}\{!\text{one}\} \\
\text{Decision} = \{!\text{one}\} \mid & \text{commit()}\{!\text{one}\} + \text{abort()}\{!\text{one}\}
\end{aligned}
$$

Each message takes an object of type Back or Succ as the argument to which the result shall be returned. The single state descriptor !one of each of these types is used up when a result is sent; hence, only a single answer to each message is allowed. The exclamation mark specifies that an answer is expected after a finite number of steps. If the answer is "prepared", a decision about the commitment or abortion of the action is demanded within a finite number of steps.

The implementation of a diary is supported by a time table of this type:

$$
\begin{aligned}
\text{TimeTable} = \quad & \{\} \mid \text{lock(Time, LockBack)} \\
\text{LockBack} = \{!\text{one}\} \mid & \text{in\_use()}\{!\text{one}\} + \text{ok(Handle)}\{!\text{one}\} \\
\text{Handle} = \{!\text{one}\} \mid & \text{unlock()}\{!\text{one}\} + \text{set(Event)}\{!\text{one}\}{\to}\{!\text{one}\} + \\
& \text{get(GetBack)}\{!\text{one}\}{\to}\{!\text{one}\} \\
\text{GetBack} = \{!\text{one}\} \mid & \text{back(Event)}\{!\text{one}\}
\end{aligned}
$$

For each access to the diary, a lock for the corresponding slot in the time table is requested. If the slot is not in use, a handle for the lock is returned. All set- and get-operations are addressed to this handle. The state descriptor !one of Handle is used up when "unlock" is sent. "set" and "get" require that !one is in the activating set, but the clause "$\to$\{!one\}" adds !one to the activating set so that an arbitrary number of these messages (terminated by "unlock") can be sent.

For a distributed diary, the same types can be used. The message "consult" can be handled by the local diary. For the other messages, all distributed copies of the diary have to return "prepared(Decision)" before the action can be committed.

When implementing the distributed diary, it turns out that the type Succ is not sufficient if the possibility of site failures is considered. We have to add a time-out:

$$
\begin{aligned}
\text{Succ} = \{!\text{one}\} \mid & \text{prepared(Decision)}\{!\text{one}\} + \text{failed()}\{!\text{one}\} + \\
& \text{time\_out()}\{!\text{one}\}
\end{aligned}
$$

A corresponding extension of Decision also is necessary.

Conclusion Conventional types are not sufficient for concurrent and distributed systems, where the acceptability of messages can depend on object states. The process type model ensures statically that all sent messages are understood even if the set of acceptable messages changes dynamically. The model ensures that messages are handled in the same logical order they were sent. Unexpected behavior caused by not-understood messages and out-of-order-execution cannot occur. It is possible to ensure that servers return answers to clients within a finite number of steps. Only one kind of possibly infinite blocking can occur: A server waits for the next message from a client. Therefore, deadlocks can be prevented. Wherever deadlock prevention is in conflict with high flexibility needed in some part of a system, deadlock prevention can be selectively disabled. Process types are a promising approach to a system combining selective deadlock prevention with strong typing, subtyping, genericity and separate compilation. We think that it is more appropriate to ensure statically that some kinds of deadlocks cannot occur and all sent messages are understood than to use behavioral subtyping, which ensures only that subtypes do not allow more deadlocks and "message-not-understood-errors" than supertypes.

4 Conclusion

4.1 Methodology and Models

The contributions to the "methodology and models" group, along with the discussions thare were held during the workshop, helped highlight a set of common opinions and concerns shared by the authors :

In several issues, the conventional OO methods and techniques were felt to be satisfactory, and consistently used by the authors. For instance, the analysis of the problem domain was considered well covered by "standard" methods such as OMT or UML, and several authors (Diagne, Restrepo) explicitly use them in the first steps of their proposed approach. Likewise, the basic notions used for structural OO models (encapsulation, inheritance, etc.) were used as a basis for initial design.

In other issues, a strong case was made that formal approaches coming from other realms might very well complement and enhance OO methods. Diagne, for example, advocates the use of Well Formed Petri nets, along with their analysis and proof techniques. Demartini integrates the use of model checking tools in the development life-cycle of concurrent and distributed Java applications.

Another opinion raised by the contributions is that the inherent complexity of concurrent and distributed OO application calls for high-level models of the concurrent and cooperative behaviour of objects : Berger proposes the ICM model which decouples the reactive behaviour of objects from their intrinsic behaviour, Demartini defines the Automaton Object as an extension of the java

RMI model, while Sadou uses the Competence Pool abstraction to address such issues.

Finally, several questions were hardly evoked by the the authors, and are felt to be still controversial and problematic : how to deal with the very variable latency encoutered in wide area networks such as the Internet ? At wich level should we deal with the problem of partial failures, inescapable in any large scale distributed application ? What about load balancing and scalability ? Such issues are still widely open for research, and might well prove the be the next major challenges in integrating distributed OO applications and formal approaches.

4.2 Formal Models

The topics covered by the contributions are relatively large within the formal model domain. Almost all aspects usually covered by such approaches in the software life cycle have been studied. Of course, formal specification is the basis of all contributions but specification is used in different way, Robben uses formal models for describing the semantics of a programming language while Peter uses a formal models for abstracting the behaviors of classes into type descriptions. The other contributions uses formal models as a description tool within the modeling phase of the development process.

Abstraction is a key word of all contributions, in the sense that managing and describing the system under development at the highest possible level of description is claimed as the only way for dealing with complexity. The kind of complexity that is discussed is: complexity of the proofs of properties by Smith, complexity of the type checking of Peter or complexity of the subtyping relation proof of Vachon.

The support for incrementality in the development process is also well covered by some contributions. For instance Smith use refinement in order to reach a concrete implementation in an model based approach. Incremental safe composition of components is one objective of the approach of Peter. Generally, incremental approaches are dealing with some kind of optimization of the proof process. This is performed by reducing proof of properties of one specification to the proof of validity of the incremental development steps.

To conclude this workshop produced very fruitful discussions and provided to participants complementary directions for future reflections.

Acknowledgments

We thanks Charles Lakos for his summary of the contributions during the workshop.

References

1. http://ltiwww.epfl.ch/sCxx.
2. G. Agha, P. Wegner, and A. Yonezawa. *Research directions in concurrent object-oriented programming*. The MIT Press, 1993.

3. Gul Agha and Fiorella De Cindio, editors. *Object-Oriented Programming and Models of Concurrency*. University of Torino, 1995. Workshop within "16th International Conference on Application and Theory of Petri Nets, Torino, Italy, June 26–30".

4. Gul Agha and Fiorella De (Organizers) Cindio. The second workshop on object-oriented programming and models of concurrency within "the 17th international conference on applications and theory of petri nets osaka, june 24, 1996, http://wrcm.dsi.unimi.it/ petrilab/ws96/home.html", 1996.

5. Olivier Biberstein, Didier Buchs, and Nicolas Guelfi. Coopn/2: A concurrent object-oriented formalism. In *Proc. Second IFIP Conf. on Formal Methods for Open Object-Based Distributed Systems (FMOODS)*, pages 57–72, Canterbury ,UK, March 1997. Chapman and Hall, London.

6. K. P. Birman. The Process Group Approach to Reliable Distributed Computing. *Communications of the ACM*, 36(12), December 1993.

7. S. Black. Objects and LOTOS. In S. Vuong, editor, *Formal Description Techniques II (FORTE'89)*. North-Holland, 1990.

8. H. Boehm. Verifying and validating software requirements and design specifications. *IEEE Software System Design*, 1(1):30–37, 1984.

9. G. Booch. *Object-Oriented Design*. Benjamin/Cummings Redwood City, CA, 2nd edition, 1993.

10. G. Booch and J. Rumbaugh. Unified method for object-oriented development. Teaching documentation set, Rational Software Corporation, Santa Clara, USA, 1997. Version 1.0.

11. Didier Buchs and Nicolas Guelfi. CO-OPN: A concurrent object-oriented Petri nets approach for system specification. In M. Silva, editor, *12th International Conference on Application and Theory of Petri Nets*, pages 432–454, Aahrus, Denmark, June 1991.

12. D. Caromel. Toward a method of object-oriented concurrent programming. *Communications of ACM*, 36(9):90–116, Sept. 1993.

13. P. Casadessus. *Conception et mise en oeuvre d'un noyau transactionnel dans un environnement parallèle*. Thèse de doctorat, Université de Paris 6, Novembre 1994. 172 pages.

14. S. Chiba. Open C++ release 1.2 Programmer's guide. Technical report, Department of Science, university of Tokyo, 1993.

15. G. Chiola, C. Dutheillet, G. Franceschinis, and Haddad S. On well-formed coloured nets and their symbolic reachability graph. In *Application and Theory of Petri Nets 1990*, Lecture Notes in Computer Science. Springer-Verlag, June 1990.

16. S. Christensen and L. Petrucci. Towards a modular analysis of coloured Petri nets. In *Proceedings of the International Conference on Application and Theory of Petri Nets*. Springer-verlag, June 1992. Sheffield, UK.

17. R. Cleaveland, J. Parrow, and B. Steffen. The concurrency workbench: A semantics-based tool for the verification of concurrent systems. *ACM Toplas*, 5(1):36–72, January 1993.

18. P. Coad and E. Yourdon. *Object Oriented Analysis*. Prentice Hall, Inc., second edition, 1991.

19. J. C. Corbett. Evaluating deadlock detection methods for concurrent software. *IEEE Transactions on Software Engineering*, 22(3), March 1996.

20. E. Cusack, S. Rudkin, and C. Smith. An object-oriented interpretation of LOTOS. In S. Voung, editor, *Formal Description Techniques II (FORTE'89)*. North-Holland, 1990.

21. E.W. Dijkstra. Hierarchical ordering of sequential processes. In C.A.R. Hoare and R.H. Perrot, editors, *Operating Systems Techniques*. Academic Press, New York, 1972.

22. Stéphane Ducasse, Mireille Fornarino, and Anne-Marie Pinna. A Reflective Model for First Class Relationships. In *Proceedings of OOPSLA'95*, pages 265–280, 1995.

23. R. Duke, G. Rose, and G. Smith. Object-Z: A specification language advocated for the description of standards. *Computer Standards and Interfaces*, 17:511–533, 1995.

24. J. Rumbaugh et al. *Object-Oriented Modeling and Design*. Prentice Hall International, Englewood Cliffs, NJ, 1991.

25. C. Fischer and G. Smith. CSP and Object-Z: Finite or infinite trace semantics. In *Formal Description Techniques and Protocol Specification, Verification, and Testing (FORTE/PSTV'97)*. Chapman and Hall, 1997.

26. Svend Frolund. *Constraint-Based Synchronization of Distributed Activities*. PhD thesis, University of Illinois at Urbana-Champaign, 1994.

27. Joseph A. Goguen and José Meseguer. Order-sorted algebra I: Equational deduction for multiple inheritance, overloading, exceptions, and partial operations. *TCS: Theoretical Computer Science*, 105(2):217–273, 1992. (Also in technical report SRI-CSL-89-10 (1989), SRI International, Computer Science Lab).

28. J. Gosling, B. Joy, and G. Steele. *The Java Language Specification*. Addison-Wesley, Inc., 1996.

29. J. Gray. *Operating Systems: An Advanced Course*, chapter Notes on Database Operating Systems. LNCS Vol 60, Springer Verlag, 1978.

30. J. Gray, editor. *Transaction processing : concepts and techniques*. Morgan Kaufmann Publishers, San Francisco (California), 1993. 1070 pages.

31. T. Haquet and B. Cazaux. Flo++ dépendances entre objets distants. Rapport de projet de fin d'étude, ESSI, 1997.

32. W. Harrison and H. Ossher. Subject-oriented programming (A critique of pure objects). In *OOPSLA'93*, pages 411–428, Washington DC, October 1993. ACM SIGPLAN Notices Vol.28, n. 10.

33. C.A.R. Hoare. Monitors: An operating system structuring concept. *Communications of the ACM*, 12(10), October 1974.

34. Ian M. Holland. Specifying reusable components using Contracts. In O. Lehrmann Madsen, editor, *Proceedings of ECOOP'92*, volume 615 of *Lecture Notes in Computer Science*, pages 287–308. Springer-Verlag, 1992.

35. G. Holzmann. *Design and Validation of Computer Protocols*. Prentice Hall, Inc., 1991.

36. G. J. Holzmann. *Design and Validation of Computer Protocols*. Prentice Hall, AT&T Bell Laboratories, 1991.

37. J-M. Ilié and K. Ajami. "model checking through symbolic reachability graph. In *Proceedings of CAAP'97*. Springer Verlag, April 1997.

38. Ivar Jacobson, Magnus Christerson, Patrik Jonsson, and Gunnar "Overgaard. *Object-oriented Software Engineering; A Use Case Driven Approach*. Addison-Wesley, Wokingham, England, 1992.

39. K. Jensen. *Coloured Petri Nets: Volume 1; Basic Concepts, Analysis Methods and Practical Use*. EATCS Monographs on Theoretical Computer Science. Springer-Verlag, Berlin Heidelberg New York, 1992.

40. Alain Karsenty. *GroupDesign: un collecticiel synchrone pour l'édition partagée de documents*. PhD thesis, University of Paris XI Orsay, France, 1996.

41. Bent Bruun Kristensen. Object-oriented modeling with roles. In *Proceedings of the 2nd International Conference on Object-Oriented Information Systems (OOIS'95)*, Dublin, Ireland, 1995.

42. K. Lano and H. Haughton, editors. *Object-Oriented Specification Case Studies*. Object-Oriented Series. Prentice-Hall, 1993.

43. Barbara H. Liskov and Janet M. Wing. A behavioral notion of subtyping. *ACM Transactions on Programming Languages and Systems*, 16(6):1881–1841, November 1994.

44. S. Maffeis. *Run-Time Support for Object-Oriented Distributed Programming*. PhD thesis, University of Zurich, February 1995.

45. T. Mayr. Specification of object-oriented systems in LOTOS. In K. Turner, editor, *Formal Description Techniques (FORTE '88)*. North-Holland, 1989.

46. R. Milner. *Communication and Concurrency*. Prentice Hall International, 1989.

47. Robin Milner. The polyadic π-calculus: a tutorial. Technical Report ECS-LFCS-91-180, Laboratory for Foundations of Computer Science, Department of Computer Science, University of Edinburgh UK, October 1991. Also in *Logic and Algebra of Specification*, ed. F. L. Bauer, W. Brauer and H. Schwichtenberg, Springer-Verlag, 1993.

48. D. Moldt. *Höhere Petrinetze als Grundlage für Systemspezifikationen*. Dissertation, Universität Hamburg, Fachbereich Informatik, Vogt-Kölln-Str. 30, 22527 Hamburg, Germany, August 1996.

49. Sape Mullender. *Distributed systems*. ACM press, Frontier series, 1989.

50. T. Murata and M. Notomi. Hierarchical reachability graph of bounded nets for concurrent software analysis. *Transactions IEEE on Software Engineering*, 5(20):325–336, 1994.

51. Oscar Nierstrasz. Regurlar types for active objects. In *Object-Oriented Software Composition*, chapter 4, pages 89–121. Prentice-Hall, 1995.

52. David Notkin, David Garlan, William G. Griswold, and Kevin Sullivan. Adding Implicit Invocation to Languages: Three Approaches. In Shojiro Nishio and Akinori Yonezawa, editors, *First International Symposium on Object Technologies*, volume 742 of *Lecture Notes in Computer Science*. ACM, October 1993.

53. Johan Van Oeyen, Stijn Bijnens, Wouter Joosen, Bert Robben, Frank Matthijs, and Pierre Verbaeten. A flexible object support system as run-time for concurrent object-oriented languages. In Chris Zimmerman, editor, *Advances in Object-Oriented Metalevel Architectures and Reflection*. CRC Inc, May 1996.

54. R. Orfali, D. Harkey, and J. Edwards. *The Essential Distributed Objects Survival Guide*. J. Wiley & Sons, Inc., 1996.

55. Benjamin C. Pierce and David N. Turner. Pict: A programming language based on the pi-calculus. Technical report in preparation; available electronically, 1996.

56. Xavier Pintado. Gluons: a support for software component cooperation. In Shojiro Nishio and Akinori Yonezawa, editors, *First International Symposium on Object Technologies*, volume 742 of *Lecture Notes in Computer Science*, pages 43–60, 1993.

57. Franz Puntigam. Type specifications with processes. In *Proc. of the 8th International Conference on Formal Description Techniques for Distributed Systems and Communication Protocols (FORTE'95)*, Montréal, Québec, Canada, October 1995. IFIP WG 6.1.

58. Franz Puntigam. Coordination requirements expressed in types for active objects. In Mehmet Aksit and Satoshi Matsuoka, editors, *Proceedings ECOOP '97*, number 1241 in Lecture Notes in Computer Science, Jyväskylä, Finland, June 1997. Springer-Verlag.

59. Wolfgang Reisig. Petri nets and algebraic specifications. In *Theoretical Computer Science*, volume 80, pages 1–34. Elsevier, 1991.

60. Bert Robben, Frank Piessens, and Wouter Joosen. Formalizing correlate - from practice to pi. In *Proceedings of the BCS-FACS 2nd Northern Formal Methods Workshop*, 1997. To be published electronically by Springer-Verlag, http://www.springer.co.uk.

61. J. Rumbaugh, M. Blaha, W. Premeralani, F. Eddy, and W. Lorensen. *Object-Oriented Modeling and Design*. Prentice Hall, Englewood Cliffs, New Jersey 07632, 1991.

62. J. Rumbaugh, M. Blaha, M. Premerlani, F. Eddy, and W. Sorenson. *Object Oriented Modeling and Design*. Prentice Hall, Inc., 1991.

63. G. Smith. A semantic integration of Object-Z and CSP for the specification of concurrent systems. In *Formal Methods Europe (FME'97)*. Springer-Verlag, 1997.

64. G. Smith and J. Derrick. Refinement and verification of concurrent systems specified in Object-Z and CSP. In *First IEEE International Conference on Formal Engineering Methods (ICFEM'97)*. IEEE Computer Society Press, 1997.

65. S. Stepney, R. Barden, and D. Cooper, editors. *Object-Orientation in Z*. Workshops in Computing. Springer-Verlag, 1992.

66. K.J. Sullivan and D. Notkin. Reconciling environment integration and software evolution. *Transactions on Software Engineering and Methodology*, 1(3):228–268, July 1992.

67. A. Valmari. Compositional analysis with place-bordered sub-nets. In *Proceedings of the International Conference on Application and Theory of Petri Nets*. Springer-verlag, June 1994. Zaragoza, Spain.

68. Gert Weckx. Een gedistribueerde agenda. Master's thesis, Dept. Computerscience, K.U.Leuven, 1995-1996.

69. Peter Wegner and S. Zdonik. Inheritance as an incremental modification mechanism or what like is and isn't like. In *Proceedings of ECOOP'88*, volume 322 of *Lecture Notes in Computer Science*, pages 55–77, Oslo, Norway, 1988. Springer-Verlag.

70. C.H. West. Protocol validation by random state exploration. In *Protocol Specification, Testing and Verification, VI*, pages 233–242. North-Holland, Amsterdam, 1986.

71. J. M. Wing. A specifier introduction to formal methods. *IEEE Computer*, 23, September 1990.

FAMOOS Workshop on Object-Oriented Software Evolution and Re-engineering

Eduardo Casais[1], Ari Jaaksi[2] and Thomas Lindner[3]

[1] Nokia Research Center
P.O. Box 422, 00045 Nokia Group, Finland
eduardo.casais@research.nokia.com
[2] Nokia Telecommunications
P.O. Box 779, 33101 Tampere, Finland
ari.jaaksi@ntc.nokia.com
[3] Forschungszentrum Informatik
Haid-und-Neu-Strasse 10-14, 76131 Karlsruhe, Germany
lindner@fzi.de

1. Overview

Over the years, a large body of complex and expanding object-oriented software has accumulated, whose evolution and maintenance is placing an increasing burden on software developers. Dealing with large-scale, mature object-oriented systems and frameworks, and endowing them with flexibility is therefore a key area for the success of future software development projects.

The goal of the workshop was to establish a working dialogue about how to deal with the drawbacks of ever-growing object-oriented legacy systems. It brought together researchers, practitioners, and tool providers, and promoted the generation and exchange of ideas among participants, thus giving new impulses to enhance the state of the art in the re-engineering of object-oriented systems.

The workshop built upon two important related achievements:

- A workshop on the same topic held at OOPSLA'96, and its seminal precursor on object-oriented legacy systems held at OOPSLA'95.
- The work done in FAMOOS[1], a project carried out within the ESPRIT IV programme.

In order to produce useful results regarding the issue of software adaptability to customer requirements and markets needs, the workshop focused on the following topics:

- experiences on re-engineering large object-oriented systems;
- documentation and re-use of object-oriented systems;
- analysis of object-oriented systems with respect to re-usability and flexibility;
- abstract models of object-oriented systems;
- methodological support for the transformation of object-oriented systems into frameworks;

---

[1] FAMOOS is project no. 21975; the partners are Nokia (Finland), Daimler-Benz (Germany), TakeFive Software (Austria), FZI (Germany), SEMA Group (Spain) and the University of Bern (Switzerland).

- metrics to measure the need for, the progress of, and improvement to object-oriented design;
- tools supporting all of the above activities.

All position papers have been published on the world-wide-web site http://www.fzi.de/ecoop97ws8. The attendance at the workshop, and the organization of a similar event at ESEC/FSE'97 demonstrate that the topic is now an established, active field of research in the object-oriented community.

2.   Workshop Presentations

Eliezer Kantorowitz started the presentations with a report on two new concepts to estimate the effort taken to build and then enhance an object library, called *implementation* and *extension complexity*. The ensuing discussion highlighted the need to provide similar concepts to handle unanticipated extensions which do not fit in the pre-defined architecture of a library.

Tamar Richner followed by showing how a formal characterization of circular dependencies helps in understanding and improving an existing object-oriented system without having to resort heavily to domain experts. An interesting question is whether one can avoid dependency analysis altogether through other higher-level techniques.

Oliver Ciupke discussed the results of applying graph analysis tools to evaluate the architecture of a large system, discover modularization and coupling problems, and suggest improvements. Raising the level of abstraction afforded by basic graph techniques is a burning issue to be addressed in further work.

Tarja Systä presented SCED, a tool that addresses a similar issue: recovering design information about the dynamics of a legacy system. SCED works by instrumenting the events of the system, generating various scenarios (represented as message sequence charts), which are then compiled into a state diagram. Handling such dynamic aspects was considered by the workshop participants as a major issue in object-oriented re-engineering.

Roland Trauter discussed the potential role of UML to integrate object-oriented re-engineering tools on top of standard repositories. He concluded that UML still lacks many features that would make it suitable for this purpose, and even as a design method: UML focuses on notations, whereas the main issue is to support software engineers when they take design and architectural decisions.

Koen de Hondt, presenting the work of Kim Mens and Tom Mens, classified the various ways to combine behavioural and structural software descriptions. Reuse contracts constitute one interesting approach, which serves to detect the impact of design decisions on an object-oriented library and to preserve its consistency.

Markku Ruonavaara elaborated on his experience in building large-scale systems by observing that time-to-market is the decisive factor in object-oriented development, while architecture and reuse are secondary. As such, what is needed is to be able to quantify economically the cost and benefits of architectural rework, as well as to formalize and streamline good design heuristics.

Akila Sarirete discussed class similarity measures derived from the comparison of method identifiers. The outcome is a clustering of classes according to their similarity, which gives hints to software engineers as to the conceptual organization of the library. It was noted that conceptual similarity, rather than just syntactical matching, requires that a library implements a consistent naming scheme.

Serge Demeyer proposed to re-engineer by in first recovering the design of the software into a rich, descriptive model, and then analysing this model and detecting anti-patterns to be corrected. Major issues are expressing the information extracted from the code at the appropriate abstraction level, and the difficulty to recover behavioural information.

Hélène Bachatène concluded with a survey of the major issues in object-oriented maintenance. Experience shows that organizational and educational issues are paramount. On the technical side, solutions are the reliance on the best available tools, their effective integration, and keeping documentation and code consistent — for example by embedding documentation in the code. At the methodological level, analysis and design patterns should increase the effectiveness of object-oriented design and maintenance.

3. Perspectives on Methods

The state of the art in object-oriented re-engineering consists mostly of a variety of isolated techniques; some more comprehensive approaches have been proposed, but empirical data about their advantages and shortcomings is still limited [Cas95]. A systematic evaluation of available techniques being beyond the scope of the workshop, the participants tried instead to clear up important methodological issues. The discussion highlighted the following aspects:
- The concepts used in object-oriented re-engineering are often overloaded, which hinders the comparison and evaluation of different approaches.
- New directions in system analysis and abstraction could bring substantial benefits during re-engineering.
- Re-engineering must be properly embedded in an iterative software development process.

Re-engineering is generally viewed as the transformation of a system's architecture to a more flexible one. In order to handle behavioural aspects, state diagrams are very often relied upon. Unfortunately, both "state diagram" and "architecture" are heavily overloaded terms. First, different words are needed to cover the various meanings attached to the term "architecture":
- All the high-level design.
- The design decisions that involve many people.
- Dynamic as opposed to static structures.
- Documentation that has a long-term validity even during the maintenance phase.
- Or simply the aspects of software development that cause the most difficulties.

The notion of "state diagram" itself needs to be standardized; in this respect, OOAD methods have taken quite different positions on what is to be achieved with state diagrams:

- Showing the processing steps performed in response to the events that an object receives.
- Specifying equivalence classes for attributes and the transitions between them.
- Defining when certain operations are legal and when they are not (interface or protocol definition).

Besides this clarification of the terminology, the workshop participants identified promising approaches to tackle re-engineering tasks.

The first approach is static analysis of object-oriented systems. Despite the importance of behavioural aspects when dealing with software restructuring, static analysis has a major role to play. Simple changes, such as modifying class and method names to make them more descriptive and consistent — for example by having the names of graphical user interface components end in "View" — are very effective. The experience of the participants confirms what has been documented in the literature [Mey90]. Re-engineering tools must provide such facilities — as is already the case with the refactoring browser [RBJ97]; other useful pattern matching and search engines are glimpse and Alta-Vista (in its local version).

A further technique, dynamic abstraction, should allow software engineers to explore and view object-oriented software from totally new perspectives:
- Collecting and manipulating method calls as objects. Scenarios and state diagrams built out of these reified method invocations would constitute the dual view of the traditional state diagrams where nodes correspond to classes and objects.
- Weighting associations between classes based on the number or frequency of method invocations, for example to suggest effective client-server decomposition.
- Providing powerful query facilities to extract and represent information about dynamic relations and method invocations.
- Combining simple pattern matching (looking for branches and loops in the source code) with coverage analysis (with tools like tcov) in order to produce state diagrams giving information about the actual transitions occurring at run-time.

A final methodological question is how to embed re-engineering in an iterative development process. The fundamental necessity of re-engineering can be justified by the impossibility to elaborate a perfect architecture or design that will accommodate all unanticipated changes [JoFo88]. The integration of re-engineering activities in the normal development process is however not obvious. Two ways are proposed:
- Resources and time for re-engineering are assigned to each phase in the development cycle; this can be described as a continuous re-engineering process.
- Re-engineering corresponds entirely to the first phase of each cycle.

In both cases a top-down re-engineering approach is effective: first determine the target, ideal design, then adjust the existing code to it.

4. Perspectives on Tools

The participants considered the re-engineering life-cycle proposed by the workshop organizers. The life-cycle can be decomposed into the phases of *model capture* (design recovery), *problem detection*, *problem analysis*, *system reorganization*, and *change propagation*. The ensuing discussion focused on two issues:

- Understanding and recovering design information about an existing system.
- Characterizing the design problems and the appropriate tools to solve them.

Poor documentation, complex code, and the unavailability of the original system designers constitute major hindrances right at the beginning of a re-engineering project. Tools are therefore necessary to support the exploration and understanding of the system to be re-engineered. Based on their concrete experience in re-engineering projects, the participants suggested the following approaches:

- Installing the system in a clean-room environment, and relying on test runs to understand the way it operates, its architecture and its underlying model. The results of these test runs enable software engineers to refine their intuitive understanding of the system and of the application domain.

  A problem with this approach is that it does not seem to scale up, although it is very useful for systems up to about 50000 lines of code.

- Using multi-dimensional browsing tools to explore the internals of the system, visualize it at various degrees of abstraction, and explore relationships between components [Tai97].

  Browsing is an indispensable technique to be used in combination with other approaches. However, the lack of dynamic visualization and browsing facilities currently restrict the scope of the explorations, and hence provide a limited view of the behavioural aspects of a system. On-going work by some of the workshop participants (Tarja Systä f.ex.) is actually addressing these issues.

- Building a prototype of the target system, on the basis of the requirements and the concepts of the application domain. Through successive comparisons with the legacy system, the prototype is refined and completed until the core problem and the corresponding design solutions have been identified.

  Rapid prototyping for object-oriented re-engineering is still very much an experimental method. It is appealing to view the prototype as the backbone of the re-engineered system and try to integrate some parts of the old software into it, but incompatibility issues make this approach often unfeasible.

Overall, scalability (how to understand really large systems comprising millions of lines of code) is a core problem of the model capture phase. Advances in multi-dimensional and behavioural browsers, collaborative tools (design recovery is fundamentally a group activity), and rapid prototyping are needed to cope with it.

An object-oriented system can exhibit a wide range of design problems; a re-engineering environment must provide the appropriate tools to tackle each one of them in an optimal way. The workshop participants summarized their findings in the following list:

- Cleaning up code without sacrificing performance.

  Software developers can use refactoring tools, especially those that eliminate code redundancy in an object-oriented hierarchy [Moo96]. Experiments show that such reorganizations may actually improve the performance of the system.

- Incorporating new requirements seamlessly.

  The problem is to avoid an inadequate implementation of the new requirements that would increase the entropy of the system, and to weed out too specific requirements. Appropriate tools are pattern matching and impact analysis utilities (such as provided by the refactoring browser), reuse contracts (to detect violations of design constraints and assumptions), as well as metrics (to measure the extension and implementation complexity of new functionality f.ex).

- Improving code quality.

Quality assessment tools, lint-like utilities, source code beautifiers, and other code transformation utilities are widely available; in addition, "purifiers" pin-point problems with memory management, which is especially relevant for programming languages without automatic garbage collection such as C++.

- Reducing build times.

Special utilities to analyze and optimize dependencies between files are envisioned (f.ex. to streamline the structure of include files in a C++ library), but reliance on scaleable configuration management and version control tools is a more feasible approach in the short term.

- Porting the system to a new platform.

The identification of platform-dependent parts prior to their subsequent isolation in subsystems is supported by dependency analysis facilities and graph visualization tools.

- Unbundling features.

The same techniques as those used to deal with portability apply. However, whereas in the latter case one usually attempts to structure a system into hierarchical layers ("horizontal" subsytems), unbundling results in components that are on the same level of abstraction ("vertical" subsystems).

- Integrating software with other components.

The approaches of choice are software buses with communication and encapsulation facilities (notably CORBA), as well as special-purpose software adapters for libraries.

- Scaling up software.

The issue is more methodological than tool-related. Solutions are provided by techniques to evaluate the complexity of algorithms, the utilization of specific architectures, and the definition of scaleable data formats (to avoid the millennium bug f.ex). Profilers serve to identify bottlenecks, and modelling and simulation tools to assess the overall scalability of a system.

- Making a system distributed.

Wrappers and middleware (CORBA f.ex.) are possible approaches.

- Ensuring the configurability of a system.

Possible techniques are wrapping the software with scripts that can be customized, providing hooks and bindings in the software for external scripts (Tcl, shell, SQL, etc), or building the system on a reflective platform.

Dependency analysis tools play a major role in the re-engineering life-cycle. A question is whether pattern-matching operations (to look for specific design patterns or anti-patterns) could provide higher-level, more directly useful results than abstract graph analyses and visualizations. Obvious obstacles are the intractability of pattern-matching when examining behavioural, rather than just structural properties, and the difficulty to raise the abstraction level from language idioms to architectural patterns.

5. Concluding Remarks

The evolution and re-engineering of object-oriented software is a complex problem, affecting an increasing number of organizations, and which requires a pragmatic methodology and scaleable tool support. Further research has to address the following key issues:

- Visualization and manipulation of dynamic system aspects during browsing.
- Raising the level of abstraction when examining and browsing source code.
- Formalization of re-engineering knowledge and heuristics.
- Effective tool interoperability, including interoperability between forward and reverse engineering environments.
- Establishment of organizations to handle re-engineering, and synchronize this activity with maintenance and development tasks.
- Migration to an incremental software development approach (evolutionary design).

The workshop participants brought forth a number of promising ideas — many of them clearly speculative — which deserve further investigation. It is expected that the preliminary results of applying these novel ideas will be presented at the next FAMOOS workshop.

References

[Cas95] E. Casais: Managing Class evolution in Object-Oriented Systems. In O. Nierstrasz and D. Tsichritzis, eds., *Object-Oriented Software Composition*, Prentice Hall, Englewood Cliffs, 1995, pp. 201-244.

[JoFo88] R. E. Johnson and B. Foote: Designing Reusable Classes. *Journal of Object-Oriented Programming*, vol. 1, June/July 1988, pp. 22-35.

[Mey90] B. Meyer: Tools for the New Culture — Lessons from the Design of the Eiffel Libraries. *Communications of the ACM*, vol. 33, no. 9, September 1990, pp. 68-88.

[Moo96] I. Moore: Automatic Inheritance Hierarchy Restructuring and Method Refactoring. In *SIGPLAN Notices*, vol. 31, no 10 (special issue on OOPSLA'96), October 1996, pp. 235-250.

[RBJ97] D. Roberts, J. Brant and R. Johnson: A Refactoring Tool for Smalltalk. *TAPOS* vol. 3, no. 4, 1997.

[Tai97] A. Taivalsaari: Multidimensional Browsing. In *Proceedings SEE Conference*, Cottbus, Germany, 8-9 April 1997, pp. 11-22.

On Implementation and Extension Complexities

Eliezer Kantorowitz

Computer Science Department,
Technion – Israel Institute of Technology, 32000 Haifa, Israel
kantor@cs.technion.ac.il

Summary

A software system may be considered as an implementation of a number of different algorithms. An evaluation of the time and space complexities of all the algorithms of the system may be employed to detect possible performance problems. There are, however, situations where the costs of computations are acceptable, but the costs of implementation and of later extensions of the system are unacceptably high. In order to check whether a given algorithm may involve such implementation or extension costs, the concepts of *implementation complexity* and *extension complexity* were introduced in [Kant97]. The implementation and extension complexities of a given algorithm may usually be estimated in a few minutes. The implementation and extension complexities may therefore be employed together with the time and space complexities for detecting and avoiding problematic algorithms. This paper starts with the definition of the concepts, and then gives some examples.

The outcome of poor programming is unpredictable. Sound programming practices are therefore assumed. This means that all methods are small and simple such that they may be quite easily verified. The focus is, therefore, on algorithms involving a number of different methods residing in a number of different classes. Correct implementation of such algorithms is difficult because all the involved classes must be considered simultaneously. These classes must be considered when extending the algorithm to support a new class. Our hypothesis is therefore that the number of different classes involved is the principal parameter for estimating the amount of code segments that implements or extends the algorithm. This is expressed by the following definitions:
- The domain of an algorithm is the set of all the classes employed by the algorithm.
- The size of the domain of an algorithm, n, is the number of different classes in the domain of the algorithm.
- The implementation complexity of an algorithm is an indicator of the number of code segments required to implement the algorithm as a function of the size of its domain. A code segment may be a function or any other unit of code. It is not an accurate estimate as may be achieved by an elaborate software metrics analysis [Fent91].
- The extension complexity is a measure of the number of code segments required in order to extend the domain of an algorithm with a single new class.

The first example regards the change propagation algorithm that motivated the introduction of these concepts [Kant97]. This algorithm is employed in a CAD system for calculation of the effects of changes in the design. The legacy algorithm had an implementation complexity of $O(n^2)$. The amount of code was therefore considerable and it was difficult to debug. The extension complexity of the legacy algorithm was $O(n)$. The costs of extensions grow linearly with n and it was not feasible to extend them beyond 9 different classes. A new algorithm was therefore developed; it had an implementation complexity of $O(n)$ and an extension complexity of only $O(1)$. It was quite easy to extend the number of classes from the original $n = 9$ to the required $n = 85$. The effort required to add a class was roughly constant, confirming the extension complexity of $O(1)$.

The above example suggests that an extension complexity of $O(1)$ is desirable in evolving systems. We define therefore a *simple algorithm* as an algorithm whose extension complexity is $O(1)$. The following theorem has been proved:

Theorem: An algorithm having an extension complexity $O(1)$, i.e. a simple algorithm, has an implementation complexity of $O(n)$.

It can be shown that an implementation complexity of $O(n)$ does not imply that the extension complexity is $O(1)$. The extension complexity is in this sense a more fundamental concept than the implementation complexity. We shall therefore, in the following example, only check if the algorithms have an extension complexity $O(1)$.

The next example shows that polymorphism facilitates the design of simple algorithms. Consider, for instance, a superclass `Shape` from which we derive the subclasses `Square` and `Circle`. The superclass has a virtual method `area()` which has different concrete implementations for `Square` and `Circle`. Consider an algorithm `total_area` for the calculation of the sum of the areas of all `Shape` objects, i.e. both `Square` and `Circle` objects. To evaluate the extension complexity of this algorithm, the case of adding one new class, say `Triangle`, is considered. In order to extend the `total_area` algorithm one new method `Triangle.area()` must be implemented. The extension complexity `total_area` algorithm is thus $O(1)$, i.e. the algorithm is simple.

References

[Kant97]   E. Kantorowitz: Algorithm Simplification Through Object Orientation, *Software Practice and Experience*, vol. 27, no. 2, February 1997, pp. 173-183.

[Fent91]   N. E. Fenton: *Software Metrics a Rigorous Approach,* Chapman & Hall, New York, 1991.

Analyzing Dependencies to Solve Low-Level Problems*

Tamar Richner and Robb Nebbe

Institut für Informatik (IAM), Universität Bern
Neubrückstrasse 10, 3012 Bern, Switzerland
(richner,nebbe)@iam.unibe.ch , http://iamwww.unibe.ch/~(richner,nebbe)/

Summary

We have identified two levels of restructuring in the re-engineering of object-oriented legacy systems: high-level restructuring is concerned with improving the overall architecture of the system, whereas low-level restructuring deals with repairing local problems which are symptoms of bad style. We propose to characterize these low-level problems as patterns of dependencies between classes as an aid in detecting and resolving them. In this paper we briefly present low-level problems and give two examples of how these can be characterized as specific dependency patterns.

In the FAMOOS project we observed the following low-level problems in the industrial case studies:

misuse of inheritance: inheritance is used as a way to add missing behaviour to a superclass, instead of modeling the problem domain. This results in deep and narrow inheritance hierarchies.

missing inheritance: code duplication is used instead of subclassing, and long case statements are used instead of method dispatching.

misplaced operations: operations are defined outside of the class to which they should belong.

violation of encapsulation: classes frequently give access to private data, through the C++ friend mechanism.

missing encapsulation: classes are used as a structuring mechanism to encapsulate unrelated functions.

Solving these problems requires restructuring the code to a new, functionally equivalent system, analogous to the normalization of relational databases: the organization of the information is improved without changing the information content. Since most low-level problems can be characterized without domain-specific knowledge, their detection could be automated, and their resolution at least partly automated.

Low-level problems often manifest themselves as the presence of undesirable dependencies among classes. A tangle of dependencies in the code impedes understanding and maintenance of the software, especially for large projects. It is therefore important to minimize dependencies to the essential ones required

---

* This research is supported by ESPRIT IV project no. 21975, and by Swiss National Science Foundation grant MHV 21-41671.94 (to T.R.)

to reflect the software design, and to avoid circular dependencies which are an obstacle to modular compilation and testing [Sou94] [Lak96].

We thus characterize the low-level problems as patterns of dependencies among classes. These patterns of dependencies could be detected through query modules on a representation of the code. Furthermore, each pattern (or rather anti-pattern), in defining a problem, also suggests a solution. We give two examples:

Dependency Pattern: a class A has several unrelated clients, each using only a part of A's interface.

Symptom of: missing encapsulation

Solution: the interface of A is partitioned into groups of methods used by different kinds of clients. Class A is then factored out into several separate classes.

Dependency Pattern: Circular dependencies between two classes

Symptom of: misplaced operations

Solution: create a new class which links the two dependent classes and whose methods break the circular dependencies

Similarly, other dependency anti-patterns are symptoms of misuse of inheritance (partial dependencies between clients and parts of the inheritance tree), missing inheritance (similar clients use different inheritance trees) and violation of encapsulation. We can thus characterize the different kinds of low-level problems as patterns of dependencies between classes. These dependency anti-patterns can then be detected in the code and the appropriate solution propagated using semi-automatic refactoring operations [JO93].

There are several issues to be addressed in implementing such low-level restructuring operations. First, we must refine the characterizations and catalogue the kind of information required to define each of these dependency patterns. We expect that a static analysis of the code would suffice. A second issue is which representation is best suited for query modules or recognizers [HYR96] to detect these patterns: a graph structure of dependencies may be a more appropriate representation than the abstract syntax tree. Thirdly, it remains open to what extent solutions can be propagated automatically using refactoring operations.

More general issues have to do with the benefit that we derive from 'repairing' low-level problems in re-engineering large industrial applications, where such static dependencies are only a small part of the problem. Ideally, we would like to be able to evaluate the importance of a problem to determine if it is worth solving or worth detecting in the first place.

References

[HYR96] D. Harris, A. Yeh, and H. Reubenstein. Extracting architectural features from source code. *Automated Software Engineering*, 3(1):109–139, 1996.
[JO93] R. Johnson and W. Opdyke. Refactoring and aggregation. In *Proceedings of ISOTAS '93 LNCS 742*, pp. 264–278, 1993.
[Lak96] J. Lakos. *Large-Scale C++ Software Design*. Addison-Wesley, 1996.
[Sou94] J. Soukup. *Taming C++*. Addison-Wesley, 1994.

Adding Architecture to Design

Markku Ruonavaara

Nokia Telecommunications
P. O. Box 759, 33101 Tampere, Finland
markku.ruonavaara@ntc.nokia.com

Summary

The need for architectural rework in existing software systems is often a consequence of lacking architectural design in the earlier life phases of the software. Adding architecture to existing designs is a difficult task and it calls almost invariably for tearing down existing structures. Even carefully thought out architectures tend to degenerate over time as the requirements of the system evolve, the complexity of the system increases and the effort required for maintenance and testing grows.

The challenges in architectural restructuring of legacy systems are to find out the current structure of the software, to find the right solutions matching the new requirements and to implement them at an acceptable cost. Architectural rework is hard to justify economically because often in large systems the effort required is large, involves a large number of people and provides little or no immediate added value to the end customer in the short term.

There are many commercially available tools for code reverse-engineering that are evidently useful in architecture rework. The tools reveal the dependencies between code level entities such as classes and methods. This is not however the whole picture; compile- and link-time dependencies are not the only significant relationships between system components. In large systems there are typically also dependencies that could be called data and run-time dependencies. *Data dependencies* between the parts of a system are caused by common data: relational database, flat files or any other type of external shared data. Data dependencies may cause very tight coupling between parts of the system. This coupling is totally invisible to code level analysis tools. *Run-time dependencies* are caused by the interaction of processes in the system at run-time, e.g. service usage via passing operating system messages. These dependencies cannot generally be found on the code level.

Often one of the goals of reorganisation is to minimise dependencies. The goal is not however zero dependencies but a manageable set of dependencies. In architectural sense the compile and link-time dependencies are the most restrictive concerning flexibility to change the structure of the system. Alterations of structure require recompilation and re-linking and thus changes to binaries. Data and run-time dependencies are more dynamic by nature and allow more flexible reorganisation and customisation.

In large-scale software production documenting the architectural decisions is the cornerstone of any systematic architecture work. Documentation is essential because it makes the architecture explicit and thus communicable. But even representing architectures is not a trivial task. One of the dilemmas is the concept of architecture itself; it is not evident what is meant by "architecture". There is a large variety of definitions starting from sophistic "architecture is what architects do" to lengthy, extremely abstract ones in encyclopaedic style.

Experience has shown that updating the design documentation as the design evolves is a tedious task. The current design methods do not really support system evolution. They are most applicable with the initial design but designing the later increments that enhance the initial one is not that well supported. In incrementally built systems the architecture solutions can be seen to span several increments. The problem of design (and architecture) documentation could be eased by attempting to record matters that remain over increments in architectural documentation that is updated as needed and leaving the increment-specific documents unmaintained because it has little value in maintenance. This raises some new questions in practise: what design information should be included in architecture documentation and maintained at each increment, what design decisions are specific for an increment and need not be kept up to date? And the next question is: could that architecture documentation or parts of it be generated on demand by reverse-engineering tools?

Solving all the problems above still leaves us the actual architecting, how to find the right architectural solutions that remove the deficiencies of current structure and stand the test of time and changing requirements. Little methodology for that purpose is available; architecting seems to be a very heuristic activity. Heuristics are not quite intangible in the methodological sense though, e.g. design patterns are a way of formalising heuristics for software design.

Conclusion. The architecture of large incrementally developed systems degenerates inevitably over time as the size of the system grows. Investments in architectural rework are needed to keep the maintenance and testing costs tolerable and to avoid loosing competitiveness in business. The challenges in restructuring large systems are various: reverse-engineering the current system, expressing architectures, finding the corrective actions and finally maintaining the achieved improvements.

The purpose of this paper is more to ask questions rather than to give answers. I would like to underline that architectural restructuring is not only a technical problem but also an organisational, managerial and methodological question. Tools for supporting this work are available but the greatest potential for improvement seems to be on the process side.

Analysis of Object-Oriented Programs Using Graphs

Oliver Ciupke

Forschungszentrum Informatik
Haid-und-Neu-Straße 10–14, D-76131 Karlsruhe, Germany
ciupke@fzi.de

Summary

Complex interdependencies between different parts of a system are a major problem for the maintenance, evolution, and reorganization of large programs. In an object-oriented system, such dependencies exist due to different kinds of interrelationships between the different kinds of entities which make up the system.

Reengineering large object-oriented systems requires methods and tools for analyzing these dependencies. Such analysis can help:

- to understand such systems
- to detect and locate architectural and design problems
- to predict the effects of reorganizations

Graph theory is well understood and encompasses a large number of concepts, methods and algorithms which can be applied for these purposes. Graphs are already widely used in an informal way as a notation for the design of programs. Examples for this are most modelling languages, such as the UML [BR97]. Graphs can also be used in a formal way to describe the complex dependency relationships in an object-oriented system.

Formally, a directed 1-graph is defined by a set of nodes V and a set of edges E, where E is a relation over V. In an object-oriented system, the nodes which represent the entities being considered can be

- *static*: classes, methods, attributes, local variables of methods, packages[1], etc.
- *dynamic*: objects, processes, etc.
- *physical*: source code files, externals such as database tables or resource files

or any combination (union) thereof. The union of methods and attributes is e.g. known as "members" in C++ or "features" in Eiffel. Relations between those entities can be:

- *static*, if they connect static entities: has attribute of type, has method, has parameter of type, returns result of type, has, inherits from, overwrites, contains call to, uses (reads or writes) attribute of type, and several others

---

[1] also referred to as subsystems or modules

- *dynamic*, if they connect dynamic entities: calls method, accesses (reads or writes), creates
- *partially dynamic*, if they connect dynamic entities to static entities, e.g. is of dynamic type

Depending on the question to be answered, different kinds of nodes and edges can be combined in order to form a new graph. For example, the set of methods which can possibly be called from a given method are the methods reachable by the relation $contains\_call \cup overwrites^T$.

For the purpose of analysis, *queries* can be performed on the graph model. These queries are relational algebraic expressions. They can be written down in an query program using a graph library, as SQL statements or even as Prolog programs.

Graph theory, especially with respect to relational algebra, is covered in [SS89] and [Har69], among others.

In order to support the suggested method, a *tool–set* was implemented for facilitating analysis and visualization. Several tools and programming libraries already exist for parsing and examining code, and manipulating and visualizing graphs. Thus, our approach was to build an environment to integrate those tools and implement missing functionality, rather than to build one single monolithic tool. This way, we were able to

- visualize object-oriented systems in an improved way compared to existing reengineering tools
- detect problems by performing queries on graphs
- implement object-oriented metrics in the form of simple queries
- visualize the results of queries

Our approach was evaluated by elaborating a list of design problems and possible solutions for an industrial case-study.

References

[BR97] Grady Booch and James Rumbaugh. Unified modeling language, 1997. Version 1.0.
[Har69] Frank Harary. *Graph Theory*. Series in Mathematics. Addison-Wesley, 1969.
[SS89] Gunther Schmidt and Thomas Ströhlein. *Relationen und Graphen*. Mathematik für Informatiker. Springer-Verlag, 1989.

Extracting State Diagrams from Legacy Systems

Tarja Systä and Kai Koskimies

Department of Computer Science, University of Tampere,
P.O. Box 607, FIN-33101 Tampere, Finland
{cstasy,koskimie}@cs.uta.fi

Summary

A basic problem of reverse engineering is to understand legacy systems and derive abstract characterizations of poorly documented software. In the case of object-oriented software, the static structure (e.g. inheritance and association relationships) can usually be understood easily, and it can be extracted from existing software using automated tools. This is due to the fact that the static aspects of object-oriented programs are more or less explicitly indicated in the source. Understanding and characterizing the dynamic behavior of such systems, in contrast, is usually much more difficult because of the gap between the static source text and the run-time behavior of the executable program. However, the dynamic behavior of a program is equally important as its static specification for understanding the software. Dynamic characterization is particularly important for those parts of a system which are mainly understood by their dynamic behavior, like various kinds of controllers, drivers, etc.

For instance, assume that the control unit of an elevator needs to be re-engineered, and that this software lacks all documentation. We can identify certain classes in the source that presumably represent various kinds of controller objects, but on the basis of the source we can only observe that they react on certain kinds of events in a particular way, depending on their current state, and that they in turn send certain events to other objects. However, it is extremely difficult to infer the general behavior of such objects in the form of, say, state diagram on the basis of static information only. The situation is somewhat better if the source is systematically written to reflect the structure of a state machine, but this is often not the case.

To solve this problem we have combined two existing techniques in our experimental system: the production of scenario diagrams from running systems, and the synthesis of state diagrams from a set of scenario diagrams. Scenario diagrams (sometimes called interaction diagrams or event trace diagrams) are a popular graphical notation for describing the interactions of a set of objects and actors during a particular usage of a system. Scenario diagrams are traditionally used as analysis and design documents (e.g. [Rum91]), but recently they have been used also for animating or visualizing the dynamic behavior of a running system ([KoMö96], [LaNa95], [SSC96]). We have taken the visualization of the run-time behavior of object-oriented programs one step further: not only scenarios but also the final specification of the dynamic behavior, i.e. the state diagram, is composed automatically as a result of the execution of a target system. This step is made

273

possible by the technique recently developed for automatically synthesizing state diagrams from scenario diagrams ([KMST96]).

Roughly, our solution works in practice as follows. The source program is first instrumented with code that registers the events and conditions concerning interesting objects. The event/condition sequence is produced at the run-time on the basis of the instrumentation code and fed to an existing system, SCED [KMST96], using a small intermediate program, called Program Tracer. This program merely analyzes the event/condition sequence and sends it further to SCED in a proper format. SCED, in turn, constructs scenario diagrams describing the interaction of a set of objects implied by the event/condition sequence. At any point, SCED can be asked to synthesize the general behavior of an object as a (minimal) state diagram, given a set of scenario diagrams in which the object participates. Thus, we can run the instrumented target system with various input for a while, and at the same time observe the interaction of the interesting objects as scenario diagrams. Then we can select one of the objects, and ask the system to produce a state diagram for it. Depending on how covering the input was, a more or less complete state diagram is shown by the system.

Currently the source code has been instrumented manually. However, the instrumentation does not seem to require techniques that could not be automated. One possibility to avoid source code instrumentation would be the usage of a debugger; the contents of the log file produced by the debugger can then be examined and analyzed instead of the source code. The disadvantage of this approach is that the user of such a system would be tied up with a certain debugger. Another approach would be the modification of the Java virtual machine itself, hence allowing the monitoring of the dynamic behavior of any compiled Java program. The great advantage of this is that the source need not be modified or even available. The usability of these possible approaches needs further investigation.

References

[KMST96] K. Koskimies, T. Männistö, T. Systä, and J. Tuomi: *SCED: A Tool for Dynamic Modelling of Object Systems*, University of Tampere, Dept. of Computer Science, Report A-1996-4.

[KoMö96] K. Koskimies and H. Mössenböck: Scene: Using Scenario Diagrams and Active Text for Illustrating Object-Oriented Programs. In *Proc. International Conference on Software Engineering* (ICSE '96), Berlin, March 1996, pp. 366-375.

[LaNa95] D. Lang and Y. Nakamura: Interactive Visualization of Design Patterns Can Help in Framework Understanding. In *ACM SIGPLAN NOTICES*, vol. 30, no. 10, October 1995, pp. 342-357.

[Rum91] J. Rumbaugh, M. Blaha, W. Premerlani, F. Eddy, and W. Lorensen: *Object-Oriented Modeling and Design*, Prentice-Hall, 1991.

[SSC96] M. Sefika, A. Sane, and R. H. Campbell: Architecture-Oriented Visualization. In *ACM SIGPLAN NOTICES*, vol. 31, no. 10, October 1996, pp. 389-406.

Combining Software Descriptions

Kim Mens, Tom Mens, Patrick Steyaert, and Koen De Hondt

Programming Technology Lab, Vrije Universiteit Brussel,
Pleinlaan 2, B-1050 Brussel, Belgium

Summary

Object-oriented software can be described in many different ways. In this extended abstract of [MMSH97] we focus on the question how these different software descriptions can best be combined in order to facilitate reuse and evolution.

Structural vs Behavioural Descriptions. When considering reuse and evolution of a software system, both its structure and behaviour are important. *Behavioural* software descriptions express how the system operates and how its components interact. *Structural* descriptions declare how the different system parts are arranged. Both kinds of descriptions are strongly correlated. By structuring the system in a certain way, a particular behaviour may become easier to design or implement. Conversely, to obtain a particular behaviour, sometimes the structure needs to be adapted.

But what is the "best" way to combine structural and behavioural software descriptions? Methodologies like OMT use *separate models* for describing a system's structure and behaviour, leading to a better understanding of the system by providing complementary views. However, because of the limited interaction between both views it is difficult to predict how changes to the behaviour affect the structure and vice versa. With *loose coupling* of behaviour and structure, as advocated in the Demeter method [Lie96], the behaviour usually does not need to be adapted when the structure evolves. Conversely, when the behaviour itself evolves one needs to investigate only the impact on the corresponding parts of the structure. Some methodologies (e.g., reuse contracts [SLMD96]) make explicit the strong correlation between structure and behaviour, by providing a *single model* in which both the structure and behaviour of a system can be described.

Essential vs Implementation-Specific Descriptions. *Essential* software descriptions focus only on those aspects of a system that are crucial to its design. The remaining descriptions are called *implementation-specific*. There is a delicate trade-off between how much essential and how much implementation-specific descriptions should be included in the design. Too many implementation-specific descriptions are undesired as they clutter the design with unnecessary details. Too little implementation-specific descriptions will make it harder to detect and solve some conflicts that might arise during system evolution.

Many approaches do not explicitly distinguish essential from implementation-specific descriptions, making it hard to recognise the "core" system design. Reuse contracts [SLMD96] take the opposite approach and mainly focus on the structure and essential behaviour of a system, while ignoring implementational aspects. A third possibility is to use layering mechanisms to achieve a gradual transition from high level essential descriptions to low level implementation-specific descriptions (e.g., nested state diagrams).

Static vs Dynamic. *Static* descriptions correspond to compile-time aspects of a system. Therefore, when a system is documented by or annotated with static descriptions, many evolution conflicts can be detected already at compile-time. Since *dynamic* descriptions also take run-time aspects into account, they can aid in finding the remaining conflicts that can be detected only at run-time. Most of the current approaches focus either on static descriptions (e.g., reuse contracts) or on dynamic descriptions (e.g., state diagrams) but do not combine both, unless in separate models (e.g., OMT). An alternative approach would be to combine both kinds of descriptions somehow in a single model.

Declarative vs Operational. Most of the models mentioned above use *operational* descriptions (*how* the system functionality is achieved). An alternative is to provide *declarative* descriptions (*what* the system does), as is the case with pre- and postconditions in Eiffel. At this point it is not yet clear which alternative (if not both) is most promising with respect to software evolution.

We think the question of *how software can best be described in order to facilitate reuse and evolution* is an important question the object-oriented software reuse community should think about to get a better insight in the software evolution process. Many ways of describing software are available that often focus on complementary aspects. Combining these different software descriptions is not trivial. Therefore, the following questions need to be answered. *Which of the complementary descriptions is best (if not both)? If both are needed, what is the best way to combine them, or to integrate them into a model? What are the repercussions of the made choices on reusability?* Answering these questions is far from easy, as they strongly interact with each other.

References

[Lie96]   K. J. Lieberherr. *Adaptive Object-Oriented Software. The Demeter Method with propagation patterns.* PWS Publishing Company, 1996.

[MMSH97] K. Mens, T. Mens, P. Steyaert, and K. De Hondt. Combining software descriptions. Vrije Universiteit Brussel, Technical report vub-prog-tr-97-06, 1997.

[SLMD96] P. Steyaert, C. Lucas, K. Mens, and T. D'Hondt. Reuse Contracts: Managing the Evolution of Reusable Assets. In *Proceedings OOPSLA '96, ACM SIGPLAN Notices*, pages 268–285. ACM Press, 1996.

Re-engineering with UML

Roland Trauter

Forschungszentrum Ulm, Daimler-Benz AG,
Wilhelm-Runge-Strasse 11, 89081 Ulm, Germany
trauter@dbag.ulm.DaimlerBenz.com

Summary

UML Version 1.0 has been submitted as proposed OOAD standard to OMG by Rational in January 1997 [BJR97]. Due to considerable weaknesses, this version could not become the expected standard and the work on a new version had to be started. I actually do not expect that this version will be the definitive standard. But it can be expected that UML version $x.y$ will be the forthcoming OOAD standard of OMG as there is no serious competitor in sight. Considering the popularity UML has already gained during the last year, and considering the consortium that stands behind UML, there is no doubt that this standard will clearly dominate the market. The main purpose of this OOAD standard is to ensure interoperability between different OOAD tools and the various methods they support. In a first step, the interoperability is restricted to a transfer of models between the tools.

A standard for OOAD is at first glance clearly related with a forward engineering approach. However, there is also a clear link to a re-engineering approach which is a combination of a forward and a reverse engineering approach. The actual difference between forward and reverse engineering is the direction of workflow, while both activities can use the same set of models. Thus, UML is also relevant for reverse engineering and re-engineering.

Currently most CASE tools, programming environments and reverse engineering tools have their own proprietary repository (file system or database). As no tool vendor has the "all-encompassing" ideal tool-set, user organizations typically work with several isolated tools with redundant, not integrated data and no tool co-operation. The typical solution offered today is an individual transfer of data for each pair of tools. This may be an easy solution from the technical viewpoint; it is however not acceptable from the economical viewpoint, because this transfer has to be done for each pair of tools over and over again with each new tool or tool version. This is a poor strategy and clearly a nonsense.

A better solution is a repository with a standard information structure shared by all tools. The problem of earlier and current repository products was and remains so far the lack of a widely accepted standard for the information structure, so that each of them has currently its own proprietary structure. It is therefore quite natural that there is a lack of tools that work on these repositories.

This situation will probably change quite soon. With a forthcoming OOAD standard based on UML, there is a standard information structure available that can be derived from the UML meta model. As stated before, an OOAD standard is also relevant for re-engineering tools and it is therefore no longer acceptable that each of these tools stores its information in its own home-made file system or database. They can as well co-operate and supplement each other via a standard information structure. We therefore have to clarify to which extent UML is currently able to support re-engineering.

UML, or with its full name Unified Modelling Language is not a method, it is, as its name says, a modelling language, which consists of a set of related modelling elements with an assigned semantic. The modelling elements define the meta-model for which OMG wants to establish a standard that allows tool interoperability. Additionally, a changeable notation and a sample of diagram types are also part of the UML 1.0 documentation. The heuristics or the process to build models with the UML elements is not part of UML.

After this first positioning of UML, its use for re-engineering is apparent. The UML modelling elements can provide the standardized information structure where different re-engineering tools can store the information they have extracted or assembled in interaction with the tool user. UML does however provide no rules, algorithms or heuristics for re-engineering operations!

Hence, UML does not help in re-engineering itself but provides a way for tool integration and efficient work distribution. Of course, UML itself is not the necessary standard information structure, but it is the starting point.

To derive this standard information structure it is necessary to use a subset of UML that is really needed to build re-engineering models. To check whether we have all these elements, we can start with the most widely used programming languages which have a defined set of elements. By building models on higher abstraction levels we use only a subset of these elements. Exactly these are the elements that we should pick from UML. When we have identified this UML subset we have to decide on an implementation for this meta-model, which finally provides the tool integration we need.

References

[BJR97]   G. Booch, I. Jacobson and J. Rumbaugh: *The Unified Modeling Language for Object-Oriented Development*, Documentation Set Version 1.0, Rational Software Cooperation, 1997.

Evolution of Telecommunication Software Using OO : Organisational and Technical Issues

Hélène Bachatène and Pierre Arnaud

Alcatel Research Division, AAR/12
route de Nozay, 91460 Marcoussis, France

Summary

This paper summarises important issues and experiences encountered during object-oriented activities carried out in business divisions (switching systems, mobile systems). These activities considered re-engineering and evolution of large software, and were driven by three major requirements:

- Enforce existing object-oriented methods and notations, to help the definition and implementation of traceable development and maintenance processes.
- Define a documentation process which reflects the major decisions (enrichment, new design, performance issues, …), to help understanding the system before subsequent re-engineering/evolution.
- Define the responsibilities involved in the object-oriented process, and the necessary synchronisation points to master iterations during development or evolution.

The following issues relate to the management of object-oriented projects for evolution or re-engineering. Developing for evolution starts with *requirements analysis*. Modelling the domain imposes early decisions on the future of domain objects, their role and cardinality. Later, the design highlights other decisions too, but some of them are closely related to analysis hints or decisions. Following organisational problems may spoil the analysis activity:

- *Object-oriented analysis* is felt to be too fastidious and too costly by project management. Because a good OOA activity has a substantial impact on the maintenance and re-engineering processes, OOA must gain a better place in a development-for-evolution process. More generally, project planning for object-orientation must prove a commitment to analysis efforts. If not desired, domain analysis may be skipped, and design may always be re-considered, until totally losing the control out of the product. Even then, re-engineering in the context of a new staff will need either the gurus or an updated version of domain analysis.
- *Understanding and managing requirements* is a critical task: in the absence of links to existing requirements (functional or not), software re-engineering or enrichment (e.g., the implementation of a new requirement) may be very complex. The presence of a product guru or of documented traces (implemented or not) helps to reduce risks. This implies the assignment of responsibilities, and important manpower for the capture, structuring and management of requirements, which deserve as much attention as the analysis activity itself.

Managing iterations is another key issue. The definition of an iteration varies from project to another, and frontiers between analysis and design vary as well. This endangers checkpoints and synchronization or common parts. [FaCl96] proposed hints which may help to reduce such risks.

Tools (selection and administration) outline a third key issue. Managing for a state of the art of tools is the traditional way to select the more adapted ones. However, once selected and installed, the evolution, customization and integration in a larger environment highlights a tasks and responsibility which deserve a 100% attention. This responsibility is seldom emphasized in resource planning, although it has direct impacts on the development process.

The following points outline the major issues that deserve more technical emphasis from developers, tool vendors or research community to help object-oriented development and evolution:

- *Documentation*: specifications and designs are usually documented, but related decisions are seldom documented. This makes implementing new requirements critical as long as the impact on the existing software is unknown.
- *Formalisms and consistency of integration*: although object-oriented models pay attention to software behavior, the links with structural properties are not supported by tools. Multiple integration proposals define how to tackle concurrency, safety, reliability and timing aspects [AwZi97], but these approaches deserve more effort to reach the maturity required by industrial applications [RaTs96].
- *Code generation* from behavioral specifications is not emphasized in almost all object-oriented CASE tools. Neither is round-trip. Both activities deserve more attention in order to support and speed up a re-engineering/evolution activity.
- *Testing tools* : syntactical checks are not sufficient to track errors; there should means to test object-oriented specifications and document tests as well.
- *Traceability*: Integrating requirement management tools in a complete environment requires the definition and implementation of upward and backward traces.

References

[AwZi97]   M. Awad and J. Ziegler: A Practical Approach to the Design of Concurrency in Object-Oriented Systems. To appear in *Software Practices and Experiences*, John Wiley, 1997.

[FaCl96]   M. E. Fayad and M. Cline: Managing Object-Oriented Software Development. *IEEE Computer,* September 1996.

[RaTs96]   C. V. Ramamoorthy and W. T. Tsai: Advances in Software Egineering. *IEEE Computer,* 1996.

Design Pattern Restructuring

Serge Demeyer, Theo-Dirk Meijler and Matthias Rieger

Software Composition Group, University of Berne
Neubrückstrasse 10, 3012 Bern, Switzerland
{demeyer,meijler,rieger}@iam.unibe.ch
http://iamwww.unibe.ch/~{demeyer,meijler,rieger}

Summary

The ability to re-engineer object-oriented systems has become a vital matter in today's software industry. Early adopters of the object-oriented programming paradigm are now facing the problem of transforming their object-oriented "legacy" systems into full-fledged frameworks. As proclaimed by the industrial partners in the FAMOOS project[1], re-engineering object-oriented programs exceeding 10000 lines of poorly documented code requires support from tools as well as methodologies.

This document focuses on one particular aspect of object-oriented re-engineering, we refer to as *design pattern restructuring*. Our work envisions a re-engineering tool that supports the detection and reparation of certain design anomalies, based on a catalogue of anti patterns [Koen95] associated with appropriate design pattern [GHJV95] counterparts.

As an example of the envisioned tool support, consider the following code which instantiates classes in a widget library depending on a selected look and feel.

```
1. Window* newWindowWithScrollBars (LookAndFeel lookAndFeel,
2.     int top, int left, int bottom, int right)
3. {
4.   Window *window;
5.   ScrollBar *scrollBar;
6.   switch (lookAndFeel) {
7.     case presentation_manager:
8.       window = new PMWindow(top, left, bottom, right);
9.       scrollBar = new PMScrollBar(top, right-20,
10.        bottom-20, right);
11.      window->addWidget (*scrollBar);
12.      scrollBar = new PMScrollBar(bottom-20, left,
13.        bottom, right-20);
14.      window->addWidget (*scrollBar);
15.      break;
16.    case motif:
17.      ...;
18.    case macOS:
19.      ...;
20.    };
21.   return window;
22. };
```

---

[1] see http://iamwww.unibe.ch/~famoos/

This code — a case statement branching on the value of a type tag — is a typical anti-pattern (see [Cop92] for a discussion of the drawbacks), which can be restructured using an "Abstract Factory" into the code below.

```
1.  Window* newWindowWithScrollBars
2.        (AbstractWidgetFactory& factory,
3.        int top, int left, int bottom, int right)
4.  {
5.    Window *window;
6.    ScrollBar *scrollBar;
7.    window = factory.makeWindow(top,left, bottom, right);
8.    scrollBar = factory.makeScrollBar (top, right-20,
9.      bottom-20, right);
10.   window->addWidget (*scrollBar);
11.   scrollBar = factory.makeScrollBar(bottom-20, left, bottom,
12.     right-20);
13.   window->addWidget (*scrollBar);
14.   return window;
15. };
```

This kind of restructuring operation cannot be performed by typical refactoring tools ([Cas92][JO93]), because they would not be able to guarantee the preservation of semantics. Thus, to implement design pattern restructuring, we must abandon the notion of "preservation of semantics" altogether. We are currently continuing our work with FACE ([MDE97a][MDE97b][Mei93][Rie97]) to experiment with detecting anti-patterns and applying the appropriate design pattern restructuring. Similar kinds of experiments ([Brown][FMW97][JaZü97]) point out that it is at least worthwhile to explore this trail.

References

[Brown]   K. Brown: *Design Reverse-Engineering and Automated Design Pattern Detection in Smalltalk*. Thesis. See http://www.ksccary.com/kbrown.htm

[Cas92]   E. Casais: An Incremental Class Reorganization Approach. In *Proceedings ECOOP'92*, Lecture Notes in Computer Science 615, Springer-Verlag, pp. 114-132.

[Cop92]   J. O. Coplien: *Advanced C++ Programming Styles and Idioms*. Addison-Wesley, 1992.

[FMW97]   G. Florijn, M. Meijers, and P. Winsen: Tool Support for Object-Oriented Patterns. ECOOP'97 Proceedings.

[GHJV95] E. Gamma, R. Helm, R. Johnson, and J. Vlissides: *Design Patterns*. Addison-Wesley, 1995.

[JaZü97] J. Janhnke and A. Zündorf: Rewriting poor Design Patterns by good Design Patterns. To be presented at *the ESEC/FSE'97 Workshop on Object-Oriented Re-engineering*. See http://iamww.unibe.ch/~famoos/ESEC97/

[JO93]   R. E. Johnson and W. F. Opdyke: Refactoring and Aggregation. In *Object Technologies for Advanced Software — First JSSST International Symposium*, Lecture Notes in Computer Science 742, Springer-Verlag, Nov. 1993, pp. 264-278.

[Koen95]   A. Koenig: Patterns and antipatterns. *Journal of Object-Oriented Programming*, March-April 1995.

[Mei93]   T. D. Meijler: User-Level Integration of Data and Operations Resources by Means of a Self-descriptive Data Model. Ph.D. dissertation, Rotterdam, The Netherlands, 1993.

[MDE97a]   T. D. Meijler, S. Demeyer, and R. Engel: Class Composition in FACE, a Framework Adaptive Composition Environment. In *Special Issues in Object-Oriented Programming*, Max Mülhäuser (ed.), dpunkt.verlag, 1997.

[MDE97b]   T. D. Meijler, S. Demeyer, and R. Engel: Making Design Patterns Explicit in FACE. To appear in the *proceedings of the ESEC/FSE'97 Conference*.

[Rie97]   M. Rieger: *Implementing the FACE Object Model in C++*. Masters Thesis, IAM, University of Bern, 1997. Available via http://iamwww.unibe.ch/~rieger/

Similarity Measures for the Object Model

Akila Sarirete and Jean Vaucher

Département d'Informatique et de Recherche Opérationnelle,
Université de Montréal
C.P. 6128, Succursale Centre-Ville,
Montréal, Québec, Canada, H3C-3J7
email: {sarirete,vaucher}@iro.umontreal.ca

Summary

In order to improve the design and understanding of class libraries, researchers have proposed automatic class hierarchy redesign methods [Cas92], [GM93], [Anq96]. Generally, the restructuring process is done within a single library and is based on syntactic matching of class signatures derived from visible class attributes.

The present paper deals with another kind of matching, semantic or conceptual matching, and a similarity measure for object-based systems is proposed. This measure is based on the semantic relations between the words which identify concepts in the object model. Wordnet, a widely available computer thesaurus, has been used to provide semantic relations between terms. The similarity measure is applied to class libraries by combining it with other metrics based on the structure of the objects. The similarity measure and its derived metrics are used to improve the reusability process in object-based libraries.

The similarity measure is defined as a function S between two names (concept identifiers) N_1 and N_2. We assume that identifiers (names) can be divided into two categories: simple ones and compound ones. A simple name is some word with a sense in the English language or for the person who wrote it. It can be an abbreviation of some word like CL which means *Class*. Further, we assume that compound names can be split into simple ones by a heuristic on letter case or human intervention. For example, *remove_key* constitutes a compound name and is split into two simple names: *remove* and *key*.

Below, we consider the different computation cases of the similarity S:

- if N_1 and N_2 are identical then $S(N1, N2) = 1$; otherwise:
- if N_1 and N_2 are compound names as $N_1 = N_{11}\_N_{12}\text{-....-}N_{1n}$ and $N_2 = N_{21}\_N_{22}\text{-....-}N_{2m}$ then $S(N_1, N_2) = \frac{1}{l} \sum_{i=1, j=1}^{n,m} k_{ij}$ i.e the average similarity between all word pairs where $k_{ij} = S(N_{1i}, N_{2j})$ and $l = n * m$;
- if N_1 and N_2 are simple names, the computation of S is based on Wordnet semantic relations [Mil95] (synonymy, hypernymy and antonymy). S can be computed as follows:
  - if N_1 and N_2 are hypernyms then $S(N_1, N_2) = 1/2^n$ where n is the number of levels between N_1 and N_2 in the concept hierarchy of Wordnet

- if N_1 and N_2 are synonyms then $S(N_1, N_2) = 1 - \frac{1}{2^d}$ where d is the number of common concepts between the two names
- If N_1 and N_2 are antonyms then $S(N_1, N_2) = -1$

Based on the similarity measure S between names, we defined some metrics which help the comparison of two classes C and C_i. One of these measures is based on the neighbouring classes of the compared classes (super, sub and sister classes). It is defined as a contextual similarity: $Sim\_Parents(C, C_i) = \|Sup_C \cap Sup_{Ci}\| + \|Sub_C \cap Sub_{Ci}\| + \|Sister_C \cap Sister_{Ci}\|$. The other measure is based on the number of equivalent attributes between C and C_i ($\|Att_C \cap Att_{Ci}\|$).

Using the above measures and the similarity S, we made some tests on existing class libraries for data structures. We considered, in our experiments the *Settools* classes (9 classes)[Kir94] which we compared to three other libraries: *Structures* (17 classes) and *Containers* (24 classes) two other versions of *Settools* written in the Simula language; and basic classes of YACL library (64 classes) written in C++ by Sridhar [Sri95]. For each *Settools'* class, we defined a number of relevant answers and computed the similarity with the other classes of the existing libraries. The results demonstrated that the defined measures give relevant information comparing it to some traditional information retrieval measures [SM83]. [SV97] gives further discussion on results.

Using this method, a designer can browse class libraries efficiently and compare them to his specifications and needs. Future work is being done on larger hierarchies like Java Generic Library to improve the results.

References

[Anq96] Nicolas Anquetil. *Contributions à l'amélioration des modélisations à objets.* PhD thesis, Université de Montréal, Novembre 1996.

[Cas92] Eduardo Casais. An Incremental Class Reorganization Approach. In O. Lehrmann Madsen, editor, *ECOOP'92 Proceedings*, volume 615 of *Lecture Notes in Computer Science*, pages 114–132. Springer-Verlag, 1992.

[GM93] Robert Godin and Hafedh Mili. Building and Maintaining Analysis-Level Class Hierarchies Using Galois Lattices. *ACM SIGplan Notices*, 28(10):394–410, 1993. OOPSLA'93 Proceedings.

[Kir94] Bjørn. Kirkerud. *Programming with Simula Language*. Addison-Wesley Publishing Company, 1994.

[Mil95] George A. Miller. Wordnet: A Lexical Database for English. *Communications of the ACM*, 38(11):39–41, November 1995. Avalaible on web site: http://www.cogsci.princeton.edu/wn/.

[SM83] G. Salton and M.J. McGill. *Introduction to Modern Information Retrieval*. McGrawHill, New York, 1983.

[Sri95] M.A. Sridhar. *Building Portable C++ Applications with YACL (Yet Another C++ Library)*. Addison Wesley Publishing Company, 1995. Available on web site: http://www.cs.sc.edu/sridhar/yacl.html.

[SV97] Akila Sarirete and Jean Vaucher. Similarity measures for object-based representation systems. In *Second International KRUSE Symposium, Knowledge, Retrieval, Use and Storage for Efficiency*. Simon Fraser University, August 1997.

Modeling Software Processes and Artifacts

Introduction to ECOOP'97 Workshop 10
Jyväskylä, Finland, June 9, 1997

Klaas van den Berg
Twente Research & Education on Software Engineering
Faculty of Computer Science, University of Twente
P.O. Box 217, 7500 AE Enschede, the Netherlands
e-mail: vdberg@cs.utwente.nl

1 Introduction

The workshop on *Modeling Software Processes and Artifacts* has been attended by 16 researchers from 10 different countries. It explored the application of object technology in process modeling. The workshop was organized by *Mehmet Aksit, Klaas van den Berg* and *Pim van den Broek* (University of Twente), *Leon Osterweil* (University of Massachusetts), *Karl Lieberherr* (Northeastern University) and *Francesco Marcelloni* (University of Pisa), and was chaired by Mehmet Aksit. After the introduction by Klaas van den Berg and the invited lecture by *Reidar Conradi* (Norwegian University of Science and Technology), a number of participants presented their position papers and there was ample time for discussion. In this introduction, we first give an overview on some background work, and describe the aims, aspects and approaches in software process modeling, and then we shortly comment on the position papers in this reader.

2 History

Software process modeling has relatively a short tradition. Nowadays, there are several workshops and conferences being held yearly. The first international workshop ISPW-1 was held at Runnymede, UK, in 1984 [17]. At ISPW-6 in 1990 [11], an example was presented of a software process, which is being used as baseline for the comparison of software process models and environments. The first international conference on software process modeling, ICSP-1, was held at Redondo Beach, CA, USA, in 1991 [16]. European workshops on software process technology started at Milan, Italy, with EWSPT-1, also in 1991 [15]. Conferences on software process improvement SPI are closely related to the area of process modeling. At the International Conference on Software Engineering ICSE, there are also regularly contributions on process modeling topics. Some special issues of magazines were devoted to this area (1991, *Software Engineering Journal* 6(5); 1993, *IEEE Transactions on Software Engineering* 19(12)). Although there is no long research tradition in this area, there is already a vast amount of literature available and many research groups are active [18]. In Europe, the PROMOTOR Working Group co-ordinated several projects [8]. We briefly now describe some modeling issues, serving as background to the current workshop.

3 Aims

Curtis et al. (1992) [6] give the following overview with objectives and goals of software process modeling:

- Facilitate human understanding and communication: requires that a group is able to share a common representational format
- Support process improvement: requires a basis for defining and analysing processes
- Support process management: requires a defined process against which actual process behaviours can be compared
- Automatic guidance in performing process: requires automated tools for manipulating process descriptions
- Automatic execution support: requires a computational basis for controlling behaviour within an automated environment.

Obviously, automated process enactment requires a more detailed and formalised model then a model just aiming at human understanding the process.

4 Aspects

The goal of process improvement has been incorporated in the SEI Software Maturity Model and several key process areas have been identified [14]. These areas can be classified in addressing the following categories or aspects:

- Managerial, such as project planning, subcontract management.
- Organisational, i.e. process definition, change management.
- Engineering aspects: requirement analysis, design, coding, testing, etc.

It is clear that these aspects are present in software process modeling in general, as in the reference model for process technology presented by Christie et al. (1996) [5]. They distinguish four main elements: the enterprise operations, the process development, the enactment technology and the process assets. The enterprise operations deal with the process effectiveness of organisations, and the technology that exists to support that effectiveness. The process development deals with the construction of process technology assets. These assets support the organisational process activities. The enactment technology deals with the technology components that need to be in place for the construction of effective process enactment systems. The process assets are the parts in the process, which have to be designed for reuse and placed in an asset library.

5 Approaches

Basic concepts in software process modeling are the artifacts (i.e. the (sub-) products) and activities or process steps, which produce externally visible state changes to the artifacts [4][7]. Another important concept is the meta-process: the part of the process in charge of maintaining and evolving the whole process, i.e. the production process, its meta-process, and the process support.

As in traditional modeling techniques, one can focus on the data in the process, the artifacts, or on the transformation functions, the activities. Products and processes are dual entities. Some approaches in software modeling are process-centered and other approaches are product-centered. The relative merits of both approaches may become apparent in applying the approach to the Software Process Example [11].

6 Issues

Two of the key process areas in the capability maturity model at level four are the Quantitative Process Management, aiming at controlling the process performance quantitatively, and Software Quality Management, aiming at a quantitative understanding of the quality of the software products [14]. Attributes of process and product entities have to be identified and measures have to be defined and validated. However, many attributes are inherently uncertain [10]. Moreover, there are many ambiguities in the process steps. The quantitative support has to cope with uncertainty and ambiguity. Software products are evolving rapidly due to changing requirements, requiring a high adaptability of the products and composability of solutions. The productivity in software development heavily relies on the reusability of products and subproducts on all levels of the development: not only reuse of code, but also of design (for instance by design patterns), frameworks and software architectures. The products must be very adaptable to facilitate customization to new requirements.

7 Object Technology

Object technology has been used in process modeling at various levels. In an assessment of project within the PROMOTOR Working Group [8], it appears that object technology is used in the modeling phase of the basic components, in process modeling languages, in supporting tools and enactment engines, and in meta-processes. Object technology has some obvious advantages [3]. Objects provide structural and behavioural views of the system architecture; they provide reusability and encapsulation in design methods, and concurrency in complex systems. However, there are several obstacles in using traditional object oriented techniques [2]. Composition filters provide composable solutions [1], notably on concurrency and synchronisation.

8 Themes and Position Papers

In this workshop we consider software process modeling in the context of object technology. We can distinguish the role of object technology in the actual software development (analysis, design, implementation, etc.) as well as in the modeling and support of this development process. Both can be object-oriented or not. We focus on the OO-modeling and support of the software development process, on which OO-techniques are being used for what purpose, their strengths and weaknesses.
In the invited lecture, *Reidar Conradi* and *Chunnian Liu* give an overview of process-centered software engineering environments in the context of software process improvement. *Francesco Marcelloni* and *Mehmet Aksit* address the problem of uncertainty in object-oriented methods. They propose the use of fuzzy logic to handle this problem. *Wiebke Reimer* and *Wilhelm Schäfer* describe - in the position paper presented by *Thomas Schmal* - an extension to the object-oriented process modeling language ESCAPE, which copes with process and configuration management. *Pavel*

Hruby discusses the advantages of a product based development process. In the paper on active software artifacts, *Mehmet Aksit et al.* propose a framework for software production in which decisions made by software developers are incorporated into the software itself - the active artifacts - making the software more reusable and adaptable. *Jean Bézivin* uses object composability techniques in the definition of process models. *Jun Han* discusses the integration of process and artifact modeling using object technology. Finally, *Ilia Bider* and *M. Khomyakov* include business processes in the object-oriented process model to handle dynamic and distributed planning.

9 References

[1] Aksit, M, Wakita, K., Bosch, J., Bergmans, L., & Yonezawa, A. (1993). *Abstracting Object Interactions using Composition Filters*. In ECOOP '93, Workshop on Object-Based Distributed Programming, LNCS 791, pp. 152-184, Springer, Berlin.

[2] Aksit, M. & Bergmans, L. (1992). *Obstacles in Object-oriented Software Development*. OOPSLA '92, ACM SIGPLAN Notices Vol. 27, No. 10, pp. 341-358.

[3] Aliee, F.S. & Warboys, B.C. (1995). *Applying Object-Oriented Modelling to Support Process Technology*. Proceedings IDPT-Vol. 1 A. Ertag et al., Eds., Austin Texas.

[4] Conradi, R., Fernström, C. & Fuggetta, A. (1994). *Concepts for Evolving Software Processes*. In: Finkelstein et al. (1994), pp 9-31.

[5] Christie, A.M., Earl, A.N., Kellner, M.I. & Riddle, W.E. (1996). *A Reference Model for Process Technology*. In: Montangero (1996), pp. 3-17.

[6] Curtis, B., Kellner, M.I. & Over, J. (1992). *Process Modeling*. Comm. ACM, Vol. 35 No 9, pp. 75-90.

[7] Feiler, P.H. & Humphrey, W.S. (1992). *Software Process Development and Enactment*, (CMU/SEI-92-TR-04, ADA258465). Pittsburgh, PA: SEI, Carnegie Mellon University.

[8] Finkelstein, A., Kramer, J. & Nuseibeh, B. (1994). *Software Process Modelling and Technology*. Wiley, New York.

[9] Fuggetta, A. & Wolf, A. (1996). *Software Process*. Wiley, Chichester.

[10] Huff, K.E. (1996). *Software Process Modeling*. In: Fuggetta & Wolf (1996), pp. 1-24.

[11] Kellner, M.I., Feiler, P.H., Finkelstein, A., Katayama, T., Osterweil, L.J., Penedo, M.H. & Rombach, H.D. (1990). *Software Process Example*, Proceedings ISPW-6, T. Katayama Ed., IEEE Computer Society Press.

[12] Montangero, C. (1996). *Software Process Technology*. Proceedings 5th European Workshop, EWSPT'96, LNCS 1149, Springer, Berlin.

[13] Lonchamp, J. (1994). *An Assessment Exercise*. In: Finkelstein et al. (1994), pp. 335-356.

[14] Paulk, M. C. et al. (1993). *Capability Maturity Model for Software*, (CMU/SEI-93-TR-24), *Key Practices of the Capability Maturity Model*, (CMU/SEI-93-TR-25), Version 1.1, Pittsburgh, PA: SEI, Carnegie Mellon University.

[15] *Proceedings of the First European Workshop on Software Process Modeling* (1991), Milan, Italy.

[16] *Proceedings of the First International Conference on the Software Process* (1991), IEEE Computer Society, Washington, DC.

[17] *Proceedings of the First International Software Process Workshop* (1984), ISPW-1, Runnymede, UK, IEEE Computer Society.

[18] See for instance: http://hamlet.cogsci.umassd.edu/SWPI/1docs/SPResearch.html

Revised PMLs and PSEEs for Industrial SPI

Reidar Conradi
Norw. Univ. of Science and Technology
N-7034 Trondheim, Norway
conradi@idi.ntnu.no

Chunnian Liu
Beijing Polytechnic Univ.
Beijing 100022, P.R. of China
bpvliu@public.bta.net.cn

1 Introduction

In the last decade, there has been much interest in *software process improvement (SPI)* [PWCC95]. Such improvement is supposed to lead to better product quality, better productivity, lower time-to-market, better predictability, etc. etc.

Many *Process-Centered Software Engineering Environments (PSEEs)* have been designed and prototyped by researchers [FKN94]. A few of these have become commercially available. However, concrete benefits of PSEEs for software practitioners have not been properly validated by industrial case studies or experiments. On the other hand, there is a growing interest in workflow technologies, often applied to more automatable office processes. In addition, there is much recent technology for distributed computing and CSCW, and all this may be exploited in PSEEs to a larger extent.

The **goal of this paper** is to (re)assess the focus and technology base of PSEEs against the needs of industrial SPI. Revised requirements for effective and practical SPI support will be formulated, e.g. for process modeling languages (PMLs) and their PSEE realization. The overall role of a PSEE to achieve effective and validatable SPI will also be elaborated.

2 PMLs/PSEEs vs. Real SPI: Status and Experiences

SPI has organizational / human components ("humanics"), as well as technical ones. In addition, we must consider possibly continuous changes in problem focus and requirements, caused by customer and market pressure.

Presently, process follow-up in software engineering projects is done according to a fairly coarse-level process model, often a project plan through PERT charts. Companies usually have own project or quality handbooks – sometimes shelves of these – serving as company standards, and often coming out of ISO-9001 certification efforts. Many organizations – such as the Norwegian software houses Telenor FoU, NOVIT, Computas and ISI – have recently converted their project handbooks into web-based documents. The notation used in these documents is informal flow diagrams and prose, such as at AT&T, NASA-SEL, and Statoil of Norway. The simple flow formalisms seem adequate for both modeling and analysis.

In the PhD thesis of Høydalsvik [Høy97], it is claimed that existing PSEEs have not shown overall cost-effectiveness for process modeling, as present PMLs are too weird.

On the other hand, use of conventional project management tools, such as MS/Project, is hampered by massive and unpredictable process evolution during project execution, e.g. because of unstable requirements.

The starting point for more industrial SPI is therefore:
- rather informal process modeling,
- almost no computer-assisted process enactment,
- problems to follow-up real process evolution,
- few on-line and shared experience databases,
- coarse-level and project-oriented metrics,
- a need to cover all SPI meta-phases in Plan-Do-Check-Act (PDCA),
- a need to disseminate SPI results to all personnel.

On the other hand, there is:
- increased use of web-based project handbooks,
- a growing use of distributed technologies,
- a growing process awareness.

Our strategy must be an incremental improvement of this technology base to initiate, support and sustain real SPI. We must also continuously validate the given process technology against industrial needs, by careful and metrified studies recorded in an experience database.

3   Revised Requirements for PMLs

Almost every process modeling research group has developed their "own" PML. We can, of course, subjectively compare these PMLs according to some "wish lists" (most of them are 4-5 years old). However, there are few usage reports to quantitatively or qualitatively assess the different PMLs. In addition, the quality of a PSEE that implements a given PML may dominate over PML-specific features.

Below we will very briefly summarize the key PML requirements, based on our own and others' experiences, and contribute some final advice. The software process has two main components: a production process and a meta-process, and both must be modeled.

First, there are distinct meta-process phases to be supported, each with different emphasis. For example, the Quality Improvement Paradigm (QIP [Bas93]) with six phases (S1–S6) in the style of PDCA:

S1. Establish baseline of e.g. last 5–10 projects.
S2. Set quantitative improvement goals.
S3. Plan a revised and metrified process.
S4. Execute process, with measurement collection.
S5. Analyze results.
S6. Package results for future reuse and learning.

Secondly, there are distinct process categories, each with different needs for PSEE support [CE94]:

- **Development tasks**, performed by a single person or by a team – some are more creative tasks (design work), others being more routine.

- **Clerical tasks**, performed similarly.
- **Planning and coordination tasks**, performed similarly.

Finally, there are some technical or domain-specific demands:

- **Coverage of the core process elements (five)**, being activities/tasks/roles, products (artifacts), humans, tools, and projects. For activity modeling it is common to use task networks / state charts, rule-based reasoning, concurrent programs, or hybrids of these [CLJ91].
- **Coverage of the core meta-process**: i.e. incremental evolution with delayed binding and filling-in of details, and later on-the-fly changes in the model. This often means an interpretative language, cf. PROLOG and Java.
- **Coverage of auxiliary process elements (at least six)**: work contexts, metrics and quality models, versioning and transactions, cooperation patterns, tool interfaces, and user interfaces.
- **Abstraction and reuse facilities**: Multiple abstraction levels, modularization, customization etc. to support model engineering.
- **Multiple and possibly conflicting views**, e.g. the view of a developer or tester, the view of a project manager or designer, or the degree of process conformance. Views represent a well-known though hard problem, Simple views can be alternative representations of model elements, e.g. duplicate tool descriptions inside a DBMS schema or process model, or alternative process perspectives shown in a user interface.
- **Understandability**: Clarity, simplicity and a user-friendly notation.
- **Formalization**: minimal, orthogonal and analyzable models.

Discussion:

Language design is difficult, so what to consider most and first? Indeed, what constitutes a high-quality process model, and what are the corresponding demands for a "good" modeling language? Further, what are the special requirements for a PML compared to other modeling languages, e.g. for enterprise modeling or for conceptual modeling? Lastly, we do not completely control the design space, since the process owner already may have invested in certain process/project models and tools. Thus interoperability of (sub)models and tools should be emphasized.

In [CL95], it was discussed to have an extensible core PML. Outside this comes a spectrum of either "compatible" (with overlapping or connected domains) or "non-compatible" sub-languages (with disjoint domains), to express e.g. metrics, cooperation, or versioning. In [ACF94], the experiences in building and designing three PSEEs (EPOS, OIKOS, SPADE) were discussed, and with similar advices for the PMLs. In [SO97], a new PML called JIL is proposed, with rich mechanisms for process control, composition, evolution.

As a conclusion, we may state that the underlying linguistic paradigm for a core PML is not paramount. More important factors are:
- Standardization on common platforms (for reuse),
- Interoperability and modularity of process elements,
- User interface with comprehensible process views,

– Easy user-level evolution of the process model,
– Validation of PML functionality to actual processes.

4 A Revised Focus and Architecture of PSEEs

In general, we know how to build an open-ended and robust PSEE. Its main components are:
– a process model in some repository,
– a process engine to interpret the process model,
– a tool interface towards development tools,
– a similar interface towards a product workspace,
– a user interface towards human process agents, and
– a tool interface against other process engines.
There may be a project hierarchy of models and corresponding engines. Again, the underlying PML concepts are rather independent of the PSEE architecture.

The Process Engine stands in architectural layers, such as:
4. Project management, of high-level process.
3. Process Engine for medium-level process.
2. Transaction and Version Manager.
1. DBMS, for data modeling and basic facilities.

In addition we must relate to "standards", such as web, Java and CORBA, and modern principles for building federated and distributed systems etc. Indeed, the new possibilities facilitated by the web and the previous comments on requirements give rise to the following, proposed PSEE architecture:

- **The main view of the process model should be simple flow diagrams**, represented by web-documents (in *html*), and possibly versioned. The process model should be annotated with (hidden) pre/post-conditions, scripts etc. for formal analysis and computerized enactment.
- **A central experience base**, with reusable process models, product models, and quality models (e.g. metrics and error distributions). These can partly be web-documents and partly be information contained in a full-fledged DBMS such as Oracle. Central SPEG (Software Process Engineering Group) people and other project managers are the users of the base.
- **Local project databases**, similarly.
- **A set of process tools for model editing, presentation, query, analysis and synthesis**, working upon the above databases and producing web-documents. This set-up conforms to modern principles for building client/server systems.
- **Decentralization and distribution** of such models and associated metrics through the web.
- **Using Java as a bottom-level PML**, with standard interpreters as Process Engines to execute "active" applets (process scripts) on process model documents. During execution, coordination messages are issued towards other tools, agents and process engines in a non-intrusive way.

- **Local product workspaces (WS)**, with normal development tools. Often the WSs are web-based also, and there are upcoming versioning standards for web-documents.
- **Process model evolution**, by incremental and interpretative execution of such process models.

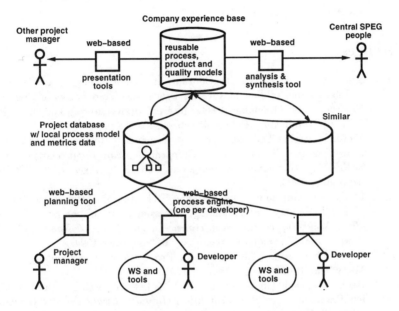

Fig. 1. Proposed process support architecture on the web.

Figure 1 shows the resulting PSEE architecture. This PSEE has a low start cost, both wrt. commitment, training and tool support on standard platforms. It can reuse existing process handbooks on the web, and make them "active". It can gradually phase in use of metrics as part of the process model. Overall distribution and reuse of models is generally supported.

5 Conclusion

It is crucial to couple further PML/PSEE work with actual SPI support. However, practical PMLs and their PSEEs must cover more than "concurrent programming".

We propose to let our SPI work be done in the context of the Norwegian SPIQ project (SPI for better Quality) in 1997-2001. Here, 15 companies will work

together with NTNU and other R&D institutions, and many of these already
have web-based project handbooks.

This effort will be coordinated with a basic research project project, CAGIS
(Cooperating Agents in the Global Information Space) in 1996-1999, dealing
with web-based process, transaction and document models.

Acknowledgements

Thanks for stimulating discussions to participants of the five European Software Process Workshops and to colleagues in the PROMOTER(2) ESPRIT Basic
Research Actions, in the years 1991–97.

References

[ACF94]   Vincenzo Ambriola, Reidar Conradi, and Alfonso Fuggetta. Experiences
and Issues in Building and Using Process-centered Software Engineering
Environments, December 1994. Internal draft paper V3.0, Univ. Pisa /
NTH in Trondheim / Politecnico di Milano, 28 p.

[Bas93]   Victor R. Basili. The Experience Factory and its Relationship to Other Im-
provement Paradigms. In *Proc. European Software Engineering Conference
(ESEC'93), Garmisch, Germany*, pages 68–83. Springer Verlag LNCS 717,
September 1993.

[CE94]   Reidar Conradi and Jacky Estublier. The Major Software Process Cate-
gories: Taxonomy and Technology Assessment. In *Magne Haveraaen (ed.):
Proc. Norsk Informatikk Konferanse – NIK'94, 14–16 Nov. 1995, Molde.
Tapir Forlag, Trondheim.*, pages 53–66, November 1994.

[CL95]   Reidar Conradi and Chunnian Liu. Process Modelling Languages: One or
Many? In *[Wil95]*, pages 98–118, 1995.

[CLJ91]   Reidar Conradi, Chunnian Liu, and M. Letizia Jaccheri. Process Model-
ing Paradigms. In *Proc. 7th International Software Process Workshop –
ISPW'7, Yountville (Napa Valley), CA, USA, 16–18 Oct. 1991, IEEE–CS
Press*, pages 51–53, 1991.

[FKN94]   Anthony Finkelstein, Jeff Kramer, and Bashar A. Nuseibeh, editors. *Software Process Modelling and Technology.* Advanced Software Development
Series, Research Studies Press/John Wiley & Sons, 1994. ISBN 0-86380-
169-2, 362 p.

[Høy97]   Geir Magne Høydalsvik. *Experiences in Software Process Modelling and
Enactment.* PhD thesis, IDI, NTNU, March 1997. 237 p. (IDI-rapport
6/97, dr.ing. thesis 1997:32 at NTNU).

[PWCC95] Marc C. Paulk, Charles V. Weber, Bill Curtis, and Mary B. Chrissis. *The
Capability Maturity Model for Software: Guidelines for Improving the Software Process.* SEI Series in Software Engineering. 640 p. Addison–Wesley,
1995.

[SO97]   Stanley M. Sutton and Leon Osterweil. The Design of a Next-Generaton
Process Language. In *Proc. ESEC'97/FSY'97 (forthcoming)*, Zuerich,
September 1997. (Preliminary version, 26 p.).

[Wil95]   Wilhelm Schäfer, editor. *Proc. Fourth European Workshop on Software
Process Technology (EWSPT'95), Noordwijkerhout, The Netherlands. 261
p.* Springer Verlag LNCS 913, April 1995.

Applying Fuzzy Logic Techniques in Object-Oriented Software Development

Francesco Marcelloni[1] and Mehmet Aksit[2]

[1] Department of Information Engineering, University of Pisa,
Via Diotisalvi, 2-56126, Pisa, Italy.
email: france@iet.unipi.it
[2] TRESE Project, Department of Computer Science University of Twente,
P.O. Box 217, 7500 AE Enschede, The Netherlands.
Email: aksit@cs.utwente.nl, www server: http://wwwtrese.cs.utwente.nl

1 Introduction

In the last several years, a considerable number of object-oriented methods have been introduced to create robust, reusable and adaptable software systems [1], [2], [3], [4]. Object-oriented methods define a considerable number of rules which are generally expressed by using two-valued logic. For instance, an entity in a requirement specification is either accepted or rejected as a class. We consider two major problems in the way how rules are defined and applied in current object-oriented methods. The first problem, termed quantization problem, is a natural result of the incapacity of two-valued logic to express the approximate and inexact nature of a typical software development process. The second problem, termed contextual bias problem, arises because most of methods are not able to model the effects of the context on the validity of the method. To reduce these problems, we propose a new fuzzy logic-based object-oriented software development technique. This technique is not specific to a particular object-oriented method, but can be used to evaluate and enhance current methods. In addition, the application of fuzzy logic-based reasoning opens new perspectives to software development, such as fuzzy artifacts and accumulative software life-cycle.

2 Problem Statement

2.1 The Quantization Problem

Object-oriented methods exploit object-oriented concepts through the application of a large number of rules [1], [2], [3], [4]. For example, OMT [4] introduces rules for identifying and discarding classes, associations, part-of and inheritance relations, state-transition and data-flow diagrams. Basically, these rules are based on two-valued logic. However, two-valued logic does not provide an effective means for capturing the approximate and inexact nature of a typical software development process. Let us consider, for instance, the following rule, termed *Candidate Class Identification*, which is typically applied to identify a candidate class:

IF AN ENTITY IN A REQUIREMENT SPECIFICATION IS RELEVANT
AND CAN EXIST AUTONOMOUSLY IN THE APPLICATION DOMAIN
THEN SELECT IT AS A CANDIDATE CLASS

The software engineer has to determine whether the entity being considered is relevant or not for the application domain. The software engineer may conclude that the entity partially fulfils the relevance criterion, and may prefer to use expressions like the entity is 70% percent relevant or substantially relevant. However, two-valued logic forces the software engineer to take crisp decisions, such as accepting or rejecting the entity as a class and, then, to quantize the available information into fixed levels. This quantization process results in a high quantization error and consequently in loss of information because the partial relevance of the entity is not modeled and cannot be considered explicitly in the subsequent phases. Referring to the area of digital signal processing where quantization errors have been extensively studied, the root mean square value of the quantization error can be also formulated for the software development process. For instance, we evaluated that the information contained in the conclusion inferred from rule *Candidate Class Identification* is only 71.7 percent of the available information present at the input of the rule. Further, we verified that coupling of rules, which is typically adopted in software development methods, increases dramatically the loss of information.

2.2 The Contextual Bias Problem

Contextual factors may influence validity of the result of a rule in two ways. Firstly, the input of a rule can be largely context-dependent. In the rule *Candidate Class Identification*, the relevance and autonomy of an entity depend on the perception of the software engineer. Secondly, the validity of a rule may largely depend on factors such as the application domain, changes in user's interest, and technological advances. Unless the contextual factors that influence a given rule are defined explicitly, the applicability of that rule cannot be determined and controlled effectively.

3 Our Approach

In the previous sections, we discussed the quantization and the contextual bias problems. An obvious solution to reduce the quantization error is to increase the number of quantization levels. In the *Candidate Class Identification* rule, the relevance of an entity can be expressed only as relevant or not relevant. To increase the number of quantization levels, we have to split the range of relevance into more levels such as *weakly, slightly, fairly, substantially* and *strongly* relevant. This transformation is not forced as a software engineer naturally expresses these gradual perceptions. Although each level can correspond to a crisp set, we observed that, for most of the inputs, the transition between membership and non-membership appears gradual rather than abrupt. On the other hand, in two-valued logic defining this crisp boundary is necessary because a proposition can be either true or false. It is therefore worth to investigate other forms of logic than two-valued logic, such as fuzzy logic.

In fuzzy logic, the concept of vagueness is introduced by the definition of fuzzy set. A fuzzy set S of a universe of discourse U is characterized by a membership function which associates with each element y of U a number in the interval $[0, 1]$ which represents the grade of membership of y in S [5]. Based on the definition of fuzzy sets, the concept of linguistic variables is introduced to represent a language typically adopted by a human expert. A *linguistic variable* is a variable whose values, called *linguistic values*, have the form of phrases or sentences in a natural or artificial language [5]. For instance, the relevance of an entity in a requirement specification can be modeled as a linguistic variable which might assume linguistic values *weakly, slightly, fairly, substantially*, and *strongly* relevant.

Each linguistic value is associated with a fuzzy set representing its meaning. To represent multiple levels conveniently, also rules have to be modified and expressed in terms of fuzzy logic. For instance, the *Candidate Class Identification* fuzzy rule is:

IF AN ENTITY IN A REQUIREMENT SPECIFICATION IS *Relevance_Value* RELEVANT
AND CAN EXIST *Autonomy_Value* IN THE APPLICATION DOMAIN
THEN SELECT IT AS A *Relevance_Value* RELEVANT CANDIDATE CLASS

Here, an entity and a candidate class are the concepts to be reasoned, and *Relevance_Value* and *Autonomy_Value* indicate the domains of properties *Relevance* and *Autonomy* of these concepts. Assume that *Relevance_Value* and *Autonomy_Value* represent the sets of values { *Weakly, Slightly, Fairly, Substantially, Strongly*} and {*Dependently, Partially Dependently, Fully Autonomously*}, respectively. Each combination of relevance and autonomy values of an entity has to be mapped into one of the five candidate class relevance values. This requires 15 rules (*subrules*) in total. An example of subrule is the following:

IF AN ENTITY IN A REQUIREMENT SPECIFICATION IS STRONGLY RELEVANT
AND CAN EXIST FULLY AUTONOMOUSLY IN THE APPLICATION DOMAIN
THEN SELECT IT AS A STRONGLY RELEVANT CANDIDATE CLASS

We would like to point out that the shift from two-valued to fuzzy logic rules in software development is quite natural. This is because most object-oriented design rules are applied to uncertain and vague domains.

To reduce the contextual bias problem, the influence of the context on the results inferred from the design rules has to be formulated. By increasing the number of quantization levels, contextual factors such as, for instance, software engineer's perception, affect less the inputs of the rules. Further, the effect of contextual factors on the validity of a rule can be reduced by modeling the influence of the context explicitly. This can be obtained by adapting the meaning of linguistic values based on contextual factors, that is, by translating, compressing or dilating the corresponding membership functions. The degree of translation, compression or dilation has to be related to the contextual factors. In general, it is not possible to formalize analytically this relation and therefore heuristics have to be adopted. Since rules defining the effect of contextual factors are typically expressed in terms of linguistic expressions, fuzzy logic is again used to implement these rules. The linguistic values inferred from these rules determine the type and the degree of transformation of the membership functions.

4 Evaluation of the Method

As well as reducing the quantization error, the increase of the number of quantization levels coupled with the use of fuzzy logic allows a software engineer to deal with design rules expressed in more familiar way. Further, the conclusion inferred from each design rule is not an crisp decision on maintaining or eliminating an artifact. Two-valued logic, not being able to express intermediate levels, causes the elimination of artifacts even if all the relevant information is not collected. In the fuzzy logic-based method each artifact (called *fuzzy artifact*) collects fuzzy information and survives during the whole software process. From this viewpoint, the fuzzy logic-based method can be considered as a learning process; a new aspect of the problem being considered is learned after the application of each rule. Only when all the relevant information is collected, a fuzzy artifact can be transformed into an artifact and then maintained or eliminated.

It follows that during the development process an entity can be considered, for instance, both as an attribute and as a class. It is the learning process which tips the scales in favour of one or the other concept, deciding for the elimination of one of the two fuzzy artifacts. To avoid early elimination of artifacts means, however, to increase the cost of the development process. A possible CASE environment has to maintain all the fuzzy artifacts in each phase of the development. Anyway, most concepts will be likely to have the lowest grade of property values. This makes it possible to minimize storage requirements by registering only the artifacts that have a grade of property values over a fixed threshold. Similar to designing digital signal processing systems, the fuzzy logic-based method provides a unique opportunity to tune the quality of the development process with respect to memory and processing costs.

References

1. Booch, G.: Object-Oriented Design with Applications. The Benjamin/Cummings Publishing Company, Inc. (1991).
2. Coleman, D. et al.: Object-Oriented Development, The Fusion Method. Prentice Hall (1994).
3. Jacobson, I., Christerson, M., Jonsson, P., Overgaard, G.: Object-Oriented Software Engineering – A Use Case Driven Approach. Addison-Wesley/ACM Press, (1992).
4. Rumbaugh, J., Blaha, M., Premerlani, W., Eddy, F., Lorensen, W.: Object-Oriented Modeling and Design. Prentice-Hall, Inc., (1991).
5. Zadeh, L.A.: Outline of a New Approach to the Analysis of Complex Systems and Decision Processes. IEEE Transactions on Systems, Man, and Cybernetics **SMC-3** 1 (1973) 28-44.

Towards a Dedicated Object Oriented
Software Process Modelling Language

Wiebke Reimer, Wilhelm Schäfer, Thomas Schmal
{wiebke|wilhelm|schmal}@uni-paderborn.de
Dep. of Computer Science, Software Engineering Group
University of Paderborn, D-33095 Paderborn

Abstract

This paper reports our experience in designing the executable object-oriented software process modelling language *ESCAPE+*. Starting with a flexible, OMT-like language, we extended the run-time system with specific process and software configuration management functionality which is accessible to process engineers through particular pre-defined classes.

Motivation

The enormous increase in complexity and size of software products leads to increasing problems of management of large sets of documents, consistency preservation of frequently changing document versions, and coordination of team work. Software configuration management (SCM) and Software Process Management are complementary methodical approaches to keep these problems under control. They can be exploited best in the form of a process modelling language (PML) which encompasses SCM aspects, instead of basing one of the approaches on top of the other. Executable PMLs enable the construction of process-centred software development environments. That is, the run-time system of the PML provides process support in accordance with the specified process model (PM).

Like with any language, it is important that there be common understanding of a PML among its designers, implementors and users. *Designers* define the PML. *Implementors* develop tools for the PML, such as process model editors, static and dynamic analysers of (executable) PMs, and, not to forget, the run-time system itself. *Users* of the PML, called *process engineers*, specify PMs. The syntax and semantics definition that designers provide for implementors and process engineers must be as precise as possible in order to avoid the ambiguities and subtleties common to natural language. Only this enables the effective use of the PML: creating, understanding, reusing, modifying and analysing PMs. It can even enable a (partly) generation of PML tool implementations.

We distinguish between the *static* and the *dynamic semantics* of a language. The latter is "the meaning" of a phrase in that language. The former, also called context-sensitive syntax, defines constraints on the well-formedness of a phrase which go beyond context-free grammar.

Object-oriented languages allow for reusability through class libraries. Specialization and instantiation are examples for re-use mechanisms. Often it is not easy to properly use a library class: There are (not explicitly stated) restrictions on both the *static* properties and the *dynamic* behaviour of a using class. That is, the pre-defined library elements carry a specific semantics. We argue for promoting these elements into the language in order to be able to define and automatically control such static and dynamic semantics constraints.

In this paper we investigate the PML *ESCAPE+*. We start by describing its predecessor *ESCAPE* which is very flexible but provides only a few dedicated concepts to define process management. *ESCAPE+* is an extension of *ESCAPE* which includes pre-defined library classes that have a particular, complex semantics. For example, a number of classes define a general model for SCM. This is comparable to "OO-Frameworks" (which are, unlike Design Patterns, executable). In order to ensure the correct usage of these pre-defined elements we defined a dedicated, very rigorous inheritance model which became an integral part of the new language, namely *ESCAPE+*.

Where we started

ESCAPE [Jun95] is an executable object-oriented PML which enables the construction of a flexible process-centred software development environment. As a modification of OMT [RBP+91] it incorporates the flexibility and power of object oriented specification. Several real-world PMs have been specified in *ESCAPE*, like e.g. the configuration management process of a large local computer vendor.

A PM in *ESCAPE* consists of three parts: The Object Model defines static properties such as inheritance hierarchies of document classes, association types, attributes and methods applicable to instances of a class. The Coordination Model contains a statechart for each document class. The Organisation Model defines role types and their responsibilities. In contrast to OMT, *ESCAPE* defines in detail the static semantic constraints between all these parts and thus makes them amendable to automatic control.

Looking at the PMs specified in *ESCAPE* we have made the following observations:

- We identified sub-models which are part of almost every PM, with very few variations between the different occurrences. Especially, software configuration management had been specified in a very similar manner in these PMs.
- There were many constraints on how to correctly re-use pre-defined classes.

Where we are now

The design of *ESCAPE+* was oriented towards the following objectives which emerged from the above observations:

- We wanted to make SCM and other recurrent process management concepts an integral part of the run-time system. This relieves process engineers from modelling these complex, but apparently relatively fixed parts of a PM. Further, it enables to provide more sophisticated and efficiently implemented support without introducing low-level, procedural programming language constructs into the PML.
- The pre-defined functionality should be customizeable.
- The constraints on how to correctly customize should be automatically controllable.

To attain these aims, we took the following approach: We pre-defined several classes which have a particular process- or SCM-related dynamic semantics. This semantics is not modelled in the PML but hard-coded in the run-time system.

Fig. 1 shows an excerpt of the Object Model where pre-defined classes are shaded.

As an example for pre-defined *process-related semantics* take class FullyGeneratedDoc. At run-time, an instance of this class is automatically created when Generate is executed on an instance of a class to which the former has an association edge of type generated-from. For the specialized classes this means that compiling (com-

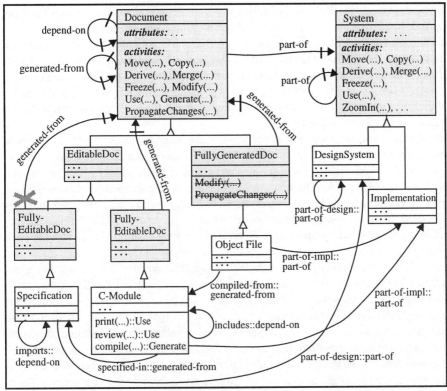

Figure 1: An Object Model with pre-defined and specialized classes

pile) a C-Module creates an instance of ObjectFile and relates the two instances by a compiled-from-edge. Class System implements an aggregate type. Some activities in System and Document perform aggregate-related functionality, such as moving a component from one aggregate to another (Move).

Activities Derive and Freeze manipulate version histories, i.e. they implement pre-defined *SCM-related semantics*. The statecharts of pre-defined classes restrict their instances' behaviour to an order of activity calls which is sensible w.r.t. SCM. E.g. deriving a new version from a document can only be done after it has been frozen, and once it has been frozen, it can no longer be modified. Versioning is also provided for class System, which enables to build hierarchical configurations.

In order to provide this complex built-in functionality, we must ensure that any class, any activity a.s.o. specified by the user can be classified w.r.t this base functionality. We achieve this by *(a)* requiring that classes defined by the process engineer be derived (directly or indirectly) from a pre-defined class, and by *(b)* defining a rigorous inheritance model. By doing so, the pre-defined classes have become an indispensable part of the run-time system and are thus part of the PML.

Briefly, this inheritance model allows for *specializing* or *deleting* model elements, but *not* for *adding* new ones. This holds for Object Model elements such as activities, attributes, association roles, and for elements of the Coordination Model such as states, transitions, transition labels etc. Requiring that user-defined elements be *specializations* of pre-defined ones allows us to associate a pre-defined semantics with them.

An example for this can be seen in class C-Module. The inherited pre-defined activity Use has been specialized into two activities print and review. This means that with regard to the pre-defined process-semantics, both activities behave like Use. Yet in C-Module's statechart, the process engineer can distinguish between them and specify, for instance, that printing a C-Module is allowed at any time, whereas a review cannot be made until editing is finished.

On the other hand, we must also allow for *deleting* inherited properties: Since we prohibit extensions to a PM, the pre-defined PM must include whatever can make sense in a user-defined PM. Not all these pre-defined elements must appear in a user-defined PM, but some of them do. Therefore most PM elements are attributed either mandatory or optional (which is not always shown in Fig.1). mandatory elements must not be deleted. Note that unlike the multiplicity of association roles in OMT, this is a type-level constraint. When specializing such an element, the constraint can be strengthened from optional to mandatory, but not the other way round.

In Fig. 1, the short line crossing one side of an association edge defines that this association role is optional. generated-from, for instance, is pre-defined in class Document with both roles being optional. For class FullyEditableDocument, the outgoing association edge is deleted. Partly- and FullyGeneratedDocs, in contrast, must have an outgoing association edge of type generated from, therefore the corresponding document types redefine the outgoing association role as being mandatory. The other association role remains optional, meaning that not every class derived from Document must be target of an associate edge derived from generated-from. Association compiled-from in class ObjectFile is a user-defined specialization of generated-from.

ESCAPE+ is subject of a forthcoming dissertation [Sac97]. In [NSS96] we presented an earlier version of *ESCAPE+* which did not yet fully incorporate the rigorous inheritance model, thus still imposing implicit specialization restrictions.

References

[Jun95]   G. Junkermann. A Dedicated Process Design Language based on EER-models, Statecharts and Tables. In *Proc. of the 7th Int. Conf. on Software Engineering and Knowledge Engineering*, Rockville, Maryland, USA. 1995

[NSS96]   O. Neumann, S. Sachweh, W. Schäfer. A High-Level Object-Oriented Specification Language for Configuration Management and Tool Integration. In C. Montangero, ed., *Proc. of the 5th European Workshop on Software Process Technology*, p. 137–143. Springer Verlag, Nancy, France, Oct. 1996.

[RBP+91] J. Rumbaugh, M. Blaha, W. Premerlani, F. Eddy, W. Lorensen. *Object–Oriented Modeling and Design*. Prentice Hall, Englewood Cliffs, N. J. 07632, 1991.

[Sac97]   S. Sachweh. *KoKoS – Ein kooperatives Konfigurationsmanagementsystem*. PhD thesis, Univ. of Paderborn, Germany, to appear in 1997.

The Object Model for a Product Based Development Process

Pavel Hruby
Navision Software A/S, Frydenlunds Allé 6, 2950 Vedbaek, Denmark
E-mail: ph@navision.com, homepage: www.navision.com

Abstract

The traditional workflow process model is typically illustrated with a graph of activities, tasks, deliverables and techniques. From an object-oriented perspective, every identifiable concept can be depicted with an object, and from this same perspective, evolution can be demonstrated with object interactions. There are at least two ways to describe the software development process using an object-oriented model. The first, an activity-based approach, uses activities as objects, tasks as object operations and deliverables as operation postconditions. The second, a deliverable-based approach, uses deliverables as objects, tasks as object operations and activities as object states. Techniques are considered the implementation of operations in both cases. The article will:

a) compare activity-based and deliverable-based object models of development processes and

b) describe our experience with a deliverable-based object model that we used for about one year when we developed an application used for financial management.

The Workflow Model

This section defines the terminology used throughout this article. *Tasks* (in this article) are small behavioral units that usually result in a deliverable. Some examples of tasks are: construction of a use case model, construction of a class model and writing of code. *Techniques* are formulas for performing tasks, for example, functional decomposition, using CRC cards, and programming in Smalltalk. *Deliverables* are final or intermediate products resulting from software development, for example, a use case model, a class model, or source code. *Activities* (in this report) are units that are larger than task units. Activities typically include several tasks and deliverables. Some examples of activities are requirements analysis, logical design and implementation.

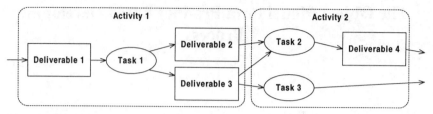

Fig. 1. Workflow model of a development process.

The Object-Oriented Model – with Activities as Objects

In an activity-based approach, the activities are modeled as objects, and tasks are modeled as their object operations. Project deliverables are postconditions of object operations. A good example of the activity-based approach is the OPEN Project Specification [2]. In this model, we see the following potential problems:

1. When setting up a new project, it can be difficult to determine the appropriate set of tasks leading to the delivery of the completed product. First of all, it would require a detailed knowledge of the entire method, and secondly, such a set of tasks would strongly depend on various project characteristics, for example, the project size.
2. Because the list of activities and tasks is determined by the method, using modified activities or tasks requires a modification of the process model.
3. The model is not fail-safe. If an activity or task is omitted in the project plan, there is typically no warning that something is missing.

The Object-Oriented Model – with Deliverables as Objects

In a deliverable-based approach, the deliverables are modeled as objects. These objects are instances of deliverable classes that determine behavior, attributes, semantics and relationships.

Deliverables have two kinds of *methods*. They have one or more *constructors*, which are one or more tasks used to create the deliverable, and *quality-assurance* methods which are, for example, completeness and consistency checks.

Deliverables have numerous *attributes*: name, kind, description, references to other deliverables, project, subsystem, increment identification, responsible developer and other attributes such as who created and modified the deliverable and when.

The attributes *kind* and *name* taken together are the key that uniquely identifies the deliverable in the data dictionary. The attribute *description* typically contains a UML diagram, a table or a text. The choice of a suitable representation is left up to the judgement of the developer and depends on the specific situation.

Each design increment is described by a single deliverable referred to as "Increment Context", that corresponds to "Task" in Microsoft Project used for project planning. "Increment Context" deliverables exists throughout the entire life cycle of the increment (from requirement analysis to implementation and testing. This is an important factor that makes management of incremental development easier.

305

Note that design deliverables may relate to more than one increment context documents. For example, different developers may work with the same class model in the scope of different increments, or more typically, class model can be reused within different increments.

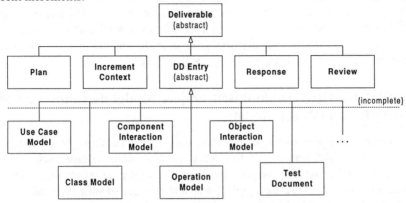

Fig. 2. Inheritance diagram showing the classes of deliverables used in the development process. The incompleteness of the inheritance tree allows for flexibility throughout the process and for the exact matching of project deliverables to different kinds of processes. The class DD Entry has abstract constructor and abstract quality criteria defined in derived classes.

Experience with the Deliverable-Based Process Model

We have used the described process model in several projects since the summer of 1996. Using the object model above, we have developed a process [4], based on the Fusion method [1], extended of the use cases and requirements analysis and made minor modifications to match the UML notation and incremental development. We used Lotus Notes as a repository for project deliverables as well as the data dictionary.

The main benefit of using these tools was flexibility – in notation, in the kinds of deliverables in the repository and in the possibilities provided for modifying the process according to the size and character of the increment.

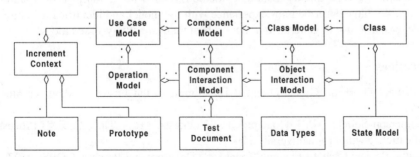

Fig. 3. Structure of typical references between analysis and design deliverables. In principle a deliverable can have bidirectional link to any other document or documents, to enable maximal flexibility.

After half a year, we had about 350 documents in the repository with the following distribution: increment context, 36%; note, 15%; use case model, 10%; component interaction model, 14%; component model, 4%; operation model, 5%; object interaction model, 3%; class model, 6%; class, 5%; state model, 1% and data types, 1%. The relatively large number of increment context documents can be explained by the fact that some minor increments were sufficiently defined by their increment context documents together with note documents and did not need to aggregate a full set of analysis and design deliverables.

Benefits of a Deliverable-Based Object Model as Compared to an Activity Based Object Model.

1. *It is easier to define a set of deliverables than a set of activities*. In a small project, it is often sufficient to produce only context, plan, source code and user documentation. As the project grows, the number of kinds of deliverables increases and always reflects project state and possible specific demands.
2. *The model is flexible*. The final product is not always a code. It could be another process, such as testing or version-control process. The deliverable-based object model can be easily adopted for different kinds of projects, just by defining the methods and attributes of the deliverable classes.
3. *The model provides good management support for incremental development*. The increment is described by a single document that remains throughout the increment's life cycle.
4. *The model is robust and consistent*. In an activity-based object model, an activity might be omitted during project planning, but in a deliverable-based model, the deliverable that is necessary for the development cannot be omitted because of the constructor and quality methods of related deliverables.

Conclusions

We have described a deliverable-based object-oriented model for the description of a software development process. Its main artifacts are deliverables, modeled as objects with constructor and quality-assurance methods and with a number of specific attributes. We have described our experience with the model and identified it as more flexible, easier to use in general, and more robust than an activity-based model.

References

[1] Coleman, D. et al.: Object-Oriented Development: the Fusion method, Prentice Hall 1994
[2] Henderson-Sellers, B., Graham, I., Younessi, H.: The OPEN Process Specification, Swinburne University 1997
[3] Hruby, P.: The Object-Oriented Model for a Development Process, OOPSLA'97
[4] Hruby, P.: The Fusion Process from an Object-Oriented Perspective. Submitted to the Fusion Newsletter.

Active Software Artifacts

Mehmet Aksit[1], Francesco Marcelloni[2], Bedir Tekinerdogan[1],
Klaas van den Berg[1] and Pim van den Broek[1]

[1]TRESE project, Department of Computer Science,
Centre for Telematics and Information Technology, University of Twente,
P.O. Box 217, 7500 AE Enschede, The Netherlands.
email: {aksit I bedir I vdberg I pimvdb }@cs.utwente.nl
www server: http://wwwtrese.cs.utwente.nl
[2]Department of Information Engineering, University of Pisa,
Via Diotisalvi 2, 56156 Pisa, Italy
email: france@iet.unipi.it

Abstract. There are many similarities between industrial goods manufacturing and software development processes. This paper first briefly analyzes the recent developments in goods manufacturing, and then identifies the equivalent techniques in software technology. It is claimed that products developed during software manufacturing must be modeled as active artifacts. As a possible approach in this direction, an object-oriented artifact production framework is presented and evaluated.

1. Manufacturing Techniques and Software Engineering

Despite of all the efforts made, developing cost-effective software systems remains a difficult task. There are many similarities between industrial goods manufacturing and software development processes, and therefore it may be worthwhile to compare these disciplines together. The progress made in industrial goods manufacturing can be roughly classified as mechanized and computerized techniques.

The mechanized manufacturing age started with the introduction of production lines. Compared to the early techniques, the production lines approach has increased the efficiency of manufacturing incomparably because production facilities could be shared, managed and automated. In this approach, however, to be able to have a cost-effective production, goods have to belong to the same product line, require similar production facilities, and the number of manufactured goods must be large enough.

During the last decade, software engineering research activities have shown many similarities with the mechanized goods manufacturing techniques. For example, to be able to specify software product lines, software architecture specification techniques have been developed. Software development methods have allowed software engineers to share the same notation, rules and processes. Component-based development techniques have enabled standard software parts to be developed and reused. Due to continuous increase in complexity of software systems, however, it looks like those goals in cost-effective software development remain equally challenging as before.

308

Let us now consider computerized goods manufacturing techniques, which have been introduced to deal with similar problems like we face today in software engineering. Firstly, computer aided design environments have been developed with increasingly high-level semantic support, such as calculating the mechanical properties of the materials used. In addition, a substantial progress has been made in design automation techniques. Secondly, to be able to increase the flexibility of the production processes, computer integrated manufacturing techniques have been developed. These aim at smooth integration of various phases in the manufacturing process. Finally, to simplify the maintenance activities, design and production information have been captured and included in the delivered products as built-in information so that service engineers can retrieve this information whenever necessary.

These recent developments in goods manufacturing imply the following equivalent techniques for software industry: computer-aided design of software systems and design automation, computer-integrated manufacturing of software systems and integrating design and manufacturing information with software products.

To realize computerized software manufacturing processes, first of all, every generated product, such as architecture specification, analysis and design models, design decisions, documentation and software components must be considered as an artifact. This is necessary for reasoning about software artifacts and their manufacturing processes. Secondly, these artifacts have to be designed as *intelligent* software modules. Being intelligent means that every artifact defines its own rules for its creation, definition of parts, quality control and coordination with other artifacts. If artifacts are designed as intelligent software modules, they may actively assist software engineers. Thirdly, artifacts must record their context and interdependencies. This helps software engineers walk through the related artifacts, for example, from executable software modules to architecture specification artifacts. Finally, because of the complexity of the problem, artifacts must be extensible and use open-ended protocols so that new artifacts can be introduced whenever necessary.

2. The Artifact Production Framework

To create reusable artifacts and open-ended protocols, we adopted object-oriented modeling principles. For uniformity, each artifact in production is derived from the super class ArtifactInProduction. As shown by Figure 1, class ArtifactInProduction is composed of two interacting parts: Producer and Controller. The part Producer carries out the artifact production process, and the part Controller is responsible for the quality of the artifact.

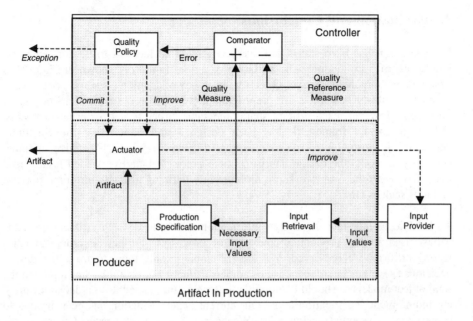

Fig. 1. Structure of an artifact in the production process.

To initiate the production process, the corresponding Input Provider supplies the pre-artifacts. Pre-artifacts are the necessary sub-products to produce an artifact. Once the pre-artifacts are supplied, the necessary information is retrieved from them. The subpart Input Retrieval describes the sequence of actions needed to implement the retrieve protocol. For example, assume that the software engineer is identifying a *class*. This requires a pre-artifact of type Entity-in-a-Requirement-Specification. To be able to reason about a class, the *relevance* and *autonomy* values of the supplied entity must be retrieved.

The subpart Production Specification defines a set of production rules which describe how the retrieved information is transformed into an artifact. For example, if an entity is *relevant* and *autonomous*, then the corresponding class can be identified. Further, the subpart Production Specification defines rules to collect the quality measures. The part Controller compares the quality measures to the reference measures and generates an error signal. This signal is examined by the subpart Quality Policy to decide which action to take. We consider here three possible actions: raise an exception (when the error is too high), improve (when the error is acceptable, but should be lowered) and commit (when the error is negligible). The exception message is captured by an external controller, which can be a software engineer or a higher-level control subsystem. The messages *improve* and *commit* are processed by the subpart Actuator. If the message is *improve* then Actuator requests the *input providers* to improve the quality of the information, whereas in case of *commit* the produced artifact is delivered. Notice that complex production systems can be defined by creating chains of artifacts in production.

3. Evaluation and Conclusions

In section 1 it has been stated that every generated artifact has to be defined as an intelligent software module. The artifact production framework shown in Figure 1 is designed as a generic active object with its own creation, quality control and interaction rules. These rules are preprogrammed based on the type of artifact to be produced. However, each artifact shares the same structure and external protocols. This experimental framework has been designed and built using the Smalltalk language [1]. Most adopted rules are expressed using fuzzy-logic [4]. This was found necessary to model the design heuristics more precisely than two-valued logic based rules. To verify the framework, we are currently defining artifacts for some popular methods such as OMT [5].

To be able to integrate the design information and context, each artifact stores the values used in the production and control processes. Further, interdependencies among artifacts are preserved. We are developing some tools to trace the design decisions as well as interdependencies among artifacts. For example, starting from the final object models, it should be possible to trace all the related design decisions up to the requirement specification level. Our current experimentation has been limited to some simple cases and design rules. We have initiated a pilot project to apply the framework in an industrial application called Integrated New European Car Dealer Information System [2].

Similar approaches have been proposed in the literature to cope with the complexity of software production. For example, at the Software Engineering Institute, a research activity on product-line systems has been established [6]. Further, there are active groups carrying out research activities on the so-called Automated Software Engineering [3]. However, to the best of our knowledge, fuzzy-logic techniques implemented in an active object-oriented framework have not been realized before.

References

1. J.B.W. van Dongen, An Object-Oriented Production Framework for Software Development, M.Sc. Thesis, University of Twente, June 1997
2. INEDIS project description, University of Twente, 1996.
3. Journal on Automated Software Engineering, Kluwer Academic Publishers, ISSN 0928-8910.
4. F. Marcelloni and M. Aksit. Applying Fuzzy Logic Techniques in Object-Oriented Software Development, to be published in this volume.
5. J. Rumbaugh et al. Object-Oriented Modeling and Design, Prentice Hall, 1991
6. Software Engineering Institute, Product-Line Systems, http:// www.sei.cmu.edu/technology/product_line_systems/

General Software Process Organization in the OSMOSIS Project

Jean Bézivin

Laboratoire de Recherche en Sciences de Gestion, Université de Nantes,
2 rue de la Houssinière, BP 92208 Nantes cedex 03, France
tel : (33) 2 40 37 30 59
email : jbezivin@acm.org

Abstract. A general life cycle reference model called J^3 is sketched here as a possible alternative to more conventional organization schemes, giving rise to a regular organization of processes and products in the object-oriented software development cycle. This is based on a clear identification and characterization of all these processes and products in the lifecycle and contradicts somewhat the so-called seamlessness property of object-oriented development techniques. The J^3 organization framework is one of the main components of the OSMOSIS research workbench. It proposes a general "model driven development process" that may be used independently of the various deployed tools (UML, Corba, Java, etc.).

1. Introduction

Transitioning from procedure-oriented to object-oriented (OO) development methods may prove to be much more difficult than foreseen. One of the reasons is that we may be too shy in giving up traditional ways of thinking. Sticking to the classical Analysis-Design-Implementation software development cycle is probably misleading and dangerous.

In order to investigate some of the issues related to the transition from procedural to OO-based methods, we have been building and using an experimental research platform named OSMOSIS (Bézivin95). The kernel of this system is made of a minimal representation support called sNets, a typed, reflective and modular kind of semantic networks. Using this meta-notation in a systematic way lead us to view the complete OO development cycle as a network of interconnected processes producing or consuming information sets called products (or artifacts or models). Each such product is based on a corresponding <u>ontology</u>, specifying the concepts that may be used and the possible relations between these concepts.

So our main starting point is that there is not one unique space for the entire development cycle but, on the contrary, a lot of spaces with different semantics and it is highly dangerous to confuse them. For example (Figure 1), in the domain business space, we are dealing with <u>concepts</u> and <u>specialization</u> of concepts, while in the design space we are dealing with <u>design classes</u> and <u>inheritance</u> and in a given implementation space we may be dealing with <u>Java classes</u> for example and <u>extension</u>

relations between them. Of course, some similarities between entities and relations of different spaces will exist, but these may be less straightforward than the ones suggested by the example of Figure 1.

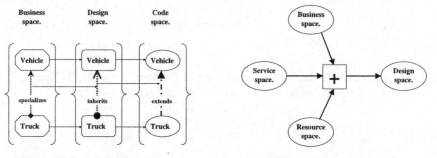

Figure 1 Multiple spaces   Figure 2 Essential spaces

The four essential development spaces are presented in Figure 2. Entities from the business space are called <u>business objects</u>. Entities from the resource space are called <u>technical objects</u>. Entities from the service space are called <u>requirement scripts</u> and may be viewed as a generalization of use cases. Design is the process that results in the creation of the design space or model. Our definition of design is an activity that has the purpose of combining together business objects and technical objects in order to fulfill some particular needs expressed by requested services in the service model.

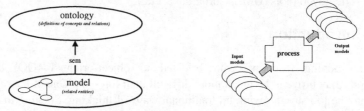

Figure 3 Ontology-based modeling   Figure 4 Processes and models

Many proposals have been centered around a unique object notation or a family of strongly-related object notations for all software development tasks. This movement has used the seamlessness argument, i.e. the supposed property of continuity between different object models. In this view one could progressively build an analysis model from the observation of the real world and then progressively shift from this abstract description to more concrete design or implementation models. We have found many difficulties in putting this method to work and this is why we have been investigating, in the OSMOSIS project, another organization mainly based on <u>model transformation</u>. In this scheme the basic paradigm is no more the classical <u>refinement</u> used in procedural techniques, but rather the <u>composition</u> much more adapted to object-oriented environments (Nierstrasz95). The preciseness of the approach is based on the systematic application of ontology-based modeling to the complete development cycle, i.e. working only with models (spaces) rigorously defined by ontologies (Figure 3).

2. In Search of a General Organization

As an alternative to the classical Analysis-Design-Implementation, we borrow ideas from three different sources to build a simplified organization framework called J[3]. We call *vertical* axis what Jackson calls coupling between the *world* on one side and the *machine* on the other side (Jackson95). The "world" may be associated with the business model. It embodies all possible statements of problems. On the other side, the "machine" corresponds to the domain of resources, mainly computer resources that may be used to build the solution. We call *horizontal axis*, the path from goals to solutions and more precisely we suppose that goals are expressed as extended "use cases" and solutions as design pattern instances (Gamma94). We have here two spaces (service and design) and a process path between them (the design process). As a matter of fact, this is a very simplified presentation because the design process may itself be decomposed in several sub-processes. Also the service model is the result of a less formal activity corresponding to final user interviews and workshops (user needs modeling).

J[3] is thus the proposed synthesis between these ideas and may be regarded as the cross-shaped organization resulting from the superposition of the vertical axis (the Jackson axis) and the horizontal axis (that we call the Jacobson/Johnson axis).

So, these are the three first spaces : world, machine and service corresponding to business analysis, resource analysis and service analysis. The fourth one (design space) is composed of design frames linking together, in a given pattern arrangement, various business and technical objects.

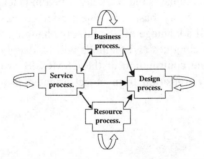

Figure 5 Basic processes in the J[3] approach.

The OSMOSIS platform proposes an idealized regular development scheme composed of processes and products. Each model has a specific ontology defining the associated concepts and relations. This allows a much more precise identification of the role of each process in the production of some products, based on the utilization of other products (Figure 4). As a central example, this has permitted to define much more precisely the design process as an activity producing the design model and based on several other well identified products: service, business, resource but also design pattern spaces. The originality of the J[3] scheme mainly lies in this definition of the design process. Around this part of the software production scheme, many other processes and models are being defined like testing, performance measurement, etc.

A process view of J^3 is sketched in Figure 5. We see there the four basic <u>cyclic</u> processes and some of the dependencies between them. At the top, there is the business modeling, aiming at producing such products as domain ontologies, workflow or other enterprise models. At the bottom we find resource modeling which sometimes means building higher abstractions of underlying hardware/software platforms, but which more usually corresponds to the discovering and understanding of already available API's, OS and other libraries. On the left we find service modeling. Much has been said in this area about "use case engineering", but this process of service modeling has a wider scope for eliciting, identifying and specifying the various facets of user requirements. Last but not least, the design process is driven by the various services that have to be implemented. For each such service, a pattern space is first searched and then business and technical objects are linked to the resulting frame in order to prepare for implementation of the selected service.

The four cyclic processes should be viewed as concurrently executing and synchronized. For example, if a given business or technical object is mentioned by a service, but not yet available in the corresponding development space, a synchronization protocol is applied in order to query for a rapid development of the corresponding item. Similarly, the achievement of a service specification may trigger the search or development for the corresponding design frame.

3. Conclusions

J^3 borrows ideas from many recent trends in object technology, but above all, the main source of inspiration remains the work described in (Jackson95) which may well provide the preliminary theory basis for object-oriented development that we still need, in order to take full advantage of the rapidly changing tools and environments. Software development techniques and methods will be deeply affected by the arrival of object technology. The contribution of the OSMOSIS project may be viewed as facilitating the necessary transition from object-oriented programming to ontology-driven modeling.

References

[Bézivin95] Bézivin, J. **Object-Oriented Requirement Elicitation in the OSMOSIS Project** IEEE International Symposium on Engineering of Computer-Based Systems, Tucson, (6-9 March 1995), p. 289-298.

[Gamma94] Gamma, E. & Helm, R. & Johnson, R. & Vlissides, J. **Design Patterns Elements of Reusable Object-Oriented Software** Addison Wesley Professional Computing Series, (1994), 395 p.

[Jackson95] Jackson, M.A. **Software requirement & Specifications A lexicon of practice, principles and prejudices** Addison Wesley, ACM Press, (1995), 228 p.

[Nierstrasz95] Nierstrasz, O. & Tsichritzis, D. **Object-Oriented Software Composition** Prentice Hall, (1995), 361 p.

Object-Oriented Modelling of Software Processes and Artifacts: Promises and Challenges

Jun Han

Peninsula School of Computing and Information Technology
Monash University, McMahons Road, Frankston, Vic 3199, Australia
phone: +61 3 99044604, fax: +61 3 99044124, e-mail: jhan@monash.edu.au

1 Introduction

Over the years, there have been significant efforts in modelling and representing software processes and artifacts, especially in the software engineering environments community, eg, [6, 4, 5]. It has long been recognised that focusing on the artifacts alone does not deliver the full benefit for software practice since software development should follow an orderly process. On the other hand, considering processes without much regard to the artifacts is also limited, eg, in dealing with fine-grained technical processes. As such, a promising direction is to integrate the modelling and representation of software processes and artifacts. Encapsulation of data and behaviour is one of the key characteristics of the object-oriented approach. As such, it seems natural to use the object-oriented approach to model software artifacts and processes in an integrated manner. Due to the specific nature of software processes and artifacts and the limitations of the object-oriented approach, however, object-oriented modelling of software processes and artifacts still requires much investigation.

In this paper, we outline *some* of the issues, promises and challenges in developing integrated models of software processes and artifacts in the object oriented approach. It also aims to achieve uniform treatment of fine-grained processes and high-level processes. The discussion is set in the context of our preliminary work in integrating software processes and artifacts [3], based on our approach to representing software artifacts [1, 2], and oriented towards full-fledged modelling and representation of software processes and artifacts.

In section 2, we briefly discuss some of the basic characteristics of software processes and artifacts. Then in section 3, we contemplate an object-oriented approach to modelling software processes and artifacts, and identify the relevant issues, promises and challenges.

2 Characteristics of Software Processes and Artifacts

The software process in general relates to all activities involved in the development and maintenance of a software system. The process has different characteristics in different phases and at different granularity levels. While acknowledging that there are other classifications, here we distinguish two types of process:

1. *fine-grained process* concerning the manipulation of an artifact's content, and
2. *high-level process* concerning the scheduling and coordination of activities performed on one or more whole artifacts.

It should be noted that an atomic activity in the high-level process may correspond to a complicated fine-grained process. In general, there may be hierarchical organisations of activities where higher-level activities are lower-level processes.

Software artifacts are the products of the software process, and their structures and contents are determined by the project. Therefore, software processes and artifacts should be treated together with equal importance. Besides, it is felt that the prominent role that tools take in some of the existing process modelling approaches is unnecessary and rather a hindrance to properly address certain issues such as fine-grained processes.

The next section will introduce some additional characteristics of software processes and artifacts, including views, active artifacts, informal communications, and modelling styles.

3 O-O Modelling of Software Processes and Artifacts

In modelling software processes and artifacts, we focus on the following aspects: fine-grained processes, high-level processes, and artifacts reflecting necessary process features. We aim to achieve integrated modelling of processes and artifacts, and uniform treatment of fine-grained and high-level processes. As mentioned above, the object-oriented approach seems natural in meeting these objectives. In general, the object oriented approach suggests that we model artifacts and their manipulation (ie, process) in an integrated manner. That is, the definition of an object in the model should involve the structural and behavioral aspects of the artifacts.

Artifact Structures. The structural formulation of an artifact should take into account the following factors: its components, the relationships among the components, and the consistency constraints about the components and their relationships. As such, this formulation presents a static definition of what a *consistent* artifact of this kind is. To a certain degree, the captured relationships form a static reflection of some process characteristics such as traceability of the process [3]. The consistency constraints are additional information about the artifact structure. They further restrict the space of the artifacts that can be constructed, and can assist the developer in understanding and constructing the artifacts. A corresponding model for artifact structures has been proposed in [1].

The current object-oriented approach can readily cope with the definition of components. However, the support for the specification of relationships and constraints are somehow limited, ie, they are not treated as first class. We believe that first-class treatment of relationships and constraints in modelling is necessary and beneficial.

Fine-Grained Processes. A fine-grained process deals with the manipulation of an artifact. It should be defined in terms of the operations that can be applied to the artifact structure, and the (sequencing) rules that govern their application. In general, it is the the developer who drives the manipulation process of a specific artifact by applying the operations as required. However, rules do exist regarding the applicability of operations at a given time, and the sequencing of the operations. While operations can be readily defined, the rules can not be *easily* specified in a formal notation in the current object-oriented approach (although there are notations like state transition diagrams).

High-Level Processes. High-level processes focus on scheduling and coordination of activities performed on whole artifacts, and should be defined based on the group of relevant artifacts. The grouping of the artifacts together with their relationships and constraints forms the structure of the *high-level object* that the high-level process applies to. The high-level process is defined in terms of the activities performed on the component artifacts, and the (sequencing) rules that govern the individual activities. As stated earlier, the current object-oriented approach does not provide *effective* support for the specification of process rules.

Among the artifacts manipulated by a high-level process may be a *process-oriented* artifact, such as a project plan. The process may manipulate the internal components of such artifacts, eg, making changes to a project plan. An operation applied to a process-oriented artifact may not only cause changes to its content, but also cause "executional" effects to the project. That is, the content change to the artifact will be interpreted (or executed) in the project in the sense that it effects process changes. (But there is no such effect from content changes of an ordinary artifact such as a design document.) Because of their executional effects, we call the process-oriented artifacts *active artifacts*. In addition, relationships originating from active artifacts may also have executional effects, and are consequently called *active relationships*. In general, it is not clear how to *naturally* model active artifacts and relationships in the current object oriented approach.

As mentioned earlier, object oriented modelling of artifacts and processes may take a hierarchical form. One level provides the *context* (eg, resources) for the next lower level. The contextual relationships between the levels need to be further investigated. Besides, the top-most level should give a high-level view of the project and how it starts and progresses.

Further Issues. Following the grouping of a number of artifacts into a high-level object in relation to a high-level process, it is possible for an artifact to appear in a number of high-level objects in the sense that each object context offers a specific perspective of the artifact from the relevant high-level process viewpoint. The consistency and relationships among the perspectives of an artifact need to be further investigated.

Another issue of interest is the process modelling style. One may model the *explicit* sequencing relationships of activities and operations in an imperative manner. For *implicit* sequencing based on status or content change of artifacts, it seems more natural to use an event-based approach. How to naturally integrating these two styles poses another challenge for process modelling.

Process modelling in general should also deal with the issues of informal discussions and negotiations in the context of supporting coordination and communication. How to handle these issues in the object oriented approach presents yet another challenge.

4 Conclusions

In this paper, we have briefly analysed a number of issues in using the object-oriented approach to model software processes and artifacts. The major issues identified include: relationships and constraints as part of artifact structures (to capture process characteristics), fine-grained processes, high-level processes, active artifacts and relationships, hierarchical multi-perspective modelling, process modelling styles, and the treatment of different forms of coordinations and communications. In general, the object-oriented approach provides a way to integrate process and artifact modelling and to treat fine-grained and high-level processes in a uniform manner. While some modelling requirements can be readily met by the current object-oriented approach, others are identified as requiring further investigation.

Acknowledgments. The author would like to thank Se-Ill Choi, Hardeep Singh, Jim Welsh and Yun Yang for their discussions in formulating some of the views expressed in this paper.

References

1. J. Han. Software documents, their relationships and properties. In *Proceedings of 1st Asia-Pacific Software Engineering Conference (APSEC'94)*, pages 102–111, Tokyo, Japan, December 1994. IEEE Computer Society Press.
2. J. Han. A document-based approach to software engineering environments. In *Proceedings of 5th International CASE Symposium*, pages 128–133, Changsha, China, October-November 1995.
3. J. Han and J. Welsh. Methodology modelling: Combining software processes with software products. In *Proceedings of 17th Annual Computer Science Conference*, volume 3, pages 601–610, Christchurch, New Zealand, January 1994.
4. ICSP. *Proceedings of 4th International Conference on the Software Process*. IEEE Computer Society, Brighton, UK, December 1996.
5. C. Montangero, editor. *Proceedings of 5th European Workshop on Software Process Technology (LNCS-1149)*. Springer, Nancy, France, October 1996.
6. H. Weber, editor. *Proceedings of 5th ACM/SIGSOFT Symposium on Software Development Environments (SEN, 17(5))*. ACM Press, Tyson's Corner, Virginia, December 1992.

Object-Oriented Model for Representing Software Production Processes

I.Bider (IbisSoft, Stockholm, email: info@ibissoft.se)

M.Khomyakov (M7, Moscow, email: ari@online.ru)

1. Requirements for Object-Oriented Process Model

Software production, as any other business process, consists of two parts: a creative part, and a routine one. The creative part is about finding the best way to approach the problems a software system should solve. The routine one is to complete all activities needed for producing software, e.g., coding, compiling, linking, testing, bug fixing, etc. Both parts need management. However, the creative part is very much dependent on the individuals in charge of the overall system architecture, just good management can't solve the problems of good design. The creative part, though the proportion of it in the software industry might be greater than in other industries, doesn't solve all the problems of software production. All routine operations should be properly carried out in order for a software project to succeed. These operations are easier to formalize, and thus model.

The quality of the software production process has direct impact on the quality of the resulting software system, and may be, at least partially, evaluated by studying this system. Probably, the most important factor of the software system quality is the quality of its structure. This parameter may be roughly measured as the total amount of program code. Another way of measuring the structural factor may be by measuring the reusability level of the basic program units, e.g., objects, functions, etc. (here, we mean the reusability of the basic units inside the same system). However, good software structure alone doesn't guarantee the quality of the system. Another important factor is how well the software system structure reflects (or models) the application domain it is aimed to work in. This factor affects the tolerance of the system to changes in the specifications (which usually occur on all stages of the software production process), and its possibility to acquire new functionality without major restructuring, i.e. system adaptability.

The factors mentioned above, which characterize reusability, and adaptability, reflect the quality of the creative part of the software production process. It's difficult to measure them directly, especially the second one. But those parameters can be evaluated indirectly by taking into account all the routine operations completed. For example, poor adaptability will result in major restructuring of the system during it's lifetime when new functionality is added.. This will immediately result in the rapidly growing number of routine operations performed during the system lifetime. Poor reusability will affect the reported problems/bugs ratio. The better reusability, the more chances that fixing one bug will result in solving many reported problems.

Thus, one legitimate approach to evaluating the quality of software processes and systems is by studying all the operation performed in the frame of the process during the system's lifetime. To effectively use this approach we need:

- A model that gives us a structured representation of all routine operations performed during the system's lifetime
- A way to gather all information that we need to put in the model.

The amount of information that will be needed for this approach is enormous and there is no chance to collect it in any other way than by registering all of them in the computer. We need a system that will register information about all activities completed in the production process. To motivate people using the system, it should not only register operations, but should also help to perform and manage them. Ideally, we need a system that helps individuals with all aspects of their routine work which usually consists of:

- execution of routine activities, like writing documentation, coding, compiling
- registration of the activities performed.
- planning of new activities.
- communication with colleagues concerning the above activities.

And we need a kind of a formal model to build this system upon, and the same model may help us to analyze the information gathered by the system, and indirectly measure the quality parameters of the production processes.

2. Object-Oriented Model for Business Processes

2.1 Bit of History

The authors' interest in management automation goes back to 1984 when we started our own CHAOS project, where CHAOS stands for Concurrent Human Assisted Object Systems. The ultimate goal of the project was to create methods and programming environment for design and implementation of distributed management automation systems. As the only business process well known to us at that time was software development, we always have in mind the task of building a computerized secretary for a programmer.

Our theoretical model was first tested in practice in 1989-90 when we were developing an application for supporting sales and marketing activities of a trading company. The system was called DealDriver to highlight that it helps the workers to "drive" their deals from the beginning to the end which is receiving payment. For this project, we devised a practical object-oriented model for representing business processes which is described in more details in [1,2]. During the project we also developed homemade object support tools which included Hi-base - an object-oriented historical database, and Navi - an object oriented user-interface system.

The object model and support tools were later successfully used for modeling business processes in other application domains. We believe that our practical model (with some modifications) can be adjusted to modeling software production processes.

2.2 Practical Model

Business processes are represented in our model as objects which we call organizing objects (or orgobjects for short) to stress their importance in organizing all activities of the business process. The state of an orgobject reflects the current state of the business process; the consecutive order of all its previous states shows the evolution of the process in time. The orgobject's state, sometimes together with its history indicates what further steps should be completed to transfer the object to the final state which means that the goal of the process has been reached.

Object is a central notion of the model. Not only are business processes represented as objects, but also all other entities of the application domain, such as software modules, the project's personnel, etc., are also represented as objects. Objects are complex and dynamic. The *complex* nature of objects is reflected by *links* that show the inclusion of one object into another. The *dynamic* properties of objects are expressed by concepts of *history, events*, and *activities*.

History is the time-ordered sequence of all the previous states of objects. *Events* present additional information about transitions from one state of the object to another, like date and time when the event had occurred, date and time when the event was registered in the system (may differ from the previous one), the person whose actions caused changes in the object (if applicable), etc. *Activities* represent actions that take place in the world of application domain, like performing a software module compilation. In the model, the activity moves an orgobject to the next stipulated state.

Our model implements an approach to management of routine work that we call a process-oriented management. The main characteristics of this management scheme is dynamic and distributed planning. *Dynamic planning* involves planning only the first few activities at the first stage. As soon as one or several of these are completed, new activities are planned with regard to the emerging state of the relevant orgobject. *Distributed planning* implies that the worker who has completed a planned activity himself plans the subsequent activities, thus there is no central planning. Moreover, he/she can assign these new activities not only to himself, but to other people too.

The principle of dynamic and distributed planning is realized in our model by a notion of planned activity. A *planned activity* is an object that contains such information as type of activity (compilation, etc.), planned date and time, deadline, reference to the person who is responsible for performing the activity, etc. Planned activities are included in the orgobjects which they will affect when executed. All planned activities included in the given orgobject compose the immediate plan of the process evolution. When executed, a planned activity changes the orgobject to which it belongs. This change may include adding new planned activities and deleting the old ones thus helping the user to modify the process plan.

2.3 Some Advantages of Practical Model

- Orgbjects provide a perfect insight into the process' state of affairs. The information stored in the objects is of great help to the management staff as it permits to evaluate the state of any process quickly (without going into t history).
- Histories make it easy to trace all the activities completed within the given process, which helps to draw up plans for complicated cases. They are also a very important source of data for all kinds of process evaluation and statistical analysis.
- The project staff becomes goal- and process conscious as it is easy for any person to overview all the activities (one's own and those of others) completed in the process he/she is involved in. The history of an old orgobject is useful for "learning by example", which may help to find solutions in difficult cases.
- Distributed planning is a very powerful tool for coordinating the work which makes unnecessary the intensive communication among the workers engaged in the same processes
- Since all the information on the past activities is being stored, the management is in a better position to resolve various kinds of conflicts.

3. Possible Application to Object-Oriented Software Development

When applying our model to a new application domain, the following tasks should be completed:

- orgobjects to represent the production processes should be designed
- simple activities that moves the process to its final goal should be identified
- rules for chaining these activities should be figured out and implemented in additional actions behind each of the activities identified

Though we started our work with the idea to create a secretary for a programmer, we never had a chance to try our model for this domain so far. However, object-oriented software is already structured in terms of objects. Thus the most elementary business process could be the one that concern the full life-cycle of a software object. An orgobject to represent this process would include all the components of the software object, e.g.: *source file, include file, documentation file*, etc., together with immediate activities planned: *compile, adjust documentation, include in the next test release*, etc.

The advantage of the software production with respect to our model is that most of the routine operations completed in the frame of this process are executed in the computer. This makes it possible to achieve the maximum automation of the process in the support system.

References

1. Bider,I. ObjectDriver - a Method for Analysis, Design and Implementation of Interactive Applications. In Data Base Management. Auerbach RIA Group, February 1997.
2. Bider,I. Developing Tool Support for Process Oriented Management. In Data Base Management. Auerbach, RIA Group, February 1997.

2nd Workshop on Component-Oriented Programming (WCOP'97)[1]

Summary

Jan Bosch

University of Karlskrona/Ronneby
Dept of Computer Science
Ronneby, Sweden
Jan.Bosch@ide.hk-r.se

Wolfgang Weck

Åbo Academy
Dept of Computer Science
Åbo, Finland
Wolfgang.Weck@abo.fi

Clemens Szyperski

Queensland University of Technology
School of Computing Science
Brisbane, Australia
C.Szyperski@fit.qut.edu.au

WCOP'97, held together with ECOOP'97 in Jyväskylä, was a follow-up workshop to the successful WCOP'96, which had taken place in conjunction with ECOOP'96. Where WCOP'96 had focused on the principal idea of software components and their goals, WCOP'97 was more directed towards composition and other topics, such as architectures, glue-ing, component substitutability, evolution of interfaces, and non-functional requirements.

WCOP'97 had been announced as follows:

COP has been described as the natural extension of object-oriented programming to the realm of independently extensible systems. The most prominent examples of such systems are constructed around compound document models such as OLE, OpenDoc, JavaBeans, or Netscape ONE and rest on object models such as SOM/CORBA, COM or Java's virtual machine. WCOP'97 intends to address their methodological and theoretical underpinnings.

COP aims at producing software components for a component market and for late composition. Composers are third parties, possibly the end user, who are not able or willing to change components. This requires standards to allow independently created components to interoperate, and specifications that put the composer into the position to decide what can be composed under which conditions. These needs raise open

---

1. The workshop reader contains short versions of the workshop papers. Full length papers have been published in the TUCS General Publications Series, Vol. 5, ISBN 952-12-0039-1, 1997. (http://www.tucs.abo.fi/publications/general/G5.html).

research questions like what kind of standards are needed and how they should be defined. Or what information specifications need to give, how this information should be provided, and how correct implementation and usage of specifications could be verified or enforced.

16 position papers were submitted to the workshop and formally reviewed. 12 papers were accepted for presentation at the workshop and publication with the proceedings. Still, 25 participants from 13 countries were counted at the workshop.

During the morning session, participants presented their work, which covered a wide range of topics. A major theme was how to select components for composition in a specific situation. Such a selection must rest on two pillars. Firstly, the selected components must be compatible with each other. Secondly, characteristics that are not part of the standardized component interface may decide which component to pick from otherwise equal ones. Examples are time or resource requirements, fault tolerance, degree of distribution, etc.

To address the compatibility of components, various approaches and philosophies were presented. An important property of component-oriented programming is that a single specification may be supported by multiple implementations. However, problems may arise if individual implementations depend on the implementation of other components. These dependencies may cause conflicts, which can often only be detected when the composed system is analysed as a whole.

One solution is that dependencies on other components as well as known conflicts with other components become part of a component's specification. Reuse Contracts [de Hondt et al.] have been proposed as a tool for this. They also allow the composer to decide quickly whether a given set of components may conflict.

[Mikhajlov & Sekerinski] suggest to define rules that, if being followed, exclude conflicts in principle. These rules affect the design of specifications, the implementation of components, and the implementation of a component's clients. For inheritance between classes of objects, such rules can be derived formally.

A third approach is to accept that components will have some dependencies that are not part of a specification and hence cannot be checked by the composer. The component creators, however, are aware of these dependencies. Thus, this knowledge, available during component creation time, has to be maintained and made accessible to system composers. [Murer] suggests that this requires tool support.

Finally, a component may not be applicable in a specific situation as it is. In these cases, it needs to be adapted, which can be done either by modifying the program's source code or by wrapping it. Both approaches have their disadvantages. Alternatives on a middle ground are needed. [Bosch] proposes the use of component adaptation types that can be superimposed on components.

One aspect of specifications is that they embody a contract between programmers of service providing components and service clients. Because it is impossible to test a provider component against all clients and vice-versa, it must be decided without testing both whether a specification is implemented correctly and whether a client uses it correctly. For this, formal methods are helpful, but need to be made applicable in practice. [Büchi & Sekerinski] address the problem of poor scalability by specification statements, which are used in refinement calculus.

The second mayor theme of the presented work were properties of components that are not part of the (functional) standard interface. One may want to add such properties to existing components when putting them together to a complete system. This allows the system's composer to pick those properties that are actually needed in the specific situation. [Troya & Vallecillo] discuss some technical precautions for this, such as a specific communication mechanism. An example of such add-on properties are mechanisms for run-time fault management in distributed systems. [Baggiolini & Harms] propose to use wrappers for providing monitoring, diagnosis, or failure correction.

Components that are otherwise interchangeable will distinguish themselves by some important (unchangeable) properties, such as resource requirements. It is an important task to select the right components, meeting possible constraints imposed by the deploying system or the problem to be solved. [Lalanda] suggests that this selection may be best made at run-time, and proposes a special architecture.

Some of the work addressed other topics than these two main themes. Workflow systems seem to lend themselves to component-oriented software, because of their configurability and building-block-like structure. [Schreyjak] proposes a special component framework to support component-based workflow systems. One way of composing systems is by expressing relations and cooperation between components in a special language. [Steensgaard Madsen] proposes an interpreted language, in which the commands are components. Such language interpreters are specialized for an application domain and need to be generated automatically. [Weck] discusses the problems of code inheritance across component boundaries, such as the danger for unwanted dependencies. Instead, inheriting classes need to refer to specifications of base classes. With this, inheritance can be replaced by object composition without sacrificing the possibility of static analysis, yet being more flexible.

Because of the many participants, during the afternoon session the workshop was split up into discussion groups. The participants expressed interest in four areas: Components, Architectures, Non-Functional Requirements, and Glue. The following are short summaries, based on presentations and notes provided by different participants of the discussion groups.

Components: As a start, it was recognized that what makes something a component is neither a specific application nor a specific implementation technology. In this sense, "anything" may be cast into a component. To provide access to something about which so little is known, an interface needs to be provided. Interfaces are mainly seen as a collection of "Service Access Points", each of them including a semantics specification. The main purpose of components is reuse of both implementations and interfaces. For effective implementation reuse, the aforementioned independence from implementation technology is particularly important. Two kinds of life cycles are to be distinguished: that of the interface and that of the component itself. The latter is shorter than the former, because the interface exists as long as any implementation is around. For interfaces, formalization of semantics is necessary. Even more important, the interoperation between components must be described. On the technical level, one needs a binary interoperation standard and a mechanism to map semantics specifications to implementations using this binary standard.

Architecture: Architecture describes compositions of components, and therefore relationships between them. This requires consideration of the component's interfaces. Architecture is to be stated in terms of interfaces rather than component implementations. In contrast, if architecture would be seen just as design patterns for composition, a concrete architecture may not be realizable because the components at hand may not fit together (architectural mismatch). On the other hand, in a given architecture, components are replaceable by others implementing the same interface. Thus, architecture represents the longer lasting and slower changing design as opposed to component implementations. More precisely, an architecture consists of a collection of interfaces that represent slots to be filled (or roles to be played) by components. Some supporting white-box implementation, for instance, a kernel, may be bundled with a given architecture.

Non-Functional Requirements: Examples of systems currently under construction were collected together with their specific non-functional requirements. For instance, an avionics system that plans trajectories of a plane and must react to route problems (such as a storm or being low on fuel) must be fast (2-3 second response time) and must adapt itself to many different situations that might arise. Secondly, a system for numerical computing on parallel processors must run fast on a given parallel machine. It also must be quickly portable to run on a new machine. Thirdly, software for controlling a kidney dialysis machine must be responsive (quickly read various sensors and updates actuators), flexible (to adapt easy and reliably to changes in hardware, such as a new pump model, or medical practice, such as a new protocol for dialysis), and demonstratable (to be shown to a regulatory agency to convince them of its safety and benefit). There are different ways of meeting non-functional requirements, depending on the type of requirement. Some are automatically satisfied if each component of the system is properly designed. Others arise out of the interaction of components, and can only be addressed at that level, not at the level of individual components. Four ways of providing non-functional properties could be found. One can parameterize components so that specific properties can be requested of them; or one can reorganize the components to deal with the property; or one can design an overall architecture that is responsible for the property and that can provide it if the components adhere to the architecture; or, finally, a meta-level mechanism can provide access to the component interaction to deal with the property. The latter is similar to aspect-oriented programming.

Glue: By glue, the participants understood middleware that is used to connect existing components. Examples are Tcl/Tk, scripting mechanisms, even make files. Some support for typing would be nice to have but hard to achieve due to the vast variety of types components may introduce. In general, the glue is more flexible than the components glued together, and thus should use a dynamic language. In connection with the discussion on architecture, it turns out that components are sandwiched between architecture and glue. To be accessible from within a given scripting environment, the components must meet some architectural requirements, like accepting messages sent by the script interpreter. Thus, the script (glue) builds on components that in turn are built for the scripting architecture.

Toward Automatic, Run-Time Fault Management for Component-Based Applications

Vito Baggiolini and Jürgen Harms

Centre Universitaire d'Informatique,
Rue Général-Dufour 24, 1211 Genève 4, Switzerland.
{vito,harms}@cui.unige.ch

Abstract. Although components are well tested and intrinsically more reliable than custom-made software, applications built of components generally lack global verification (especially if they are independently extensible) and are subject to distributed failure scenarios. We discuss a simple component framework based on a data flow architecture that addresses these problems and allows for building failure-resilient applications. We illustrate the characteristics that make this architecture particularly suitable for automatic fault management and explain the mechanisms we use for detecting, diagnosing and correcting faults at run-time.[1]

1 Introduction

Components are mature and reliable pieces of software, that are extensively tested and have many less bugs than custom-made code. However, applications built from independently extensible component frameworks are subject to run-time failures, because they lack global testing and verification [1, 2].

We propose to handle such failures at run-time by integrating *fault management* functionality into the component framework. It is our goal to develop fault management solutions that are re-usable for different applications and allow to automate the process of failure handling. For this, we advocate a component framework containing (1) "application components", i.e., the building blocks for the primary application functionality and (2) "management components" that are capable of handling typical failure scenarios. Applications are constructed out of the application components (furtheron simply called "components") and made failure-resilient by addition of management components.

Our ultimate research goal is the generic fault management of *distributed* applications [3]. Currently, network management paradigms and technology is used in this area [4, 5]. In our opinion, however, this approach is not a good basis for automatic management, amongst others, because management functionality is typically added as an afterthought to existing applications. We believe instead that fault management functionality must be integrated into an application to be effective, and that fault management must be considered as a software design

---

[1] This work was funded by a research grant of the Swiss National Science Foundation, Project No. 2129-04567.95

criterion right from the start if re-usable fault management solutions shall be obtained. Components seem to us the best underlying technology for this.

2 A Manageable Data Flow Architecture

Our work is based on a data flow architecture. Data flow architectures consist of interconnected filter components that accept data items on one side, carry out transformations on them and push them out on the other side. This push-paradigm results in a flow of data items through the application.

Our framework contains active and passive components. Active components act as the "motors" of the application. They contain a thread and an incoming queue in which upstream components can deposit data items, which are then pushed, one at a time, through the passive components. Passive components carry out the data processing.

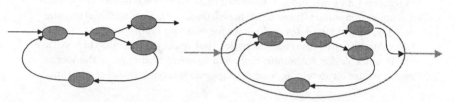

Fig. 1a) Graph of elementary components   Fig. 1b) Composite component

Components are connected together using a registration scheme. Connections are normally set up when the application is started, but they can be freely modified at run-time. While components could in principle be interconnected to arbitrary graphs, they are typically grouped into composite components. These have the same behavior as elementary components, they are also connected to each other and can again be grouped into higher-level composites. This results in a hierarchical design with clear abstraction layers. Figure 1a shows an simple example of interconnected components that are grouped into a composite component in Figure 1b.

The following characteristics make this architecture suitable for management. (1) It is highly modular and the components can be manipulated independently. (2) The dependencies between the components are clear and can be easily traced during failure diagnosis. (3) The application structure is straightforward and homogeneous through all abstraction layers. Elementary and composite components all use the same processing paradigm and the only way they interact is by forwarding data items. Management is therefore simpler: the application is easier to model; there are fewer possible failure scenarios and consequently a smaller set of management algorithms is necessary to handle them.

3 Generic Fault Management Strategies and Algorithms

Based on the above component framework, fault management essentially works as follows: *monitoring* detects potential failure symptoms as early as possible;

diagnosis traces the fault symptom back to the faulty component(s) and identifies the failure scenario, and *fault correction* eliminates the fault by acting on the faulty component(s) or on the application structure.

In the following, we explain a number of fault management strategies and algorithms that are specific to the proposed framework, but at the same time generic to all applications built from it.

Monitoring. In order to detect suspicious situations as fast and close to the cause as possible, monitoring should ideally be carried out almost continuously and "everywhere" in the application. However, only a very limited overhead can be tolerated, and the mechanisms must be carefully chosen. We use the following light-weight mechanisms. (1) *Data consistency checks* integrated into the data items are executed every time the data item enters a component. They use simple assertions on invariant characteristics of the data. (2) *Hop counters* contained in the data items are incremented for every component the data items pass through, enabling the detection of loop failures[2]. (3) The *queue lengths* of the active components are monitored to detect bottleneck conditions. (4) *Time-out mechanisms* keep components from getting stuck while forwarding data items, and help to detect deadlocks.

In addition to the above, components provide *self-test routines* that are executed from time to time (possibly when the application is idle). They assert amongst others that the component has enough resources and that its configuration and internal data structures are consistent.

Diagnosis. Diagnosis starts when a failure symptom has been discovered. Its goal is to establish a hypothesis about the fault type and the involved component(s), that serves as a basis for carrying out corrective actions. Diagnostic activities include "isolation testing" of data items and components, inspection of the data stream between components, tracking of dependency paths and analysis of the application structure.

- *Isolation testing* is a form of black-box testing; it does not use the integrated test functions of data items or components. To test a component, a "test suite" of specifically crafted data items are sent through it. For this purpose, the component is temporarily disconnected from its neighbors and taken out of the data stream (hence the name "isolation testing"), so that the tests can be carried out in the "live" execution environment without affecting the rest of the application. A similar procedure is used for testing data items: they are sent through a diagnosis component that is specially tailored for their type and capable of finding inconsistencies in their contents.
- *Data stream inspection* is used for instance for diagnosing incompatibility between two components. A diagnosis component is inserted between the two components to determine which one of them is behaving faultily. In a similar

---

[2] loop failures subsist when data items are continuously forwarded in a circular manner between a set of components.

way, a component's behavior can be assessed by observing its interactions with all neighbors.

- *Dependency paths* are explored to trace back a fault symptom to the actual fault. For example, if a corrupt data item has been detected, it is likely that it has been corrupted by a previous component and the dependency path must be followed upstream. Conversely, if there is a bottleneck scenario, the downstream dependencies must be followed to find the component that slows down processing.
- *Structural analysis* is used to diagnose deadlocks and loops, which can happen when components are connected to cycles. Deadlocks happen if too many data items are present in a cycle of components; data items keep looping in a cycle due to erroneous forwarding decisions. In this case, all components that are part of the loop must be identified, as well as those components where data items flow into and out of the loop.

Fault correction. Once the fault has been identified, corrective actions must be taken to eliminate it. Note that failures *inside* a component, e.g. design flaws or programming errors, cannot be corrected at run-time. Failure correction is thus limited to the following options: (1) re-configuration, re-initialization or substitution of a component and (2) reconfiguration of the application structure.

Examples of *component reconfiguration* are: augmenting the number of slots in the in-queue of an active component; switching to a resource-conservative mode in case of a resource shortage; insertion of additional active components in a composite component to enhance throughput. If a component is found to be buggy, it can be substituted by a compatible replacement component.

Management actions aimed at the *reconfiguration of the application structure* include for instance: de-coupling of incompatible components by insertion of a management component in between; insertion of additional components in parallel to an overloaded component to alleviate bottlenecks; insertion of buffer components into a loop to limit the potential of deadlocks happening.

4 Prototype Implementation

We have implemented a prototype of an E-mail relay based on our framework. It is composed of approximately thirty elementary components grouped into nine composite components. Each of the latter implements a piece of high-level functionality (like the SMTP protocol engine, aliasing of addresses, formatting of the message body, etc.). In its current implementation, our prototype contains a central management component with a user interface that gives a human manager access to the composite components and to all the elementary components they contain.

Presently, only monitoring is done automatically. The detected fault symptoms are dispatched to the management component, and the human manager can manually diagnose them at run-time by invoking methods on the components, just as an automatic management component would do. This approach has proven to be very useful for the design and testing of management algorithms.

5 Conclusions

There is an interesting symbiosis between component-oriented programming and automatic fault management: Component-based applications can benefit from run-time fault management to handle failure situations resulting from the lack of global testability. Fault management, in turn, profits from many characteristics of components as described in the paper.

We find the idea of adding re-usable management components to a framework very promising, and we expect that with a mature framework of this type, applications can be made failure-resilient with little additional effort. It should be feasible to build applications that recover from most typical problems automatically - we estimate that over 90% of the problems[3] can be solved without human intervention. For the remaining cases, the human manager (e.g. a system administrator) will not have to troubleshoot problems from scratch, but s/he will be able to build on the diagnosis already made by the fault management components.

The data flow paradigm is particularly suitable for fault management and it allow various kinds of applications to be built. Nevertheless, we do not expect all developers to use this paradigm, just for the sake of manageability. Our long-term goal is therefore to extend our approach to other paradigms and architectures. For the moment, we are working on the implementation and automation of our algorithms in the form of re-usable components. In parallel, we are extending the fault management to a *distributed* data flow application, namely a network of the E-mail relay prototypes mentioned above.

References

1. C. Szyperski, "Independently Extensible Systems - Software Engineering Potential and Challenges", Proceedings of the 19th Australasian Computer Science Conference, Melbourne, Australia, January 1996.
2. W. Weck, "Independently Extensible Component Frameworks", in M. Muehlhaeuser (ed.): Special Issues in Object- Oriented Programming, dpunkt Verlag, Heidelberg, 1997.
3. J. Harms, C.F. Tschudin, "Generic fault management of heterogeneous distributed applications", Request for Funding, NFRS Project 2129-04567.95, Geneva, 1995. *http://cuiwww.unige.ch/Telecom-group/members/vito/GFM.html.*
4. G. Genilloud, M. Polizzi, "Managing ANSA Objects with OSI Network Management Tools", in Proceedings IEEE Second International Workshop on Services in Distributed and Networked Environments, Whistler, British Columbia, 1995.
5. J.W. Wong et al. "Distributed Applications Management Using the OSI Management Framework", Technical Report 448, University of Western Ontario, Canada, January 1995.

---

[3] 90% with respect to their frequency, not 90% of all possible failure types.

Formal Methods for Component Software:
The Refinement Calculus Perspective

Martin Büchi and Emil Sekerinski

Turku Centre for Computer Science, Lemminkäisenkatu 14A,
20520 Turku, Finland, {mbuechi, esekerin}@abo.fi

Abstract. We exhibit the benefits of using formal methods for constructing and documenting component software. Formal specifications provide concise and complete descriptions of black-box components and, herewith, pave the way for full encapsulation. Specifications using abstract statements scale up better than pre-postconditions and allow for 'relative' specifications because they may refer to other components. Nondeterminism in specifications permits enhancements and alternate implementations. A formally verifiable refinement relationship between specification and implementation of a component ensures compliance with the published specification. Unambiguous and complete contracts are the foundation of any component market.

1 Introduction

The separation of specifications/interfaces and implementations of components is a prerequisite for the establishment of component software. It alleviates the necessity to distribute source code, thereby protects the implementation know-how and avoids overspecification. Overspecification basically prohibits future enhancements and alternate implementations. Furthermore, separate specifications enable the component integrator to understand the functionality without having to examine the source code.

The lack of easily and quickly understandable, concise, and complete specifications is the chief reason, why the advantages of the separation between specifications and implementations are not commonly exploited. Most current interface-description languages (IDLs) are limited to expressing syntactical aspects such as number, names, and types of parameters only. The IDLs completely ignore the behavior of components which is usually given as incomplete, ambiguous, partly overspecific, and often outdated textual description[1]. Incompleteness forces the component integrator to derive additional properties by trial and error which might be invalidated in future versions of the component. Ambiguity often remains undetected in an informal setting and causes mysterious errors. Overspecification unnecessarily restricts future enhancements. Incompleteness, ambiguity, and overspecification hinder alternate implementations — the ground stone of any component market.

Formal specifications can solve these problems. The creator of a component can test, whether based solely on the specification the component may be appropriately

---

[1] We denote by interface the syntactical aspects only and by contract both the interface and the behavioral specification.

used. Ambiguities can be detected by consistency proofs. Overspecification can more easily be detected in a concise formal language. Formal verification, here in the form of refinement proofs, guarantees that the implementation actually behaves as specified. Furthermore, a specification which is created before the component is implemented, can facilitate a structured development and, thereby, create more general, robust and efficient components and often also helps to save costs. The adaptation of formal specifications has been slow because of difficult notations which differ too much from implementation languages and lack of tool support, but also due to ignorance and prejudice.

Section 2 makes a plea for formal specifications as contracts, Sect. 3 shows why nondeterminism is also relevant for practitioners. Refinement between specifications and implementations to ensure compliance and refinement between different versions of a specifications are the topics of Sect. 4. Section 5 points to related work and Sect. 6 draws the conclusions.

2 A Plea for Formal Contracts

Vendors of integrated circuits provide data sheets and, quite commonly, also an executable specification in form of a VHDL program. They describe all relevant information for deployment, such as form factor, voltage, and signal delay in a standard way, that does not require interpretation or understanding of the physics required to build the chip. Contrast this with the typical description of an ActiveX software component: Incomplete plain textual descriptions augmented with a formal part that merely describes the number and types of parameters. The customer has no possibility to verify in advance whether the desired part meets the requirements. He often spends hours of trial and error to find out how the component must be used. He relies on testing of a few cases as the only way to gain confidence. Nobody and nothing guarantee that he uses only functionality which will continue to exist in future versions. Hence, there is an urgent need for better contracts! A good contract is clear, complete, and concise. A bad contract is ambiguous, misses important points, lays down irrelevant details, and is unnecessarily long. That current contracts, respectively in our terminology interfaces with textual addition, are too weak has also been acknowledged at WCOP'96 [9]. The lack of standardized contracts for software components is due to the high degree of freedom compared to hardware, the immaturity of the field, the difficulties in automated verification, and the — partly unnecessary — complexity and ill-definedness of common programming languages, which further complicates verification.

Jézéquel and Meyer [4] recently argued that the crash of the Ariane 5 was due to a reuse specification error. A poorly documented limitation in a component originally designed for the Ariane 4 with different physical requirements caused the error. Jézéquel and Meyer conclude, that reuse without a contract is sheer folly. Yet, contracts are the most important non-practice in component software. Clearly, white-box components do not solve these problems for large systems as they overwhelm the designer with details, rather than providing suitable abstractions.

A simple and popular form of contracts is that of pre- and postconditions. If a component is used in a correct manner, it has to satisfy its contract, i.e. establish the promised postcondition. If, however, its preconditions are not met, it has no obligations whatsoever and is free to behave arbitrarily.

Pre- and postconditions that are only checked at runtime — as it is usually the case — help to locate errors, but do not prevent them as static analysis does. Furthermore, these runtime checks are often removed from the final version for efficiency reasons. A program can still fail at a customer's site with input values which have not been tested. Because of the deficiencies of run-time only checking, programmers are not inclined to use specifications at all.

Pre- and postconditions being predicates, they cannot contain calls to other methods, except pure functions. This means that using pre- and postconditions one has to reinvent the wheel afresh for each method, rather than being able to build upon other specifications. Specifications in form of abstract statements are not affected by this scalability problem. Consider the partial specification of component Buffer using abstract statements:

```
component Buffer ...
  b : set of Item
  print(d: Device) = for all x in b do d.print(x) end
end Buffer
```

If we were to specify the same component using pre- and postconditions, we would have to expand the definition of the base type Device's print method incurring a number of disadvantages. The specification of how print ultimately sets the pixels on a device would be rather lengthy and not of our interest here. We loose the information that a method of d is invoked. Reasoning about the program, we cannot use the knowledge that d is of (behavioral) subtype of Device with a more deterministic specification. Pre-postcondition specifications contradict encapsulation and specialization.

Specifications by abstract statements come close to contracts as proposed by Helm et al. [3]. Contracts of Helm et al. specify "behavioral dependencies" between objects in terms of method calls and other constructs. Contracts are expressed in a special purpose language and then have to be linked to the underlying programming language. By contrast, we like to see abstract statements as a moderate extension of the underlying programming language for expressing contracts.

Changes to the specification of the print method, e.g. improved version decreasing nondeterminism, are not automatically reflected in the specification of Buffer. Pre-postconditions do not support 'relative' specifications in the sense of relying on previous specifications. The loss of self-containedness of abstract statement specifications can easily be compensated by a specification browser supporting in place expansion or hypertext-like facilities. Abstract statements also lend themselves to grey-box specifications, which reveal parts of the internals, such as call-sequences [10].

The process of writing a formal specification often leads to more generally useful, easier to integrate, and longer-lived components. Rough edges, special cases, and anomalies resulting from implementation difficulties and lack of overview during implementation can often be detected and eliminated by a specification.

For example, the above specification of Device states that for all elements in b, the method print is called in an arbitrary order. No element is printed twice, since a set contains an element at most once. If this is desired, we should have used a bag (multiset) rather than a set. If we like that the elements are printed always in the same order, we should have used a sequence rather than a set and an iteration in print. The specification also states that printing an empty buffer is a no–op rather than an error.

A component should not only formally specify its own contract, but also the (minimal) contracts of its required components. A calendar component might require a database component which satisfies a certain contract [1,11]. The component integrator can choose such a component, or — in a more dynamic scenario — the calendar component can 'shop' for the desired component at runtime. Formal specifications of required and existing components simplify also the creation of wrappers/adaptors.

3   Nondeterminism: Avoiding Overspecification

Nondeterminism is an approach to deliberately leave a decision open, to abandon the exact predictability of future states. As such, nondeterminism appears to be neither commonly desirable nor is it used in implementation languages. On the other hand, nondeterminism is a fundamental tool for specifications to avoid laying down unnecessary details.

A nondeterministic specification leaves more choice for the implementation, which can be used for optimizations. Even if this degree of freedom is not used in the envisaged first implementation, it greatly increases the likelihood that future enhancements and alternate implementations can be made compliant with the specification. The earlier specification of the component Buffer is an example.

Nondeterminism often enhances the comprehensibility of specifications because the reader does not have to wonder why something has to be exactly in a certain way, when other choices would be as good. Many things are actually nondeterministic and should be acknowledged and specified as such.

Nondeterminism from an outside perspective often stems form information hiding, where the actual implementation is deterministic. A SQL database query without any sorting options returns an arbitrarily sorted list of records; a square root function returns an arbitrary value satisfying the specified precision. Both implementations are deterministic, but the outcomes are determined by hidden state components and implementation details.

We can also interpret nondeterminism as 'free will' of a component which can in no way be influenced from the outside. Writing a combined specification consisting of existing components and a custom 'glue component' which we implement ourselves, we have to distinguish between two forms of nondeterminism. Nondeterminism within existing components which is beyond our control, called demonic nondeterminism, and nondeterminism in our custom component which we can control in our favor, called angelic nondeterminism. In this sense, we can consider program execution as a game, the rules of which are given by the specification [2]. Demonic choices are moves made by an opponent (the existing component), and angelic choices are our moves. The combined specification is correct, if we can make moves such that we can achieve the desired goal, no matter what the opponent does. Hence, such a combined specification can help to decide whether a given component is suitable to solve a certain task.

4 Refinement: Ensuring Compliance with Specification

Employing formal specifications, we want to make sure that the implementation actually complies with its specification or, more precisely, is a refinement thereof [2]. A statement T refines a statement S, if considering the observable input-output behaviour, the output of T for a given input would be possible with S as well. Taking the possibility of nondeterminism into account, we formally define that $S \sqsubseteq T$ (S is refined by T) as

$$S \sqsubseteq T \stackrel{\text{def}}{=} \forall q.wp(S,q) \subseteq wp(T,q)$$

where q is a set of states and $wp(X,q)$ denotes the weakest precondition of q with respect to statement X, i.e., the set of states from which X is guaranteed to terminate in a state of q.

Refinement is reflexive, transitive, and antisymmetric. Assume that we have specifications S1 and S2, where $S1 \sqsubseteq S2$, and implementations I1 and I2, where $S1 \sqsubseteq I1$ and $S2 \sqsubseteq I2$. Then $S1 \sqsubseteq I2$ holds because of transitivity, but $I1 \sqsubseteq I2$ does not hold. No refinement relationship holds between two implementations of the same specification. Hence, it is important that clients only rely on properties guaranteed by the specification. Testing cannot uncover reliance on unspecified implementation features, only formal analysis can.

5 Related Work

Related work includes the Interface Specification Language developed at CSTaR Software Engineering Lab [5], the work of the Composable Software Systems group at Carnegie Mellon [8], and the research conducted by the Object Systems Group at the University of Geneva [7]. Bertrand Meyer propagates design by contract for component software, albeit of a less formal nature [6].

6 Conclusions

We have argued that only formal contracts paired with refinement can guarantee full encapsulation of software components, which is the base for improved and alternate implementations. Formal contracts lead to a more structured development, more orthogonal and, hence, longer-lived and more generally useful components, often at a lower cost.

Nondeterminism is a necessity for providing freedom of implementation. Refinement guarantees that implementations adhere to their specifications and that new versions are plug-compatible. Abstract statements do not have the scalability problems of pre-postcondition specifications because they allow for external calls.

Formal methods are needed to compensate the loss of the closed-world assumption and the impossibility to test a component in all possible environments. They are, however, no universal panacea nor is their application very simple, but we regard them as a necessity for the establishment of component software.

337

The paper presented at the workshop (http://www.abo.fi/~mbuechi/) contains more material on refinement and also includes sections on the specification of invariants and temporal properties and on the design of specification languages, which are left out of this version.

Acknowledgments We would like to thank the referees, Wolfgang Weck, Ralph Back, and Lars Nielsen for their comments.

References

1. Ásgeir Ólafsson and Doug Bryan. On the need for "required interfaces" of components. In M. Mühlhaeuser, editor, *Special Issues in Object-Oriented Programming*, pages 159–165. dpunkt Verlag Heidelberg, 1997. ISBN 3-920993-67-5.
2. R. J. R. Back and Joackim von Wright. *Refinement Calculus: A Systematic Introduction.* Springer Verlag, to appear 1997.
3. Richard Helm, Ian M. Holland, and Dipayan Gangopadhyay. Contracts: Specifying behavioral compositions in object-oriented systems. In *Proceedings of OOPSLA/ECOOP '90 Conference on Object-Oriented Programming Systems, Languages and Application*, pages 169–180, October 1990.
4. Jean-Marc Jézéquel and Bertrand Meyer. Put it in the contract: The lessons of ariane. *IEEE Computer*, pages 129–130, January 1997.
5. W. Kozaczynski and J. O. Ning. Concern-driven design for a specification language. In *Proceedings of the 8th International Workshop on Software Specification and Design*, Berlin, Germany, March 1996.
6. Bertrand Meyer. *Object-Oriented Software Construction.* Prentice Hall, second edition, 1997.
7. Oscar Nierstrasz and Dennis Tsichritzis, editors. *Object-Oriented Software Composition.* Prentice Hall, 1995.
8. David Garlan, Daniel Jackson, Mary Shaw, and Jeannette Wing. Composable software systems, 1996. http://www.cs.cmu.edu/~Compose/.
9. Clemens A. Szyperski and Cuno Pfister. Component-oriented programming: WCOP'96 workshop report. In M. Mühlhaeuser, editor, *Special Issues in Object-Oriented Programming*, pages 127–130. dpunkt Verlag Heidelberg, 1997. ISBN 3-920993-67-5.
10. Martin Büchi and Wolfgang Weck. A plea for grey-box components. In *Foundations of Component-Based Systems '97*, 1997. http://www.abo.fi/~mbuechi/.
11. Amy M. Zaremsky and Jeannette M. Wing. Specification matching of software components. In *SIGSOFT Foundations of Software Engineering*, October 1995. Also CMU-CS-95-127.

Reuse Contracts as Component Interface Descriptions

Koen De Hondt, Carine Lucas, and Patrick Steyaert

Programming Technology Lab
Computer Science Department
Vrije Universiteit Brussel
Pleinlaan 2, B-1050 Brussel, Belgium
www: http://progwww.vub.ac.be/
email: kdehondt@vub.ac.be, clucas@vub.ac.be, prsteyae@vub.ac.be

Abstract. Current interface descriptions are poor in describing components, because they only provide an external view on a component and they do not lay down how components interact with each other. Suggestions to improve component interface descriptions at last year's workshop are reconsidered and reuse contracts are put forward as a solution that goes one step further.

1 Introduction

One of the major issues at last year's Workshop on Component-Oriented Programming was the need for more information about how a component relies on its context, than traditionally provided by the current state of the art interface description languages.

Ólafsson and Bryan [3] argued that, apart from the provided interface, a component interface description should also state the "required interfaces". A required interface is the interface of an acquaintance component that is required to enable a component to interact with that acquaintance component.

Although they argue that required interfaces are essential to understand the architecture of a component-based system, we claim that they in fact contain too little information to get a good understanding of the architecture, since an interface does not say what actually happens when one of its methods is invoked. For instance, an interface does not state the call-backs to the originating component. In our opinion, what is crucial in order to get a good understanding, is a description of the interaction structure, or the software contracts in which components participate. For this reason required interfaces are also insufficient to support component composition correctly, for they allow the composition of components that have compatible provided and required interfaces, but not the correct interaction behavior. We believe that information on interaction structure should be part of the interface of a component, so that it can be used to make the architecture clear, to help developers in adapting components to particular needs, and to verify component composition based on their interface instead of auxiliary (and perhaps informal) documentation.

In this paper, reuse contracts [4] are applied to the domain of components. It will be shown that reuse contracts are not interface descriptions to which components have to comply exactly. Instead they can be adapted by means of reuse operators. These reuse operators state how a reuse contract is adapted. By comparing reuse operators applied to a reuse contract, conflict detection can be performed and composability of components can be validated. This capacity makes reuse contracts more than just enhanced interface descriptions.

2 Reuse Contracts

Essentially, a reuse contract is an interface description for a set of collaborating participant components. It states the participants that play a role in the reuse contract, their interfaces, their acquaintance relations, and the interaction structure between acquaintances. Reuse contracts employ an extended form of Lamping's specialisation clauses [1] to document the interaction structure. While Lamping's specialisation clauses only document the self sends of an operation, specialisation clauses in reuse contracts document all inter-operation dependencies. In their most basic form, specialisation clauses in reuse contracts just list the operation signatures, without type information or semantic information, such as the order in which operations are invoked.

Reuse contracts are defined formally by Lucas [2]. Since such formal specifications are hard to read, a visual representation of reuse contracts was developed. A participant is depicted by a rectangle containing the participant's name and interface. An acquaintance relationship is depicted by a line connecting two participants. Invoked operations, together with the operations that invoke them, are notated along this line. For clarity, the line can also be annotated with the name of the acquaintance relationship. As a shortcut, self-invocations are notated in the interface of a component, instead of along an acquaintance relation with itself.

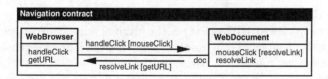

Fig. 1. Example Reuse Contract

Figure 1 shows a reuse contract for navigation in a web browser. `handleClick` on `WebBrowser` invokes `mouseClick` on `WebDocument`. `WebDocument` invokes its `resolveLink` operation when the mouse was clicked on a link (the details of the detection of the link is of no importance here). `resolveLink` invokes `getURL` on `WebBrowser` in order to get the contents of the web page pointed to by the link. For simplicity, no arguments of operations are shown here.

A reuse contract documents the assumptions each participant makes about its acquaintances. For instance, in Fig. 1 the `WebBrowser` can safely assume that the `WebDocument` may invoke `getURL` when it invokes `mouseClick`. When a component developer builds a component, he can rely on these assumptions to implement the component according to the participant descriptions. However, requesting that a component is fully compliant with the interface and interaction structure descriptions, would make reuse contracts too constraining, and consequently too impractical to use. Instead, components may deviate from the reuse contract, but the component developer has to document how they deviate exactly, so that this information can be used later on to perform conflict checking.

Therefore, reuse contracts are subject to so-called reuse operators, or modifiers, actions that adapt participants and the interaction structure between these participants. In practice, a developer performs several adaptations at once in order to reuse a component. A few basic reuse operators were identified into which such adaptations can be decomposed [2]. More general adaptations are aggregations of the basic reuse operators. Each reuse operator has an associated applicability rule, that is, a reuse operator can only be applied when certain conditions apply. Applying a reuse operator on a reuse contract results in a new reuse contract, called the derived reuse contract.

Typical reuse operators on reuse contracts are extension and refinement, and their inverse operations, cancellation and coarsening. These operators come in two flavors: one flavor handles the operations on a participant, while the other flavor handles the operation on the context of a reuse contract, being the set of participants and their acquaintance relationships. A participant extension adds new operation descriptions to one or more participants in a reuse contract. A context extension adds new participant descriptions to a reuse contract. A participant refinement adds extra operation invocations to the specialisation clauses of already existing operations. A context refinement adds extra acquaintance relationships to a reuse contract.

The top of Fig. 2 shows how a web browser component with a history to store the already viewed URLs changes the original reuse contract given in Fig. 1. This new reuse contract is the result of applying the following reuse operators to the original reuse contract: a participant extension to add `addURLtoHistory` to the interface of the browser component and a participant refinement to add `addURLtoHistory` to the specialisation clause of `getURL`. Note that the browser component's name has changed to `HistoryWebBrowser`. This is achieved through a renaming operation.

The bottom of Fig. 2 shows another adaptation of the original reuse contract. The rationale behind this adaptation is that the new document component, called `PDFViewerPluginDocument`, only contains links that point to places within the PDF document and the targets of these links can thus be retrieved by the component itself. This retrieval is achieved with a new operation `gotoPage` instead of delegating this responsibility to the browser component through `getURL`. Therefore the original navigation reuse contract is adapted as follows: a participant coarsening removes the invocation of **getURL** from the specialisation clause of **resolvelink**, a participant extension adds the new operation **gotoPage** to the interface of **PDFViewerPluginDocument**, and a participant refinement adds the invocation of **gotoPage** to the specialisation clause of **resolvelink**. A renaming operation is also required to change the name of the document component.

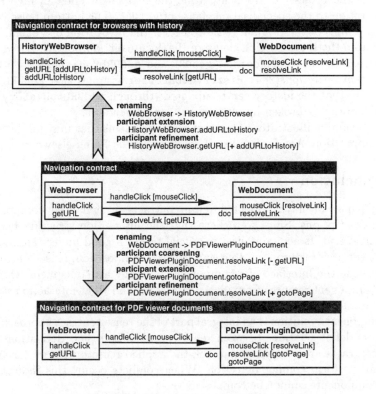

Fig. 2. Two adaptations of the original reuse contract

3 Component Composition

When a reuser now wants to combine the **HistoryWebBrowser** with the **PDF-ViewerPluginDocument**, he runs into trouble, because his application will not behave correctly. Since link resolving is done by the **PDFViewerPluginDocument** instead of by the **HistoryWebBrowser**, the **HistoryWebBrowser**'s history will not be updated when the user clicks on a link in a **PDFViewerPluginDocument**.

With standard interface definitions, this problem would not have been detected until the application was running, because **HistoryWebBrowser** and **PDF-ViewerPluginDocument** have compatible provided and required interfaces.

With reuse contracts however, this problem is detected when the two components are composed. By comparing the reuse operators that were used to derive the two reuse contracts in Fig. 2, one can easily determine what inhibits composition of `HistoryWebBrowser` and `PDFViewerPluginDocument`. The top reuse contract is derived by applying a combination of an extension and a refinement on the original reuse contract. The extension adds `addURLtoHistory` to the interface of the browser component, while the refinement adds an invocation of this operation to the specialisation clause of `getURL`. The bottom reuse contract is a coarsening of the original reuse contract: the invocation of `getURL` was removed from the specialisation clause of the document component. Based on this comparison we can conclude that `getURL` and `addURLtoHistory` have become *inconsistent operations*[2][4]: `HistoryWebBrowser` assumes that `getURL` will be invoked, so that the history can be updated (through `addURLtoHistory`), while this assumption is broken by `PDFViewerPluginDocument`.

This example illustrates but one of many problems that may inhibit component composition. A complete list of conflicts can be found elsewhere [2].

4 Conclusion

In this paper we have presented reuse contracts as enhanced component interface descriptions. Since we believe that the interaction structure between a component and its acquaintances is crucial to get a good understanding of the component architecture, and to ensure correct composition, reuse contracts not only provide the interface of a component, but they also document what interface a component requires from its acquaintances and what interaction structure is required for correct inter-component behavior.

Component evolution is an integral part of the reuse contract approach. Reuse operators define relations between reuse contracts and their derivations. When reuse contracts are evolved in parallel, the applied reuse operators can be compared to perform conflict detection. When conflicts occur, this indicates that some components cannot be composed.

References

1. John Lamping: Typing the specialization interface. Proceedings of OOPSLA'93 (Sep. 26 - Oct. 1, Washington, DC, USA), volume 28(10) of ACM Sigplan Notices, pages 201–214. ACM Press, October 1993
2. Carine Lucas: Documenting Reuse and Evolution with Reuse Contracts. PhD thesis, Vrije Universiteit Brussel, 1997
3. Asgeir Ólafsson and Bryan Doug: On the need for "required interfaces" of components. In Max Mühlhäuser, editor, Special Issues in Object-Oriented Programming, Workshop Reader of the 10th European Conference on Object-Oriented Programming, ECOOP'96, Linz, pages 159–165. dpunkt Verlag, 1997
4. Patrick Steyaert, Carine Lucas, Kim Mens, and Theo D'Hondt: Reuse contracts: Managing the evolution of reusable assets. In Proceedings of OOPSLA'96 (Oct. 6-10, San Jose, California), volume 31(10) of ACM Sigplan Notices, pages 268–285. ACM Press, 1996

A Control Model for the Dynamic Selection and Configuration of Software Components

Philippe Lalanda

Thomson-CSF Corporate Research Laboratory
Domaine de Corbeville
F-91404 Orsay, France

Abstract. Component-oriented programming is becoming increasingly important in the software-intensive industry. However, there is currently little guidance for software developers on how to compose software components in order to produce running applications. We believe that the development of domain-specific software architectures (DSSA) provides a way to integrate properly software components developed by different organizations.

The purpose of this paper is to present an architectural approach that permits the development and exploitation of DSSAs. This approach builds on a model of dynamic control that permits to select and configure software components both statically and dynamically.

1   Introduction

The industry of software-intensive systems is facing today both economical and technical challenges. On one hand, shrinking budgets and sharp competition require to reduce significantly development and maintenance costs, shorten lead time, and improve predictability. On the other hand, the size and complexity of systems have dramatically increased in the past few years. This has brought considerable problems in terms of suitability, efficiency, scalability and portability.

Component-oriented programming, which amortizes development costs on several systems, is therefore becoming increasingly important. The key paradigm of this approach is megaprogramming [1], that is the ability to define a system by putting together software components. However, component-oriented programming raises several important issues. In particular, we believe that unguided composition of software components is unlikely to produce running applications and that an architectural framework is necessary to integrate components. A domain-specific software architectures (DSSA) provides such a framework. It takes into account the domain under consideration and provides the computational framework necessary to solve typical problems of the domain. It describes the type of components that can be integrated in the system, their possible connections, and the rationale under their collaboration.

The purpose of this paper is to present an architectural approach that permits the development and exploitation of DSSAs. This approach builds on a model of dynamic control that permits to select and configure software components both statically and dynamically. We will show that it permits the integration of software components developed in separate projects, while ensuring overall architectural coherence.

2 Domain-specific software architecture

Domain-specific software architecture [2] is a subdomain of software architecture where a reference architecture, partly abstract, is developed in a well understood domain. A DSSA comprises:

- a reference architecture describing a general computational framework,
- a component library containing reusable chunks of domain expertise,
- an application configuration method for selecting and configuring components within the architecture to meet particular application requirements.

A DSSA thus provides a framework for top-down design. It actually permits to develop and reuse a pool of components (assets) pluggable in the architecture, and to generate new applications by selection/composition of components based on application requirements.

Generic architectural models have been proposed recently to support the development of DSSAs. GenVoca [3] is a domain-independent model for defining scalable families of hierarchical systems as compositions of reusable components. A reference architecture in GenVoca is made of *realms*, that is sets of reusable components that export and import standardized components organized into semantics layers, and design rules to identify (and then preclude) illegal components combination. An application is obtained by combining subsystems, that is combinations of components of the same realms. This approach, which makes the assumption that a system can be expressed as a combination of primitive components (it is actually an equation), seems to be limited to specific domains. Rapide [4] constitutes a more general approach. It is a computer language for defining and executing models of system architecture. An architecture is defined by a set of modules and their interconnections, with no restriction on their organization. Communication between modules are explicitly defined by connections between module interfaces. Interfaces specify both the operations a module provides and the operations it requires from other modules. In this approach, components communicate directly. Selected components can introduce new requirements for capabilities other component implementations will need to satisfy. The integration of components is therefore not straightforward and depends on the current system's configuration.

3   Blackboard-based control

We have been developing and experimenting with a domain-independent control model that permits to:

- define DSSAs made of independent software components,
- select and configure software components both statically and dynamically.

Our approach builds on a model of dynamic control [5] where a system has (a) a repertoire of independent domain and control components; (b) a control plan expressing its desirable behavior; (c) a meta-controller that chooses at each control cycle the currently enabled component that best matches the current control plan.

Domain and control components are kept in a library. Domain components are concerned with the solving of a particular problem. They retrieve data from a shared knowledge base and write their contribution to the problem solving in it. Control components deal with the management of the system control plan. They can replace the current plan, postpone it, refine it, *etc...*
Each component has a set of triggering conditions that can be satisfied by particular kinds of *events*, that is global changes in the system resulting from external inputs or previously executed components. When an event satisfies a component's triggering conditions, the component is enabled and its parameters bound to variable values from the triggering situation. At each control cycle, many competing components may be enabled and the system must choose among them. To support this control decisions, each component has an interface that describes the kinds of events that enable it, the variables to be bound in its enabling context, the task it performs, the type of method it applies, its required resources (e.g, computation, perceptual data), its execution properties (e.g, speed, complexity, completeness), and its results properties.

A control plan describes the system's intended behavior as a temporal graph of plan steps, each of which comprises a start condition, a stop condition, and an intended activity in the form of a tuple (task, parameters, constraints). Control plans do not refer explicitly to any particular component in the system's repertoire. They only describe intended behaviors in terms of the desired task, parameter values, and constraints. Thus, at each control cycle, the system has a plan of intended action, which intentionally describes an equivalence class of desirable behaviors and in which currently enabled specific components may have graded degrees of memberships.

The meta-controller attempts to follow the current control plan by executing the most appropriate enabled components. Specifically, the meta-controller configures and executes the enabled component that: (a) is capable of performing the currently planned task with the specified parameterization; and (b) has a description that matches the specified constraints better than any other enabled component that also satisfy (a). If the selected enabled component is a control component, the control plan is updated. Otherwise, a domain component is executed in order to contribute to the problem solving process.

This generic architectural model supports the development of a wide variety of DSSAs. The dynamic control model provides a framework in which appropriate sets of components can be selected and configured at both design time and run time. The integration of components is actually very simple since components are considered independently and are only characterized by their own properties. At run-time, if useful new application-relevant component should become available, the new components can be substituted for old ones or added to the knowledge base alongside the old ones, without interrupting system operations. The architecture's event-based enabling of components, its plan-based meta-control choices among competing components, and its effort to retrieve necessary knowledge from the shared knowledge base are not preprogrammed to require any particular components.

4 Domain of Experiments

We have been developing DSSAs in several domains. In particular, our approach has been applied to autonomous office robots. Detailed results about these experiments can be found in [6]. We are now conducting experiments on the planning and real-time updating of aircraft missions. We give in this section a brief description of the purposes and main features of such a system, and explain why it has been chosen as a viable domain for the building of a DSSA.

The primary goal of a mission planning system is to provide the aircraft's automatic pilot with a multi-dimension trajectory. A *nominal* trajectory is computed off-line before the mission starts. As the mission progresses, the goal of the mission planning system is to check the consistency between the expected plane position as given by the nominal trajectory and its actual position. If some deviation is detected, the system has to analyze the discrepancy and generate a new trajectory fulfilling the mission goals as well as possible.

Numerous components are involved in mission planning systems. First, many components specialized in the computation of trajectory are available, depending on the requirements (speed, fuel preservation, discretion, *etc*...), the target plane, or the trajectory's dimensions that are needed. There are also diverse plans expressing various ways to react to unexpected events depending on the pilot's profile, mission objectives, planes characteristics, *etc*....

This domain is ideally suited for building a DSSA for several reasons:

- the domain is well understood and the basic technology is relatively stable,
- there are several existing systems and a need for many new applications,
- common abstractions and features can be identified across different systems,

– domain-specific components are available and variability can be expressed at the architectural level with a variation in components.

Strategies necessary to react to unexpected components have been encapsulated in control components which transform them into control plans. Algorithms specialized in trajectory calculations have been wrapped up in domain-specific components. According to the principles previously presented, the architecture supports both design time and run-time configuration. At design time, one can select plans and calculating algorithms required to tackle a given application. At run-time, new components can be integrated in order to provide new reactions to a given situation or new ways to compute a trajectory, or simply to replace outdated components.

5 Conclusion

The lack of architectural perspective acts as a brake on wider use of reusable components. The general DSSA approach provides a coherent computational framework where software components can be plugged with confidence. Our generic architectural model permits the design and implementation of DSSAs in many domains. It makes use of the basic blackboard organization in order to enable the integration and interoperation of diverse components. The additional features of the dynamic control model provide the necessary additional support for flexible run-time configuration and meta-control. This approach has been successfully applied to diverse domains like autonomous robots and monitoring systems and is now used for the planning and real-time updating of aircraft missions. It has allowed us to integrate smoothly legacy code with newly developed components and to select and configure them for specific applications.

6 References

References

1. B.W. Boehm and W.L. Scherlis, *Megaprogramming*, Proceedings of the DARPA Software Technology Conference, April 1992.
2. E. Mettala, *Presentation at ISTO Software Technology Community Meeting*, June, 1990.
3. D. Batory, V. Singhal, J. Thomas, S. Dasari, B. Geraci, and M. Sirkin, *The GenVoca Model of Software-System Generators*, IEEE Software, September 1994.
4. D. Luckham, J. Kenney, L. Augustin, J. Vera, D. Bryan, and W. Mann, *Specification and Analysis of System Architecture Using Rapide*, IEEE Transactions on Software Engineering, vol. 21, number 4, April 1995.
5. B. Hayes-Roth, *A blackboard architecture for control*, Artificial Intelligence, num. 26, 1985.
6. B. Hayes-Roth, P. Lalanda, P. Morignot, M. Balanovic and K. Pfleger, *A domain-specific software architecture for adaptative intelligent system*, IEEE Transactions on Software Engineering, 1995.

Design and Evaluation of Distributed Component-Oriented Software Systems

Michael Goedicke and Torsten Meyer

University of Essen,Mathematics and Computing,D-45117 Essen,Germany

Abstract. In this contribution we consider an approach to describe the architecture of distributed software systems. This approach is based on a component model of software which contains additional information about distribution. Using the design description as a basis a distributed object-oriented implementation compliant with OMG's CORBA standard can be generated automatically. We discuss how a performance model can be derived systematically from the architecture description. Thus the design of complex, hierarchically structured distributed software systems can be assessed wrt. e.g. response time of remote operation invocations [1].

1   Introduction and Related Work

The design of the software architecture of distributed software systems with complex client-server relationships is still a major problem. In this contribution, we present our architectural framework for developing component-oriented distributed systems. We sketch how distributed architectures can easily be designed using our architecture description language Π. The step to implement a distributed architecture is realized by transforming software components in Π to distributed objects according to the Object Management Group's standard CORBA (Common Object Request Broker Architecture). Since the resulting implementation structure corresponds to the design structure, knowledge about the execution of the distributed system may feedback thus giving new insights at the design and requirements stage.

Related research w.r.t. self-contained and independent software components is done in many places. A prominent example is ROI (Regis Orb Implementation), an integration of the architecture description language REGIS/DARWIN with IONA Technologies CORBA implementation ORBIX (cf. [2]). In contrast to Regis/Darwin, Π has a richer language for describing semantic properties in interfaces. Architectural support on top of CORBA is also provided in [9] using design patterns and application frameworks (cf. [5], [1]). As patterns and frameworks are often specialized w.r.t. sets of horizontal functionalities or vertical areas of application domains, our approach is more general. Our approach is based on formally specifying software architecture while patterns and frameworks are less rigorously founded.

---

[1] This work is partly funded by the DFG project QUAFOS, contract MU1158/2-1.

In chapter 2 we show how the design of distributed component-oriented software systems can be described using the Architecture Description Language Π. It is also briefly shown how Π and CORBA are integrated. We introduce our concept for simulation-based evaluation of the design architecture in chapter 3.

2 The Architecture Description Language Π

In this chapter we will present Π, our Architecture Description Language (ADL), which supports the design of distributed component-oriented software systems. It provides concepts for separating the development of distributed independent software components from the interconnection and configuration of such components: although component dependency requirements can be stated with a single independent component, the explicit connection structure can be defined at a different point in the design process [6].

According to [7] a software *component* is a unit which provides its clients with services specified by its interface and encapsulates local structures that implement these services. It may use services of other components to realize the exported ones. Each component encapsulates one or more Abstract Data Types (ADTs), hence an object-based structuring of the whole architecture is enforced. Collections of components connected via use relations are called *configurations*. Also, configurations have in principle the same interfaces to their environment as single components and thus may be used as components hierarchically.

In Π, each component is described by four sections. The *export section* gives an abstract image of the component's realization; the abstract data types stated here are public and may be used by other components. The *body section* describes the realization of a component; here, the construction of the exported abstract data types is encapsulated. According to the concept of formal import, only requirements to imported abstract data types are specified in the *import section*. While configurations of components are built, the import section has to be actualized with export sections of potential server components via use relations. Finally, in the *common parameters section* abstract data types are stated which are imported and exported unchanged.

Π is a multi-formalism language and single views can be seen as overlapping partial specifications of a component. Each section can be specified by four views: the *type view* describes the component's invariant properties (according to execution of operations) by means of algebraic specification techniques, the *imperative view* defines imperative operation signatures and algorithms, the *concurrency view* specifies possible orderings of operation executions, the *interaction view* encapsulates information according to distribution of components.

Due to the fact that in Π each component specification is parameterized by its formal import it can be used with different parameter actualizations. A component developed and viewed in isolation is some kind of component template in contrast to the same component used within the specific context of the other components. Different instantiations of a component which can be connected via use relations are called *component incarnations* and the isolated component template is called *Concurrently Executable Module* (CEM). Thus, our approach takes an open world perspective: according to the concept of formal import a clear distinction can be made between the independent development of self-contained CEMs and the connection of component incarnations. During the development of a single CEM only requirements to imported services are described, the actual mapping from a component incarnation's requirements to services offered by potential server incarnations is made within the component connections. Within a configuration of component incarnations not all open imports have to be actualized. They can be connected to the import requirements of the entire configuration in order to allow other components to be linked to the configuration at a different time.

A distributed software system can now be described as a configuration of distributed components which communicate via local or remote use relations (cf. [8]). For each remote use relation between two distributed components, a communication protocol and functional as well as non-functional attributes for this protocol can be specified. Further, non-functional requirements regarding remote use relations and the performance of potential server components can be stated with a client component. The remote use relation is only valid for that component, if its performance attributes satisfy the component's performance requirements.

The tool PiLS (*Π*-Language Syntax Editor) allows editing and visualizing of *Π*-configurations. In addition a distributed object oriented implementation based on the Object Management Group's standard CORBA can be generated from a *Π* architecture description automatically. Details regarding our *Π*/CORBA integration concept can be found in [8].

3   Performance Evaluation of the Design

In addition to functional requirements, also non-functional requirements (e.g., response time, throughput, etc.) have essential impact on the design of distributed systems. This is true a priori, i.e. the analysis and assessment of a components' performance should be possible while the entire design architecture is still unfinished, as well as a posteriori, i.e. measuring the efficiency of the components' implementations.

Using the *Π* language, the functional behaviour of distributed components and their connections can be described as well as performance-related attributes of this architecture. For functional as well as performance-related evaluation, we use the Queuing Specification and Description Language QSDL [3]. QSDL is an extension of the ITU's Specification and Description Language SDL for evaluating systems wrt. non-functional properties. The transformation of a QSDL-specification to an executable program for simulation and validation of the specified system is performed automatically by the tool QUEST that has been developed at the University of Essen. By executing the simulator, stochastic performance measures can be gained.

We have identified interfaces between the component model in Π and the system specification in QSDL using ViewPoints a method engineering and integration framework. Thus performance requirements of a software system identified in its component model can be evaluated in its corresponding QSDL-system. The simulation results can be transferred back to the Π world by means of the ViewPoint framework. Details according to the ViewPoint framework can be found in [4], while our Π/QSDL integration concept is described in [3].

Within a QSDL specification, measurement of performance-related system properties is done with the help of the *sensor* concept. A sensor can be placed anywhere in the QSDL-system and collects information about system events during the simulation of the QSDL-system (e.g., a counter for signal throughput of a communication channel). QSDL provides a standard sensor library for the most usual performance attributes and also allows individual user-defined sensors. Finally, the evaluation results can be visualized using the QUEST tool.

In Π, the concept for a remote use relation's performance attributes is adapted to QSDL's sensor concept and the interaction view's performance requirements are sensors extended by a compare operator and a concrete value (e.g., response time $\leq$ 10 ms). Thus bidirectional relations of performance-related system properties between Π and QSDL can be identified: performance attributes grasped in the architecture design can be evaluated and also the results of the evaluation may feedback to new insights in the development cycle's requirements stage.

4 Conclusions

In this paper we sketched how distributed component-oriented software architectures can be designed and evaluated based on a concept of independently created and interconnected software components. We covered some important aspects of the design stage of the development cycle with the architecture specification language Π and used the OMG standard CORBA for the implementation stage. We closed the gap between design and implementation by providing an integration concept for Π and CORBA.

We also discussed how performance-related requirements regarding distributed communication can be integrated into the Π design model. Such a design model may be analysed quantitatively in order to gain information about the distributed system's functional and non-functional behaviour. This information may either justify design decisions or may lead to changes in the design architecture.

5 Further Work

We have completed the automated transformation from distributed Π specifications to OMG/IDL and the target language C++ for object implementations including runtime support. We use Sun SparcStations with Solaris and SunSoft's

CORBA realization NEO. While tool support exist for both the Π-language and QSDL separately, we are also researching on implementing our Π/QSDL integration concept.

For developing large dynamic evolving systems it is also important to overcome the closed world assumption not only at design stage, but also within the distributed CORBA implementation and the QSDL performance model. Currently we are researching how to use dynamic invocation within the architecture's CORBA implementation in order to access newly added objects at runtime. While the evaluation of a QSDL-system always requires an environement (at least an abstract description of a load generator), QSDL-processes can be created dynamically.

6   Acknowledgments

The Π-language was developed while the first author was with H. Weber, now head of the Fraunhofer Institute ISST Berlin/Dortmund. His inspiration is gratefully acknowledged.

References

1. Bosch,J., Molin,P., Mattsson,M., and Bengtsson,P.O. (1997): Object-Oriented Frameworks - Problems & Experiences, submitted.
2. Crane,J.S., and Dulay,N. (1997): A Configurable Protocol Architecture for CORBA environments, Proc. of ISADS 97, Berlin, Germany.
3. Diefenbruch,M., and Meyer,T. (1996): On Formal Modelling and Verifying Performance Requirements of Distributed Systems, Proc. IDPT 96, ISSN 1090-9389, Austin, USA.
4. Finkelstein, A., Kramer, J., Nuseibeh, B., Finkelstein, L., and Goedicke, M. (1992): Viewpoints: A Framework for Integrating Multiple Perspectives in System Development, Intl Journal of Software Engineering and Knowledge Engineering, vol. 2, pp. 31-57.
5. Gamma,E., Helm,R., Johnson,R., and Vlissides,J. (1995): Design Patters: Elements of Reusable Object-Oriented Software, Addison-Wesley, Reading,Massachusetts.
6. Goedicke,M., Cramer,J., Fey,W., and Große-Rhode,M. (1991): Towards a Formally Based Component Description Language - a Foundation for Reuse, Structured Programming Vol. 12 No. 2, Berlin: Springer.
7. Goedicke, M., and Schumann, H. (1994): Component-Oriented Software Development with Π, ISST report 21/94, Fraunhofer Institute for Software-Engineering and Systems Engineering.
8. Goedicke,M. and Meyer, T. (1997): A concept for the interaction of components, report Π-2 DFG project QUAFOS, University of Essen.
9. Mowbray,T.J., and Malveau,C. (1997): CORBA Design Patterns, Wiley Computer Publishing, New York: John Wiley & Sons, Inc.
10. Object Management Group, Inc. (1995): The Common Object Request Broker Architecture and Specification, revision 2.0.

The Fragile Base Class Problem and Its Impact on Component Systems

Leonid Mikhajlov and Emil Sekerinski

Turku Centre for Computer Science, Lemminkäisenkatu 14A,
20520 Turku, Finland, {lmikhajl, esekerin}@abo.fi

Abstract. In this paper we study applicability of the code inheritance mechanism to the domain of open component systems in light of so-called *fragile base class problem*. We propose a system architecture based on *disciplined inheritance* and present three check lists for component framework designers, component framework developers, and its users.

1 Introduction

One of the most important characteristic features of open component systems is the late integration phase. End users obtain components from the software market and integrate them into their system. In general, parties developing the components are unaware of each other as well as of the end users that are going to integrate these components.

The component oriented paradigm stemmed from the main principles of object orientation. Such concepts as encapsulation and subtyping are intrinsic to component development. One of the key ideas in object-oriented development is the construction of new objects by incremental modification of existing ones. Apparently, the possibility of constructing new components by reusing previously designed ones is highly desirable. The primary reuse mechanism employed in object-oriented languages is (code) inheritance. Whether the inheritance mechanism can be used in component system development and whether it can extend over component boundaries is unclear and requires close consideration.

In this paper we consider the so-called *fragile base class problem* and its influence on application of inheritance over component boundaries. At first glance the problem might appear to be caused by inadequate system specification or user assumptions of undocumented features. We consider an example which demonstrates that this is not the case and that the problem can be very concealed.

We propose a disciplined approach to inheritance which allows safe implementation reuse and provides high degree of flexibility. Our proposal is based on the research described in [4], where we abstracted the essence of the problem into a flexibility property and explained why unrestricted code inheritance violates this property. We also suggested five requirements, justified by orthogonal examples, for disciplining inheritance. Then we formally proved that these requirements are sufficient for the flexibility property to hold.

354

Here we present three check lists, for component framework designers, component framework developers, and its extenders. By verifying that every requirement in the corresponding list holds, all parties can make sure that they successfully avoid the fragile base class problem.

2 The Fragile Base Class Problem

The fragile base class problem becomes apparent during maintenance of open object-oriented systems. Imagine that a customer has obtained a certain component framework consisting of a collection of classes. In this framework inheritance is employed as the primary implementation reuse mechanism. The customer, willing to make slight modifications to the functionality provided by a framework class, inherits from it and overrides several methods. So far everything works fine and objects generated from the resulting class are perfectly substitutable for original ones generated from the framework class. When framework developers release a new version of their system, naturally they claim that the new version of the system is fully compatible with the previous one. Unfortunately, soon after obtaining the new version of the framework, the customer discovers that some custom extensions are invalidated. The following example, adopted from [8], illustrates the presented scenario. In this example a class *Bag* belongs to a framework, *CountingBag* is its custom extension, and *Bag'* is a revision of the *Bag*.

$$Bag = \textbf{class}$$
$$b : bag\ of\ char$$

$$init \mathrel{\widehat{=}} b := \|\ \|$$
$$add(\textbf{val}\ x : char) \mathrel{\widehat{=}}$$
$$\quad b := b\ \cup\ \|x\|$$
$$addAll(\textbf{val}\ bs : bag\ of\ char) \mathrel{\widehat{=}}$$
$$\quad \textbf{begin var}\ y\,|\,y \in bs\cdot$$
$$\quad\quad \textbf{while}\ bs \neq \|\ \|\ \textbf{do}$$
$$\quad\quad\quad self.add(y);$$
$$\quad\quad\quad bs := bs - \|y\|$$
$$\quad\quad \textbf{od}$$
$$\quad \textbf{end}$$
$$cardinality(\ \textbf{res}\ r : int) \mathrel{\widehat{=}}$$
$$\quad r := |b|$$
$$\textbf{end}$$

$$CountingBag = \textbf{class}$$
$$\textbf{inherits}\ Bag$$
$$n : int$$

$$init \mathrel{\widehat{=}} n := 0;\ super.init$$
$$add(\textbf{val}\ x : char) \mathrel{\widehat{=}}$$
$$\quad n := n + 1;\ super.add(x)$$

$$cardinality(\ \textbf{res}\ r : int) \mathrel{\widehat{=}}$$
$$\quad r := n$$
$$\textbf{end}$$

$$Bag' = \textbf{class}$$
$$b : bag\ of\ char$$

$$init \mathrel{\widehat{=}} b := \|\ \|$$
$$add(\textbf{val}\ x : char) \mathrel{\widehat{=}} b := b\ \cup\ \|x\|$$
$$addAll(\textbf{val}\ bs : bag\ of\ char) \mathrel{\widehat{=}} b := b\ \cup\ bs$$
$$cardinality(\ \textbf{res}\ r : int) \mathrel{\widehat{=}} r := |b|$$
$$\textbf{end}$$

It is easy to notice that if *Bag'* is used as the base class for *CountingBag*, the resulting class returns the incorrect number of elements in the bag.

Apparently, inheritance is responsible for the problem. Different kinds of problems connected to inheritance have been widely discussed in the literature [7,10,2]. The source of these problems can be traced back to the fact that inheritance violates encapsulation [7]. In a closed system (at least in theory) encapsulation can be compromised in order to achieve the desired degree of flexibility. Correctness of the resulting system can be verified on the integration phase. Since in open systems it is impossible to conduct a global integrity check, it becomes impossible to guarantee the overall correctness of the system. Therefore, the fragile base class problem is of particular importance for open component systems. If this problem were not considered at the design stage, it is too late to try to amend it during exploitation.

The problem of safe modification of base classes in presence of independent extensions deserves a separate name. We have encountered the name Fragile Base Class Problem in the technical literature describing component standards [11,1]. Although we have noticed slight deviations from our understanding of the problem, we think that this name expresses the essence of the problem rather well.

3 Component Framework Architecture Based on Disciplined Inheritance

First let us briefly introduce the used terminology. When an extension class invokes its base class method, we say that an *up-call* has occurred; when a base classfragile invokes a method from a class derived from it, we refer to such an invocation as a *down-call*. A call of a method from another method in the same class is referred to as a *self-call*. We refer to an invocation of a base class method by an extension class as a *super-call*.

We suggest a component framework architecture based on *disciplined inheritance* which relies on inheritance for implementation reuse. Every class in the framework is to be represented by two, an interface definition class augmented with specifications of the intended functionality and its default implementation. We refer to the augmented interface class as a specification class. The default implementation remains completely hidden behind the specification class. Therefore, the user of the framework can rely only on the information provided by the specification class. When reusing the framework, the user derives an extension class from an appropriate framework class. However, what the user sees is just the specification class. This specification class is too abstract to be executed and at run time is substituted with its default implementation.

With such a component framework architecture its designers, developers, and extenders should follow the check lists presented below. These check lists emerge from the formal study of the fragile base class problem undertaken in [4]. By verifying that every item in the corresponding list holds, all parties can make sure that they successfully avoid the problem. First we present the *check list for framework designers*:

1. The framework designers should decide whether they want to fix the data representation of the framework class. In some languages [9] this decision can be expressed by putting the declaration of the instance variables in a *private* or *protected* section of the class definition. Private attributes are only accessible by methods of the same class, while protected attributes can be accessed by the extension class as well. When instance variables of the specification class appear in the protected section, implementation class must have the same data representation. When instance variables of the specification class are declared in the private section, implementation class can change the data representation. If future extensions are expected to require more freedom in modifying the class state than is allowed by the class client interface, the class can provide a number of low-level state modifying methods. Since having these methods as a part of the class client interface may be inappropriate, we suggest declaring them as protected [7].
2. Specification class method bodies must indicate all *self* method calls.

Now let us consider the *check list for framework implementors*:

1. The implementation class can change the data representation of the specification class only if it is declared as private.
2. A method of the implementation class may self-call only those methods that are self-called by its counterpart in the specification class.
3. When verifying that some method of the implementation is a refinement of a matching method in the specification, instead of considering the bodies of the self-called methods, one should consider the bodies of the corresponding methods in the specification.

And finally let us consider the following *check list for framework extenders*:

1. A method of an extension class may only self-call those methods that are self-called by its counterpart in the specification class, or it may make up-calls to these methods. Plus, an extension method may always make up-calls to its counterpart in the specification class.
2. When verifying that some method of the extension is a refinement of a matching method in the specification, one should disregard the fact that due to dynamic binding the base class can make down calls to the extension class methods. One should consider that the base class calls its own methods instead.
3. The extension class may not establish an invariant binding values of inherited instance variables with values of its own instance variables.

4 Conclusions

We have discussed the fragile base class problem and its impact on component systems. The name fragile base class problem was introduced while discussing component standards [11,1] since it has critical significance for component systems. Modification of components by their developers should not affect component extensions of their users in any respect. First of all, recompilation of derived classes should be avoided if possible [1]. This issue constitutes a syntactic aspect of the problem. While being apparently important, that problem is only a technical issue. Even if recompilation is not necessary, component developers can make inconsistent modifications. Such inconsistent base class modifications constitute a semantic aspect of the problem, which is the focus of our study. This aspect of the problem was recognized by COM and Oberon/F developers [11,5]. They see the root of the problem in inheritance violating data encapsulation and choose to abandon inheritance, by employing the forwarding architecture. Although solving the problem, this approach comes at the cost of reduced flexibility.

We formulate an architectural approach based on disciplined inheritance combining flexibility of an ordinary inheritance architecture with safety of a forwarding architecture. We also present guidelines for constructing component systems employing inheritance and avoiding the fragile base class problem.

The fragile base class problem in our formulation (although they do not refer to it by this name) is considered by Steyaert et al. in [8] and by Kiczales and Lamping in [3]. The first paper is most closely related to our work. The authors introduce *reuse contracts* "that record the protocol between managers and users of a reusable asset". Acknowledging that "reuse contracts provide only syntactic information" they claim that "this is enough to firmly increase the likelihood of behaviorally correct exchange of parent classes". In our opinion such syntactic reuse contracts are insufficient to guard against the fragile base class problem.

The objective of the paper by Kiczales and Lamping is to develop a methodology for informally specifying a framework, so that the specification would accurately describe its functionality and provide the framework user with appropriate leeway for extending and reusing it. However, their recommendations are based only on empirical expertise. We believe that such methodology should be grounded on a mathematical basis and developing it constitutes the ultimate goal of our research.

Effects of disciplining inheritance the way we propose on component and object-oriented languages and systems require separate consideration and constitute the subject of our future research. The other research direction is in generalizing the results by weakening the restrictions we have imposed on the inheritance mechanism.

References

1. IBM Corporation. IBM's System Object Model (SOM): Making Reuse a Reality. *IBM Corporation, Object Technology Products Group*, Austin, Texas. http://www.developer.ibm.com/library/ref/reference.html
2. Walter L. Hürsch. Should Superclass be Abstract? *Proceedings ECOOP'94, M. Tokoro, R. Pareschi (Ed.), LNCS 821, Springer-Verlag*, Bologna, Italy 1994, pp.12–31.

3. Gregor Kiczales, John Lamping. Issues in the design and specification of class libraries. *OOPSLA '92 Proceedings,* pp. 435–451, 1992.
4. Leonid Mikhajlov, Emil Sekerinski. The Fragile Base Class Problem and Its Solution. *TUCS Technical Report No 117, Turku Centre for Computer Science*, Turku, June 1997.
5. Cune Pfister, Clemens Szyperski. Oberon/F Framework. Tutorial and Reference. *Oberon microsystems, Inc.*, 1994.
6. Dick Pountain, Clemens Szyperski. Extensible Software Systems. *Byte Magazine,* 19(5): 57–62, May 1994. http://www.byte.com/art/9405/sec6/art1.html.
7. Alan Snyder. Encapsulation and Inheritance in Object-Oriented Programming Languages. *OOPSLA '86 Proceedings,* pp.38-45, 1986.
8. Patric Steyaert, Carine Lucas, Kim Mens, Theo D'Hondt. Reuse Contracts: Managing the Evolution of Reusable Assets. *OOPSLA '96 Proceedings,* pp. 268-285, 1996.
9. Bjarne Stroustrup. The C++ Programming Language. *Addison-Wesley,* 1986.
10. David Taenzer, Murthy Gandi, Sunil Podar. Problems in Object-Oriented Software Reuse. In *Proceedings ECOOP'89, S. Cook (Ed.), Cambridge University Press.* Nottingham, July 10-14, 1989, pp.25-38.
11. S. Williams and C. Kinde. The Component Object Model : Technical Overview. *Dr. Dobbs Journal,* December 1994.

The Challenge of the Global Software Process

Tobias Murer

Computer Engineering and Networks Laboratory, ETH Zuerich, Switzerland

Abstract. The emerging technologies such as software components and the Internet challenge the way software is produced and marketed. The social, technical and organizational aspects of the software business will change significantly compared to the traditional understanding. Discussions about software components are often mainly limited to the technical aspects of interoperability. The purpose of this position paper is to motivate for a broader interdisciplinary discussion about components including technical aspects, but also organizational, social and even marketing aspects. We investigate these various aspects to develop the concept of a software engineering environment capable to face the outlined challenge.

1 Introduction

Software components are a promising paradigm shift and could answer the software crisis by attacking the conceptual essence of the difficulties inherent in the nature of the software. Compared to other engineering disciplines where components are used successfully and decide the business success, software component technology is not yet mature. Discussions about components are often mainly limited to the technical aspects [3] of interoperability. Contrarily, industry reports to be more challenged by organizational or social aspects when using components in large software projects. Cox [1] argues that the difficulties we have long experienced in the software field including our efforts to reuse software components are the result of a "technocentric" view of software development. I agree and provocatively add that component research issues do not differ significantly from object research issues from a technical point of view. The specific nature and challenge of components become only visible if we accept software production and markets to happen in a complex socio-technical system. Thus, to take full advantage and to evolve the paradigm shift we need to go beyond objects. The investigations should encompass technical but also social, organizational and market issues. This also allows to distinguish components from objects in an attempt to gain a more specific focus on what components are all about.

The emerging technologies such as software components and the Internet will have an increasing impact on the way software is produced and marketed. Traditional approaches of the software business are substituted or complemented by various new approaches closely related to the underlying emerging technology. Although the changes are triggered by technical issues the software component business is not restricted to a technical challenge. Technical aspects like interoperability issues are certainly critical for a successful deployment of the component business. But the significantly changing organizational and social aspects facing the problem of the decentralized management of software processes and products shared world-wide among heterogeneous organizations are also a difficult task. Even marketing aspects tightly correlated with the emerging technologies should be investigated carefully to establish the various new business opportunities. We investigate these various aspects in the GIPSY (Generating Integrated Process support SYstems) project to develop the concept of a software engineering environment capable to support the development and maintenance of high quality software components in a global context. Thus, our concerns are issues that are relevant for software engineering environments. This paper intends to motivate for a broader interdisciplinary discussion about components and outlines the organizational aspects of software components.

2 Organization

To understand the software component business we should carefully observe other engineering disciplines where components play a key role. Car manufacturers for example are managing a complex network of enterprises delivering the various components of a car just in time to be put together to the final product. The various nodes of this network have to co-operate tightly on a high level to assure a high quality work including the areas of development, production, maintenance and marketing. Therefore, enterprises weaken their boundaries and appear as one unitary organization from the viewpoint of an external observer and build a so-called 'virtual organization' [4]. This flexible and dynamic organization concept has many advantages, single nodes can for example be exchanged by alternative enterprises. The organizational and social aspects of such a heterogeneous virtual organization are an immense challenge since the organizations differ typically in many aspects such as location, technology, methods, culture, policy, strategy, skill, quality and more.

The analogy to the software component business is obvious: Different component producers need to co-operate tightly on a high level to assure proper component interoperability by sharing and linking their development processes resulting in tightly co-operating virtual organizations. But compared to the car manufacturer there are two major differences that make virtual organization within the software component business much more challenging to manage. The car manufacturer keeps its organizational structure quite stable once developed and the applied composition techniques are more advanced. Within the software component business the product has a more dynamic nature and virtual organizations are formed more dynamically. Component producers form a virtual organization with the goal of building a configuration of properly interoperating components. In fact, for every client that likes to use a set of interoperating components, there is a virtual organization of component producers co-operating to meet this specific requirement. As a vision, the development efforts of many individual component producers together may be regarded as one large global development process consisting of many linked processes. Managing such a software process on a high level across enterprise boundaries within a virtual organization is an enormous challenge since the various process parts are managed decentralized and linked into the global context of the virtual organization.

Besides components Java also popularized concepts like 'write once, run everywhere' and the distribution of software components across the Internet. Components are collected from different nodes of the global Internet and configured on the client machine to support a certain task. Everyone knows the problem of hyperlinks in the World Wide Web pointing to nowhere. The obvious reason for that is the decentralized management of link configurations by every web participant not controlled by any organization or policy. Whereas web surfers are just upset about the missing links, the consequences in the component business are more dramatic. If a client intents to collect a configuration of components from different locations of the web, every component should be available at the right version and the configuration should be confirmed from the virtual organization of the involved component producers as a stable package of properly interoperating components. Missing versions and incorrectly configured sets of components can not be accepted within the software component business. Versions and configurations need to be available, persistence and stable. Assigning expire dates to components and valid configurations should be considered. In addition, versions of compilers and runtime systems should also be kept, especially if we think about software only compiled and distributed on demand.

The consequences seem to be significant, if we focus on the responsibility of providing component interoperability. If a producer for example releases a new version of an operating system, everyone hopes ('plug and pray' mentality) that actual software versions running on top of the new release of the operating system still work properly. In fact, every software running on top of an operating system is invalidated after a new release of the operating system until the component producer establishes a new link from its component to the new version of the operating system confirming proper interoperability. The complex network of component versions, configurations and dependencies updated decentralized is difficult to control. This world-wide global configuration management system for products is a severe organizational challenge. Introducing a simple version concept to Java is definitely a first step to face the challenge [5].

3   Facing The Challenge

As outlined above, the decentralized management of products and processes and organization forms within a virtual organization represents a severe challenge with a significant impact on the concepts of supporting tools. The difficulty mainly comprises the heterogeneity of the virtual organization, since the participating autonomous organizations vary in many respects including various locations, cultures, policies, strategies, methods and more.

We are investigating the concept for a software engineering environment (SEE) framework capable to support the global software process within a virtual organization. We believe that the outlined significantly changing challenge force the requirements for a SEE to be revised compared to traditional concepts. A

SEE should more support between the nodes of the organization than within the nodes where autonomy is particularly preserved. There is a strong need for a common understanding of organization to be shared among the participating organizations. Thus, a SEE should enable communication about organization rather than forcing the various nodes to use sophisticated models.

We believe organizational integrity to be the most important design issue of a SEE aimed to face the outlined challenge. Organizational integrity encompasses the common understanding of the structure and evolution of product, process and organization form shared among all development process participants including users and tools. A promising and rather obvious approach to handle organizational integration is to achieve structural unity among the three main organizational structures [6] by using similar structures to manage the organizational aspects of product, process and organization form. We use a simple 3D model to represent structure (2 dimensions) and evolution (3rd dimension) of a software product and its process. Development processes of different components that interoperate in a certain way are linked together. The links are established on different layers with respect to the history dimension, thus indicating which versions of the components interoperate. Whereas this approach promises a rather easy way to obtain organizational integrity, its limitations are also clear. To gain structural unity each structure has to sacrifice some of its specific characteristics. We believe that gaining organizational integrity by sacrifying sophisticated aspect-specific structures is the better choice than vice versa to face the outlined challenge.

4 Markets

All aspects of the traditional software business such as software engineering, maintenance, distribution and marketing are challenged by the emerging technologies. Because of the impact of the emerging technologies on component marketing aspects a tight cooperation between component development and marketing is required to establish the various new business opportunities triggered by the technology shift. The emerging technology gives highly skilled small competitors the chance to compete on the global market. Components allow small competitors to provide a solution for a specific need, there is no need for a single provider to offer an integrated all inclusive product. Such monolithic products can be substituted by competitive configurations of components provided by virtual organizations dynamically built among small providers within virtual organizations. The Internet is the perfect platform for cooperation and marketing to reach the global market with only low investment. The component market may transform the producer-driven software market into a customer-driven one. Publishing and connecting processes in a global context opens up many business opportunities. For example, an electronic product catalogue with interoperability, version and configuration information about components could be built on top of the model introduced above and could be an important part of a virtual software house of components on the World Wide Web (software offers, catalogue, on-line consulting, distribution, updating, pay-per-use and more). Such an interactive catalogue could be provided with the outlined method. Attractive 3-dimensional navigation through virtual software stores may be performed in order to find consistent combinations of components.

5 Conclusions and Outlook

All aspects of the traditional software business are significantly challenged by emerging technologies such as software components and the Internet. There are major changes of the social, technical and organizational aspects of the software component business compared with traditional approaches, especially, if the focus is put on the use and development of components within virtual organizations. The decentralized management of products, processes shared among heterogeneous virtual organizations is challenging but essential for the development and marketing of high quality software components in a global context. To face the challenge future SEEs need to provide more support between groups across organizational boundaries and less within groups where skill and motivation of group members decide the success and not a sophisticated tool. The software engineering environment community should carefully consider these changing aspects for the concept of SEEs.

A simple model needs to be defined enabling organizational integration within virtual organizations, which encompasses the common understanding of the structure and evolution of product, process and organization form shared among all process participants (users and tools). We propose a similar 3D model to represent the structure and evolution of a software product and its process. This leads to the structural unity of product, process and organization form, which we believe to provide organizational integrity. This simple model could be the underlying concept of future SEEs supporting software process and configuration management within virtual organizations.

References

1. B.J. Cox. *No Silver Bullet Reconsidered* American Programmer Magazine, November 1995
2. T. Murer, D. Scherer, A. Wuertz. *Improving Component Interoperability Information* Workshop Reader ECOOP 96, June 1996, pp. 150 -158
3. C. Szyperski, C. Pfister. *WCOP'96 Workshop Report* Workshop Reader ECOOP 96, June 1996, pp. 127 - 130
4. W. Davidow, M. Malone. *The Virtual Organization : structuring and revitalizing the corporation for the 21st century* Burlingame, 1992
5. M. Jordan, M. Van De Vanter. *Modular System Building with Java(TM) Packages* Proc. Software Engineering Environments Conference (SEE97), April 1997
6. T. Murer, D. Scherer. *Structural Unity of Product, Process and Organization Form in the GIPSY Process Support Framework*, Proc. Software Engineering Environments Conference (SEE97), April 1997

Coupling of Workflow and Component–Oriented Systems

Stefan Schreyjak

University of Stuttgart, 70565 Stuttgart, Germany

Abstract. The use of component–oriented systems in a workflow system solves several problems of today's workflow systems like e. g. lacking adaptability. For that purpose, however, both systems must be modified and coupled in a two level system. In this paper several modifications are proposed that will improve the systems' cooperation, like the creation of interfaces and the provision of a process context, as well as the introduction of interactively changeable views in the application.
Keywords: workflow system , components, user adaptation

1 Introduction

A *workflow management system* [5] is a software system for the coordination and cooperative execution of business processes in distributed heterogeneous computer environments. The objectives of a workflow system are in a first phase the modelling of the structure of an enterprise and of the sequence of all business procedures, and in a second phase the controlling, supervising and recording of the execution of all modelled processes. All sequential or parallel relationships between process steps are specified in *business process* models or *workflows*. It is determined for each step which work objects (data and documents) and which human, technical and organizational resources are necessary for the execution. A process step, also called *activity*, is a piece of continuous work executed by one person. The *actor* of an activity can use an interactive application program to fulfil the objective of the activity.

Components are reusable software building blocks which can be assembled or disassembled in an application without violating its integrity. A *component–oriented system* is an architecture for a software system which provides the infrastructure for components. An implementation of this architecture consists of an application development environment and a runtime environment for components. A *component–based system* uses components only in the development environment.

Workflow systems and component–oriented systems have similar assignments and use similar technical approaches to facilitate the development of applications. But they differ in the application domain and in the magnitude of the application. Workflow systems control enterprise–wide applications that consists of activities. Component–oriented systems control local applications that consists of software building blocks. This paper is going to show how both systems can benefit from each other.

After describing some problems of current workflow systems these problems are used to motivate the use of component–oriented programming in workflow systems. A pure combination of both systems is insufficient, instead a coupling of the systems is demanded. This is proved by proposing a solution approach for each itemized problem. In the last section all essential ideas are summed up.

2 Problem Description

The use of current workflow systems reveals some problems. In this section all those problems are discussed which can be solved or reduced using component–oriented programming.

Adaptability Problem in Activities

Before the emergence of workflow systems, business processes were realized with big monolithic business applications. In order to preserve marketability, business processes must be adaptable to the actual market situation. These requests for change must be implemented by programmers of business application vendors. Hence, adaption is costly, time–consuming and expensive.

These facts have resulted in the development of workflow systems. Hereby, business processes are divided into a function–oriented part — the work steps — and a process–oriented part — the relationship between the steps. Because of the abstract representation of the workflow, the user can adapt the workflow more easily than programmers can adapt monolithic business application. Workflow systems, however, only allow adaption in the process–oriented part.

Heterogenous System Environments

Workflow systems are used in a very heterogenous infrastructure of computer equipments, which is grown by and by. Hence, workflows have to be platform independent. The specification is already platform independent, but the applications are not. Therefore, an activity needs one platform specific application for each platform. Every application used in a workflow system needs to exist in several portations: one application for each platform. Alternatively, applications with similar functionality have to exist for each platform. This approach is unsatisfying, costly and expensive.

Incomplete Reuse of Workflows

The reuse of workflows in a different company requires the possibility of adapting the workflow by the user and the possibility to run the applications on all used platforms. As a consequence of the two subsections above reuse of workflows is not really possible.

Unspecific Applications

Workflow systems are especially useful when workflows are executed often. Therefore, the applications should be accommodated very well to their operation area in order to achieve high productivity. But customized applications must be bought expensively from software vendors. Instead, generic standard applications are often used. But these applications can only be limited incompletely to their task domain. The user is allowed to do much more than he should. The workflow system has only few possibilities to check what is done in activities. The incomplete adaption to the task domain makes the task more costly and error prone than necessary.

No Mutual Profit of Services

Standard applications have no knowledge about their use in a workflow system. So they cannot use services offered by the workflow system. Vice versa, the workflow system sees activities as black boxes. It is not able to control the applications in the activities. As a consequence of this lacking arrangement, services may be implemented twice.

3 Using Workflow and Component Systems Together

3.1 Combining Workflow and Component Systems

An approach is to use component–oriented programming for the development of applications in activities. Workflow systems are a large and rewarding application domain because the complexity of program logic in activities is typically low and often similar. It turns out quickly that today's systems are not prepared satisfactorily for that use if they are not modified for that purpose. So, the combination of these unmodified systems shows the problems mentioned above in a different perspective:

- A simple combination does not eliminate the problem of lacking mutual profit.

- Now, the user has the possibility to create customized applications with components providing standard functions. Unfortunately for every new adaption (like a different color) a new additional application is needed. In addition, applications cannot be customized dependent on the task domain (e. g. a certain activity in a process).

- The problem of heterogenous system environments is not solved if the components remain platform dependent.

- Reuse will be possible when the problems of heterogeneity and adaptation will be solved.

- The applications in the activities can be adapted by the user if component–oriented systems are used. This is not valid for a component–based system! Indeed the possibility to adapt applications is not supported very well from today's component systems. The user cannot adapt an application easily:

Functionality dealing with the cooperation of components can only be gathered with difficulty. Events and callbacks are used as a communication technique. The code of these callbacks is spread over all components. Therefore, the user must accumulate the knowledge of the structure of a component–application in a reengineering phase by himself.

The replacement and addition of components is not supported in an adequate way by today's component systems. There are no integrity checks whether all required interfaces and preconditions are met when using a the new component. The user has to test it by himself.

The glue code is necessary for the creation of callbacks and allows the cooperation of components. Glue code is usually written in the same language with which the component is implemented, and not in a language which is tailored to user skill. Most of all the code must be interactively testable.

3.2 Coupling Workflow and Component Systems

The combined use of unmodified systems solves the problems mentioned only partly. Therefore, it has to be examined if it would not be more successful not only to combine but also to couple both systems. In such a coupling both systems can be modified and enhanced with additional functionality to solve these problems. Objective of the coupling is to allow transfer and adjustment of similar technologies for a redundance–free partitioning of responsibilities and to allow a highly effective cooperation. The coupling results in a two level system where each single system can be used on its own, too.

In the following subsections, a solution is proposed for each problem mentioned. Also, some technical aspects concerning implementation aspects are discussed.

To: **No Mutual Profit of Services**

Both systems must be modified in a way that they offer their services in public interfaces. Double implementations can be avoided if it is defined which system implements the service and which system uses the service. An example for such an API are controlling functions for components. A controlled abort, a resume, as well as storing and loading of component states are important functions to support error handling of the workflow system [4].

An example for the distribution of functionality is the transport of software. With the help of internet protocols a workflow system can transport and install applications at the actor's computer [3]. This functionality can also be used for the transport of components, just like the loading of java applets in a html–page.

To: **Unspecific Applications**

Component–oriented applications need to be aware of the surrounding process to be able to customize to a specific task. This can be achieved with a process context.

A *process context* is a logical storage used by components to store and retrieve data. The workflow system provides and manages different contexts. Contexts can be defined through conditions. For example, a person can form a context, but also a workflow instance or an activity in a workflow template. The concept of a process context allows *context sensitive* applications.

A component can store the attributes' values, configuration scripts or other data in the context. For example, a context sensitive command history can be implemented. Default values in data entries are another example. Thus, an actor can use the old data he had typed in last time using this application.

To: **Heterogenous System Environments**

The problem of heterogeneity can be overcome if the component system and the components are implemented in a platform independent programming language (like Java, Tcl/Tk or Python).

To: **Adaptability Problem in Activities**

Analogous to the modelling of workflows, application must be modelled to allow easy–to–use adaption for the users.

The user can change an application built with components on three adaption levels: The first level is limited to changes of the component server attributes. On the second level glue code used for the component communication can be adapted to change the cooperative behaviour of the component–application. These two levels can be controlled by the process context. On a third level the user can replace and add whole components and change the structure of the component–application.

To perform this adaption work the user needs easy–to–use editor tools. Graphical methods are necessary to describe the functionality of the whole application on a level of high abstraction. The understanding of a component–application's functionality can be improved by the introduction of views. A *view* shows a certain aspect of the application. The user can use a view to change something interactively in the component–application.

Adaptations made by the user have to be stored. The scope of adaptations may differ. Global adaptations are valid for all users, while local adaptations are only visible in a certain context.

4 Conclusion

In today's workflow systems the adaptability of workflows ends at platform dependent activities. This results in bad reusability. Furthermore, control over applications is minimal and applications cannot use workflow services. Therefore, potential for automatism is not used.

A first approach to improvement is to use component–oriented systems in activities. But a simple combination of unmodified systems does not succeed satisfactorily. There is a need for higher coupling.

The creation of a two level system–coupling requires several modifications in both systems. The following modifications have been proposed in this paper. The introduction of interfaces will allow redundance–free partitioning of system tasks. The introduction of a process context will enable the use of highly specific applications (context sensitive applications). By using interactive editable views, modelling the functionality of an application built of components, the user can more easily adapt these applications.

References

1. R. M. Adler. Distributed coordination models for client/server computing. *IEEE Computer*, 28(4):14–22, April 1995.
2. F. Leymann. Workflows make objects really useful. In *Proceedings of the 6th International Workshop on High Performance Transaction Systems* , 1995.
3. S. Schreyjak and H. Bildstein. Beschreibung des prototypisch implementieren Workflowsystems Surro. technical report No 1996/19, Universität Stuttgart.
4. S. Schreyjak and H. Bildstein. Fehlerbehandlung in Workflow–Management–Systemen. technical report No 1996/17, Universität Stuttgart.
5. WfMC. Workflow management coalition specification — terminology and glossary.

A Generator for Composition Interpreters

Jørgen Steensgaard-Madsen

Department of Information Technology
Bldg. 344, DTU, DK-2800 Lyngby
Denmark

Abstract. Composition of program components must be expressed in some language, and *late composition* can be achieved by an interpreter for the composition language. A suitable notion of component is obtained by identifying it with the semantics of a generalised structured command. Experiences from programming language design, specification and implementation then apply. A component can be considered as defining objects or commands according to convenience.

A description language including type information provides sufficient means to describe component interaction according to the underlying abstract notion of components. Actual compositions can be type checked before execution.

Keywords: Interpretation, polymorphism, modularity, reuse.

1 Introduction

An application program may contain an *interpreter* that maps *commands* into computations which are characteristic for the program's application domain. The set of acceptable commands is called the *command language*. Typically an interpreter is programmed to operate in a cyclic fashion: read a command, perform the computation, repeat. The term *command language interface* is used to describe this situation.

Interpretation seems also to be relevant for late composition of independently developed components: some expression is needed to indicate an actual composition and the set of possible expressions forms a language.

The various tasks involved in the construction of a command language interface can best be compared to the design of a programming language and the implementation of a corresponding compiler/interpreter. In itself the design of a decent programming language is no simple task and neither is the construction of an interpreter or compiler. Tools exist for the construction part, but these are targeted primarily at computing science specialists.

This abbrieviated short paper describes an effort to generate interpreters for composition languages. It is partly justified by the view that a portable interpreter construction tool with its language family may form a standard for a component market.

Figure 1 shows the overall structure of the intended system. The achievements can be summarised as follows:

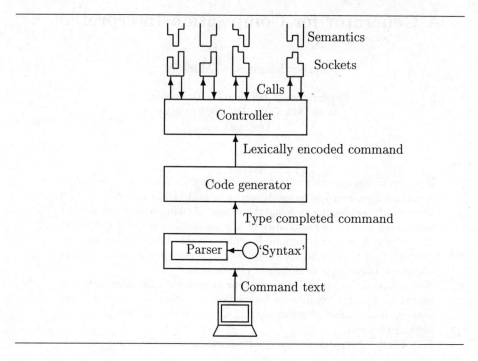

Fig. 1. System structure

- A particular language is described by a set of *signatures.*
- A generated *translator* augments commands with type information.
- A *code generator* encodes commands for interpretation.
- An abstract *controller* interprets encoded commands as socket calls.
- A *dispatcher generator* that generates sockets that interface semantics.
- A *skeleton generator* maps signatures to empty semantics routines.

The short paper contains an introduction to the language family with emphasis on use, illustrations of component descriptions, a short description of a related system development discipline, various observations for discussion, and finally it relates this to some work of others. The structure is maintained here, where explanationes have been shortened.

2   Weak Abstraction Languages

A family of languages, called *weak abstraction languages,* has been identified and a tool for generating interpreters for them has been developed. The languages are intended to describe combination of commands with their semantics written in another language. In principle the components that implements the semantics may be written in different languages. An example:

```
program{
  listpackage a;
  induction(1::2::3::4::nil) {
    a.split(problem) {0} {hd+result(tl)}
}}
```

This is a small program that uses three components: a statement-like component program{...}, a class-like `listpackage` to introduce the type of lists with polymorphic operations on them, and finally `induction` with traits that makes it both class- and statement-like. The program uses induction over a list of integers to find the sum of the lists' elements. The short paper provides more details.

The example is a toy program, primarily of academic interest. However, the general principles have been used in serious applications like a compiler and a document preparation system.

Each language can be characterised semantically as a particular set of higher-order, polymorphic functions that can be freely combined within the limits determined by a type system. Syntactically the languages unify the notions of statements and objects.

3 Description of Weak Abstraction Languages

Usually a language is described by a set of production rules that form the grammar of the language. A weak abstraction language is essentially described by a number of *signatures* which can be conceived as its grammar.

A signature is similar to the description of a routine in a typed, polymorphic programming language. It associates a name with a number of *types, places* and *parts* that must be filled in when it is used in a command. Types are filled in automatically. The others may be filled in with *values* or *command sequences.*

Consider the description of the `induction`-component used above:

```
SIG induction OF DATA,V (value:DATA)
    [justification(problem:DATA)
      [result(subproblem:DATA):V]:V
    ]:V;
```

A signature in a bracket describes a part. Parts similar to those of ordinary structured statements have names (here written in italics for help only.) Uses of `induction` have the form

   induction(*value*){*justification*}

The names `problem` and `result` may be used in the *justification*-part of a command and they can be compared to member names of a class.

Types are not used in commands, but can appear in error messages. Type variability is supported: `induction` may be applied to values of type `DATA` for various instantiations of `DATA`. The `listpackage` introduces a `List` type-constructor and binary operators, like `::`, that can be used on operands of type `A` and `A List`, say, for various instantiations of `A`.

Part names (those in italics) are very useful in an informal explanation:

Provided the *justification*, for some intended f, computes
$f(0)$ when problem=0 and
f(problem), assuming result(i) = f(i) for 0<=i<problem
then induction(*value*){*justification*} will compute $f(value)$.

This applies when DATA is instantiated as integer. It will be the user's responsibility to apply induction only for appropriate instantiations of DATA. Note that the names problem and result are introduced implicitly with *justification* as their scope. This mechanism is called *implicit name introduction*.

4 System Development Discipline

When a system can be identified with an interpreter for a particular weak abstraction language, an effective system development discipline can be prescribed. System and language design become closely connected: useful components correspond to semantics of useful commands.

The construction of interpreters for composition of components has been automated. The steps needed to *modify* an actual system are:

1. Copy a language core to a new development directory.
2. Add signatures to a file and generate empty semantics.
3. Modify the semantics and generate a system.
4. Test for adequacy.

Once developed and tested within one system a component can be transfered to another in object form. Incremental development is assumed to dominate.

As mentioned previously semantics routines can be plugged into sockets and tools exists to generate both the base containing the socket interface and empty semantics routines that fit into the sockets. It means that a particular language can be tested as soon as it has been described formally, i.e. programs can be expressed and considered as pseudocode in an early phase. Furthermore, the tests become more and more meaningful as the individual components are developed.

Very few systems will probably be developed from scratch since most will contain some primitives of general interest, e.g. if- and while-commands.

5 Discussion

A component may be considered (and defined as) class-like when that point of view seems adequate. A component's signature is similar to a template but signatures is a more powerful notion.

A supplier may contribute to a system with a precompiled component in object module form accompanied by a signature for it. Integration will be straightforward according to the description of system development.

A fixed number of component definitions is assumed in the described system. Modification of a component involves re-integration of the entire system. Further investigations are needed if modification, removal or addition of a component should be allowed on the fly.

The techniques used for composition of components combine the mechanisms of structured statement composition and implicit name introduction (ordinarily associated only with abstract data structures.) Both mechanisms can be explained simply in terms of higher-order constructs. The techniques are well understood and acceptable with respect to efficiency.

Late composition of components via an interpreter is particularly interesting when it conforms to general programming language principles, because *early composition* then should be an alternative choice. It will provide the freedom either to pay composition costs once for a fixed composition, or to pay it repeatedly for the sake of flexibility. In both cases a supplier might be able to contribute the same component in object module form only, so the choice can be left to the composer.

6 Related Work

Any program that takes text as input can be considered an interpreter, although often with a very primitive input language, similar in nature perhaps to assembly languages. No sharp dividing line seems useful to distinguish those with a flexible command language. One conclusion could be that language interpretation should be essential knowledge for all programmers of systems that take text as inputs.

One example of a set of tools to provide a command language interface is Tcl [3]. It is untyped and has rather unusual scope-rules. Its success, not the least to define the language Tk for the application domain of building graphical user interfaces, witnesses to the value of having a command language interface for an application domain.

An interpreted, general programming language may of course be used to develop application systems. This may lead to nice systems provided the language is seen as pleasing, that the possible cost of changing existing programming habits is not considered too high, and that the resulting programs meet the users' expectations with respect to performance. The application area of Tk has been approached in this way by using the languages Scheme [1] and ML [2] as interfaces to the semantics underlying Tk.

The form of signatures presented has its roots in the design of a general programming language that has been described in [4].

References

1. W. Clinger and J. Rees. Revised(4) report on the algoritmic language scheme. *ACM Lisp Pointers IV*, 1991.
2. R. Milner, M. Tofte, and R. Harper. *The Definition of Standard ML*. MIT Press, 1990.
3. J. K. Ousterhout. *Tcl and Tk Toolkit*. Addison-Wesley, 1994.
4. J. Steensgaard-Madsen and Lars Møller Olsen. Definition of the programming language Modef. *Sigplan Notices*, 19(2), 1984.

On the Addition of Properties to Components

Jose M. Troya and Antonio Vallecillo

Dpto. de Lenguajes y Ciencias de la Computación.
Universidad de Málaga. Campus de Teatinos. 29071 Málaga. Spain.

Abstract. The design of components for open systems has led to the
study of new systems and their properties. Most of these systems try
to facilitate the design of components by incorporating new features,
services and utilities that solve the basic problems of open systems: heterogeneity, partial knowledge of the components, and dynamic changes
in the system's configuration. However, our approach is not focused on
the system but on the components themselves. This paper defines the
properties that components of those systems should have and introduces
a framework to implement them.

1 Introduction

There is now an increasing interest in the study of Open Systems, and in particular in the Independently Extensible systems [5] as the base for a component
market. In this market users are able to buy or rent reusable components off the
shelf and compose them to build their applications.

Extensible systems allow new functionality to be added at run time. Independently Extensible systems allow extensions of the system to be developed
by different people in ignorance of each other [6]. In these systems, the key
are the software components, individual units that can be reused by any end-
user to build up his system. Usually users are third parties willing to compose
them without modifications. The study of the properties that systems should
have to allow late composition of components is an active area of research, and
Component-Oriented Programming (COP) is proving to be a natural extension
of Object-Oriented Programming (OOP) for these types of systems.

So far, most of the efforts have been invested in improving the systems,
incorporating the services and facilities that allow components to run on them
more easily and to adapt to their changes. Examples of these systems are Hector
or ASX, or component architectures as Infospheres, Java™ Beans or IBM Aglets.
In them, the system developer can count on a good set of tools that allow
a better design and implementation of components. However, all the facilities
not directly offered by the system have to be taken over by the components
themselves, which forces each designer to add them to its components in an
individual fashion and therefore with no guarantee of modularity, portability,
or openness. In general, system restrictions should be incorporated, if possible,
separately from the component's code; hardwiring time or other constraints into
the component's code jeopardizes reusability and may bring other undesirable
results, as for instance mentioned in [2].

Our approach is not so much focused on the system itself, but on the components. We need to incorporate the desired properties to them, in a modular and independent fashion. This leads to a methodology for the design of components, whereby components can be designed to concentrate *just* on their goal (i.e. their computational aspects) without taking into account other particular issues of the systems they will run on. When an end-user buys or rents a component to build up his application, he may buy as well some add-on properties to the component, like time control if his application is time-critical or robustness if his running environment is unsafe. In this way, components are designed independently from the systems they will run on, and the components they will compose with. Later, the appropriated properties to cope with the system's requirements can be added to them.

With this in mind, our proposed solution is based on a tripartite structure "components/add-on properties/systems" instead of the standard pair "components/systems". Systems have just to provide the supporting infrastructure for components to work and interoperate among themselves. The add-on properties are abilities that components can incorporate to adapt to the systems. Separating these concerns allows a modular and independent addition of properties to components, benefitting a simpler design and the reuse of components.

Our contribution is twofold. On one hand we have identified some basic properties that allow components to achieve their goals in open and changing environments. And on the other, we also introduce an architecture to define and implement properties in a modular and independent fashion. To support the model we have built a general framework that allows the definition, design and implementation of properties.

2 The Properties

We have identified three main properties: Autonomy, Robustness and Competitiveness. Each one deals with specific problems of the open and extensible systems, like dynamic re-configuration, error detection and recovery, maintainability and adaptability. *Autonomy* can be defined as the ability of a component to take its own decisions in an independent way (however, by autonomous we do not mean self-sufficient or self-reliant). *Robustness* guarantees reliability and secure access. And *Competitiveness* provides the component with a general philosophy of survival in terms of a resistance and durability.

Being such a general and complex abilities, the key idea is to define them in terms of the composition of "smaller" basic properties. Thus, we can define the property of **Autonomy** as the composition of other three properties:

- *Independence*: The component should be self-governed, able to discover the services it needs and free to decide the solutions to hire in each situation.
- *Adaptability*: The component should be able to accommodate to different interfaces and protocols, and to changes in the requirements. It has to be composible, flexible, versatile and extensible.

- *Self-Protection*: The component should protect itself against external failures and unforeseen circumstances. The component cannot depend on the rest of the components' behavior and well-functioning.

Robustness is achieved through the composition of three basic properties:

- *Integrity*: The component has to offer a robust behavior under a variety of circumstances, different inputs and different uses of its interface, valid or invalid ones. This property checks pre-conditions on the incoming messages, verifies (and puts right) the order in which they are received and the time interval between them, etc.
- *Secure Access*: Every access to and from the component must be authorized. Unlawful entries and illegal outputs have to be detected and banned. Signatures can be added and later checked using this property, and encryption mechanisms can be used. System *laws* can be not only defined with this property, but also enforced.
- *High Availability*: The component should protect itself against failures in the processes or machines executing it.

Finally, **Competitiveness** can be expressed in terms of:

- *Best Effort/Least Losses*: The component should try its best to satisfy its users in terms of response time, functionality and quality of the services provided, whilst maintaining its suffering and losses to a minimum when servicing requests.
- *Durability*: The component has to incorporate mechanisms to be able to be renewable, keep itself updated and improve over time.

3   The Model and its Implementation

3.1   Components

In general, components can be seen as encapsulation of programs. The *"capsule"* abstracts the program functionality, offers a common interface to the program services, hides their implementation and allows the composition and coordination of components. The idea we use to implement each property is by adding *"layers"* to the capsule. Each layer acts as an active *wrapper* that captures and modifies the program's inputs and outputs, offering to the outside world an interface with the given property. Please note that in our scheme the behavior of a layer is not passive or merely computational as if it were a filter: as a result of an incoming message the layer may send one or more messages to the system, wait for their responses and build up from them the message that will be finally passed to the component. Besides, the layers can be "composed" so the component can have multiple properties or abilities simultaneously.

3.2   Communication Mechanisms

To implement this scheme we need a system's computational model that allow components to communicate, and define the minimum requirements to do so. We have chosen a very simple one that just contains the functionality required for our purposes. It tries not to be a novelty but a tool easy to implement in different existing systems.

At a low level, our model is based on components that communicate using message queues (mailboxes). Each component belongs to its *domain*: the address of the machine (or net of machines) where it lives. We shall use Internet domains as valid component domains, and name them accordingly. This allows the easy integration of our model with the WWW and the usage of some of its services, like name servers. Each mailbox will have a unique global address (`mb@domain`), given by its name "mb" and its domain name "@domain". If the domain is omitted, the current domain name is used. If the mailbox name is omitted, we refer to *all* mailboxes currently at that domain. This mechanism allows sending broadcast messages to a domain.

There are two basic communication primitives: `Send` and `Receive`. The first one sends a message to a mailbox address, and the second one reads a message from a mailbox. `Receive` is a blocking operation in case the mailbox is empty, while `Send` is non-blocking. This model allows the use of formal reasoning methods, similar to the ones outlined in [3].

3.3   Controllers

Controllers are the special processes that *wrap* the component and modify its behavior. They intercept all incoming and outgoing events by accessing its message queues, and treat them according to their strategy. They are analogous to decorators or adapters [4], meta-actors [1], or filters [2].

To specify controllers we need to define the messages they deal with and the operations they use to handle these messages. We have defined a general scheme that can be gradually specialized: first to specify the controllers that implement each property, and then to particularize them when being added to a precise component in a given system. The more basic scheme of a controller is as follows:

```
public class Controller {
    public void Deliver(Msg m) {    // Captures outgoing messages.
        Outq.Queue(m);
    }
    public void Received(Msg m) {    // Captures incoming messages.
        Inq.Queue(m);
    }
    public void TimeoutExp(Msg m) { // Captures timeout conditions.
    }
}
```

The first method is invoked by the system every time the component wants to send a message out to a mailbox. Method `Received` is invoked on the receipt of a message and `TimeoutExp` allows the controller to know that a sent out message does not get an answer when expected. In general, properties do not need to deal with time; however, they can be aware of these situations with this mechanism.

Once the controller has dealt with an incoming message, its result is put back into the component's incoming message queue `Inq`. Symmetrically, the controller deals with the outgoing messages before they go out, leaving the result of the treatment in the `Outq` queue. In case of having several controllers chained together (due to a composition of properties), the end of each `Inq.Queue` operation causes the invocation of method `Received` in the next controller and the end of each `Inq.Queue` operation causes the invocation of `Deliver` in the next one.

3.4 A Framework for Adding Properties

Based on this scheme we have developed a framework for designing, implementing and composing properties. The use of a Component Framework as a "white-box component that reveals part of its internal configuration, establishes configuration rules, and may enforce some of these rules" [6] fits like a glove to our ideas. It is not the typical framework for the development of open and distributed systems and applications, as in the case of Hector, ASX or others. Our framework goes in a different direction: it provides the support to our methodology for designing components.

Its structure is the following. The communication basic model sits on the lower level, serving as interface between the components and the system. Apart from sending and receiving messages, the model incorporates the possibility of attaching controllers to mailboxes, which is the way properties are added to components. The framework handles the controllers' composition and all message passing among them. The user just configures its preferences when attaching the controllers. The properties described here are provided with the framework and their controllers, but they can be easily modified, as well as new properties can be easily defined, implemented and included in the framework.

References

1. G. Agha, W. Kim and R. Panwar. *Actor Languages for Specification of Parallel Computations.* In DIMACS, 1994.
2. L. Bergmans and M. Aksit. *Composing Synchronization and Real-Time Constraints.* In JPDC, No. 36, pp.32–52, Academic Press Inc., 1996.
3. K.M. Chandy and A. Rifkin. *Systematic Composition of Objects in Distributed Internet Applications: Processes and Sessions.* Proceedings of the 30th HICSS, Hawaii, 1997.
4. E. Gamma et al. *Design Patterns.* Addison-Wesley, 1995.
5. C. Szyperski. *Independently Extensible Systems —Software Engineering Potential and Challenges—.* Proceedings of the 19th Australasian Computer Science Conference, Melbourne, 1996.
6. W. Weck. *Independently Extensible Component Frameworks.* In Special Issues in O.O. Programming –Workshop Reader of ECOOP'96. Max Muehlhaeuser (ed.). Dpunkt Verlag, 1997

Adapting Object-Oriented Components

Jan Bosch

University of Karlskrona/Ronneby, Department of Computer Science and Business
Administration, S-372 25 Ronneby, Sweden, e-mail: Jan.Bosch@ide.hk-r.se,
www:http://www.pt.hk-r.se/~bosch

Abstract. component-based software development is one of the more
promising approaches to reuse existing software. However, "as-is" reuse
seldomly occurs and reusable components generally need to be adapted.
Component adaptation techniques should be transparent, black-box, composable, configurable, reusable and efficient to use. Unfortunately, existing component do not these requirements. To address this, this paper
discusses superimposition, a black-box adaptation technique that allows
one to impose predefined, but configurable types of adaptation functionality on a reusable component. In addition, three categories of typical
adaptation types are discussed, related to the component interface, component composition and monitoring.

1 Introduction

Component-oriented programming is receiving increasing amounts of interest
in the software engineering community. The abstract, naive view of component
reuse is that the component can just be plugged into an application and reused
as is. However, "as-is" reuse is very unlikely to occur and in the majority of
the cases, a reused component has to be adapted. Adapting a component can
be achieved using *white-box*, e.g. *inheritance* or *copy-paste*, and *black-box*, e.g.
aggregation or *wrapping*, adaptation techniques.

In this paper, we argue that the aforementioned techniques are insufficient
to deal with all required types of adaptation without experiencing, potentially
considerable, problems. To address these problems, we introduce the notion of
superimposition, a technique to impose predefined, but configurable, types of
functionality on a component's functionality. The notion of superimposition has
been implemented in the layered object model (LAYOM).

2 Component Adaptation Techniques

Based on our experience, we believe that a component adaptation techniques
should fulfil the following requirements:

- **Transparent**: Both the user of the adapted component and the component
  itself should be unaware of the adaptation in between them.

- **Black-box**: The adaptation technique should requires no knowledge of the internal structure of the component, but is limited to the interface of the component.

- **Composable**: The adaptation technique should not require redefinition of the component when composed with it.

- **Configurable**: Adaptation often consists of a generic and a specific part. The technique has to provide sufficient configurability of the specific part.

- **Reusable**: Although the specific part cannot be reused, the adaptation technique should allow for reuse of the generic part.

- **Efficient**: The adaptation technique should require little understanding of the adapted component's internals and be easy to use.

Traditional adaptation techniques can be categorised into white-box and black box adaptation techniques. *White-box* adaptation techniques require understanding of the internals of the component. Two instances of white-box adaptation are *copy-paste*, i.e. copying the code of a component and using it to define a new component, and *inheritance*, which makes the state and behaviour of the reused component available to the reusing component. *Black-box* adaptation techniques allow the software engineer to adapt components solely based on the externally visible interface. Two instances of black-box techniques are *aggregation*, i.e. define existing components as part of a new component, and *wrapping*, which also encapsulates the component but with functionality for forwarding, with minor changes, requests from clients to the wrapped components.

In table 1, an overview of the conventional adaptation techniques is presented that indicates how well each technique fulfils the specified requirements. From the table, one can identify that some requirements are dealt with well by the black-box techniques but not so well by the white-box techniques and visa versa. Since no technique fulfils all requirements, we investigate *superimposition* as a novel technique to component adaptation.

Table 1. Conventional adaptation techniques versus the identified problems and requirements

Requirement	Copy-Paste	Inheritance	Aggregation	Wrapping
transparent	+	+	-	-
black-box	-	-	+	+
composable	-	-	-	+
configurable	-	-	-	-
reusable	-	-	+/-	+/-
efficient	-	+	+	-

3 Component Adaptation through Superimposition

We discuss superimposition as a novel technique to adapt components in a component-based system. The notion underlying superimposition is that a component and the functionality adapting the component are two separate entities on the one hand and need to be very tightly integrated on the other hand. We believe that, in addition to a set of reusable components, a set of reusable component adaptation types is required. These adaptation types should be configurable and composable with each other to allow for complex component adaptations.

During our work on component adaptation, we have identified three typical categories of component adaptation. Below, each of these categories is discussed in more detail.

Changes to Component Interface A typical situation in component-based system construction is when a component in principle could be reused in the system at hand, but its interface does not match the interface expected by the system. In such situations, the interface of the component needs to be adapted to match the expected interface. Typical examples of component interface adaptation are: *changing operation names, restricting parts of the interface* and *client- and state-based restriction*

Component Composition Components are intended for composition to form larger structures. Sometimes, the components have to composed such that the resulting structure seems a single component from the system's perspective. Three types of component adaptation relevant for component composition are: *delegation of requests, component composition* and *acquaintance selection and binding*.

Component Monitoring Component monitoring implies that other components are in some form notified or invoked when certain conditions at the monitored component occur. Three examples of monitoring are: *implicit invocation, observer notification* and *state monitoring*

4 Superimposition using the Layered Object Model

Since traditional object and component models are unable to implement component adaptation through superimposition, more advanced models are required. One such model is the **layered object model** (LAYOM) that we have been working on for several years. LAYOM provides direct language support for superimposition and most of the component adaptation types are available as layer types.

The layered object model is an extended component object model, i.e. it defines in addition to the traditional object model elements, additional parts such as layers, states and categories. In figure 1, an example LAYOM object is presented. A *state* in LAYOM is an abstraction of the internal state of the object. An *acquaintance* category is an expression that defines a set of components that are treated similarly by the component.

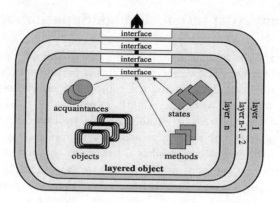

Fig. 1. The layered object model

Layers are the entities that provide superimposition functionality to components. Layer classes have, among others, been defined for the representation of relations between classes and objects, design patterns, acquaintance handling and superimposing behaviour. Since layers intercept messages sent to and from the component, layers are able to superimpose certain functionality on the component. An example is the *Adapter* layer type, shown below. An instance of class *Adaptee* is declared and a layer of type *Adapter* is added to object. The layer will intercept the messages sent to the object and change certain message selectors so that the component can interpret them. Due to reasons of space, the facilities for component adaptation provided by LayOM are only discussed very brief. We refer to [1, 2] and to the indicated WWW page for more information.

```
// object declaration
adaptedAdaptee : Adaptee with layers
adapt : Adapter(accept mess1 as newMessA, accept mess2, mess3 as newMessB);
end;
```

5 Related Work

The notion of adapting reusable components to match the requirements of the application at hand is not extensively studied in the component-based software engineering community. Some object models provide *before* and *after* facilities that allow the software engineer to add pre- and post-behaviour to the execution of an operation in a component. The notion of superimposition has earlier primarily been used in the context of distributed systems, e.g. [3] and [7]. There it is used to indicate the additional, superimposing control over some algorithm. Since superimposition is a novel technique, no existing implementations of superimposition exist besides the layered object model. However, meta-object protocols, e.g. [8], can be viewed as types of superimposing behaviour for object-oriented systems. In general, reflective languages such are suitable to implement superimposition.

6 Conclusion

Component-based software engineering requires component adaptation techniques that are transparent, black-box, composable, configurable, reusable and efficient to use. Conventional techniques for adapting components do not fulfil most of the identified requirements. In this paper, a component adaptation technique, *super-imposition*, was discussed. An object superimposition S of B over O is defined as the additional overriding behaviour B over the behaviour of a component object O. Example types of adaptation behaviour are related to component interface adaptation, component composition and component monitoring. Superimposition is implemented as a language construct in the layered object model (LAYOM) through the notion of layers. The extended expressiveness of LAYOM provides the software engineer with powerful component adaptation types through superimposition.

References

1. Bosch, J.: Design Patterns as Language Constructs,' Accepted for publication in the *Journal of Object-Oriented Programming,* November 1996.
2. Bosch, J.: Object Acquaintance Selection and Binding, *submitted,* August 1997.
3. Bougè, L., Francez, N.: A Compositional Approach to Superimposition, *Proceedings POPL'88,* pp. 240-249, 1988.
4. Gamma, E., Helm, R., Johnson, R., Vlissides, J.O.: Design Patterns - Elements of Reusable Object-Oriented Software, *Addison-Wesley,* 1994.
5. Goldberg, A., Robson, D.: Smalltalk-80 - The Language, *Addison-Wesley,* 1989.
6. Helm, R., Holland, I., Ganghopadhyay, D.: Contracts: Specifying Behavioral Compositions in Object-Oriented Systems, *Proceedings OOPSLA '90,* pp. 169-180, 1990.
7. Katz, S.: A Superimposition Control Construct for Distributed Systems, *ACM Transactions of Programming Languages and Systems,* Vol. 15, No. 2, April 1993.
8. Kiczales, G., des Rivires, J., Bobrow, D.G., The Art of the Metaobject Protocol, *The MIT Press,* 1991.
9. Lieberman, H.: Using Prototypical Objects to Implement Shared Behavior in Object Oriented Systems, *Proceedings OOPSLA '86,* pp. 214-223, 1986.
10. Reenskaug, T., Wold, P., Lehne, O.A.: Working With Objects: The Ooram Software Engineering Method, *Prentice Hall,* 1995.

Inheritance Using Contracts
& Object Composition

Wolfgang Weck

Turku Centre for Computer Science (TUCS) & Åbo Akademi, Turku, Finland

Abstract. Normal class-based code inheritance across component boundaries creates a dependency between the involved components. To avoid this, a specification of the inherited class must be part of the respective component's contract and the inheriting class must be specified with reference to this specification only. With this, inheritance can be replaced by object composition without sacrificing the possibility of static analysis, yet being more flexible.

1   Introduction

Object-oriented programming is a foundation technology for components. A typical component will specify a couple of classes or objects. To access services, other components will obtain objects from the providing component and send requests to them. In a running system, the hierarchy of components is complemented by a mesh of objects.

Object reuse and modification is a key tool for component reuse. In this paper we investigate language support for inheritance across component boundaries under the aspect of late composition. We do, however, not discuss the semantical problems of inheritance, such as the fragile base class problem.

2   Object Composition versus Class Composition

Two notions of classes and inheritance exist in the object-oriented programming community. Many programming languages and their underlying models are *class-based* (e.g. Eiffel, C++, Java, or Smalltalk). Others, such as Cecil [5] or Self [11] are *prototype-based*.

Class-based approaches abstract from the many instances of objects by grouping them into classes. All the objects of one class have the same attributes, accept the same messages, and exhibit the same behavior. Every new object is created as an instance of some specified class, and it will remain an object of this class throughout its life time.

With prototype-based approaches, objects are created by cloning an existing object, the prototype, and modifying the clone. Here, classes are sometimes seen as a dynamic equivalence relation that can be infered at run time. By modifying an object's state or structure, objects can be migrated from one class to another at run time. This approach has the advantage of being more flexible. It allows to change the behaviour of objects or to assign class membership via predicates on the state [4].

The flip side of this flexibility is that static checking and reasoning becomes almost impossible. It may not even be clear, which messages a given object accepts, unless its complete history is examined. In a closed system, complete flow analysis may allow to make up for this [1], but in an extensible system this is not possible anymore [9].

With object-oriented programming, it is common to express composition and reuse by means of *inheritance*. In short, some inheriting entity inherits from one or several inherited entities by copying their implementation and modifying it.

The above two views on object-orientation use inheritance between different kinds of entities. Class-based approaches support inheritance between classes, whereas prototype-based approaches support inheritance between objects. The latter is, for instance in Self [11], implemented through reference to a *parent object*, to which the handling of unknown messages is delegated.

Class-based approaches fix the inheritance relations at compile time. Since inheritance relates to implementation, class-based inheritance fixes the implementation to be inherited at compile time, i.e. before composition time in a component-oriented context. This makes state-of-the-art class-based inheritance unsuitable across components, because we want to delay the selection and binding of the base-class implementation until composition time.

Thus, depending on the view, object-oriented programming either supports static analysis or the possibility to compose implementations later than at compile time, but not both. A question of interest is, whether a middle ground can be found, on which you get both static analysis and late composition of implementations. Such a middle ground would be necessary for component-oriented programming to allow for inheritance across components.

3   Contracts Separate Specification from Implementation

On the component level, the above dilemma between static analysis and late composition is well known. There, the answer is the definition of contracts, which specify the obligations component providers must meet and the expectations component clients may have. For every component, it must be documented according to which contracts it offers or requires services. Two components can be composed, if one offers services that are requested by the other component according to the same contract. Each component can be analyzed separately, based on the contracts it participates in. At composition time, one only needs to check whether the two components actually claim to stick to the same contract. If they don't, the composition can be rejected.

In short: at compile time only specifications are bound, whereas implementations are bound at composition time. The contract provides the necessary separation of the specification from the implementation.

The practical effect of this separation is that static reasoning is still possible, because the yet unknown partner can be substituted by the contract. Still, bindings between implementations are established only at composition time, retaining full flexibility of selecting components to the composer. With components we managed to eat the cake and have it too.

4 Class Composition With Contracts

The same technique can be used with inheritance. Instead of refering to an implementation, the inheriting class refers to a contract only. The contract states what to expect from the inherited class; the inheriting class can be statically analyzed. We get the safety we want.

Only when an object is instantiated, the binding to a concrete base class implementation must be established. Any class meeting the required contract can be bound. In addition to safety, we get the late composition we want.

Class inheritance with contracts is implemented in IBM's SOM and in modular object-oriented programming languages, such as Modular Smalltalk [13] or Oberon-2 [7]. These languages feature separate constructs for modules and classes. Modules are separately compilable, similar to Modula-2. It is possible to compile several modules implementing the same interface. This allows for alternative implementations of the same specification.

With modular object-oriented programming, only one component (module) per contract can be used in a running system. As a consequence, all classes meeting a given contract have the same implementation. It is just that this implementation is selected very late.

5 Object Composition With Contracts

Can we get rid of the aforementioned restriction and support different implementations of a contract simultaneously? One could allow several modules implementing the same interface to coexist in a running system. This would collide with some assumptions being generally made about modules and also would require a way to refer to the different module implementations. Currently, identifications are made by refering to the module name, i.e., the contract, which is implemented by exactly one module.

Alternatively, when we separate subclassing from subtyping, as in Sather [10], types can be seen as contracts and classes as implementations to be bound later. Further and in contrast to Sather, subclasses would have to be specified by reference to a type (contract) instead of a class (implementation).

With this, the base classes to be used with an object would need to be specified at object allocation time; the allocation procedure would need to accept the respective additional parameters.

This can be taken one step further by composing objects instead of classes: one can specify a base object instead of a base class when allocating an object.

If a contract is used to specify statically the properties required from the parent object, and if the parent object is bound for ever when the refering object is created, static analysis is possible to exactly the same degree as with class-based inheritance with contracts. Though each object may be of a class of its own now, the same information as before is available from the object itself and the contract specifying the parent.

To retain the full amount of static information as with class inheritance, we must prohibit to re-assign the parent or base object. Otherwise, unexpected changes of state and/or behaviour of the composed object could occur.

This construction is indeed on a middle ground between static class inheritance and full dynamic inheritance as used with prototype-based object-orientation. Compared to the former, we gain flexibility, even more than with class composition based on contracts. Compared to prototype-based object-orientation, we get more static information because of two restrictions. First, not any object can be used as parent: it has to satisfy the required specification. Second, the parent, once assigned, cannot be changed anymore. Still, we get much of the flexibility of prototype-based object-orientation, because the user can interactively specify the parent object.

We take it as strong support of our proposal that it implements the formal model used by Cook and Palsberg to describe inheritance [6]. There, inheriting classes are specified as *wrappers* that only refer to the base class' signature. A concrete base class is bound at instantiation time only.

An implementation inbetween our proposal and Self was proposed as "Delegation Through a Pointer" to be added to C++ [8]. Compared to Self, the pointer to the parent object is typed. Viewing types as approximations for specifications again, we see that one of our two restrictions applies. The parent has to meet a certain specification. In contrast to our's, Stroustrup's proposal would still allow to re-assign the parent object.

An implementation that fixes the parent object can be found in Modula-3 [3]. Its allocation procedure allows to specify a list of methods to be bound to the new object. However, the base object's class (i.e. its implementation) is fixed statically by the type of the variable passed to *NEW*. Thus, Modula-3 does not allow a dynamic selection of the parent object at run time. In this sense, it is less flexible than our construction.

An implementation of our proposal can be done similar to aggregation in Microsoft's COM. With the right language support, the needed run-time data structures would be generated by the compiler.

6 Summary

To be applicable as a foundation technology for component-oriented programming, object-oriented programming with inheritance must support a middle ground between class-based and prototype-based object-orientation. Traditional class-based object-orientation is not flexible enough, unless class specifications rather than implementations are bound at component manufacturing time. On the other hand, prototype-based object-orientation is too flexible, thereby prohibiting effective static analysis.

As the above middle ground we suggest syntactical support for inheritance but using only a specification of the base class together with an implementation as object composition "under the hood". The compiler would have to hide the details of the latter to assert that the objects are not composed arbitrarily. In particular, the parent object must match the specification. Also, the compiler would have to prohibit that the parent object is re-assigned, once the composed object has been created.

This scheme allows for full static analysis, limited only by the amount of information stated with the specification of the inherited object. It gives the best possible flexibility, since the selection of the inherited code is delayed not only until component composition time, but until object generation time. The latter allows even the user to pick the code to be bound.

References

1. Agesen, O., Palsberg, J., Schwartzbach, M.I.: Type Inference of SELF: Analysis of Objects with Dynamic and Multiple Inheritance. In Proc. of ECOOP'93, LNCS 707, Springer-Verlag Berlin, ISBN 3-540-57120-5, pp. 247-267.
2. Brockschmidt, K.: Inside OLE 2. Microsoft Press, ISBN 1-55615-618-9, 1994.
3. Cardelli, L., Donahue, J., Glassman, L., Jordan, M., Kalsow, B., Nelson, G.: Revised Modula-3 Report. SRC Rep. 52, Digital Systems Research Center, Palo Alto, 1989.
4. Chambers, C.: Predicate Classes. In Proc. of ECOOP'93, LNCS 707, Springer-Verlag Berlin, ISBN 3-540-57120-5, pp. 268-296.
5. Chambers, C.: The Cecil Language, Specification and Rationale, Version 2.1. Department of Computer Science and Engineering University of Washington, Seattle as available at April 25, 1997 from http://www.cs.washington.edu /research/projects/cecil/www/Papers/cecil-spec.html.
6. Cook, W., Palsberg, J.: A Denotational Semantics of Inheritance and its Correctness. In Proc. of OOPSLA'89, SIGPLAN Notices 24:10.
7. Mössenböck, H.: The Programming Language Oberon-2. Structured Programming 12:4, 1991.
8. Stroustrup, B.: Multiple Inheritance for C++. Proc. of EUUG Spring Conf., 1987.
9. Szyperski, C.: Independently Extensible Systems - Software Engineering Potential and Challenges. In Proc. of the 19th Australasian Computer Science Conference, Melbourne, Australia, 1996.
10. Szyperski, C., Omohundro, S., Murer, S.: Engineering a Programming Language: The Type and Class System of Sather. In Proc. of the International Conference on Programming Languages and System Architectures, LNCS 782, March 1994.
11. Ungar, D., Chamber, C., Chang, B.-W., Hölzle, U.: Organizing Programs Without Classes. In Lisp and Symbolic Computation, July 1991 4:3, Kluwer Academic Publishers, pp. 223-242.
12. Wirth, N., Gutknecht, J.: Project Oberon. The Design of an Operating System and Compiler. Addison-Wesley New York, ISBN 0-201-54428-8, 1992.
13. Wirfs-Brock, A., Wilkerson, B.: An Overview of Modular Smalltalk. In Proc. of OOPSLA'88, SIGPLAN Notices 23:11.

The 7th Workshop for PhD Students in Object-Oriented Systems

Frank Gerhardt – fg@acm.org
Lutz Wohlrab – lwo@informatik.tu-chemnitz.de
Erik Ernst – eernst@daimi.aau.dk

It is a tradition at ECOOP conferences to have a workshop for PhD students, conducted by the network of PhD Students in Object-Oriented Systems (PhDOOS). The purpose of this network is to help leveraging the collective resources of young researchers in the object community by improving the communication and cooperation between them. In a year of the PhDOOS network the workshop is the main event where we meet face-to-face. Between workshops we stay in touch through our mailing list. More information on the PhDOOS network can be found at http://purl.org/net/PhDOOS.

The workshop was a little special compared to the other workshops at ECOOP. Where other workshops typically center on a well-defined topic chosen at the outset, the technical topics of this workshop were derived from the research interests of the participants. Since the workshop had 36 participants, we partitioned the main group into several subgroups, each having a more focused research area as topic. The work in these subgroups had been prepared extensively by the participants. A little less than half of the participants had submitted a position paper. Everybody had prepared a presentation of his or her research work—a longer presentation for those participants with a position paper, and a shorter one for those who just provided a short abstract of their research work. The position papers have been published at Århus University; information about how to obtain this report is given at the end of this introduction.

The technical sessions in subgroups were an important part of the workshop, but there were also other activities. In plenary sessions we heard two invited speakers, had a writer's workshop, and discussed issues related to the network itself. We also had a discussion about the conditions of being a doctoral student in various countries, as a followup to an email based discussion about this shortly before the workshop.

Our invited speakers were Prof. Mehmet Aksit from the University of Twente and Prof. Peter Wegner from Brown University. They spoke about their academic lives in retrospect, their current and future research, and the PhD-getting process in general. We were impressed by wide range of experience they demonstrated and thankful for the personal remarks they made regarding our profession. We think it is invaluable to get this insight when starting a career in academia or industry.

There were a couple of plenary sessions dealing with the network itself. We felt that the network is too inactive during the year, and that communication needs to be improved. The ECOOP workshop is good, but there ought to be more of other things, too. To make this happen, the activities in the network should become a natural and indispensable part of the daily work of the members, as opposed to a beautiful idea that we can play with after having finished our real work...

We picked up the idea from the year before to review each other's papers. While the previous approach intended to have reviews only before each ECOOP conference, we now want to start a continuous review process. It should be convenient and a good habit for members of the network to receive valuable feed-back from other members of the network about articles, books, or selected parts of such written work, before submitting them to a conference or publishing them. We also have to make sure that the authors feel assured their work is not "stolen" by anybody in this process. Since cooperation is a basic tool in research today, keeping the work secret is not an option. On the contrary, as soon as many people know that a particular idea or approach originally came from one group of persons, it will in fact be *better* protected again "theft" than without this community awareness. The network is a great resource of knowledge and inspiration, we just have to push a little bit to make it visible, accessible and useful for each member.

Another idea was to use the Internet more intensively to get in touch on a regular basis. Real meetings are great, but difficult to arrange. Therefore we want to try out "vitual meetings" using technologies like IRC or conferencing groupware. Whether in real life or via network cables, meeting other people and getting to know them is a necessary precondition for good, lively cooperation.

Finally we had to find the organizers of next year's workshop. Erik and Frank will continue for one more year. They are joined by Luigi Benedicenti (`Luigi.Benedicenti@dist.unige.it`). The homepage of the 1998 workshop is `http://purl.org/net/PhDOOS/1998`. If you want to join the network, take a look at `http://purl.org/net/PhDOOS`.

The remainder of this chapter is devoted to the presentation of the techical discussions which took place in the workshop subgroups. Each group has presented itself in one section.

Each section starts with a group summary. The summary should work as a reader's guide for you, to quickly find out what has been discussed in the group. After the summary each section contains a number of subsections, each written by one member of the group.

In each subsection, a participant presents his or her own research, as it was presented and discussed at the workshop. The presentation is approximately one page long; it is not supposed to be an ultra-compact research article, but rather an appetizer which would give you an opportunity to look closer at somebody's work using the provided URLs and similar references. The addresses of the participants are listed separately at the end of this chapter.

As mentioned above, the workshop also accepted submission of position papers. These position papers have been published and are available as the technical report DAIMI PB-526, Department of Computer Science, Aarhus University. It will also be made available in an electronic format, please contact the library of the department at `library@daimi.aau.dk` about this.

1 Applications & Frameworks

Krister Ahlander, Tero Ahtee, Wade Holst,
Kitty Hung, Selma Karadurak, Roger Kehr,
Palle Nowack, Stefan Tai

In this sub-group, individual research and work on different aspects of frameworks was discussed to identify commonalities and differences in our understanding of frameworks for software development. The presentations and discussions focused on five major areas namely: (1) methodological and life-cycle issues for business object architecture; (2) software architectural abstractions for object-oriented programming frameworks, and for distributed object systems with integration platform technologies; (3) design patterns for product prototyping; (4) specific framework developments supporting configuration management, efficient method dispatch techniques for compiler development and for solving partial differential equations; and (5) conceptual framework to test OO CASE tools.

The individual presentations: Krister's research aims at a OO framework for solving partial differential equations (PDEs) numerically, extensible both with respect to the description of the PDEs as well as the description of the numerical methods used for solving the PDEs. Tero uses a framework approach to develop evaluation criteria of OO CASE tools and his framework describes evaluation procedures with a sorted hierarchical checklist and test diagrams recommended for evaluation. Wade has developed a framework for table-based method dispatch based on a few fundamental algorithms acting as template methods. The algorithms are incremental in nature, and can be used to provide dispatch even in languages that add classes and methods at run-time. Kitty has developed a Business Object Architecture (BOA) framework and implemented it through a Dynamic Systems Development Method (DSDM) life-cycle environment with emphasis on end-users' involvement. Selma's adoption of framework technology is predominately on a design patterns level to support Rapid Product Prototyping (RPP). Roger develops a concrete framework for OO system configuration management. A delegation-based object model is used to explore the inherent redundancy in configuration problems. The next step is to extend it from a concrete system to a more general framework. Palle presented an approach towards raising the level of abstraction when describing and organising OO frameworks based on the notions of architectural units and relations. Stefan is developing a software architectural framework supporting the design of distributed heterogeneous object systems of combined forward and reverse engineering. Object models and integration platform technologies such as CORBA are considered.

In summary, the general framework idea is commonly used for supporting and enclosing OO models ranging from conceptual design to physical implementation. Distinctively, frameworks are treated as skeletal support and basis for model construction. Agreed within our sub-group benefits of frameworks are that they support our conceptualisation and design approaches for specific application domains.

1.1 Krister Ahlander: OO Design of a framework for PDE Solvers

I develop an OO framework for building PDE Solvers, (programs that numerically solve Partial Differential Equations). Traditionally, this is a highly algorithmic problem, which usually yields a FORTRAN function library. However, my aim is to create a software framework that is more flexible and more extensible than such a library. Therefore, I have used OO methodologies such as OMT, Booch, and OOSE/Objectory. Further, I have used C++ as implementation language. The major problems I address are how to design the framework so that it is possible to extend it with new kinds of PDE problems to solve numerically, as well as new numerical methods to solve the PDE problems with.

In an earlier project, Cogito/Solver[1], a framework for PDE in one spatial dimension was developed. It was demonstrated how objects representing the PDE problem as well as objects representing the numerical method could be combined and executed in run-time, thus making it possible to compose and solve problems interactively. An OO database was used to achieve higher flexibility.

Currently, I work on the extension of these ideas to several space dimensions, using the Overture class library as efficient lower level tools. I have also extended the scope so that coupled PDE in several space dimensions may be treated. I have found that the dynamical model of an OO methodology has provided many important contributions to achieve the necessary decoupling of the participating objects.

1.2 Tero Ahtee: Evaluation of OO-CASE Tools by a Test Specifications Model

The target of my research is to find out how the evaluation of CASE tools could be improved.

Phases of CASE tool evaluation according to ISO [ISO94] are:

- preparing for evaluation
- evaluation
  - measurement
  - rating
  - assessment
- reporting

The evaluation (and selection) of a suitable CASE tool is problematic to almost all organizations. Nowadays tools' properties are tested quite randomly, in very few cases there are planned test models. With a general test specifications model organizations would get quite a wide overview of tool's properties and functions in short time before they choose a tool.

When organizations are choosing CASE tools, they usually don't have time enough to perform complete benchmarks or field tests. Because of that, organizations may run into great difficulties later, when they suddenly realize that

---

[1] http://www.tdb.uu.se/research/cogito/

their tool is not suitable for the intended use. The problem of buying 'wrong' or 'insufficient' CASE tool is obvious.

If organizations could have a pre-defined test specifications model, they could test the candidate CASE tools with it. The testing process would be quite comprehensive and quick. The additional advantage is, that in case of testing several tools, the results of different tests are at least somehow comparable.

In larger organizations this evaluation problem has been taken more seriously. It is the middle-size and small organizations that do not use thorough evaluation strategies while choosing CASE tools.

A solution to this evaluation problem might be a Test Specifications Model (TSM). It contains

- questionnaire about the tool
- checklist about the tool characteristics
- checklist about what the tool is like in test use
- method-dependent part of diagrams (a test model), e.g. OMT

By using a TSM, organizations could use their evaluating time and efforts better. The cost/benefit ratio would be better because of precise test procedures. The evaluation would last shorter time, and the evaluator gets printed diagrams and reports as documents.

My idea is, that organizations should use a test specifications model; with which they try to draw the same diagrams and do the same tasks with the tool as in the TSM are. If they can draw all of the diagrams completely, the tool might be good. If they fail, they see the disadvantages of the tool. While doing that users test the coverage and user friendliness of the tool. Users get a wide inside look about tool's capabilities in a relatively short time. The 'failure' of the tool does not mean that it is useless - it may still be suitable; many organizations do not need all the brilliant drawing features of an versatile CASE tool.

For more information please see http://www.cs.tut.fi/~tensu/Eval-CASE.html

1.3 Wade Holst: Efficient Method Dispatch in Object-Oriented Languages

Object-oriented languages have various properties that provide them with highly desirable features, like abstraction, modularity, information hiding and code reuse. However, these same properties have an impact on execution performance because they introduce the need for *method dispatch*: run-time determination of the method to invoke at a particular call-site. Although the method to invoke can sometimes be established at compile-time, such optimizations are not always possible. Furthermore, object-oriented languages are highly variable in how certain concepts are implemented. Some languages restrict the flexibility or generality of the language in order to ensure more efficiency, while others place more emphasis on language expressiveness. This variability can have a profound effect on the method dispatch techniques appropriate for the language in question. My research is concerned with three distinct but related issues associated with method dispatch: 1) efficient method dispatch in the broadest possible category of object-oriented languages, 2) how to efficiently maintain the minimum amount of information necessary to perform method dispatch, and 3) when and how run-time method dispatch can be avoided.

Object-oriented languages can be categorized in a variety of ways. From the perspective of method dispatch, two issues are extremely important. The first issue is whether the language has the ability to add classes and selectors at runtime (we call such languages *schema-evolving* languages, and they are contrasted against *schema-static* languages). A broad category of dispatch techniques have not previously been applicable to schema-evolving languages. Some of my research demonstrates how such techniques can be applied, by making the algorithms *incremental* (they modify the information each time a class or selector is added to the environment. The second issue is whether the language is *single-dispatching* or *multiple-dispatching*. Most languages are single-dispatching, and thus a dedicated *receiver* class and selector are sufficient to identify an address to invoke. On the other hand, multiple-dispatching languages use the dynamic types of all arguments (along with the selector) to determine method addresses.

There are a variety of well-established method dispatch techniques for single-dispatching languages. Different techniques provide different trade-offs between dispatch speed and memory utilization, and varying performance on schema-evolving versus schema-static languages. Part of my research has extended a broad category of single-dispatching techniques to schema-evolving languages. My future research will involve using these techniques to provide efficient multiple-dispatching techniques.

Published papers and additional details can be found at `http://www.cs.ualberta.ca/~wade`.

1.4 Kitty Hung: "Is there life after death?": The Rejuvenation of Life-cycle in a Dynamic Business Object Architecture

In recent years, Business Object technology is considered to be one of the ideal approaches to deliver solutions to achieve the objective of Software Best Practice (SBP). However, the current phenomenon has shown that the strategies proposed only see the business from the IT developers' pair of "tinted glasses" with the developers looking at the business from their own perspectives. The influence of business end-users over SBP has since been neglected. Business end-users hold business knowledge and they pose to be the most ideal candidates as business information providers and system testers and responders.

Dynamic Systems Development Method (DSDM) is derived from the concept of Rapid Application Development (RAD) with additional principles emphasising on user's involvement. DSDM provides an ideal environment to enable developers to produce quality software while deliver on time and within budget through the techniques of: joint requirement planning (JRP), joint application development (JAD), function points, time-boxing, clean room technique, feasibility studies, business studies, functional model iteration, system design and build iteration, implementation. The holistic approach of DSDM is to form a vehicle to drive the developers and end-users together. Traditionally, developers tend to put a subjective view on their work presuming this is what the real world needs. A fundamental assumption of DSDM is that nothing is built perfectly first time. As a result all steps can be revisited as part of its iterative approach. Therefore the current step needs be completed only enough to move to the next step. DSDM not only provides a life-cycle but also the necessary controls to ensure its success.

This paper attempts to integrate two of the existing techniques namely: (1) Business Object Architecture (BOA) and (2) Dynamic Systems Development Method (DSDM) life-cycle environment to develop a Dynamic Business Object Architecture (DBOA). The DBOA model contains business objects holding business knowledge. The architectural design of the BOA makes the business object components easy to be reused. The rejuvenation of life-cycle through different stages of prototyping is to enable the developers to build a model at an early stage of the project before any significant investment is incurred and allows the developers to modify the system throughout the development phases. The holistic approach of DSDM through substantial user involvement has brought the business end-users and software developers together to achieve the objective of SBP. CAD Consultants Ldt. (a credit insurance agent)'s system has been used in this paper as a case study of our development work.

1.5 Selma Karadurak: Using Design Patterns in Object Oriented Product Prototyping

Principal Objective This research is based on the application of design patterns to object oriented rapid product prototyping. The principal objective of this proposal is to test the idea that using design patterns [Gamma95] in rapid prototyping will provide a reliable and adaptable standard method for producing a product prototype which can be easily extended, modified and re-used. I propose to integrate object oriented tools and techniques with design patterns in order to support the design of physical artefacts such as HI-FIs, video recorders and car radios. The use of design patterns should be an invaluable aid to interactive rapid product prototyping since it is often limited by its supporting tools and techniques.

Prototyping and Design Patterns Using prototyping creates a bridge between industrial designers and software developers in order to provide the production of well-designed products which meet the expectation of customer needs. This reduces the cost and risk involved in developing software systems. Without the supporting tools and techniques rapid prototyping can be lengthy, costly and inefficient.

The life-cycle of object oriented prototyping is an evolutionary software development process which makes modifications and extensions easy to manage. Unfortunately, this process might eventually result in irrational software since new classes which are introduced to satisfy additional requirements or modifications could lead to inflexible class hierarchy. In order to make software more re-usable, refactoring should take place. This involves rearranging class hierarchy and considered to be time-consuming. Design patterns make program extensions and modifications easier and safer by clearly indicating the 'hook' for the new classes (i.e. 'Abstract Factory' design pattern) thus reducing the amount of later refactoring. Therefore, using design patterns in evolutionary rapid prototyping enhance software quality by solving the fundamental forces such as reusability, extendibility and adaptability.

Conclusion Reusability is the key issue in rapid prototyping. Using object oriented tools and techniques does not automatically result in reusable software components. The intention is to create objects which can be reused with no modification or only a little modification. Well-analysed object oriented techniques and proper use of tools such as design patterns are the key to successful reusability in object oriented rapid prototyping. This should allow the developers to "build the right system" and "support the next system" rather then just "build the system right" which does not always reflect user needs as it should. These ideas will be tested by constructing an interactive prototyping tool for physical artefacts that utilises the tools and methodologies investigated throughout the project.

References

[Gamma95] E. Gamma, R. Helm, R. Johnson, J. Vlissides: *Design Patterns – Elements of Reusable Object-Oriented Software*. Addison-Wesley, 1995.

1.6 Roger Kehr: Scot – A System Configuration Tool Based on Prototypical Objects and Constraints

The SCOT system is the central configuration repository within a larger project concerning network and system configuration management. It does not deal with concrete operating systems or physical devices. Instead it offers a flexible object-oriented framework for modeling configuration data and logical assertions, called predicates, on top of the data.

It uses a prototype-instance based object model. Objects represent hosts or services from a system configuration point of view. Prototypes with delegation allow for a flexible and dynamic description of configuration data avoiding redundancy.

In this model collections of objects are represented as first-class objects computed by a functional query on objects which is automatically maintained and updated by the system. These collections are to some extend comparable to views in RDBMS and implement the concept of predicate types in SCOT.

Appropriate mappings may be added to transform the configuration data into a representation suitable for further processing by operating systems or other applications. These mappings are expressed using generic functions that implement multi-method dispatch on collections and individual objects.

It supports the specification of consistency checks on objects and collections using user-definable predicates in a functional query language and uses one-way constraints (data flow graphs) for the efficient re-evaluation of these predicates. Appropriate exceptions are raised if the system enters invalid states probably resulting in misconfigurations. Predicates can also be used to model systems at various stages between a pure object-based model and a class-based model.

Objects are organised in a hierarchical namespace similar to a hierarchical file system. A versioning system for objects is under investigation.

The system aims at a more general framework for configuration tasks. Future work will be based on experiences with the current prototypical implementation.

1.7 Palle Nowack: Framework Description & Organization

Reuse is considered part of an efficient software development process. The architecture of a software system is an important aspect of its design; it is the aspect that developers, users, and maintainers most rely on, as it represents the stable, invariable part of the system. Hence, is is very desirable to reuse previously developed architectures. The use of object-oriented frameworks amongst other things exactly allows this, but the architecture is only implicitly represented in the framework code.

In general, it is very hard to deduct the analysis and design information used to develop a framework, from the framework code. More specifically, the architectural design of the framework is hard to trace. There is a large conceptual gap between the abstract design-level description of a framework's architectural organization and it's representation (the large amount of complex code making up the framework implementation). When applying or maintaining a framework, the success of design and implementation decisions is very dependent on whether they conform to the existing architecture of the framework.

Instead of relying solely on extensive framework documentation, we propose to investigate an alternative representation of frameworks based on architectural and organizational aspects[2], abstracting away from both algorithmic and data structural issues. The description should be applicable both on an informal design as wells as on a formal implementation level. Specifically we propose the development of the Framework Architecture Ensemble, which consists of a conceptual model, a design notation, a description language, and some parts of a development and application methodology.

The *conceptual model* defines the notion of *architectural units* and *architectural relations*. We organize a framework into architectural units, which we relate with architectural relations. An architectural unit describes a parametric component of a framework, by describing fixed as well as variable aspects of a part of the framework. In this sense it resembles an adaptable framework *hot-spot* as expressed by meta patterns. The set of architectural relations will be designed based on the abstraction mechanisms known from conceptual programming and

---

[2] Further described on http://www.cs.auc.dk/~nowack/phd/researchIndex.html

the notion of reusable frames. The *design notation* provide means for describing a concrete framework architecture as a collection of architectural units and relations. The *description language* describes more rigorously the framework architecture, and it can be interpreted and/or translated, supporting the development of a framework architecture and the production of framework code. The *methodological* parts of the approach in this project includes description of steps that guides a framework developer and user through the development of an architecture, as well as the maintenance and use of it. Most importantly it describes the notion of problem domains and software domains, and provide a conceptual framework for an architecture-centered approach to framework development and use.

1.8   Stefan Tai: A Software Architectural Framework for Modeling Integrated Object Systems

Distributed object technologies as exemplified by integration platforms like the OMG's CORBA support *continuous software engineering*: the integration of diverse old and new software applications into a long-lived software environment. Technologies like CORBA can be considered as *enabling* technologies facilitating the development of distributed, *integrated object systems (IOS)* since

- technical aspects of distribution and heterogeneity are mostly transparent to the system designer but shifted to supporting platform services, and
- object-oriented concepts are promoted: all diverse integrated software entities are considered *objects* that interact through message passing.

However, for expressing the software architecture of today's complex systems that are continuously built using object integration platforms, *high-level software architectural mechanisms* are needed. The conventional class-based object model of common design modeling languages is too low-level because

- the *class* concept (as originated in object-oriented programming languages) serves only for describing program-level objects, but not *components* in the sense of applications (system-level objects),
- the *message passing* model only specifies interactions involving two (program-level) objects at a time, but not higher-level, complex *collaborations* between multiple system-level objects (where typically several, possibly ordered program-level object interactions occur).

Based on concepts of software architecture, object-oriented methodologies, and reference models for distributed object computing, we introduce a conceptual framework of *components, connectors,* and *component schemes* to effectively structure and abstract integration and interoperation between system-level objects in IOS.

A *component* models an integrated object that consist of a number of internal (local) and external (facade) program-level objects. Components are described by an *interface specification* (a set of interfaces), a *representation* (an internal object-oriented scheme), and a *representation map* (an external object-oriented scheme). A *connector* abstracts component integration and interaction (structural and behavioral relationships) and describes a pattern for component interplay. Connector specifications comprise *roles*, *role interfaces*, and *interaction protocols*. *Component schemes* interprete connectors for specific components: they describe the mapping of responsibilities to component elements.

Our conceptual framework mediates between different object granularities of system-level and program-level objects, structures all relevant design information according to design *rationales*, and strongly supports modeling complex component dependencies and interaction models that are inherent to IOS.

For more information, please see `http://cic.cs.tu-berlin.de/~stai/`.

2 Languages and Distributed Systems

Lourdes Tajes-Martinez, Bart Vanhaute,
Martin von Löwis, Marc Geilen, Gautier Koscielny,
Nils Fischbeck

This group focussed mainly on distributed systems but had very different views of this topic. Lourdes Tajes-Martinez investigates the basis of distributed systems: the group she is working with develops an object-oriented operating system and studies security and synchronisation aspects. A flexible security system for mobile agents is developed by Bart Vanhaute. Martin von Löwis and Marc Geilen take part in the development of tools and methodologies for the specification and validation of real-time distributed systems. The grouping of objects in competence pools is studied by Gautier Koscielny and Nils Fischbeck investigates object oriented languages in its ability to be used for the specification of telecommunication applications.

Based on these different viewpoints much discussion time was absorbed by understanding each others topic and especially its application field. However the discussion was fruitful since it allowed each group member to think of his PhD work in other terms than usually. Major differences in the approach to solve a problem where identified, e.g. Marc Geilen considered pre- and postconditions vital for the formal verification of distributed system whereas Martin von Löwis chose to validate a system by simulation.

Since the presented topics are very different a summary of each's work is following:

Lourdes Tajes Martinez: The main goal of the project I'm working on is the design of an object-oriented operating system that will offer a "world of objects" where the only abstraction is object. This operating system will be based on an object oriented abstract machine that will offer support to the OS object model. The main characteristics the OS must offer are security, persistence, distribution and concurrency. The concurrency model is partially supported by the abstract machine and is based on active objects that encapsulate computation as well as state, synchronous invocation of methods and the tagging of methods as exclusive or concurrent.

Bart Vanhaute: My work tries to use meta-level concepts as a basis for designing an open and flexible security system for multi-agent systems. This approach has the advantage that security policies and mechanisms can be separated into a meta-level while normal computation is kept at the base-level. An important issue here is the identification of what basic facilities the execution environment should provide, and how safeness can be guaranteed with them. These basic services together constitute the the trusted computing base (TCB) and they will then be used to construct more high-level services like migration and secure communication.

Marc Geilen: In my PhD work I am focussing on languages, algebras and semantics for modelling and specification of concurrent real-time systems. I took part in the development of a specification and simulation environment that has been built for POOSL, the language we work with. Future research will include the search for a understandable object-oriented language / logic in which requirements and properties can be expressed formally. This formalism can then serve as a basis for formal proofs or validation / verification tools, such as mappings to formalisms suitable for formal verification or automatic validation of simulation results.

Martin von Löwis: When designing distributed systems, various specification techniques are employed. Formal methods support accepted validation techniques. Object-oriented methods simplify the specification process. Ideally, both approach could be combined, as attempted in SDL. For complex systems, the verification using proofs is not widely used because it is too difficult. Validation using simulation and similar approaches seems to be more promising.

Gautier Koscielny: Various distributed object applications use many different objects which provide common facilities. We propose to gather these objects bearing a common "know-how" relation into sets named competence pools. Our aim is to develop new applications based on pre-existent groups of objects, *i.e.* to allow a dynamic re-use of active objects. Thus, a competence pool represents a logical and dynamic organisation of distributed objects able to solve specific problems and may be shared by different applications. The main advantage of our approach is to raise the abstraction's level of the cooperation between objects.

Nils Fischbeck: Telecommunication systems place special requirements on a language for design and implementation since they must satisfy real-time constraints, mostly use asynchronous communication and involve the transport of variable or constant stream of data. Currently used languages for the design and implementation of telecommunication systems are SDL, ROOM or CHILL. All of these languages miss features some telecommunication systems need to be adequately modelled. In my PhD theses I will provide a classification of language features and identify missing language constructs. The final goal is the creation of a new language that fills the identified gaps and aligns well with the Object Definition Language currently developed by ITU-T.

2.1 Lourdes Tajes Martinez: Adding concurrency to an object-oriented operating system

This abstract presents SO4, a research project in Oviedo University. The main goal of this project is the design of an object-oriented operating system. This new OS will recognize objects as the unique entities that exist in the system and method invocations will be the only valid operations. SO4 offers the abstraction of a virtually infinite object space where all the objects created in the system exist, without differences between user objects and system objects. This uniformity will allow changing, removing or adding objects providing a specific or improved functionality.

One of the most important features of this OS is to be based on a reflective object-oriented abstract machine. This machine supports objects as the only abstraction and will offer the basic support to the OS object model. In the design of the OS we will pay special attention to key features such as security, persistence, distribution and concurrency.

Concurrency in SO4 In SO4, concurrency is defined as the ability to serve simultaneous method invocations in a number of objects, granting object consistency. We try to endow the system with a concurrency model that achieves the following objectives: i) Maximize the parallelism degree in a secure way. We have to allow concurrency between objects and between methods of an object, in the most secure way. ii) Simpleness. SO4 concurrency model tries to achieve a balance between the maximization of the parallelism and conceptual simplicity.

Concurrency model i) Active objects. Abstract machine offers the abstraction of self-contained objects, so the adoption of an active model is a natural decision. Objects are active and encapsulate computation completely. Conceptually, they have a virtual multiprocessor for multiple threads, with the needed concurrency control mechanisms for integrity preservation. Other OS like Guide or Clouds have chosen a passive model. ii) Synchronous invocation. When a method is invoked in a object, the caller is blocked during the resolution of this invocation. But other actions can take place in the caller and in the callee object. iii) Exclusive and concurrent methods. Every method defined in an object must be tagged as exclusive or concurrent. An exclusive method modifies the object state and cannot coexist with any other method in the object. Objects behave like monitors when dealing with this kind of methods. Concurrent methods do not modify its state, so they are compatible with other concurrent methods. This scheme has become very popular because Java implements a similar model.

Implementation Incorporating the concurrency model in the abstract machine may be a more simple and efficient solution than one that introduces parts of it in the machine and the rest as objects of the operating system. The abstract machine will take charge of the message passing and, in passing, take care of the security. Once the object has been located, the abstract machine studies its execution environment, and it decides if the method execution takes place immediately or if it must be enqueued.

402

References URL http://www15.uniovi.es/~lourdes.

2.2 Bart Vanhaute: An open and flexible security system for distributed agent applications

The widespread use of the Internet has accelerated the emergence of a new programming model that is based on mobile agents. An agent is an autonomous entity, with its own execution context. In order to perform its task, it can travel from host to host. A typical example of such an agent is an information scavenger that roams the network in search for information, like e.g. the cheapest place to buy some product.

This new concept requires a security model that goes beyond the models that have been used in classical client-server applications. An agent should not be able to compromise the integrity of the host it is executing on, nor should that host be able to corrupt the agent. Also, measures must be taken such that one agent can not obtain or corrupt private information of another agent.

In this PhD research, an open and flexible security system for mobile agent environments will be studied. Traditional systems generally have fixed system-wide policies, employ fixed algorithms, etc. In a more open strategy, it is the application programmer who can specify the policies and security algorithms of his/her agents. This approach has two important benefits. First, the programmer is less bound to decisions taken by the environment, giving more flexibility in his/her implementation. Second, a more fine grained control is achieved in the access specifications of agent services.

In the building of flexible and reusable systems, separation of concerns is a key issue. When security issues can be kept largely independent of the application code, it becomes feasible to reuse these separate secure components across different applications and to maintain security policies in a controlled manner. A meta-level architecture makes it possible to separate the main computation of an agent from other aspects. For every object, there are one or more meta-level objects that control the behaviour of this base-level object. If for instance another object sends this object a message, a meta-level object will intercept the message and can decide whether to allow the operation belonging to that message to be invoked or not.

As a basis for this realisation, a more formal model of agent interaction and execution is appropriate. This should allow us to reason about properties of sets of agents, such as mutual trust and authenticity, and derive and prove such properties.

2.3 Martin von Löwis: Simulation of Distributed Systems using SDL'92

In my master's thesis, I worked on an object-oriented methodolody for the development of telecommunication services, especially broadband ISDN services. Part of the methodology is use of appropriate specification and programming languages. For the telecommunications domain, the ITU Specification and Description Language is a possible candidate.

Another requirement for a methodology is the availability of tools in order to edit, analyse and process the specifications and implementations. Since my master's thesis, I concentrated on the development of tools for processing SDL specifications. My major interestest is in the simulation of SDL and other languages used to describe telecommunication protocols and services [3].

Simulating a telecommunication system is an important step in validating it. Since it is usuable unfeasable to analyse all possible states and interactions in the distributed system, only a subset of the interactions can be validated. On the other hand, it is not always possible to analyse these interactions in the target system: The experimentation environment might be limited, or it might not be possible to produce a certain input sequence because not all of the target environment is available during development.

Instead, the simulation is a means to perform an as detailed analysis of the specification as desired, at an acceptable cost. This involves distribution in two aspects: the simulated system is distributed, and so might be the simulator. The former fact results in requirements for data analsysis and presentation, the latter one in requirements for effective scheduling and data collection strategies.

Not only the specification being simulated might be written in a object-oriented specification technique: The simulator might make use of distributed object interfaces as well. Currently, a certain large-grain clustering of object interfaces is being performed on the simulation environment. For example, the simulator proper and the debugger user interface are separate tools communicating via ILU. Future work will concentrate on identifying and implementing finer-grained distribution of the objects involved. This work primarily has to deal with the speed-up due to multi-processor execution and the slow-down due to the extra communication overhead. Once the SDL simulator is significantly finished, my work will target other specification techniques.

2.4 Marc Geilen: Object-Oriented Specification and Design of Real-Time Hardware Software Systems

Information processing systems are often concurrent, distributed, reactive real-time systems, which consist of both hardware and software. In the Information and Communication Systems Group, an object-oriented methodology is being developed for specification and design of parallel and distributed communicating software/hardware systems[4]. This methodology combines both informal methods and an (executable) formal specification language POOSL (Parallel Object Oriented Specification Language). Its rigorous formal model allows the use of formal tools, e.g. simulation or verification.

---

[3] URL:http://www.informatik.hu-berlin.de/~loewis/sdl/

[4] [PVS95] van der Putten, P.; Voeten J. and Stevens, M. "Object-oriented co-design for hardware/ software systems" Proceedings of Euromicro'95

In order to make the language more suitable for real-time systems, it has been extended with primitive operators that allow the expression of timing properties of the system, such as delays, time-outs, watchdogs. Timing concepts of real-time process algebras have been studied and used for the extension of the language POOSL, whose concurrency and communication model is similar to CCS.

Real-time systems generally require high levels of reliability and safety. At the same time concurrent and distributed systems are known to be very hard to understand and design. Methods for verification and validation are important for building correct systems.

Exhaustive formal verification is often impossible because of state space explosion. Asynchronously operating processes cause the number of possible system states to grow exponentially with the size of the system. Therefore, validation is frequently performed by means of simulation of an executable model. Although simulation does not give full coverage and therefore cannot prove a system to be correct, it is applicable to large and complex systems.

A specification and design environment has been implemented in smalltalk-80. In this environment, communicating concurrent systems can be specified in POOSL and subsequently their behaviour can be simulated. The simulation results can be inspected in different representations, to assure correctness of the behaviour.

This way, a formal operational model can be constructed of the behaviour of a system. The requirements however are mostly expressed informally in natural language. As a consequence, the correctness of the behaviour can only be verified manually by inspection of simulation results.

To be able to formally validate a design, a language is being designed in which requirements of concurrent communicating real-time systems can be expressed formally. Such a modal logic could be used to create tools for automatic verification or validation of the formal model against the formally expressed properties.

In contrast to existing logics, the language should furthermore fit to the object-oriented paradigm and support hierarchy and modularity. Preferably, it should also be readable and simple, since experience shows that modal logics tend to be extremely difficult to use.

2.5 Nils Fischbeck: Requirements for an Object-Oriented Language for the Design and Implementation of Telecommunication Systems

Object-oriented languages are widely used in the design and implementation of telecommunication systems. Since the ITU-T specification and description language SDL was designed for this application field it is used in numerous projects. New emerging languages like ROOM claim a growing share of the market. Telecommunication systems place special requirements on a language for design and implementation since they must satisfy real-time constraints, mostly use asynchronous communication and involve the transport of variable or constant stream of data. Also new design methodologies like ODP and TINA-C put new requirements on the language. At Humboldt-University the SDL tool environment SITE has been developed for the design and implementation of telecommunication software. This environment has been used for the simulation and implementation of B-ISDN protocols and Intelligent Network services. During these projects it was realized that SDL lacks some features for an appropriate modelling of the applications.

In my PhD thesis I define a consistent set of terms which classify the requirements of telecommunication systems. Part of these definitions is the notion of active and passive objects and a structural and hierarchical composition. Languages for telecommunication systems should support multiple threads which supply the execution context for active objects. Communication between objects can take place asynchronously and synchronously. Objects are allowed to communicate at interfaces only. I evaluate existing languages according to these requirements.

In a first step SDL has been studied. This language lacks interface definitions, special kinds of asynchronous communication and a unified hierarchy definition. The evaluation of other languages will follow. The final vision is the definition (or identification) of a language ideal for the purposes defined by the special application field telecommunication systems.

3 Meta-Aspects and Distribution

Arno Bakker, Laszlo Blum, Fernando Sánchez,
Maria D. Fondón, Dario Álvarez, Juan M. Murillo,
Stephan Reitzner, Lutz Wohlrab, Michael Zastre

Papers and presentations given by members of this group covered, in the context of object-orientation, a range of meta-programming and distributed programming issues. "Meta" refers to "meta-programming", or "programming-about-programming", with the investigators interested in facilitating code re-use in the difficult areas of operating, distributed, mobile object and multi-media systems. Since distributed systems programming can be considered "meta", especially when mechanisms of distribution are kept hidden from algorithms using the system, this area of research was included in the group. Discussions held during the workshop's technical sessions benefited the working group participants; the results of these gentle but forceful debates will ultimately emerge in the full papers made available through the World Wide Web by the authors. An overview of the individual presentations follows.

- **Arno Bakker**: *Developing Wide Area Applications using Distributed Shared Objects*. Wide area applications are developed via a distributed shared objects framework (GLOBE). Contribution of research is to develop model for building such systems through composition; scaleability, latencies, reliability, availability are all issues during system construction. A research goal is the discovery of frameworks comparing the different, extant models existing for distributed objects

- **László Blum**: *A Synchronization-Scheme Using Temporal Logic.* Temporal logic is used to specify properties of method calls, with possible inheritance anomalies in systems identified at their specification stage. TL expression are gathered together into *synchronization sets*, with sets used as guards before methods. Ultimate aim is to provide tools such that a system can be proven to have good synchronization (flow control) properties (or the absence of bad ones), while at the same time keeping functionality and synchronization issues separate.

- **Fernando Sánchez Figueroa**: *Composition Language for Different Aspects through Abstract State Information.* Basic behavior is separated from synchronization code, hence leading to polymorphic *and* dynamic synchronization choices. That is, synchronization code can be re-used, and policies changed, on-the-fly. The goal of research is to build a visual programming tool combined with a composition language.

- **María Ángeles Díaz Fondón**. Part of team at the University of Oviedo investigating an object-oriented operating system on top of an object-oriented abstract machine. Security model is a capability based, where all object references must contain the appropriate capability. Ph.D. research will look into the effect of this homogeneous protection mechanism on top of the homogeneous object model.

- **Darío Álvarez Gutiérrez**. Part of team at the University of Oviedo (see entry for M.D. Fondón). The research group is examining persistence, distribution, security and concurrency in an object-oriented system, with the ultimate research goal to eliminate differences between OS, user and machine objects. D. Álavrez's research contribution is in the implementation of orthogonal persistence for this system.

- **Juan Manuel Murillo Rodriquez**: *The Coordination Aspect in Object-Oriented Concurrent Programming.* Synchronization is considered as an *aspect*, hence reducing code complexity when one object affects another. Examples abound in multi-media systems where inter-stream coordination is necessary, but object interactions to maintain this coordination cannot be easily encapsulated into a single control object. Aim of research work is to ensure any uses of aspects to separate coordination from processing is kept transparent.

- **Stephan Reitzner**: *Splitting Synchronization from Algorithmic Behavior.* Main contribution of work is to show that annotations in base class code can be used to highlight synchronization events relevant ("of interest") to that same code. These events are mapped to synchronization objects. *Inheritance constellations* involving these synchronization objects have been examined for published inheritance anomalies, of which none appear. Further research remains in examining the effect of typing these annotated classes; a current project is to introduce these base class annotations and synchronization objects into a system such as *MetaJava*.

- **Lutz Wohlrab**: *A Means for Mastering the Adaptation of Object-Oriented Operating Systems.* Configuration and adaptation management problem in large systems is addressed by this work. Main contribution is in the combination of an expert system *within* the operating system to record what runtime environment objects need (e.g. versions numbers of server objects they depend upon). OS functionality in C++ is kept separate from the information expressed in Prolog.
- **Michael Zastre**: *Mobile Objects – the Next Generation.* Aim of work is to examine what is gained by adding mobile object to distributed programming systems. Only by keeping the mobile object interface open can a system designer make appropriate decisions about transport, security and method binding issues. The system could be used conceivably for prototyping applications having their functionality extended on-the-fly while running a remote sites. Major goal of research is to examine where the *meta-programming* boundary should lie.

3.1 Arno Bakker: Developing Wide-Area Applications Using Distributed Shared Objects

In the GLOBE project, our research concentrates on the development of a single unifying paradigm that can be used for developing wide area distributed applications. The paradigm must support many different kinds of applications in a flexible, yet efficient way.

The research to be done by A. Bakker concentrates on expanding our current object model to support application development through composition. We are seeking for suitable mechanisms that will allow us to build a large-scale wide area application as a collection of distributed shared objects, but which itself appears as just another distributed shared object. The following research issues are to be addressed:

A Model for Object Composition. There are different ways objects can be grouped together. Research should concentrate on developing a suitable model for object composition, and expand the current concept of a distributed object with mechanisms that support that model.

Dynamic adaptation. A large-scale wide area application should be dynamically adaptable by adding or removing components. In the case of object compositions, this means that it should be possible to add, remove, or change a constituent distributed object without affecting clients that are presently bound to the composed object. Research should concentrate on developing facilities that will allow an object composition to be changed while it is being used.

Object management. Object management in the present model is relatively simple: objects are named and registered with a naming and location service. This is not enough for composed objects, in which case the internal organization should be known as well. It is yet unclear what kind of mechanisms are needed so that management of large-scale object compositions scales to wide area networks. Research should concentrate on identifying and devising facilities that support object management.

Proposed mechanisms are to be validated through prototype implementations. It is also expected that the applicability of the extended object model is demonstrated by a prototype application.

3.2 Laszlo Blum: A Synchronization-Scheme Using Temporal Logic

Keywords: inheritance, inheritance anomaly, object models, synchronization-schemes, temporal logic, specification, verification.

In the beginning my PhD work, I was interested in the different kinds of object models of distributed systems. I find the reflective model of actors to be the best for describing these systems. Using synchronization policies for choosing methods often leads to inheritance anomalies, described in [Mat93b]. To avoid these anomalies, new synchronization schemes need to be introduced. In the literature, many of the given schemes are suitable for avoiding most of these anomalies[Mat93][McH91][Tom89]. I think that the question of how to completely avoid history sensitiveness anomalies still remains open. We propose a new synchronization-scheme in [Blu97] to largely reduce the above-mentioned anomalies especially the last one. Our model is based on the reflective model. The abstraction level of the model is very high because we use temporal logic formulas for synchronization. Separating implementation code and the synchronization code is straightforward in building robust distributed applications, as mentioned in [Bah95]. In our model, we can inherit both implementation and synchronization code, in addition we can completely redefine the synchronization. Firstly, we want to apply this model to specifying objects and verifying whether the object has correct synchronization. We saw in [Ara95] that temporal logic is suitable for describing the behaviours of objects, thus we wonder how to apply our model to describe larger systems. I am also interested in theorem provers, like HOL, by which one can reason about distributed systems [Bus95]. In the future, I would like to deal with the problem of the possibility to adapt our scheme to HOL to reason about the correctness of the synchronization of a system.

References

[Ara95] C. Arapis: A Temporal Perspective of Composite Objects. In O. Nierstrasz & D. Tsichritzis, editors: *Object-Oriented Software Composition*, pp. 123-152, Prentice Hall 1995.

[Blu97] L.Blum, L. Kozma: *Implementation Problems of a New Synchronization Scheme*, Fifth Symposium in Programming Languages and Software Tools, Jyvaskyla 1997.

[Kes93] Y. Kesten, Z. Manna, H. Mcguire, A. Pnueli: A Decision Algorithm for Full Propositional Temporal Logic. In *5th Conference on Computer Aided Verification*, pp. 97-109, LNCS 697, Springer-Verlag, 1993.

For more information, please visit http://www.vein.hu/~bluml/refer.htm.

3.3 Fernando Sánchez: Composition language for different aspects through abstract state information[5]

Adaptability has become one of the most important research areas in O-O systems in the last years. It tries to cope with an efficient system evolution and it can be defined as the ability to deal with new/changing requirements with minimum effort (number of modules that are created or modified when changes in the requirements are necessary).

The solution that O-O languages provide for building adaptable software is the use of traditional composition techniques such as inheritance, delegation and parts-of relations. These mechanisms work well when the aspects of the application are general and simple. This is the case of data structures and behavior. However, when the application domain becomes more and more complex, new aspects must be introduced in order to cope with the changing requirements. These include, for instance, aspects related to synchronization, coordinated behavior, real-time, distribution, etc. In this case, the current composition techniques do not provide enough support for adaptability.

The problem is that in the conventional object model, the different aspects involved in an application are not clearly/cleanly separated. Consequently the introduction of new requirements affecting a single aspect may involve the modification of other different aspects, thus expanding the number of components that must be changed or modified. And this situation is clearly against the definition of adaptability given before.

My contention is that the problem is not the composition techniques in themselves but the bad design of the components they have to compose. Several research works have indicated that the separation of concerns is the key concept to achieve the right design of components. This is one of the main reasons why the area of composability is gaining more interest. Composability can be defined as the ability to put together a piece of software from several components. By component I mean an entity able to encapsulate any valid software abstraction. So, whereas adaptability is the aim, composability is a way to get it.

The idea is to separate concerns into different components and later on to compose them through a composition language. In my proposal the solution for the separation of concerns relies on the use of abstract state information. For this purpose I have developed what I have called the Disguises Model where a suitable syntax is provided for specifying different aspects (synchronization, real-time, coordination, distribution, etc) into different components. Currently the DM has only been developed for the synchronization aspect. In order to compose these components my current work is focused on the development of a composition language to be able to obtain flexible and adaptable object-oriented applications in the sense that their components can be removed, replaced or reconfigured without affecting the diverse parts of the application. The use of abstract state information in the composition language will allow the development

[5] This research work is being developed with the support of the CICYT, Spain, under contract TIC96-0551

of polymorphic solutions and the achievement of dynamic change of concerns (changing policies at run-time).

3.4 María Ángeles Díaz Fondón: A Protection Mechanism for an Object-Oriented Operating System Based on an Abstract Machine

Oviedo3 is an environment based completely in the object-oriented paradigm. The goal of the system is to offer a single object space where objects possibly placed in different machines exist indefinitely, and co-operate using messages. The basis is an OO operating system that transparently provides objects with a set of important features such as orthogonal persistence, distribution, concurrency and security. The technique chosen to structure the OS is to use an OO abstract machine that brings a number of benefits for the construction of the OS. The machine offers the basic homogeneous object model and support to all objects of the rest of the system. In addition, the machine is given a reflective architecture so that there is no difference between user objects, objects providing OS functionality and machine objects.

One of the problems faced in an object environment like this is protection. A mechanism that ensures that only authorised objects are able to invoke a given method on an object should exist. We pursue a homogeneous protection mechanism with the same access control for every object in the object space. Every invocation to any method of an object should be controlled.

Capability-based protection is used in some operating systems such as Amoeba, Grasshopper, Clouds and Mungi. Capabilities are like access cards that should be shown when invoking a method on an object. The capability holds the identification of an object and information about which methods are allowed to be invoked on it.

This protection mechanism fits very well into the object model. The use of an abstract machine helps the design of a single and uniform protection mechanism. The two fundamental ideas proposed for object protection are i) Capabilities as object references. Machine object references are converted to capabilities, without modification of the object model. ii) Protection mechanism in the innermost level of the system. The security should be introduced in a uniform way in the heart of the system, making the message passing mechanism check the protection information contained in the capability. An exception raises if no valid rights are held. Design modifications in the machine should be considered to accomplish this.

A combination of the advantages of both segregated and sparse capabilities is expected. On one hand, the machine guarantees capabilities can not be tampered with or altered without permission. On the other, capabilities are stored as normal references in every object (including "user" objects).

The capability-based protection mechanism together with the rest of the system contributes to a very flexible computing environment, easily adaptable and extensible, but in a secure way controlled by the machine protection mechanism.

For references: URL http://www15.uniovi.es/~fondon/.

3.5 Darío Álvarez Gutiérrez: Complete Persistence for an Object-Oriented Operating System Using a Reflective Abstract Machine

An approach to solve problems derived from an uneven adoption of the object-oriented paradigm in computing systems is to move the OO support to a common place into the operating system. Oviedo3 is a research project that tries to build an experimental integral object-oriented system in which all components including the operating system itself, share the same object-oriented paradigm.

One technique to structure this OO operating system which may offer many advantages is to use an OO abstract machine as the substrate of the OOOS. The machine provides portability and a standard object model for the system. Functions of the OS are provided by normal objects, which extend the functionality of the abstract machine. Key features are complete persistence, distribution, security and concurrency.

The goal is a single object environment with no distinctions between user, OS and machine environments. The computing environment is simply a set of homogeneous objects following an OO model, which live until no longer needed (persistence feature of the OS) and interact in a secure way regardless of physical location (distribution feature of the OS). Object-orientation is used consistently throughout the whole system. OS and machine objects can be reused, extended and adapted just like any user object. To yield such uniform system a reflective architecture is proposed for the machine.

Some important aspects that should be researched when designing this abstract machine are i) How to support the OS and integrate the hardware consistently into the object model of the system, and transparently with OS objects. ii) Which particular object model to support. It should accommodate more than one programming language, be not very complex and retain significant semantic information. Initially a standard model with global object identity, inheritance, etc. but also with aggregation and generic relationships is used. iii) Architecture of the machine itself. The external architecture exposed for reflection should be carefully designed, as it will be used for user and OS objects. Ideally the implementation design should be the one exposed, but a simpler design perhaps will be easier to use. Currently a machine with two areas, one for instances and the other for class information is being explored. iv) How to better solve implementation questions such as the representation of the object model, implementation of reflection, efficiency, etc.

The persistence support mechanism of the operating system will be implanted to evaluate these expected advantages. A set of OS objects will transparently extend the functionality of the abstract machine providing complete persistence to the rest of the objects. One working design is based on a "persistence object" which is activated by an exception raised by machine objects when objects must be written to stable storage and vice versa.

For references: URL http://www15.uniovi.es/~darioa/

3.6 Juan M. Murillo: Coordination in object-oriented concurrent programming languages[6]

In the last few years, the separation of concerns has been recognized as the most adequate and elegant software engineering approach for designing complex object-oriented software systems. In this kind of system, programmers express and reason about the different concerns involved in the application they want to design. This mechanism increases flexibility, adaptability, reusability and favors the composability of object-oriented programs. Moreover, separation of concerns has been successfully applied for separating the basic object behavior of an object from special concerns such as synchronization and real-time, and it has been used to deal with inheritance anomalies in concurrent object-oriented languages.

More recently, it has been recognized that the coordination aspect presents the same problems as the forementioned aspects from the reusability and extensibility points of view. However, it offers more difficulties than may appear at first glance because multi-object coordination involves the synchronized interaction among several active objects in order to obtain a single goal. The reasons for this are twofold: first, high-level mechanisms are not provided by the conventional object model for the abstraction of the coordinated behavior among various objects because objects only interact through message passing. The semantic of this process only involves two partner objects. Second, the coordination aspect is not localized in a single object but is spread among sets of interacting objects making more difficult not only to extend and reuse the coordination algorithms but also to reason about them by itself.

Having this background in mind and taking into consideration these difficulties the main goal of our works is to propose a language mechanism to deal with the separation of the coordination aspect, and subsuming proposals which fails in reusability and expressive power. This mechanism is based on abstract state information and the novel concept of state notification. State notification allows an object to monitor and synchronize with abstract state changes of other objects. It is important to note that state notification does not require the explicit collaboration of the requested objects.

In our research group, we are also working in separation of the synchronization concerns in the realm of COOP. Then, the following question is now underlying: What are the consequences when different concerns are composed in the same object? Are there any rule that allows speak about this interaction? In this sense, would it be possible to formulate an arithmetic of the composition of concerns? This is the next step in our work.

3.7 Stephan Reitzner: An Event Model for Synchronizing Concurrent Objects

In concurrent object-oriented environments objects can be accessed concurrently by multiple threads of control. A concurrent programming language has to pro-

[6] This research work is being developed with the support of the CICYT, Spain, under contract TIC96-0551

vide means for preventing inconsistent object states in case of concurrent invocations. This protection is called concurrency control, the implementation of which is called synchronization code. It is commonly accepted that the synchronization code should be separated from the algorithmic code of an object. The critical point is connecting the two separated parts. Some approaches made a static connection, which creates so called inheritance anomalies.

My basic idea is to model concurrency control of an object by a second object, which is called the *synchronization object*. The protected object—further called the *algorithmic object*—is processed concurrently. Each time a critical point of the algorithmic code is reached, a method of the synchronization object is invoked. This method invocation is suspended in the synchronization object as long as the necessary synchronization constraints are not fulfilled. A possible implementation would be to insert code for the method invocation in the algorithmic code. This was considered bad because it would reduce the flexibility of the whole mechanism. My solution is to insert another layer which separates the synchronization point in the algorithmic object from the invocation of the corresponding synchronization method. This layer is made up by an event mechanism. I have identified certain events of an algorithmic object at which a synchronization call may be useful. Examples of such events are entering or leaving a method. The connection between the events being raised and the invocations which have to be performed is established by the *event mapping*. The mapping fulfills two tasks: First, it defines the type of the synchronization object, and second, it specifies which methods of the synchronization object are responsible for catching particular events.

When inheriting from a synchronized class, it is obvious that the synchronization behaviour of the new subclass may change. This is expressed by a two-way inheritance. On one hand, the algorithmic behaviour can be refined by deriving a subclass from the algorithmic class. On the other hand, the modified synchronization behaviour of the subclass is accomplished by deriving a new synchronization subclass. Again, the new relationship between these two derived classes is expressed by defining a new event mapping. To simplify the formulation of a new mapping it is possible to inherit the event mapping of the base class and modify it to meet the new synchronization requirements. It is possible to define event methods for the new events of the subclass, but it is also possible to modify the mapping of base-class events to refer to other event methods. The new methods in the synchronization subclass meet the changed synchronization requirements of the algorithmic subclass. This mechanism dramatically reduces the number of inheritance anomalies that can occur when inheriting from a synchronized class.

3.8   Lutz Wohlrab: A Means for Mastering the Adaptation of Object-Oriented Operating Systems

The trend in object-oriented operating systems goes towards more and more fine-grained structures. This imposes great problems for systems not statically tailored and dynamically adaptable. The number of set screws to be adjusted and entities to be managed explodes. To get such a system set up, optimised, and

414

to keep it running would require a lot more administrator's expertise than even todays all-purpose operating systems. To make fine-grained, highly adaptable object-oriented operating systems feasible in practice, we need new means for mastering adaptation.

Today configuration data is usually shattered over several configuration files, directories, or databases. Configuration and setup utilities write into these without checking for discrepancies. Errors are detected no sooner than the erroneous configuration data is actually used and something does not or ceases to work. This is because there is no instance which is an organic part of the operating system and responsible for the integrity of its configuration.

The adaptation manager is introduced as an active instance, shielding the configuration of the operating system as a whole, checking new configuration knowledge before accepting it, putting together the best available runtime environment for the applications. From the applications' point of view the adaptation manager is a special meta object. For programs which want to alter or adapt the system's configuration, it replaces the files they directly wrote into. Being an active instance, it is able to reject the alteration if errors can be detected in it.

The adaptation manager needs to be able to perform meta-computation over configuration data, to check whether consistency rules are violated or other actions have to be done before the new data can be accepted. These tasks resemble that of an expert system for system administration. Since many expert systems have been built successfully using Prolog, the adaptation manager was designed as an object encapsulating a Prolog inference machine. Both configuration data, consistency and other rules are taken down in the shape of Prolog clauses.

The technology of the adaptation manager is being investigated under the object-oriented operating system CHEOPS[7] and Linux. Aspect-orientation and a "configuration aspect" is considered as a means for programmers to describe the runtime environment needed for the applications without mixing up configuration code with the functionality of the programs.

3.9 Michael Zastre: Mobile Object Systems: The Next Generation

Mobile objects fit into the matrix of internetworks, large data sources, and powerful network clients. The union of mobile code, state plus data has many applications, such as distributing control in workflow or groupware systems. The next generation of these systems of travelling objects must address two groups of issues. *Mobile Objects in-the-small* is the name I give to concerns over mobile object construction and arrangement. *Mobile Objects in-the-large* is my term for the issues involving large systems of mobile objects (dozens to hundreds) interacting together. Mobile Object technology promises to become ubiquitous. Before this happens, however, I believe that at least two aspects require much further research:

---
[7] CHemnitz OPerating System

- *Mobile objects-in-the small*: programming environment support for developing mobile object systems, such as for the construction, transmission, reception, and resource management of these objects, *where the system developer determines the implementation decisions underlying the mobile object system itself.* This constitutes an *Open Mobile Object System (OMOS)*.
- *Mobile objects in-the-large*: tools for specifying and exploring the interactions of large (dozens) and very large (hundreds) of systems of mobile objects whether these objects enter a network from outside an enterprise, or originate from within the same intranet.

These should be the characteristics mobile object's next generation of languages and systems. It includes concerns over how these systems can be validated from the specification and synthesis of the mobile and interacting portions of an object graph given a database of application domain knowledge. I explore these two aspects of next generation systems in more detail, using a workflow example for motivation. Standard meta-programming facilities are re-cast into the mobile agent support environment (e.g. for memory management, run-time stack examination, heap manipulation), and I propose additional facilities. Specification of mobile object interactions and expressibility of their properties, and currently technology's bearing on these, is discussed, and future work suggested. A schematic for a system synthesis tool is also presented. All discussions are ultimately aimed at the research and development of an integrated set of mobile object system construction tools.

More information is available at `http://gulf.uvic.ca/~zastre/mobs`.

4 Debugging and Testing, and More

Luigi Benedicenti, Christian Bunse,
Eyðun Eli Jacobsen, Yvan Labiche

Since this group covered quite different areas it is a little difficult to pinpoint an overall subject. However, the members of the group work with topics associated with the investigation and management of existing software systems, focusing on debugging, testing, reading source code, or on the relationship between a programmer's view of a piece of software and the conceptual model which is actually supported by the programmer's tools. Another common point of interest is that the techniques in focus are applied to ensure or enhance the quality of the software being produced or maintained.

Luigi's research focuses on the impact of reuse on object-oriented programming. Reuse is a significant attribute in the calculation of productivity in programming projects, and the selection of such a single, important aspect as reuse makes it possible to compare the productivity characteristics of different programming paradigms. To do this, code measures must be defined to find a relation between productivity and reuse, a complex task. However, a set of metrics have been identified that manage to define reuse and productivity in terms of elementary (measurable) attributes of the source code. This makes it possible to apply statistical analysis techniques and find candidate relations.

Eyðun Eli Jacobsen presents a view on software systems which emphasizes that a software system shapes the user's conceptual model. Regarding a software developer as a user, there is a gap between the conceptual model of a software development system and the software developer's conceptual model of a software system. To minimize this gap, an extension of software development systems to support architectural abstractions is needed, and a two level model is proposed, consisting of a program level and an extract level.

A central topic in Christian Bunse's research is reading techniques for object-oriented source code. Inspection of source code is a form of verification widely believed to be effective for finding defects. Even though object-orientation provides many benefits for software development, there is little available material on applying reading techniques in this context. Special considerations are needed, however, since inheritance, genericity, dynamic dispatch and polymorphism cause new problems in source code inspection. Moreover, programming style guidelines are less well-defined and thus harder to enforce using inspection. The aims of this research is to define a reading technique for object-oriented source code and to provide tool support for the application of this technique.

Yvan Labiche works with testing in the context of object-oriented software systems. For critical systems, which need a certification, the testing process is an important task. But procedural testing techniques are not well-suited for object-oriented software. There is an inherent difference between the procedural and the object-oriented approach to structure and behaviour. New, useful features such as encapsulation, inheritance, and polymorphism imply new problems for the testing process. Hence, the primary questions with which this research is concerned are: What are the new problems raised? How can the usual solutions for the testing process be applied, or extended, or exchanged with new approaches? Finally, how can the new object-oriented mechanisms be used to help us in the testing process?

4.1 Luigi Benedicenti: An experimental protocol to measure the impact of reuse on Object Oriented versus traditional programming

This dissertation discusses, evaluates and assesses the impact of reuse on Object Oriented programming, comparing it to the results obtained by traditional programming. The Object Oriented paradigm should grant its users a more effective way to address the problem of programming in the large, groupware, and multi-team frameworks.

More specifically, the current belief is that Object Oriented programs achieve a higher level of reuse than conventional ones, thus improving the development time and therefore the time to market.

However, there is no specific evidence of such fact, mainly because case studies are not aimed towards this goal, but rather to measure the efficiency of each programming paradigm. I feel that it is very difficult to aggregate every contributing factor to a single, meaningful parameter. Therefore, my research is directed towards the evaluation and assessment of a single factor, in the hope to find a vector of characteristics that can be used effectively to compare the different paradigms of computing.

In particular, my research focuses on reuse as a significant attribute in the calculation of productivity.

This task is not an easy one, and requires some careful planning. First of all, it is necessary to find a measurement protocol that can be effectively applied to both Object Oriented programs and conventional ones; this involves an initial hypothesis. Then, the protocol has to be applied to real world examples. Finally, the measures collected will be compared, and the results yielded will confirm or confute the initial hypothesis.

Since code is the result of every programming effort, it will be the only item used in measures. The measures computed on code are of two kinds: measures of program size (LOC), and measures of reuse. The reuse level is computed by means of a method by Frakes and Terry that defines how to calculate internal reuse level and frequency, and external ones.

These measures are then coupled with effort measurements, that are the chief interesting attribute for productivity, and defect density, which instead is correlated with quality as perceived by the programmers.

The experiment consists of the calculation of a set of measures for both object oriented and conventional code, and then the search for a model (possibly a simple linear correlation) that puts productivity, quality, and reuse into relation.

The resulting model, if there will be one, will enable programmers to choose between different paradigms on the basis of the kind of program they have to produce: the model will be implemented in a Decision Support System.

The achievement of the measures is possible only when a statistically significant amount of code will pass through the analyser. This will be possible with the completion of special measurement tools that are able to measure chunks of code and that use Internet to facilitate the measuring process. In fact, in this way the measurement takes place remotely, directly on the computer that contains the source code, and only the results are sent to the server. This avoids security problems.

4.2 Christian Bunse: An Effective Inspection Technique for Object-Oriented Code

Reading (Inspection) of software artifacts and especially of source code is one form of verification which is widely believed to be an effective means for finding defects. At the same time, the object-oriented paradigm is cited as providing many benefits for developing software. However, there is little available material on applying reading to object-oriented software.

There are properties of object-oriented languages that can hinder the inspection of code written in that languages. (1) The search for the definition of class features can be impeded by inheritance. (2) Genericity can be problematic: When inspecting a single class, a 'huge' number of classes may have to be inspected in parallel, because of the dependencies on the behavior of the instantiating classes. (3) A major problem when inspecting object-oriented code are the differences between static code structure and dynamic, runtime system structure. (4) Furthermore at runtime, dynamic binding and polymorphism combine to hinder the static prediction of which methods will be invoked. (5) Recent experiences show that object-oriented systems tend to consist of a large number of small methods, which distribute functionally related code over a wider area than procedural systems. This also increases the number of relationships that exist within the system which have to be understood. (6) Besides defect identification inspections are normally used to enforce quality-guidelines (e.g. developing standards). For object-oriented code these guidelines are less well defined than those of procedural code, and may be difficult to enforce during inspection. All these difficulties contribute to the fact that 00-code is difficult to inspect.

The aim of this research is to define a reading technique for object-oriented code which overcomes or at least tackles the problems stated above. Therefore work is/was done in the following areas[8]:

1. A detailed analysis of existing reading techniques was performed, examining the strengths, weaknesses, and prerequisites of the techniques with respect towards the application on object-oriented code.
2. Currently a systematic reading technique is defined. The main idea behind it is to visualize code properties at different levels of abstraction. For each level reading effort is directed towards specific properties.
3. By having defined the reading technique itself a tool has to be developed to support it. The tool will concentrate on a specific programming language, in order to be able to perform the final step of this research.
4. The final step of this research will be the conduction of a controlled experiment to validate the newly defined reading technique, and to show that the technique is 'superior' over existing reading technique as 'ad-hoc' or 'checklists' in terms of efficiency and effectiveness.

4.3 Eyðun Eli Jacobsen: Bringing Architecture to Software Development

Traditionally software has been designed with focus on algorithms and on components making up the system. Today software is to an greater extent being designed with focus on the user's experience with the software. Attention is paid to the nature of human-computer interaction and the metaphorical spaces that users inhabit when using a piece of software—the design of software is the design of the user's conceptual model.

A software developer is a user who uses software to develop new software. In order to make a development system comfortable and productive to use we

---

[8] Further information can be found at: http://www.iese.fhg.de/AboutUs/Staff/ bunse.html and http://www.iese.fhg.de/Competences/ISE/CR

must pay attention to the user's conceptual model when designing the software development system.

A software development system can be oriented towards several sets of concepts; examples include classes and objects, functions, and logical assertions. In the study we will mainly consider object-oriented software development.

Software development with classes and objects is now so well-understood that software developers are extending their design language. A software developer's design language is the set of abstractions over structures in a software system. The elements finding way to software developers' design language are new concepts that express archetypical patterns of class and object relations and collaborations. These patterns are not dependent on a specific software system, but occur across many software systems. This evolution is reflected in recent books on object-oriented programming.

The patterns of class and object collaborations can be regarded as examples of architectural abstractions. The notion of an architectural abstraction is a more general concept regarding abstraction over structures in software systems, and as such it is a more convenient concept when discussing extensions of a design language as it covers other kinds of abstractions than just class and object relations and collaborations.

With the arrival of new architectural abstractions comes also an increased distance between a software developer's design language and the conceptual model represented by his software development system. The more abstract or complex the new concepts are, the longer the distance between languages becomes. The distance between the languages is problematical since developing software involves both languages and translations between these, and the longer the distance between languages, the harder it is to develop software using the specific software development system.

The subject for this Ph.D.-study is therefore the understanding of architectural abstractions and of software development systems based on objects and classes. The goal of the project is to describe a model for architectural abstractions and, if successful, to describe a software development system in which architectural abstractions are part of conceptual model represented be the software development system.

For more information please see `http://www.cs.auc.dk/~jacobsen`.

4.4 Yvan Labiche: On Testing Object-Oriented Programs

The object-oriented paradigm is a new technology for producing software. This new technology has many benefits for parts of the entire software development cycle (analysis, design and implementation phases): the object-oriented development process is iterative, the object-oriented paradigm emphasize reuse, the items of interest are always the objects... Thus, engineers and managers want to use this technology in their own field. But, for critical systems, which need a certification, the testing process is an important task.

Then, the testing techniques for object-oriented programs should be studied even though some people can think the object-oriented paradigm seams to be the panacea. By applying usual testing techniques (i.e. those for procedural programs) for object-oriented programs one found two major problems. First, procedural testing techniques are not well-suited for object-oriented ones: there is an intrinsic difference between the procedural and the object-oriented approach (structure vs. behavior). Second, the new useful features introduced (such as encapsulation, inheritance, or polymorphism) imply new problems for the testing process: problems of observability, for example.

Then we are interested in studying these new mechanisms with the tester viewpoint in mind through three major questions. What are the new problems raised? How usual solutions for the testing process can be applied (or extended) or do we have to find new ones? and, How object-orientedness (the new mechanisms) can help us for the testing process?

For more information please see http://www.laas.fr/~ylabiche/english.

5 Programming Languages

Walid Al-Ahmad, Carlos Canal, Amnon Eden,
Erik Ernst, Tracy Gardner, Frank Gerhardt,
Markus Knasmüller, Albertina Lourenci, and
Mads Torgersen

This group has nine members who share an interest in object oriented programming languages. Within this broad topic a wide range of issues are addressed, from support for the use of existing languages to the development of new languages. The participants are at various stages in the PhD getting process, some have almost finished and others are just getting started. The different viewpoints within the group are illustrated below using a number of topics that emerged during the workshop.

Concerning the decision as to whether or not to create new languages, the entire spectrum is represented: Mads wants to create an entirely new language, and Markus and Erik are enhancing the semantics of existing languages without changing their syntax significantly. Carlos, Walid and Tracy work with the concept of inheritance, but the design or redesign of a programming language will not be the main contribution of their PhD projects. Frank is concerned with large scale porting of software and other aspects of legacy software management, he does not even want *others* to invent new languages. Albertina takes an interdisciplinary approach—being an architect—and brings such things as catastrophe theory, graph theory, and semiotics into an evaluation of existing programming languages; using those theories in computational modelling forces designers to perceive jumps in the design reasoning and to sort out design and nondesign activities.

Almost everybody is working with *inheritance*; this concept has so many interpretations and ramifications and such a great a potential for development that everybody seems to have a different approach to it. This also indicates that inheritance, despite being well established and having undergone intense debate, is still immature and in need of further research. In prototype based languages *delegation* plays a similar role, and the future might bring even more related concepts. Tracy is building an overview of all the variants and aspects of inheritance, and hopes to divide it into several simpler, well–defined, practically manageable concepts—analogous to the process which once developed the powerful but unwieldy GOTO statement into several more structured flow–of–control constructs. Walid is also working with inheritance at large, developing support for restriction inheritance as well as extension inheritance. Carlos is working with the behavior conformance aspect of inheritance, using an Architectural Description Language beeing developed from the π-calculus to specify large software systems at the level of interfaces. Frank researches into the same interplay between inheritance and behavior correctness in his work with porting large software systems from Smalltalk to Java in an industrial setting. Erik has developed an inheritance mechanism based on constraint solving; one explicit inheritance operation may entail many implicit inheritance operations, so this enhances the expressivity of the inheritance construct. Albertina prefers prototype based object oriented languages due to their malleability and flexibility; inheritance is not even present here, but delegation and 'traits' objects are used for similar purposes. Finally, Mads defines inheritance by means of certain predicates, such that two classes may be related by inheritance whether or not the more specialized class was specified by (direct or indirect) derivation from the more general one. His object model is inherently distributed.

The eventual client of any research into programming languages must be software developers (and this usually means industry) but the time–frame for knowledge to filter down to the bleeding–edge varies considerably depending on the nature of the research. Frank is associated with a large industrial company, and his work is constantly intertwined with software engineering efforts which are carried out on a commercial basis. The other members of the group are not directly associated with industrial companies, but some must still consider software developers as their target audience. Markus and Erik are each working with one particular language and have implemented enhancements, such enhancements must be a well-chosen improvement from a programmer point of view. Albertina uses the language Self to represent and implement the domain dependent model level of an ecodesign model for the development of sustainable cities, and this of course has a practical aspect. Tracy is concerned with understanding the conceptual relationships that software developers wish to model using inheritance mechanisms; her work has implications for software developers and programming language designers. Walid's work concerns the design of language mechanisms that could be added to existing languages. The usage of process algebras seems to place Carlos in a theoretical camp which is far removed from industry, but for specification and verification purposes, such process algebras may indeed be applied in an industrial setting, especially if there is good tool support. Mads is so far away from a completed language design that his work will not be of interest to industry for some time.

Of course there are also aspects which are special for each member of the group. Markus works with transparent persistence of objects in Oberon, and with automatic support for the evolution of types of persistent objects. Frank is working at Mercedes-Benz, looking at the real world every day. Albertina is an architect, and now and then the rest of the group does not understand what she is saying. Mads is taking a very radical approach, trying to construct a new language with genuinely new ideas from scratch. Walid works with the details of language mechanisms but still wishes to apply the results to many languages. Erik works with the language BETA, and the special richness of this environment makes it harder to apply the results to many languages. Carlos is trying to combine process algebras and object orientation for the specification of architectural aspects of software. Finally, Tracy differentiates and develops the inheritance concept quite independently of individual languages, and then hopes to be able to use the results in existing languages.

The following subsections are the individual abstracts of the members of the group. They are very short descriptions of the research work of each person, but they should be sufficient to provide an overview and give a few pointers to more detailed information.

5.1 Walid Al-Ahmad: Concepts of Object-Oriented Programming: Shortcomings and Perspectives

One of the key mechanisms of the object-oriented paradigm is the concept of inheritance. The current object-oriented languages have not provided adequate support for some important issues related to inheritance. This is mainly due to the fact that the goals of inheritance are not yet completely reached. In other words, there is still no universal consensus on the definition and mechanisms that must support inheritance.

The purpose of this research is to shed light on the shortcomings, mainly concerning inheritance, facing the current object-oriented languages. It intends to identify the problems, highlight their importance and relevance to the software community, and finally set a sound and concise plan to alleviate them.

We believe that a distinction must be made between two separate language mechanisms for inheritance: one to support extension inheritance and the other to support specialization inheritance. As such, this research will probe into the ramifications of this approach and pinpoint the necessary requirements to fully support each of the two kinds of inheritance. We will illustrate as well how the solutions worked out during this research could be incorporated in major object-oriented languages, in a way that is in line with the language philosophy and design goals.

5.2 Carlos Canal: An Object-Oriented Architecture Description Language

Software Architecture (SA) refers to the level of design in which the system is represented as a collection of interconnected computational and data components.

Although object-orientation can be applied to different levels of abstraction, in SA the more general term *component* is preferred, allowing to consider not only objects but also architectures and interaction patterns as first-class concepts of a software architecture. Most object-oriented concepts can be directly applied to the so called component-oriented paradigm.

However, object-oriented specifications often fail to describe the requirements of behaviour that a component imposes to those connected to it. Traditionally, the interface of an object has been described by the signature of its methods, with no explicit description of the interaction patterns, that is the sequence in method invocations, that must be followed to achieve a correct behaviour of the system.

On the other hand, process algebras are widely accepted for the specification of software systems, in particular for communication protocols and distributed systems. Their formal basis permit analysis of equivalence, deadlock freedom and other interesting properties. In this field, we consider that the π-calculus, a simple but powerful process algebra, is very well suited for describing complex interactions among components. However, the π-calculus is a low-level notation, which makes difficult its direct application to the specification of large systems. Hence, a higher level notation is required.

My PhD. work focuses on the development of formal notations and methods for SA. Its final goal is the definition of an Architecture Description Language (ADL) which incorporates concepts from the object-oriented paradigm, using the π-calculus as its formal basis.

Using this ADL, the interface of a component will represented by a set of *roles*, written in π-calculus. Each role describe the interaction pattern that the component follows with respect to another one. Since we usually want to connect components whose roles match only partially we have defined a relation of compatibility among roles which ensures that the connection is deadlock-free. Reusability and incremental development are addressed by the definition of a relation of inheritance, such that compatibility is closed under inheritance. Role inheritance allows to replace any component in a system by another one whose roles derive from those of the former. This replacement can be done without rechecking the compatibility of the system.

5.3 Amnon H. Eden: Tool Support for Design Patterns Application – Precise Specification of Design Patterns

Our research focuses on the precise specification of design patterns. At the first stage of research we investigated tool support for the specification and application (implementation in code) of patterns; our approach employed an algorithmic description of patterns, and was implemented by metaprogramming techniques. For details about this part of our research please see:

References

[EdGiYe97] Amnon H. Eden, Joseph (Yossi) Gil and Amiram Yehudai: *Precise Specification and Automatic Application of Design Patterns.* Accepted at Automatic Software Engineering – ASE'97.

The article is available in postscript at http://www.math.tau.ac.il/~eden/ precise_specification_and_automatic_application_of_design_patterns. ps.Z, and in rich text format at http://www.math.tau.ac.il/~eden/precise_ specification_and_automatic_application_of_design_patterns.rtf.zip.

We now seek a declarative language that should allow simple recognition of design patterns, i.e., tracking "patterns" in existing programs. The difference from past similar attempts is that our specification is expected to be also constructive, that is, we require a decidable and efficient algorithm to exist such that a pattern specification can be used to derive the steps necessary to be taken to modify (parts of) an existing program to follow this pattern (i.e., implement it). We currently investigate the usefulness of AI techniques, such as planning, in the solution of such problems and in the specification of a formal pattern language.

5.4   Erik Ernst: Constraint Based Inheritance

Traditionally, in object-oriented languages which support a strict, static type-analysis, inheritance lets you specify a new class incrementally by one or more super-classes and an enhancement, like e.g. (in pseudo-C++):

```
class D : public B {..};
```

D is declared to be a class which is derived from B as specified in the block {..}. Both B and D denote compile-time constant classes, and only *one* new class is created, namely D. My research work generalizes this, starting from the language BETA which I consider very well-designed. The generalization supports inheriting from classes only partially known until run-time. It also supports creating several new classes for each visible occurrence of inheritance. This is because the inheritance mechanism is constraint based: Pull a string somewhere, and the rest of the system adjusts until all constraints are satisfied. Even though this sounds very dynamic, the generalized language has strict static type checking, just like BETA.

BETA unifies many concepts including class, procedure, function, and process into the very general *pattern* concept. The language has general block structure (true closures) and virtual patterns (specializable pattern attributes). It provides all the common object-oriented facilities such as (single) inheritance, virtual methods, genericity, exceptions, and more. It also supports coroutines, threads, behavioural inheritance, method closures (hence futures), and types as first class values. In BETA there are *non-fixed* types. A declaration has a *fixed* type iff the type analysis yields the same result, no matter from where it is referred. The statically known type of a virtual pattern in BETA depends on the position in the source code where it is referred, so it is non-fixed. Another example of a non-fixed type is "like Current" in Eiffel.

I have generalized BETA such that non-fixed and dynamic patterns can be inherited from. Moreover, the semantics of virtual patterns has been generalized: A further-binding of a virtual pattern is a lower-bound *constraint* on the structure of that virtual pattern. As a result, one inheritance operation may imply many, because new constraints propagate to dependent patterns. It is possible to design type constraint graphs such that some patterns can be extensively—"deeply"— modified by a simple top-level operation. This potential for far-reaching impacts is known precisely at compile-time, hence safe. As a by-product of constraint based inheritance comes a multiple inheritance mechanism.

How would one use this? The constraint based inheritance enhances the support for *combination* and hence allows a deeper *separation* of concerns—just like inheritance did, compared to no inheritance. It is e.g. possible to create a set of "roles" which can be "played" by existing patterns, supporting some design patterns directly.

The generalized BETA language has been implemented by means of an interpreter; for more information (and possibly download) see http://www.daimi. aau.dk/~eernst/gbeta/.

5.5 Tracy Gardner: Developing effective inheritance paradigms for software construction

The benefits of inheritance are many and well known, but unfortunately, simply using inheritance does not lead to well designed, easily maintainable systems with high levels of reuse. A major factor in the difficulty of using inheritance, even in the presence of the many guidelines and heuristics on the subject, is that there is no single correct way to use inheritance. Inheritance mechanisms are powerful constructs that have been put to many (valid) uses by innovative software developers.

Although inheritance can be put to various uses, good applications of inheritance have one thing in common: they are based on an underlying conceptual relationship. Unfortunately, even if the designer of a system has a clear understanding of the relationship he is modelling with inheritance, that reasoning does not become part of the resulting system. This lack of information makes systems using inheritance difficult to understand which hinders maintenance, testing and reuse (the very tasks that inheritance is supposed to facilitate). Different forms of inheritance have different implications for each of these areas of software development.

The aim of this research is to identify the conceptual relationships that are implemented (with varying degrees of success) using inheritance mechanisms, and then to provide 'development patterns' detailing how these relationships should be used throughout the software development process. As far as possible this work is based on improving the use of inheritance in existing languages, but where existing languages prove insufficiently expressive improvements will be suggested.

A number of conceptual relationships have been identified and their respective roles during software development have been investigated. In each case the reason why inheritance has been chosen to implement the relationship has been determined and the appropriateness of available inheritance mechanisms has been assessed. The role of each relationship throughout the software lifecycle has also been considered. Current work concerns providing formal definitions that capture the intuition behind the informal definitions developed so far.

This research began in October 1995 and is being carried out under the supervision of Claire Willis (`C.P.Willis@maths.bath.ac.uk`); funding is via an EPSRC studentship.

Information concerning the progress of this work can be found at `http://www.bath.ac.uk/~maptag/Work/work.html`.

5.6 Frank Gerhardt: Retargeting Object-Oriented Legacy Systems

My PhD research addresses the co-evolution of object-oriented applications and their underlying implementation technology (programming language and class library/framework).

Object techonology (OT) has introduced a vast number of programming languages during the last decade. This period is sometimes called the "language war". Many of these languages have been implemented commercially. Because of the lack of standards vendors usually implemented proprietary dialects. Commercial implementaitons often included a vendor-specific class library.

Many companies adopted OT to build system which were not feasable otherwise. The most promising languages were chosen to implement these systems, especially C++ and Smalltalk. Today companies find that their software infrastructures consists of diverse implementation technologies. Some of them even "died", e. g. two major dialects of Smalltalk. From a strategic point of view these technologies should be replaced by current technologies and the diversity should be reduced towards more standardization of platforms.

An engineer who attempts the migration from one platform to another, e. g. Smalltalk to Java, will encounter three kinds of problems: 1. Differences similar to those between 3GLs (different basic types, control and data structures; presence of static typing, automatic memory management etc.). 2. Differences related to object-oriented concepts (polymorphism, inheritance, reflection). 3. Differences in the architecure of the class libraries/frameworks (architectural mismatch). The last category of problems is by far the most challenging one.

So far I examined new research areas for their applicability to these problems. Particularly I'm interested in aspect-oriented programming, adaptive programming, generative programming, intensional programming, reflection, architectural understanding, architecture description languages, design patterns, re-engineering and modeling (UML).

My goal is to devolop a method for retargeting object-oriented applications. This method will be based on a conceptual framework for explaining the differences between development platforms (problem areas). Within this framework I want to describe the tasks necessary to adapt an application to a new platform (transformations). The essential quesitons are: "In general, what are the differences between two platforms and how can they be overcome?" and "What has to be done to retarget a given application?"

5.7 Markus Knasmüller: Oberon-D

While object-orientation has become a standard technique in modern software engineering, most systems lack persistency of objects. This is rather surprising because many objects (e.g. objects in a graphical editor) have a persistent character. Nevertheless, most systems require the programmer to implement load and store operations for the objects. In this work we demonstrate the seamless integration of database functionality into an object-oriented development environment, in which the surving of objects is for free.

The idea is to offer the impression of an indefinitely large dynamic store on which all objects live. It is not necessary to distinguish between "internal" and "external" objects. All objects can be referenced and sent messages as if they were in main memory. The underlying language does not have to be extended.

Persistence is obtained by a persistent heap on the disk. Persistent objects are on this heap, while transient objects are in the transient memory. Transient and persistent objects can access each other mutually. Accessing a persistent object leads to loading the object into the transient heap. If it is not accessed from transient objects any more, it will be written back to the persistent heap. An object is persistent if it can be reached from a persistent root. Every object may become a persistent root if it is registered with a special function. If not defined otherwise, all objects referenced by a persistent root directly or indirectly are automatically persistent as well. Persistent objects which are not referenced by other persistent objects are reclaimed by a Stop & Copy garbage collector. This algorithm uses two heaps (files) and copies all accessible objects from the full *fromHeap* to the empty *toHeap*.

Other database features are embedded in this persistent environment. Schema evolution, for example, is done during the persistent garbage collection run. In this phase it is checked, if the type definition of any object was been modified. If this is the case the object is read from the *fromHeap* by using the old type definition and is written to the *toHeap* by using the new type definition.

Furthermore, an Oberon-2 binding for ODL/OQL is implemented as a part of this work. ODL is a specification language for defining interfaces to object types that conform to the Object Model of the Object Database Management Group. OQL is an object query language supporting this model.

A proof-of-concept implementation has been done in the Oberon system, which offers powerful mechanisms for extending software in an object-oriented way. However, any other object-oriented operating system which offers garbage collection and exception handling can be used instead. Please refer to http://www.ssw.uni-linz.ac.at/Projects/OberonD.html.

5.8 Albertina Lourenci: The Hermeneutic Nature Of An Ecodesign Model And Self

The mainstream formalist computer science pays little attention to the domain dependent knowledge. Worse the communities from applied fields lag behind in either modeling the intrinsic activities of specific domains or building bridges to computer science. Yet an emergent hermeneutic computer science seems willing to bridge this gap. The object-oriented paradigm is a transition between both trends. Recently it has been introducing design patterns and the prototype-based paradigm that clearly grasp a more interpretative nature of the phenomena around us. The Model of Primary, Secondary and Tertiary Waves (MPSTW) for the design and planning of sustainable cities derived from the application of catastrophe, semiotics and graph theories stresses the hermeneutic nature of the design dovetailing its immanent and transcendent aspects. Its fundamental unit is the eco-system with hyphen that defines the urban ecosystem and is defined by the ecosystem, blending design and planning. A finer granularity the subeco-system with hyphen corresponds to the elements of the architectural design, namely environmental comfort, activities, structural system, and so on each one viewed as processes of interaction of the architectonic object with the environment and design processes, corresponding respectively to the primary and secondary waves. The former are depicted through the hypotheses homeostasis, continuity, differentiation and repeatability. The latter are part of the submodel of the architectonic sign where architectural design is viewed as a language with its planes function and form and its stratas substance of the function, form of the function, substance of the form and form of the form. It triggers off a new geometric modeling based on tilings, discrete groups of the plane and fractals. Its granularity match the levels of granularity of the prototype based object oriented programming language Self. The independence of each element or process suggests an object. Each object accepts or delegates tasks to each other.

For more information please see
http://www.lsi.usp.br/~lourenci/ecoop97.html.

5.9 Mads Torgersen: Generalizing Object-Oriented Languages

Currently there are many ongoing discussions within the object-oriented language design community over "which construct to use" for various purposes. The reason that these debates pervade is that both parts usually have very strong arguments.

Notorious controvercies include

- Overwriting or extension-based subclassing
- Genericity with parameterized or virtual classes
- Single or multiple inheritance
- No-, co- or contravariance on input types
- Structural or declarational (name-based) subtyping
- Full or partial (or no) static type safety

Merely putting all approaches into the same language is either directly impossible or leads to immensely complex languages. When taking a step back, however, and looking at what people want to *achieve* with their favourite construct, it is often possible to reconcile the approaches combining the benefits of both in a more abstract and general feature.

As part of my research I aim to take part in such a reconciliation within specific issues. As a longer term goal this generalization and unification process is intended to converge into an abstract language or family of languages with the ability to faithfully express (as opposed to emulate) the vast majority of object-oriented programming constructs (including all those listed above).

Such a language will be a useful tool for analytic and comparative purposes, and whereas it might turn out to be impratical or inefficient to implement directly as a programming language, it may act as an inspiration in the creation of such languages.

My main inspiration is the conceptual modelling perpective - the fact that people organize and exchange knowledge via the construction and use of *concepts*. This has often been taken to imply that language construction should be based on human *intuition*. Intuition however is vague, subjective and error prone (which has often been turned against the modelling perspective as such). Rather I advocate a notion of *common sense*, which taken literally does not deny the need for logical soundness but requires the inner logic of a model to be accessible - indeed *sensible* - also to non-specialists.

Experience shows that the answer to "Yeah. But what does it *mean*?" often contains the key to new solutions which are simpler and easier to reason about, yet far more general, powerful and expressive.

At present draft solutions exist for the reconciliation of all the above controversies. A proposal for a fully statically type-safe combined solution to genericity, covariance and self recursion based on the BETA notion of virtual classes is currently being prepared for submission.

Author Information

Krister Ahlander,
krister@tdb.uu.se
Department of Scientific Computing,
Box 120, 751 04 Uppsala, Sweden

Tero Ahtee,
tensu@cs.tut.fi
Tampere University of Technology,
Software Systems Laboratory, Finland

Walid Al-Ahmad,
walid@cs.kuleuven.ac.be
Department of Computer Science,
Katholieke Universiteit Leuven,
Belgium

Arno Bakker,
arno@cs.vu.nl
Department of Mathematics and
Computer Sciences, Vrije Universiteit
Amsterdam, The Netherlands

Luigi Benedicenti,
Luigi.Benedicenti@dist.unige.it
Via Opera Pia 13, 16145 Genova, Italy

Laszlo Blum,
bluml@almos.vein.hu
Department of Mathematics and
Computer Science, University of
Veszprem, Hungary

Christian Bunse,
bunse@iese.fhg.de
Fraunhofer Institute for Experimental
Software Engineering (IESE),
Sauerwiesen 6, 67661 Kaiserslautern,
Germany

Carlos Canal,
canal@lcc.uma.es
Dept. of Computer Science and
Languages, University of Málaga,
Spain

Amnon H. Eden,
eden@math.tau.ac.il
Department of Computer Science, Tel
Aviv University, Tel Aviv 69978, Israel

Erik Ernst,
eernst@daimi.aau.dk
Department of Computer Science,
University of Århus, Denmark

Nils Fischbeck,
fischbec@informatik.hu-berlin.de
Department of Computer Science,
Humboldt-University Berlin, Germany

María Ángeles Díaz Fondón,
fondon@pinon.ccu.uniovi.es
Department of Computer Science,
University of Oviedo, Spain

Tracy Gardner,
maptag@bath.ac.uk
School of Mathematical Sciences,University of Bath, UK

Marc Geilen,
geilen@ics.ele.tue.nl
Department of Electrical Engineering,
Eindhoven University of Technology

Frank Gerhardt,
fg@acm.org
Daimler-Benz AG (IO/TM), E702,
D-70546 Stuttgart

Darío Álvarez Gutiérrez,
darioa@pinon.ccu.uniovi.es
Department of Informatics, University
of Oviedo, Spain

Wade Holst,
wade@cs.ualberta.ca
Department of Computer Science,
University of Alberta, Canada

Kitty Hung,
hungks@sbu.ac.uk
South Bank University, UK

Eyðun Eli Jacobsen,
jacobsen@cs.auc.dk
Department of Computer Science,
Aalborg University, Fredrik Bajers Vej
7E, 9220 Aalborg Ø, Denmark

Selma Karadurak,
karadura@lgu.ac.uk
London Guildhall University, CISM

Dept.,100 Minories, Tower Hill,
London, EC3N 1JY, United Kingdom
Roger Kehr,
kehr@informatik.th-darmstadt.de
Department of Computer Science,
WG Distributed Systems, Technical
University of Darmstadt
Markus Knasmüller,
knasmueller@ssw.uni-linz.ac.at
Department of Practical Computer
Science, University of Linz, Austria

Martin von Löwis,
loewis@informatik.hu-berlin.de
Institut für Informatik, Humboldt-
Universität zu Berlin, Germany
Yvan Labiche,
ylabiche@laas.fr
LIS-Aerospatiale, LAAS-CNRS, 7
Avenue du Colonel Roche, 31077
Toulouse Cedex, FRANCE
Albertina Lourenci,
al@sc.usp.br
Faculty of Architecture and Urbanism,
University of São Paulo, Rua
Maranhão 88, Higienópolis, São Paulo,
SP, CEP: 01240-000

Lourdes Tajes Martinez,
tajes@pinon.ccu.uniovi.es
Department of Computer Science,
University of Oviedo, Spain
Juan M. Murillo,
juanmamu@unex.es
Department of Computer Science,
University of Extremadura, Spain

Palle Nowack,
nowack@cs.auc.dk
Department of Computer Science,
Aalborg University, Fredrik Bajers Vej
7E, DK-9220 Aalborg Ø, Denmark

Stephan Reitzner,
reitzner@cs.fau.de
Dept. of Computer Science, Univ. of
Erlangen-Nürnberg

Fernando Sánchez,
fernando@unex.es
Department of Computer Science,
University of Extremadura, Spain

Stefan Tai,
stai@cs.tu-berlin.de
Technical University Berlin, Sekr.
E-N 7, Einsteinufer 17, 10587 Berlin,
Germany
Mads Torgersen,
madst@daimi.aau.dk
Computer Science Department, Århus
University, Denmark

Bart Vanhaute,
Bart.Vanhaute@cs.kuleuven.ac.be
Department of Computer Science,
Catholic University of Leuven, Belgium

Lutz Wohlrab,
lwo@informatik.tu-chemnitz.de
Chemnitz University of Technology,
09107 Chemnitz, Germany

Michael Zastre,
zastre@csr.uvic.ca
Department of Computer Science,
University of Victoria, Canada

Object-Oriented Real-Time Systems: Workshop Report

Leonor Barroca[1], Eugene Durr[2], and François Terrier[3]

[1] Dept of Computing, The Open University
U.K.
[2] Dept. Computational Physics
Utrecht University
The Netherlands
[3] LETI/DEIN (CEA - Technologies Avancées)
France

Abstract. We report here on the workshop on object-oriented real-time systems. The papers presented and the subsequent discussion in the workshop covered a wide range of issues. There is a fast growing expertise relating to the application of object-oriented technology to real-time systems and this year's workshop was a clear evidence of that.

1 Introduction

As the advantages of object technology have become more widely known, objects are being applied more and more in real-time systems, but there are many specific real-time problems that still need to be addressed from an object-oriented perspective. In particular:

- How to manage specific real-time issues in object-oriented methods?
- How to capture and specify time constraints?
- How to adapt analysis models for real-time systems?
- How to design solutions which effectively take care of the real-time aspects?

¿From the implementation perspective, real-time object-oriented languages, code generation from design models, and patterns and frameworks specific to real-time systems still raise questions for further research. Validation and testing has to address dynamic behaviour and the fulfillment of time constraints. Finally, object-oriented real-time kernels and mapping of object-oriented designs to existing kernels are also an important points to be considered.

2 Contents

The workshop gathered participants from both academic institutions and industry. The attendees were half the authors of papers and half informal attendees. Presentations and discussions can be grouped into two main domains of interest:

 – system modelling, and
 – implementation

Methods for real-time systems were an important issue addressed by about half of the papers. There is a major requirement for any method for real-time: to allow for the definition of time constraints, their incorporation in the design of the system's architecture, and also the need to analyse the code produced and verify that these time constraints are kept. However, there is still a need to capture and represent time at the requirements level and this issue was not covered by any of the presentations. There was discussion about the importance of the analysis phase, and the need for either analysis patterns for real-time systems or the use of analysis methods that lead to architectures as provided by the design methods. The presentations addressing this subject are the three following:

 – Lano and Goldsack (Imperial College, United Kingdom) discussed the benefits of combining real-time design methods with formal notations. Real-time design methods provide a set of guidelines on decomposing a system and structuring a design; the use of a formal notation provides a basis for reasoning about the system's behaviour and the specifications can themselves be animated. The combination of the two gives a precise meaning to a well structured design. The combined notations are HRT-HOOD and VDM++ and the use of VDM++ allows for a systematic refinement of designs transforming time in a continuous domain into discrete time representation. The main drawback of this approach is still the lack of support tools for reasoning with VDM++.
 – The presentation by Amador (ESA, The Netherlands) focused also on design methods, in this case HRT-HOOD and the ESA experience on its application on the development of the European Robotic Arm. The design proceeds in an incremental way starting from a physical architecture that fixes the structure of the system to which functional detail is added in several iterations.
 – Zamperoni (Bosch Telecom, Germany) in his position paper raised a set of questions for discussion. Namely, the need to specify behaviour using notations that support time ordering and communication, and that are amenable to code generation. An important issue raised by this presentation was the need of good integration between the different techniques and notations used.

Implementation of real-time systems with object-oriented technology was covered by the second half of the papers. A new tendency can be noticed in this year's workshop: a strong interest in mechanisms allowing an object-oriented implementation of industrial and distributed real-time systems. The four presentations addressing these questions were the following:

 – Rioux and Vanuxeem (CEA-LETI, France) dealt with the implementation of real-time objects and how to relieve the programmer from the difficulties of real-time. Supported by the Class-Relation method and based on the active object concept it proposes an architecture for parallel execution of controllers and objects in an efficient way. Each object has a mailbox and three controllers (for state, concurrency, and scheduling).

- Toinard and Chevassus (Labri, University of Bordeaux, France) discussed an architecture for application in computer integrated manufacturing. Communication between objects is supported by a multicast memory with variables updated periodically with a multicast. This solution guarantees time properties to be asserted as well as ordering to be constrained.
- Cornilleau and Gressier-Soudan (CNAM-CEDRIC, France) also dealt with the problem of spatial and temporal consistency in distributed real-time databases. They propose Temporal Causal Consistency to support updating of variable's values, in fieldbus environments, maintaining consistency.
- Maisonneuve (Alcatel Alsthom Research, France) discussed the drawbacks of CORBA for real-time and presented work in development to provide real-time and dependable computing services to extend CORBA. A framework for telecom applications had been designed, based on these extensions, to support real-time applications.
- Barry (OTI, Canada) presented experience in using a Smalltalk environment for real-time embedded systems.

3 Conclusions

The workshop focused mainly on design methods, architecture issues for efficiency and consistency, and on implementation. There are three issues that have not been addressed in this workshop and are still opened for further research:

1. the need to capture and specify time requirements earlier than design in the development;
2. the need for automatic techniques and tools for validating and testing the real-time behaviour of the systems modelled and their implementation; and
3. the reuse of model and implementation in real-time system development (including patterns and frameworks for both analysis and design).

Formalising Real-Time System Design

K. Lano, S. Goldsack

Dept. of Computing, Imperial College, 180 Queens Gate, London, SW7 2BZ

Abstract. This paper identifies ways in which formal real-time notations (VDM^{++}) real-time design methods (HRT-HOOD) and simulation
tools (gPROMS) can be combined in practical developments.

The benefits of such a combination include that a precise semantics can
be attached to specifications in HRT-HOOD using the VDM^{++} notation
and that HRT-HOOD guidelines on structuring and decomposition can
be used for VDM^{++} specifications and designs. Abstract real-time specifications can also be animated at an early development stage to validate
them against requirements.

1 Combining HRT-HOOD and VDM^{++}

1.1 VDM^{++}

The VDM^{++} method is a formal object-oriented method for concurrent and
real-time systems. Details of the syntax and semantics of VDM^{++} are given in
[4].

The key elements of VDM^{++} used for defining real-time systems are *time
variables*, which represent continuously varying quantities, and *whenever* statements, which define responses to events [3]:

```
whenever P
also from δ ==> Q
```

asserts that for any time point **t** at which **P** becomes true, within δ time units
of **t**, **Q** will be true[1].

1.2 HRT-HOOD

HRT-HOOD [2] is a design method for hard-real time systems, using Ada-like
modules. HRT-HOOD defines objects as either **Passive**, **Active**, **Protected**,
Cyclic or **Sporadic**. For example, a **Protected** object may have limited forms
of synchronisation constraints, but does not spontaneously call operations of
other objects – such calls are always in response to calls on itself. Such categories
can also be assigned to classes in VDM^{++}: classes with time variables can be
considered to be **Active**, for instance. We will annotate VDM^{++} classes with
their HRT-HOOD category.

---

[1] We will use a slight extension of this notation, in which **Q** may contain "past state"
values $\overleftarrow{v}$ denoting the value of v : T at the time that **P** became true. This abbre-
viates a formula $\forall w : T \cdot w = v \Rightarrow$ (whenever **P** also from δ ==> $Q[w/\overleftarrow{v}]$).

Only Cyclic, Passive, Protected and Sporadic objects will be present at the terminal level in the development of a program using HRT-HOOD, Active objects are not permitted because they cannot be fully analysed. Cyclic objects are used for time-driven activities, whilst Sporadic objects are used for event-driven activities. Protected objects encapsulate shared data using permission guards to block concurrent callers where necessary to protect the integrity of this data.

1.3 Formalising HRT-HOOD Object Types in VDM^{++}

Cyclic objects can be represented by VDM^{++} classes with a periodic thread:

```
class Cyclic
instance variables ...
methods
  m() ==
      Code executed periodically
thread
  periodic(Period)(m)
end Cyclic
```

We can express temporal constraints such as a period $\mathbf{P}$ of execution, and deadline $\mathbf{D}$ for periodic method $\mathbf{m}$ of cyclic objects, via statements:

```
inv objectstate ==
  whenever P | now
  also from D  ==>  #fin(m)  =  #fin(m)‾ + 1
thread
  periodic(P)(m)
```

The invariant asserts that "within $\mathbf{D}$ time units of any time $\mathbf{t}$ which is a multiple of $\mathbf{P}$, there will have been one more completed execution of $\mathbf{m}$ than at $\mathbf{t}$".

$\mathbf{P} \mid \mathbf{now}$ denotes that $\mathbf{P}$ divides the current time. A more sophisticated approach would allow a degree of approximation to a multiple of $\mathbf{P}$:

$$\exists \mathbf{n} : \mathbb{N} \cdot \mathbf{n} * \mathbf{P} - \epsilon < \mathbf{now} < \mathbf{n} * \mathbf{P} + \epsilon$$

for a small value $0 < \epsilon < 1$.

$\#\mathbf{fin}(\mathbf{m})$ counts the number of completed executions of $\mathbf{m}$, whilst $\#\mathbf{act}(\mathbf{m})$ counts the number of initiated executions of $\mathbf{m}$.

We assume that the class is *fully mutex*: at most one method invocation can be executing at any time. In general ASATC operations of the cyclic object could interrupt the periodic activity, however two invocations of $\mathbf{m}$ cannot overlap in their executions, so the above **whenever** statement remains meaningful for all forms of cyclic object.

2 Refinement and Design

There is already a set of design transformations that can be applied to sequential and discrete VDM^{++} systems, such as *annealing*, the replacement of instance variables by supplier objects. In this section we formalise design steps which involve a transformation from a continuous model of the world to a discrete or hybrid model.

A common form of transformation from continuous to discrete views of a system starts from a class which abstractly describes a reaction to an event (eg.: a requirement to establish some condition $E(ot)$ of an output time variable within δ_0 time units of some condition $C(it)$ becoming true of an input time variable):

```
class ContinuousController   /* Active */
time variables
input it :  X;
      ot :  S;
effect it, ot   ==
  whenever C(it) also from δ₀ ==> E(ot)
end ContinuousController
```

If we can assume that C remains true for at least $t_C > 0$ time units from the points where it becomes true, and C remains false for at least $t_C > 0$ time units from when it becomes false, then we can define a sampling approach:

```
class AbstractController   /* Active */
-- refines ContinuousController
time variables
input it :  X;
      ot :  S;
effect it, ot  ==
  whenever C(it) ∧ (P | now) ∧
           (now  > 0  ⇒  ¬ C(it(now − P)))
  also from δ ==> E(ot)
end AbstractController
```

where:

- $P \le t_C$: no $C := \mathbf{true}$ or $C := \mathbf{false}$ events are missed;

- $\delta + P \le \delta_0$: response is within δ_0 as required.

$\delta < P$ is needed for schedulability.

We can deduce that the abstract requirements are met, as follows:

- If $C(it)$ is true at **now** and $\mathbf{now} - P$ then it is true at every point in between these times – otherwise there is a time t with $\mathbf{now} - P \le t \le \mathbf{now}$ at which $C(it)$ becomes false, and therefore remains false until $t + t_C$, which is $\ge \mathbf{now}$, a contradiction.

- Likewise if $C(it)$ is false at **now** and $\mathbf{now} - P$, it must be false at all intermediate points.

This shows that responses are carried out exactly to the events required by the **ContinuousController**. The choice of δ ensures that they are carried out in the required time.

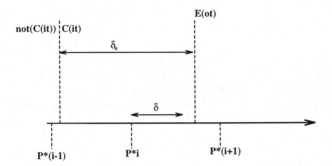

Fig. 1. Periodic Refinement

Figure 1 shows the rationale for this design step.

AbstractController is then implemented by a cyclic class:

```
class ConcreteController  /* Cyclic */
-- refines AbstractController
instance variables
  id, old_id : X;
  j : ℕ;        /* Counts cycles */
  x_sensor : @XSensor;
  ot_obj : @SClass;
inv objectstate ==
  whenever P | now
  also from δ ==>
        #fin(react)  =  #fin(react) + 1;
init objectstate ==  j := 0
methods
  react()  ==
     (dcl id : X := x_sensor!sample_x();
     if (j > 0 ⇒ ¬ C(old_id)) ∧ C(id)
     then ot_obj!achieve_E(v);
     j := 1;
     old_id := id)
thread
  periodic(P)(react)
end ConcreteController
```

XSensor encapsulates the **it : X** time variable. Objects of this class periodically sample the **it** value from **x_sensor**, compare the truth of **C(id)** with the truth of **C(id)** on the previous cycle, and if there has been a change, execute a method to achieve the condition **E** on the **ot** variable encapsulated in **ot_obj**.

A similar refinement can be undertaken in the case that we choose an interrupt strategy for communicating the occurrence of the **C(it) := true** event to the software control system.

3 Case Study

3.1 Requirements

The system to be controlled is a pasteurisation plant [7]. This involves a large number of separate processes, devices and sensors, and we will focus only on one process here, the delivery of raw milk from tankers into an input holding tank. Figure 2 shows the elements of this part of the system.

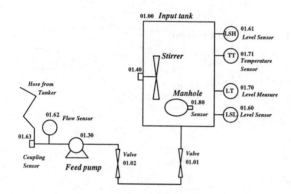

Fig. 2. Layout of Input Holding Tank

The processing is as follows: the process is initiated by the operator entering the "ST RP IN" command at a central console, the tanker being connected (sensor 1.63 energised), and then a local pushbutton being pressed to start the process. The holding tank must not be completely full (sensor 1.61 energised) and the manhole in 1.00 must be closed (sensor 1.80 energised).

If all these conditions are met, the valves 1.01 and 1.02 are opened (energised) to allow flow from the intake line into the tank, and pump 1.30 is switched on (energised). The system must react to certain conditions within deadlines:

1. if the manhole is opened (sensor 1.80 becomes de-energised) then valve 1.01 and pump 1.30 must be signalled to become de-energised within 100ms;

2. similarly in the case that the tanker disconnects (sensor 1.63 de-energised) during filling;

3. if the level reaches 100%, then these components must be de-energised within 2000ms, and similarly if sensor 1.61 becomes de-energised or sensor 1.62 de-energised (flow ceases).

On termination the system must de-energise valves 1.01, 1.02 and switch off pump 1.30.

A stirrer in the tank (item 1.40) must be on if the tank level is over 30% full, and off if the level is below 25% full.

3.2   Specification and Design

An initial model 0 [3] specification of the combined environment and control system is given by the **InputRoute_0** class:

```
class InputRoute_0 /* Active */
values             /* Milliseconds in processor */
  ms : ℕ = ...  /* clock ticks */
types
  SState = ENERGISED | DEENERGISED
time variables
    level : ℝ;   /* Between 0 and 100 */
    probe_161 : SState;
    sensor_180 : SState;
    sensor_163 : SState;
    sensor_162 : SState;
    valve_101 : SState;
    valve_102 : SState;
    pump_130 : SState;
    stirrer_140 : SState
assumptions ==
    d level
    ------ > 0  ⇒  valve_101 = ENERGISED
      dt
      /* The level can only be increasing   */
      /* if valve_101 is open                */
effects ==
  (whenever sensor_180 = DEENERGISED
   also from 100 * ms ==>
          valve_101 = DEENERGISED ∧
          pump_130 = DEENERGISED)   ∧

  (whenever level ≥ 100
   also from 2000 * ms ==>
          valve_101 = DEENERGISED ∧
          pump_130 = DEENERGISED)   ∧

  /* Effects clauses for other requirements */
end InputRoute_0
```

All time variables are **outputs**, since this class represents the overall behaviour that the user expects from the combined controller and environment. In the abstract specification of the controller, the sensor variables will become inputs.

In order to meet the timing requirements we can either choose a sufficiently rapid sampling of the input data, or use interrupts from the hardware wrapper to communicate critical changes in their values to the controller. To illustrate the process, we choose sampling for the **level** variable, and interrupts for the manhole sensor 1.80.

We separate the **level** into an environment class:

```
class Level  /* Active */
time variables
```

```
    level :  ℝ
methods   /* Return "current" level value */
  get_level() value ll :  ℝ  ==
      [ext rd level
        post ∃ t :  ℝ  ·  ‾now‾  ≤  t  ≤  now  ∧
                          ll  =  level(t)]
```

end **Level**

The assumption on the **level** variable now belongs in a *workspace* class which defines the links between the environment and controller.

Similar classes are defined to encapsulate the **sensor_180**, **probe_161**, **sensor_162** and **sensor_163** time variables.

The abstract specification of the controller is:

```
class Controller_0    /* Active */
values
   τ :  ℕ  =  undefined   /* Sampling period */
time variables
   input sensed_level :  ℝ;
   input sensed_180 :  SState;
   ...
effects
  (whenever sensed_180  =    DEENERGISED
   also from 100 * ms ==>
          valve_101  =    DEENERGISED  ∧
          pump_130  =    DEENERGISED)   ∧

  (whenever τ  |  now   ∧    sensed_level  ≥  100  ∧
           (now  >  0   ⇒    sensed_level(now − τ)  <  100)
   also from τ/2 ==>
          valve_101  =    DEENERGISED  ∧
          pump_130  =    DEENERGISED)   ∧
   ....
end Controller_0
```

A workspace class **Model_1** defines the connection between these classes, and represents the initial refinement of **InputRoute_0**.

We can then use the design pattern for periodic sampling given above, to refine **Controller_0** class by a cyclic class.

A further refinement step moves the level sampling out into a special purpose cyclic class, which reduces the controller to being a **Protected** object.

Figure 3 shows part of the HRT-HOOD decomposition of the final level of design presented here.

Notice that all the classes which are within the software development are now non-active, as required by the HRT-HOOD development method.

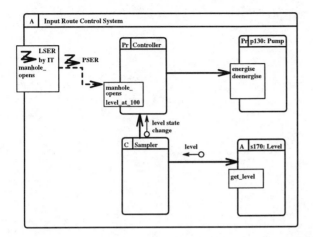

Fig. 3. Part of HRT-HOOD design decomposition

4 Simulation using gPROMS

In [5] we show how the gPROMS dynamic simulation system [1] may be used to validate abstract VDM++ specifications, including hybrid classes with **whenever** statements. The structuring of gPROMS simulation specifications into modules corresponds to object structuring in VDM++, with data *streams* between modules corresponding to (sampled) time variable connections between VDM++ objects.

A detailed specification of the dynamic behaviour of the environment can be given, in addition to continuous or discrete descriptions of the controller.

In [5] we give an example of a simulation of the cat/mouse system described in [6]. This is given as a model 0 VDM++ system with corresponding simulation (an example of one case of behaviour is given in Figure 4), and as a model 1 system where the mouse and cat components are separated. An extract from the gPROMS description of model 1 is:

```
MODEL Cat
PARAMETER     /* Constants */
  Cat_Speed      AS REAL
VARIABLE     /* Time variables */
  Cat_Velocity    AS Velocity
  Mouse_Dist, Cat_Distance  AS Distance
STREAM     /* Links to other modules */
  Input: Mouse_Dist AS DistStream
  Output: Cat_Distance AS DistStream
SELECTOR   /* Discrete state variable */
  Cat_State  AS (Running,Failed,Catches)
            DEFAULT Running
SET
  Cat_Speed      := 6;
EQUATION
```

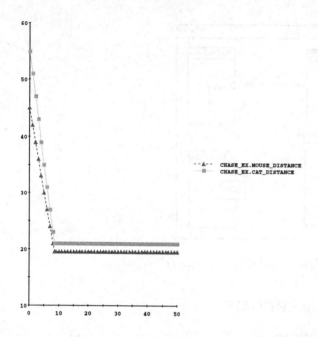

Fig. 4. Transition to Caught state

```
$Cat_Distance = Cat_Velocity;

CASE Cat_State OF
    WHEN Running : Cat_Velocity = -Cat_Speed;
        SWITCH TO Failed
            IF (Mouse_Dist <= 1) AND
                (Cat_Distance - Mouse_Dist > 1.5);
        SWITCH TO Catches
            IF Cat_Distance - Mouse_Dist <= 1.5;
    WHEN Failed : Cat_Velocity = 0;
    WHEN Catches : Cat_Velocity = 0;
    END
END # Cat
```

$ denotes the differential wrt time. The **Cat** module corresponds to a VDM^{++} class definition in which "streams" are time variables and $\epsilon = 1.5$, $\ell = 1$:

```
class Cat
...
time variables
    input mouse_dist : Distance;
    cat_velocity : Velocity;
    cat_distance : Distance;
    cat_state : CState;
```

445

```
effects cat_distance, cat_velocity ==
   cat_velocity = d cat_distance/dt;
effects cat_state, cat_distance,
        mouse_dist, cat_velocity ==
  (whenever cat_distance − mouse_dist ≤ ε
   also from δ ==> cat_state = < catches >) ∧

  (whenever mouse_dist ≤ ℓ ∧
          cat_distance − mouse_dist > ε
   also from δ ==> cat_state = < failed >);
   ⋮
end Cat
```

There is a similar module for the **Mouse**.

The translation from VDM^{++} to gPROMS model notation should be largely automatic, because of the structural and conceptual similarities of the two notations. A translator is currently under development.

Conclusions

We have shown that VDM^{++} can be combined with the real-time design method HRT-HOOD in order to enhance the precision of this method. Timing constraints for HRT-HOOD objects can be formally expressed in VDM^{++}, allowing implementations to be verified against these objects.

Simulation of abstract continuous and hybrid VDM^{++} classes can be carried out using a translation to the gPROMS tool.

References

1. P I Barton, E Smith and C C Pantelides. Combined Discrete/Continuous Process Modelling Using gPROMS, 1991 AIChE Annual Meeting: Recent Advances in Process Control, Los Angeles, 1991.
2. A Burns and A Wellings. HRT-HOOD: A structured design method for hard real-time systems. *Real-Time Systems*, 6(1):73–114, January 1994.
3. E Durr, S Goldsack, and J van Katjwick. Specification of a cruise controller in VDM^{++}. In *Proceedings of Real Time OO Workshop, ECOOP 96*, 1996.
4. K. Lano, S. Goldsack, J. Bicarregui, S. Kent, *Integrating VDM^{++} and Real-time System Design*, Z User Meeting 1997, LNCS.
5. K Lano. *Refinement and Simulation of Real-time and Hybrid Systems using VDM^{++} and gPROMS*, ROOS project report GR/K68783-13, November 1996, Dept. of Computing, Imperial College.
6. Z Manna and A Pnueli. Time for concurrency. Technical report, Dept. of Computer Science, Stanford University, 1992.
7. PRESTO P4 Project. *Integrated Design of Control and Automation Systems*, PRESTO Document 200197A11, Centre for Process Systems Engineering, Imperial College, 1997.

Object-Oriented Real-Time Software in the European Space Agency

Jorge Amador Monteverde

Software Engineering and Standardisation Section
ESA-ESTEC
Keplerlaan 1 - 2200 AG Noordwijk - The Netherlands
Tel.: (31) 71 565 4388
Fax: (31) 71 565 5420
E-mail: amador@wm.estec.esa.nl

Introduction: Overview of ESA on-board software systems development

ESA on-board software is mostly real-time and embedded, performing a variety of tasks to control and monitor the functioning of a satellite. Typically, it can be divided into the following categories:

- On-board Data Handling (OBDH): mission critical, usually hard real-time, with both cyclic and sporadic activities, with different deadlines and priorities.

- Attitude and Orbit Control Software (AOCS): mission critical, but is usually soft real-time. It is essentially cyclic software.

- Payload software: It is (usually) not mission critical, and its real-time features depend very much on the specific case.

The majority of on-board software being developed in ESA projects is designed with the HOOD method, and coded in Ada.

HOOD[1] (Hierarchical Object-Oriented Design) was developed under ESA contract, and is based on Booch's OOD. It is mainly oriented to the design of embedded Ada software. It provides good support for the design of concurrent systems, although it is weaker on the modelling of real-time properties.

The Ada RTS (i.e. tasking) is hardly used, RT operating systems being preferred. It was mainly due to the big overheads (both in performance and memory) of the commercial Ada RTSs, although this situation has changed (better RTSs and also the introduction of the ATAC chip, which provides Ada tasking support on chip level).

Resource budgets have to be defined and adhered to throughout the project, however, validation of real-time (and in general, non functional) requirements is usually done at testing, with little or no effort in the early phases.

R&D for on-board software: OORT technology

Obviously, the situation presented above leads to high development costs and high risk in ESA's projects. Therefore, a number of R&D activities have been and are being carried out to improve that situation.

As it was seen that real-time requirements were not modelled nor validated properly during the early development phases, explicit actions were taken at both method and tool level, to provide a comprehensive set of techniques and tools for real-time embedded software development and early validation. This was done in the frame of OO techniques which were already in use (i.e. HOOD).

The following is a summary of the most relevant results.

HRT-HOOD[2] ('93)

It is an extension to the HOOD method specially well suited for hard real-time systems. It provides:

- explicit recognition of the types of typical hard real-time systems' activities (i.e. cyclic, sporadic, resource monitors),

- the integration of scheduling paradigms in the design process,

- explicit definition of the application's timing requirements and criticality for each activity,

- decomposition to a software architecture that easily allow the processor allocation, schedulability and timing analysis,

- facilities and tools to allow static verification of real-time properties early in the design process.

HRT-HOOD supports computational models that allow: co-existence of both cyclic and sporadic activities, interactions between concurrent activities, a blocking approach suitable to avoid unbounded delays and prevent priority inversions, off-line schedulability analysis. Although it is open to any scheduling model, work has focused on the RMS and DMS algorithms. The HRT-HOOD method extends HOOD's object model (which has Passive and Active objects as the main building blocks) to include Protected, Sporadic and Cyclic objects, and defines rules for their usage. A formal mapping to Ada95, allowing automatic code generation, is also defined.

HRT-HOOD provides a very good integration of state-of-the-art techniques for real-time systems design and validation (e.g. DMS) with an industrial design method, and that without imposing a given computational model. That is a strength of HRT-HOOD compared to other methods like ROOM, which imposes a reactive computational model.

On the other hand, HOOD and HRT-HOOD provide a clear separation between an object's interface (its operations and the calling constraints on its operations) and its internals (i.e. attributes and operations implementation). This allows to perform the real-time analyses based only on the objects' interfaces, as well as automatic code generation for those (validated) interfaces.

HRT Support Tools[3]('96)

A set of tools supporting the HRT-HOOD method and the off-line static verification of hard real-time properties have been defined and produced:

- Worst Case Execution Time (WCET) analyser: it is integrated with an Ada compiler (Aonix's AdaWorld) for ESA's SPARC processors (ERC32)

- Schedulability Analyser, and Schedulability Simulator, freeware available from Spacebel, in Belgium.

- HRT-HOOD tool[4]: it is an extension of an existing HOOD tool to support the HRT-HOOD method. It also integrates the three tools defined above, providing a complete and integrated environment for HRT systems design. It also generates Ada95 code automatically out of the verified system.

Implementation experience: the European Robotic Arm (ERA)

ERA is intended to be used in the construction of the Russian segment of the International Space Station Alpha. The ERA project selected HRT-HOOD as the design method for the ERA Control Computer (ECC) Software. It is being written in Ada with an estimated size of 60000 SLOC. It is a hard real-time system, with around 30 concurrent objects (including cyclic, sporadic and protected objects). It has three main components, developed by three independent companies, one them centralising the real-time verification activities (i.e. schedulability analysis) of the whole system.

Its development follows an incremental approach, with 4 consecutive versions, where the physical architecture and a minimal functionality is fixed in V0, including the real-time feasibility verification, and further versions add more functionality to that fixed structure. This approach is possible thanks to HRT-HOOD's clear distinction between the object's interface and implementation, described above.

The early verification approach for real-time has been (and is) of great help to the ECC SW development. It has allowed to assess how changes both in the real-time requirements and in the execution environment (including a change in the processor) impacted the design, and that in a minimum amount of time (usually less than half a day).

Current and future directions

Reusable on-board real-time software components

Space software architectures at ESA are very similar between missions. It is clear that reusable components are not only code, but also design and analysis objects. The main problem now is the reuse granularity. Although generic architectures look very promising from a 'static' point of view, it is very difficult to include dynamic aspects, specially real-time in such architectures in a generic way. It is preferred to have libraries of small components with well defined static and dynamic (including real-time) properties, which can then be combined to build the final system. The use of full OOP features like inheritance and dynamic binding is considered a key feature for the extensibility and adaptability of those components to changing requirements, and is currently under investigation.

Integration of HRT-HOOD and Formal methods

Formal methods are seen as an excellent tool for functional requirements specification and validation, but not so much for real-time requirements, where specific techniques are available (e.g. DMS theory). The integration of formal methods and tools (SDL) for functional requirements specification with HRT-HOOD technology for real-time design is currently under development.

References

1. HOOD Technical Group, "HOOD Reference Manual release 4", September 1995.

2. "HRT-HOOD -- A Structured Design Method for HRT Ada Systems", Reference Manual Version 2.0 University of York, September 1993.

3. T. Vardanega, "Tool Support for the Construction of Statically Analysable Hard Real-Time Systems in Ada", Proceedings of the 17th Real-Time Systems Symposium, IEEE, December 1996.

4. "HRT-HoodNICE: A Hard Real-Time Software design Support Tool", Final Report, ESTEC Contract No. 11234/94/NL/FM(SC), Intecs Sistemi, March 1996.

Scheduling Mechanisms for Efficient Implementation of Real-Time Objects

Laurent Rioux, Patrick Vanuxeem, François Terrier

LETI (CEA - Technologie Avancées) DEIN - CEA/Saclay, F-91191 Gif / Yvette Cedex France
Phone/FAX: +33 (0)1 69 08 62 59 / 83 95; E-Mail: Francois.Terrier@cea.fr

Abstract:
This paper deals with the implementation of complex object oriented applications on shared memory multiprocessor machines. For this, we propose to use the real-time object paradigm. Real-time behaviour of these applications is specified by assigning deadline, periodicity or priority constraints to the messages. In this approach real-time objects messages are processed by independent threads. This produces a messages scheduling problem where messages (tasks) have dependency and resource constraints. The architecture proposed allows to parallel the controls and the treatments of the different messages. To ensure a good performance, we propose also here a new thread manager to ensure a high reactivity of the object when it receives a message. This architecture permits a real-time parallel control into each object that provides a high parallelism into application (Treatment and Control).

1 Introduction

The concurrent object model provides multitasking capability, along with modularity and reusability, which are a great challenge for real-time applications. The active object paradigm allows us to design an application as a set of autonomous entities which simplifies multitasking problems, since they become local to each of the entities [9] [1]. Moreover, real-time constraints of the applications requires very precise control, particularly deadline and inter-task synchronisation.

In our project, we use a real-time extension of the active object model. As in most real-time extensions of the active object model [12] [6] [10], we have chosen to attach different timing constraints to the message: the client (emitting object) imposes its constraints and the server must do all that is necessary to respect them [5] [4]. In this model, the notion of message passing is associated with the notion of task (for each message, a thread is attached for the message processing). First, we present the context of this study and then, all components of this architecture and finally the scheduling mechanisms.

2 Context Presentation

The active object can be roughly seen as composed by a mailbox, a concurrency and thread manager. ACCORD project [13] [14] proposes its extension to real-time by attaching deadline constraints to the messages and by associating the task notion with the execution of a method [5] [4]. Such objects will be called **real-time objects**. To develop application with such objects, ACCORD provides a real-time object oriented application workshop [14]. This workshop comprises three modules:

- **Modelling**: this module is used to model the real-time application in terms of interacting real-time objects.
- **Development**: this module is used to develop the different methods of real-time objects. Code generation is used to introduce all mechanisms to transform an object into a real-time object.
- **Runtime**: this module is constituted by several classes libraries: the real-time object kernel, the operating system interface (virtual machine), ...

All modules are supported by a case tool based on the *CLASS-RELATION* method: the *Objecteering* tool of *Softeam*.

3 An Architecture for Real-Time Objects

The problem consists in managing the constraints set of a real-time application running on a multiprocessor and multithread operating system. Three parts of the problem can be distinguished:

1. Control of the different states of the objects (objects' processing capacity).
2. Intra-object concurrency control (access to the attributes).
3. Scheduling control on Processor resources.

The problem may therefore be divided into three steps, each one dedicated to a type of constraint and performing a kind of filtering on the whole problem and defining a pipelined control architecture. Each real-time object contains a mailbox that receives messages and three controllers as shown in *Figure 1*:

- **A state controller**: it manages the internal state of the object and controls the execution of the different methods altering the object state.
- **A concurrency controller**: it controls the concurrent execution of the messages so that no concurrency problem can arise within a given state.
- **A scheduling controller**: it schedules the different messages sent to the object.

These three controllers access to the information stored in a passive object. This object provides all the data for defining the behaviour of the object methods in order to ensure their control.

3.1 Principle of the Architecture

When a message is received in the mailbox, it is sent to the state controller (1), which checks its acceptability according to the current state of the object. If possible, a thread is attached to the message (to process it), otherwise it is either delayed, or an error is generated. To decrease the amount of thread creation (generally costly), a thread manager is created when loading the application. This manager owns a pool of threads and can attach them to the methods to execute. If during the execution of the application, all the threads are used (in execution), it can create a new one dynamically. This mechanism is used to prevent the starvation problem in processing resources (thread). This new thread will not be returned to the pool at the end of its execution to avoid overloading the operating system with useless threads. After this step, there will be no messages that cannot be executed in the current state of the

452

object. Hence, the message is passed to the concurrency controller (2) which will manage the concurrency at the attribute level following the usual protocol of « *n readers, 1 writer* »: it is possible to read attributes in parallel but not to modify them (and only them). Once intra-object concurrency problems have been resolved, the messages whose executions are parallel are passed to the scheduling controller (3). It must be underlined that this approach is based on real-time objects, there is no global data shared by several objects, thus messages of different real-time objects have no concurrency constraints and can be processed in parallel.

The scheduling controller will schedule the messages along with all the other message in the application. This planning is performed globally in order to manage the processor resource efficiently. Hence the processor controller is in charge of sending message processing orders (i.e.: start, suspend or resume) to the Operating System. In order to schedule subsequent messages, each controller receives and handles the "end of treatment" message of the object it controls.

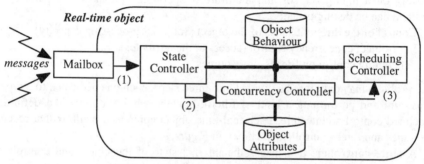

Figure 1: Structure of a Real-Time Object

3.2 The Behaviour Class

To perform a specific solution to each object, we have defined a passive object attached to each of the real-time object. This object is defined by a class called *Behaviour*. This object contains the behaviour information about the real-time object methods. This enables each controller to adapt its control to each processed message and to provide a specific solution corresponding to the needs of the real-time object.

This information is accessible in read mode, parallel execution of the controllers into each object is possible. Consequently, a message being processed by a controller will not be slowed down by the arrival of another message in the object (as long as another processor is available). The overhead introduced by the use of this passive behaviour-control object is small and allows the dynamic adaptation of the object processes scheduling to its execution context.

All of the information contained in this object is defined during the application design, in particular, the developer will be ask for specifying the behaviour of the object methods. Using this information, a C++ automated code generation will create the passive object inside the real-time object. The state controller and concurrency controller are detailed in [11].

3.3 Scheduling controller

The scheduling controller receives only concurrent and pre-emptable messages. Synchronisation problems of messages with a reply (dependency) have been managed before, through deadline propagation at message passing [3] [14]. So, from its point of view, the utilisation of a classical real-time scheduling algorithm is possible. In our approach, we have chosen the EDF (Earliest Deadline First) algorithm [8] [7] with deadline propagation, because it is optimal for these kind of tasks, if the scheduling criterion is satisfied [2]. Since the message scheduling problem has been solved (from the scheduler point of view), we propose that this scheduling controller should be integrated into each object. In order to propose better scheduling solutions, we propose to give to the scheduling controller, the access on the behaviour information of the scheduled messages. Then, to preserve the object encapsulation, the scheduling methods will be fully integrated to the real-time object itself.

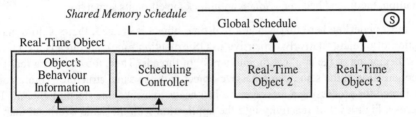

Figure 2: Architecture for Global Scheduling

For that, the schedule plan is placed in a passive object shared by all the real-time objects. This schedule is accessed by all the scheduling controllers of the application via a semaphore, Ⓢ , in order to ensure the integrity and consistency of the plan.

4 Threads Manager

The applications targeted by this architecture can be dispatched on several on several address spaces. Hereafter, we call « *zone* » an address space with some threads for execution. An object *ThreadsManager* has been defined to manage and optimise the threads used into each « *zone* ». All threads are associated to an object (*Thread*) encapsulating a thread pointer, a thread status, a specific mailbox and a semaphore to synchronise the thread execution. There is only one *ThreadsManager* object by « *zone* ». The state attribute indicates the thread status into the thread manager:

* « *busy* »: the thread is used for a message (for its control or its execution).
* « *idle* »: specifies that the thread is free and it can be used for a new message. This thread is locked on a semaphore, that ensures, it will not use the processor resource while it remains idle.

When the *ThreadsManager* is created (at the beginning of the application), it creates all the *Thread* instances. But before this, the *ThreadsManager* blocks all semaphores, so that, each thread gets lock by its semaphore. To unlock one thread, the application must write on its mailbox. From the control point of view, messages received by the real-time objects have a specific semantic and management: they must be processed in parallel with the rest of the application. They will be called here after a « *request* ». A request is defined by a class *Request* containing the following attributes:

- A reference to the target real-time object having to support the processing.
- The processing real-time constraints of the message.
- The message identification, the value of each method parameter.
- A reference to the *Thread* instance that performs the message.

When the *ThreadsManager* receives a request, it searches an idle thread, puts the request into its specific mailbox and unlocks the semaphore. The thread chosen become « *busy* », reads its specific mailbox, analyses the request content and executes the associate method code. Before execution, the thread pointer is saved into the request (by the thread itself) that allows to access from a given request to the *Thread* instance in charge of its processing. The *ThreadsManager* uses this pointer to suspend or resume the request thread, it must just know the request. At the end of a message execution, the thread become « *idle* » and blocks itself on its semaphore.

One must underline here that, when a real-time object is created, there is no dynamic creation of thread (relatively expensive in OS execution time): all threads are created at the beginning of the application into a pool of threads. Then, the cost for a real-time object creation is the same like a passive object with the same structure. To allocate a new thread for processing a message, we just needs to awake one sleeping thread. This ensures a high level of reactivity into the application with the same overhead than for classical multitask programming. Then, the designer do not need to discern high frequency object with others.

5 Multi « *Zones* » Scheduling Management

Some mechanisms around the *Schedule* and *MailBox* objects aims at multi « *zones* » scheduling management. To ensure the global consistency of the scheduling, the *Schedule* which contains request and « *zone* » information is placed in shared memory. That allows each scheduling controller to know all the real-time constraints of the requests to take into account in the scheduling algorithm. A semaphore controls the sequential access to the schedule. Moreover, during the execution of the application, a scheduling controller of a given real-time object can need to suspend or resume some requests processed in other real-time objects (i.e.: threads). If the request is within the same « *zone* » than the scheduling controller, it has a direct access to the corresponding thread. But when the request is in a different « *zone* » (i.e.: thread in other process), the scheduling controller will use also the shared memory to inform the other « *zone* » that there is a scheduling action to do. For that purpose, each *ThreadsManager* instance in a « *zone* » has a specific mailbox in shared memory which is a *ThreadsManagerMailbox* instance (see *Figure 3*).

Any scheduling controller of a « *zone* » can put in a mailbox (not its own) some messages defining a scheduling action to do in an other « *zone* ». Each *ThreadsManager* instance has a control thread at the maximum priority, locked and waiting on its own mailbox semaphore in shared memory.

ZONE 1   SHARED MEMORY   ZONE 2

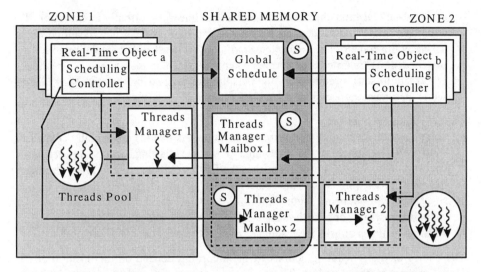

Figure 3: Control Thread Architecture with Mechanisms for Scheduling

When the scheduling controller wants to suspend or resume a request (i.e. thread) in an other «zone», it puts the scheduling actions («resume» or «suspend» or «start») and the request reference within the *ThreadsManagerMailbox*. The request reference is available from the shared memory schedule. After, the scheduling controller unlocks the semaphore attached to the *ThreadsManagerMailbox*. Then, the unlocked control thread of the target «zone» pre-empts (because it has higher priority than all other threads) and executes the scheduling action specified into its *ThreadsManagerMailbox*. After, it locks itself on the semaphore and the operating system suspends automatically this thread. In the initial «zone», the thread of the scheduling controller continues its execution and after, it is ready to send some other scheduling actions to other «zone»s. In the case of multiprocessor machines, the scheduling can put more than one message into *ThreadsManagerMailbox*, then the control thread can execute more than one order on different requests in its «zone».

6 Scheduling Algorithm

The used scheduling algorithm **EDF** (*Earliest Deadline First*) performs the global requests scheduling. Its principle is based on the management of a global requests list ordered following their growing absolute deadlines. The global request with the earliest deadline in the list is always executed first. *An extension to this algorithm to a multi-processors machine case is proposed by starting the first P requests of the schedule when P is the processors number.* The scheduling algorithm is decomposed into scheduling orders, treatments and actions. The **scheduling orders** are in input of the algorithm while the **scheduling actions** are in output. Scheduling orders are:

- **schedule**: inserts a request in the schedule depending on its deadline. It is performed when a request is accepted by the concurrency controller.
- **reschedule**: reschedules a request depending on its new deadline. This order is performed when a request R_n with an earlier deadline d_n occurs while a request R_i

of the same real-time object with a greater deadline d_i is currently in execution. To complete ASAP the request R_i, a rescheduling of R_i with a new deadline dn is asked by the concurrency controller. Starting of R_n is asked at completion of R_i.

- **unschedule**: This order is performed when a service completion occurs or when it is too late to start a request, i.e. the deadline for processing the request is missed while the request processing has not been started.

The scheduling actions are:

- **start**: asks the beginning of a service execution. As threads are initially created in « *suspended* » state, at the first time a service starting occurs a « *resume* » operation is realised. This distinguishes the first « *resume* » operation for starting a message processing from the others. This allows to unschedule a service suspended without being started before.
- **suspend**: suspends or asks the suspension of a service execution.
- **resume**: resumes or asks the resume of a service execution.

The choice of the scheduling actions by the algorithm depend on the position of the global request in the schedule. These actions concern either the request which has requested the scheduling action or an other request in the schedule. In another hand, this action depends if the calling service request and the service request to be started, are in the same « *zone* » (intra « *zone* » scheduling context) or in different « *zones* » (inter « *zone* » scheduling context).

Finally, the scheduling controller may be qualified of scheduling manager, parallel or sequential, multi « *zones* », multi real-time objects, multi global requests.

7 Summary of Mechanisms

This section proposes an analysis overview of the operating system mechanisms requested for processing a real-time object message. Two cases are envisaged: the *best case*, where the real-time object receiving the message is ready to process it immediately; and, the *worst case*, where the message has to wait that the several possible constraints for processing would be released before to be processed.

The *best case* is defined as following: the application is composed by only one « *zone* »; the object state is good; no concurrency problem (i.e. resource attributes are available); the processor resource is available. On sending the request, the caller automatically select a thread and resumes it. This thread pre-empts the caller, because it have a higher priority (control priority). It executes the state controller operations, then it reads the object state data in critical section (all data concerning object state, concurrency or attributes and the schedule are accessed and modified in critical section to ensure the integrity of the data while parallel accesses). Assuming, we have no state problem, then it continues its control. It manages the concurrency at the attributes level. Assuming, also that there is no concurrency problem, it modifies the attributes access list in critical section and arrives in scheduling controller operations. Then, it updates in critical section the schedule. Assuming that all processors are available, then it executes the methods attached to the message. After the method execution is completed, the thread suspends itself and resumes a pending thread.

The **worst case** corresponds to the following situation: the application is multi
« *zones* »; object state is not good; attributes are used by an another method; processor
resources are used by other message in another « *zone* ». First, a thread *T* is resumed
by the caller emitting the message. This thread *T* pre-empts the caller, because it have
a higher priority (control priority). It executes the state controller operations, but the
object state is not according with the method state, then *T* suspends itself. When
another message modifies the object state, it makes a « *resume* » on the thread *T*. If the
new state is according with the message, *T* continues and executes the concurrency
controller operations. But, as some attributes are used, then *T* suspends itself again.
When another message completes its execution, it liberates the used object attributes
and makes a « *resume* » on *T*. Assuming the attributes are now free, *T* continues its
controls and executes the scheduling controller operations. The processor resource is
used by another message *M* from another « *zone* » *i*. Then, the scheduling controller
puts a « *suspend* » order in the *ThreadsManagerMailbox* of the other « *zone* » *i* and
unlocks the cross-process semaphore associated to this *ThreadsManagerMailbox*.
After, the *ThreadsManager* of the « *zone* » *i* pre-empts the processings, executes the
order « *suspend* » and locks itself on its semaphore (waiting an another order). Now,
the resource processor is available, the thread *T* can execute the associated message.
When it completes its execution, it updates the information inside its object and
executes all « *resume* » according the modification into the object and locks itself with
its semaphore in the *ThreadsManager*.

The first table below summarises for both cases the operations performed by the
operating system. The second give timing evaluations allowing to compare relative
costs of the operations. The data used are these given for the given VxWorks on a
68040/33 MHz machine with cache memory enable. The execution time unit used for
evaluating the ratios is the semaphore lock (with contention).

OS operation	VxWorks	
Lock (local) semaphore	8 μs	1
Unlock (local) semaphore	15 μs	2
Thread suspend or resume	10 μs	1
Message processing system cost for *best case*	158 μs	20
Message processing system cost for *worst case*	228 μs	29

Because VxWorks is a single process OS, it provides no cross-process semaphore.
Thus, the worst case is considered with real-time object being in the same « *zone* ».
For Solaris 2.5, timing data are either not provided either unclear, so we have not
included them in this table. However, one can consider from the constructor data that
locks and unlocks on cross-process semaphore (C-P locks & unlocks) are two times
more expensive than on local one (i. e., 105 μs instead of 48 μs). In any case we must
remember that manual programming of the same functionality in an application would
need a quite similar sequence of operations and thus this cost is not a cost induced by
the object orientation but by the application requirement : *dynamic activation of tasks
(here, message passing to real-time objects) that can share data (here, the object
concurrency constraints) with dynamic and contextual conditions that can inhibit the*

task activation (here, the object state constraints) and with deadline constraints (managed by the global schedulers).

Real-time object control operations	Best case op.	Worst case added op.
Message send	1 resume	
1 Create a request and select a free thread for the message	*resumes* a thread	
Message receipt by the RT object	3 lock & unlock	+ 3 resume, 4 suspend 2 C-P locks & unlocks
1 State constraints analysis *When state constraints are OK*	*lock & unlock*	+ *suspend* self thread + *resume* a thread
2 Concurrency constraints analysis *When concurrency constraints are OK*	*lock & unlock*	+ *suspend* self thread + *resumes* a thread
3 Update the schedule plan	*lock & unlock*	+ *C-P lock & unlock suspends* self thread
a Send order to the other « zone »		+ *C-P lock & unlock suspend* self thread
b When a processor is free → The message is processed		+ *resume* a thread
Message processing end:	3 lock & unlock semaphore, 1 resume	
1 Update the schedule plan	*lock* semaphore & *unlock*	
2 Update the list of used attributes	*lock* semaphore & *unlock*	
3 Update the object state	*lock* semaphore & *unlock*	
4 Activate next message processing	*resume* a thread	

8 Remarks

In this architecture, when the application creates a real-time object, it provides a new source of parallelism. More the machine can perform parallel processing and more an application with a great number of real-time objects can take benefit of the material resources. Small passive objects may be encapsulated into a greatest real-time object, this design implies the serialisation of the treatments delegated to the encapsulated passive objects. As for classical multitasks architecture, the processing execution time of each tasks (messages) should remain great in regards to the internal mechanisms of the operating system. So, when a real-time object provides methods implemented with few instructions (e.g., just returning a value) the execution of this method will be performed under the control mechanisms of the real-time object but in the thread of the caller. This avoids architecture overhead for small operations. Sometimes, the designer can need shared passive objects (i.e. with concurrency control but without creation of parallelism). These objects will be declared as *« protected objects »* and will exploit the state and concurrency control modules of the real-time objects without the elements dedicated to the thread management.

This architecture does not provide specific solution for solving the deadlock problem due to eventual dependency existing between different objects. This problem has to be analysed and solved at the design step by dedicated mechanisms based on knowledge on application structure and properties.

9 Conclusions and Future Works

The major advantage of this architecture is that all the controllers are encapsulated in the objects which permits their parallel execution and favours parallel processing of messages. Since the controllers have been designed to be multithread, this ensures parallelism also for the control. Hence the message control will not slow down the application specific treatments, nor will be slowed down by the arrival of other messages. The overhead due to real-time dynamic scheduling is limited. We have a minimum time to create a new message. Moreover, this architecture optimises scheduling communications between different « zones ». Distribution is being contemplated but in a static (logical) way, i.e. without any migration of objects (usually time consuming). Moreover, in most applications, hardware resources are managed by specific machines and their control cannot therefore migrate to other machines. The scheduling problem is then local to each site and our architecture is able to manage such distributed applications. This architecture is being implemented in C++ with the CLASS-RELATION object-oriented method and evaluated on SUN Sparc 10 bi-processors machine with Solaris 2.5. The first results are demonstrate the feasibility of the architecture. We are now studying an extension of the architecture to inter-site management (distribution) and especially transaction problems.

10 Bibliography

1. Atkinson, C., *Object-oriented reuse, concurrency and distribution : an Ada-based approach*. 1991. Addison-Wesley.
2. Chetto, H. , Delacroix, J. *Minimisation des Temps de Réponse des Tâches Sporadiques en présence des tâches périodiques*. in *Conf. on Real-Time Systems*. Paris, France, 1993.
3. Chetto, H., Silly, M., Bouchentoul, T., *Dynamic scheduling of real-time tasks under precedence constraints*. Real-Time Systems, 1990. Vol. 2: p. 184-194.
4. Fouquier, G., *Programmation temps réel à objets : études et propositions*1996, Mémoire de thèse de l'Université d'Orsay, Paris XI, 1996.
5. Fouquier, G., Terrier, F. *Introducing priorities into a C++ based actor language for multithread machines*. in *Conf. TOOLS PACIFIC'94*. Melbourne, Australia, 1994.
6. Ishikawa, Y. et al. *Object-oriented real-time language design: Constructs for timing constraints*. in *ECOOP &OOPSLA'90*. Ottawa, 1990. V25 ACM SIGPLAN Not. p.289-298.
7. Leung, J.Y.T., Merill, M.L., *A Note on Pre-emptive Scheduling of Periodic Real-time Tasks*. Information Processing Letters, 1980. Vol. 20(3): p. 115-118.
8. Liu, C.L., Layland, J.W., *Scheduling algorithms for multiprogramming in a hard real-time environement*. Journal of the ACM, 1973. V20(1): p. 46-61.
9. Nierstrasz, O. *Active objects in Hybrid*. in *Conference OOPSLA'87*. 1987. Vol. 22. ACM SIGPLAN Notices: p. 243-253.
10. Nigro, L., Tisato, F., *RTO++: A framework for building hard real-time systems*. Journal of object-oriented programming (JOOP), 1993. (May): p. 35-47.
11. Rioux, L. et al. *A control architecture for C++ real-time objects*. in *Conf. TOOLS Pacific'96*. Melbourne, Australia, 1996: p. 61-73.
12. Takashio, K., Tokoro, M. *DROL: An object-oriented programming language for distributed real-time systems*. in *Conf. OOPSLA'92*. V27. ACM SIGPLAN Not. p.276-294.
13. Terrier, F., Fouquier, G. *Vers des objets temps réel*. in *Object Expo*. Paris, France, 1995.
14. Terrier, F. et al. *A Real Time Object Model*. in *TOOLS Europe'96*. Paris, France, 1996.

An Object Communication Architecture for Real-Time Distributed Process Control

Christian Toinard[1] and Nicolas Chevassus[2]

[1] LaBRI/ENSERB, 351 cours de la Libération, 33405 Talence Cedex, France
[2] AEROSPATIALE - Centre Commun de Recherches,12 rue Pasteur, BP 76, 92152
Suresnes Cedex, France
e-mail: toinard@labri.u-bordeaux.fr, NICOLAS.CHEVASSUS@siege.aerospatiale.fr

Abstract. We consider the automation and supervision software applications that are the first levels of the Computer Integrated Manufacturing hierarchy. We define that the application requires time properties (a bounded time exchange and/or a time validity) and ordering properties (a causal and total order). We explain the interest and the difficulties to get these two properties in an asynchronous context. Our communication architecture is composed of three asynchronous systems. A field bus provides mainly time properties for the automation. A client-server system allows exchanges between the automation and the supervision. The multicast memory system provides order and time validity properties for both the supervision and the automation.

1 Problems solved by the communication architecture

The automation requires time properties. For example, when a tank is full, a signal is raised by a sensor object and communicated to a remote actuator object that stops filling the tank. This signal must be communicated in a bounded time otherwise the tank overflows. Moreover, the actuator object must know the time validity of the signal in order to run an emergency processing when the time validity is false. The command of a valve and the resulting indication of opening are two process events that are causally related. Generally, a causal order is used for satisfying the causality between the events. In [7], we show that either a causal order or a total order can be used. Moreover, a total order helps to get a fault tolerant behavior. At the supervision level, an alarm notification and a cancelation are two causally related events. An operator must observe these events according to their causal relation in order to know that the alarm has been canceled. Again, a causal order or a total order can be used. Moreover, a total order allows the operator to observe the process events in the same order on redundant workstations. The alarm can be processed late if the system fails to perform the exchange quickly. The time validity of the alarm variable can be managed for warning the operator of a possible missing (late) information. The application can require simultaneously time and order properties.

Now, we explain the difficulties to get both time and order in an asynchronous system. At the automation level, the asynchronous Factory Instrumentation Protocol (FIP) field bus [12] performs a bounded time update for multiple copies of a variable and provides the time validity to the consumers of the variable. A bus controller avoids the competition for the bus and an update is performed through two broadcasts. The update is performed periodically. FIP is an asynchronous system because no global time is defined and the update succeeds in the requested period when no transmission error occurs (otherwise, the update can occur late and the bounded time exchange is not satisfied). The FIP standardization does not define an order property. In [8], we use a formal result [3] to show that FIP provides a causal and total order at a low production speed. For a higher production speed, a solution [9] is defined but we lose the time properties. So, we show the difficulties to get both time and order properties with an asynchronous field bus. Generally, at the supervision level, multicast systems built in an asynchronous environment provide order properties [4] [6] [11]. One layer of protocol is defined for the causal order and another one for the total order.

The asynchronous hypothesis is interesting because it corresponds to many commercial networks like Ethernet, Transmission Control Protocol/Internet Protocol (TCP/IP) and many field buses. Generally, field buses provide time properties and multicast systems, defined in asynchronous context, provide ordering. So, we see the interest of a proposition for time and order properties in the asynchronous context. With the propositions in a synchronous context like [1] [2], we have to pay for special hardwares or softwares in order to get a global time.

2 An architecture for the automation and the supervision

A memory exchange allows efficient communications for automation, client-server and supervision domains.

The automation classically uses a memory service through a field bus. In that case, the multiple copies define the *automation memory*.

For client-server exchanges between the supervision and the automation, a memory access is also classically used and a variable exists in a single copy on the remote server. Like defined in [10], a supervision object (client) accesses to an automation variable (server) through a Common Object Request Broker Architecture (CORBA). A variable is an object with read/write methods. Conversely, an automation object calls a supervision variable through CORBA. CORBA solves the heterogeneity problem and runs over a standard TCP/IP network.

This paper complements these two first systems previously studied. We propose a *multicast memory* that satisfies the supervision requirements. Multiple copies of the same variable are managed. Read and write operations are provided on a variable.

CORBA is used as an integration tool for the multicast memory system. A variable is a CORBA object that is designated with a name. This name corresponds to a group of copies. Two methods allow read and write operations. A variable can be written by multiple producers and read by multiple consumers. Each station runs a memory server that performs the multicast memory service for the local consuming and producing clients and manages a copy of the requested variables. A client calls some methods that are executed by the memory server. Read method is executed locally by a memory server that returns the value to of its copy to the client. The memory server performs a write method by multicasting an update to a group of memory servers. For this purpose, it is interesting that the CORBA system allows to send a request to a group. Each server of the group received the update and manages a copy of the corresponding variable. CORBA allows the update to be processed by heterogeneous servers.

The memory service allows to get the time validity of a variable. The basic idea is to associate a variable with periodic constraints. One period is defined for production. One period is defined for the network. The variables with periodic constraints define the *(periodic) multicast memory*. The producer must write the variable periodically according to the production constraint of the variable. As each write is performed like an update, the variable is periodically updated. A consumer gets a production validity and a network validity when reading a variable through two status that are maintained by each memory server of the group. These status are computed by the server using two local timers. A first timer is set according to the production period on a server. When the producing client writes, the timer status (on or off) is transmitted by the server in the update and the timer is restarted. This production status allows a server to know the production validity. On a receiving server, a second timer is set according to the network period. When a time out occurs, the network status becomes false. When an update is received, the timer is restarted. A server returns the two time validity status to a consuming client. With the network status, a consuming client knows if the update has been performed since the last one within the network constraint. With the production status, a consuming client knows, when reading, whether the producer wrote at time. The semantics is not far from the time validity of the FIP field bus.

The multicast memory provides a causally and totally ordered service. For this purpose, a third indication method is proposed. The indication method returns the name of the next ordered variable that can be read. Thus, a consuming client can read orderly the indicated variables. The multicast memory uses a server of order like defined in [3]. We build a totally ordered multicast. In order to perform the update, a memory server addresses an update request to the server of order. Then, the server of order sends the update to the group of memory servers. Two messages are required for an update: one point to point message with one local sequence number and one broadcast on the underlying network (or a multicast on the underlying network) with one global sequence number (or a vector of global sequence numbers). A receiving server reorders the updates according to their global sequence numbers like defined in [3]. The solution can be improved according to the data size. We get a causal property by proof [3].

Thus, a consumer reads the values in a causal and total order according to the indications and gets the time validity of the read values. No bounded time update can be guaranteed. The system can recover from the transmission errors (i.e. the server of order performs retransmissions).

The automation can use the multicast memory and compensate for lack of ordering (at a high production speed) with the automation memory. The multicast memory can be faster than the automation memory but without guarantee. The automation gets the time validity in a rather close way, than the automation memory. Moreover, the multicast memory performs a redundancy for the automation memory. Thus, the automation gets a redundant communication channel. The time properties of the multicast memory are not far from the automation memory and the automation can use it for a rescue processing.

3 Conclusion

We tackle three needs: real time properties, integration of existing solutions and standard components. We define a memory service. An automation variable gets a bounded time update (when no transmission error occurs) and a time validity with a standard field bus. This automation memory provides a causal and total order at a low speed. Client-server exchanges are performed through CORBA. Here, a multicast memory allows causally and totally ordered reading of variables and provides a time validity. The multicast is used by the supervision and offers a complementary quality of service for the automation. Moreover, the automation can use it as a redundant memory. A unique interface with read/write CORBA methods is defined for the three systems.

References

1. Cornilleau, T., Gressier-Soudan, E., Horn, F., Lizzi, C.: Cohérence causale temporelle. Proceedings Real Times Systems, Paris (1997)
2. Cristian, F.: Synchronous atomic broadcast for redundant broadcast channels. Journal of Real-Times Systems **2** (1990) 195-212
3. Florin, G., Toinard, C.: A new way to design causally and totally ordered multicast protocols. ACM Operating Systems Review **26, 4** (1992)
4. Friedman, R.: Using Virtual Synchrony to develop Efficient Fault Tolerant Distributed Shared Memories. TR95- 1506 Cornell University (1995)
5. OMG: The Common Object Request Broker: Architecture and Specification. Document Number **91.12.1**, John Wiley & Sons (1992)
6. Van Renesse, R., Hickey, T. M., Birman, K.P.: Design and performance of Horus: a lightweight group communications system. TR **94-1442**, Cornell University, (1994)
7. Toinard, C.: Protocoles pour diffusion ordonnée: Chapter in Réseaux de Communications et conception de protocoles, Hermès (1995)
8. Toinard, C., Chevassus, N.: De nouvelles architectures de communication pour le contrôle de procédé industriel: vers une répartition massive et tolérante aux fautes. Proc. Real Times Systems, Paris, (1996)
9. Toinard, C., Chevassus, N.: Une nouvelle architecture de communication pour le temps réel réparti. Proc. Real Times Systems, Paris (1997)
10. Toinard, C., Chevassus, N.: CORBA for distributed and fault tolerant process control. ECOOP97 Workshop CORBA: Implement. Use and Evaluat., Finland (1997)
11. Amir, Y., Dolev, D., Kramer, S., Malki, D.: Transis: A communication subsystem for high availability. Annual Symp. on Fault Tolerant Computing Number 22, (1992)
12. UTE: Norme 46-602, FIP Couche application. (1990)

RT-Objects Based on Temporal Causal Consistency: A New Approach for Fieldbus Systems

T. Cornilleau, E. Gressier-Soudan
Cnam, Laboratoire Cedric, 292 rue St Martin 75141 Paris Cedex 03 FRANCE
vercor@cnam.fr, gressier@cnam.fr

Abstract : We describe a new object-oriented approach for fieldbus systems. It shows how Temporal Causal Consistency applies to fieldbus environments and how it can be used to support real-time objects for control process applications.

1. Introduction

Fieldbuses are used to build control process applications that share real-time variables among different entities. Fieldbus environments offer an industrial distributed data base management facility [7]. We describe a new object-oriented approach for fieldbus systems based on Temporal Causal Consistency (TCC) that applies to fieldbus environments. This scheme can support real-time objects [11] for control process applications. TCC emerges from the study of consistency management in the field of distributed shared memory. It extend Causal Consistency proposed by Ahamad et al. [1] with real-time constraints as deadlines and lifetimes associated to shared data [3].

Fieldbuses [11] are currently presented as networks that link raw devices like actuators, sensors, to process controllers. Fieldbuses are layered communication architectures that correspond to the communication layers 1, 2 and 7. It is a classical message passing oriented solution. This classical approach has several drawbacks. It is difficult to implement shared variables based applications using message passing based systems. Application designers have to translate variables access into message requests. The consistency of shared variables offered to applications in fieldbuses systems is supposed to be strong : every entity sees the same value everywhere. Else, they see an undefined value if a variable has not been refreshed before an associated timeout. Shared variable consistency management in fieldbuses requires intensive update messages. It is bandwith consuming. The fieldbus message-oriented programming interface is not suited to the design of safe object-oriented applications with modern methodologies. We provide a brand new point of view for fieldbus systems based on a distributed system approach. We provide an answer for each previous given drawback. We propose a distributed shared variables framework to support applications. It is very close to the simple shared variable programming paradigm. It provides a better support for the distributed real-time database model of fieldbus systems. We propose a weaker consistency model based on causal relationships between variables accesses. Using this approach, spatial and temporal properties are defined uniformely among all variables. We present an original object-oriented distributed system design of fieldbus systems : application entities are supported as real-time active objects, the distributed data base is supported by a sub-system managing the distributed shared and consistent real-time variables.

2. Fieldbus Environment Model

The fieldbus communication model between Manufacturing Devices and Application Entities is "shared variable oriented". We chose the Factory Instrumentation Protocol

(FIP) architecture as a starting basic model [7]. We are interested by FIP because it makes the hypothesis of a real-time synchronous communication model. It makes an explicit reference to time properties for data. Real-time constraints are : variable timestamping, acuracy, freshness, validity, and deadlines. This simplifies the use of temporal causal consistency for fieldbus environments.

Variable basics : Variables are : simple (booleans, integers, reals, strings), structured types (arrays, records, lists...). Variables can be replicated or not depending on sharing patterns. There is only one writer per variable, unless fault tolerance is required. Addressing variables doesn't need to specifiy a destination host or an application. An important aspect of fieldbuses is that variables are named explicitly and globally in the fieldbus environment, like it is in distributed systems. Two models are encountered to modify variable values : aperiodic state changes (event driven model) or periodic produced values (state driven model). FIP communication services ensure two important properties : the spatial and the temporal consistency of distributed shared variables. A status field is associated to each variable replica to characterize its temporal consistency. If a value is too old or if the delivery of the variable value misses its deadline, its status becomes false, the variable cannot be consummed anyway. To ensure spatial consistency, the value of replicated variables has to be the same everywhere. This requirement is called strong consistency. As described below, our model is weaker, we stress that the corresponding spatial consistency that we propose is better suited to real-time environments.

Interaction basics : Interaction models in fieldbus environments are the producer/consumer and the client/server models.

Application basics : Real manufacturing devices or process control entities, use fieldbus services to access local or remote variables values : they can read or write them. There is always two local copies of a variable on a site : the application private copy and the communication environment copy. When an operation is performed, the private copy (local) is always accessed. The fieldbus communication system handles the update of the communication system copies independently of local accesses. During a remote access all the distributed copies in the fieldbus network environment are updated. Hight level entities can be notified of changes. Entities are synchronous or asynchronous. Synchronous entities execute when they receive an update notification about the local copy of a data. Asynchronous entities execute indepently from the network. They work with their private copy. When they need the copy of the communication environment, they perform an explicit swapping request, called resynchronization. In the following, we will consider only synchronous application entities. So, we do not need two local copies of the same variable on a site in our architecture.

3. Supporting application RT-Objects with Temporal Causal Consistency

We describes now an object-oriented approach of the previous model based on the distributed shared memory paradigm. Control process applications use two kinds of data: variables and process components abstractions. Variables describe data in a way that is very close to the process while components abstractions represent application elements. The two levels are complementary sides of the same environment. The set of variables defines a Distributed Real-Time DataBase (DRTDB) while the component abstractions can be implemented as active objects that perform read or write within the DRTDB. In the following, we are going to describe how this architecture is handled in our design and how it can be used for fieldbus environments.

Underlying System Support : In our design, we suppose that communications are deterministic, real-time constraints on communications are expressed in terms of Quality of Service [2]. Inter-process communication mailboxes use directly the communication channel. We expect that site kernels support deadline scheduling for message delivery. Clocks of kernels are synchronized [8] either by hardware or by software. Our solution can be implemented with current on-the-shelf hardware and software components as PC boards, ATM networks, real-time kernels.

Real-Time Objects : Classical application entities in networked architectures correspond, in our proposal, to active real-time objects [9]. These active objects are called real-time objects. A real-time object interfaces the DRTDB with process devices as board, computer, programmable logic controller... or with application software components. A real-time object is local to a site. It needs a subset of the DRTDB variables to perform its computation. During its computation, it reads or writes these variables locally. It reads a variable if it is its consumer. It writes a variable if it is its producer. Each variable is replicated on the site that needs it. For a variable read, if the variable has a true status, the real-time object can read it, else it triggers a read fault that the DRTDB subsystem handles. For a variable write, a real time object requires the ownership of the variable locally. A site owns a variable when it grants the write access, only one site at a time is the owner of a variable. When it gets the ownership, it can modify it. The resolution of a read or a write fault triggers message exchanges between the current owner of the variable and the requiering real-time object. This fault handling model use less network and system bandwith than the broadcast of new values in traditionnal fieldbuses. More than one real-time object can write a variable in our environment. We suppose that a deadline is associated to each variable operation, it can vary along application lifetime. The DRTDB subsystem ensures that a fault is solved before the associated deadline expires, else the status of the variable becomes false, and the corresponding real-time object has to retry its access. Deadlines insure accuracy. We expect that deadline failures are avoided by a correct performance study at the design phasis of the application. The deadline feature allows to ensure the temporal consistency property required by fieldbus systems.

Distributed Real-Time Database : DRTDB management is based on TCC [3]. Causal Consistency (CC) [1] is derived from causal message delivery [6] : a write access corresponds to a message send and a read access corresponds to a message delivery. CC ensures that a read operation issues a value associated to the most causally recent write. With CC, a site is ensured that any data read will not return a value causally older than an already known value. CC handling does not need invalidation messages as required for strong consistency, data invalidations are deduced from variables causal relationship patterns. Current CC implementations allow one writer and many readers simultaneously [4]. CC is a weaker consistency than the strong consistency offered by fieldbus systems but it still matches applications spatial consistency requirements. TCC extends CC by adding lifetimes to variables values, a variable value cannot be read past its lifetime, its status becomes false. This scheme provides freshness to applications. Moreover, it ensures the liveness of the DRTDB system. The lifetime can be changed along application cycle of life too. Real-Time Objects access local DRTDB variables, the underlying TCC management sub-system performs variable updates and invalidations transparently.

4. Conclusion

Temporal Causal Consistency ensures a temporal and weak spatial consistency for the DRTDB associated to a fieldbus environment. Our scheme fits the producer/consumer model : writers create values that readers use, values come to the readers in a bounded time, and values expire past their lifetime. Our proposal is based on a copy-on-access model while classical fieldbus environments require continuous broadcast of modifications. Consequently, we do not need any broadcast facility. However, to ensure fault tolerance or availability, our proposal can be extended with a multicast facility: each time a consumer makes a read, all other consumers can get the same required data.

The full implementation is under development. Current work has improved standard causal consistency implementation based on logical time. Causal consistency is built on top of the Chorus micro-kernel [4] using system memory servers. This step asserted the global behaviour of our prototype. To implement temporal causal consistency, we will replace version counters by physical time issued by synchronized clocks. Deadlines and lifetimes associated to data have to be added.

A distributed system approach is adopted also in [10]. Their main goal is to offer fault-tolerance properties. Whilst our proposal is based on a distributed shared memory approach, these authors handle the real-time database of a fieldbus system with ordered multicast group communications. Additionnally, we can extend our model with object oriented industrial messaging services provided through an object request broker [5].

References

1. Causal Memory - M. Ahamad, J.E. Burns, P.W. Hutto, G. Neiger - 5th Int. Workshop on Dist. Alg., pages 9-30 - Springer-Verlag - 1991
2. A Quality of Service Architecture. A. Campbell. PhD Thesis. Lancaster University. January 1996. England.
3. Cohérence Causale Temporelle. T. Cornilleau. E. Gressier-Soudan. F. Horn. C. Lizzi. RTS'97. Paris. January 1997.
4. Etudes des Cohérences Mémoire Uniformes - Cohérence Causale: mise en oeuvre sur CHORUS et extensions. T. Cornilleau. PhD Thesis. Cnam. Paris. January 1997.
5. COOL-MMS: a CORBA approach to ISO-MMS. G.Guyonet, E. Gressier, F. Weis. ECOOP'97. Workshop : CORBA: Implementation, Use and Evaluation. Jyväskylä. Finland. June 1997.
6. Time, clocks, and the ordering of events in a distributed system - L. Lamport - Communications of the ACM, 21(7):558-565, July 1978.
7. Le bus de terrain FIP. P. Leterrier, J-P. Thomesse. Personnal Communication. 1991.
8. B. Liskov. "Practical Uses of Synchronized Clocks in Distributed Systems". Distributed Computing. Vol. 6, p211-219, 1993.
9 A Real Time Object Model. F. Terrier, G. Fouquier, D. Bras, L. Rioux, P. Vanuxeem, A. Lanusse. Conference on Technology of Object-Oriented Languages and Systems. Prentice Hall Editor. Paris. France. 1996.
10.An object communication architecture for RT distributed process control. C. Toinard, N. Chevassus. ECOOP'97. Workshop : OO Technology and Real Time Systems. Jyväskylä. Finland. June 1997.
11.http://cran.esstin.u-nancy.fr/CRAN/Cran/ESSTIN/FieldBus.html

Configuring Realtime CORBA Systems for Telecom Applications

Julien Maisonneuve

Alcatel Telecom Research Division

Abstract. This paper presents the main features of a programming environment for distributed real-time applications. The originality of the approach lies within the integration of a software development cycle and a set of tools to build and configure complete application images on various platforms with no code modification. The outcome of this work is composed of two prototypes, one of which is relying on CORBA and is highly portable.

1 Introduction

Telecom systems are an area where a lot of stress is put on software. Today, as systems grow in complexity and number, additional requirements are appearing : they must be highly available, tolerate various failures, be highly interoperable, scale gracefully over distributed architectures, allow for partial software evolution and replacement and provide interoperability with myriads of legacy systems.

Traditional real-time system development involved a lot of experience and tuning, leading to low productivity in the design of these systems. The explosive growth and complexity of current telecom software systems renders this approach less and less practical, as these techniques are not well scalable. This problem is aggravated by the increased demand for high productivity and flexible services that characterizes the competitive telecom market.

New Object-Oriented technologies seem to open a promising way to better structure software systems in general, and give interesting results in a lot of domains. They offer an opportunity to improve the structuring and modularity of telecom systems, and allow smoother evolution and portability. There are however specific requirements to telecom applications that need to be addressed.

We introduce a development framework based on a software development methodology and a set of services adapted to the telecom environment. Its originality lies in a comprehensive approach to development and focus on telecom applications requirements.

2 The CORBA approach

Among the popular approaches, CORBA provides very useful properties like distribution transparency and broad interoperability. However, the behavior of CORBA in realtime settings is insufficiently specified. To avoid these problems, one must pay close attention to elements that impact real-time performance such as thread control and memory management. Additionally, the communication model underlying traditional ORBs lacks support for elaborate interactions (beyond the synchronous/asynchronous dichotomy) or specialized communication protocols and offers incomplete support for managing communication failures. Ongoing proposals will answer some of these problems, but there is a need for a comprehensive approach to simplify the development process, still very complex in CORBA.

Real-time systems have specific communication needs that are not always adapted to the original CORBA model based on client-server interactions. Specifically, asynchronous calls are predominant, but with specifications in excess of what is specified for CORBA's oneway invocations. Deferred synchronous invocations are also required, and CORBA offers them only through the impractical DII.

While CORBA provides useful tools to build distributed applications, it is not sufficient to build correct and fault tolerant applications alone. A number of proposals addressing some of the shortcomings are under review, but will probably not constitute a coherent framework adapted to telecom fault-tolerant applications development.

3 Our Approach

We are working on a support framework for dependable real-time applications. Our objective is to integrate the benefits of Object-Oriented technologies and distributed systems in telecommunication applications. We use CORBA as a foundation to provide distribution transparency and provide additional services for real-time and dependable computing. In the same way, we try to provide a high degree of fault-tolerance transparency.

This framework was originally developed on a proprietary platform and a new implementation has been developed with COOL/ORB, leveraging advantages of CORBA while preserving the benefits of a well-specified telecom environment. COOL/ORB is a CORBA-compliant ORB aimed at the embedded and real-time market.

We are working in collaboration with Chorus Systems to tailor COOL/ORB in order to provide adequate support for real-time operation. Particular attention has been paid to invocation scheduling , priority management and ORB timeliness. We also designed mechanisms to help fault tolerance and recovery capabilities within the ORB framework.

Our approach is designed to provide a comprehensive approach along the development cycle, taking into account development and integration aspects and managing real-time constraints. It offers a structuring model, tools and runtime environment for building dependable and fault tolerant applications. It helps isolating the application environment from the underlying system and hardware architecture, enhancing portability and reusability. It also helps in deploying the same application on different target platforms with minimal modifications.

The development approach emphasizes the definition of static properties in the application to help both sizing and static property verification in the system.

4 Development process

Telecommunication applications are usually developed in roughly 3 steps. The first is specification where functional modules are identified. The second is deployment where an actual configuration using the software modules defined in the first step is set up and mapped on a hardware platform. The third step is the application execution, likely in an hostile environment with little support from the outside to overcome problems and errors.

Our architecture respects this structuration by decoupling the component development and configuration steps.

The development phase consists in defining software components along with their interfaces. It consists in building object classes, defining their interfaces in traditional CORBA IDL, and specifying object properties (related to persistence, concurrency,...) and module dependencies in an Object Description Language (ODL). The ODL is specialized for the purpose of the framework.

The deployment phase specifies how components should be plugged together (logical mapping), how they are mapped on an hardware architecture (physical mapping) and how they share resources (locked memory, threads, priorities). It also specifies which modules are initially created and where, and how many dynamic instances may be created. This is done with a specialized configuration language (CDL), which is based on on a set of attributes defined at the application, node, capsule and object level.

The execution phase benefits from the fault-tolerance mechanisms built within the architecture and from additional guidelines imposed on the module programmers.

5 Support for Fault Tolerance

The framework supports semi-transparent fault tolerance. Applications objects are checkpointed on stable storage when requested. When a capsule crashes, it is restarted in a restoration state, from which the application can rebuild its own state using the stored data. The runtime ensures that the communication channels with other capsules remain valid through capsule restoration.

The ODL specifies the dependable state of each object, and checkpoint methods to save it to stable storage (checkpoint functions will later be generated automatically from data declarations). It also specifies what action should be invoked in the event of a crash. This allows the application to master its own recovery process from checkpointed data on a per object basis.

6 Key Concepts

The programming model is composed of several elements :

- capsules (akin to processes)
- nodes (akin to processors)
- objects (concurrent or not)
- logical object identifiers

Objects are instantiated within capsules and are designated with logical identifiers. They can be invoked from any other capsule transparently. Objects can be created in any capsule by type-specific factories. The creation capsule selection being dynamic, it allows load sharing between nodes. The creation policy (what is created where, associated resources) is defined within the system configuration.

7   The programming environment

The programming environment enriches the CORBA environment and IDL compiler with an ODL compiler and a configuration management tool.

The runtime is responsible for the respect of the specific object properties specified in the configuration step (realtime constraints, concurrency). It handles the creation, destruction and locking of objects, the management of resources and of logical object identifiers.

The ODL and IDL compilers generate skeletons for user programs in conformance with the specification. The configuration tool allows to connect components together and map the resulting application on a specific hardware configuration, taking into account specific real-time and capacity constraints.

8   Conclusion

We have designed a framework for telecom applications that takes advantage of distributed Object-Oriented technologies such as CORBA, adding concerns for dependability, fault-tolerance and real time. Two separate implementations now exist, one on a proprietary platform and the other on a tailored CORBA ORB. Test applications are being developed to assess the validity of the architecture.

The current research areas are to integrate more formal aspects of the software development process within the framework. We are looking into the integration of development methods (such as specification languages or OMT). We are also integrating test methodologies and to support them in the runtime by providing specialized hooks. There is ongoing work on object-oriented database integration, group-based fault-tolerance policies and coexistence of applications developed within and outside the framework.

New Complexities in the Embedded World – The OTI Approach

Kim Clohessy, Brian Barry, and Peter Tanner
Object Technology International Inc.

1. Complexity – The Emerging Embedded Problem

The embedded software world is facing a significant increase in complexity. Walk through an embedded-systems conference or scan the trade magazines and you will see the arrival — with a vengeance — of a new generation of high-performance, highly integrated microcontrollers from almost all the main silicon vendors. These new, low-cost devices are accelerating the competitive pressures to deliver embedded products that have more features while at the same time are more user friendly. Customers want more integration and connectivity throughout their systems. They expect flexible and configurable products. Products that were once stand-alone applications are now expected to be components of larger systems. There is also a growing need for dynamically downloadable application components. To make the software developer's job even harder, add the need for application portability and the demand for customizations. Then add the emphasis on "time to profit." Hardware costs will no longer preclude the delivery of such solutions. The limiting factor will be software.

It is becoming painfully clear that the current methodologies that most embedded-system developers use will not keep pace with the complexity of these demands, and the embedded problems were difficult problems to begin with. The complexity problem is not simply a design problem; complexity is present throughout the life cycle of the product — from determining product requirements through design, build, debug, test, configuration of product lines, customizations, and upgrades over the life of the product family. New approaches are required to deal with this complexity.

2. Dealing with Complexity

There is currently no silver bullet [1] in the offing; however, progress is being made with methodologies and tools that will help deal with the complexity. The change with the largest potential effect is the ability to move from low-level programming to the ability to build software systems by integrating components. This is the same move that we saw in the hardware world. However, this move needs an infrastructure that properly deals with components and provides the tools to create, exchange, browse, experiment with, debug, test, and glue together these components into larger components and then into systems.

What characteristics will be needed in these new approaches and tools?

First, designing from the ground up is no longer viable: reuse is not just nice to have, it is a necessity. The new approach needs tools — not just languages — that deliver reuse. The tools must address rapid development as well as the lifecycle management of application code. The tools must help the developer to explore the problem through prototyping and modeling. The tools must be more than just procedures; they must allow developers to get products rapidly built, tested, and shipped. The tools that will be successful will be the tools that allow smaller teams of domain experts to build and deliver high-quality, extensible software. The tools must provide real portability because market pressure and hardware advances will require approaches that permit easy migration from one hardware platform to another. The tools must be based on higher-level languages that scale down to these new embedded platforms. These approaches must handle continuous improvement comfortably. The tools must look beyond holding the line; they must address the need to deliver more features faster and do so using fewer resources.

In this paper, we discuss some of these requirements and then describe the approaches that OTI took with **ENVY**/*Embedded*, a Smalltalk-based development and execution environment for real-time embedded systems.

3. New Ways of Organizing to Deal with Complexity

OO methodologies address complexity by encouraging developers to view embedded systems as groups of interacting real-world objects. This approach provides a more natural way to think about a system and makes embedded systems easier to understand, reason about, and discuss. It results in software partitioning that is more flexible. Ultimately, with experience, it delivers real reuse, which is the greatest potential source of productivity gains. However, OO methodologies are not enough. Tools are required that span the design, prototyping, development, execution, and maintenance processes.

3.1 Browsing Tools to Permit Reuse

Rapid deployment of embedded systems will result in large parts of the system being constructed from reusable components, many of which may come from third-party sources. This means that the development process is, in large part, a process of browsing components and their interfaces to determine how they are to be used. In addition, this development process requires the ability to quickly and cheaply experiment with the components. Application developers need to be able to evaluate a component against possible use cases and to experiment with alternatives.

Eventually, we expect that software component interfaces will undergo the same evolution as hardware component interfaces: evolve from discrete, non-standard interfaces to well-documented, standard interfaces. This will make it possible to make automatic or assisted tools for integrating and assembling components.

3.2   Higher-Level Languages for More Productivity

Dynamic languages such as Smalltalk and Java are demonstrably more productive than C, C++, and assembly language. However, developers are unnecessarily afraid of perceived performance penalties. In typical embedded real-time systems, we claim that the 90/10 rule applies: 10 percent of the code is truly time critical; 90 percent is associated with functions such as configuration control, user interfaces, report generation, and so on. These functions usually need to run at human interface speeds (hundreds of milliseconds) rather than hardware interface speeds (in the millisecond and microsecond ranges).

We are not claiming that all systems or system problems can be solved at the component level and written in Smalltalk or Java. There will still be a requirement to build glue logic to hold the components together. And there will always be parts of the system that need low-level coding in C or assembly language. High-performance interrupt service routines are an example where specially crafted, low-level code is often desirable. Embedded development tools must support the ability to mix languages and use 5GLs alongside 3GLs. The aim is to use the most productive language possible at all times. The development environment must be able to cope with these situations and must be able to manage multiple languages with ease.

3.3   Modeling to Deal with Complexity

Engineers need a well-integrated capability to model both the system under development and its associated operating environment. Modeling allows information about the hardware and the environment to be captured and used in testing the application software. It also has the benefit of supporting hardware/software co-design by allowing testing or experimentation even before the target hardware is available. Modeling, done carefully, can allow hardware to be properly sized. It can provide data from "what if" scenarios for determining initial hardware requirements or assessing the effect of additional features or options.

With modeling, actual hardware interfaces and low-level drivers are replaced with simulations that can be driven programmatically. The operation of the application software can be observed. Modeling allows large parts of the application code to be tested on the development workstation. This process achieves the desirable objective of minimizing the amount of untested code that goes to the target.

3.4   Rapid Development Environment

There is a pressing requirement to make workstation-style, rapid application development (RAD) tools (which support interactive, incremental development, and visual programming) accessible to developers of real-time embedded software. These tools must accommodate the range of real-time operating systems (RTOS) that are in common use.

3.5   Complexity and Lifecycle Management

Unlike most workstation software applications, embedded systems have expected lifetimes of from ten to fifteen years or longer. Lifecycle management of systems and components needs to deal with the problems that accumulate over such long periods: changes in target hardware, updated requirements and test suites, and bug fixes. Developers must cope with the reality that not all installations are upgraded synchronously, so different software versions must be concurrently supported in the field. Upgrading existing systems to new versions of components often requires that new glue code be written to retrofit existing interfaces. Over the lifecycle of a product, the application software may need to be re-hosted to new hardware. This may be necessary to achieve cost reductions or to meet a new price performance point. Good configuration management and design partitioning will allow such changes to be accommodated by replacing only the low-level components. Multiple line-ups and associated test software need to be managed, now across multiple platforms.

3.6   Portability

Software represents a repository of corporate intellectual capital and can be the focus of major investment even in non-software companies. It must be possible to amortize this investment over different platforms and different generations of the same platform; that is, the software must be portable. Development environments must deal with the complexities associated with portability and facilitate concurrent development for multiple, dissimilar platforms. The development environment must maximize the opportunity to share code between platforms and must provide tools to help the developer to manage specializations. In addition, the development tools themselves should be portable across multiple platforms.

Portability is also a prerequisite for the development of a third-party market for components. Portability is required to make it economically viable for a producer to create high-quality, supported components.

3.7   Quality

Formal quality systems require sophisticated configuration management and tracking systems. The development environment should be able to provide both developers and management with information about problem areas, frequency of changes, components that are getting a large amount of attention, and other metrics. The development environment should be able to track problem reports and link them to fixes. Development environments should be able to collect and organize quality metrics automatically.

3.8   Organizing Teams for Component-Based Development

If we accept that real progress will come only when we start integrating components, we must begin to structure software development teams as component producers and component consumers (integrators). Component producers develop general-purpose components that can be reused profitably across multiple products or projects. The producers are responsible for building well-designed, high-performance, well-tested components that support a broad range of anticipated requirements. Such components should come with well-documented interfaces, regression tests, and sample use cases or examples.

Component integrators will tend to be domain experts who understand their customers' end-use issues. Their job is to configure components to meet these requirements. In much the same way that hardware engineers use hardware components, software integration engineers *reuse* software components. They do not rewrite components or add features or functions. Instead, they report deficiencies and feature requests back to the component builders.

Examples of components include:

- persistent storage (for example, file subsystems)
- communication subsystems
- embedded user interfaces
- voice-recognition subsystems
- text-to-speech subsystems
- specialized math functions
- motion controllers
- telephony call processing

3.9   Application Packaging

We can anticipate that increased use of software components will tend to increase the memory footprint. Users will demand more function; more function will require additional or modified components to be added to the system. Over time, components themselves will become more full featured and hence larger. Consequently, it is important, especially for embedded systems, that it be possible to strip out the pieces of a component that a particular application does not use in order to minimize the footprint. We refer to this process as *application packaging*. Successful application packaging also requires that the components themselves be in a form that facilitates packaging.

4. The ENVY/Embedded Approach

OTI's experience with embedded systems dates to the mid-1980s and the Actra research project at Carleton University. The project focused on the development of a multiprocessor Smalltalk that was based on Harmony, which is a multitasking, multiprocessor RTOS [2, 3]. This research led to **ENVY**/*Embedded*, which entered commercial use around 1990. Since that time, the product has matured into a full-featured, cross-development environment that merges the capabilities of its sister product, IBM's VisualAge for Smalltalk, with traditional, embedded, cross-development facilities. (VisualAge for Smalltalk supports application development for PCs, workstations, servers, and mainframes.)

ENVY/*Embedded* has a toolkit that addresses the needs previously described. The tools include:

- A full Smalltalk development environment that supports all the expected interactive facilities, including editing of code and data during program execution using the Smalltalk debugger. After ten years in commercial use, Smalltalk sets the standard for incremental, interactive, development environments.

- **ENVY**/*Developer*, a collaborative team programming environment with tools for version control and configuration management. The tools address many of the requirements for component management previously described. An optional capability manages the organization and integration of C or C++ code within the Smalltalk environment.

- Cross-development tools for packaging, remote debugging, and managing multi-platform Smalltalk images via LANs or other communication links.

- Execution profiling and analysis tools.

4.1 Why Smalltalk?

Smalltalk [4] provides a mature platform for component-based development; it is highly portable; and it facilitates modeling, experimentation, and RAD. It interoperates with lower-level languages such as C and assembly languages. It has excellent facilities for integrated source-level debugging and profiling; it has exceptional tools for configuration management and version control.

In 1996, the Smalltalk community celebrated its 25-year anniversary. Smalltalk has evolved from a bulky, slow, personal tool into a robust, industrial-strength application-development environment. Over this time, little has changed in the language itself; it is quite stable and an ANSI committee (X3J20) will likely propose a Smalltalk standard later in 1997. While the language is static, there have been major improvements in the implementations of Smalltalk products and development tools. Smalltalk is now on mainframes, workstations, and a variety of embedded platforms.

4.2 The Virtual Machine

Like Java, Smalltalk uses a virtual machine (VM) that executes the bytecode representation of the application. The VM can be executed from ROM as can much of the application image, which is an ability that is a key requirement for very small, cost-sensitive or power-sensitive embedded systems. Although VMs must be tailored to each platform, OTI has developed a proprietary process to rapidly port VMs for new platforms. The process is a necessity if companies are to take advantage of new, lower-cost or more powerful processors as soon as they come on the market. The success of the process is evident by the wide range of supported processors (PPC, iX86, MC68K, PA-RISC, SPARC, ALPHA, and MIPS). The VM can run with an operating system (besides the usual commercial OSs, a number of embedded operating systems such as QNX, OSOpen, VxWorks, and OS9 are supported), or in a bare configuration with no OS. The choice depends on many factors, such as the need to use existing code, the availability of hardware drivers, the available memory, customer preferences, and the need to minimize software royalty charges.

One of the significant benefits of Smalltalk is that the VM takes care of the memory management functions (using garbage collection). The VM allocates and initializes space for new objects and, when objects are no longer needed, the VM reclaims the memory. There are no pointers and therefore or pointer errors. Doing away with memory leaks and pointer errors typically reduces the debugging time by more than half. Memory management consumes approximately three percent of the processor, depending on the rate that objects are created and destroyed.

4.3 Process Model

Smalltalk has its own process model and facilities to handle external interrupts. Processes (more similar to threads) can be created at one of seven priority levels. Processes support the usual thread operations such as suspend, resume, and terminate. The process model can also be subclassed to suit the application. It is relatively easy to make the transition from Smalltalk to C or to assembly language. Typically, C functions and macros are provided to convert objects into C data types and to create and manipulate Smalltalk objects in C. Smalltalk objects can be marked as fixed (which guarantees that the garbage collector will not move them) and hence allows direct access to system memory or memory-mapped I/O. User-written C functions can be easily linked with the VM and accessed from Smalltalk. This permits the use of existing code and third-party C libraries. In a typical embedded system, 90 percent of the system is in Smalltalk, with the balance (including interrupt service routines, drivers, and time-critical functions) in C or assembly language.

4.4   The Development Tools Offer the Real Gain

The real productivity gains are derived as much from Smalltalk, the development environment, as from Smalltalk, the language. The development environment itself is actually an executing Smalltalk program. The developer sees workspaces and a set of browsers. Pieces of code can be written and executed within a workspace, making experimentation a natural mode of working. The advantages of **ENVY**/*Developer* as the source-management tool are well known and apply equally to embedded development.

4.5   Component Support

In **ENVY**/*Developer*, classes must be organized along functional lines into components. There is normally a base component, sometimes referred to as the kernel, that contains an extensive set of base classes (collections, magnitudes, streams) that are used to build other components.

Smalltalk environments all have a set of browsers that are used to create and organize code. They are also used to browse existing classes and the methods in those classes. Most Smalltalk environments come with an extensive library of classes. For Smalltalk environments that use the **ENVY**/*Developer* management tools, the browsers are also used to manage the components that are available to the developer. These components are kept in a database (called a library) that is shared by all the members of the development team. The components contain the source code and the compiled bytecode. The library may contain several versions of a component. A developer can browse the components in the library and choose to load a particular component into his development image. This allows the developer to experiment with the component, understand its interfaces, and determine its suitability. Developers can also browse changes between different versions of the same component.

New components or new versions of components can be imported into the developer's library. In the MIS Smalltalk world, there is a growing base of third-party component builders that are marketing their components in this format. This can be expected to happen in the embedded world as well.

4.6   Smalltalk Supports Experimenting and Rapid Prototyping

Because the development environment is active, experimenting with components and code fragments is straightforward. Arbitrary pieces of code can be typed or pasted into a workspace, highlighted, and executed. Smalltalk is a dynamically linked language and code is compiled as it is written. Methods are compiled and linked when they are saved, and this usually occurs in a fraction of a second. An integrated debugger can be used to step through the code, set breakpoints, inspect objects, and even change intermediate results. Methods can be changed within the debugger and, if there were no side effects, can even be re-executed. All this experimenting is done within a code-management system that allows developers to comfortably keep track of their prototyping.

4.7   Integrated Profiling Tools

A set of integrated profiling tools has been developed for **ENVY**/*Embedded*. Code can be selected and executed within the environment. While the program executes, the VM collects trace data, which can be displayed in a numbers of ways. The developer can identify which sections of the application are consuming time and can experiment with changes. Some applications involve interaction with external events and some may vary from run to run. Results from different experiments can be retained for comparison. Similar tools allow memory use to be profiled as well. For embedded applications, memory will often prove to be a resource that is even more critical than time.

4.8   Smalltalk Runtime Systems

Smalltalk development is usually done on a host platform, although for targets with sufficient resources (such as memory, input devices, and display), self-hosted, in-target development can be an option. A target image is created on the host for execution on a target runtime environment. The target runtime environment is a VM and supporting interfaces that have been ported to the target platform. The target platform may be an RTOS or it may be without one. When using an RTOS, the VM runs as an OS task or process. This means that Smalltalk can be added to and mixed with existing code

The **ENVY**/*Embedded* VM is designed to be ported quickly and has a well-defined interface to the underlying platform or RTOS. A basic port requires implementation of only basic memory calls (such as malloc() and free()), timer functions, and general serial I/O functions. More capable ports require network interfaces, file systems, and possibly GUIs.

Debugging facilities on target systems vary in complexity. They range from TTY debugging (a combination of single-stepping and print statements) through to full, cross-development tools that have all the functions expected in workstation debugging, such as code browsing, code substitution, and control facilities.

At runtime, execution begins at a defined startup method similar to a C main() function. A typical embedded system goes through some initialization. It then looks for external events and responds to them.

Because Smalltalk is dynamically linked, it is an ideal runtime system for building downloadable systems. Many portable and hand-held devices will need to support dynamically loadable applications or application components for reasons of size, distribution, or maintenance. Smalltalk provides most of the underlying language technology to deliver this.

5. Future Directions

The barriers to using Smalltalk in embedded systems are coming down in time to meet the growing complexities and challenges that threaten to submerge the embedded world. Through their experiences using **ENVY/***Embedded* to develop PBXs, oscilloscopes, cell phones, and factory automation equipment, OTI and its customers have shown that VM-based OO systems can be used to develop complex systems. The project teams that use this approach are enthusiastic and are experiencing the productivity gains that OO development environments have demonstrated in other areas. Future developments will further define the component model and enable easier and perhaps automatic assembly of components.

Other areas of research include continued improvement of the profiling tools — they can never be good enough. It is also important to expand the support for modeling to make it easier to create models and to work with models. This is a area that is suitable for providers of third-party components.

Smalltalk is, of course, not the only dynamic OO language that is targeted at embedded systems. Sun Microsystems has announced its plans for embedded Java. Java's architecture is similar to Smalltalk: in a very real sense, Java is Smalltalk with a veneer of C++. But tools that support team development and a component-based approach are only now starting to appear for Java, and the tools are mainly for workstations. Embedded Java VMs are slow and tools are lacking. But we expect that the situation will improve as the technology matures over the next few years. Undoubtedly, the Java community will follow the same path that embedded Smalltalk set and will put these tools and improvements in place in the years to come.

6. References

[1] Cox, B., "What if there is a Silver Bullet," Byte Magazine, 1986.

[2] Barry, Brian M., Prototyping real-time embedded systems in Smalltalk. Proceedings of OOPSLA '89, New Orleans. ACM SIGPLAN, 1989.

[3] Barry, Brian M., "Real-time object-oriented programming systems," American Programmer, October, 1991.

[4] Goldberg, A. and Robson, D., Smalltalk-80: Language and its implementation. Addison Wesley, 1983.

Aspect-Oriented Programming
Workshop Report

Kim Mens[1], Cristina Lopes[2], Bedir Tekinerdogan[3], and Gregor Kiczales[2]

[1] Vrije Universiteit Brussel,
Department of Computer Science, Programming Technology Lab,
Pleinlaan 2, B-1050 Brussel, Belgium
[2] Xerox PARC, Systems and Practices Laboratory,
3333 Coyote Hill Rd, Palo Alto, CA 94304, USA
[3] University of Twente,
Department of Computer Science, Software Engineering,
P.O. Box 217, 7500 AE Enschede, The Netherlands

Abstract. Whereas it is generally acknowledged that code tangling reduces the quality of software and that aspect-oriented programming (AOP) is a means of addressing this problem, there is — as yet — no clear definition or characterisation of AOP. Therefore, the main goal of the ECOOP'97 AOP workshop was to identify the "good questions" for exploring the idea of AOP.

1 Introduction

Mechanisms for defining and composing abstractions are essential elements of programming languages. They allow programs to be composed up from smaller units, and they support design styles that proceed by decomposing a system into smaller and smaller sub-systems.

The abstraction mechanisms of most current programming languages — subroutines, procedures, functions, objects, classes, modules and API's — can all be thought of as fitting into a generalised procedure call model. The design style they support is one of breaking a system down into parameterised components that can be called upon to perform some function.

But many systems have properties that do not necessarily align with the system's functional components. Failure handling, persistence, communication, replication, coordination, memory management, real-time constraints and many others are aspects of a system's behaviour that tend to cut-across groups of functional components. While these aspects can be thought about and analysed relatively separately from the basic functionality, programming them using current component-oriented languages tends to result in these aspects being spread throughout the code. The source code becomes a tangled mess of instructions for different purposes.

This "tangling" phenomenon is at the heart of much needless complexity in existing software systems. It increases the dependencies between the functional components. It distracts from what the components are supposed to do. It introduces numerous opportunities for programming errors. It makes the functional components less reusable. In short, it makes the source code difficult to develop, understand and evolve.

A number of researchers [KLM+97] have begun working on approaches to this problem that allow programmers to express each of a system's aspects of concern in a separate and natural form, and then automatically combine those separate descriptions into a final executable form using automatic tools. These approaches have been called aspect-oriented programming (AOP).

In this workshop, rather than focussing on the idea of automatic weaver tools, a more general notion of AOP was adopted: AOP was regarded as a general concept or mechanism to solve the problem of modelling the different aspects of concern in a system. The purpose of the workshop was to bring together researchers and practitioners working in the area of AOP or related areas to discuss the current status of AOP research.

2 About the Workshop

The second workshop on *aspect-oriented programming* was organised by Cristina Videira Lopes, Gregor Kiczales, Kim Mens and Bedir Tekinerdogan on June 10 during the 11th European Conference on Object-Oriented Programming in Jyväskylä, Finland. (The first AOP workshop — the "AOP friends meeting" — was held at Xerox PARC in conjunction with OOPSLA'96.)

All participants were encouraged to submit a short position paper and the workshop was organised around the common tendencies detected in these position papers, such as:

1. What exactly are *aspects*? How can they be identified or characterised? [Meu97,MJV+97]
2. What is the difference between an aspect and a *component*? How do components and aspects interact? [HOT97,Lam97,Van97]
3. How to *weave*? (I.e. how to merge the base component program and the different aspect programs into a final executable form.) [Lam97]
4. Need for a theoretical foundation for AOP. [Meu97]
5. How to expand the use of aspects to other phases of the software development life-cycle: requirements, analysis, architecture, design, implementation, maintenance, ... [Aks97,HOT97,MJV+97,Mul97,Wer97]
6. What are the relationships or differences between AOP and other approaches or programming paradigms and especially between AOP, reflection, open implementations and meta-object protocols? (For example, is AOP better than a general framework like reflection?) [CES97,Meu97,DC97,MJV+97,Lam97]
7. Visual representations of AOP. (For example, visual presentation of relationships between components/aspects, graphical representations of aspects and aspect weaving, ...) [HOT97,Van97,Wer97]

8. Whereas the topics enumerated above are of a more general nature, many position papers mentioned specific concerns such as feedback on specific aspects and domains for AOP:
   - How to express the "coordination" aspect in concurrent OO? [HPMS97]
   - "Synchronisation" is not a single aspect but should be separated in several more specific aspects. [HNP97]
   - How to specify "failure detection" and "failure handling" in distributed OO using AOP? [Roy97]
9. Another important question which was not raised in any position paper is how to prove that AOP is good (i.e. better than existing approaches).

The goal of the workshop was not to find a definite answer to the above questions, but to use them as a general starting point for discussions. During the workshop, participants were encouraged to come up with other relevant questions and issues. The main purpose of the workshop was to identify the good questions that can lead to a characterisation of what AOP is and is not about.

3 About the Participants

During the warm up session, the participants were asked to introduce themselves, give a short summary of their position statement and optionally raise some questions for discussion.

- Many participants suggested new domains where AOP might prove useful such as distribution and mobility, automatic failure detection, coordination, synchronisation, load balancing, ...
- A number of other participants mentioned their interest in reuse and evolution issues, and the relation between AOP and current research issues in the reuse world.
- The relationship between AOP and composition mechanisms was also deemed interesting by many people.
- Peter Werner and some others stated that apart from aspect-oriented "programming", also aspect-oriented "modelling" and aspect-oriented "design" are important. This remark is strongly related to common tendency 5.
- Some people were a little sceptic. Sathoshi Matsuoka wondered whether AOP languages are needed at all, or whether we can suffice with conventional OO techniques and existing computational models. Wolfgang De Meuter mentioned that it might be possible to model AOP by means of meta-level programming (rather than considering meta-level programming a subset of AOP).
- Most of the participants talked about AOP in a general sense. Mira Mezini's statement that "AOP is not a programming paradigm but a design framework for separation of concerns" reflected this general understanding about AOP during the workshop.

4 Selected Presentations

Some of the submitted position papers raised more interest than others, especially the ones that made more general observations about AOP. Five authors were selected to present their position statement in more detail.

4.1 Aspects Should Not Die

Bert Robben [MJV+97] starts out with a discussion on the nature of aspects:

1. All aspects should be considered equally important within the context of a single application. This encourages aspectual decomposition from the very beginning.
2. What is the domain of aspects? Do they only deal with run-time properties (such as performance enhancement) or also with elements of the problem domain?
3. What is the appropriate abstraction level at which to describe aspects? Using separate high level declarative aspect description languages seems more appropriate than using the same language as the component language.
4. How and when do aspects show up during the development cycle? During which stages are they manifest as separate entities? Up to which point are the aspects orthogonal?

Next, the above mentioned issues were used to compare AOP with related approaches such as meta-object protocols and open implementations. As an example, consider Table 1 which compares the manifestation of aspects during different development stages for each of the approaches.

Table 1. Manifestation of Aspects

Development Stage	Traditional	MOP, OI	AOP now	AOP tomorrow
modelling	implicit	explicit	explicit	explicit
description	hard-coded	some aspects	explicit	explicit
run-time	fuzzy	some aspects	weaved	some explicit, some weaved

As can be seen from the last column in Table 1, the same issues were also used as a basis for identifying some possible future trends in AOP research. For example, it was argued that aspects (or at least some of them) must survive in the executable code if dynamic behaviour is to be supported.

In current AOP, aspects are only explicit until weave-time. An aspect weaver takes the aspect descriptions and tightly interconnects them with the application's functionality. In tomorrow's AOP at least some of the aspects (e.g., load balancing) should survive at run-time, to ensure maximal flexibility and to allow an aspect to adapt itself based on execution time information. Aspects that can be statically dealt with (e.g., synchronisation) can still be woven as before.

4.2 A Comparison of AOP-related Approaches

Krzysztof Czarnecki [CES97] discussed some problems with currently existing
object-oriented technologies based on a comparison of different approaches from
3 different research communities:

1. Software Reuse,
2. Formal Transformational Development (generative programming),
3. OO and Adaptability Research.

The approaches were compared using the following criteria:

- Is the configuration time static or dynamic? (I.e. construction time or run
  time?)
- Which kinds of design knowledge can be expressed?
- Which kinds of optimisations are possible? (Global versus local and static
  versus dynamic.)
- What coordination mechanisms are used? (In other words, what are the *join
  points*?)
- Which concerns can be addressed?

He also argued that, to some extent, all discussed approaches (including
AOP) strive towards reaching the same common goals:

- obtaining a (more) direct correspondence between requirements and code
  segments;
- raising the abstraction level;
- improving adaptability, extensibility and reusability;
- achieving a "complete" separation of concerns;
- achieving a "complete" separation of concerns *and* at the same time achieving high performance.

The important contribution of AOP could be to make these ideas practicable
in industry.

4.3 Issues in Aspect-Oriented Software Development

Mehmet Aksit [Aks97] argued that aspect-oriented programming must be considered in a broader context. It is common practice to decompose software development activities into various phases, like requirements specification, domain
analysis, architecture definition, design, implementation and maintenance. These
phases are defined based on the viewpoints of the software engineer (analysis deals with what to do, design with how to do it, etc.). Since the concerns
adressed in each of these phases have a major impact on the final structure and
quality of software, they must be recognised as aspects. Going from one phase
to another is then actually an aspect weaving process.

We can *identify* aspects by considering software development as a problem
solving activity. The problem is typically represented by the requirement specification for which we try to find (software) solutions. The solutions are inherently

defined by the requirement specification and the domain knowledge. Aspects and aspect weaving processes have to be derived from the canonical models of these solutions. So clearly, aspect identification should start in the requirements specification and domain analysis phases, and not in the implementation phase. Aspects identified in the upper level phases of software development will have impact on the following phases. However, each subsequent phase may add new aspects and/or refine the existing aspects.

From the perspective of adaptability and reusability, mapping these solution techniques to the conventional object-oriented language mechanisms performs unsatisfactorily. Especially, multiple views, synchronisation and conditionally changing behaviour cannot be implemented well. Inheritance-based solutions perform better, but they cannot implement dynamically changing behaviour. The conventional object-oriented model requires 3 to 5 times more method implementations than the ideal case. The composition-filters model provides almost an ideal solution. In the composition-filters approach, the basic behaviour is implemented by using any programming language, and the additional aspects are defined in the filters. However, the composition-filters model is not capable of expressing aspects and weaving process at the design-level. Therefore, new techniques must be defined for design-level aspects and aspect weaving processes. Important characteristics of design level aspects are that they are mostly based on uncertain factors and that they are conflicting, context-dependent and non-deterministic.

4.4 Monads as a Theoretical Foundation for AOP

One of the reviewers qualified Wolfgang De Meuter's position paper [Meu97] as "an interesting beginning to the semantics of AOP and AOP in a functional programming setting".

The author proposes a theoretical foundation for AOP, based on the notion of *monads* known from functional programming. Aspects can be thought of as monad transformers, the base component program as a monadic style program and aspect weaving as monad transformation. The join points correspond to the "bind" operation on monads in combination with the other monadic operations.

As an experiment, De Meuter implemented a Fibonacci method to which the "aspects" of result caching and concurrent computation were added in a monadic way. These experiments indicate that the monad concept might be a very good candidate to give a formal semantics to AOP languages.

Besides providing a theoretical foundation for AOP in general, the proposed theory could also be regarded as a way of introducing AOP in the functional programming paradigm. An aspect-oriented program in a functional programming language would be nothing more than a monadic style program.

4.5 The Interaction of Components and Aspects

One of the realities of AOP is that aspect code and component code interact. It is this interaction that makes weavers necessary and that makes AOP interesting.

Different AOP approaches can be classified in terms of what the join points are and how the components and aspects interact.

John Lamping [Lam97] made a first classification of AOP approaches based on how the aspect behaviour and component behaviour are combined. In other words, how does the aspect code and the base code fit together? He distinguished between 3 ways of combining aspect and component behaviour, and gave some examples for each of them.

Juxtapose. Interleave doing aspect and component behaviour. In other words, the structure of the woven code looks basically like the base code, with aspect code added at the join points. (E.g., Iguana, Oz, composition filters, monads, coordination.)

Merge. As opposed to juxtaposition, when merging, a combination of aspect and component descriptions can be merged into a single action. (See the numerical code example in [KLM$^+$97])

Fuse. An example of fusing can be found in the image processing example of [KLM$^+$97] (loop fusion), where a single action is a combination of both aspect and several component level descriptions. In other words, several component level and aspect level descriptions can be fused into one single action.

A second classification can be made based on what kind of contextual information is needed. What kind of information about the context of execution of the component code is needed to choose the aspect behaviour? (I.e., what kind of information *not* maintained by the aspect code is needed by it?) Again, several kinds of contextual information can be distinguished:

Local. Composition filters and Oz only use information that is lexically nearby. In the image processing example, on the contrary, non-local information is needed: in order for a loop fusion aspect to fuse two loops it must examine two loops from the component code, which may potentially not even be adjacent in the component code.

"History". E.g., composition filters.

"Future". E.g., image processing, monads.

"Simultaneous". E.g., Iguana, coordination.

5 Afternoon Session — General Discussion

During the afternoon, about 40 participants joined in a plenary discussion of the following topics:

1. How do aspects and components interact?
2. Is aspect-orientation bound to object-oriented programming?
3. Are general purpose aspect languages possible or useful?
4. Can current technologies be used for AOP or do we need yet another technical development? (What existing techniques for manipulating computations exist?)
5. How can aspects be identified?
6. Which concerns does or should AOP separate?
7. Which problems can AOP solve? What are the hard problems?

5.1 Interaction of Aspects and Components

The first discussion was a continuation of John Lamping's presentation 4.5.

Mehmet Aksit did not completely agree with the classification that composition filters can depend on local contextual information only, as global objects can also be composed locally. Furthermore, composition filters do not only allow juxtaposition of aspect and component behaviour, but also merging. If the aspect code can be inferred in the compiler it can be merged with the base code.

There was also an undecided discussion on whether MOP should be considered an example of juxtaposition or merging.

5.2 Is Aspect-Orientation Bound to Object-Oriented Programming?

Now let us turn to the question of whether aspect-orientation is bound to object-oriented programming. In fact, this question can be decomposed in two questions:

1. Is aspect-orientation bound to object-orientation?
2. Is aspect-orientation bound to programming?

From the conceptual viewpoint, it is generally agreed that the object-oriented paradigm can model real world entities in a neat and understandable way. However, object-orientation lacks in adequately solving the problems which arise when different concerns, like real-time, synchronisation and coordination need to be composed together (and with the real world entities).

The reason for these modelling problems is the lack of expressive solution models and the lack of adequate composition mechanisms for such concerns. We cannot easily map the cross-cutting concerns to concepts of the conventional object model and we are not able to compose them in an orderly way. Aspect-orientation arose from the need to solve these modelling problems and accordingly addresses two basic issues. Firstly, how should we separate the real world concerns? Secondly, how should we compose these concerns at compile-time and at run-time?

Aspect-orientation advocates the use of expressive models for both components and concerns. By mapping real world concerns to aspects the cross-cutting behaviour of the different concerns will be eliminated and accordingly software systems will be better maintainable and adaptable. Clearly, like object-orientation is not bound to programming only, aspect-orientation can also be considered as a modelling technique and a mechanism which applies to all the phases of the entire software development cycle. Consequently, we can speak of aspect-oriented analysis (AOA), aspect-oriented design (AOD), aspect-oriented programming (AOP).

Further, we can state that aspect-orientation is not bound to object-orientation only. All existing programming paradigms like procedural, functional, logical and object-oriented paradigm provide models to express real world entities. In aspect-orientation conceptually an explicit distinction is made between *aspect languages* with which cross-cutting concerns are expressed, and *component languages* with which real world entities and the basic computation functionality are expressed. Each aspect should be expressed in its own natural language. As such, in addition to the basic computation language we may for example have specific aspect languages for concurrency, real-time and coordination concerns. Conventional languages may equally both be used as component languages and aspect languages. The component and aspect languages might even be the same. The choice of the language inherently depends on the problem and additional context parameters. The fundamental point however is that aspect orientation intrinsically advocates the use of those languages — possibly from different paradigms — that are most natural for the task at hand. In this sense we could say that aspect orientation is rather independent of the existing paradigms.

5.3   General Purpose Aspect Languages

Would it be *possible* to get an aspect language that is general purpose to the same degree that an OO language is general purpose? The advantage of using a general purpose language such as, for example, C++ is that everyone knows it and can understand it. It is a common way of expressing the semantics and freezes the patterns of usage that programmers are used to.

But do we *want* general purpose aspect languages or do we prefer many different aspect languages? In general there is a trade-off between using a single general purpose or many specific aspect languages. Mehmet Aksit gave the example of composition languages. If all composition filters are written in the same language as the base program, the weaving is much easier. But now suppose you want to deal with real-time filters. First the composition language will need to be extended to deal with real-time aspects, but all the rest will become more difficult as well. With separate languages you only need one extra language in which to describe the real-time aspects.

There are some other advantages to using many different aspect languages rather than a single general purpose language. When using appropriate aspect languages the aspect code will be more concise and easier to understand, and will limit the programmer to mess up. General purpose languages for aspects are not good because they do not allow to describe the aspects at the right abstraction level. A related motivation for using different languages is that lots of aspects have to do with control flow. This can be modelled very well by means of constraints but poorly by imperative code. Hence the subject matter of aspects is different than the subject matter of components and it is probably better to use different languages.

Having different aspect languages is neither necessary nor sufficient for AOP. Indeed, in some cases it may be convenient to write both the aspects and the component program in the same language, whereas in other cases using different aspect languages seems more advantageous.

But if you use a number of aspect languages, eventually they will need to be translated into a single language. Which facilities or features does this language need to provide? Current AOP languages do not seem to require anything special, as long as the output language is low level enough. But can we have a high enough level output language? Is it possible to make a general purpose intermediate aspect language so that it is easy to translate into any other language?

And even if you do not want a general purpose aspect language, can we provide general aspects weavers, or do we need domain specific weavers?

As a final remark, it should be remembered that the "generality" of aspect languages and aspect weavers will always apply only to some extent. Therefore, it might be better to talk about the scope of generality of an aspect language or weaver.

5.4 Reflection versus AOP

In the context of discussion topic 4 there was some discussion on how much help can be expected from reflective techniques. Reflection certainly seems to be a sufficient mechanism for AOP, but many regard it as too powerful: anything can be done with it, including AOP. When using reflection, will the aspect-oriented program be safe or efficient enough? Is reflection required to make the program adaptable enough? More research is needed here.

Someone argued that reflection is too powerful because of its focus on mechanisms rather than on the structure of the meta-level. In other words, what is missing to constrain the reflective power is a composition methodology at the meta-level.

5.5 Identification of Aspects

How can aspects be identified? What aspects should we be looking for? What other domains are there?

Someone suggested that when a problem is decomposed in subproblems, every subproblem can be considered as an aspect. However, this *cannot* be the case as aspects are not packaged in one component but come out of the interactions between components. (Kiczales mentioned that this is also the reason why subjectivity does not feel like aspects.) In fact, this is precisely a characterisation of the difference between aspects and components. Components are those things you obtain when breaking something in pieces of functionality, whereas aspects are those things that remain and are difficult to describe locally with respect to those components. However, it is possible that with another choice of components some aspects become components and vice versa.

If we want to identify aspects, it would be a great help to have explicit software entities that map onto the aspects. For example, in the functional programming paradigm, programs can either be structured according to the values they consume or according to the computations they consume. The latter style of programming is called *monadic programming* [Meu97]. These two styles of functional programming seem to correspond to component programs and aspect programs, respectively. Furthermore, AOP is about having both kinds of programming styles simultaneously. This is the same in monadic programming where you still need the component way of programming as well. So there seems to be a close correspondence between AOP and monadic style functional programming.

5.6 Separation of Concerns

With AOP we want to separate out different aspects at a more convenient abstraction level. Furthermore, we want to describe these aspects independent of the components in the base program and use weavers to avoid having to visit all components. AOP typically tries to separate some of the concerns that component-based technologies are not good in decomposing. But AOP should not be seen as a *complete* separation of concerns: the aspects still have to do with the components. You still have to look at the components, but not at everything, only at the things you want to see. Achieving a complete separation is not only hard, it is not even a goal: if you would have complete separation, the things that are separated would not be part of the same system anyway. But the question remains how much we want things to be separated.

5.7 Which Problems to Solve with AOP?

The last discussion topic regarded application domains for AOP. Which problems can AOP solve? What are the hard problems? Due to a lack of time only one interesting new application domain for AOP was suggested.

No position paper mentioned the use of AOP for writing web-software, where many components are being updated and changed at different rates. Although AOP is not an approach specific to this area, one might wonder whether an AOP approach could be of value here. One important issue when writing web-software is to be able to control the *interaction* between the objects. (You want to control the interaction between the objects rather than the objects themselves, because you do not own the objects.) At first glance, AOP seems a useful approach because it is good in addressing such a non-local thing.

6 Concluding Remarks

AOP defines a new concept, called aspect, that enables us to talk about an important new kind of modular unit in system designs and implementations. Aspects are intended to work together with traditional notions of components, including modules, objects, API's and the like, but typically address concerns that cut-across groups of these components. Aspect-oriented programming is a style of programming in which aspects and their interactions with components are clearly identified. Aspect-oriented programming can include specific aspect languages to program the aspects, or can be done with existing programming languages and coding idioms that make the aspects more clear.

With this as our background, it is clear that a lot of work remains to be done. Some of the key issues that were addressed during the workshop are summarised below:

Need for more technical research. Whereas there seems to be a common intuition on what AOP actually is, it is equally clear that the technical precision behind that intuition needs to be worked out. For that, a complete catalogue should be made of the precise technical problems that need to be solved.

Need for AO*. From the discussion on the use of aspects throughout the software life-cycle we can deduce that there is not only a need for Aspect-Oriented Programming (AOP), but also for Aspect-Oriented Analysis (AOA), Aspect-Oriented Design (AOD), Aspect-Oriented Modelling (AOM), and so on. AOP should be scalable to these domains.

Need for AOP metrics. To justify the claim that AOP actually makes building real software easier, measurable results for AOP are needed. (Metrics of code tangling.)

Can existing technologies be used for AOP? During the workshop there was a lot of discussion about the relation between reflection and AOP. The key question here is how much of the technology that is needed for AOP (or AO*) is already available. Is there really a need for a new technical development, or is (for example) reflection or meta-programming already sufficient?

Need for comparisons between AOP and related approaches. As people will want to know whether AOP is new or whether it is nothing more than a new name for an old thing, comparisons between AOP and related work (such as composition filters and subject-oriented programming) are important.

Need for a theoretical foundation. It is obvious that lots of research is needed on theoretical foundations for AOP, for example, monads.

Separation of concerns in AOP. It should be made clear what we set the goal of separation of concerns to be: what are the concepts we want to separate, and how much do we want them to be separated?

Is AOP bound to OO? This is only a rhetorical question as we clearly want AOP *not* to be bound to OO only. The right question to ask is what communities we should be talking to about this idea and for help with this idea.

Other future work. Apart from the general considerations above, some more specific questions and topics to be investigated are:
- What is the domain of aspects?
- How to identify aspects?
- Aspect description languages.
- Orthogonality of aspects.
- Translation techniques.
- How to weave? What should a weaver do?
- Run-time versus earlier time aspects.
- How to specify join points?
- General purpose or domain specific AOP?
- Aspects applied to existing libraries.
- How to deal with evolution?
- Visual representations of AOP.

7 Acknowledgements

We express our gratitude to the reviewers of the submitted position papers: Mehmet Aksit, Lodewijk Bergmans, Pierre Cointe, Theo D'Hondt, Karl Lieber-herr, Carine Lucas, Calton Pu and Michael VanHilst.

We would also like to thank the participants who sent in a position paper as well as all other participants who joined the discussions in the afternoon sessions of the workshop: Vito Baggiolini, Per Brand, Vinny Cahill, John Dempsey, Ulrich Eisenecker, Marc Evers, Bjorn Freeman-Benson, William Harrison, Juan Hernández, David Holmes, Wouter Joosen, J. S. Madsen, Francesco Marcelloni, Satoshi Matsuoka, Frank Matthijs, Jürgen Müller, Juan Murillo, James Noble, Harold Ossher, Michael Papathomas, John Potter, Fernando Sánchez, Patrick Steyaert, Peri Tarr, Kresten Krab Thorup, Klaas van den Berg, Pim van den Broek, Willem van den Ende, Bart Vanhaute, Michael VanHilst, Peter Van Roy, Pierre Verbaeten and Peter Werner. Special thanks to Mehmet Aksit, Bert Robben, Krzysztof Czarnecki, Wolfgang De Meuter and John Lamping who presented their position statement at the workshop as well.

References

[Aks97] Mehmet Aksit. Issues in aspect-oriented software development. Position paper at the ECOOP'97 workshop on Aspect-Oriented Programming, 1997.

[CES97] Krzysztof Czarnecki, Ulrich W. Eisenecker, and Patrick Steyaert. Beyond objects: Generative programming. Position paper at the ECOOP'97 workshop on Aspect-Oriented Programming, 1997.

[DC97] John Dempsey and Vinny Cahill. Aspects of system support for distributed computing. Position paper at the ECOOP'97 workshop on Aspect-Oriented Programming, 1997.

[HNP97] David Holmes, James Noble, and John Potter. Aspects of synchronisation. Position paper at the ECOOP'97 workshop on Aspect-Oriented Programming, 1997.

[HOT97] William Harrison, Harold Ossher, and Peri Tarr. The beginnings of a graphical environment for subject-oriented programming. Position paper at the ECOOP'97 workshop on Aspect-Oriented Programming, 1997.

[HPMS97] Juan Hernandez, Michael Papathomas, Juan M. Murilli, and Fernando Sanchez. Coordinating concurrent objects: How to deal with the coordination aspect? Position paper at the ECOOP'97 workshop on Aspect-Oriented Programming, 1997.

[KLM+97] Gregor Kiczales, John Lamping, Anurag Mendhekar, Chris Maeda, Cristina Lopes, Jean-Marc Loingtier, and John Irwin. Aspect-oriented programming. In ECOOP'97 Proceedings, Lecture Notes in Computer Science, Springer-Verlag, pages 220–242, 1997.

[Lam97] John Lamping. The interaction of components and aspects. Position paper at the ECOOP'97 workshop on Aspect-Oriented Programming, 1997.

[Meu97] Wolfgang De Meuter. Monads as a theoretical foundation for aop. Position paper at the ECOOP'97 workshop on Aspect-Oriented Programming, 1997.

[MJV+97]   Frank Matthijs, Wouter Joosen, Bart Vanhaute, Bert Robben, and Pierre
           Verbaeten. Aspects should not die. Position paper at the ECOOP'97 work-
           shop on Aspect-Oriented Programming, 1997.
[Mul97]   Jurgen K. Muller. Aspect-design in the building-block method. Position
           paper at the ECOOP'97 workshop on Aspect-Oriented Programming, 1997.
[Roy97]   Peter Van Roy. Using mobility to make transparent distribution practical.
           Position paper at the ECOOP'97 workshop on Aspect-Oriented Program-
           ming, 1997.
[Van97]   Michael VanHilst. Subcomponent decomposition as a form of aspect-
           oriented programming. Position paper at the ECOOP'97 workshop on
           Aspect-Oriented Programming, 1997.
[Wer97]   Peter Werner. Position statement submitted to the ECOOP'97 workshop
           on Aspect-Oriented Programming, 1997.

All position papers submitted to the workshop are available on the web-site
http://wwwtrese.cs.utwente.nl/aop-ecoop97/

Workshop on Object Orientation and Operating Systems

Preface

The most discussed topics and aims in operating system research are flexibility, adaptability, and scalability. Usual general purpose systems suffer from not being the optimal support for most applications due to different application demands. Thus, there is a large conformity that an operating system should be very flexible to be scalable in the extend of its functionality. This way it can be adapted or it can adapt itself to changing application needs.

Another large conformity lies in the technique which is today most suitable to realize systems with these characteristics: the object orientation. Object orientation offers a high abstraction level and the language feature of dynamic binding – C++ is still playing the leading role – is a good point of departure for operating system developers to embody adaptation functionality.

A gain of flexibility often contains the danger of usability loss. The more functionality can be subject of adaptation, the more difficult it may be to find the optimal operating system variant. It cannot be the user's job, who usually neither knows nor cares about the operating system structure, to control the availability of operating system features. Therefore, configuration is a main issue in many operating system projects.

In our workshop on object orientation and operating systems we brought together fourteen researchers and developers for discussing aspects for the application of object orientation to operating systems. Seven papers were presented and one invited talk was given. Most of the papers resp. their authors originate more or less from concrete operating system development projects.

Today's operating system research always means to look at distributed environments, too. In terms of object orientation it is therefore necessary to deal with distributed and concurrent object models and languages. The first paper reports research activities in this field of object orientation. Experiences with taking advantage of the consistency techniques known from distributed shared memory systems for a distributed object model are documented here.

Another important keyword which is widely used in many projects on adaptable operating systems is reflection. In reflective systems functional and non-functional code, the *meta-level*, are separated. The meta-level controls – and adapts – the nature and extent of the functional code. The second paper is about reflection in conjunction with the Java programming language, which is more and more upcoming also in the field of operating systems.

The next paper also deals with reflection. It originates from a project developing a native object oriented operating system kernel. The project members research in extending operating system adaptability to the very fine-grained level of classes. The granularity of especially dynamic adaptations in the operating system sector was often rather coarse. The paper describes an approach to this problem based on the runtime availability of structuring informations.

The fourth paper coming from the same project like the previous turns to the problem of configuring adaptable operating systems. Here, for realizing dynamic adaptation, ideas from artificial intelligence are called on. Configuration and adaptation are eased by a small expert system which is an organic part of the operating system.

Another approach to configure the adaptability of an operating system is presented in the fifth paper. It is firstly emphasizing static building of the system from a huge number of given operating system classes. This way a system is tailored to the application needs. The concepts are based on source code annotations describing the characteristics of the implemented operating system facilities.

The sixth paper votes for an object oriented abstract machine on top of which the operating system runs. The architecture of the abstract machine is designed to work reflectively. An object model is laid down in the abstract machine which makes a homogeneous view of different kinds of objects available to the operating system. For the system this abstraction has got the advantage of being very flexible especially relating to its basic features security, persistence, distribution, and concurrency.

A more general discussion on object models and the distinction to separated execution models is given in the last workshop paper. The author also prefers the meta-level approach similar to the reflective architectures mentioned above. In contrast to these systems an advanced model of *containers* is proposed.

The workshop was concluded by an invited talk which lead over to a detailed final discussion. The invited talk was given by Prof. Wolfgang Schröder-Preikschat (http://irb.cs.uni-magdeburg.de/~wosch), University of Magdeburg, Germany. He reported on his experiences in designing and implementing object oriented operating systems. The central approach of his work is the *family concept* for designing the systems. The family concept corresponds very well to an object oriented realization. Actually the main target is downward scalability, i.e. to find a minimal basis of the operating system family members which should be as small as possible. This way it will become possible to build operating systems also for smallest embedded and real-time systems with extreme conditions e.g. on memory consumptions. For this purpose it is necessary to join a very complex design with large class hierarchies with a very simple and therefore efficient realization and representation of the built operating system. Consequently, configuration is also very important for this operating system construction set.

Finally we would like to express our gratitude to the authors, the lecturers, the workshop participants and especially the organizers in Finland who all helped to make the workshop a successful event.

August 1997

Henning Schmidt, University of Potsdam
Frank Schubert, Chemnitz University of Technology
Lutz Wohlrab, Chemnitz University of Technology

Applying Distributed Shared Memory Techniques for Implementing Distributed Objects *

Antonio J. Nebro, Ernesto Pimentel and José M. Troya

Depto. de Lenguajes y Ciencias de la Computación, Universidad de Málaga
E.T.S.I en Informática. Campus de Teatinos.
E29071- Málaga (SPAIN)
e-mail: {antonio, ernesto, troya}@lcc.uma.es
Phone: +34 5 2133310
Fax: +34 5 2131397

Abstract. In this paper we study how the potential advantages of distributed shared memory (DSM) techniques can be applied to concurrent object-oriented languages. We assume a DSM scheme based on an entry consistency memory model and propose an object model that can incorporate that DSM scheme. The object model is characterized by the requirement of explicitly enclosing object invocations between acquire and release operations, and the distinction between command and query operations. Details of a thread-based implementation are discussed, and results show that significant speed-ups can be obtained. We also conclude that using kernel-level threads can lead to better performance, and the overhead versus user-level threads is negligible.

1 Introduction

Distributed shared memory (DSM) is a model for interprocess communication in distributed systems that simplifies distributed programming by offering a programming model similar to concurrent programming in shared memory systems. A DSM system logically implements a shared memory model on a physically distributed memory system. Thus, distributed programs do not use message passing primitives, such as send or receive, but some form of **read** and **write** primitives.

There are three main issues that characterize a DSM system [13]: the level where the DSM mechanism is implemented, the algorithms for implementing DSM, and the memory consistency model of the shared data. At the implementation level there are three main approaches: hardware, software and hybrid. Several basic algorithms for implementing DSM are described in the literature [15], but the most widely used ones employ replication techniques to enhance the performance of language and system implementations. The use of replication introduces the inconsistency problem, which occurs when a process writes

---

* This work was funded in part by the "Comisión Interministerial de Ciencia y Tecnología" (CICYT) under grant TIC94-0930-C02-01.

replicated shared data. So, it is necessary to define a memory consistency model [10], i.e., a contract between the programs and the memory defining the behavior of the memory when the programs satisfy the contract. The choice of the memory consistency model has a tremendous influence on performance, because the stronger the consistency model is, the more numbers of messages it generates. The problem is that, in general, the programming model becomes more complicated when the consistency model is weaker. Thus, choosing a memory consistency model is a trade-off between increasing concurrency and programming model complexity.

We can classify software DSM systems, independently of their memory consistency model, in page-based (IVY [9], Clouds [7]), shared-variable based (Munin [6], Midway [1]) and object based (Orca [3], Linda [5]). This ordering shows an advance in the direction of higher-level programming models. All these systems have a similar programming model, where parallel (distributed) programs are composed of a set of processes that access some kind of shared information. The aim of our work is to advance one more step and consider a programming model in which a parallel program is composed only of concurrent objects, following a concurrent object-oriented approach.

The idea is to consider objects as information units shared by other objects and apply DSM techniques to allow efficient implementations. Thus, several issues must be considered. As we mentioned before, the choice of the memory consistency model is very important because of its influence on performance and programming complexity. We choose entry consistency, a weak memory model that matches the one used by shared memory parallel programs, which use critical sections to guard shared data accessing [1]. Additionally, we have to deal with a problem not encountered in classical DSM systems, like the presence of synchronization constraints.

In modern operating systems a process is defined as an address space plus multiple threads of control. Threads present some characteristics which make them suitable for obtaining efficient implementation of distributed objects, as code sharing and communication through shared memory. Thus, an interesting topic which should be analized is the influence of kernel-level versus user-level threads on performance.

The rest of this paper is organized as follows. The object model we define is described in Section 2. In Section 3, we discuss some implementation issues. Performance results are shown in Section 4. Related work is commented on Section 5. Finally, conclusions and future research are outlined in the last section.

2 Object Model

We want to study the applicability of DSM concepts to implement a system based on distributed objects. Instead of assuming an existing object model and studying how to benefit from DSM approaches, we make our approach from the opposite side. We assume a software DSM scheme where objects can be replicated and the consistency model is entry consistency, and we define an object model satisfying the requirements of the DSM scheme.

A commonly accepted definition of a concurrent object-oriented programming model does not exist. For this reason, we assume a generic definition of object. We define an object as an entity that have three basic components: a set of private state variables, an interface and a set of synchronization constraints. The state is hidden and can be accessed through the operations defined in the class interface. Synchronization constraints prevent the acceptance of operations when these are not allowed. Objects are the building blocks of parallel programs, which are collections of objects that communicate among themselves invoking the operations defined in their interfaces.

Using a C++ like notation, the classical example of a bounded buffer could be written as follows:

```
ConcurrentObject IntBuffer
  { int buffer[DIM] ;
    int in, out, count ;
  public:
    IntBuffer() ;
    int head(); bool is_full(); bool is_empty(); int free_slots(); // Queries
    void put(int); void delete();                                  // Commands
  constraints:
    disable put when (count == DIM);
    disable delete, head when (count == 0); } ;
```

According to entry consistency, shared data have to be associated a synchronization variable. In our case, each object, replicated or not, has an associated implicit lock, and three operations are predefined: **acquire_exclusive**, **acquire_non_exclusive** and **release**. Whenever an object tries to invoke the operations of another one, it must enclose those operations between an acquire operation and a release operation. Thus, we establish a common mechanism for inter-object communication.

If an operation cannot be accepted because of a synchronization constraint, the acquired object must be temporarily released to give to a different object the possibility of changing the state. The original object will resume its activity later, when the operation is enabled. This implies that the previous acquisition must be reestablished.

We assume that the programmer has to decide if an object is replicable or not. Depending on the program, an object could be replicated if the average number of method invoking that do not modify the state variables is high. However, the hiding information principle states that perhaps the programmer does not know how an object operation is implemented, making it difficult to decide when an object can be replicated. Also, the correct use of the **acquire_exclusive** and **acquire_non_exclusive** operations requires us to know about the behavior of operations as regards the state variables.

For these reasons, operations can be classified in two categories: commands and queries. A **command** is an operation that modifies the state of the object, without returning information about it. A **query** is an operation that returns some information about the object, without modifying its state. This distinction, already stated in [11], avoids side effects; therefore, queries imply pure read accesses and commands imply pure write accesses. Queries and commands present different behavior. Commands are asynchronous, so the invoking object can continue its execution in parallel with the invoked object. Queries are synchronous, so the invoking object must wait for the response of the invoked object.

The distinction between commands and queries disallows the definition of a `get()` operation, in the case of the bounded buffer object. Instead, a pair of `head()` and `delete()` operations must be issued. In these circumstances, there is no possibility of obtaining unexpected results, because the bounded buffer object must be previously acquired in exclusive mode. As objects can have synchronization constraints, there is no guarantee that the set of operations invoked between an acquire-release pair be performed atomically. This issue is not within in the scope of this paper, and so will not be addressed here.

3 Implementation

We have implemented a thread-based prototype. It has been coded in C++ [14] and consists of a runtime system and a set of base classes that must be inherited by the classes used in the distributed programs. It runs on SUN UltraSPARC workstations on top of two networks: a 10 MB/sec ethernet and a 155 MB/sec ATM network. The implementation employs the socket interface for inter-node communications and the Solaris 2 thread package. This thread package is characterized by supporting both user-level and kernel-level threads, called unbound and bound threads, respectively.

The protocol used for object replication is based on that of Midway [1], but with several differences. The main replica of a replicable object resides in the same node as the last object that acquired it in exclusive mode. As in Midway, the location of this replica is done by using a distributed queuing algorithm. However, the invalidation scheme is simpler, because the request for replicas is always sent to the main copy, simplifying the invalidation process. An important difference is that we consider the object state as a whole, so we do not use logical clocks to determine if some state variables have been updated more recently than others. The motivation of these differences is that we are in the early stages of our implementations and we prefer simpler solutions when possible. In any case, we think that most objects in distributed programs will be fine or medium grained, so the use of logical clocks will be justified only in some kind of applications. Furthermore, the bandwidth of existing networks suggests that it is possible to reduce the complexity of some distributed algorithms at expenses of increasing communication.

4 Performance

To measure the performance of the current implementations, we have coded a parallel program that multiplies square matrices of integers. The parallel algorithm is based on dividing the result matrix in 4^N square submatrices and computing them in parallel.

The program is composed of the following objects:

- Two replicable matrix objects, the matrices to multiply, and a non-replicable matrix object, the result matrix. The interface of these objects has three operations: `read_item`, `write_item` and `write_submatrix`.
- A multiplier object per submatrix. These objects compute a submatrix of the result matrix when their `compute` operation is invoked. The computed submatrix is written back to the resulting matrix by invoking the `write_submatrix` operation in exclusive mode. After that, the `finish` operation of the master object is invoked.
- A master object reads matrices from a file, creates the remaining objects, starts the computation, detects the termination of the program, and displays the result matrix. The master object detects the termination when its `finish` operation has been invoked as many times as the number of multiplier objects.

The multiplier objects acquire the matrices to multiply in non-exclusive mode, which implies that those matrices are transferred into a node when the first acquire access is performed. Matrix objects have not synchronization constraints. Therefore, their state variables can be directly accessed. The number of multiplier objects depends on the value of N. Thus, we can measure the performance of the parallel program when increasing the number of multipliers, while decreasing the grain of the computation they perform.

4.1 Speed-ups

In Table 1, we present the results of multiplying square matrices with a size ranging from 400 to 1000 when running the program on the ethernet and ATM networks. Each object is assigned to a bound thread. The speed-up is calculated dividing the time obtained by a classical sequential matrix multiply algorithm by the time obtained by the parallel program. Time is measured after reading the matrices, and when the computation termination has been detected. The value of N is 1, when using two and four nodes, and 2, when using eight nodes. By way of comparison, the Midway system yielded speed-ups of 1.96 and 3.79 for a two and four processor matrix multiply, respectively, using an ATM network [2]. These programs multiply two 512x512 floating matrices.

ETH	2 Nodes	4 Nodes	8 Nodes	ATM	2 Nodes	4 Nodes	8 Nodes
400	1.59	2.57	2.90	400	1.63	3.09	4.57
600	1.72	3.05	4.03	600	1.77	3.44	6.10
800	1.85	3.34	4.71	800	1.88	3.68	6.68
1000	1.91	3.52	5.27	1000	1.94	3.79	7.12

Table 1. Speed-ups of parallel matrix multiply

4.2 Kernel versus User-level Threads Comparison

As objects are implemented using threads, it is interesting to compare the performance of the same parallel program using kernel-level and user-level threads. A priori, user-level threads have the potential advantages of being more efficient and less resource consuming, while user-level threads are more heavyweight but are scheduled in a preemptive way, without blocking the rest of threads of the same process.

In Table 2, we show the results (in seconds) obtained from running three versions of the parallel multiply program using four nodes and the ATM network. Each column contains the results of multiplying a 400 x 400 integer matrix, using 4, 16 and 64 multiplier objects. So, we increase the concurrency level and the number of messages, while the computational time is maintained constant. In the SOC_b version a bound thread is assigned to each multiplier, while unbound threads are used in the SOC_{ub} version. The results obtained by the SOC_b version follows a predicted behavior: time increases as the number of objects and communications do. The cost of increasing the number of objects is in the order of 1.2 seconds, comparing the four versus the sixty four multipliers executions. This represents a difference of about 7.5%.

	4 Multipliers	16 Multipliers	16 Multipliers
SOC_b	15.6	16.2	16.8
SOC_{ub}	28.9	18.5	19.0
SOC_{ub}^{*}	15.8	16.5	16.7

Table 2. Results of multiplying a 400 x 400 matrix using four nodes

The results of the SOC_{ub} version are influenced by the invoking order of the compute operations and the First Come First Served (FCFS) scheduling policy applied to the unbound threads. The SOC_{ub}^{*} is a variant of the SOC_{ub} version, where the CPU is explicitly yielded when a submatrix row is computed. The times obtained show similar results when comparing with the SOC_b version.

In Table 3, we show the measurements obtained using only one node. In this case, the SOC_{ub} always performs better than the SOC_b version, but the differences are minimum. An interesting result is that the overhead of increasing the number of objects is negligible, on the order of 0.7%.

	1 Multiplier	4 Multipliers	16 Multipliers	64 Multipliers
SOC_b	56.1	56.2	56.3	56.5
SOC_{ub}	55.9	56.0	56.1	56.2

Table 3. Results of multiplying a 400 x 400 matrix using one node

If we analize the results obtained from running the parallel matrix multiply program, we could conclude that using kernel-level threads have more advantages than using user-level threads. The preemptive scheduling policy increases the concurrency level, allows the overlapping of computation and communication, and the overhead of kernel-thread management in a node is insignificant. However, user-level threads require fewer resources and the concurrency level can be increased yielding the CPU voluntarily. This solution is not satisfactory if the programmer has to modify the default scheduling policy by annotating the programs explicitly with thread primitives. Nevertheless, compiler techniques could be applied to overcome this inconvenience.

5 Related Work

The object model we present is related with the extension of Eiffel proposed by Meyer [11], in the sense that there is a query-command distinction and the objects must be acquired to be accessed by other objects. Acquire accesses are done implicitly using argument passing as the mechanism. The aim of this work is to define a satisfactory integration between object-oriented programming and concurrency.

In other works related to Eiffel extensions [8] [4], the programmer must specify the policy that governs the scheduling of the incoming requests to concurrent objects. We prefer to maintain the object as simple as possible, so we define an implicit scheduling policy that is common for all the objects.

Midway [1] [2] was the first system based on entry consistency, although it also supports processor and release consistency. In Midway, parallel programs must be annotated with special code to declare synchronization variables, shared data and associations among them. These associations are dynamic and can change during the program's execution. On the contrary, in our proposal all the objects can be shared and have an implicit lock. This lock is part of the object, and cannot be associated to another object. Other issues have been compared in Section 3.

6 Conclusions and Future Work

We have presented an object model that fits into an entry consistency DSM scheme. This model is well-suited for the efficient implementation of objects in distributed systems, since it allows object replication. The main difference from other DSM systems is that we assume a concurrent object-oriented programming model, where parallel programs are only composed of concurrent objects. We conclude that entry consistency requirements can be held by this object model, associating an implicit lock to each object and distinguishing between command and query operations. Object accesses must be enclosed between a pair of acquire, in exclusive or non-exclusive mode, and release operations.

Implementation details have been discussed, and some results, using a parallel matrix multiply program, show that significant speed-ups can be obtained with our proposal. We have compared the using of kernel-level versus user-level threads. We conclude that kernel-level threads can lead to better performance, and getting similar results with user-level threads would require the explicit annotation of programs with low-level thread primitives.

Future work will be related to implementing a suite of parallel applications to evaluate all the characteristics of the object model. The parallel matrix multiply program does not use, for example, synchronization constraints. Comparative studies have to be carried out at the programming level and performance.

References

1. Bershard, B. N., Zekauskas, M. J. "Midway: Shared Memory Parallel Programming with Entry Consistency for Distributed Memory Multiprocessors". Tech. Report CMU-CS-91-170. 1991.
2. Bershard, B. N., Zekauskas, M. J., Sawdon, W. A. "The Midway Distributed Shared Memory System". Compcon 1993.
3. Bal, H. E., Kaashoek, M. F., Tanenbaum, A. S. "Orca: A Language for Parallel Programming of Distributed Systems". IEEE Transactions on Software Engineering. Vol. 18, No. 3, March 1992.
4. Caromel, D: "Toward a Method of Object-Oriented Concurrent Programming". Communications of the ACM, Vol. 36, No. 9. September 1993.
5. Carriero, N, Gelernter, D.: "How to Write Parallel Programs". The MIT Press. 1990.
6. Carter, J.B., Bennet, J.K., Zwaenepoel, W.: "Implementation and Performance of Munin". Proc. 13th Symp. on Operating Systems Principles, ACM, pp. 152-164, 1991.
7. Dasgupta, P., LeBlanc Jr., R. J., Ahamad, M., Ramachandran, U.: "The Clouds Distributed Operating System". IEEE Computer, vol. 24, no. 11. 1991.
8. Karaorman, M., Bruno, J.: "Introducing a Concurrency to a Sequential Language". Communications of the ACM, Vol. 36, No. 9. September 1993.
9. Li, K., Hudak, P.: "Memory Coherence in Shared Virtual Memory Systems". ACM Trans. on Computer Systems, vol. 7. Nov. 1989.
10. Mosberger, D.: "Memory Consistency Models". Operating Systems Review, ACM Press. Vol. 27, No. 1. January 1993.
11. Meyer, B: "Systematic Concurrent Object-Oriented Programming". Communications of the ACM, vol. 36, no. 9. September 1993.
12. Papathomas, M.: "Concurrency Issues in Object-Oriented Languages". Tech. Rep. Centre Universitaire Informatique. University of Geneva, D. Tsichritzis, Ed., 1989.
13. Protic, J., Tomasevic, M., Milutinovic, V.: "Distributed Shared Memory: Concepts and Systems". IEEE Parellel and Distributed Technology. Summer 1996.
14. Stroustrup, B.: "The C++ Programming Language. Second Edition". Addison-Wesley. 1991.
15. Stumm, M., Zhou, S.: "Algorithms Implementing Distributed Shared Memory". Computer, Vol. 23, No 5. May 1990.

MetaJava - A Platform for Adaptable Operating-System Mechanisms

Jürgen Kleinöder, Michael Golm

University of Erlangen-Nürnberg, Dept. of Computer Science IV[1]
Martensstr. 1, D-91058 Erlangen, Germany
{kleinoeder, golm}@informatik.uni-erlangen.de

Abstract. Fine-grained adaptable operating-system services can not be implemented with today's layered operating-system architectures. Structuring a system in base level and meta level opens the implementation of operating-system services. Operating-system and run-time services are implemented by meta objects which can be replaced by other meta objects if the application requires this.

1 Introduction

This paper describes the MetaJava system, an extended Java interpreter that allows structural and behavioral reflection.

MetaJava was built to achieve the following goals:

- It must be possible to separate the functional, application-specific concerns from non-functional concerns, such as parallelism or fault tolerance.
- The reflective architecture must be general; different problems, such as persistence, distribution, replication, or synchronization must be solvable in it.

The paper is structured as follows. We first introduce the concepts of reflection and metaprogramming in Section 2 and the computational model of MetaJava in Section 3. Section 4 explains how object-oriented meta-level architectures can be applied to the structuring of operating-system mechanisms. Section 5 addresses the problems that had to be solved for the implementation of MetaJava. Section 6 discusses related work and Section 7 concludes the paper and suggests future work.

2 Reflection and Metaprogramming

In the past, programs had to fulfill a task in a limited computational domain. As applications have become increasingly complex today, they need more capable programming models, which support mechanisms of modern run-time environments, such as multithreading (synchronization, dead-lock detection, etc.), fault tolerance, distribution, mobile objects, extended transaction models, persistence, and so on. Many ad hoc extensions to languages and run-time systems have been

---

1. This work is supported by the *Deutsche Forschungsgemeinschaft DFG* Grant *Sonderforschungsbereich SFB 182*, Project *B2*.

508

implemented to support some of these mechanisms. But such proceeding does not meet the very diverse demands, different applications make on their run-time environment. Instead it is desirable to provide an application with means to control the implementation of its run-time mechanisms and to add own modifications or extensions if necessary. Reflection is a fundamental concept to get influence on properties and implementation of the execution environment of a computing system.

Smith's work on 3-LISP [20] was the first that considered reflection as essential part of the programming model. Maes [13] studied reflection in object oriented systems. According to Maes *reflection* is the capability of a computational system to "reason about and act upon itself" and adjust itself to changing conditions. *Metaprogramming* separates functional from non-functional code. *Functional code* is concerned with computations about the application's domain (*base level*), non-functional code resides at the *meta level*, supervising and managing the execution of the functional code. To enable this supervision, some aspects of the base-level computation must be reified at the meta level. *Reification* is the process of making something explicit that is normally not part of the language or programming model. The advantages of the separation in base level and meta level are outlined in [9].

As pointed out in [3] there are two types of reflection: structural and behavioral reflection (in [3] termed computational reflection). Structural reflection reifies structural aspects of a program, such as inheritance and data types. The Java Reflection API [21] is an example for structural reflection. Behavioral reflection is concerned with the reification of computations and their behavior. The main focus of MetaJava is to provide behavioral reflection capabilities.

3 Computational Model of MetaJava

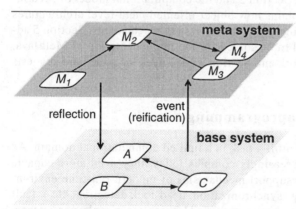

The computations of objects A, B, and C raise events that transfer control to the meta level. The meta objects influence the computation of A, B, and C.

Fig. 1 Computational model of behavioral reflection

Traditional systems consist of an operating system (OS) and, on top of it, a program which uses the OS services through an application programmer interface (API). Additional services may be provided by a run-time layer between OS and application.

As OS and run-time services supervise and manage state and execution of applications, their functionality corresponds to that of a meta level as defined in the previous section.

In our reflective model the system consists of a meta system and the application program (the *base system*). The program may not be aware of the meta system.

enter-method(object, method, arguments) method is being called at object with arguments
load-class(classname) class classname is being used for the first time and must be loaded
create-object(class) an instance of class is being created
acquire-object-lock (object) the lock of object is being acquired
release-object-lock(object) the lock of object is being released
read-field (object, field) the field of object is being read
write-field (object,field, value) value is being written into the field of object

Fig. 2 Events generated by a base-level computation

The computation in the base system raises events (see Fig. 1). These events are delivered to the meta system. The meta system evaluates the events and reacts in a specific manner.All events are handled synchronously. The base-level computation is suspended while the meta object processes the event. This gives the meta level complete control over the activity in the base system. For instance, if the meta object receives a *enter-method* event, the default behavior would be to execute the method. But the meta object could also synchronize the method execution with the execution of another method of the base object. Other alternatives would be to queue the method for delayed execution and return to the caller immediately, or to execute the method on a different host. What actually happens depends entirely on the meta object used. The currently defined events are listed in Figure 2.

A base object also can invoke a method of the meta object directly. This is called explicit meta interaction and is used to control the meta level from the base level.

Not every object must have a meta object attached to it. Meta objects may be attached dynamically to base objects at run time. This is especially important if a distributed computation is controlled at the meta level and certain method arguments need to be made reflective. As long as no meta objects are attached to an application, our meta architecture does not cause any overhead. So applications only have to pay for the meta-system functionality where they really need it.

Currently meta objects can be attached to references, objects, and classes. If a meta object is attached to an object, the semantics of the object is changed. Sometimes it is desirable only to change the semantics of one reference to the object — for example, when tracing accesses to the reference, or when attaching a certain security policy to the reference [18]. Attaching a meta object to a class makes all instances of the class reflective.

To fulfill its tasks the meta object has access to a set of methods which can manipulate the internal state of the virtual machine. These methods are called the *meta-level interface* (MLI) of the virtual machine. Architecture and terminology of the Java VM are described in detail in [12]. A list of the most important methods of the MLI is given in Figure 3.

---

void **attachObject** (MetaObject meta, Object base)
> Bind a meta object to a base object.

Object **continueExecution** (EventMethodCall event)
> Continue the execution of a base-level method. This calls the non-reflective method. No event is generated, otherwise the reflection would not terminate.

Object **doExecute** (EventMethodCall event)
> Execute a method. Contrary to the previous method, this one calls the method as if it were called by an ordinary base object.

Object **createNewInstance** (EventObjectCreation event)
> Create a new instance of a class. The class name is passed as String (as part of the event parameter).

void **installBytecode** (Object ref, String method, byte code[])
> Installs code as new method bytecode. Together with addConstantPoolItem this method is used to generate a stub method in the place of the original method.

String **retrieveObjectLayout** (Object ref)
> Returns the types of all fields of object ref. This method is used together with getFieldObject, getFieldInt, getFieldFloat, setFieldObject, etc., to access fields of arbitrary objects.

Object **getField** (Object ref, String fieldName)
> Returns the contents of field fieldName of object ref. Name and type of all fields (object layout) can be retrieved with retrieveObjectLayout.

void **setField** (Object ref, String fieldName, Object obj)
> Sets the contents of field fieldName of object ref to object obj.

int **addConstantPoolItem** (Class c, CPItem i)
> Adds an item to the constant pool of class c.

Fig. 3 Selected methods of the meta-level interface of the MetaJava virtual machine

---

4 Metaobjects for open operating-system implementations

In a Java environment, most mechanisms and policies that are traditionally regarded as operating-system or run-time–system services are provided either by the virtual machine itself or by native libraries. As these services are implemented in C and the flexibility and comfort of a Java environment is not available for them, it is not easy to adapt them to special application needs or to transparently add new services. MetaJava provides an architecture for an open implementation of most mechanisms and policies that are currently a fixed part of the virtual machine, such as memory management, garbage collection, thread management and scheduling, or class management. The virtual machine has to provide merely a very primitive implementation of a few basic mechanisms, such as thread switching, and simple policies to get the first metaobjects up and running (e.g. a simple class loader to install classes from a local disk). More complex mechanisms and policies can be implemented as Java metaobjects, which can use the basic mechanisms via the meta-level interface.

511

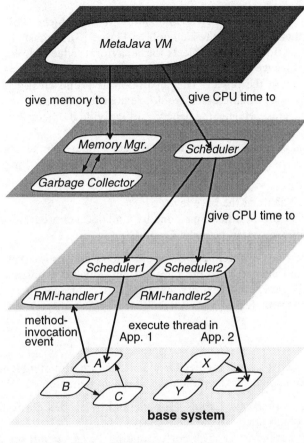

give memory to

give CPU time to

give CPU time to

method-
invocation
event

execute thread in
App. 1   App. 2

base system

Fig. 4 Hierarchy of meta levels

If several applications are executing within one Java machine, application-specific metaobjects lead to a hierarchy of metaobjects (Fig. 4). Global metaobjects give the resources to applications, application-specific metaobjects control the resource usage within the application. Of course, even application parts may employ their own metaobjects, if necessary.

In addition to the mechanisms listed above, a broad range of extended run-time services can be implemented by metaobjects: persistence, object migration, object replication [10], just-in-time compilation, active objects [5], asynchronous method invocations, transactions, synchronization, various security policies, and so on.

5   Implementation

Integration into Java. The initial version of MetaJava used a shared library to extend Sun's Java Virtual Machine (JVM). The further development required extensive changes to the JVM, so we decided to build our own virtual machine, the MetaJava Virtual Machine (MJVM). The MJVM is a superset of the JVM. It uses the same class-file format and executes the same bytecode set as the JVM, but provides a meta-level interface to the virtual machine (Fig. 3).

We did not change the Java language or the class-file format, so off-the-shelf development tools can be used.

This section outlines the changes to the JVM that were necessary to enable our reflective model. A more detailed description can be found in [11].

5.1 Shadow classes

The purpose of a metaobject is to change the semantics of one object. This change should not affect other objects of the same class. Ferber [3] suggests to use classes for structural reflection and metaobjects for behavioral reflection. We do not adopt this model because we think that classes (conceptually) should contain complete information about the object. The separation as proposed in [3] seems only be justified by the fact that classes are not related to individual objects but to all instance of the class. Hence, the behavior of individual objects can not be changed by customizing classes.

We introduce shadow classes to solve this problem, which is inherent in class-based languages. A shadow class C' is an exact copy of class C with the following properties:

- C and C' are undistinguishable at the base level
- C' is identical to C except for modifications done by a meta-level program
- Static fields and methods are shared between C and C'.

The base-level system can not differentiate between a class and its shadow classes, so the shadowing is transparent to the base system. Several problems concerning class data consistency, class identity, garbage collection, code consistency, and memory consumption had to be tackled to ensure this transparency.

5.2 Event Mechanism

Shadow classes allow us, to transparently modify the class structure of individual objects. This is the base mechanism for the reification of object behavior.

- *Reification of incoming method invocations:* The method bytecodes are replaced by a stub code, which jumps to the meta space.
- *Reification of outgoing method calls:* The corresponding *invokevirtual* opcodes are replaced by stub code.
- *Reification of instance variable accesses:* The corresponding *putfield* and *getfield* opcodes are replaced by stub code.
- *Reification of object locking:* The MJVM uses a function pointer in the class structure to acquire or release an object lock. This pointer normally refers to a function that implements locking and unlocking. When a metaobject registers for the lock events, the MJVM redirects this pointer to the metaobject's event handler.
- *Reification of class loading and object creation:* Class loading and object creation is reified similar to object locking. The MJVM class structure contains a pointer to the class-loader/object-creation function. If a metaobject registers for this event, the pointer is redirected to the metaobject.

5.3 Metaobject Attachment

Attaching to objects: The MJVM uses an object store with object handles. A handle contains a pointer to the object's data and a pointer to the object's class.

When a metaobject is attached to an object, a shadow class is created and the class link of the object is redirected to this shadow class.

Attaching to references: When a metaobject is attached to a reference, the object handle is copied and the class pointer in the handle is changed to point to a shadow class. After copying the handle, it is no longer sufficient to compare handles when checking the identity of objects. Instead, the data pointers of the handles are compared.

6 Related Work

There have been described several reflective systems with related goals and properties as MetaJava. However, non of the systems provided the performance and flexibility, the MetaJava has achieved with the techniques described in this paper. A system with strong emphasis on performance is OpenC++ [2]. OpenC++ supports class based reflection. A method declaration can be annotated in the base-level class and invocations of this methods are later reified. More flexible tailoring mechanisms are provided by CodA [14] and AL-1/D [16]. CodA tries to identify the basic building blocks of an object-oriented run-time system. Because CodA is based on Smalltalk, it focuses on message exchanges and separates the subsequent actions in a message exchange from each other. Al-1/D separates different views of a base-level system. One view is concerned with the language semantics, another with resource management, and so on.

7 Project Status and Future Work

We are working on several other applications of the MetaJava architecture. We implemented metaobjects for remote method invocation, replication, and active objects. Further projects for meta objects include support for security policies [18], concurrency control [17], and distribution configuration.

The ultimate goal of our work is making reflection an integral part of the programming model and support composition of meta-level systems. One major issue is to develop concepts to make the attachment of the meta objects to software modules configurable and to keep such configuration statements out of the functional code of the application program. This can only be achieved by providing language support for specifying information about base-level objects.

To keep the security and robustness of the Java system, one must be able to specify the rights of metaobjects.

Currently the MetaJava system allows to modify the object model and implement extended object models. Further development will aim at providing the meta system access to core operating system facilities - for example, by extending the JavaOS operating system.

Information about the current project status is available at http://www4.informatik.uni-erlangen.de/metajava/.

8 References

1. C. Chambers. *The Design and Implementation of the Self Compiler, an Optimizing Compiler for Object-Oriented Programming Languages*. Ph.D. Thesis. Stanford University. March 1992.

2. S. Chiba and T. Masuda. Designing an Extensible Distributed Language with a Meta-Level Architecture. *ECOOP '93*, Kaiserslautern, Germany, LNCS 707, Springer-Verlag, pp. 482–501.

3. J. Ferber. Computational Reflection in class based Object-Oriented Languages. *OOPSLA '89*, New Orleans, La., Oct. 1989, pp. 317–326.

4. J. Fabre, V. Nicomette, T. Perennou, R. J. Stroud, Z. Wu. Implementing fault tolerant applications using reflective object-oriented programming. *Proc. of the 25th IEEE Symp. on Fault Tolerant Computing Systems*, 1995.

5. Michael Golm, Jürgen Kleinöder. *Implementing Real-Time Actors with MetaJava*, Tech. Report TR-I4-97-09, Universität Erlangen-Nürnberg: IMMD IV, Apr. 1997

6. W. L. Hürsch, C. V. Lopes. *Separation of Concerns*. Technical Report NU-CCS-95-03, Northeastern University, Boston, February 1995.

7. G. Kiczales. Beyond the Black Box: Open Implementation. *IEEE Software*, Vol. 13, No. 1, Jan. 1996, pp. 8-11.

8. G. Kiczales et al. *Aspect-Oriented Programming*. Position Paper for the ACM Workshop on Strategic Directions in Computing Research, MIT, June 14-15, 1996 (http://www.parc.xerox.com/spl/projects/aop/).

9. J. Kleinöder, M. Golm. MetaJava: An Efficient Run-Time Meta Architecture for Java. *IWOOOS '96*, Oct. 27-18, 1996, Seattle, Washington, IEEE, 1996.

10. J. Kleinöder, M. Golm. *Transparent and Adaptable Object Replication Using a Reflective Java*, Tech. Report TR-I4-96-07, Universität Erlangen-Nürnberg: IMMD IV, Sept. 1996

11. M. Golm, J. Kleinöder. *MetaJava—Design and Implementation of a Platform for Adaptable Operating-System Mechanisms*, Tech. Report TR-I4-97-10, Universität Erlangen-Nürnberg: IMMD IV, Jun. 1997

12. T. Lindholm, F. Yellin. *The Java Virtual Machine Specification*. Addison-Wesley, Sept. 1996.

13. P. Maes. *Computational Reflection*. Technical Report 87_2, Artificial Intelligence Laboratory, Vrieje Universiteit Brussel, 1987.

14. J. McAffer. Meta-Level Architecture Support for Distributed Objects. *IWOOOS '95*, Lund, Sweden, IEEE, 1995, pp. 232–241.

15. P. Mulet, J. Malenfant, P. Cointe. Towards a Methodology for Explicit Composition of MetaObjects. *OOPSLA '95*. pp. 316-330

16. H. Okamura, M. Ishikawa, and M. Tokoro. Metalevel Decomposition in AL-1/D. *International Symposium on Object Technologies for Advanced Software*, Kanazawa, Japan, LNCS 742, Springer-Verlag, Nov. 1993.

17. S. Reitzner. *Splitting Synchronization from Algorithmic Behavior*. Technical Report TR-I4-08-97, University of Erlangen-Nürnberg, IMMD IV, April 1997.

18. T. Riechmann. *Security in Large Distributed, Object-Oriented Systems*. Technical Report TR-I4-02-96, University of Erlangen-Nürnberg, IMMD IV, Mai 1996.

19. F. B. Schneider. Implementing Fault-Tolerant Services Using the State Machine Approach: A Tutorial. *ACM Computing Surveys*, Vol. 22, No. 4, Dec. 1990, pp. 299-319.

20. B. C. Smith. *Reflection and Semantics in a Procedural Language*. Ph.D. Thesis, MIT LCS TR-272, Jan. 1982.

21. Sun Microsystems. *Java Core Reflection, API and Specification*. February 4, 1997.

A Reflective Architecture for an Adaptable Object-Oriented Operating System Based on C++

Frank Schubert

Chemnitz University of Technology, D-09107 Chemnitz, Germany
fsc@informatik.tu-chemnitz.de

Abstract. The paper presents an approch for achieving dynamic adaptability in operating system by means of an object-oriented system architecture. The concept is based on the ideas of reflection and runtime representations of abstractions and was realized in C++.

1 Introduction

Todays operating systems have to support applications and hardware with highly specialized requirements. Traditional all-purpose operating systems can't be an optimal runtime environment for all the diverse applications. Therefore, instead of huge universal operating systems small tailored systems are needed to provide exactly the services and properties really required in a concrete situation.

In the field of software development the object-oriented paradigm has been widely accepted as powerful method to achieve adaptability. Hence, if the set of required properties remains the same during the whole runtime of a system, object-oriented frameworks like PEACE [13], Choices [11] or Tigger [2] are well suitable to manufacture tailored operating systems. However, once booted, such a system can not be adapted to changed requirements ($\rightsquigarrow$ *static adaptability*). If rebooting is not acceptable (due to the required availability or the effort for rebooting) a way for dealing with future requirements by dynamic modification of the running system is needed ($\rightsquigarrow$ *dynamic adaptability*). Several commercial systems (Solaris, AIX, etc.) and a lot of research systems (e. g. Spin [1] and Apertos [16]) are already dynamically modifiable. Also some of the named frameworks have been extended to support dynamic adaptation (e. g. PEACE [12] and Choices [10]). However, possible modifications are often highly restricted and complicated to perform. Even though a system has been structured in an object–oriented manner and implemented in an object-oriented language, during runtime usually nothing of that structuring information is still available. After compiling and linking the system, there is no knowledge about classes, class membership, etc. Therefore, some operating systems are constructed as object management systems (e. g. BirliX [7] or Clouds [5]). They are able to manage objects in various ways and to use objects as the basic components for service providing, adaptation, migration, etc. However, the resulting object structure differs considerably from the structures used during software development (source-code level). Because of the often very heavy-weight objects (private address space and own thread of control) no fine–grained adaptation is possible.

In the CHEOPS[1] project we are applying an approach for a reflective, object-oriented system architecture, to support fine-grained, dynamic adaptability. It is based on the idea to close the gap between models and abstractions used during development (design and implementation) and the identifiable entities in the running system (see also [4]). By retaining most of the structuring information about classes, objects, and the relations between them it should be possible to perform the same extensions and modifications as have been done to the system's description (source code) within the running system itself.

2 Reflection and Runtime Representations of Abstractions

A clear and well comprehensible system architecture forms the general basis for each modification of a system. To perform the same steps of adaptation in the running system as have been done at source-code level we need an open architecture that fulfills the following requirements:

- The identifiable objects in the running system have to be the same (in granularity and functionality) as at description level, modeled by means of an object-oriented programming language.
- *Meta-level informations* as available classes, class hierarchy (*is-a* relations), *using*-relations, correlation of objects to classes, and affinity relations between objects have to be still available in the running system.
- *Meta functionality* as creation, destruction, storage and life-time management of objects as well as object invocation mechanisms (all usually performed by the run-time environment) has to be opened up and assigned to identifiable entities in the system.

The solution is based on the concepts of *reflection* and *run-time representations of abstractions*. Reflection has been introduced by Brian Smith [14]. Later the ideas have been broadened to the object-oriented world by Pattie Maes [9]. The concept can be shortly outlined as the ability of objects (so called base-level objects) to know about their run-time environment (also called *infrastructure* or *meta level*) and to be able to make that environment to the matter of computation itself. In this way objects are able to change their (meta-)properties by

---

[1] CHEOPS – **CHE**mnitz **OP**erating System

modifying the meta level. In an object-oriented system the meta level itself may be also composed by objects.

Although the most work in the field of reflection has been done related to several programming languages (e. g. the meta-object protocol of CLOS [8]) Apertos has shown that the concept is also suitable for an operating systems architecture. In our opinion the pre-condition for applying reflection within a running system is the availability of identifiable system components as run-time representations of the meta-level abstractions used during development. According to that we propose to transform classes into the running system and to assign them all the tasks resultant from the requirements above.

3 The Class-Object Architecture of CHEOPS

Dynamic adaptation in CHEOPS is done by adding or exchanging classes and objects during the system's runtime. Therefore, as explained above we need a representation of classes within the running system, the so called *class objects*. To distinguish the base-level objects from the class objects the former are called *regular objects* (see Fig. 1). A class object is an identifiable object within the system. One class object exists for each description-level class in the system. The class object manages the objects belonging to its class. and is responsible for:

- creation and destruction of objects,
- object management (registering, localization),
- service negotiation,
- access control (e. g. by access control lists or capabilities),
- supporting object exchange by using the knowledge about the class hierarchy (abstract classes, polymorphism).

Class objects are part of the infrastructure of regular objects and therefore influence their meta properties. To modify these meta properties we would have to modify the class objects. For example, if object A invokes a service of object B, the real invocation has to be performed by the infrastructure, precisely by the class object of object B. Dependent on the class object, object invocation will be performed by a simple call, by a remote procedure call (RPC), or by sending a message, etc. To A and B this can be absolutely transparent. The functionality for performing object invocation could be modified, for instance to add access control or parameter conversion, without any notification to the communicating objects.

Class objects are specific for each class. As each object is described by its class, for each class object a class description, the *class-object class (COC)*, exists as well ($\leadsto$*meta-meta level*). Based on the class definition of regular objects, this class-object class is generated automatically (at source code level) by the *COC-generator*.

The automatically genereateted classes are able to deal with the basic tasks of the class object. To extend or to change that functionality, the developer could specialize the class-object class by derivation.

Class-objects can be added or removed to/from the system dynamically. Loading classes and creating class objects is based on dynamic linking and supported by the so called *class-object manager (COM)*.

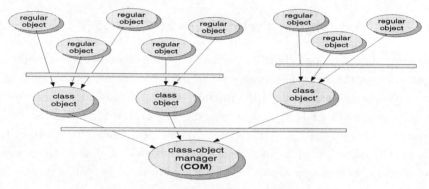

Figure 1. The Class-Object Architecture

The COM exists right from the start within the system and is responsible for loading new classes (loading the class and the class-object class, creating the class object), removing classes, exchanging classes, and managing the class hierarchy.

While adding a new class is a simple kind of extension (always possible), removing a class is only allowed, if currently no objects of that class exist. Exchanging classes can be used, for example, for correction of programming errors in an existing class. In this case the class object of the old class has to provide a service to determine and store the current state of all its objects. The new class object has to use these data to reconstruct all objects. This kind of services is not part of the COC created by the current version of the COC-generator and have to be added by specialization of the COC.

4 Realization Based on C++

4.1 Language and Restrictions

The realization of the shown approach is based on the C++ programming language. The decision to use this language was influenced, among others, by the following advantages:

- C++ compilers and appropriate development tools (e. g. class browsers) are available for a lot of hardware platforms,
- a lot of implementations in the field of system software and operating systems (e. g. Choices) have been done in C++ and show its suitability for constructing efficient systems.

Dynamic adaption in CHEOPS is based on adding, removing or exchanging classes and objects. If a new created object of a derived class has to substitute an old one, the new object generally can't be stored at the same place, because of different object sizes. Furthermore, objects have to be able to migrate into other infrastructures to change their meta properties. Therefore, *location transparency* for all those objects is needed. To avoid direct access to objects and influenced by the idea to use the C++-calling mechanism for virtual methods to implement our alternative object invocation mechanism we have decided to make some restrictions to the used language (e. g. no public data members, virtual methods only). Furthermore, because of the resulting equivocations and their tricky implementation no multiple inheritance is allowed.

4.2 Implementation

Basics

The platform of our implementation is formed by the CHEOPS kernel. It is running stand-alone on Intel-based PC's (protected mode) and provides the basic functionality for memory management, thread management and message passing. On that base the class-object manager runs as kernel thread. To be able to load and reload classes during runtime it contains a small set of functions to support the dynamic linking process based on ELF's (Executable and Linking Format) position-independent code.

The COC-generator as well as all the other necessary development tools are running on top of Linux. By using an implemented communication mechanism (based on UDP) the COM is able to communicate with an special module-loader process to transfer compiled object modules into the CHEOPS kernel. After that, the object module is transfered to the CHEOPS-kernel and the modifications are performed dynamically. One of the resultant advantages is the very short turn-around time during the incremental kernel development, because frequent rebooting is not necessary.

However, the system developer has to do several steps to add a new class to the system. As usual the developer has to create a class definition and implementation at source code level. After that he can build the class-object class by using the COC-generator. This class can be specialized by derivation as necessary. Finally the class-object manager loads the code of the class and the generated class-object class into the system and instantiates the class object.

All further tasks for managing objects of the loaded class have to be done by the new class object. For the implementation of class objects we have modified the mechanisms for object identification and method invocation.

Alternative Object Access resp. Method Invocation

All dynamically created C++ objects are referenced through the address of their data area. Calls to virtual methods are performed indirectly via a virtual method table (VMT) referenced by a special component in the object's data area.

To obtain location transparency for objects we have modified this mechanism. Because different kinds of objects have to be handled differently (e. g. local or remote objects), potentially each object has to get its own VMT to meet the object's special requirements. Grouping of objects within the class to use the same VMT is possible. The Class-objects manage all necessary information about the objects of its class. The creation mechanism for objects was modified in such a way, that it delivers not a pointer to an object but a pointer to an object description entry managed by the class object. As the first component in each object description entry the pointer to the (modified) VMT is stored so that the compiler generated method invocation is still working.

Figure 2 demonstrates the resulting procedure of method invocation. In the current implementation the COC-generator creates a class-object method corresponding to each method of the appropriate class. The new VMT refers to the class-object method instead to the object's method. Within that class-object method decisions can be made, how to proceed with the object's method invocation. Using the object description entry, the class object can detect if the object exists locally or remotely, if the caller and the callee are related to the same or to different threads, etc.

A typical sequence of actions could be as follows:

1. register object invocation, for logging objects state,
2. check access permissions
3. check object's location and object-activity relations,
4. invoke method, either by a simple call or by an RPC,
5. register end of method invocation,
6. deliver output parameters.

To change, extend or reduce these steps, the system developer has to specialize the automatically generated class-object class and to tell the class-object manager to use this new class instead. For instance, in the current implementation only synchronous method invocation is supported, performed by a local call or an RPC. If it is necessary to modify this meta property of objects, the class object has to be modified (changing infrastructure).

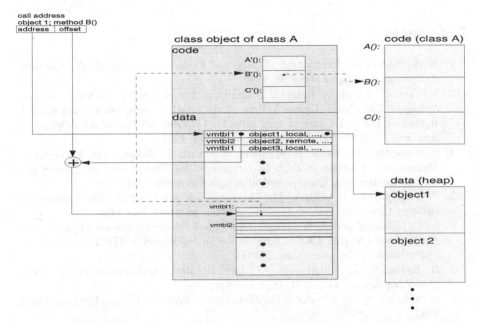

Figure 2. The Modified Structure for Object Invocation

A similar approach to achieve dynamic adaptability by modifying the management and the invocation structure of C++ objects has been presented by the Object Binary Interface approach [6]. However, in contrast to that work, our approach is based on using the available C++ compilers without the necessity of compiler modifications.

5 Future Work

During the next time some experiments with the implemented class objects have to be performed, in order to gain more experiences. The most suitable default COC functionality has still to be determined. This is necessary to prevent, that always specialized COC's have to be written. Till now, the whole prototype is located in a single address space and is running entirely in kernel mode. The support for application layer processes is still under construction. One further field of our investigations is the support of adaptation management by means of the class-object architecture [15]. Beyond this, we plan to perform a series of efficiency tests, in order to determine where the overhead introduced by the class objects is too big to be compensated by their advantages. The result of these tests will consist of guidelines, which components may be implemented based on the class-object architecture and which parts have to be realized in a traditional manner.

References

1. B. Bershad at al.: *Extensibility, Safety, and Performance in the SPIN Operating System.* proceeding of SOSP'95, 1995.
2. V. Cahill, C. Hogan, A. Judge, D. O'Grady, B. Tangney, and P. Taylor: *Extensible Systems – The Tigger Approach.* Proc. of the SIGOPS European Workshop 1994.
3. B. Gowing and V. J. Cahil: *Making Meta Object Protocols Practical for Operating Systems.* IWOOOS '95, Workshop Proceedings, 1995.
4. S. Graupner, W. Kalfa, F. Schubert, R. Vogel, J. Werner, and L. Wohlrab: *Dynamische Adaption in Betriebssystemen – Das Cheops Projekt.* Chemnitzer Informatik–Berichte, Technische Universität Chemnitz, 1996.
5. P. Dasgupta, R. J. LeBlanc, M. Ahamad, U. Ramachandran: *The Clouds Distributed Operating System.* IEEE Computer, pp.34-44, Nov.1991.
6. T. C. Goldstein and A. D. Sloane: *The Object Binary Interface – C++ Objects for Evolvable Shared Class Libraries.* Technical Report SMLI TR–94–26, Sun Microsystems Laboratories, Inc., 1994.
7. H. Härtig, W. E. Kühnhauser, W. Lux, W. Reck: *Architecture of the BirliX Operating System.* GMD, St.Augustin, 6p., 1990.
8. G. Kiczales et. al.: *The Art of the Meta-Object Protocol.* Cambridge: MIT Press, 1993.
9. P. Maes: *Concepts and Experiments in Computational Reflection.* OOPSLA 87 conference proceedings, pp. 233-240, 1987.
10. P. Madany, N. Islam, P. Kougiouris, and R. H. Champbell: *Practical Examples of Reification and Reflection in C++.* International Workshop on Reflection and Meta-Level Architectures, pp. 76-82, 1992.
11. V. F. Russo: *An Object-Oriented Operating System.* PhD Thesis, University of Illinois, 154p., 1991.
12. H. Schmidt: *Dynamisch veränderbare Betriebssystemstrukturen.* PhD Thesis, University Potsdam, 1995.
13. W. Schröder–Preikschat: *Design Principles of Parallel Operating Systems – A PEACE Case Study.* Technical Report 93–020, ICSI Berkeley, 1993.
14. *Reflection and Semantics in a Procedural Language.* PhD Thesis, Massachusetts Institute of Technology, 1982.
15. L. Wohlrab: *Configuration and Adaptation Management for Object-Oriented Operating Systems.* ECOOP 97 workshop "Object-Orientation and Operating Systems", Jyväskylä, Finland, 1997.
16. Y. Yokote: *Kernel Structuring for Object–Oriented Operating Systems: The Apertos Approach.* Sony CSL, Technical Report SCSL–TR–93–014, 1993.

Configuration and Adaptation Management for Object-Oriented Operating Systems

Lutz Wohlrab**

Chemnitz University of Technology, 09107 Chemnitz, Germany

1 Introduction

The requirements to be met by computers and their operating systems rapidly increase in both number and variety. Embedded systems, servers, and personal workstations, and so forth demand different support by the operating system to carry out their tasks effectively.

Because of their increased modularity, object-oriented systems can more easily be tailored to meet specific hardware and user requirements. Among them, the trend goes to more and more fine grain, leading to an increased level of adaptability. This, however, results in an exploding number of objects constituting an operating system.

Even today's off-the-shelf operating systems consist of a large number of components, each of which in turn introduces some new shell variables, registry entries or whatever kind of set screws to adjust. A greater number of these set screws, without suitable means for a human administrator to remain master of them, would mean to build operating systems so much adaptable, that no one could possibly adapt them properly. That would be quite a Pyrrhic victory.

Operating systems for dedicated machines like controlling devices or game consoles are best tailored statically using object-oriented frameworks. This way whole families of operating systems emerge, for example Choices [Rus91,CIRM93], PEACE [SP93,BBC+96], and Tigger [CHJ+94]. Being custom-made by the manufacturer they need no, or at least less adjusting of configuration and tuning parameters. However, operating systems for personal computers and servers can hardly be statically tailored.

One of the approaches to reduce the costs of ownership for universal operating systems are so-called no-administration operating systems. The no-administration operating systems of uniform clients within a network get their software from a special server automatically. This addresses networks with quite homogeneous clients, such as installed in a bank. If the computer hardware and the user requirements within the network are too heterogenous, this concept is hard to apply. It then degenerates to what we know as remote administration. Besides, the administration of servers is not addressed. Therefore, we need other more general solutions to ease maintenance of computer systems.

Some operating system distributions already have installation tools which are able to check mutual dependencies between software packages and do some

---

** lwo@informatik.tu-chemnitz.de

configuration tasks automatically. These tools are great helpers for installations from scratch and updates of packages. The human administrator, however, faces tough problems, if these tools alter something in the configuration they better did not touch. For instance, configuration parameters of manually installed software. That is because these tools are not really an organic part of the operating system, but act upon separate databases containing the knowledge about dependencies between packages and necessary configuration steps. So we need something beyond these utilities, which is an organic part of the operating system and thus enabled to prevent configuration conflicts, from whatever source (administrator, application, installation tool) they may originate.

Administration tasks get a lot tougher than described till now, if requirements for the system core change at runtime and rebooting is out of question. This is easily the case with server machines (which have to be highly available), with multi-tasking systems on workstations (frequent reboot is just a nuisance), and even with operating systems under development (changing a kernel module instead of re-making the whole kernel reduces turn-around-times considerably).

Bearing all the discussed issues in mind, we decided for our CHEOPS[1] operating system, to design a so-called adaptation manager as its specific organic component responsible for configuration and adaptation issues.

The remainder of this paper is organised as follows. Section 2 shows how the adaptation management component fits into the object model of the CHEOPS system, how it is supposed to get its knowledge base filled, and how it exploits the knowledge. Section 3 sketches where to get and how to represent the knowledge. Related and future work is discussed in the last two sections.

2   The Adaptation Manager in CHEOPS

To provide fine-grained dynamic adaptability, the CHEOPS object management architecture allows to retain a lot of information from the source code level and to use it to make the system flexible to an unusual extent. Although many operating systems are coded in an object-oriented language (in most cases, this means C++), at runtime only a few deal with objects of the same granularity as at compile-time. So different notions of objects coexist in these projects: a runtime notion (e.g. active objects, consisting of processor context, message queue, code and data) and a notion during development (e.g. "traditional" objects just consisting of code and data). In order to make it easy to evolve an operating system during runtime, we propose straightforward mapping of development time notions into runtime abstractions. This way the same entities are dealt with when specifying, designing, implementing, and (last, but not least) running a system.

To make this straightforward mapping possible, CHEOPS objects are passive at the outset, are instances of a class, and encapsulate code and data. The representation of classes at runtime are the CHEOPS class objects. Such a class

---

[1] CHemnitz OPerating System

object exists at most once in each object-management hierarchy. Class objects are managed by a class object manager as depicted in Figure 1.

Other than, for instance, in Choices [MIKC92] CHEOPS class objects are specific

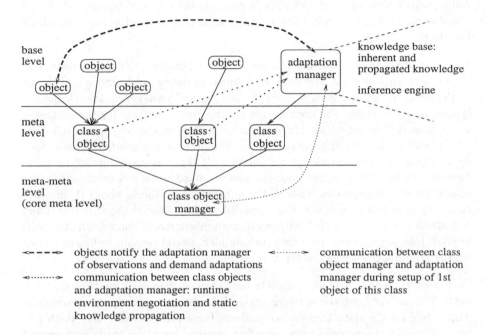

<div></div>	
◄- - -► objects notify the adaptation manager of observations and demand adaptations	◄·······► communication between class object manager and adaptation manager during setup of 1st object of this class
◄·······► communication between class objects and adaptation manager: runtime environment negotiation and static knowledge propagation	

Fig. 1. Adaptation manager and CHEOPS object management hierarchy

for each class. That means, they are instances of a class object class especially created for a given class.

Being the specific meta objects for objects of the same class, class objects are responsible for the execution environment of these objects. To ensure the objects get what they want, CHEOPS class objects negotiate with the adaptation manager till an acceptable solution is found.

CHEOPS class objects, too, can be used to plug in observer and filter objects. Since the VMT's of the class are managed by the class object, it is able to redirect calls for any of its objects and methods to other objects. Further, it can call pre-methods and after-methods before and after letting the real method execute.

Let's have a look on a simple example: an operating system on a PC with several I/O devices like sound card, network adapter and modem. These devices compete for IRQ numbers. If the default values do not match, the cards usually have to be programmed or jumper-ed. If the system knew of all the drivers that and what IRQ they want to use, it could at least easily detect conflicts and re-program a card or advise the user to re-jumper a card. With the adaptation manager, this means the following: both the IRQ the device wants to use and the range of IRQs it is capable of using are reported to the adaptation manager. Since the adaptation manager is connected with the system's resource management, a driver is not allowed to do anything till the IRQ wanted is reserved for it. If conflicts appear, the adaptation manager checks all IRQ ranges given by the drivers running and decides about a solution. With programmable cards, this could result in letting special objects re-program the cards. Without, this would result in an alert for the administrator and an appropriate advice how to adjust the IRQs.

Every time the first instance of a class has to be created, the appropriate class object is created, too. At this time, as detailed in the example above and shown in Figure 1, the class object teaches the adaptation manager all knowledge the system needs to create the appropriate runtime environments for the instances of the class it is representing. Having learned its lesson, the adaptation manager tries to ensure that the appropriate runtime environment is created. This is done by checking the new knowledge for conflicts. If there exists a conflict, it takes measures to dissolve it. In our example, this meant to find a new solution for IRQ allocation and to negotiate with all the affected class objects about it, in order that they switched to another IRQ if possible and told about their success. Only if matters can not be settled without human interference, the administrator is alerted. Like a good error message, such an alert would contain sufficient advice for the administrator what to try and do.

However, during their work objects may wish to change its runtime environment. For instance, let the network traffic increase significantly on a computer which, besides the data transfer, compiles a large piece of software. With less network traffic, there need only very few physical memory pages be reserved for incoming packets. The rest can be used by the compiler objects. As soon as the network traffic increases significantly, there needs to be more reserved, since throwing away packets en mass and getting them sent again would be very inefficient.

With the adaptation manager being always present and being an active entity, these adaptations can for the first time made happen automatically. This is another fact which clearly distinguishes the adaptation manager concept from what's custom today: just config files or registry databases would never be able to do this job.

One could suspect, that for yet another active component of the operating system, needing valuable resources, there would have to be a performance penalty paid for. Compared with a well optimised system, a performance penalty certainly has to be paid for it. But to optimise a system is a hard task, so a lot of today's installations are far from being well optimised. In these cases, having software which sees to optimisation automatically as far as possible, will result in a performance gain. Besides, sheer computing performance is not the main concern of most computer owners. They mostly want to get their work done and the costs of ownership to be low.

3 Appropriate Knowledge Bases

Considering knowledge bases, two great questions are to be answered: how the knowledge is to be represented and how it is to be obtained.

3.1 Knowledge Representation and Integrity

For our project, we decided that we would represent the knowledge in Prolog clauses. There are a couple of arguments in favour of Prolog: Prolog is the most widely used and the oldest of representation languages for unstructured knowledge. Hence, the amount of experience existing regarding the realisation of expert systems with Prolog is the greatest. Since we do not want to conduct AI research but depend on AI researchers' expertise, this was a point for Prolog. Another plus was the availability of free Prolog interpreters with good C interfaces for a variety of platforms, since we had to embed it into an operating system.

However, using Prolog means, too, that the provider of rules and facts is not forced to stick to some scheme of knowledge representation (except bringing it into the shape of clauses). Therefore, the adaptation manager has to verify new clauses closely before accepting them as correct. If we weren't strict about that right from the beginning, we would scarcely get an advantage (regarding consistency) over databases like the Windows registry. How this verification looks like depends on the clauses to check. By default, functor name, arity, and slot values all are subject to it. What the adaptation manager does if this examination fails, too, is dependent on what check failed. Normally, the clause is rejected as incorrect and, consequently, no objects of the class in question are created. An exception from this default, for example, are environment settings about file and directory locations: there is always only one "official" environment predicate describing a certain location, for instance, the location of the default editor. If not set with the force options, other predicates are automatically redirected to the "official" predicate. This way all applications use the same default editor, unless forcibly configured otherwise. Changing the default editor for all applications means just one alteration in the system's configuration. Further, the applications can configured separately to use an editor other than the default one easily.

3.2 Knowledge Acquisition

The configuration knowledge which formerly went into various files, databases, or directories the adaptation manager gets from the class objects. For whatever it needs to know about the current system dynamics, such as the current workload, it questiones appropriate system observer objects, or is notified by them.

Setting up automatic adaptation or optimisation cycles based on such observer objects and the adaptation manager is a very hard task. Automatic adaptation cycles are not suitable if the overhead needed for observing and finding a (possibly new) optimal solution (almost) exceeds the gained benefit. Ensuring this needs a lot of expertise about the dynamic behaviour of system components and about efficient algorithms to detect workload situation changes.

In respect to its acquisition, there are two different kinds of knowledge about dynamic behaviour of software components: the first is computable independent of execution, the other only obtainable through observation. An example for the first kind of knowledge is information about code page access behaviour: knowing the size of a page frame on the target machine, the compiler is able to compute information about the page most likely accessed next, depending on a currently accessed page. In contrast to this, information about compute time consumption, for instance, belongs to the second kind.

Obtaining knowledge by observation of running software components today is very limited. Usually it consists of periodically checking a small set of parameter values and using (heuristic) conditions indicating the need for a certain change. There are no tools to help an administrator or a programmer to find easily computable conditions for the optimisation of system parameters, they have to find all of them themselves. So we liked to know whether mathematical tools, machine learning methods, neural nets, or evolutionary algorithms could be of use in this context.

Therefore, we started an experiment using the Linux paging system (which is optimisable by roughly two dozen parameters) as object for finding optimisation rules. A Linux kernel compilation provided the workload on the test PC, a 486 equipped with 20 MB of RAM. We logged page in/out and swap in/out events. Since logging into a file proved not tolerable in this context, we cut 4 MB of RAM off the memory management, logged the events into this RAM portion and wrote the data to disk after the experiment cycle was finished. This way we ensured that the kernel worked like on a machine with 16 MB, pretty undisturbed by the logging. The resultant logs we tried to analyse using various tools.

Mathematical analysation (test for periodic paging load values via Fourier analysis) did not even discover regular cron job peaks. If there is a periodic occurrence of a similar load at all, the intervals are too long to be discovered with reasonable effort.

On neural nets, the effect was comparable to this: Because of the intervals with the same workload being extremely different in length, the net forgets everything it would need before the next interval even began. So-called recurrent neural nets which can handle data vectors of different length are available. But alas, they just assume the longest possible vector (equivalent to a time interval with us) and consume that much computing power, that it was not possible for us to proceed with this idea. However, AI specialists are working on these problems, so there might be a new type of neural net able to cope with input vectors very much different in length available sometime. Till then we will have to seek for a reasonable workaround, for instance, pre-computations which do not discard too much of the information contained in the original input vectors and unify the length.

With machine learning algorithms the input data, too, proved to be too complex. Evolutionary algorithms we did not try so far, since they aim at finding an optimal solution rather than recognising a pattern. Using them at most will result in finding an optimal set of parameters for the workload given during the experiment as a whole.

It has to be concluded that observing software components as a black box and deriving rules for optimal set screw settings will remain a great challenge, even with today's AI tools at hand. Therefore, the bulk of the rules in the knowledge base will be statically obtained knowledge originally provided by programmers and administrators. It will be provided either in Prolog clauses or in some configuration script language and transformed to clauses by a compiler or a runtime gateway like the /proc filesystem under Linux.

4 Related Work

[Hec91] introduces the concept of adaptiveness in an operating system using a knowledge base. From his point of view, the system consists of execution base, observation base and knowledge base. Observation base components notify the knowledge base of system state changes. Reflecting, the knowledge base may then give orders to the execution base. For the sake of efficiency, we do not require every runtime observation/environment change go via the adaptation manager. If some environment parameter, such as a scheduling time slice length, has to be adapted constantly according to a certain policy, we let an object do this directly as long as the system has to use this scheduling policy. Heck's work focuses on adaptiveness as the main purpose of the knowledge base, whereas our scope includes the system's configuration as well.

Apertos [Yok92] as the first reflective object-oriented operating system is related to CHEOPS in that respect, that both of them are object-oriented operating systems enabled to reflect about their own behaviour. However, they significantly differ in architecture: real Apertos objects are generally active, CHEOPS objects are passive until they get a thread attached temporarily. In CHEOPS, a single instance (the adaptation manager) does or controls reflective operations. In Apertos, this task is divided among reflectors. CHEOPS objects are managed by special class objects. In Apertos, this task is partly assigned to the reflectors and partly to the MClass meta-space.

Choices objects and class objects [MIKC92] are passive. However, in Choices class objects are not instances of a class object class especially tailored to the class of the objects they are representing. As in Apertos, the reflection approaches discussed are non-centralistic in respect to the operating system.

Lots of other work, especially about reflective and adaptive algorithms, could be discussed here, because the CHEOPS adaptation manager is able to integrate them rather than making every decision itself.

5 Future Work

The CHEOPS system is being implemented at three points in parallel. As of now, a part of the system core is already running on bare i486 hardware, the object management (tools for automatically generating raw class object classes and the class object manager) is implemented as a prototype running on top of Linux. The current prototype of the adaptation manager is implemented as a combination of a daemon and a dynamically loadable Linux kernel module. After the evaluation phase, the last two components will be ported to the native kernel.

At least the adaptation manager prototype will be further developed under both systems. We are interested in how this new technology is usable under "old" operating systems, especially how applications unaware of the existence of the adaptation manager can still use old configuration interfaces (/etc, for instance) and the system can profit from adaptation management. Therefore, the most pressing work is to further populate the till now sparsely filled knowledge base. In order not to program the whole knowledge base manually, new interface and development tools (e.g. gateway functions for some /etc config files) will have to be designed and programmed.

References

[BBC+96] R. Berg, L. Büttner, J. Cordsen, E.-M. Luther, H. Schmidt, and F. Schön. PEACE – Beispiel einer anwendungsorientierten Betriebssystemstruktur. *it+ti*, February 1996. Sonderheft Betriebssysteme.

[CHJ+94] V. Cahill, C. Hogan, A. Judge, D. O'Grady, B. Tangney, and P. Taylor. Extensible systems – the Tigger approach. Technical Report TCD-CS-94, University of Dublin, Trinity College, Department of Computer Science, Distributed Systems Group, September 1994. *Proceedings of the 6th ACM SIGOPS European Workshop*, ftp://ftp.dsg.cs.tcd.ie/pub/doc/TCD-CS-94-07.ps.gz.

[CIRM93] R. H. Campbell, N. Islam, D. Raila, and P. Madany. Designing and implementing Choices: an object-oriented system in C++. *Communications of the ACM*, 36(9):117–126, September 1993.

[Hec91] A. Heck. *Adaptive Betriebssystemkonzepte.* PhD thesis, Technische Hochschule Darmstadt, Fachbereich Informatik, 1991.

[MIKC92] Peter Madany, Nayeem Islam, Panayotis Kougiouris, and Roy H. Campbell. Practical examples of reification and reflection in C++. In *Proceedings of the International Workshop on Reflection and Meta-Level Architectures*, pages 76–82, November 1992.

[Rus91] V. F. Russo. *An object-oriented operating system.* PhD thesis, University of Illinois, 1991.

[SP93] W. Schröder-Preikschat. Design principles of parallel operating systems – a PEACE case study. Technical Report TR-93-020, International Computer Science Institute, Berkeley, California, USA, 1993.

[Yok92] Yasuhiko Yokote. The Apertos reflective operating system: the concept and its implementation. Technical Report SCSL-TR-92-014, Sony Computer Science Laboratory, October 1992. *Proceedings of the Seventh Annual Conference on Object-Oriented Systems, Languages, and Applications (OOPSLA'92)*, ftp://ftp.csl.sony.co.jp/CSL/CSL-Papers/92/SCSL-TR-92-014.ps.Z.

An Approach for Managing Highly Configurable Operating Systems

Danilo Beuche
danilo@first.gmd.de

GMD FIRST, Rudower Chaussee 5, 12489 Berlin, Germany

1 Introduction

Building a small and well adapted operating system for a particular problem class is one thing, building the same for a wide range of problems another.

Embedded systems e.g. are becoming more and more complex, and the assembly style programming which is quite usual in this context does not allow a quick adaption of old sources to a new problem which is only slightly different. Similar problems arise in massively parallel systems. The operating system should support every application optimal i.e. have no feature that is not used by the running application. Different application have different needs, one uses only a single task, other are doing full multitasking. All these operating systems have so much in common, that it pays off to share those common parts. Both kinds of adaption are solvable through use of object-oriented designs. But object-orientation is often said to bear too much overhead to be practical for systems with very limited resources. We claim that this is not true. With C++ very small systems can be built without compromising the principles of full object-orientation if a family based approach is used.

The operating system family PEACE [SP94] is an example for that kind of software. The goal is to support massively parallel execution of programs. The code is completely written in C++. PEACE shows that it is possible to build very efficient operating system platforms with object-oriented implementations.

The disadvantage of family based designs is the complex configuration of such systems. PEACE has 170 classes, which can be combined to 20 family members. It runs on four processor types using various underlying hard- and software platforms. This gives us more than 80 different sets of source code. Most source code is shared among the family members, but there are e.g. deviations in the inheritance path or different implementations of the same method in the family members.

One of the most important problems in object-orientation is to automatically combine classes and objects to a semantically correct system. Different approaches for solving that problem are known, most of them work on top of and independently from the implementation.

We propose a different solution. We try to annotate information about system components were it belongs to, in the class definition. This is done while maintaining full compatibility with existing tools as compilers, class browsers and so on. We use this information to mark functional components which consist of classes realizing one dedicated system function, e.g. a communication subsystem. For a given subsystem different variants may exist, each supporting different features. Externally stored information is used to represent relations between subsystems and system features. To generate a specific system we choose a set of system features. This set, combined with the description of relations and the annotated class definitions, is used to determine the classes plus the correct implementation variant that has to be used. All information is analyzed by a configuration tool, which is able to generate makefiles or other descriptions needed to build the system.

2 Problems

In order to build operating systems which have the properties

- small memory usage
- low overhead
- accommodation of a wide range of applications

the use of a program family [Par79] design is one solution.

An program family consists of entities called extensions which can be combined to form *family members*. The power of the program family approach derives from the ability to combine the *extensions* in manifold ways and thus construct different family members. Each family member supplies exactly the needed features to optimally support a given application. The functionalities common to all family members are called the *minimal subset* of system functionalities of that program family.

Managing the source code is an important problem when using family based designs as the same sources combined in several ways give the different family members. The use of tools which deal with configurations of program families can ease the handling of such problems. Users specify the needs and requirements for their customized operating systems. These tools then choose the right combination of the extensions and generate the appropriate family member.

It is important to make configuration and generation of family members feasible for the user of the operating system family because good adaption requires good knowledge about the problem to be solved. This knowledge is often available from the user only. To make optimal adaption feasible each system component (i.e. system extension in program families) must be as small as possible. In complex systems like PEACE this leads to a great number of family members, so it is not realistic to get all family members build by the family developers and give it precompiled to the user.

The major problem with building tools which simplify the configuration of complex operating system families is the loss of information when design structures are implemented. The information represented by conventional OO-languages covers only the code generation and simple software structures like modules or packages. In case of operating system families the knowledge

– which classes belong to a specific extension
– and the dependencies of extensions

are lost.

While it is possible to use hierarchical file system structures to group classes for an extension in a single directory, there is no easy way to express dependencies of extensions. But even the idea to use one directory per extension turns out to be a problem if one looks at the implementation of PEACE for example. Extensions may need different implementations if they are used on different platforms or as parts of different family members. The differences are usually very small which means that the source code would be almost the same in each directory for the extension variants. This may cause consistency problems e.g. when changes to the sources are made.

But the loss of dependency information has to be considered more seriously. Only valid combinations of system extensions will lead to a working family member, otherwise either compilation fails or in the worst case the operating system will behave unexpectedly. This problem is much like building a house from pre-fabricated elements as windows, doors, wall parts and so on. One can combine the single small elements in many different ways but only if one follows the general rules of house building and the specific rules for the chosen elements one gets a house where people can live in.

For managing operating system families we need a way of expressing similar rules to support easy configuration which yields optimal adapted family members.

3 Approach

To perform optimal configuration of an operating system family we use the following information:

– description of capabilities supported by the operating system family
– description of requirements of used hard- and software platforms
– assignment of class definitions to extensions
– dependencies of capabilities, requirements and extensions

Usual development tools and OO-languages are not able to represent this information, therefor we developed a language called ALC for that purpose. The language may be embedded into other OO-language to annotate e.g. class definitions or used stand alone e.g. for system descriptions and similar purposes.

The language consists of only two different kinds of statements: *attribute definitions* and *attribute instances*. Attribute definitions are used to name and structure information entities, e.g. to describe a system capability or system extension. Attribute instances or for short *attributes* represent a specific value out of the value range of an attribute definition. In the example below, we show the definition of an attribute that represents the processor types supported by an operating system and an annotated C++ class definition. The first statement is given in a pure ALC syntax, the second statement is the same definition given as valid C++ class definition. The last line shows how to annotate a C++ class definition with an attribute.

```
attribute enum mini::Machine { i386, i860, ppc };

class miniMachine: public enumAttribute {
        enum Values { i386, i860, ppc };
};

class cpuRegister { ... } /*! Machine = i386 !*/;
```

Each configuration information element (description of a system capability, a system requirement or a component) has to be represented by an appropriate attribute definition. To assign class definitions to components the C++ declarations have to be annotated with attributes. This is done through comments in which attribute instances are embedded. The dependencies are expressed in a separate language which allows manipulation of sets of attributes. The attribute definitions, the annotation of sources and the dependency description has to be done by the system developers. The attribute definitions are stored in a data base called the *type repository* and the dependencies are put in a file called dependency script.

The central element in the configuration process is the *type repository* which stores attribute and class definitions. The repository may be searched for definitions that match user defined conditions, e.g. annotation with a specific attribute. Unlike in C++ or other OO-languages a class definition in the repository may exist in different variants to support different implementations of a class. The complete, annotated source code of the operating system family is parsed by a tool called *analyzer* and then stored in the type repository. This is shown in the upper part of Fig. 1.

A user of the configuration system specifies the capabilities the family member should have. Furthermore the system requirements of the target computing platform must be specified. The configuration tool uses this information to check if a family member can support this configuration and if so, generate the necessary information to build it.

The first step in this check is to evaluate the operating system family dependencies with the user specified attribute set. The result is a set of needed components, supported system capabilities and requirements. In the next step the repository is searched for the needed system components and their classes. Within a component classes may uses classes from other components. All used components are added to the set of needed components. During the search for classes of an component only compatible class definition variants are included. For compatibility all attributes of the class must have the same value as given in the set of system capabilities and requirements. If an class attribute does not occur in this set, it is simply ignored.

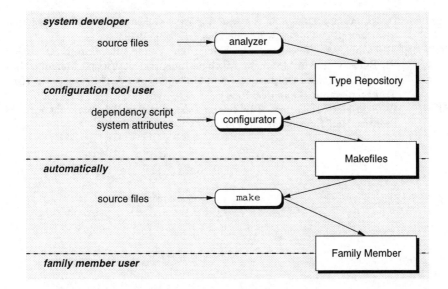

Fig. 1. Flow of configuration information

The result of the retrieval is an extended set of needed system components and a set of class definitions (with possibly more than one variant). The class definition set is used to build a C++ class graph. If this can be completed successfully, the last step is to generate a description with the information how to build the family member. This could be project descriptions like makefiles.

A prototype implementation of the configuration tools is described in [Beu97].

4   Conclusion

We presented a method for configuring an operating system family which allows optimal adaption to the applications needs. This configuration process is strictly separated from the actual building of the operating system. The configuration is done statically to avoid the overhead introduced by dynamic configuration support in traditional operating systems like Mach [RTY+88] or Linux.

The approach presented deals only with static, pre-runtime configuration. Planed enhancements will include interactive evaluation of the user needs and a graphical interface for the configuration tools. While not planed, it is also possibly to support other OO-languages apart from C++ with only minor modifications in the configuration process and tools.

References

[Beu97]   D. Beuche. Konfigurierung objektorientierter Programmfamilen in C++. Master's thesis, Technische Universität Berlin, 1997. english title: "Configuring object oriented program families in C++".

[Par79]   D. L. Parnas. Designing Software for Ease of Extension and Contraction. *Transaction on Software Engineering*, SE-5(2), 1979.

[RTY+88] R.Rashid, A. Tevanian, M. Young, D. Young, R. Baron, D. Black, W. Bolosky, and A. J. Chew. Machine-Independent Virtual Memory Management for Paged Uniprocessor and Multiprocessor Architectures. In *IEEE Transactions on Computer*, 1988.

[SP94]   W. Schröder-Preikschat. *The Logical Design of Parallel Operating Systems*. Prentice Hall International, 1994. ISBN 0-13-183369-3.

An Object-Oriented Abstract Machine as the Substrate for an Object-Oriented Operating System

Darío Álvarez Gutiérrez, Lourdes Tajes Martínez, Fernando Álvarez García,
María Ángeles Díaz Fondón, Raúl Izquierdo Castanedo, Juan Manuel Cueva Lovelle
Department of Computer Science, University of Oviedo
Calvo Sotelo, s/n, 33007 OVIEDO - SPAIN
{darioa,tajes,fag,fondon,ric,cueva}@pinon.ccu.uniovi.es

Abstract: *Using an object-oriented abstract machine brings a number of benefits for the construction of an object-oriented operating system. In this paper we describe the structure of an abstract machine designed for this task. This machine provides the basic object model and support for the rest of the system. Among other options, we propose a reflective architecture as a collaboration mechanism between the machine and the OS. Finally, we show how using this architecture based on the abstract machine improves and facilitates the construction of operating system features like orthogonal persistence, object distribution, concurrency and capability-based security, giving a flexible integral OO computing environment.*

1 Introduction

The adoption of the object-oriented paradigm is not done in an integral way in all the system components. This produces a serious impedance-mismatch and interoperability problem, for the paradigm changes and/or object translations made depending on which element to work with. The result is a proliferation of additional software layers trying to alleviate these problems, but introducing in fact extra complexity in the system.

An approach in order to solve this problem is to move the OO support for the rest of the system to a common place into the OS. Oviedo3 [1] is a research project that tries to build an experimental integral object-oriented system based on that foundation. All components: user interfaces, applications, languages, compilers, databases... and the operating system itself share the same object-oriented paradigm.

The object-oriented operating system (OOOS) is the basis for this integral system. It provides only one abstraction: objects. Objects can only create new objects from a class or send messages to others. We believe an operating system should supply transparently the following features for the objects of this integral system: a capability-based protection mechanism, complete persistence, object distribution and concurrency. There are operating systems exploring these topics. The distributed OS Amoeba explores sparse capabilities in an object-based environment, and Mungi is a distributed single address space persistent OS with password capabilities. Another OS focusing on persistence is Grasshopper. Nevertheless, we think this particular mix of properties is very adequate for an integral OO system, and worth to research jointly in the context described below.

One technique to structure an OOOS aimed to support an integral OO system which offers many advantages is to use an OO abstract machine as the substrate of the OOOS. This machine offers the basic object model and support to all objects of the rest of the system. The OS functionality is given by a set of user objects not different from any other object.

2 The Object-Oriented Operating System

The heart of the Oviedo3 system is the operating system, named SO4 [1]. The OS offers the abstraction of a single object space where objects exist indefinitely, virtually infinite, and where objects placed in different machines cooperate transparently using messages. Besides, the OS transparently achieves a set of important features: security, persistence, distribution and concurrency. In sections below, each one is analyzed in depth.

The master guidelines of the design of SO4 are:

- Object as the only abstraction. Only objects, of any granularity, exist.
- Intentionally "standard" object model, with the more common features found in OO programming languages: encapsulation, inheritance, and polymorphism [2].
- Exclusively OO working mode. An object can only create classes inheriting from others, create objects from a class, and send messages to other objects.
- Simpleness. To adhere to the above guidelines, achieving maximum simpleness.

Some important characteristics we wish to impose on objects, in accordance with these guidelines:

- Homogeneous objects. There are no special objects. OS objects themselves are not different from other objects.
- Transparency. Objects must not be aware of the existence of OS mechanisms to achieve features as persistence, message passing, distribution, etc.
- Self-contained objects. Objects encapsulate all the information about it, including computation. The behavior must not be dependent on other objects.
- Complete semantics. Objects have all the semantics embedded in the object model. They are not considered just as a contiguous memory space.
- Object identity. Each object has a unique identifier, which is used as a reference is the only means to access it. The concept of memory address space does not exist.

3 The Object-Oriented Abstract Machine

Using an OO abstract machine as the substrate for structuring the OOOS has many advantages. This machine supporting the OS should supply the essence of the aspects mentioned above: a simple self-contained homogeneous object model, with the object identity used as the unique access reference. This will be the only system abstraction.

Next, the overall organization of the Carbayonia abstract machine is shown. It has been designed specifically to support the OS as described above. This organization may be considered as a reference for the features that an abstract machine should have to support this kind of object-oriented OS. Other abstract machines could also be adapted for this purpose. Indeed, due to the popularity of the Java language, and the recent availability of public specifications we are considering the adaptation of the Java Virtual Machine [3].

The machine supports an object model with the following features: Object identity and abstraction, encapsulation, inheritance, and also generic and aggregation relationships between objects and, finally, polymorphism or message passing.

Figure 1 shows the architecture of the Carbayonia abstract machine [1], consisting of four areas: class area, references area, instance area, and system references area.

The class area maintains the description of each class. A set of primitive classes is permanently defined. The references area stores the references. Every reference has a type (relates to the class area) and points to an object of this type (relates to the instance area). The instance area stores objects created. And the system references area contains references with specific functions in the machine.

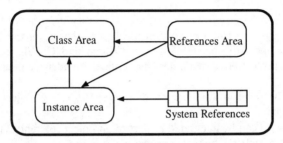

Fig. 1. Architecture of the Carbayonia abstract machine.

Each area can be considered as an object in charge of the management of its data.

The main characteristic of the machine is that every action upon an object is made using a reference to it.

The machine language is a pure OO low level language. It allows class declaration, method definition and exception handling. There are a number of classes built into the class area of the machine, with "Object" as the root class.

In the following, we will refer to objects in general, making no distinction between objects and classes.

Some of the preliminary advantages derived from using an abstract machine in general for this OS support task are:

- Impedance mismatch is removed. There is a common object model for the system, supplied by the machine for every object, including OS ones.
- Portability and programming language independence. Once an object is created in the machine, it is independent from the programming language used to define it.
- Implementation of OS features. In sections below OS features are described, and how they benefit from the use of the abstract machine.

4 Abstract Machine and OS Relationships. Reflectivity

The abstract machine can be considered as a kernel for the OS, supplying a basic support for objects, which will be extended by the OS to incorporate additional features. The machine should supply mechanisms to accomplish this. We consider three mechanisms basic for this, which should be present in the machine. These mechanisms can be used alone or in combination:

- Internal modification of the machine to adapt its inner workings to ease the implementation of a feature.
- Extension of the functionality of the basic classes. To add new attributes and methods to enlarge the functionality of the basic classes.
- Reflective architecture. To allow OS objects to collaborate with the machine when it cannot accomplish a task by itself by means of a reflective

architecture[4]. The machine should be given an architecture where the machine objects are exposed as normal objects. When a machine object can not continue for some problem, it raises an exception, which activates an OS object. This object will collaborate with the machine, intercommunicating with its objects to solve the problem, treating them just as other normal objects.

5 Security

Many operating systems use a protection mechanism based on the Lampson access matrix. Systems like Amoeba, Grasshopper, Mungi and Clouds use some kind of capability-based protection, while others like Guide, Amadeus, etc. use access control lists.

We intend to have a homogeneous access for every object based in two fundamental ideas:

- Capabilities [5] can be integrated as part of an object reference. They introduce a minimal overhead and the object model is not modified.
- Protection mechanism in the innermost level of the system, making the message passing mechanism check the protection information contained in the capability.

We propose to embody the protection management at the abstract machine level, converting references into capabilities, adding protection information to its contents.

New operations must be added to the machine, as well as modifying others to take into account the new role of references as capabilities.

Now, the machine must check the access rights after locating the object using its identifier in the capability. An exception is raised if no valid rights are held.

Thus advantages of both segregated and sparse capabilities [6] are combined. The machine guarantees capabilities can not be tampered with or altered without permission. Only the operations provided by the machine can be used to handle capabilities. Besides, neither the object model nor the way of using objects changes and the protection mechanism is transparent for the rest of the system. On the one hand, by using capabilities, the objects are not aware of the management of its protection. On the other, using capabilities as normal references in user structures facilitates system use, because there is no special way to access the segregated area where capabilities are stored.

6. Persistence

The function of the persistence system in SO4 is to provide a unique virtual persistent memory for objects, extending transparently the instance area by means of secondary storage. It creates a single persistent virtual space for objects. The main features desired are:

- Complete Orthogonal Persistence [7]. Every object is always persistent.
- Stability and Resilience [8]. The system must be able to resume operation after an unexpected system failure.

Some features of the abstract machine are very adequate to give support for persistence to the system:

- Unique object identifier. It is part of the references used in the objects. It eliminates pointer swizzling in disk swaps, as there is only one identifier for all situations.

- Self-contained Objects. A single operation stores the object on disk, including its computation, which is also encapsulated.

Putting together the above aspects a number of final advantages are achieved:

- Single memory abstraction. A single persistent virtual space replaces the duality of short-term and long-term memory, easier to understand and use for programmers and users.
- Continuous system and environment. The complete persistence of self-contained objects makes a truly continuous environment for every object, including OS ones.
- More intuitive interfaces. The system and the continuous environment permit interfaces closer to the user perception of the object functioning in the real world object. Disconnection, intended or not, does not alter their state.
- Virtual persistent distributed space. Together with the distribution system and using unique identifiers, a single distributed persistent object space among the machines of the system is created.

A way to support persistence is to use the exception ability of the machine to activate a "pager object" extending the instance area in a reflective way. Causes of activation may be object fault, object replacement, or arbitrary stabilization (figure 2).

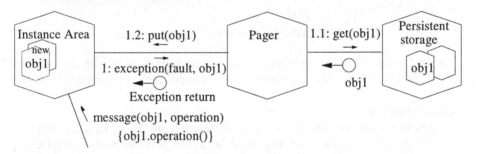

Fig. 2. Object Fault.

7 Distribution

On a distributed architecture consisting of several machines, the distribution system [9] allows inter-object communication without regard to its location, and provides mobility mechanisms with the maximum degree of transparency.

The goals of the distribution system [1] can be reduced to:

- Access and location transparency [10]. To provide a location service that delivers the messages to the objects, regardless of its location.
- Object mobility and load balancing.

Some of the features of the abstract machine imply several immediate advantages for distribution:

- Unique object identifier. Objects are always referenced and accessed in the same way regardless of their location.
- Self-contained objects. Moving an object between machines is achieved just by moving its encapsulated state that includes the computation.

Combining these aspects some advantages are obtained:

- Single object distributed space.
- Performance improvement, by balancing the load of the whole system using object mobility.
- Reliability improvement, using a replication mechanism (as in Chorus or Clouds), possibly in combination with the persistence mechanism.

The use of a location object server as in the Clouds system and a load-balancing object is an approach to implement distribution.

Figure 3 shows a possible scenario of invoking a method in an object and the interaction between the persistence and distribution mechanisms.

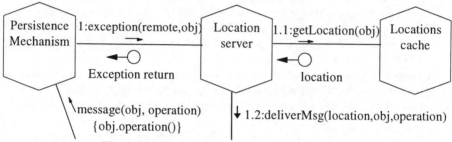

Fig. 3. Delivering a message for a remote object

A load-balancing object implements the object mobility policy of the system, based mainly on the load of every machine and the interaction with remote objects.

8 Concurrency

We try to endow the system with a *simple* concurrency model [1] that achieves the *maximization of the parallelism degree* in a secure way, allowing concurrency between objects and between methods of the same object, in the most secure way.

These are the main aspects of the concurrency model proposed for the system:

- Multithreaded active objects [9, 11]. Active objects that encapsulate computation are a natural extension of the self-contained object model provided by the abstract machine. Conceptually, they have a virtual multiprocessor for multiple threads, with the needed concurrency control mechanisms. Other existing OS such as Clouds and Guide chose a passive object model and supply an abstraction like process or thread to provide computation.
- Synchronous invocation [11]. For simpleness reasons, a thread of an object is blocked during the invocation of a method of another object.
- Exclusive and concurrent methods. When defining a method, it must be tagged as exclusive or concurrent. An exclusive method modifies the state of the object and cannot coexist with any other thread in the object. Objects behave as monitors when dealing with this kind of methods. Concurrent methods do not modify its state, so their threads are compatible with other concurrent threads. This approach has become very popular and recently languages such as Java have a similar concurrent model [12].

A set of objects provides the concurrency mechanism functionality. It seems more adequate to include some of this functionality in the machine and the rest in objects providing OS functionality. Method execution ability and the characterization of methods as exclusive or concurrent is offered by the machine. OS objects will implement concurrency policies.

9 Reflective abstract machine + OOOS: very flexible integral OO computing environment

The reflective architecture of the machine makes machine objects usable just like any other objects. This yields a computing environment seen as a set of homogeneous interacting objects. Thus the separation among base machine, operating system and user applications is removed: a single integral OO computing environment (figure 4).

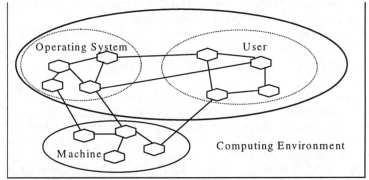

Fig. 4. Computing environment composed of a set of homogeneous objects

In this computing environment, the OS, user applications, and even the base machine itself, take advantage of the OO paradigm, including areas such as flexibility, extensibility and reusability:

- Removal of non-necessary objects. Customized computing environments can be built as needed.
- Object replacing. It is possible to dynamically replace an object for another providing the same services in a different way.
- Reusability. Every object is organized into a class hierarchy. This allows code reuse, using the inheritance of the system. It is not necessary to re-implement functionality already present in other objects (even from the OS or the machine itself).

The combination of the three above elements produces a very flexible computing environment, easily adaptable and extensible, but in a secure way controlled by the machine capability protection mechanism.

There are other research projects with this goal of an integral OO system. Tunes [13] and Merlin [14] are systems which share this approach of using reflective architectures to obtain such environments, organized around the SELF language in the case of Merlin, and with a new language developed for Tunes.

10 Conclusions

The combination of an OO abstract machine offering object support with an OO operating system implemented as a set of objects is a promising way of structuring

OO integral systems. Advantages such as portability, language independence and impedance mismatch removal are complemented with improvement and ease of implementation of the functionality of the OOOS.

A reflective architecture for the abstract machine is one of the most important mechanisms the machine must provide to qualify as a substrate for an OOOS.

The most relevant aspects of the OOOS are security, persistence, distribution and concurrency. The design decisions presented for every of these aspects, coupled with the OO abstract machine will give the user a computing environment completely based on the object oriented philosophy, more flexible, coherent, intuitive and easier of use, removing most of the problems of existing systems.

Oviedo3 is a research project at the University of Oviedo that intends to develop an experimental integral object system with this structure, using the Carbayonia OO abstract machine and the SO4 OO operating system.

A first version of the abstract machine (developed under Windows NT) is complete. The detailed design of the operating system components has now begun, for a subsequent implementation on the abstract machine.

References

[1] Cueva Lovelle, J.M., and others, Sesión "Sistemas Operativos Orientados a Objetos: Seguridad, Persistencia, Concurrencia y Distribución" (Object-Oriented Operating Systems: Security, Persistence, Concurrency and Distribution), II Jornadas sobre Tecnologías Orientadas a Objetos, Oviedo, Spain, March 1996. (in spanish).
[2] Booch, G. "Object-Oriented Analysis and Design with Applications", 2nd edition, Benjamin Cummings, 1993.
[3] Sun Microsystems Computer Corporation, "Java Virtual Machine Specification, Version 1.0 Beta", URL ftp://ftp.javasoft.com/docs/vmspec.ps.z, November 1996.
[4] Maes, P. "Concepts and Experiments in Computational Reflection", Proc. OOPSLA, pp 147-155, 1987.
[5] Dennis, J.B., and E.C. Van Horn, "Programming Semantics for Multiprogrammed Computations", Communications of the ACM, Vol. 9, N.3, 1966.
[6] Anderson M., and C. Wallace, "Some comments on the implementation of capabilities", The Australian Computer Journal, 1988.
[7] Atkinson, M.P., P. Bailey, K. J. Chisholm, W.P. Cockshott, and R. Morrison, "An Approach to Persistent Programming", The Computer Journal, vol 26, 4, pp 360-365, 1983.
[8] Dearle, A., J. Rosenberg, F. Henskens, F. Vaughan, and K. Maciunas, "An Examination of Operating System Support for Persistent Object Systems", Proc. of the 25th Hawaii International Conference on System Sciences, Hawaii, U.S.A., pp 779-789, 1992.
[9] Chin, R.S., and S.T. Chanson, "Distributed Object-Based Programming Systems", ACM Computing Surveys, Vol. 23, N.1, March 1991.
[10] Coulouris, G., J. Dollimore, and T. Kindberg, "Distributed Systems. Concepts and Design", 2nd edition, Addison-Wesley, 1994.
[11] Papathomas, M., "Concurrency Issues in Object-Oriented Programming Languages", in Object-Oriented Development TR, Centre Universitaire d´Informatique, University of Geneva, ed. Tsichritzis, D., 1989.
[12] Sun Microsystems Computer Corporation, "The Java Language Specification", URL ftp://ftp.javasoft.com/docs/langspec-1.0.ps.Z, November 1996.
[13] The Tunes project, URL http://www.eleves.ens.fr:8080/home/rideau/Tunes/, November 1996.
[14] The Merlin Project, URL http://www.lsi.usp.br/~jecel/merlin.html, November 1996.

Objects in Different Execution Environments

Sven Graupner

Chemnitz University of Technology
Department of Computer Science, Operating Systems Group
09107 Chemnitz, Germany
E-Mail: sgr@informatik.tu-chemnitz.de

Abstract. Object-orientation (OO) is primarily a software development technique. One of its major advantages is covering all phases of software development by a widely uniform methodology: analysis, design, and programming. It is obvious to extend this into run-time systems as well, where object-oriented software structures are not adequately reflected in most cases today. Run-time or implementation details should be hidden to developers, but there might be reasons for making them explicit. This paper points out such reasons of explicit separation of Object- (OM) and Execution Models (EM). It is intended to describe the problem sphere, to classify domains of executional qualities and to derive a simple model for dealing with objects and different execution environments.

1 Object Models and Execution Models

An **Object Model (OM)** specifies general assumptions of systems composed of objects and relations, whereas *systems* actually relate to *models of real-world systems*. OO provides a common methodology for analyzing ($\rightarrow$ deriving models) and developing systems ($\rightarrow$ model and system construction):

- objects are basic system components with attributes: encapsulate states and behavior ($\rightarrow$ state transitions),
- objects partially expose attributes to other objects by interfaces,
- interacting objects define system behavior,
- equal objects share equal sets of object-attributes,
- classes describe sets of equal objects,
- inheritance relations among classes are used to centralize descriptions of common subsets of object-attributes, see also [1, 7].

Object-orientation provides a method for centralizing and classifying descriptions of *system models* with elements, attributes and relations, which can be mapped into hierarchical structures, such as class- (inheritance-) or aggregation-hierarchies. This reduces redundancy and complexity and is close to mental rules of grouping and structuring, and hence of abstraction and thinking. There are also disadvantages of hierarchical structures but these are not discussed here.

Object-orientation basically comprises two domains. First, an analytical for deriving models from parts of reality and describing them in terms of classes, objects, attributes and relations ($\rightarrow$ OOA). The second domain is construction for building first models and then information processing systems (or parts of them). During OOD, the analyzed model reflecting an application area is transformed into a *new model of an information processing system* to be made. Terms of a machine are relevant, such as states, methods, and method invocations. The same terminology is applied for both models (OOA and OOD), but referred areas are actually different. In OOP, designs are furtherly transformed into descriptions (programs) for controlling processing of abstract machines. OO methodology succeeds well over OO[ADP] because it *always refers to models* over all phases.

Object-oriented programming languages define, as every programming language, abstract machines which combine application- or object-related elements of design models ($\rightarrow$ OM: classes, class relations, objects, object relations) with processing elements of a machine ($\rightarrow$ EM: processes, states and interaction).

The **Execution Model (EM)** specifies general assumptions of information processing of a particular real (or abstract) machine with particular *"kinds of elements"* (processes, states) and *"kinds of processing"* (interaction).
OM- and EM-related aspects are not clearly separated in most object-oriented languages and systems today. OM-related parts are typically exposed in languages by means of specifying classes, objects, interaction and so forth. EM-related parts are widely kept invisible, they are implicitly assumed.

Some examples can illustrate this for C++. There is always only one thread of control in a system of C++ objects. Interaction means calling local procedures. Memory holding object states is always versatile and not permanent. Object identification is based on addresses in main memory. Addresses are unique only for one processor address space which is likewise assumed to contain all objects. Method code is fixed and cannot be changed or extended during run-time.
All these are examples of EM-related (implicit) assumptions of C++. Only some can be explicitly expressed in programs, such as storage classes for variables and objects: static, automatic, and register. Others are implementation platform-specific, but most of them are implicit and not pictured in programs.
Thinking and developing software in terms of simplified and well structured models and abstractions really eases the software development process. Insights into realization details are not desired and are not necessary in many cases.

Abstract machines defined by languages must be implemented some way. There are two basic principles. One is compiling programs (or transforming descriptions) for an abstract, object-oriented machine into programs for a lower level, not necessarily object-oriented (real) machine. The other is running an implementation of an abstract machine as a software layer upon an underlying machine. Hierarchies of machines ($\rightarrow$ layers) imply different executional qualities with each layer, and OM-related aspects usually become less represented down this hierarchy (see Fig. 2).

OM-qualities of particular object-oriented programming languages are likewise OM-qualities of abstract machines defined by that languages. The "layer-below" machines need not necessarily cover these OM-qualities and usually does not, because they are not visible to developers. Hence, OM-qualities are lost during compilation. The same holds for the second case of running an abstract machine upon a lower-layered machine. OM needs not to be applied for internal structure itself. Arguments for that are mainly efficiency and "no necessity". Higher-level structures cause more memory- and CPU-consumption and should be avoided, and representing higher level structures inside systems is also not actually necessary because they are hidden to developers.

To summarize, the mixture of OM and EM in languages results from the intersection of models (OM in OOA, OOD, OOP) with real processing (EM).

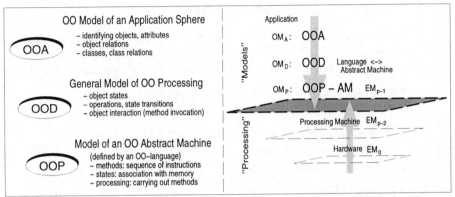

Fig.1 Different Models in OO   Fig.2 OM-Levels and EM-Layers

2   Relevance of OM and EM

The mixture of OM and EM in object-oriented languages is actually not seen as a problem by developers. It seems artificially pointing it out here in such detail. OM-related ($\rightarrow$ functional) aspects should dominate the software development process. A lot of software can be developed in terms of abstract machines without recognizing particular mappings to (or implementations of) "real" executing machines. Mappings are automated, either by compiling or interpretation.

Why should it be necessary to deal with different EM? Today, languages provide more or less comfortable facilities for expressing OM-related qualities for defining and deriving classes, creating objects, object interaction etc. But they provide fairly simple EM. The case of C++ was discussed above. EM of given languages can only be accepted if these EM are sufficient for applications. This usually holds for that class of applications the language was designed for. But there is an increasing number of applications with demands beyond, so that EM must be extended. **Extending EM** of OO programming systems is the major reason for dealing with and separating OM and EM in systems.

An example is a *"distributed system of C++-objects"* which spawns across several machines. C++ cannot capture this EM. There must be a further *"model behind"* which encloses distributed servers as basic system components. The OM, however, should remain unchanged for software developers. Another example are object-oriented operating systems with different EM in each layer. It is aspired to smooth OO structures across kernel- and application- and also inside kernel-layers. This can be achieved for OM, but EM will remain different.

Reasons can be summarized that it *could* be relevant to deal with different EM:
- distributed applications are beyond EM of many languages or systems,
- systems spawning several system layers are faced with different EM,
- application-initiated adaptations of underlying layers may change EM.

3 Execution Qualities make EM

It is difficult to identify all possible facets of executional qualities. Formalizing them is nearly impossible. Therefore, a selection should be given here which is grouped into three categories. EM-qualities basically comprise for OO systems:

- the existence of objects ("kinds" of objects),
- the effects of processes ("behavior"), and
- the global system structure.

Objects always need some kind of *"container"* to exist. Qualities of such containers have strong influence on EM.

- The **existence of objects** comprises:
  - installation of objects (type descriptions),
  - creation and destruction of objects, lifetime (persistent, volatile),
  - object identification,
  - accessibility (relation to addressing and protection domains),
  - existence in single or multiple containers (cached or replicated),
  - bound to a fixed location or migratable.

Objects are primarily considered as passive here. They are *subjects of actions* which are directed to objects. Processes are the actual processing entities in systems. Hence, there must be at least one process making a system of objects alive. Objects hold and encapsulate states and provide services upon states for processes which then carry out state transitions.

- **Kinds of processes** have strong influence on dynamic EM-qualities:
  - one or multiple processes, globally or attached to objects, with:
    - one global process among all objects ("C++"),
    - multiple global processes among all objects ("multi-threaded C++"),
    - one process attached to each object (active objects, server-objects),
    - multiple processes attached to each object (multi-threaded objects),
    - one process per method invocation (per method threads),
  - general process model: cooperative, concurrent, kind of scheduling policy,
  - relations to address spaces: globally shared, partially shared, individual,
  - access protection: objects, methods (permissions), object- or global states,
  - means of interaction: among processes or active objects.

- The **global system structure** comprises the basic system elements and their relations to objects, layers (machines), object-containers and processes:
  - layers: only one layer with one EM, multiple layers with multiple EM,
  - containers at each layer:
    - one global container for all objects,
    - multiple containers with one object each,
    - multiple containers with multiple objects,
  - relations among processes, and objects within containers.

Any OO programming language can be categorized by this points. It is understood that any particular EM cannot cover *all* qualities. The EM of C++ was kept simple ($\rightarrow$ e.g. one single process) to avoid complexity ($\rightarrow$ e.g. for synchronizing processes), because it is not necessary for most C++-applications.

4 Extending EM or OM

Complex systems require more complex EM than languages usually offer. EM must be adapted or extended to meet these requirements: objects should become persistent or should migrate, they should optionally exist with multiple replicas, or processes should be attached to objects making them active. Many other qualities are possible and might be useful for particular applications.

Approaches in languages for extending EM are as old as languages. New languages were designed or derived from existing languages in the past, especially for introducing concurrency [3]. Examples are the "concurrent"-versions of languages like C or Pascal. Proposals were made for new languages like Distributed Processes or CSP. Ada or Chill a priori considered concurrency. All these languages and extensions came up long before object-orientation.

Summarized, there are several ways for extending EM of (OO) languages: designing new languages, extending languages, and also meta-level languages. Meta-level languages are newer approaches typically in combination with object-orientation. An example is the CLOS-extension in [4].
Creating new languages with particular EM-qualities for applications has some difficulties. New languages with new syntax and semantics must be established, compilers and tools must be developed which is costly and takes time. Only a small number of languages have a real chance to become popular.
It is more easier to extend EM of existing languages than designing new ones. This was extensively done with C++ for adapting it to application requirements beyond its predefined EM-qualities. It again primarily referred to concurrency and distribution: Concurrent C++, μC++, Presto, QPC++, ACT++, or C&&. Extensions differ by kinds of extension techniques:
  - source code modifications by preprocessors,
  - (class-) libraries with side effects,
  - link-time modifications by post-processors,
  - load-time and run-time modifications.

Source code modifications and (class-) libraries are most popular techniques.

Object management systems, as operating systems, typically provide fixed EM for object-oriented applications. BirliX [2] is an example of such a system. Objects (or teams, as called here) are *always* persistent, distributed (RPC for interaction in general) and exist with individual address spaces. The problem is not this particular set of qualities, they are certainly appropriate for some kinds of applications, the problem rather is inflexibility of the *one EM* which cannot be changed or adapted. Efforts were taken for "opening up" the BirliX-kernel to introduce new or changed EM-qualities, as for object interaction by reflective techniques [8]. Many systems promoting general usability tend to apply general "super-sets" of EM-qualities, which are usually the most expensive ones on the other side. Thus, the general approach should not be providing a general, all purpose EM, it rather should be providing *general flexibility* that EM can be adapted to particular needs and environments. EM must be made explicit for that and must be identifiable in systems.

4.1 Meta-Level Approaches

Lower system-layers act as infrastructures for higher layers. They immediately set up EM-qualities. Adaptable EM can thus be achieved by adaptable "layers below" or adaptable infrastructures.

The basic idea of "meta-level" systems, abstract machines or languages is: opening up "layers below" making them changeable [4, 5]. It directly affects realizations and likewise implementations of abstract machines, which were previously closed for developers. It either concerns compilers or machine implementations. There are examples of meta-level approaches for both cases.

4.2 Conclusions for Extending EM

The essentials of extending EM in languages or systems can be summarized.

- EM enclose non-functional qualities, like concurrency, persistence, distribution or replication with different shapes in different layers.
- Executional requirements of applications are becoming more and more diverse, and applications typically require only particular subsets of them.
- Systems should provide flexibility (adaptability) instead of generality.
- Developers should remain thinking in terms of abstractions as far as possible, OM should be invariant and not overloaded with EM-extensions.
- A solution is explicitly separating OM- and EM-related parts in systems.
- Meta-level languages and systems fulfill this isolation to a certain degree. OM and EM *can be* (and *should be*) distinguished in object- and meta-levels. But the separation between 'levels" does not always refer to the separation between OM and EM-qualities in existing meta-level systems.

5 "Containers" Providing EM-Qualities

If functional- (OM) and non-functional (EM) aspects should conceptionally be distinguished, both should be assigned to separate system components. This is possible with meta-level systems by concentrating non-functional qualities in meta-levels. Most meta-level systems allow objects to control their meta-levels causing effects that are reflected back to objects. It is a matter of interpretation what "meta-levels" in systems actually are. Systems layers can act as infrastructures for superior object-spaces. Infrastructures or system layers are separated and have a "causal connection" to their objects. Hence, infrastructures can be seen as meta-levels, and infrastructures can be designed to allow objects controlling their EM-qualities to some degree. Meta-level systems explicitly support and encourage meta-level interaction to achieve higher degrees of flexibility, particularly directed to extending or adapting EM.

In Apertos [10], meta-levels are provided by meta-spaces composed of meta-objects. Objects are causally connected to their meta-spaces. This general concept depends on particular implementations. Other meta-level systems, as the CLOS-extension described in [4], "open up" their implementations, that means the abstract machine implementing the CLOS-layer. It globally affects the machine implementation and is thus globally reflected to object space.

Another variant is possible as well and should be promoted here. Not system layers provide a global EM for all objects, but so-called "containers" form the environment of existence and processing for the enclosed objects. Containers can be seen as a special shaping of meta-spaces. However, containers are not made of meta-objects. They are established by infrastructures or lower system layers and add a "third tier" to the coarser-grain "2-tier-structure" of infrastructures and object spaces. Containers allow finer-grained and individual tuning EM according to application demands directed to particular sets of objects and not globally affecting all objects.

The idea of using containers is based on observations of real systems. Objects do not exist in virtual (meta-) spaces. In Unix, they only exist within Unix-processes. If distributed systems spawn across several processes, the global system structure cannot only be based on objects,

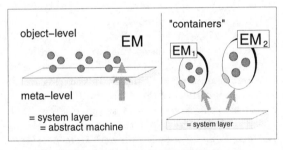

Fig.3 Meta-levels and Containers

it must also comprise processes or servers. The global system structure of the CORBA system is based on objects ($\rightarrow$ OM) and servers ($\rightarrow$ EM) containing objects [6]. There are several mappings of objects into servers. Sun's Spring-kernel also supports objects and servers [9], which is intentionally close to CORBA.

6 Summary

The idea of containers is combining servers with the ability to provide different and finer-grained EM to individual groups of objects. It is based on observations of existing object-systems, like CORBA or Spring. The step beyond "pure servers" of these systems is proposing containers (or "servers") also for comprising individual EM-qualities for enclosed objects. By this, objects can be isolated from controlling their EM by delegating this to related containers. Reasons for containers can be summarized:

- **intended goals:**
  - isolate EM from OM by a further, finer-grained level: container,
  - keep OM simple by concentrating EM in containers rather than in layers,
  - isolate objects from meta-level control by delegating this to containers,
  - individual and finer-grained EM for subsets of objects are easier to achieve;
- **practical relevance:**
  - already applied technique (layers/servers/objects),
  - simpler implementation technique compared to system layers;
- **related approaches:**
  - meta-level systems are usually 2-tier, with one global object-area and one related meta-level, containers provide individual meta-spaces.

The relevance of the proposed containers is also confirmed by current developments in CORBA. An example is the Persistence Object Service (POS). Persistent objects reside in servers that explicitly provide this particular EM-quality.

Containers are expected to provide more individual, easier adaptable EM and are an advantageous concept for structuring adaptable object-oriented systems.

References

1. Coad, P. and Yourdon, E. *Object-Oriented Design.* Yourdon Press Computing Series, 197 p. Prentice-Hall, Inc., Englewood Cliffs, New Jersey, USA, 1991.
2. Härtig, H., Kühnhauser, W., Lux, W., and Reck, W. Operating System(s) on Top of Persistent Object Systems. *Proc. of 25th HICSS*, pages 790–799, January 1992.
3. Karaorman, M. and Bruno, J. Introducing Concurrency to a Sequential Language. *Communications of the ACM*, 36(9):103–113, September 1993.
4. Kiczales, G., Riviéres, J. des, and Bobrow, D.G. *The Art of the Metaobject Protocol.* 335 p. The MIT Press, Cambridge, Massachusetts, USA, 1991.
5. Maes, P. and Nardi, D., editors. *Meta-Level Architectures and Reflection,* selected papers, 355 p., 1986. Elsevier Science Publishers B.V. 1988.
6. OMG. *The Common Object Request Broker: Architecture and Specification, Revision 2.0.* Object Management Group (OMG), 463 p., USA, July, 1995.
7. Rumbaugh, J., Blaha, M., Premerlani, W., Eddy, F., and Lorensen, W. *Object-Oriented Modeling and Design.* Prentice-Hall, 1991.
8. Sonntag, S. *Adaptierbarkeit durch Reflexion.* PhD thesis, 103 S., Technische Universität Chemnitz, Fakultät für Informatik und GMD Birlinghoven, Juni 1993.
9. SunSoft. *A Spring Collection – A Collection of Papers on the Spring Distributed Operating System.* Sun Microsystems, Inc., USA, September 1994.
10. Yokote, Y. The Apertos Reflective Operating System: The Concept and Its Implementation. *Proceedings of OOPSLA '92*, pages 414–434, October 1992.

Author Index

554

Springer
and the
environment

At Springer we firmly believe that an international science publisher has a special obligation to the environment, and our corporate policies consistently reflect this conviction.
We also expect our business partners – paper mills, printers, packaging manufacturers, etc. – to commit themselves to using materials and production processes that do not harm the environment. The paper in this book is made from low- or no-chlorine pulp and is acid free, in conformance with international standards for paper permanency.

Springer

Lecture Notes in Computer Science

For information about Vols. 1–1280

please contact your bookseller or Springer-Verlag

Vol. 1317: M. Leman (Ed.), Music, Gestalt, and Computing. IX, 524 pages. 1997. (Subseries LNAI).

Vol. 1318: R. Hirschfeld (Ed.), Financial Cryptography. Proceedings, 1997. XI, 409 pages. 1997.

Vol. 1319: E. Plaza, R. Benjamins (Eds.), Knowledge Acquisition, Modeling and Management. Proceedings, 1997. XI, 389 pages. 1997. (Subseries LNAI).

Vol. 1320: M. Mavronicolas, P. Tsigas (Eds.), Distributed Algorithms. Proceedings, 1997. X, 333 pages. 1997.

Vol. 1321: M. Lenzerini (Ed.), AI*IA 97: Advances in Artificial Intelligence. Proceedings, 1997. XII, 459 pages. 1997. (Subseries LNAI).

Vol. 1322: H. Hußmann, Formal Foundations for Software Engineering Methods. X, 286 pages. 1997.

Vol. 1323: E. Costa, A. Cardoso (Eds.), Progress in Artificial Intelligence. Proceedings, 1997. XIV, 393 pages. 1997. (Subseries LNAI).

Vol. 1324: C. Peters, C. Thanos (Eds.), Research and Advanced Technology for Digital Libraries. Proceedings, 1997. X, 423 pages. 1997.

Vol. 1325: Z.W. Ras´, A. Skowron (Eds.), Foundations of Intelligent Systems. Proceedings, 1997. XI, 630 pages. 1997. (Subseries LNAI).

Vol. 1326: C. Nicholas, J. Mayfield (Eds.), Intelligent Hypertext. XIV, 182 pages. 1997.

Vol. 1327: W. Gerstner, A. Germond, M. Hasler, J.-D. Nicoud (Eds.), Artificial Neural Networks – ICANN '97. Proceedings, 1997. XIX, 1274 pages. 1997.

Vol. 1328: C. Retoré (Ed.), Logical Aspects of Computational Linguistics. Proceedings, 1996. VIII, 435 pages. 1997. (Subseries LNAI).

Vol. 1329: S.C. Hirtle, A.U. Frank (Eds.), Spatial Information Theory. Proceedings, 1997. XIV, 511 pages. 1997.

Vol. 1330: G. Smolka (Ed.), Principles and Practice of Constraint Programming – CP 97. Proceedings, 1997. XII, 563 pages. 1997.

Vol. 1331: D. W. Embley, R. C. Goldstein (Eds.), Conceptual Modeling – ER '97. Proceedings, 1997. XV, 479 pages. 1997.

Vol. 1332: M. Bubak, J. Dongarra, J. Was´niewski (Eds.), Recent Advances in Parallel Virtual Machine and Message Passing Interface. Proceedings, 1997. XV, 518 pages. 1997.

Vol. 1333: F. Pichler. R.Moreno-Di´az (Eds.), Computer Aided Systems Theory – EUROCAST'97. Proceedings, 1997. XII, 626 pages. 1997.

Vol. 1334: Y. Han, T. Okamoto, S. Qing (Eds.), Information and Communications Security. Proceedings, 1997. X, 484 pages. 1997.

Vol. 1335: R.H. Möhring (Ed.), Graph-Theoretic Concepts in Computer Science. Proceedings, 1997. X, 376 pages. 1997.

Vol. 1336: C. Polychronopoulos, K. Joe, K. Araki, M. Amamiya (Eds.), High Performance Computing. Proceedings, 1997. XII, 416 pages. 1997.

Vol. 1337: C. Freksa, M. Jantzen, R. Valk (Eds.), Foundations of Computer Science. XII, 515 pages. 1997.

Vol. 1338: F. Plás˘il, K.G. Jeffery (Eds.), SOFSEM'97: Theory and Practice of Informatics. Proceedings, 1997. XIV, 571 pages. 1997.

Vol. 1339: N.A. Murshed, F. Bortolozzi (Eds.), Advances in Document Image Analysis. Proceedings, 1997. IX, 345 pages. 1997.

Vol. 1340: M. van Kreveld, J. Nievergelt, T. Roos, P. Widmayer (Eds.), Algorithmic Foundations of Geographic Information Systems. XIV, 287 pages. 1997.

Vol. 1341: F. Bry, R. Ramakrishnan, K. Ramamohanarao (Eds.), Deductive and Object-Oriented Databases. Proceedings, 1997. XIV, 430 pages. 1997.

Vol. 1342: A. Sattar (Ed.), Advanced Topics in Artificial Intelligence. Proceedings, 1997. XVII, 516 pages. 1997. (Subseries LNAI).

Vol. 1343: Y. Ishikawa, R.R. Oldehoeft, J.V.W. Reynders, M. Tholburn (Eds.), Scientific Computing in Object-Oriented Parallel Environments. Proceedings, 1997. XI, 295 pages. 1997.

Vol. 1344: C. Ausnit-Hood, K.A. Johnson, R.G. Pettit, IV, S.B. Opdahl (Eds.), Ada 95 – Quality and Style. XV, 292 pages. 1997.

Vol. 1345: R.K. Shyamasundar, K. Ueda (Eds.), Advances in Computing Science - ASIAN'97. Proceedings, 1997. XIII, 387 pages. 1997.

Vol. 1346: S. Ramesh, G. Sivakumar (Eds.), Foundations of Software Technology and Theoretical Computer Science. Proceedings, 1997. XI, 343 pages. 1997.

Vol. 1347: E. Ahronovitz, C. Fiorio (Eds.), Discrete Geometry for Computer Imagery. Proceedings, 1997. X, 255 pages. 1997.

Vol. 1348: S. Steel, R. Alami (Eds.), Recent Advances in AI Planning. Proceedings, 1997. IX, 454 pages. 1997. (Subseries LNAI).

Vol. 1349: M. Johnson (Ed.), Algebraic Methodology and Software Technology. Proceedings, 1997. X, 594 pages. 1997.

Vol. 1350: H.W. Leong, H. Imai, S. Jain (Eds.), Algorithms and Computation. Proceedings, 1997. XV, 426 pages. 1997.

Vol. 1351: R. Chin, T.-C. Pong (Eds.), Computer Vision – ACCV'98. Proceedings Vol. I, 1998. XXIV, 761 pages. 1997.

Vol. 1352: R. Chin, T.-C. Pong (Eds.), Computer Vision – ACCV'98. Proceedings Vol. II, 1998. XXIV, 757 pages. 1997.

Vol. 1353: G. BiBattista (Ed.), Graph Drawing. Proceedings, 1997. XII, 448 pages. 1997.

Vol. 1354: O. Burkart, Automatic Verification of Sequential Infinite-State Processes. X, 163 pages. 1997.

Vol. 1355: M. Darnell (Ed.), Cryptography and Coding. Proceedings, 1997. IX, 335 pages. 1997.

Vol. 1356: A. Danthine, Ch. Diot (Eds.), From Multimedia Services to Network Services. Proceedings, 1997. XII, 180 pages. 1997.

Vol. 1357: J. Bosch, S. Mitchell (Eds.), Object-Oriented Technology. Proceedings, 1997. XIV, 555 pages. 1998.

Vol. 1361: B. Christianson, B. Crispo, M. Lomas, M. Roe (Eds.), Security Protocols. Proceedings, 1997. VIII, 217 pages. 1998.